THE
YIDDISH HISTORIANS
AND THE
STRUGGLE
FOR A
JEWISH HISTORY
OF THE
HOLOCAUST

THE YIDDISH HISTORIANS AND THE STRUGGLE FOR A JEWISH HISTORY OF THE HOLOCAUST

Mark L. Smith

Wayne State University Press
Detroit

Copyright © 2019 by Mark L. Smith. Published by Wayne State University Press, Detroit, Michigan 48201. All rights reserved. No part of this book may be reproduced without formal permission.

ISBN 978-0-8143-4841-3 (paperback); ISBN 978-0-8143-4612-9 (hardcover); ISBN 978-0-8143-4613-6 (e-book)

Library of Congress Control Number: 2019945981

Wayne State University Press
Leonard N. Simons Building
4809 Woodward Avenue
Detroit, Michigan 48201-1309

Visit us online at wsupress.wayne.edu

CONTENTS

List of Figures ix
Note on Languages and Sources. xi
Preface xiii

Introduction: Writing Jewish History in Yiddish 1
    Yiddish, the Holocaust, and Jewish History   1
    The Prewar Foundation   4

1. The Yiddish Historians of the Holocaust 21
    Introducing the Historians   22
        Philip Friedman   22
        Isaiah Trunk   25
        Nachman Blumental   27
        Joseph Kermish   28
        Mark Dworzecki   30
    The Iron Curtain and the Yiddish Historians   31
    The Historians' Personal Relations   33
    The Absence of Women among the Historians   40
    The Historians and Yiddish   41
    The Yiddish Historians as Public Figures   53

2. Becoming Yiddish Historians of the Holocaust. 62
    The Study of Jewish Life under the Nazis   63
    The Unbroken Chain   83
        Political Continuities   86
        Personal Continuities   100
        Reintegration across the Divide   108
    A New Field of Jewish Historiography   110

3. No Silence in Yiddish..116

Against the "Myth of Silence"   117
The Continuity of Jewish Self-Expression   123
The Imperative to Publish   127
The Lay–Professional Partnership   131
The Reciprocal Relationship   142
The Voices of the Yiddish Historians   149
The Final Link in the Chain   159

4. Holocaust History as Jewish History....................162

The Early Struggle for a Jewish Orientation   165
German versus Jewish Historical Sources   182
Arguing against the Tide   190
Jewish Approaches to Holocaust History   193
The Holocaust and Prior Catastrophes   195
The Continuity of Jewish History   198
The Study of Everyday Life   210
The Topics Not Covered   214
From the General to the Specific   218

5. The Search for Answers...................................225

The Question of Questions   230
The Response   246

6. The Transmission of a Culture..........................279

Translation   279
Transition: A Case Study   283
The Turn to Original Languages   293
In the Field of Yiddish Studies   308

Concluding Thoughts 313

Bibliographies..319

Bibliography of Philip Friedman   325
Bibliography of Isaiah Trunk   341

Bibliography of Nachman Blumental   359
Bibliography of Joseph Kermish   381
Bibliography of Mark Dworzecki   396
General Bibliography   416

Index 441

FIGURES

Philip Friedman	23
Isaiah Trunk	26
Nachman Blumental and Joseph Kermish	28
Mark Dworzecki	30
Book inscription from Mark Dworzecki to Philip Friedman	34
Isaiah Trunk	36
Table of Principal Yiddish Publishing Venues of the Yiddish Historians of the Holocaust	52
Map of Contributions to *Yizkor* Books by Yiddish Historians	138
Second Academic Conference, Lodz, 1945	176

NOTE ON LANGUAGES AND SOURCES

All translations and transliterations are my own. In general, I have followed the standards of the YIVO Institute for Jewish Research in transliterating Yiddish. The few exceptions include well-known terms and names such as *yizkor* (rather than *yisker*) and Sholem Aleichem (rather than Sholem Aleykhem).

For the names of persons, I have taken the dual approach of using the conventional English spelling in the text and the transliterated Yiddish or Hebrew spelling in the footnotes and bibliography. Thus, "Rachel Auerbach" appears in the discussion, and "Rokhl Oyerbakh" appears in the footnotes and bibliography.

For well-known Polish cities, I have used their common English names (Warsaw, Lodz, and Krakow), and for others, their correct Polish spellings.

The titles of foreign-language books and articles are translated into English in the bibliography (but not in the footnotes).

I have used the anachronistic term "Holocaust" throughout, although it was used by the Yiddish historians only in their very latest works and would have been foreign to all but the longest lived. Their customary Yiddish terms for the Holocaust were *katastrofe* or *khurbn* (from the Hebrew *hurban*, destruction, which traditionally refers to the destruction of the First and Second Temples in Jerusalem), and, when writing in English, the "Destruction" or "Catastrophe" of European Jewry. Their works in Hebrew use either *hurban* or the more modern Israeli Hebrew *Sho'ah* (catastrophe).

A number of online sources are cited in the footnotes and bibliography. Instead of listing a "last accessed" date for each source, all online sources have been re-accessed and verified as of February 6, 2019.

PREFACE

The work that is placed before the reader—to use a favored expression of Yiddish writers—had its origin in a rupture of Jewish cultural continuity that occurred at the end of the twentieth century. The first stirrings of this research came at a time when the last remaining Yiddish books were disappearing from the shelves of larger urban bookstores, when public libraries were replacing their Yiddish holdings with the literatures of more recent immigrants, and shortly before Yiddish books would become the first national literature widely available online. During this brief interval, the aspiring reader of Yiddish faced a future seemingly without ready access to the printed Yiddish word.

The writer of these lines—to quote another phrase much used by Yiddish authors—resolved to resist this rupture by collecting widely, then following the age-old advice to "read widely"—and doing so in Yiddish. At the personal level, I also resolved to reverse the process described by Jeffrey Shandler in which the symbolic value of the Yiddish language has often come to outweigh its value "as a vehicle for communicating information, opinions, feelings, ideas" in the era of "postvernacular Yiddish."[1]

Reading widely led me from the classical authors to writers of prose and poetry generally, to literary history and linguistics, theater and humor, the rabbis and *rebbes*, and to the repository of them all, history. The voices that spoke most directly to me were those of the twentieth-century historians who chose to write Jewish history in Yiddish. In their much-neglected works, I had the privilege of reading the urtext before the commentary: Ginsburg and Zinberg testing the possibility of writing Jewish historical

---

1. Jeffrey Shandler, *Adventures in Yiddishland: Postvernacular Language and Culture* (Berkeley, 2006), 4.

scholarship in the language of the people; Schiper switching languages in mid-career; Ringelblum and Mahler pulling strongly to the left—and campaigning for Yiddish among a new generation of historians; Friedman holding to the center—but also in Yiddish; the Polish group drawing inward, with Tcherikower reaching for a pan-Ashkenazi history in Yiddish; Shatzky, the Yiddish Columbus, adding the New World to the territory of Yiddish scholarship; and then—suddenly—fewer voices, in more urgent discourse.

Discovering these historians through the portal of their Yiddish writings provided a specific and coherent perspective. Themes that would animate the present work soon became apparent. Two of these relate to process: that a group of historians chose to turn from other languages to their shared ancestral language; and that they conducted a public discourse intended for an educated lay readership. And two themes relate to content: that their focus was on the internal history of the Jews (rather than the history of Jewish rights and disabilities or antisemitism); and that they were engaged in an anti-lachrymose approach to medieval and other periods of Jewish history well before it was advocated by Salo Baron (who might have joined their ranks had he followed the path of his fellow historians from the Austro-Hungarian province of Galicia).

In the first years of the twenty-first century, the commentary was yet to emerge. Avrom Novershtern could call forth in conversation the few works touching on these historians—all first-person accounts destined to become primary sources but without a secondary literature. John Efron encouragingly confirmed to me that these historians "have not found their historian." The first scholars of the new century to focus on these figures (if not on the Yiddish aspect of their works) had yet to commence publishing.[2] The general neglect of these historians in the literature of the time is illustrated by the article on "Jewish Historiography" in the original English-language *Encyclopaedia Judaica* of 1972, in which historians who worked in Yiddish before World War II receive less than one-half of one sentence, and those who wrote Holocaust history no mention at

---

2. These historians include Natalia Aleksiun, Boaz Cohen, and Laura Jockusch, whose writings are cited later in this work.

all.³ A growing familiarity with their works suggested that they merited a measure of the regard they had enjoyed in their own time and language. A first fruit was the entry on prewar and postwar historian Isaiah Trunk in the 2007 second edition of the *Encyclopaedia Judaica*, for which Michael Berenbaum—in the spirit of a new age shaped in part by the gradual emergence of works from Yiddish into English—generously granted an expanded allotment of space.⁴

One of the first scholarly works to touch on the Yiddish school of historiography was the pathbreaking book by David Myers on the emergence of Jewish historical practice in Israel. Discussing the fateful divergence of institutional Jewish scholarship that occurred in 1925 with the founding of the Hebrew University and of the Yiddish Scientific Institute, he chose (to my relief) to trace the path that led to the "Jerusalem School" rather than to Vilna.⁵ With gratitude, I acknowledge his welcoming an other-than-customary graduate student into the UCLA Department of History—and I acknowledge my good fortune in having the opportunity to pursue my intended topic with the benefit of his specialization in the study of Jewish historiography and his insights into historical writing in general.

As the focus of this work shifted from the more obvious bright lights of Yiddish historical work in the interwar period to its final sparks in the postwar period (partly at the urging of Samuel Kassow, who had recently completed his comprehensive study of Emanuel Ringelblum), the focus also turned to Holocaust historiography. A fortunate consequence was that my work was drawn into the specialty of Saul Friedländer, the inaugural holder of UCLA's 1939 Club Chair in Holocaust Studies, to whom I am indebted for much wise counsel—both regarding approaches to Holocaust study and his encouragement of my own research.

I must also express my gratitude for the expertise of Peter Baldwin in the area of European historiography, of Arnold Band in the area of Jewish literature, and of Samuel Kassow in East European Jewish history in the

---

3. Cecil Roth, "Historiography," *Encyclopaedia Judaica*, ed. Cecil Roth, vol. 8 (Jerusalem, 1972), 562, 566.

4. Mark L. Smith, "Trunk, Isaiah," *Encyclopaedia Judaica*, 2nd ed., ed. Fred Skolnik and Michael Berenbaum, vol. 20 (Detroit, 2007), 160–61.

5. David N. Myers, *Re-Inventing the Jewish Past: European Jewish Intellectuals and the Zionist Return to History* (New York, 1995), 38–39.

prewar and wartime eras. To my former teacher Samuel Aroni, professor and Holocaust survivor, I extend my deep appreciation for his continuing interest in this project and long years of friendship.

A further consequence of the shift from interwar to postwar Yiddish historical scholarship is that the present project necessarily becomes the sequel to a work not yet written. Therefore, the introduction sets forth the subject of Yiddish historical writing in general—and the term and concept of "Yiddish historians." Here, I contend that the prewar historical practice of these figures established a transnational public discourse among themselves and an educated lay audience that was reenacted after World War II by their survivors and successors. One tension within this practice during the interwar period was that these historians chose to focus on the internal history of Jewish life in Eastern Europe, while the political reality of the time required engaged historical writing designed to provide arguments from Jewish history for use in the struggle for Jewish rights.

Chapter 1 introduces the five "Yiddish historians of the Holocaust"— their mutual relations, their attitudes toward Yiddish, and their status as public figures within the postwar Yiddish-speaking world. In short, the purpose is to establish the existence of a defined group of historians, with a particular approach to Jewish history, working toward the realization of a shared research agenda, for a specific audience. The succeeding chapters develop selected themes in the works and careers of the Yiddish historians.

Chapter 2, "Becoming Yiddish Historians of the Holocaust," discusses the continuities, both personal and professional, that led these historians to study the Jewish history of the Holocaust and which also rendered Yiddish historiography an appropriate vehicle for their work. Chief among these continuities were the focus on internal Jewish history and the anti-lachrymose approach to Jewish historical writing that had developed among Yiddish historians before the Holocaust and which led to their study of Jewish life, rather than death, under Nazi occupation. This chapter also explores the research interests and political stances that bridged each historian's prewar and postwar periods and animated their individual emphases in Holocaust study. The personal correspondence on which a portion of this chapter relies was generously made available by the archives staff during my various visits to the YIVO Institute for Jewish Research in New York.

The communal function of the Yiddish historians, by which they resumed the prewar tradition of Yiddish historiography as a form of public discourse, is the subject of chapter 3. This chapter discusses the relations of the Yiddish historians with their audience, exploring the interactions I describe as the "lay–professional partnership" and contesting the existence of a "Myth of Silence" in the Yiddish-speaking world. A portion of this chapter, which is called "No Silence in Yiddish," was published under the same title with research funding from the UCLA/Mellon Program on the Holocaust in American and World Culture, for which I express my appreciation.[6]

Chapter 4, "Holocaust History as Jewish History," uncovers the Yiddish historians' struggle to place the study of Jewish experience at the center of Holocaust history, and it explores the principal subjects of their research. Chief among these struggles was their resistance to the heavy hand of Soviet-imposed research objectives, designed to concentrate attention on Nazi crimes in Poland and to exaggerate the role of Communist aid to the Jews, while minimizing the study of Jewish life and non-Communist resistance. Minutes and correspondence from the archives of the postwar Central Jewish Historical Commission in Poland, which were indispensable for this research, were graciously provided by the staff of the commission's successor organization, the Jewish Historical Institute in Warsaw.

The subject of chapter 5 is the urgent wish of the Yiddish historians to use their role as intellectual representatives of the postwar survivor community to dispel the accusations of cowardice and passivity that arose in the early years following World War II against the Jewish victims of Nazism. In "The Search for Answers," I argue that the Yiddish historians fashioned both a vigorous defense, in studying the many impediments to Jewish resistance, and also a daring offense, in formulating a new definition of resistance that would expand its scope from the limited instances of armed resistance to the widespread efforts of the unarmed Jewish masses to remain alive under Nazi occupation.

---

6. Mark L. Smith, "No Silence in Yiddish: Popular and Scholarly Writing about the Holocaust in the Early Postwar Years," in *After the Holocaust: Challenging the Myth of Silence*, ed. David Cesarani and Eric J. Sundquist (London, 2011), 55–66.

Chapter 6, "The Transmission of a Culture," turns to the longer-term transmission of the Yiddish historians' work from the community of Yiddish speakers to the larger world of Jewish and general scholarship. This chapter discusses a first phase, commencing during the active period of the Yiddish historians, in which the process of cultural transmission occurred chiefly through the medium of translation. It concludes by examining a second, more recent phase marked by a turn to original languages, in which Yiddish works by these historians have lately achieved a degree of integration into the mainstream of Holocaust study.

Chapter 6 is followed by a brief statement of conclusions and a series of annotated bibliographies intended to assist in making known the writings of the Yiddish historians.

The publication of this work in its unabridged form is one of many kindnesses for which I am grateful to the staff of Wayne State University Press: to successive editors-in-chief Kathy Wildfong and Annie Martin for their warm reception of this project; to Kristin Harpster for her careful management of the publication process; to Rebekah Slonim for her precise and collegial copyediting; to Rachel Ross for the splendid appearance of the book; and to Emily Nowak and Kristina Stonehill for helping to bring the results of this collaboration to the public. My thanks to each of them.

That it has been possible to incorporate the most recent developments into the present study reflects the tempo of my work, which has alternated between two impulses. One is the imperative to present this research while it may yet be timely. The other is the knowledge articulated by Abraham Joshua Heschel, in his study of the Kotsker Rebbe, that one cannot always *davenen tsu der tsayt* (that prayer does not always come at the appointed time).[7] I express my gratitude for a family tradition that has encouraged learning and *Yidishkayt*, for my mother who has embodied and transmitted to me both of these values, and for the privilege of having reached this moment in my life and work.

---

7. Avrom Yehoshue Heshl, *Kotsk*, vol. 2 (Tel Aviv, 1973), 190.

INTRODUCTION

Writing Jewish History in Yiddish

When Philip Friedman returned to Lodz soon after the city's liberation from the Nazis, he published the notice: "Dr. Philip Friedman has returned. Persons who possess memoirs, documents, photographs, or other materials about the Jewish destruction, are invited to come," followed by his address and hours.[1] He had been a leader among the younger generation of Jewish historians in Poland before the Holocaust, and he survived the Nazi occupation in hiding. His notice foretold the opening of a new field of Jewish historical research of which he would become the chief founder.

Yiddish, the Holocaust, and Jewish History

This is the story of the concluding period in the work of the Jewish scholars I have come to know as the "Yiddish historians." The protagonists are the twentieth-century historians from Eastern Europe who chose to write Jewish history in Yiddish.

Like many concluding periods, it is also the point of beginning for a new historical moment: The historians who were survivors of the Nazi occupation of Poland conducted the principal Jewish enterprise of Holocaust research in the years immediately following World War II. Most significantly for the development of the field, they pioneered the study of the Holocaust from the perspective of Jewish experience. However, they have not been recognized as a specific group united by a commitment to

---

1. Rokhl Oyerbakh, "D"r filip fridman z"l (dermonung un gezegenung)," *Di goldene keyt* 38 (1960): 178.

Jewish historical writing in Yiddish. Nor has their work been seen as the pursuit of a shared research agenda, guided by the traditions of prewar Yiddish historical writing.

As a result, at the intersection of three areas of Jewish scholarship—Yiddish studies, Holocaust studies, and Jewish historiography (the writing of Jewish history)—we discover a group of historians whose works have yet to be explored in their original context. Increasingly, Holocaust research has turned to source materials written in Yiddish, and there is also a well-developed literature on the writing of Holocaust history. Surprisingly neglected, however, are the works of the survivor-historians who chose to study the Holocaust from the perspective of Jewish history, and did so in the Yiddish vernacular of their readers.

The origins of this neglect appear to lie in the intellectual habits of the two fields of Yiddish studies and Jewish historiography.

To the extent that the study of Yiddish culture has focused on the products of high culture (ironically so, for a language at first disparaged and later promoted as the folk idiom of Ashkenazi Jewry), such attention has concentrated largely on an expanding canon of belles lettres and polemics, stopping short of the chronologically last intellectual pursuit undertaken in Yiddish, the writing of Jewish history. This was true before the Holocaust, when the field of Yiddish studies crystallized among literary critics, linguists, and sociologists, and it remains true even as the field has attracted increasing participation by historians.

Historical work in Yiddish has been similarly unrecognized by students of modern Jewish historiography, whose focus has tended toward the sustained success stories—the century-long career of the German-Jewish *Wissenschaft des Judentums* and the ensuing academic study of Jewish history in Hebrew and English that came of age in Jerusalem and America in the early twentieth century.[2] Apart from a single article that appeared in the Yiddish encyclopedia in 1939,[3] modern historical writing in Yiddish has

---

2. On the "Jerusalem School" of historians at the Hebrew University, see David N. Myers, *Re-Inventing the Jewish Past* (New York, 1995).

3. E. Cherikover, "Yidishe historiografye," *Algemeyne entsiklopedye*, vol. Yidn I (Paris, 1939), 284–302. In a prior article, "Di yidishe historishe visnshaft in mizrekh-eyrope," *YIVO bleter* I, no. 2 (February 1931): 97–113, which covered only Jewish historical work in Russian, he announced his intention to treat each of the language traditions in turn,

not been recognized as a specific scholarly endeavor nor, accordingly, as a potential subject for study.[4] Remarkably, the special status often accorded other forms of Holocaust-related writing in Yiddish, such as memoirs, fiction, and poetry, has not extended to works of Holocaust history in Yiddish. It is this neglect of the field of Yiddish historiography in general, with specific regard to the writing of Holocaust history, that I hope to remedy.

I propose to reconstruct the post–World War II phase of the Yiddish historians' work as it relates to the Holocaust. My purpose is to recover the varied elements of their diverse and yet integrated interests and aims that have not previously been seen as a distinct approach to Holocaust historiography.

Among the accepted truths of Holocaust historiography are that it developed as an academic discipline separate from Jewish history, even among Jewish historians; that "victim" studies emerged from the shadow of "perpetrator" studies only after the 1961 Eichmann trial; that research on the Jewish Councils and wartime Jewish leadership was prompted by accusations of Jewish passivity and complicity by Raul Hilberg, Hannah Arendt, and Bruno Bettleheim in the early 1960s; and that attempts to compare the Holocaust with other historical occurrences or to "historicize" or "normalize" the events of daily life under Nazi rule by employing the customary tools of historical research must be opposed by those who would seek to defend the uniqueness of the Holocaust.

The Yiddish approach to Holocaust historiography stands in opposition to all of these ideas. The field of Holocaust research in Yiddish was created by Jewish historians who dealt at once with the Holocaust as an integral period of Jewish history. They focused on the internal aspects

---

but nothing further resulted until his 1939 encyclopedia article. The only other treatment of Yiddish historical scholarship is found in Isaiah Trunk's summary of historical work at YIVO, "YIVO un di yidishe historishe visnshaft," published in YIVO's fiftieth anniversary volume, *YIVO bleter* XLVI (1980): 242–54.

4. For example, Nokhem Shtif's well-known proposal of 1925 for the creation of a Jewish academic institute treats the writing of history in Yiddish as an end in itself, without distinct qualities. He demonstrates familiarity with the recent literature of each area of Jewish studies in Yiddish, except history. In an appendix intended to rectify hasty omissions in his original text, he introduces historical writing by Israel Zinberg, Saul Ginsburg, and Jacob Shatzky for the first time but further reveals an unfamiliarity with developments in Yiddish historiography and conflates amateur historians with those considered professionals at the time. N. Shtif, "Vegn a yidishn akademishn institut," in *Di organizatsye fun der yidisher visnshaft* (Vilna, 1925), 19–22; appendix, unnumbered thirty-fourth page.

of daily existence among Jews in the ghettos and camps under Nazi occupation and stressed the importance of relying on Jewish sources and the urgency of collecting survivor testimonies. They understood that the question of "uniqueness" was not relevant to the study of the Jewish experience of the Holocaust. The rise of broader popular and academic interest in their areas of study during more recent decades is not merely anticipated by their work, but also represents a gradual transfer of their published works and research agenda from the language community of the survivors to the general public arena.

This final, postwar period of Yiddish historiography is discussed in the absence of the prior chapters that would help to introduce the concept of the "Yiddish historians." With the hope that these earlier chapters may yet come to realization, I offer a brief overview of the historical tradition that gave rise to the Yiddish historians of the Holocaust, and following that, introduce the historians themselves.

The Prewar Foundation

The writing of Jewish history in Yiddish, as a secular, learned profession, is a phenomenon of the twentieth century. By the end of the previous century, the use of Yiddish by leading Jewish authors had transformed it from a disrespected "zshargon" into a modern literary language,[5] and it was thereafter adopted successively by folklorists, linguists, and historians.[6] The use of Yiddish for historical scholarship extends from a bicentennial article on the history of St. Petersburg Jewry, published in that city by Saul Ginsburg in 1903,[7] to the final Holocaust works of Joseph

---

5. The transformation of Yiddish from low- to high-culture status is the subject of Joshua A. Fishman, *Ideology, Society & Language: The Odyssey of Nathan Birnbaum* (Ann Arbor, 1987), and of Barry Trachtenberg, *The Revolutionary Roots of Modern Yiddish, 1903–1917* (New York, 2008).

6. See the landmark collection, Shoyl Ginzburg and Peysekh Marek, *Yidishe folkslider in rusland* (Moscow, 1901) and the first major work of original Yiddish scholarship, the philological compendium *Der pinkes*, ed. Sh. Niger (Vilna, 1913); also the retrospective discussion by Itzik Nakhmen Gottesman, *Defining the Yiddish Nation: The Jewish Folklorists of Poland* (Detroit, 2003).

7. Shoyl Ginzburg, "A bletil yudishe geshikhte tsum 200-yorigen yubileyum fun peterburg," *Der fraynd* 108 (May 27, 1903): 2–3 (signed "G—g").

Kermish that appeared in Israel in the 1980s. In retrospect, it may be said that the career of no earlier or later historian found expression in significant measure through the medium of Yiddish. Observed now, in the aftermath of the era of Yiddish historical scholarship, it would appear that occasional later writings by younger historians may be regarded not as late-burning embers but as a possible revival whose course has yet to be charted.[8]

The path of modern Jewish historical scholarship in Yiddish parallels that of Hebrew. Neither was the continuation of a medieval tradition of historical chronicles written in Jewish languages. Both are instead products of post-Enlightenment movements of Jewish national awakening that led to original scholarship in Hebrew and Yiddish by the turn of the twentieth century. The first work of the preeminent Hebrew-language Zionist historian Ben-Zion Dinur (on the biblical period of Jewish history) appeared simultaneously in Hebrew and Yiddish editions in 1919, and the author expressed his regret that "so far, unfortunately, we do not have a translation of the *Tanakh* [Old Testament] into Yiddish to which one could refer the reader."[9] His book was praised by a leading proponent of Yiddish as an example of the new trend of writing Jewish history in Yiddish.[10] That Hebrew would become the language of a Jewish state and of its national university was far from assured in 1925 when both the Hebrew University in Jerusalem and the Yiddish Scientific Institute (YIVO) in Vilna commenced their work. Although many Yiddish historians were sympathetic to Zionism and its goal of a revived Hebrew vernacular, they were convinced that the majority of Jews would remain in the Diaspora and that Yiddish would serve as the unifying force among various forms of Diaspora nationalism.[11] As a result, the path toward Yiddish was by far

---

8. Examples are the (few) articles by historians in the New Series of *YIVO bleter*, 4 vols. (New York, 1994–2003).

9. B. Dinaburg, *Idishe geshikhte (historishe khrestomatye)* (Petrograd-Kiev, 1919), preface, second unnumbered page.

10. N. Shtif, "Vegn a yidishn akademishn institut," in *Di organizatsye fun der yidisher visnshaft* (Vilna, 1925), 17.

11. On Yiddish and Diaspora nationalism generally, but without consideration of the role of historians, see Emanuel S. Goldsmith, *Architects of Yiddishism at the beginning of the Twentieth Century* (Rutherford, 1976).

the more traveled in its time by Jewish historians, although it has been the one less explored by posterity.

I have applied the term "Yiddish historians" to writers of Jewish history who chose to work primarily or substantially in Yiddish. None wrote exclusively in Yiddish, and all functioned in multilingual settings. For Jewish historians to work in languages other than Yiddish was not remarkable; it was the choice of Yiddish that carried both significance and hardship. Like the founding fathers of Yiddish literature during the second half of the nineteenth century, most turned to their ancestral mother tongue from careers in other languages. For example, Elias Tcherikower, the future head of YIVO's Historical Section, was convinced to turn from Russian to Yiddish in 1915 in New York at the age of thirty-four by his childhood friend and townsman, Ber Borochov—the early Yiddish philologist and advocate for scholarship in Yiddish. Tcherikower recounts that "from then on, I have written in Yiddish. It is unnecessary to explain what it means for a writer when he finds his language.... [I]n my intimate world this was a new chapter, the most important one."[12]

Each of the Yiddish historians worked in multiple contexts and may be viewed from varied perspectives. The better known of these historians have been the subject of much recent research (and earlier study as well). However, such research has tended to draw them to adjectives other than "Yiddish" or to subsets of their Yiddish cohorts and, thereby, to categories that create divisions rather than commonalities: They have been deemed historians of hyphenated Jewish identities, generally "Russian-Jewish"[13] or "Polish-Jewish."[14] They have been studied in relation to historical periods,

---

12. E. Cherikover, "Ber Borokhov—vi ikh ken im," *Literarishe bleter* (December 30, 1927): 1024.

13. E. Cherikover, "Di yidishe historishe visnshaft in mizrekh-eyrope [Russian-Jewish only]," *YIVO bleter* I, no. 2 (February 1931): 97–113; Isaiah Trunk, "Yidish-rusishe historyografye," *Geshtaltn un gesheenishn* (Buenos Aires, 1962), 83–107; English, "Historians of Russian Jewry," in *Russian Jewry (1860–1917)*, ed. Jacob Frumkin et al. (New York, 1966), 454–71. Naturally, several works could be placed in more than one of these categories.

14. Yeshayahu Trunk, "le-Toldot ha-historiografiyah ha-Yehudit-Polanit," *Gal-Ed* III (1976): 245–68; Maria Dold, "'A Matter of National and Civic Honour': Majer Bałaban and the Institute of Jewish Studies in Warsaw," *East European Jewish Affairs* 34, no. 2 (2004): 5–72; Michael Brenner, *Prophets of the Past: Interpreters of Jewish History* (Princeton, 2010), 106–14; and Natalia Aleksiun-Madrzak, "Ammunition in the Struggle for National Rights: Jewish Historians in Poland between the Two World Wars" (PhD diss., New York University, 2010).

chiefly those of late Imperial Russia,[15] interwar Poland,[16] and postwar Europe.[17] They have been claimed for the histories of their institutions, particularly YIVO,[18] Yad Vashem,[19] the Central Jewish Historical Commission of Poland (and its successor, the Jewish Historical Institute),[20] and the less widely known but productive Jewish Division of the Institute for Belorussian Culture.[21] Most are included in surveys of "East European" Jewish historiography.[22] Several have been the subject of individual biographies.[23]

---

15. Benjamin Nathans, "On Russian-Jewish Historiography," in *Historiography of Imperial Russia: The Profession and Writing of History in a Multinational State*, ed. Thomas Sanders (Armonk, 1999), 397–432.

16. Philip Friedman, "Polish Jewish Historiography Between the Two World Wars (1918–1939)," *Jewish Social Studies* XI (October 1949): 373–408; Artur Eisenbach, "Jewish Historiography in Interwar Poland," in *The Jews of Poland Between Two World Wars*, ed. Yisrael Gutman et al. (Hanover, 1989), 453–93; and Natalia Aleksiun, "From Galicia to Warsaw: Interwar Historians of Polish Jewry," in *Warsaw. The Jewish Metropolis*, ed. Glenn Dynner and François Guesnet (Leiden, 2015), 370–89.

17. Laura Jockusch, *Collect and Record! Jewish Holocaust Documentation in Early Postwar Europe* (New York, 2012).

18. Yeshaye Trunk, "YIVO un di yidishe historishe visnshaft," *YIVO bleter* XLVI (1980): 242–54; Lucjan Dobroszycki, "YIVO in Interwar Poland: Work in the Historical Sciences," in *The Jews of Poland Between Two World Wars*, ed. Yisrael Gutman et al. (Hanover, 1989), 495–518; Cecile Esther Kuznitz, *YIVO and the Making of Modern Yiddish Culture: Scholarship for the Yiddish Nation* (New York, 2014).

19. Orna Kenan, *Between Memory and History: The Evolution of Israeli Historiography of the Holocaust, 1945–1961* (New York, 2003); Boaz Cohen, *Israeli Holocaust Research: Birth and Evolution*, trans. Agnes Vazsonyi (Abingdon-New York, 2013).

20. Rafoel Mahler, "Di forshung fun der letster yidisher martirologye oyf naye vegn," *Yidishe kultur* 11, no. 2 (February 1949): 1–8; Feliks Tych, "The Emergence of Holocaust Research in Poland: The Jewish Historical Commission and the Jewish Historical Institute (ŻIH), 1944–1989," in *Holocaust Historiography in Context: Emergence, Challenges, Polemics and Achievements*, ed. David Bankier and Dan Michman (Jerusalem, 2008), 227–44; Mauritsi Horn, "Visnshaftlekhe un editorishe tetikayt fun der tsentraler yidisher historisher komisye baym TsKY"P un funem yidishn historishn institut in poyln in di yorn 1945–1950," *Bleter far geshikhte* XXIV (1986): 143–59; Natalia Aleksiun, "The Central Jewish Historical Commission in Poland 1944–1947," *Polin* 20 (2007): 75–97.

21. Elissa Bemporad, *Becoming Soviet Jews: The Bolshevik Experiment in Minsk* (Bloomington, 2013), 100–109.

22. Samuel Kassow, "Historiography: An Overview," *The YIVO Encyclopedia of Jews in Eastern Europe*, www.yivoencyclopedia.org/article.aspx/Historiography/An_Overview.

23. Mordecai Eliav, "Me'ir Dvorz'etzki, z"l—ha-ish, ha-hoker veha-moreh," in *'Iyunim bi-tekufat ha-Sho'ah: asupat ma'amarim le-zikhro shel Prof. Me'ir Dvorz'etzki z"l*, ed. Mordecai Eliav (Jerusalem, 1979), 11–18; Samuel D. Kassow, *Who Will Write Our History? Emanuel Ringelblum, the Warsaw Ghetto, and the Oyneg Shabes Archive* (Bloomington,

In the present study, I propose to view the Yiddish historians from the perspective of the Yiddish-speaking world with which they chose to identify in their Yiddish works. This perspective unifies the Yiddish historians' manifold valences across time periods, geographical areas, and institutional affiliations. Writing at a time in which the study of subordinate populations often emphasizes their cultural hybridity, I have preferred to follow a single linguistic thread which, though insular in one respect, expands the arena of research to the worldwide culture of Yiddish discourse.

Such an acknowledgment of context invites at least two others: At a time when the joint project of Yiddish studies and Holocaust studies—in recovering the experiences of Jewish victims and survivors—has spurred the writing of Holocaust history from below, I have chosen to concentrate on a product of high culture in Yiddish (albeit one focused on the everyday Jew and intended for a broad readership). And at a time when the most recent ferment in Yiddish studies arises from the discovery of post-vernacular Yiddish culture, I have embraced instead the last authentically vernacular phase of a public conversation commenced and defined by the first generation of Yiddish historians.

The Yiddish historians of the Holocaust inherited a tradition that began as a dissident and populist undertaking. It was the deliberate innovation of committed partisans for Yiddish, and, in each of its time periods, this approach to writing Jewish history has run counter to the prevailing linguistic current. As elites with secular education emerged among the Jews of Imperial Russia, including Russian-ruled Poland, they replicated the language pattern common to colonized and subaltern peoples: In both Russia and Poland, prominent among the first historians of the Jews were non-Jews, who wrote in Russian and Polish.[24] The earliest modern

---

2007, 2018); Roni Stauber, *Laying the Foundations for Holocaust Research: The impact of the historian Philip Friedman* (Jerusalem, 2009); Natalia Aleksiun, "Philip Friedman and the Emergence of Holocaust Scholarship: A Reappraisal," *Simon Dubnow Institute Yearbook* XI (2012): 333–46; Boaz Cohen, "Dr Meir (Mark) Dworzecki: The historical mission of a survivor historian," *Holocaust Studies* 21, nos. 1–2 (2015): 24–37; Véronique Mickisch, "Jewish Historiography between Socialism and Nationalism: A Portrait of Historian Isaiah Trunk (1905–1981)" (MA thesis, Free University of Berlin, 2017).

24. The most influential in commencing the scholarly study of Jewish history were Sergei Bershadskii (1850–96) in Russia and Tadeusz Czacki (1765–1813) in Poland.

Jewish historians adopted the language of the dominant powers as a form of cultural emulation,[25] several also converting to Christianity.[26] These early Jewish scholars were soon challenged by more nationalist-oriented historians who demanded that the Yiddish vernacular be promoted to a high-culture function as a form of national resistance or renewal.

The impetus for historical scholarship in Yiddish arose in a growing division among Jewish intellectuals over the preferred form of Jewish life in late Imperial Russia. The setting was the capital city of St. Petersburg, where the empire's principal Jewish institutions were located. On the one side were communal leaders who argued that Jewish disabilities could be removed only through full participation of Jews in Russian society, and on the other, populist thinkers who observed the resilience of other minority cultures in the empire and favored retention of a distinctly Jewish identity based on Yiddish as the national language.[27]

This division was reflected linguistically and thematically in the circle of Simon Dubnow, the preeminent Jewish historian of Eastern Europe who presided over the Jewish Historical-Ethnographic Society. In the mainstream were historians who chose to work primarily in Russian and who concentrated on external aspects of Jewish history, such as anti-Jewish legislation and the "Jewish Question" within the empire.[28] They were subtly opposed by a divergent group of "proto-Yiddish" historians, centered around Saul Ginsburg and his frequent collaborator Israel Zinberg, who focused on the internal aspects of Jewish life, particularly Jewish social and cultural history.[29] In 1903, Ginsburg had become the

---

25. These include Ilia Orshanskii (1846–75), Maxim Vinaver (1863–1926), and Julius Gessen (1871–1939), who worked primarily in Russian (as did Dubnow), while those who identified with the struggle for Polish independence, notably Meyer Balaban (1877–1942) and Moses Schorr (1874–1941), worked occasionally in Russian, but primarily in Polish.

26. Well-known converts included Daniel Chwolson (1819–1911) in Russia, and Alexander Kraushar (1843–1931) and Ludwik Gumplowicz (1838–1909) in Poland.

27. The only recent scholar who appears to have noted this division is David E. Fishman in *The Rise of Modern Yiddish Culture* (Pittsburgh, 2005), chapter 3.

28. The principal figures were the historians cited above, Orshanskii, Vinaver, and Gessen.

29. Dubnow considered Ginsburg's journal of social and cultural history, *Perezhitoye* (1908–13) to be competitive with his own more general journal, *Evreiskaya Starina* (edited by Dubnow, 1909–17); see Shimen Dubnov, *Dos bukh fun mayn lebn*, vol. 2 (Buenos Aires, 1962), 93.

founding editor of the first Yiddish newspaper in Russia and, thereafter, of leading Yiddish literary journals.[30] Both Dubnow and Ginsburg published historical journals in Russian, but the historians in Ginsburg's circle would become the first to work in Yiddish.[31]

The opening manifesto of another journal associated with Ginsburg, *Di idishe velt* (The Jewish World) refers in 1912 to the awakening of Jewish national sensibilities and the need to unite all strata of Jewish society through use of the national language.[32] Within the principal Jewish public institution of prerevolutionary Russia, the Society for the Dissemination of Enlightenment among the Jews (the OPE), Ginsburg and Zinberg sided "with that democratic wing of Jewish public activity which believed in the importance of developing the Yiddish language into an instrument of modern culture."[33] At a meeting of the OPE Executive in 1905, they had demanded the use of Yiddish in the OPE's Russian-language schools in the Pale of Settlement, and Ginsburg was physically assaulted by a member of the Executive[34] (providing early confirmation of Joshua Fishman's thesis that shifts in language status from low to high function threaten established elites).[35] Following the revolution of March 1917, Ginsburg indicated that he intended to convert his historical journal from Russian to Yiddish, under the title *Amolike yorn* (Bygone Years).

---

30. Ginsburg founded the newspaper *Der fraynd* in 1903 and its literary journal *Dos leben* in 1905, followed by a leading role in *Di yidishe velt* in 1912. Ginsburg does not appear as editor of *Di idishe velt*, but literary historian Elias Schulman says: "As a direct continuation of 'Dos leben' . . . 'Di idishe velt' began to appear in 1912." He notes that the editor is given as B. Muzikant (a name not heard before or since in Yiddish letters), "but the actual editor was S. Ginsburg." See Eliyohu Shulman, "Di tsaytshrift 'Di yudishe (idishe) velt,'" in *Pinkes far der forshung fun der yidisher literatur un prese*, ed. Shloyme Bikl (New York, 1965), 132.

31. Of the writers who appeared in their respective journals, 59 percent of Ginsburg's would turn to writing in Yiddish, while only 26 percent of Dubnow's would do so, using the criterion of their presence or absence from the *Leksikon fun der nayer yidisher literatur*, 8 vols. (New York, 1956–81).

32. Shoyl Ginzburg, "Unzer veg," *Di idishe velt* 1 (March 23, 1912): 1–6 (unsigned).

33. Max Weinreich, "Israel Zinberg 1873–1943 [sic; d. 1938]." *Historia Judaica* VI, no. 1 (April 1944): 101.

34. David E. Fishman, *The Rise*, 43.

35. Joshua A. Fishman, "Attracting a Following to High-Culture Functions for a Language of Everyday Life: The Role of the Tshernovits Language Conference in the 'Rise of Yiddish,'" in *Never Say Die! A Thousand Years of Yiddish in Jewish Life and Letters*, ed. Joshua A. Fishman (The Hague, 1981), 389 (item 4).

Had this occurred, it would have been the first historical journal published in Yiddish.[36] Ginsburg himself gradually shifted his own writing entirely to Yiddish. On the 1937 publication—in Yiddish—of his collected works, the editor of the historical journal *Fun noentn over* (The Recent Past) wrote that Ginsburg's style and mode of exposition "made him beloved and understood by a broad circle of readers" as the creator of "an invaluable '*historical folk-literature*,' a new type which we have not had until now" and, above all, that Ginsburg's "greatest purely scholarly contribution" was that "he had laid the trope for the study of our *internal* life in past times."[37]

After World War I, the center of gravity of East European Jewish intellectual life shifted briefly to Berlin with the arrival of Dubnow and other émigrés from Russia but settled decisively in newly independent Poland, which incorporated most of the former Pale of Settlement. In Poland, too, immediately before and after World War I, the language of the land prevailed among the first modern Jewish historians. A "Polish-Jewish" school of historiography was created by scholars from the older generation, such as Moses Schorr and Meyer Balaban, who would continue to publish largely in Polish as part of a nationalist movement that defined itself as both Polish *and* Jewish.[38] This school was centered around the Institute for Jewish Studies in Warsaw, founded by Schorr, Balaban, and others (which conducted courses in Polish and Hebrew), and the University of Warsaw at which Balaban had the unique honor in Poland of occupying a chair in Polish-Jewish history.[39]

---

36. Zalmen Reyzen, "Shoyl ginzburg," *Leksikon fun der yidisher literatur, prese un filologye*, vol. 1 (Vilna, 1926), 570. Instead, Ginsburg created a short-lived historical journal in Hebrew from 1918–19 with the title, *he-Avar* (The Past). The later Israeli journal of Russian-Jewish history with the same name was named in honor of Ginsburg's journal.

37. Moyshe Shalit, "Shoyl ginzburgs histor. verk, 3 bender, nyu-york 1937," *Fun noentn over* IV (1937): 340 (emphasis his).

38. For a general discussion of these historians in the pre–World War I period, see Natalia Aleksiun, "Polish Jewish Historians Before 1918: Configuring the Liberal East European Jewish Intelligentsia," *East European Jewish Affairs* 34, no. 2 (2004): 41–54.

39. On this Polish-Jewish orientation, see Maria Dold, "'A Matter of National and Civic Honour': Majer Bałaban and the Institute of Jewish Studies in Warsaw," *East European Jewish Affairs* 34, no. 2 (2004): 5–72; and Natalia Aleksiun, "From Galicia to Warsaw: Interwar Historians of Polish Jewry," in *Warsaw. The Jewish Metropolis*, ed. Glenn Dynner and François Guesnet (Leiden, 2015), 370–89.

This "Polish-Jewish" trend was opposed by Jewish nationalists who favored Yiddish, such as Emanuel Ringelblum and Raphael Mahler, and their mentor, the elder Isaac Schiper, who commenced in 1924 to reissue his earlier Polish works in Yiddish translations prepared by Ringelblum and thereafter to write in Yiddish. Historians of the newer trend embraced Yiddish as a means of promoting a specifically Jewish national solidarity and creating historical self-awareness among Yiddish-speaking Jews. Of particular importance for the growth of Yiddish historiography was the founding in 1923 in Warsaw of the study group later named the *Yunger historiker krayz* (Young Historians Circle) by Raphael Mahler and Emanuel Ringelblum, who encouraged and published work in Yiddish by the younger generation of historians, all born soon after the turn of the twentieth century.

Yiddish historical work reached maturity during the period between the world wars in the three principal centers of Yiddish culture: Poland, the United States, and the Soviet Union. Nearly all of the Yiddish historians who came of age during the interwar period had received a doctorate or *magister* (first academic) degree from universities in Eastern or Central Europe, but none achieved a university position in Poland before World War II. YIVO, the Yiddish Scientific Institute founded in Vilna in 1925 as a graduate-level institute of Jewish studies, therefore assumed the role of a shadow university for Yiddish-oriented scholars, including the Yiddish historians. In 1926, the *Yunger historiker krayz* became the Warsaw branch of YIVO's Historical Section. YIVO's journals published advanced research in Yiddish, and its *aspirantur* program offered both instructors and students a postgraduate-level experience.[40] The future Yiddish historian, Jacob Shatzky, on receiving his doctorate at the University of Warsaw in 1922, left Poland for New York and there adopted Yiddish as his language of scholarship. With the founding of YIVO in Vilna in 1925, Shatzky helped to create a branch of YIVO later the same year in New York, where he was eventually joined by Mahler in 1937, and others in subsequent years. The only Yiddish historians who were institutionally separate from YIVO were those at the Soviet academies in Minsk and

---

40. On the history of YIVO in general, see Kuznitz, *YIVO*.

Kiev which had been created in 1921 and 1926, respectively, to conduct cultural, if not national, Jewish scholarship, and which had the distinction of being the first government-sponsored institutions to function in Yiddish.

Although Vilna became the capital of organized Yiddish culture in the West, it was not the birthplace or center of Yiddish historiography. A tradition of publishing anthologies on the past and present of Jewish life in Vilna had developed during the 1920s and continued until World War II, but most of their relatively few historical articles were written by prominent physicians who had become communal leaders and amateur historians. No personal or institutional links were forged between these figures and future Yiddish historians. With one minor exception,[41] no prewar Yiddish historian was born in Vilna, lived in Vilna, or wrote about the city's Jewish history. As a result, the historians who became associated with each other through YIVO were located elsewhere throughout the three centers of prewar Yiddish culture.

Within and across these centers, the Yiddish historians conducted a transnational and pan-Yiddish scholarly enterprise that would survive the Nazis and be continued by the Yiddish historians of the Holocaust. The first volume of YIVO's *Historishe shriftn* (Historical Writings, 1929), edited in Berlin and published in Warsaw, included original Yiddish contributors from these cities as well as Vienna, New York, Odessa, and others.[42] *Di tsukunft* (The Future) of New York carried articles throughout the interwar period from that city and Russia, France, Germany, Lithuania, Poland, and Romania. At its most liberal and inclusive moment in 1928, the journal *Tsaytshrift* (literally, "Periodical") published by the Soviet center in Minsk, brought together its own ideologically committed historians with the decidedly non-Communist Ginsburg and Zinberg

---

41. The exception was Pinkhas Kon, a native of Lodz who settled in Vilna and became a lawyer and lay historian. He specialized in discovering and making known archival documents on the history of Vilna Jewry. Kon was forced to become a member of the first Vilna Judenrat and was soon executed by the Nazis. He has not received appropriate scholarly attention.

42. The American branch of YIVO did not publish a journal specifically dedicated to history but included in its *Pinkes* (New York, 1928) reviews of YIVO's publications in Vilna and of the Minsk *Tsaytshrift*.

of Leningrad and other non-Communist Yiddish historians outside the Soviet Union.[43]

The transnational scholarly discourse conducted by the Yiddish historians during the interwar period was possible only in Yiddish, the common language of East European Jewry throughout its dispersion. Although they published most of their works locally, the geographic breadth of their public conversation may be seen in their occasional long-distance exchanges. Two are representative: Schiper's major work on the history of Jewish theater, published in Warsaw,[44] was reviewed by Shatzky in New York, at first with a five-page article in a local Yiddish theater journal,[45] and then with a twenty-five-page corrective in the Vilna YIVO's *Filologishe shriftn*[46] (which carried a separate critique by YIVO director Max Weinreich[47]), and it was also reviewed by Zinberg in Leningrad with a laudatory two-part article published in Warsaw.[48] When Tcherikower in Paris published two articles in *Di tsukunft* in New York in 1939 accusing the early Maskilim (adherents of the Jewish Enlightenment) of failing to oppose the anti-Jewish policies of Tsar Nicholas I,[49] he was countered in

---

43. In 1926, the Minsk center commenced publication of the first Yiddish scholarly journal, *Tsaytshrift far yidisher geshikhte, demografye un ekonomik, literatur-forshung, shprakhvisnshaft un etnografye*, but after 1929, the Soviet Yiddish centers suffered the same Stalinist suppression of non-Russian languages as did the institutions of other minority cultures. The authoritative survey of Soviet-Jewish scholarship in all languages and periods is Alfred Abraham Greenbaum, *Jewish Scholarship and Scholarly Institutions in Soviet Russia 1918–1953* (Jerusalem, 1978). See also David Shneer, "A Study in Red: Jewish Scholarship in the 1920s Soviet Union," *Science in Context* 20, no. 2 (June 2007): 197–213; and Elissa Bemporad, *Becoming Soviet Jews: The Bolshevik Experiment in Minsk* (Bloomington, 2013).

44. Yitskhok Shiper, *Geshikhte fun yidisher teater-kunst un drame fun di eltste tsaytn biz 1750*, 2 vols. (Warsaw, 1923, 1925).

45. Yankev Shatski, "A naye idishe teater-geshikhte," *Tealit* 1, no. 3 (January 1924): 23–32.

46. Yankev Shatski, "Di ershte geshikhte fun yidishn teater: tsu d"r y. shipers verk," *Filologishe shriftn* II (Vilna, 1928): cols. 215–64.

47. M. Vaynraykh, "Tsu der geshikhte fun der eltere ahashverush-shpil," *Filologishe shriftn* II: cols. 425–28.

48. Y. Tsinberg, "Tsu der geshikhte fun der yidisher folks-dramatik," *Bikher velt* 2, no. 1 (January 1, 1929): 31–41; 2, no. 3 (March 1, 1929): 22–30.

49. E. Cherikover, "Yidishe buntn gegen di gezeyres fun nikolay dem ershtn," *Di tsukunft* (March 1939): 175–79; "Di maskilim, nikolay der ershter un di idishe masen" (July 1939): 409–13.

the same journal by two responses from Ginsburg (with whom he had worked in St. Petersburg before the revolution), writing now from his Stalin-era refuge in Lincoln, Nebraska.[50]

The principal audience for this public conversation was the Yiddish-reading public. In accord with the populist program of YIVO and of Yiddish scholarship in general, the Yiddish historians regarded their readers as both sources and consumers of historical knowledge. The lack of a Jewish national archive and the historic reliance of Jewish and gentile historians on non-Jewish sources for the writing of Jewish history had led to the famous appeal by Dubnow in 1891 for the collecting and preserving of Jewish documents. His appeal found greater response from the less assimilated masses than from the Russified Jewish leaders to whom it was directed, suggesting to Dubnow "a new audience and perhaps a following."[51] The collection process was formalized by YIVO with the creation of its *zamler* (collector) program that encouraged the public to collect sources of Jewish historical and ethnographic interest for the YIVO archives.

In turn, the Yiddish historians were ideologically committed to serving an audience of educated laypeople. Most of the publications in which their works appeared were intended for a lay audience: *Literarishe bleter* (Literary Pages), *Landkentnish* (Knowing the Land), and *Fun noentn over* in Warsaw; and *Di tsukunft* in New York. Further, the scholarly journals published by YIVO—the *YIVO bleter* (YIVO Pages) and *Historishe, Ekonomishe*, and *Filologishe shriftn* (Writings), among others—were supported by donations from the public, for whom the tangible reward was a copy of each newly published volume. The primary journal, *YIVO bleter*, for example, had 1,231 subscribers in 1935, nearly two-thirds of whom lived in the United States, followed by Poland, Argentina, South Africa, Lithuania, and Australia.[52] At YIVO's tenth anniversary conference in Vilna in 1935, Dubnow contrasted the YIVO historians with those of the Hebrew University, observing, "The difference is clear. There—research for specialists; here—for every thinking person," adding that the Jerusalem

---

50. Shoyl Ginzburg, "Vi azoy men shraybt bay unz geshikhte," *Di tsukunft* (November 1939): 662–65; "Di haskole un ihre moderne kritiker" (December 1939): 719–21.

51. Robert M. Seltzer, *Simon Dubnow's "New Judaism": Diaspora Nationalism and the World History of the Jews* (Leiden, 2014), 156.

52. Kuznitz, *YIVO*, 167.

historians' work would be redeemed "by popularizers who will make it accessible to the people."⁵³

The Yiddish historians of the Holocaust were also the inheritors of a tradition of engaged scholarship that had prevailed in Eastern Europe before World War II. In the course of the preceding two centuries, the study of Jewish history had spread from Christian to Jewish scholars, from Western to Eastern Europe, and from German to Yiddish and other East European languages. In each of these phases, the writing of Jewish history was marked by a continuing tension between "pure" and "instrumental" scholarship that was prompted by the ever-present "Jewish Question"—the debate over the status to be accorded the Jews in a given society.

Prior to the era of Jewish emancipation, the Jewish Question had been discussed primarily by Christian philologists and theologians whose view of the Yiddish language as a corrupted form of German helped to justify the exclusion of Jews from German society during the eighteenth century.⁵⁴ In the first period of modern Jewish scholarship that followed, historians of the *Wissenschaft des Judentums* movement in nineteenth-century Germany hoped to facilitate the acceptance of Jews by recasting the image of German Jewry in confessional rather than national terms. They contended that Jewish otherness had resulted mainly from a linguistic detour that led medieval Jews to depart briefly from German for Yiddish. For example, Leopold Zunz argued in 1832 that the Jews of medieval Germany "had no other language than that spoken by their Christian neighbors," that for 300 years after their migration from Germany to Poland in the fourteenth century they spoke "nearly correct German," and that only because of their exclusion from all aspects of German culture have "the Jews remained since that time behind their Christian brothers in scientific education, and this degeneration, even if only a pause, shows

---

53. Shimen Dubnov, "Der itstiker tsushtand fun der yidisher historiografye," in *Tsum hundertstn geboyrntog fun shimen dubnov*, ed. Nakhmen Mayzil (New York, 1961), 74.

54. In part, by reason of the use of the Hebrew alphabet for Yiddish writing, German-Christian Orientalists who were interested in Yiddish viewed Yiddish speakers as not only foreign, but "Oriental" (e.g., Caspar Calvör describes Yiddish as a form of German that is "entirely false, corrupt, unreadable and unintelligible") and says that Jews learn German "with difficulty because, as a foreign-Oriental people [*fremd-orientalisch Volck*], they cannot properly understand the German language," *Gloria Christi* (Leipzig, 1710) (second unnumbered page of "Erinnerung").

its disadvantaging effects first of all on language and institutions."⁵⁵ Fifty years later, Moritz Güdemann claimed that as Jews returned to Germany during the sixteenth century, their language became their impediment: "The strange dialect of those who returned must have had the result that Christians withdrew from the Jews, and had the further result that Jews held still firmer to their language which they also regarded as an inheritance from their ancestors."⁵⁶

In the succeeding century, Yiddishist historians in interwar Poland adopted the *Wissenschaft* approach to historical-critical scholarship, praising new Yiddish works that were "based on archival materials" and "*mit an aparat*" (with a scholarly apparatus), but these historians had other instrumental purposes. A chief concern of the *Wissenschaft* historians had been personal advancement. In David Myers's words, "Lacking formal institutional acceptance, they turned again and again to Wissenschaft in the hope of demonstrating their scholarly merit, and achieving ultimate social validation," whereas the Yiddish historians' turn to Yiddish could not have improved their eligibility for positions in Polish or other universities. In *Wissenschaft*, the German scholars had seen "a method and language which Jews must acquire to render themselves fit for the modern age" (in German society), whereas scholarship in Yiddish was intended to offer a parallel means of entering the modern age. To the extent that *Wissenschaft* served as "a source of identity formation," it had a goal in common with Yiddishist scholarship, but one which was not articulated by the Yiddish historians. In a single respect only—that "Wissenschaft could help to ameliorate the status of the Jews"⁵⁷—did the instrumental purposes of the Yiddish historians explicitly coincide with those of their German predecessors, but in this, too, the approach of the Yiddish historians diverged. It was not their purpose, as Michael Meyer

---

55. Leopold Zunz, *Die gottesdienstlichen Vorträge der Juden*, 2nd ed. (Frankfurt, 1892), 452.

56. Morits Gideman, *Idishe kultur-geshikhte in mitlalter (idn in daytshland dos XIV un XV yorhundert)*, trans. Nokhem Shtif (Berlin, 1922), 191 [Moritz Güdemann, *Die Geschichte des Erziehungswesens und der Cultur der abenländischen Juden während des Mittelalters und der neueren Zeit*, vol. 3 (Vienna, 1888)].

57. David N. Myers, "The Ideology of Wissenschaft des Judentums," in *History of Jewish Philosophy*, ed. Daniel H. Frank and Oliver Leaman (London, 1997), 716, 712, 712, 709.

has described one aim of the *Wissenschaft* scholars, "to show that the Jews had contributed more than their share to modern culture and to refute the resurgent claims of antisemites that the Talmud contained pernicious doctrines."[58] Rather than attempting to recast the image of Jews in a form acceptable to non-Jewish society, the Yiddish historians sought to provide arguments by which Jews could defend their economic and political rights as a national minority in Poland and other East European countries.

Nachman Meisel, editor of the leading Yiddish literary gazette in Warsaw, *Literarishe bleter*, reported on the work of YIVO's *aspirantur* program for graduate students in 1937, declaring, "What a difference between the scholarly methods of the one-time *Wissenschaft des Judentums* and current Jewish scholarship in their attachment to Jews and their position on the Jewish Question!" At a time when Jews were increasingly restricted to the back benches, if any, of Polish universities and were legislated out of traditional Jewish occupations, Meisel contends, "Current Jewish scholarship has become a weapon . . . in our difficult Jewish life; it prepares the materials that are needed in the daily fight."[59]

A call for an engaged approach to Jewish history is found, for example, in the writing of future Yiddish historian of the Holocaust Isaiah Trunk. In 1938, he demanded that the presentation of Polish-Jewish history must "clearly emphasize our nearly thousand-year rootedness in Poland, our immensely important role in the economic development of the country"—themes he would develop in his forthcoming history of the Jews of Płock.[60] A reviewer in the Warsaw daily *Haynt* (Today) declared Trunk's book on Płock to be "a clear refutation of the recent

---

58. Michael A. Meyer, "Two Persistent Tensions within Wissenschaft Des Judentums," *Modern Judaism* 24, no. 2 (May 2004): 105–19.

59. Nakhmen Mayzil, "Yidn-visnshaft oder yidishe visnshaft," *Literarishe bleter* (December 3, 1937): 780. Kuznitz ascribes the "uniformly negative view" of YIVO's founders toward *Wissenschaft* scholarship to "prevailing stereotypes and lack of familiarity," but chiefly to the need for a "rhetorical straw man" in the prior generation against which to contrast the innovations of YIVO. Kuznitz, *YIVO*, 64.

60. Yeshaye Trunk, "Bamerkungen tsum historishn opteyl fun der oysshtelung 'yidn in poyln,'" *Shul-vegn: khoydeshshrift fun der tsentraler yidisher shul-organizatsye in poyln* 6, no. 1 (October 1938): 35. Characteristically, he insists that "apologetics and exaggerations" must be avoided and that "one must let the facts and figures speak for themselves." Trunk's avoidance of overt politicization is discussed in chapters 2 and 4 below.

'achievements' of the official Polish historiography, which attempts to minimize and obscure the role of Jews in the economic history of Poland."[61] Examples of similar engagement appear in the prewar writings of each of the Yiddish historians of the Holocaust.[62] It may even be said that the preoccupation of Polish-Jewish intellectuals with the Jews' deteriorating situation in Poland after the death in 1935 of Polish leader Jozef Pilsudski, who had protected the Jews and other national minorities, may help to explain the Yiddish historians' nearly total silence on the rise of Nazism and the anti-Jewish terrors occurring in Germany and Austria. (By contrast, the debate between Tcherikower and Dubnow over the appropriate response to Nazism—which prompted Dubnow's well-known Yiddish essay, "What should one do in Haman's Times?"—was conducted entirely outside of Poland.)

Nevertheless, these outward expressions of the Yiddish historians' national-Jewish program existed only in furtherance of its underlying emphasis on studying the internal aspects of Jewish history. A decade before the establishment of YIVO, one of its future leaders, the Yiddish linguist Zelig Kalmanovitch (who would become Dubnow's Yiddish translator), set forth his desiderata for a new form of Jewish historiography. In an enthusiastic 1915 Yiddish review of a new anthology on the history of East European Jewry published in Russian, he argues that German *Wissenschaft* was not suited to the East: "Western Europe, where Jewish life consists largely of *Judaism*, cannot provide the example of writing the history of the Jewish *people* as is needed here in the East where the folk-masses live." The work he reviewed was the collaborative product of the "proto-Yiddish" historians referred to above, who later regarded it as the chief accomplishment of Jewish historiography in prerevolutionary Russia. Kalmanovitch quotes approvingly from the book's prospectus, which

---

61. A. Valdman, "700 yohr idisher yishuv in poyln," *Haynt* (March 10, 1939): 10.
62. As examples, see: Filip Fridman, "Tsvey lodzsher yidn hobn oyfgeboyt balut," *Lodzsher togblat* 64 (1932); Józef Kermisz, "Nieznany list patriotyczny rabina do Kościszki z rozu 1792," *Głos Gminy Żydowskiej* 4 (October 1937): 87–88; Mark Dvorzshetski, "A idisher prese-albom baym tsofn-yarid in poyln," *Unzer ekspres* (15 August 1930): 16, and *Haynt* (August 20, 1930): 6; Nakhmen Blumental, "Videramol vegn rasizm," *Literarishe bleter* (September 16, 1938): 607 (in which he asks after the Austrian Anschluss, "Where is today's Bialik?").

promises it will "show the actual life of the people, as the true creator and transmitter of its history," and he praises this as "the new concept innovated by the young Jewish historical science in Eastern Europe."[63]

In his editorial preface to the first volume of *Historishe shriftn* in 1929, Tcherikower insisted on a Yiddish historical science that would not "mechanically translate" from other languages, but would write *"originally"* in Yiddish.[64] Ten years later, in his article on Jewish historiography in the Yiddish encyclopedia, he summarized the distinguishing characteristics of historical writing in Yiddish as "economic history, internal life, literary history (which is entwined with pure-historical elements), Jewish social movements, history of the workers' movement, memoirs and contemporary history."[65] The central traits of this approach—emphasizing the internal life of the people, restoring agency to the Jews in history, and promoting national solidarity—became the defining characteristics of the new Yiddish historiography.

---

63. Zelig Kalmanovitsh, "A nay verk iber der geshikhte fun yuden," *Di yudishe velt* 1, no. 2 (February 1915): 199–207; 1, no. 3 (March 1915): 338–54 (emphases his); citations from 199–203.

64. E. Cherikover, preface to *Historishe shriftn* I (Warsaw, 1929), unnumbered p. I (emphasis his).

65. Cherikover, "Yidishe historiografye," *Algemeyne entsiklopedye*, vol. Yidn I (Paris, 1939), 303.

1

THE YIDDISH HISTORIANS OF THE HOLOCAUST

With the concept of "Yiddish historians" now brought to the threshold of World War II, this chapter will introduce the "Yiddish historians of the Holocaust." It will describe their mutual relations, their attitudes toward Yiddish, and their status as public figures. By doing so, I propose to remedy three oversights that I believe have led to their lack of recognition under this designation. First, they have not been seen as a specific group—a cohort of scholars whose principal bonds as historians were with each other throughout their postwar years and who shared a research agenda that transcended their individual efforts. Second, their embrace of Yiddish has not been understood as itself defining a public sphere of Holocaust discourse with an inherent range of topics, an approach to historiography, and a set of relations between historians and audience. Third, the perception (by Lucy Dawidowicz) that their works "had little resonance because of the obscurity of the journals in which they appeared, but more likely because the subject matter was still too traumatic for historical consideration"[1]—while undeniable from a certain perspective—has obscured the status of these historians as the central figures in a worldwide public conversation that existed independently of, and largely before, the generally well-known course of Holocaust research.

---

1. Lucy S. Dawidowicz, *The Holocaust and the Historians* (Cambridge, 1981), 132.

Introducing the Historians

The "Yiddish historians of the Holocaust" are those who devoted their postwar careers to researching the Jewish experience of the Holocaust and writing to a significant extent in Yiddish. There are five: Philip Friedman, Isaiah Trunk, Nachman Blumental, Joseph Kermish, and Mark Dworzecki, each of whom survived the Nazi occupation in ghettos and camps, in hiding, or by fleeing to the Soviet Union. Each historian merits an individual treatment, but as this study relates to a group phenomenon, I have preferred to allow the details of their lives to emerge within the themes to be discussed. (Additional personal information and variant spellings of their names are provided in the footnotes.)[2]

Philip Friedman

Their undisputed leader was Philip Friedman (1901–60).[3] He became the first director of the Central Jewish Historical Commission of Poland (later the Jewish Historical Institute) in November 1944, having survived the Nazis in a series of hiding places in occupied Lwów. Among his generation of young Jewish historians in interwar Poland, which included Emanuel Ringelblum and Raphael Mahler, and the other future Yiddish historians of the Holocaust, Friedman had been the most prolific in published output. He was unique in having received his education outside of Poland, earning his doctorate in Central and East European History

---

2. Spellings are available for each in Polish, Yiddish, Hebrew, and English. My choice here, for consistency and the convenience of the English-language reader, is to use the common English form of their given names, together with the spelling of their surnames that was most prevalent in English during their postwar careers.

3. Friedman was born in Lemberg (later Lwów, today Lviv, Ukraine) when it was the capital of the Austro-Hungarian province of Galicia. As often noted, this region was the birthplace of the most distinguished generation of Polish-Jewish historians, Meyer Balaban, Moses Schorr, and Isaac Schiper, and many historians of Friedman's generation, including Mahler and Ringelblum, Friedman's mentor Baron, and his younger colleagues, Blumental and Kermish. All had benefited from the more liberal educational policies of the Austrian regime, including mandatory public education, as contrasted with the quotas on Jewish enrollment in institutions of higher public instruction in the Russian Pale of Settlement. Friedman graduated from the public gymnasium in Lwów in 1919. His name appears in Polish as "Filip Friedman" and in Yiddish as "Filip Fridman."

Philip Friedman, Yad Vashem Photo Archive, Jerusalem. 5339/571.

from the University of Vienna in 1925.[4] Friedman had the most varied language output (publishing in German, Polish, Hebrew, Yiddish, and, finally, English)[5] and exhibited the broadest range of research interests, extending from the *Haskalah* (Jewish Enlightenment) in Austrian Galicia to the industrialization of Jewish workers in Lodz.

Friedman was also the only historian of his generation who might be termed a "historian's historian." Twice before the war he had proposed the creation of a worldwide union of Jewish historians, first at

---

4. His dissertation, *Die galizischen Juden im Kampfe um ihre Gleichberechtigung (1848–1868)*, was published with an American subvention arranged by Salo Baron, Friedman's former Hebrew tutor at the Juedisches Paedagogium (Jewish Teachers College) in Vienna. Friedman's professors at the university were Alfred Francis Pribram and Hans Uebersberger, who were specialists at that time in the pre–World War I foreign policy of Austria and Russia, respectively. The former was a Jewish historian, well-known for his favorable views of the Habsburg monarchy, who had written at least once on a Jewish topic, and the latter was an early advocate of the removal of Jews from university positions (and from Vienna in general) and of the Austrian Anschluss with Nazi Germany.

5. His curriculum vitae also lists ability in Ukrainian, Russian, French, and Italian. YIVO Archives, RG 1258, F 976.

the International Congress of Historians in Warsaw in 1933, and again at YIVO's tenth anniversary conference in Vilna in 1935. His proposal included a comprehensive plan for an international association of Jewish historians, including a coordinating body, central archive and library, and publishing program for scholarly and popular works.[6] After the war, he reissued the proposal to his colleagues at the CJHC. In this paper, and throughout his career, he advocated for his own approach to writing Jewish history, which focused on regional studies and favored cultural issues over class conflict. Like all of his future colleagues in Holocaust studies, he was not an adherent of the Marxist interpretation of history, and, moreover, he was outspokenly opposed to Communism and Soviet influence. He specifically contested Ringelblum and Mahler's Marxist orientation in reviews of their works, and he remained apart from their leadership of Jewish historical studies in Warsaw. Rather, in Lodz, where he taught history at the humanistic Hebrew gymnasium, he transformed the academic group of the *Landkentnish* society into the *Visnshaftlekher krayz* (Academic Circle) of the Society of Friends of YIVO in Lodz,[7] thereby creating the second academic branch of YIVO in Poland after Ringelblum and Mahler's *Yunger historiker krayz* in Warsaw.[8]

In Lodz, Friedman developed his own Jewish version of the regional approach to European historiography then practiced by historians in Western Europe. As a deliberate strategy, regionalism had emerged during the early twentieth century among historians of the Annales school in France, for whom it joined their preference for study of a sustained period (the *longue durée*) with, as Friedman described it, a broader "fight against the centralized system and against the cultural hegemony of Paris."[9] During his year as an *aspirantur* instructor at YIVO in 1935, he advocated the regional approach to Jewish history. His student, Menachem

---

6. Friedman, "Di oyfgabes fun undzer historisher visnshaft un vi azoy zey tsu realizirn," *YIVO bleter* XIII, no. 3–4 (1938): 301–12 (first published in Polish in 1933).

7. Friedman, Introduction to *Lodzsher visnshaftlekhe shriftn* I (Lodz, 1938): III–IV.

8. He had published a Yiddish version of a portion of his dissertation in the *Yunger historiker* journal in 1929 and was claimed by Mahler as a onetime member of the group in his *Historiker un vegvayzer* (Tel Aviv, 1967), 312. Friedman drew both Ringelblum and Mahler into the academic work of his organization in Lodz. See, e.g., "Visnshafts-krayz tsu forshen dos idishe leben in lodzsher kant," *Haynt* (April 4, 1934): 4.

9. Friedman, "Regyonalizm," *Landkentnish* (May 1937): 3.

Linder (who would become one of Ringelblum's chief associates in Oyneg Shabes and a founder of the Yiddish cultural organization in the Warsaw Ghetto), described him as "the theoretician of Jewish regionalism."[10] Friedman published a two-part discussion of regionalism in the *Landkentnish* journal in 1937 (of which he was a coeditor),[11] explaining both the regional approach in general and the practice of Jewish regionalism. In this, he may be unique among historians of regional historiography, who have routinely neglected its Jewish current in surveys of the field.[12] He stressed the distinction between European and Jewish regionalism— that the former was intended to counter the super-centralization of national culture occurring in many European countries, whereas the Jews in Poland had only begun to create such national cultural institutions as YIVO, and the goal of regionalism was not to resist centralization but to provide material for accurate syntheses of historical trends among Jewry at large. After the war, Friedman continued to promote Jewish regionalism, and it became a chief element in the Jewish approach to Holocaust research, albeit with a radically altered purpose (as discussed at the end of chapter 4).

Isaiah Trunk

Among the younger historians of Friedman's acquaintance in prewar Poland whom Friedman praised as practitioners of the regional approach was Isaiah Trunk (1905–81).[13] Trunk had attended the gymnasium in

---

10. Menakhem Linder, "Historish-ekonomisher regyonalizm," *Literarishe bleter* (July 24, 1936): 1–2.

11. Friedman, "Regyonalizm," *Landkentnish* (May 1937): 3–7; (July 1937): 1–3. On the place of Friedman's article in the Polish-Jewish *Landkentnish* movement, see Samuel Kassow, "Travel and Local History as a National Mission: Polish Jews and the Landkentenish Movement in the 1920s and 1930s," in *Jewish Topographies*, ed. Julia Brauch et al. (Aldershot-Burlington, 2008), 258.

12. Examples are Celia Applegate, "A Europe of Regions: Reflections on the Historiography of Sub-National Places in Modern Times," *American Historical Review* 104, no. 4 (October 1999): 1157–82; and Eric Storm, "Regionalism in History, 1890–1945: The Cultural Approach," *European History Quarterly* 33, No. 2 (2003): 251–65.

13. Trunk was born in Kutno, a city in central Poland to the west of Warsaw and north of Lodz, with a large and historic Jewish community. Trunk's father, Rabbi Yitskhok Yehuda Trunk, was the family's third rabbi in Kutno and the city's last before the Holocaust, as well as a founder of the Mizrachi Orthodox Zionist movement in Poland. His name

Isaiah Trunk, Yad Vashem Photo Archive, Jerusalem. 1592/96.

Lodz at which Friedman was an instructor, graduating in 1927 (although neither mentions knowing the other during this time). He then received his *magister* degree from the University of Warsaw as a student of Meyer Balaban, who was himself a leading practitioner and proponent of regional studies. Until the start of World War II, Trunk taught Jewish history at Jewish secondary schools in Poland. He was active in the work of the *Yunger historiker krayz* and YIVO's Historical Section, with specific engagement in Ringelblum's project for collecting and preserving the record books of Polish-Jewish communities.[14] He had published an extended positive review, also in *Landkentnish*, of Friedman's Jewish history of Lodz, expressing the hope that it would stimulate further regional scholarship and concluding that regionalism "is a rewarding field in which much can be accomplished."[15] In return, Friedman praised Trunk's

---

appears in Yiddish as "Yeshaye [or Shaye] Trunk" and in Polish as "Jeszaja Trunk." He was a cousin of the well-known Yiddish novelist and literary figure Yehiel Yeshaye Trunk, with whom he is occasionally confused in library catalogs.

14. Trunk, "Barikht fun der pinkeysim-aktsye," *Yedies fun YIVO* 83–84 (March–April 1939): 6–10 (unsigned; see Kermish, "Yeshaye trunk z"l" [1983] in the bibliography); Trunk, "Emanuel ringelblum—der historiker 1900–1944," *Di tsukunft* (April 1965): 158–59.

15. Trunk, "Poylisher mantshester," *Landkentnish* (January 1936): 7.

prewar monograph on the earliest Jewish presence in the region of Mazovia, which "allows us to deduce the beginning of Jewish settlement in the area of Lodz Province."[16] On the occasion of YIVO's fiftieth anniversary in 1975, Trunk cited the regional approach as a principal characteristic and accomplishment of the YIVO-affiliated historians and named Friedman's Lodz project in particular.[17] At the latest, Trunk became acquainted with Friedman in Warsaw during Friedman's lectureship at the Institute for Jewish Studies in 1938–39.

During the Nazi and Soviet invasions of September 1939, both Friedman and Trunk took refuge in areas of Soviet occupation—Friedman in his home city of Lwów where he found a university position (until Lwów was taken by the Nazis and Friedman went into hiding),[18] and Trunk in Białystok, where he resumed teaching at a Jewish school (until he was exiled to the Soviet Far East for refusing to accept Soviet citizenship). When Trunk was repatriated to Poland in early 1946, he reported directly to Friedman at the CJHC for work as a historian.

Nachman Blumental

Likely, though not certainly, known to Friedman before the war was Nachman Blumental (1905–83),[19] whose final prewar teaching position was also at a Jewish gymnasium in Lodz. Blumental had long acted as a *zamler* (collector) of folklore materials for YIVO, and he reported for the *Literarishe bleter* on activities of the Lodz "Friends of YIVO" headed by

---

16. Friedman, "Historishe literatur vegn yidn in der lodzsher voyvodshaft (1918–1937)," *Lodzsher visnshaftlekhe shriftn* I (Lodz, 1938): 134.

17. Trunk, "YIVO un di yidishe historishe visnshaft," *YIVO bleter* XLVI (1980): 349–50.

18. During the Soviet occupation of Lwów, Friedman served as a senior research fellow in economic history and head of the Department of Industry at the local branch of the Ukrainian Academy of Sciences, 1940–41.

19. Blumental was born in the Galician town of Borshtshiv (Borszczów, Poland; today Borshchiv, Ukraine), into a prominent family associated with the local brick factory, and graduated from the local gymnasium. One Blumental relation was the treasurer of the Talmud Torah (Jewish religious school); another founded the modern Hebrew gymnasium that attracted students from the surrounding area. Many are listed among both the victims and survivors in the town's *yizkor* book, edited by Blumental. One also served on the Judenrat. His name is occasionally misspelled "Blumenthal" in published sources. Blumental's mother was Basya Meisel.

Blumental (center) and Kermish (right) with the Polish Commission of Inquiry in Chełmno, May 1945. Yad Vashem Photo Archive, Jerusalem. 1427/358.

Friedman.[20] Both Friedman and Blumental were frequent contributors to the *Literarishe bleter*, edited by Blumental's hometown cousin, Nachman Meisel. Although Blumental's degree from the University of Warsaw in 1928 was in Polish literature,[21] his energies in writing and speaking were devoted to Jewish ethnography, specifically Yiddish literary history. He was one of the first associates to join Friedman at the CJHC in Lublin, when it was the temporary capital of Poland during the country's liberation from the Nazis.

Joseph Kermish

Joseph Kermish (1907–2005)[22] first met Friedman and Blumental in Lublin. He had received his doctorate in Polish history from the University

---

20. Blumental, "A glezl tey mit di lodzsher moler," *Literarishe bleter* (February 3, 1939): 37–38.
21. His thesis was on problems of literary composition in Polish.
22. Kermish was born in the Tarnopol region of Galicia in the small town of Złotniki (today Zolotnyky, Ukraine), and he graduated from the gymnasium in nearby Tarnopol in 1927. The Polish spelling of his name is "Józef Kermisz."

of Warsaw in 1937.[23] He became, in later terminology, a "public historian" who was employed for specific projects, including a bibliography of the Jewish history of Warsaw supported by leaders of the Warsaw Jewish Community. At the start of the war, Kermish took refuge in the Soviet zone, where he was employed from 1939 to 1941 as a teacher of history, and later principal, at a municipal gymnasium.[24] As the Soviet army retook the region in March 1944, he was "soon selected to be lecturer in history" at the officer training school of the Soviet-sponsored Polish People's Army near Zhytomyr.[25] When the school was relocated to Lublin in September 1944, he found Friedman and Blumental already at work in the single room occupied by the local Jewish historical commission,[26] and he became the founding director of the CJHC archives. Photographs of Kermish in the period 1944 to 1946, including those taken at meetings of the CJHC, show him in uniform, first as a captain and later as a major.

Together, Friedman, Blumental, and Kermish—and from 1946, Trunk—became known as the leading historians of the CJHC. Their chief non-historian colleague was Rachel Auerbach, one of the few survivors of Oyneg Shabes in the Warsaw Ghetto, who directed the oral history section of the CJHC and became associated with the Yiddish historians for the remainder of her career. Her many important writings on Holocaust topics consisted largely of personal accounts and reportage rather than historical research. On Friedman's departure from Poland in May 1946, Blumental became the director and Kermish the assistant director and secretary-general. Blumental, Kermish, and Trunk left in the course of 1950 for Israel, where they founded the research program at Ghetto

---

23. His professors had been the distinguished historians of modern Polish history, Wacław Tokarz, a non-Jew without apparent interest in Jewish history, and Marceli Handelsman, who was of Jewish origin and sympathetic to Jewish topics and had supervised the dissertations completed by Shatzky in 1922, Ringelblum in 1927, and Eisenbach in 1931.
24. In the Podolian town of Husiatyn (today Gusyatin, Ukraine).
25. "Di byografye fun d"r yosef kermish," unpublished autobiographical memoir (see "Writings about Kermish" in the bibliography). It is also the source of certain other details of his life that are not generally well known.
26. Kermish, "D"r filip fridman—der historiker fun khurbn," *Di tsukunft* (April 1975): 151. The English version of 1960 mistakenly names the city as "Lwów," but the Yiddish version says correctly "Lublin."

Dworzecki speaking at a memorial assembly in Tel Aviv for the Jews of Vilna, October 3, 1965. Courtesy Ghetto Fighters' House.

Fighters' House (Bet Lohame ha-Geta'ot). They appeared together frequently in the journal they founded for the GFH and as speakers in the public programs of the Israel Friends of YIVO, at which they previewed their forthcoming research papers.[27]

Mark Dworzecki

The fifth of the historians to be considered here is Mark Dworzecki (1908–75; pronounced "Dvorzhetski"),[28] who had been a medical doctor

---

27. "YIVO tetikayt in medines-yisroel," *Yedies fun YIVO* 50 (September 1953): 4.

28. In his later years Dworzecki wrote, "To this day I do not know where I was born. Some of my documents say Vilna; most of the others say Maytshet," the family's hometown 200 kilometers to the south (today Moučadź, Belarus). In the family history contributed by Dworzecki to the Maytshet *yizkor* book, he relates that he was descended from three generations of Dworzecki rabbis. His paternal grandfather had been a delegate to the Second Zionist Congress in Basel and had settled in Rehovot in 1926. His father, a graduate of the Slonim Yeshiva, was active in the local Zionist movement, and his mother (an architect, whose father was also a rabbi) was a *maskilah*, learned in several languages. During the latter part of World War I, Dworzecki's family lived in Maytshet, where he received a traditional religious education from the town's rabbis and took part in the cultural activities of the local Zionist organization. After the war, he returned to Vilna and graduated from the Hebrew gymnasium. See Dworzecki, "Mishpahat Dvorz'etzki," in *Sefer-zikaron li-kehilat Meytshet*, ed. Ben-Tzion H. Ayalon (Tel Aviv, 1973), 211–17 (English translation online; see bibliography). His name appears in Polish as "Mark [at times,

in Vilna before the war and survived the Vilna Ghetto and several concentration camps. On escaping from a forced march in Germany in April 1945, he settled in Paris where he immediately began writing and lecturing, and became president of the Survivors Union in France. His all-encompassing study of the Vilna Ghetto was quoted by Trunk as early as 1949,[29] and it remains one of the most ubiquitously cited sources on the history of the Vilna Ghetto.[30]

The Iron Curtain and the Yiddish Historians

Separated from this group of historians were those who remained behind the Iron Curtain in Communist Poland. The first application of the aims and methods of Yiddish historiography to Holocaust history had been the project organized by Emanuel Ringelblum in the Warsaw Ghetto under the code name Oyneg Shabes (Sabbath Joy). For the Ringelblum Archive, as the collected materials came to be known, Ringelblum and his colleagues assembled official documents, personal accounts, questionnaire responses, topical essays and sociological studies, creative works, and communications from other Jewish ghettos. These are headed by Ringelblum's own *Notes* of events, and together they exemplify the prewar Yiddish historians' commitment to engaged social history.[31] Once recovered from their underground hiding places, these materials became and have remained the core of the Holocaust collection at the Jewish Historical Institute in Warsaw.

It would satisfy the urge for historical justice to envision Ringelblum as the natural leader of the Yiddish historians of the Holocaust had he survived the Nazis—continuing the task he had begun in the ghetto—but

---

Marek] Dworzecki," in French as "Marc Dvorjetski," in Yiddish as "Mark Dvorzshetski," and in Hebrew as "Me'ir/Mark Dvorz'etzki."

29. Trunk, "Shtudye tsu der geshikhte fun yidn in 'varteland' in der tkufe fun umkum (1939–1944)," *Bleter far geshikhte* II, nos. 1–4 (January–December 1949): 254.

30. Dworzecki, *Yerusholayim d'lite in kamf un umkum* (Paris, 1948).

31. See Emanuel Ringelblum, *Ksovim fun geto*, 2 vols. (Tel Aviv, 1985); Samuel D. Kassow, *Who Will Write Our History? Emanuel Ringelblum, the Warsaw Ghetto, and the Oyneg Shabes Archive* (Bloomington, 2007, 2018); and Robert Moses Shapiro and Tadeusz Epsztein, eds., *The Warsaw Ghetto: Oyneg Shabes-Ringelblum Archive: Catalog and Guide*, trans. Robert Moses Shapiro (Bloomington, 2009).

this single change would not have sufficed to alter the course of events in postwar Poland. A more nuanced view would find inevitable the fissure that developed between the minority of Jewish survivors who favored the Communist takeover of Poland and the large majority who, returning from places of refuge in the Soviet Union, fled from further Soviet rule, as well as from continuing antisemitic violence in Poland.[32] Had Ringelblum survived, he could neither have prevented nor surmounted these events.

By 1950, each of the figures discussed here had left or resolved not to return to Soviet-led Poland. If Ringelblum had joined their exodus, it is far from certain that he could have persuaded his fellow historians to join in a common enterprise under his leadership in one or more locations. However, Ringelblum's personal history suggests he would more likely have remained in Poland. His commitment to the welfare of Polish Jewry led him to stay in Poland during the 1930s to coordinate relief work among Jewish refugees, even as his colleague Mahler left in 1937 for America—and it led him to stay again during the early days of the German invasion in September 1939 when he and his family had the opportunity to escape.

If Ringelblum had survived and remained in Communist Poland, he would have joined his fate to that of the other Jewish historians who chose to remain but soon found themselves neither free to leave nor to conduct the research of their choice. These included Ber (Bernard) Mark, Artur Eisenbach (Ringelblum's brother-in-law), and Szymon Datner, who served in succession as directors of the post-1947 Jewish Historical Institute. Despite their important early Holocaust works, these historians and their colleagues became separated from the mainstream of Yiddish Holocaust historiography and had only occasional contacts with their colleagues in the West.

---

32. Feliks Tych, director of the JHI from 1996 to 2007, indicates in his history of the CJHC/JHI that between the Kielce pogrom of July 1946 and the end of 1947, "the number of Jews living in Poland dropped from about 240,000 to 90,000, and continued to decrease until the end of 1950, when the borders were closed for Jewish emigration." See "The Emergence of Holocaust Research in Poland: The Jewish Historical Commission and the Jewish Historical Institute (ŻIH), 1944–1989," in *Holocaust Historiography in Context*, ed. David Bankier and Dan Michman (Jerusalem, 2008), 239.

During the period of Stalinist purges in the Soviet Union in the late 1940s and early 1950s, Jewish-oriented Holocaust studies in Poland were discouraged, and the narrative of Jewish resistance and non-Jewish aid to Jews was restricted to the efforts (real or fanciful) of Communist partisans and Soviet forces. Until the fall of the Communist regime in 1989, the historians of the JHI were subject to the recurring periods of antisemitic agitation suffered by Polish Jews at large. They often found it safer to divert their writing into earlier, less contentious periods of Jewish history.[33] The chronicle of their perseverance—and of their feigned but obligatory attacks on other Yiddish scholars in the West—is an important subplot in the history of Yiddish historiography, but it requires a narrative of its own. The principal discussion must, therefore, return to the historians in the West who had secured the personal liberty needed to pursue their own research agendas.

The Historians' Personal Relations

The first public record of contact between Dworzecki and another Yiddish historian is the report of "an evening dedicated to Dr. Mark Dworzecki on the publication of his book 'Jerusalem of Lithuania in Struggle and Extermination'" organized by the publisher in Paris in April 1948, at which Friedman headed a group of distinguished speakers.[34] Their personal acquaintance can be traced to August 12, 1946, the date on which Dworzecki inscribed a copy of his first book, on "medical resistance" in the Vilna Ghetto, to "Dr. Friedman, with heartfelt greeting, a chapter of history from Vilna Ghetto. M. Dworzecki. Paris."[35] Thereafter, Dworzecki corresponded with the CJHC to obtain illustrations and other materials

---

33. After the 1950s, Eisenbach returned almost entirely from Holocaust studies to his prewar concentration on nineteenth-century Jewish history, and he was dismissed as director of the JHI during the official antisemitic campaign of 1968. The JHI's journal, *Bleter far geshikhte*, suspended publication from 1969 through 1979, resuming from 1980 to 1993. Periodic turns toward safe topics may be observed in the comprehensive "Biblyografye fun di shriftn fun prof. ber (bernard) mark," *Bleter far geshikhte* XXVI (1988): 240–360.

34. "Khronik," *Kiem* (May 1948): 349.

35. Dworzecki, *Kamf farn gezunt in geto-vilne* (Paris, 1946). Punctuation added.

Book inscription from Dworzecki to Friedman, August 8, 1946. In the collection of the author.

for his forthcoming book on the ghetto as a whole. The CJHC's advance knowledge of this book made possible its inclusion in their 1947 anthology on Jewish Vilna.[36] In a letter of August 1947, he thanked the CJHC for the desired items and also for a complete set of their publications, which he promised to publicize as editor of the literary section of *Unzer vort* (Our Word) in Paris.[37] The chapter of Dworzecki's history of the Vilna Ghetto on "Social Differences in the Vilna Ghetto" appeared in Polish translation in 1948 in the Warsaw periodical *Mosty* (Bridges) of the Labor Zionist Hashomer Hatzair party, in which Blumental and Kermish frequently appeared.[38]

Relations remained close, and perhaps deepened, once all of the Yiddish historians had left postwar Europe. Blumental and Kermish remained permanently in Israel, where they became lifelong coworkers, first at Ghetto Fighters' House and then at Yad Vashem, where Blumental was a researcher and "scientific editor,"[39] and Kermish was founding

---

36. *Bleter vegn vilne: zamlbukh* (Lodz, 1947), unnumbered page headed "Bikher vegn vilner geto." Dworzecki is one of four authors listed with works on the Vilna Ghetto.

37. Dworzecki, letter "Tsu der yidisher historisher komisye in poyln" (August 19, 1947), Archives of the JHI, AZIH/CKCP/CŻKH 303XX160.

38. "Różnica socjalne w getcie wileńskim," *Mosty* (April 19, 1948): 34. Separately, a Polish translation of the section on Hebrew theater in the ghetto was announced for the same periodical, but this apparently did not occur; see "Już ukazał się miesięcznik 'Mosty' nr 2 (10)," *Mosty* (18 February/Lutego 1947): 4.

39. Blumental is described in several issues of the *Yad Vashem Bulletin* during the 1960s as "one of the first scholars to engage in the investigation of the Catastrophe.

director of the archives. Although Blumental and Kermish had not been acquainted before the war, they belonged to the same circle of young Jewish intellectuals. Thus, the Yiddish journalist Shmuel-Leyb Shnayderman (best known for discovering and editing Mary Berg's diary of the Warsaw Ghetto)[40] reported that when he visited the CJHC in 1946, he enjoyed an emotional reunion with Kermish, "my friend from student years in Warsaw," and with Blumental, "my former co-editor at the *Literarishe bleter*."[41] Blumental and Kermish were frequent coworkers of the two other prominent survivors on the Yad Vashem staff—Auerbach, who headed the oral history section, and the historian Natan Eck, who had been a classmate of Friedman's at the University of Vienna. In the well-known conflict that developed at Yad Vashem in the late 1950s between these survivors and the veteran-Israeli leadership (see the end of chapter 2), their chief supporter was Dworzecki, the leading survivor representative on the Yad Vashem directorate.

In the other postwar center of Yiddish Holocaust research, New York, the principal figures were Friedman and Trunk. Friedman arrived in October 1948 at the invitation of Columbia University on the initiative of Salo Baron, his friend and teacher from Vienna. The headquarters of YIVO had been relocated to the New York branch in 1940 by Max Weinreich, and Friedman became the head of the Historical Section. Trunk immigrated to Canada in 1953, where he was director of the Yiddishist Peretz School, a forerunner of the Calgary Hebrew Academy, and in 1954, he was invited to join YIVO in New York. His career at YIVO carried the official positions of senior research associate and chief archivist, and he was known to graduate students for his courses in Jewish and Holocaust history at YIVO and also at Columbia University. In New York, Trunk became the historian most closely associated with Friedman and, on Friedman's premature death in 1960, the leading voice of Yiddish historiography in America.

Former director of the Jewish Historical Institute in Poland. Presently, scientific editor at Yad Vashem."

40. S. L. Shneiderman, ed., *Warsaw Ghetto, a Diary by Mary Berg* (New York, 1945).

41. Sh. L. Shnayderman, *Tsvishn shrek un hofenung (a rayze iber dem nayem poyln)* (Buenos Aires, 1947), 214–15.

Isaiah Trunk (left) conducting his graduate seminar at YIVO on "Internal Conditions in the Ghettos under Nazi Rule," New York, 1973. From right to left: future Jewish historian Robert Moses Shapiro, future Yiddish translator Joachim Neugroschel, future Holocaust educator and historian Isaiah Kuperstein, and future Jewish scholar and psychoanalyst Michael Mashberg. From the Archives of the YIVO Institute for Jewish Research, New York.

Fortunately, evidence of the warm relations between the Yiddish historians in New York and Israel has been preserved in their correspondence.[42] Typical greetings between Kermish and Friedman include: "Very distinguished and dear Dr. Friedman," and "Dear and beloved friend Dr. Kermish."[43] (Apart from friendship, one notes the difference in status—reenacted between Trunk and Kermish, who also greet each other as "Dear friend," but with only Trunk, like Friedman, addressed as "distinguished.") In anticipation of his first and only visit to Israel in 1957,

---

42. The letters cited here are from the YIVO archives; Friedman's correspondence (RG 1258) with Kermish (F 116), Dworzecki (F 57), Ber Mark (F 155); Trunk's correspondence (RG 483) with Kermish (F 29), Dworzecki (F 54), Auerbach (F 27), Mark (F 7 and F 26), and Shaul Esh (F 27). On Friedman's wide-ranging network of correspondents, see Natalia Aleksiun, "An Invisible Web: Philip Friedman and the Network of Holocaust Research," in *Als der Holocaust noch keinen Namen hatte / Before the Holocaust Had Its Name*, ed. Regina Fritz et al. (Vienna, 2016), 149–65.

43. Letters dated October 28, 1954 and March 12, 1957, respectively.

Friedman writes to Kermish, "I hope to come to the Congress of Jewish Studies and for a long visit to Yad Vashem this summer, and it will be a great joy for me to see my closest colleagues and friends, especially you," and as the time drew nearer, "I am overjoyed that we will see each other after such a long time."[44]

Their correspondence includes family news and good wishes, greetings for others in the group, the housing situations encountered by Kermish and Blumental (and Auerbach) in their early years in Israel, notes on having read each other's works, and congratulations on their achievements. In 1970, Trunk informs Kermish that his son Gabriel is now living on a kibbutz in Israel, and Kermish responds, "I was pleasantly surprised and very glad to receive a visit from your son. I knew him as a small boy, and now a grown man."[45] On Trunk's research visits to Israel, he would work with Kermish in the Yad Vashem archives during the day and visit with the Blumentals at their home in the evening.[46]

Mutual assistance in professional matters was the principal topic of their correspondence. One of Friedman's chief efforts during the 1950s was the Joint Documentary Project of YIVO and Yad Vashem that originated with his own collecting of Holocaust research materials and ultimately appeared in twelve volumes from 1960 to 1973. Friedman received thousands of entries from Kermish and Blumental (and Auerbach) and ten pages of technical suggestions from Dworzecki.[47] Trunk's major study of the Judenrat (the Nazi-imposed Jewish governing councils) led to requests for information from his colleagues in Israel. One of the responses was Dworzecki's exhaustive reconstruction of the initial and ever-changing membership of the Vilna Judenrat.[48] Over the course of nearly twenty-five years, Kermish discussed with Trunk the progress of his efforts to produce a critical edition of the many publications of the

---

44. Letters dated March 12, 1957 and June 27, 1957, respectively.
45. Letters dated September 8, 1970 and July 16, 1971, respectively.
46. Gabriel Trunk, telephone conversation, May 4, 2009.
47. Despite the publicly strained relations between the Yiddish historians in the West and those remaining in Warsaw, Friedman and Trunk both exchanged letters with Ber Mark (generally over specific requests for published materials) that are notably cordial and solicitous of each other's health and professional efforts.
48. Dworzecki, "Der yidn-rat fun vilner geto," six-page typescript, dated February 4, 1966, YIVO archives RG 483, F 59.

underground press in the Warsaw Ghetto. From the late 1960s through the late 1970s, he requested and received from Trunk repeated assistance in gaining access to the publications held by the archives of the General Jewish Labor Bund. In 1970, Kermish invited Trunk to serve on the editorial committee for the project, and Trunk promptly accepted.[49]

The most remarkable, and poignant, exchange of letters is found in the Friedman–Dworzecki correspondence. On Friedman's arrival in Jerusalem in July 1957, he received a letter from Dworzecki inviting him to his home in Tel Aviv "for a glass of tea with other Jews from Tel Aviv who are concerned with Holocaust research, and who have high regard for your name." In January 1958, Friedman wrote to say how pleasantly he recalled the occasion.[50] Intervening was the first of Friedman's heart attacks, followed by the liver ailment of which he eventually died (and of which he had informed Dworzecki, the medical doctor). Following years of effort, Dworzecki succeeded in establishing the world's first chair in Holocaust studies at Bar-Ilan University—and was installed as its first incumbent in November 1959. He sent Friedman the formal announcement of the event, and Friedman replied, a month before his death, with his final letter to Dworzecki. "I rejoiced mightily that at last a chair for Holocaust research was created at Bar-Ilan and that it was placed in such good hands. You will put into your work not only your great knowledge and devotion, but also your administrative abilities."[51] In Dworzecki's response, he says that he now has the first volume of Friedman's bibliography series in hand,[52] and that he has just come from his class at Bar-Ilan: "It was Philip Friedman hour. I brought your book and showed it to the students; told what I know about you and your historical research; . . . the students were astonished with the book; I send you their collective greeting."[53] Seven days later Friedman died, and the letter bears no indication as to whether it was known to him.

---

49. Letters dated August 18, 1970 and September 8, 1970, respectively.
50. Letters dated July 25, 1957 and January 14, 1958, respectively.
51. Letter dated January 5, 1960. The letter indicates that it was typed by Friedman's secretary, apparently because of his failing health.
52. Friedman, *Bibliyografiyah shel ha-sefarim ha-'Ivriyim 'al ha-Sho'ah ve-'al ha-gevurah* (Jerusalem, 1960).
53. Letter dated January 31, 1960.

The interconnections revealed by the historians' correspondence are confirmed by their published works. They frequently cite each other's writings, especially in the first decade of their work when fewer published sources by others were available. As seen in the table on page 52, the publishing venues for these historians' works frequently overlapped, implying both a common endeavor and a shared readership that included each other. All except Dworzecki worked together in the *Pinkas ha-Kehillot* (Encyclopedia of Jewish Communities) and *Entsiklopediyah shel Galuyot* (Encyclopedia of the Diaspora) projects.[54] Blumental and Kermish collaborated on three major documentary projects in the 1960s.[55] Trunk undertook and carried to completion the Judenrat study begun by Friedman before his death. Of the forty *yizkor* books so far identified to which any of these historians contributed, six include contributions by two of the historians—with a division of labor between the prewar and Holocaust-era historical articles. At seven conferences of Jewish or Holocaust studies between 1945 and 1977, in Lodz, Paris, Jerusalem, and New York, two or more of these historians coincided as presenters and in the published papers, and at the Yad Vashem Conference on Manifestations of Jewish Resistance in 1968, organized by Dworzecki, papers were presented by all four of the historians then still living.[56] In the 1953 volumes of *YIVO bleter* and *YIVO Annual*, devoted to Holocaust studies and coedited by Friedman, contributors include Friedman, Trunk, and Kermish (who quoted Blumental in his text).

The longer-lived among the historians eulogized the departed: Trunk and Kermish published memorial essays about Friedman (as did

---

54. Contributions to the former, the *Chronicle of [destroyed] Communities*, are anonymous; those in the *Encyclopedia of the Diaspora* are listed in the bibliography.

55. Blumental and Kermish, eds., *Mul ha-oyev ha-Natzi: Lohamim mesaprim 1939–1945*, vol. 1, with joint introduction (Tel Aviv, 1961), consisting almost entirely of Yiddish narratives; *ha-Meri veha-mered be-geto Varshah / Resistance and Revolt in the Warsaw Ghetto: A Documentary History* [in Hebrew] (Jerusalem, 1965); and *Shimon Huberband, Kiddush ha-Shem—Ketavim mi-yeme ha-Sho'ah* (Tel Aviv, 1969).

56. These conferences were (with the historians' initials): Second Academic Conference of the CJHC, Lodz, 1945 (F, K, T); Conférence européenne des commissions historiques et des centres de documentation juifs, Paris, 1947 (F, K; paper by B); Second World Congress of Jewish Studies, Jerusalem, 1957 (F, K); YIVO Colloquium on the Judenrat, New York, 1967 (B, T); First Yad Vashem Conference (on resistance), 1968 (B, D, K, T); Second Yad Vashem Conference (on Jewish leadership), 1974 (D, K); Third Yad Vashem Conference, 1977 (T, K).

Auerbach),[57] and they spoke at the memorial services for Friedman in New York and Jerusalem, respectively.[58] Kermish contributed the memorial essay on Trunk that appeared in Trunk's posthumous collection of Yiddish writings.[59]

The Absence of Women among the Historians

That not any of the historians discussed here are women is both an accident of history and a reflection of their time. Had Bella Mandelsberg-Shildkroyt (an active member of the *Yunger historiker krayz*) survived the Nazis, she would likely have been among these historians. Blumental, who had been her teaching colleague in Lublin during much of the 1930s, prepared a posthumous Festschrift in Israel in 1965 of her prewar Yiddish works in Hebrew translation.[60] Had Tatiana Bernstein not remained at the Jewish Historical Institute in Warsaw when others left for the West, she too would be discussed here. More often, the custom of the times dictated that women subsume their careers within those of their husbands. Friedman's postwar wife, Ada Eber,[61] who received her doctorate in history from the University of Lwów before the war, joined the staff of the CJHC in June 1945 but worked primarily to assist her husband, also editing his writings for posthumous publication and helping to prepare the final volume of his Holocaust bibliography project (in which she is credited as "Mrs. Philip Friedman").[62] This mirrors the lifelong relationship of Friedman's friend and mentor, Salo Baron, and his wife, Jeanette, who assisted in editing Baron's works and whose editing enabled Friedman to

---

57. Trunk, "Dr. filip fridman, der historiker," *Di tsukunft* (October 1961): 390–93 and Kermish, "D"r filip fridman—der historiker fun khurbn," *Di tsukunft* (April 1975): 151–54.
58. "Memorial Meeting for Dr. Philip Friedman," *News of the YIVO* 74 (April 1960): 7*; "Azkarah le-D"r Filip Fridman," *Davar* (February 16, 1960): 3.
59. Kermish, "Yeshaye trunk z"l," in Trunk, *Geshtaltn un gesheenishn* [*naye serye*] (Tel Aviv, 1983), 7–16. English translation in Trunk, *Łódź Ghetto: A History*, trans. and ed. Robert Moses Shapiro (Bloomington, 2006), xi–xxviii.
60. Blumental, ed., Bela Mandelsberg-Shildkroyt, *Mehkarim le-toldot Yehude Lublin* (Tel Aviv, 1965).
61. See Naomi Flax Tepfer, "Dr. Ada Eber-Friedman," *Morningside Gardens News* (January 18, 1975): 3; (February 28, 1975): 3 (both formerly online).
62. Jacob Robinson, assisted by Mrs. Philip Friedman, *The Holocaust and After: Sources & Literature in English* (Jerusalem, 1973).

enter the world of English-language publishing in America.[63] Similarly, Dworzecki's posthumous bibliography and the completion of a biographical sketch of Kermish were undertaken by their respective widows.[64] The only woman regularly associated with the Yiddish historians was Rachel Auerbach, but she did not train or practice as a historian.

The Historians and Yiddish

The Yiddish historians of the Holocaust belonged to the last generation of Jewish intellectuals whose careers began in the secular, trilingual culture once idealized by Simon Dubnow.[65] It embraced three languages—Yiddish, Hebrew, and the language of the land, in their case, Polish—and, not surprisingly, it proved an unstable linguistic model. Each language became the vehicle for a competing approach to modernization as Jews transitioned from traditional small-town life to urban modernity in the period between the pogroms of 1881–82 and World War II. Proponents of Yiddish and Hebrew saw in their languages weapons against assimilation and, in turn, promoted their opposing goals of Diaspora nationalism and Zionism. In interwar Poland, networks of Jewish schools, publications,

---

63. Friedman expresses his "warm thanks to Mrs. Jeanette M. Baron for her helpful assistance in stylistic revision and correction of this paper" in his article, "The European Jewish Research on the Recent Jewish Catastrophe in 1939–1945," *Proceedings of the American Academy for Jewish Research* 18 (1948–1949): 179; similar assistance may have occurred with his articles in *Jewish Social Studies* in 1940 and 1941 while still in Europe.

64. See the bibliography of Dworzecki's works edited by his widow, Hasia, in *'Iyunim bi-tekufat ha-Sho'ah: asupat ma'amarim le-zikhro shel Prof. Me'ir Dvorz'etzki z"l*, ed. Mordecai Eliav (Jerusalem, 1979), 129–39. Regarding Kermish's unpublished autobiographical sketch, see note in bibliography. The eventual emigration from Poland to Israel of Ber Mark's widow, Esther Goldhar-Mark, who had published work of her own in the early years of the JHI, enabled her to complete her husband's final work, *Megiles oyshvits* (Tel Aviv, 1977).

65. Shimen Dubnov, *Dos bukh fun mayn lebn*, vol. 3 (Buenos Aires, 1962), 89. For discussions of this trilingualism, see Koppel S. Pinson, "Simon Dubnow: Historian and Political Philosopher," in *Nationalism and History: Essays on Old and New Judaism by Simon Dubnow*, ed. Koppel S. Pinson (Philadelphia, 1958), 50–53; Chone Shmeruk, "Hebrew-Yiddish-Polish: A Trilingual Jewish Culture," in *The Jews of Poland Between Two World Wars*, ed. Yisrael Gutman et al. (Hanover, 1989), 285–311; Benjamin Harshav, *Language in Time of Revolution* (Berkeley, 1993), 24–27; Joshua Shanes, "Yiddish and Jewish Diaspora Nationalism," *Monatshefte* 90, no. 2 (Summer 1998): 179.

and political parties affiliated with each of the three languages competed for adherents.[66]

These historians functioned in all three language systems. They learned Yiddish in their childhood homes and, as demonstrated by their writings, became proficient in academic-level Yiddish well before the opening of Yiddish schools. They graduated from secular Jewish gymnasiums with levels of Hebrew literacy ranging from excellent (Friedman, Dworzecki, and Trunk), to more than adequate (Kermish), to less fluent (Blumental). Following gymnasium, all received degrees from European universities for theses and dissertations written in non-Jewish languages.

In this trilingual environment, the historians had complicated relationships with language, as seen in two bilingual publications. The journal of the Landkentnish Society had Polish and Yiddish sections, the former tending toward Polish-Jewish acculturation and the latter toward Jewish particularism. Friedman and Trunk contributed only to the Yiddish section, as did Mahler, Ringelblum, Schiper, and the journalist Auerbach. By contrast, the publication of the Warsaw Jewish Community was also bilingual,[67] but in this case, as might be expected, a review of their contents finds that the Yiddish portion favored traditional and religious themes while the Polish one treated current issues and modern Polish-Jewish history, often in combination. Here, Friedman and Kermish wrote solely for the Polish portion, together with Balaban and Schorr (and also, one might note, Adam Czerniaków, the future leader of the Warsaw Judenrat, whose ghetto diary Kermish would later edit for publication). Such nuances of language politics resulted in an equally complicated alignment of languages among these historians in prewar Poland. Friedman's publishing was the most multilingual, with approximately one-third of his

---

66. Regarding the pre–World War I period in which the Yiddish historians themselves were educated, see Kh. S. Kazdan, *Fun kheder un 'shkoles' biz tsysho* (Mexico City, 1956), particularly chapter 9 ("Yiddish under Fire from Two Directions"); for the interwar period in Poland, see Kazdan, *Di geshikhte fun yidishn shulvezn in umophengikn poyln* (Mexico City, 1947), which treats the secular Yiddish and Hebrew schools and religious schools (but with more detailed and sympathetic coverage of the Yiddish school movements). On the Yiddish schools and their teachers, see Trunk, "Der monument fun dem yidishn folks-lerer [review of Kh. Sh. Kazdan, ed., *Lerer yisker bukh: di umgekumene lerer fun tsysho shuln in poyln* (New York, 1954)]," *Unzer tsayt* (July 1955): 49–51.

67. *Di kehile-shtime / Głos Gminy Żydowskiej.*

output in Yiddish, one-half in Polish, and the remainder in Hebrew or German. Trunk and Blumental appear to have published exclusively in Yiddish, Dworzecki primarily in Yiddish and occasionally in Hebrew, and Kermish exclusively in Polish.

Trunk and Blumental were partisans for Yiddish. In a 1938 review of his brother's Yiddish book on psychotherapist Alfred Adler, Trunk complains that scholarly works "are still an abysmal void in our literature." He argues, "The time when there was no consumer for a serious scholarly book in Yiddish is, it seems to me, already behind us," but, he claims, scholarship in Yiddish is scarce and "little is translated from foreign-language literature."[68] His own first book—on the history of the Jews in Płock—was written in Polish (for Balaban at the University of Warsaw) and was translated by Trunk into Yiddish for publication by YIVO.[69] The other prewar partisan for Yiddish was Blumental, who published an appeal in 1929 for funds for a *folks-shul*, which he celebrates as the oldest "with Yiddish as the language of instruction" in Galicia and, to his mind, the "greatest 'sight' [worth seeing] in our Galician cultural life."[70] Throughout the 1930s, Blumental himself taught Polish in a Jewish gymnasium, but his extracurricular activity was the surreptitious teaching of Yiddish language and literature to his students, and he published many articles on these topics in Yiddish periodicals.

Most complex in his prewar language relations was Dworzecki, who preached against Yiddishism—but did so in the Yiddish press. In addition to practicing as a medical doctor and publishing medical articles in Yiddish, he was immersed in Jewish public affairs, particularly Zionism, and wrote for both the Yiddish and Hebrew Zionist presses. A frequent topic of his writing was the conflict then occurring between proponents

---

68. Trunk, "Di lere vegn mentsh [review of *Alfred adler: der mentsh un zayn lere* (Warsaw, 1938) by Trunk's brother, Israel Trank (pseud. of Srul-Shiye Trunk)]," *Os* 2, no. 2 (February 1938): 43.

69. "Protokol fun der zitsung fun prezydyum fun der historisher komisye, 29ster april 1938," *YIVO bleter* XLVI (1975): 301.

70. Blumental, "Der goyrl fun a yidisher shul in a galitsishn shtetl," *Tsushtayer: draykhadoshim shrift far literatur kunst un kultur* 1 (September 1929): 64. The quotation marks in Blumental's text enclose "zeens-virdikayt," apparently to indicate its loan-status from the German *Sehenswürdigkeiten*.

of Yiddish and Hebrew in Vilna.[71] One of his most strident articles, in the Warsaw Yiddish daily *Haynt*, attacked adherents of the General Jewish Labor Bund. It was the report of a mock trial in 1929 titled, "The Bundist School System in the Dock," in which he notes that Vilna was known "as the Bastille of Yiddishism and as the spiritual center of the bitterest opponents of the Jewish national movement." He claims that YIVO, "which ignores Hebrew," is not "Yiddish" (i.e., "Jewish") but "Yiddishist" (i.e., anti-Zionist), thus partially conflating YIVO with the Bund for rhetorical effect.[72] The following year, he wrote approvingly of the founding, within the worldwide PEN Club movement, of a separate branch in Jerusalem for Hebrew writers—arguing the the Yiddish branch in Vilna had failed to represent the interests of all Jewish writers worldwide, and he published his statement in the Yiddish section of a bilingual Polish-Yiddish journal of Jewish thought.[73] Since the departure of the Russians from Vilna during World War I, the legal status of the city and its Jews had been contested, and an argument for Yiddishism was that without their own language, the Jews could not claim political, economic, or cultural rights as a national minority.[74] In 1932, Dworzecki reported in the Hebrew press that the leadership of the Union of Yiddish Writers and Journalists had proposed "to all the writers in Vilna that they should influence the Jewish public to record Yiddish in the census questions as their 'parents' language,'" to which he objected, saying they "did not have the authority to impose their view on those who hold another view."[75] It is unclear from his writings whether his own view of Yiddish was closer to Borochov's Zionism-*and*-Yiddish or Ben Gurion's Zionism-*in*-Yiddish. However, as

---

71. In Yiddish, Dworzecki wrote regularly for *Di tsayt* of Vilna. In Hebrew, he wrote as Vilna correspondent for the Warsaw daily *ha-Tzefira*, published by Zionist leader Nahum Sokolow. See, for example, his "Yeme ha-shitafon be-Vilnah," *ha-Tzefira* (April 29, 1931): 3.

72. As is well known, YIVO director Max Weinreich withdrew from the Bund to give nonpartisan leadership to YIVO. However, Dworzecki had correctly identified YIVO as an intellectual center of Diaspora nationalism. See further regarding this article and Dworzecki's politics in chapter 2.

73. Dworzecki, "Vegn yidishn un hebreyishn pen-klub," *Trybuna Akademicka* (September 1, 1930): 18–17 (Yiddish section).

74. Shmuel Kasov, "Zalmen reyzen un zayn gezelshaftlekh-politish arbet: 1915–1922," *YIVO bleter* New Series II (1994): 74ff.

75. Dworzecki, "Yeme ha-shitafon be-Vilnah," 3.

will be seen from his later work, he was—or would become—a proponent of Yiddish itself.

In contrast to the general observation that the destruction of European Jewry similarly diminished the vitality of the Yiddish language, the opposite prevailed among the Yiddish historians of the Holocaust. They belonged to that smaller class of survivors who chose to defy the destruction of the Nazi years, integrate their prewar and postwar lives, and expand their ties with fellow survivors by maintaining and augmenting their use of Yiddish. It is notable that nearly all of their letters to each other are written in Yiddish.[76]

Whereas one-third of Friedman's published output had been in Yiddish before the war, the proportion rose to one-half after the war.[77] The lesser-known aspect of Friedman's postwar career is that, apart from his teaching at Columbia University and service to YIVO, his primary employment in New York from 1949 to 1956 was as dean of the Jewish Teachers' Seminary and People's University, "the only tri-lingual Jewish teachers training institute in the United States."[78] Founded in 1918 by the Labor Zionists to supply teachers for the Yiddish school movements, it was in Friedman's words, "the only place in America where Yiddish language and Yiddish literature, Yiddish composition, grammar, Yiddish folklore and lifestyle, and Yiddish popular traditions are taught in

---

76. The exceptions are a few in Hebrew to or from Dworzecki, and a very few, generally perfunctory, between Trunk and Kermish. Most of these exceptions date from periods directly following visits to Israel by Friedman or Trunk. One other exception is that Auerbach divided her correspondence to Friedman and Trunk between official matters in Yiddish on Yad Vashem letterhead and personal letters in Polish; in general, they responded accordingly. Correspondence between Trunk and Israeli Holocaust historian Shaul Esh is in Yiddish, despite Esh's well-known partisanship for Hebrew.

77. These figures are based on Friedman's bibliography (privately published, 1955), and the posthumous continuation (presumably by his widow) held in the YIVO Archives, RG 1258, F 538, both supplemented by the additional items listed in the bibliography.

78. "Jewish Teachers Seminary Celebrates First Degree-Granting Program," *Jewish Telegraphic Agency* (January 10, 1962), www.jta.org/1962/01/10/archive/jewish-teachers-seminary-celebrates-first-degree-granting-program. Yiddish historians connected with the seminary include Shatzky, who taught there from 1925 to 1935; Bernard Weinryb, who preceded Friedman as dean; and Mahler, who serialized his wartime research project on the Karaites in Yiddish in the seminary's bilingual journal, *Gedank un lebn / The Jewish Review*.

a fundamental manner."[79] The official history of the seminary gives repeated praise to Friedman for devoting himself "heart and soul" to its welfare.[80] Friedman's installation address in February 1949 echoes the concern shared by many Jewish educators in postwar America that "linguistic assimilation" would lead directly to "total assimilation," and he rejects the view, still much debated by Yiddishists in later decades,[81] that "Jewish content can also be disseminated and deepened in non-Jewish vessels, namely, in the language of the country."[82] In his 1951 review of the most recently published volume of the Yiddish encyclopedia, he laments the lack of university-level Yiddish textbooks and relates that he tested the encyclopedia as reading material among his seminary students, who "were inspired by the articles." He concludes by recommending its use by all higher-level Yiddish schools and "Yiddish culture clubs, youth groups, and self-study circles across the country."[83] For the following volume, he contributed a lengthy article on the history of American Jewish organizations, including their efforts to help Jews during World War II.[84]

Several years after Friedman's death, Trunk found in the Jewish Teachers' Seminary the place to pursue the doctorate he had not acquired in Warsaw. It was the only institution in America that granted doctoral degrees for dissertations written in Yiddish.[85] There, in 1969, Trunk

---

79. Friedman, "Der idisher lerer seminar," *Idisher kemfer* (March 14, 1952): 11. As part of the training program for teachers in Yiddish and Hebrew schools, the curriculum also included, in Friedman's words, "intensive instruction in Hebrew studies," ranging from language to Bible to Israeli demography. In 1967, the Herzliah Hebrew Teachers' Institute was merged into the JTS&PU, and in 1979 both were merged into the Judaic Studies Department of Touro College.

80. Yisroel Shtaynboym, *Di geshikhte fun yidishn lerer-seminar un folks-universitet in nyu-york* (Jerusalem, 1979), 119–20; 135.

81. See discussions quoted within, and arising from, Janet Hadda's "Imagining Yiddish: A Future for the Soul of Ashkenaz," *Pakn Treger* (Spring 2003): 10–19.

82. Friedman, "Di tsiln un oyfgabes fun yidisher hekherer dertsyung in amerike baym hayntikn tog," *Bleter far yidisher dertsyung* I, no. 1 (June–September 1949): 52.

83. Friedman, "Di yidishe entsiklopedye—a kapitl kultur-geshikhte fun undzer dor," *Di tsukunft* (March 1951): 133.

84. Friedman, "Sotsyale un politishe bavegungen [in the US]," *Algemeyne entsiklopedye*, vol. Yidn V (New York, 1957), 42–83.

85. Between 1962, when it received degree-granting authority, and 1977, the ending date of the degrees reported in its official history, the seminary granted 18 doctorates, of which 4 were for dissertations in Yiddish, 3 in Hebrew, and the balance in English. The authors and titles are listed in Shtaynboym, *Di geshikhte fun yidishn lerer-seminar*, 62–63.

received his doctorate with a Yiddish-language dissertation on Jewish life in the ghettos of Eastern Europe under Nazi rule.[86] All of his postwar works, apart from a few prepared for Hebrew journals, were written in Yiddish and published in Yiddish or in English translation. Trunk saw the Yiddish language as not incidental, but elemental, to the history of Ashkenazi Jewry as a national group, and thus essential as a language of scholarship for the continued vitality of Yiddish culture at all its functional levels. Neither he nor the other Yiddish historians left an ideological declaration or manifesto; their ideas must be teased from their various works. Discussing the early modern period in Eastern Europe, he says, "The historical fate of Yiddish is tied to the historical fate of the Jewish folk masses. Together with the national and social awakening of the Jewish masses also began the improving fortunes of Yiddish."[87] In one of his earliest writings after leaving Poland, Trunk writes of the future of East European Jewry after the Holocaust, declaring that "the inheritance that it left us . . . [and] the ideas with which it lived its language—Yiddish, with which it breathed, shall remain a mighty chapter of our spiritual life."[88]

The first joint effort undertaken by the Yiddish historians who left Poland for Israel was the founding of the academic research program at Ghetto Fighters' House. Under Blumental's editorship, two volumes of the Hebrew journal, *Dapim* (Pages),[89] were published from 1951 to 1952 with contributions from Blumental, Kermish, Trunk, Friedman, and others. It was praised by the lay Yiddish historian Julian Hirshaut for having as its purpose "to acquaint the Hebrew reader with the accomplishments of Holocaust research" at a time when it "is well known that the majority

---

86. Trunk, "Ineveynikste farheltnishn in di getos in mizrekh-eyrope unter natsisher hershaft [Internal Relations in the Ghettos in Eastern Europe under Nazi Rule]" (PhD diss., Jewish Teachers' Seminary, May 1969, for the degree, "doctor of Yiddish literature"). YIVO Archives, RG 483, F 52 (title pages only).

87. Trunk, "A pyonerish verk in unzer historish-pedagogisher literatur," *Unzer tsayt* (November–December 1956): 52. Trunk was also punctilious in his Yiddish usage. In one instance, he wrote to the publisher of a forthcoming article to insist that his work be "published as it is written, e.g., according to the YIVO rules of spelling." Letter from Trunk to "Redaktye fun almanakh 'yidish'" (July 1, 1961), YIVO Archives, RG 483, F 26.

88. Trunk, "Tsum 10-tn yortog fun natsyonaln khurbn," *Lebns-fragn* 12–13 (April–May 1952): 6.

89. *Dapim le-heker ha-Sho'ah veha-mered*.

of our Holocaust research has until now been published in the Yiddish language."[90] But condemnation came from the well-known Yiddish literary historian Elias Schulman, who complained, "The historians and researchers who settled in Israel . . . are ignoring Yiddish and limiting themselves only to Hebrew . . . ." Blumental responded in an open letter, dispelling both misperceptions.[91] He wrote that the material was prepared "in fact, mostly in Yiddish" but handed over to the publisher, ha-Kibutz ha-Me'uhad (the United Kibbutz Movement), "which printed the journal at its own expense. And as is well known, that publisher issues books exclusively in Hebrew." Rather, he explained, he and the other editorial board members (Kermish and Tzvi Shner) "undertook various steps to publish the *Dapim* in Yiddish but regrettably could find no publisher and no sponsor who would underwrite the project."

Blumental continued to prepare his own research works in Yiddish, even at Yad Vashem, where his writing was translated into Hebrew for publication.[92] On his visit to pre-state Israel in 1947 to represent the CJHC at the founding conference of Yad Vashem, he observed that the children spoke only Hebrew but that adults spoke "a hearty Yiddish."[93] Late in life he recalled being drawn to the Bund in Israel (though not becoming a member) and to its leader Issachar Artuski, editor of the journal *Lebns-fragn* (Life Questions) in which he published many articles. He recounted that he had been invited to attend a Bund celebration, conducted by Artuski: "Everyone here spoke Yiddish. I felt as if I were in Warsaw at a Jewish mass meeting—altogether *heymish* [homey]. Also, the Yiddish-speaking orators touched on themes that were close to me in those times: Yiddish newspapers, Yiddish schools, Yiddish theater (indeed, all in Yiddish!)."[94]

---

90. Y. Hirshoyt, "Bleter far geshikhte fun umkum un oyfshtand," *YIVO bleter* XXXVI (1953): 310.

91. Blumental, "Briv in redakstye," *Lebns-fragn* 26 (June 1953): 15 (quoting and responding to Schulman's complaint).

92. Blumental, "On the Nazi Vocabulary," *Yad Washem Studies* I (1957): 182.

93. Blumental, "Di 'yad vashem'-konferents in yerusholayim [July 13–14, 1947]: ayndrukn fun nakhmen blumental oyf a tsuzamentref mit yidishe shrayber," *Dos naye lebn* (October 17, 1947): 6.

94. Blumental, "[Issachar] Artuski," in *Yid, mentsh, sotsyalist: y. artuski ondenk-bukh* (Tel Aviv, 1976), 86.

Alone among the Yiddish historians, Kermish did not express himself on the subject of language. Before the war he had published only in Polish, but after the war he immediately commenced writing in Yiddish at the CJHC in Poland. He did so again on arriving in Israel, and continued to publish in Yiddish throughout his career, despite official disapproval in the early years. In one of the occasional statements by a Yiddish historian that requires a more than superficial reading, the first article published by Kermish at Yad Vashem (in Hebrew, on the state of Holocaust research at Yad Vashem) announces that there would be a "journal and bulletin of Yad Vashem in Hebrew and in Yiddish (for the sake of the Diaspora)."[95] This subordination of Yiddish for use only in the Diaspora reflects the position of Yad Vashem's founding director, Ben-Zion Dinur. At the first meeting of the World Council of Yad Vashem in 1956, the Yiddish writer and survivor Israel Tabakman (whose memoir of Nazi-occupied Belgium would soon appear with an introduction by Blumental) was "critical of Yad Vashem for, in his opinion, not using Yiddish sufficiently." In his response, Dinur contended that "Yiddish is not given an inferior status; material in Yiddish and English is sent abroad."[96] The less well-known sequel to this interchange is that shortly before Dinur's departure as director of Yad Vashem in his much-publicized conflict with the survivor-historians, Yad Vashem established a substantive periodical in Yiddish as a forum for the survivor-historians and their readers. Parallel to the Hebrew publication that debuted in 1954 under the name *Yedi'ot* [*News of*] *Yad va-Shem*, it was titled *Yedies fun yad vashem* and appeared from 1957 to 1961. The regular contributors were Blumental and Kermish, as well as editor Natan Eck, with one article each by Dworzecki and Auerbach. Without commenting on his choice of language, Kermish himself published in Yiddish continuously from his first appearance in the Israeli literary journal *Di goldene keyt* (The Golden Chain) in 1951, to his last in 1988, and he contributed one of the few Yiddish chapters to appear in the Hebrew-language *Encyclopedia of the Jewish Diaspora*.[97]

---

95. Kermish, "la-Matsav ba-hoker ha-Sho'ah," *Yedi'ot Yad va-Shem* 1 (April 30, 1954): 9.
96. "Sesye funem veltrat fun yad-vashem [April 19, 1956]," *Yedi'ot Yad va-Shem* 10–11 (August 1956): 35 (English).
97. Kermish, "Di endgiltike tseshterung fun varshever geto" in *Entsiklopediyah shel Galuyot*, vol. XII: Warsaw 3, ed. Kh. Barlas et al. (Jerusalem, 1973), 383–406.

After the war, Dworzecki embraced Yiddish with increased fervor, while not lessening his commitment to Hebrew. One of the first articles he published after his escape from captivity, "My last days in a concentration camp," appeared in Yiddish adjacent to an announcement of his upcoming speech in Hebrew on the theme, "Cultural Work in the Vilna Ghetto (1941–1943)."[98] As early as December 1945, he expressed concern for unity between the Land of Israel and the Diaspora and set forth the novel, if not already moot, proposal: "In the Diaspora, where we carry out cultural work primarily in Yiddish, we should, for the sake of the wholeness of our culture, acquaint the people simultaneously with the age-old and new values of Hebrew." And, from the opposite side: "In the Land of Israel, where all cultural activity and agriculture and trade are forged only in Hebrew, we must ... acquaint the people with the values of Yiddish that have coalesced over recent centuries."[99] With this latter goal apparently in mind, when he was a delegate to the twenty-second Zionist Congress in Basle in 1946, he proposed the creation of a chair in Yiddish at the Hebrew University of Jerusalem, but lack of support forced him to withdraw the suggestion.[100] In his writings in Paris he continued to advocate communal unity, but by 1948 he had come to despair of a Jewish future in France and resolved to leave for Israel. He concurrently conceived a more sober assessment of the future status of Yiddish in Jewish culture, "of which Hebrew is its beginning—its continuity—its eternity." He concludes, "Yiddish is a portion of it, an inseparable ring in its age-old chain. And Yiddish will be hallowed in our inherited treasure, just as Aramaic was hallowed in our inheritance."[101]

Once in Israel, Dworzecki did not sentimentalize Yiddish but intensified his commitment to its use. He joined the Yiddish Writers and Journalists Union and was elected to the directorate, serving with Bundist leader Artuski, surviving Vilna poet Avrom Sutzkever, and leading Yiddish journalist

---

98. Dworzecki, "Di letste teg in a kontsentratsye lager," and announcement by "Berit 'Ivrit Tzarfat" (Hebrew Union of France) of a lecture by Dworzecki on "ha-'Avodah ha-tarbutit be-Geto shel Vilnah (1941–1943)," *Unzer vort* (May 25, 1945): 2.

99. Dworzecki, "Integrale idishe kultur," *Idisher kemfer* (December 28, 1945): 7.

100. "ha-Haktsavot le-hinukh ule-tarbut," *Davar* (December 24, 1946): 1. As is well known, the first such proposal for the Hebrew University was defeated in 1927, and a chair in Yiddish was not established until 1951.

101. Dworzecki, "ba-Meh Madlikin?," *Kiem* (December 1948): 698.

Mordechai Tsanin.[102] Although he had adapted enthusiastically to life in Israel, working as a doctor for the national health service and running on the *Mapai* party ticket for the Knesset, he did not adopt the widespread Israeli tendency to disparage Yiddish as the language of the Diaspora and of defeat. In an exchange published in 1958 in an Israeli Yiddish periodical, he rejected, as he put it, the "wild statement said by someone in Israel: 'With Yiddish they went to Treblinka, with Hebrew to Sinai.'"[103] His first books, written in Paris, had appeared in Yiddish and French. Writing in Israel, he was assured of publication in Hebrew but continued to seek publication in Yiddish. A letter to Friedman in 1955 sought advice in finding a Yiddish publisher for his latest book,[104] and he succeeded in securing publication in Yiddish in Israel for each of his further major works.

The cumulative result of the Yiddish historians' postwar commitment to Yiddish is seen in the table on the following pages.

Each of the major postwar Yiddish scholarly, literary, and political periodicals in Europe, Israel, and America is represented by contributions from one, and usually more than one, of the Yiddish historians. To these are added occasional appearances in other periodicals and anthologies and over seventy articles in *yizkor* books that extend their publishing venues to Mexico, Argentina, Brazil, and South Africa. Their works were reprinted across decades and continents, in a few instances apparently without the author's knowledge, and in others posthumously. The bibliography of each historian's writings prepared for the present work charts the later publishing history of each of the entries. These reveal a further process of republication and translation, continuing beyond each historian's lifetime.[105] The outstanding example is Trunk's 1962 history of the

---

102. "Yerlekhe farzamlung fun yidishn literatn un zshurnalistn-fareyn," *Lebns-fragn* 70–71 (June–July 1957): 25.

103. Dworzecki, "Kh'varf op a. shulmans artikl (a briv in redaktsye)," *Heymish* 19–20 (January 17, 1958): 16.

104. Friedman suggested YIVO, but Dworzecki found success with Y. L. Perets in Israel. Letters dated February 16, and March 4, 1955, respectively; YIVO Archives, RG 1258, F 57.

105. Especially notable as reprints are works by Dworzecki (1965) and Kermish (1978) in the 1991 anthology, *Yidish-literatur in medines-yisroel*. Translations of long duration include an article by Friedman (1952) in Horowitz's 2011 anthology, two by Trunk (1953, 1969) in Marrus's 1989 anthologies, one by Blumental (1968) in the Wellers-Klarfeld 1989 anthology, and one by Kermish (1956–57) in *Masu'ah* in 1996; all except Kermish's were posthumous.

Principal Yiddish Publishing Venues of the Yiddish Historians of the Holocaust

	Friedman	Trunk	Blumental	Kermish	Dworzecki
Poland					
Bleter far geshikhte and *Yedies* (JHI)	—	1948–49	1948–49	1948–49	—
Dos naye lebn (Official)	1945	1947–48	1945–48	1945–48	—
Yidishe shriftn (Official)	—	1949	1949	1949	
France					
Kiem [Kiyum] Unzer kiem (Leftist)	1948–53	—	1948	1953, 1965	1948–68
Israel					
Di goldene keyt (Labor Zionist)	—	1953, 1967	1953–57, 1969	1951–88	1954–71
Heymish (Leftist)	1958	—	1958	1958	1957–60
Lebns-fragn (Bundist)	—	1952–53	1953, 1958–80	—	—
Yedies fun yad vashem	—	—	1957–61	1957–61	1958
Yerusholayimer almanakh (Ex-Soviet)	—	—	—	1974–78	—
United States					
Idisher kemfer (Labor Zionist)	1949–55	—	—	—	1945–54
Folk un velt (World Jewish Congress)	1958	—	1968	—	1954, 1959
Di tsukunft (Socialist)	1949–59	1953–80	1978	1975	1946–47, 1955, 1969
Unzer tsayt (Bundist)	—	1954–67, 1979	—	—	—

Yidishe kultur (Communist)	1945	—	1945–82	—	1961
YIVO bleter; Yidishe shprakh	1950–53	1953–80	1948, 1956–63	1953	1947
Book Publishers					
Dos poylishe yidntum series (Buenos Aires)	1950	1962	1948	1964	—
Y. L. Perets Farlag (Tel Aviv)	—	1983	1960, 1981	1985	—

Lodz Ghetto, which appeared in 2006 in an English translation by his former student, historian Robert Moses Shapiro.

The Yiddish Historians as Public Figures

The Yiddish historians of the Holocaust were among the intellectual elite of postwar Yiddish-speaking survivors—for three reasons. First, they enjoyed the status accorded to national figures, largely unknown in Western Europe and America, that was customary for historians of national movements in Central and Eastern Europe.[106] For example, when Friedman wrote to the editor of an Israeli Yiddish periodical—whom he had met on his visit to Israel in 1957—to point out a factual error, his letter was published at the top of a page with a headline that appears to boast of the honor received: "A Correction from Historian Dr. Philip Friedman."[107] To this professional regard was added the rarer distinction in

---

106. This status was related to the close association between historians and emergent national movements. See, i.e., Dennis Deletant and Harry Hanak, *Historians as Nation-Builders: Central and South-East Europe* (Basingstoke, 1988); Monika Baár, *Historians and Nationalism: East-Central Europe in the Nineteenth Century* (Oxford, 2010).

107. Friedman, "An oysbeserung fun historiker d"r filip fridman," *Heymish* (December 5, 1958): 2. Friedman had met the editor, Moyshe Grosman, during his visit to Israel and had previously written to thank him for sending the publication (presumably without charge), saying that he read every issue and that it exceeded in quality many prewar publications. Letter dated April 23, 1958, YIVO Archives, RG 1258, F 364.

the Yiddish-speaking world of holding advanced degrees. In the style of Central and Eastern Europe, their names were always preceded by "Dr." or "Mgr." when spoken or printed, as in the cited example, and this was not limited to the public sphere. A cousin of Friedman's reports, "I recall meeting him on several occasions as a child. Out of respect, we always called him Dr. Friedman," adding, "I remember him as a very serious man, someone who seemed to hold the weight of the world on his shoulders."[108] Only Blumental permanently retained the status of *magister*, yet many editors prefixed his name with the honorific "Dr.,"[109] and the Israeli Yiddish journal to which he contributed most often added the inaccurate title "Prof." to the headline of his obituary.[110] In addition to these professional and academic attainments, the historians held the still rarest of distinctions: they had survived the trauma that preoccupied the postwar Yiddish-speaking world, and they offered special expertise in explaining and organizing an understanding of that trauma. Thus, the immigration of Kermish to Israel in 1950 was greeted with a feature story in the Hebrew newspaper *'Al ha-Mishmar* by Noah Gris, his former colleague at the CJHC, that integrated each of these forms of special regard in the headline, "Arrival of Shoah Researcher Dr. Joseph Kermish."[111]

The Yiddish historians of the Holocaust quickly became public figures. In the late 1940s, Friedman and Dworzecki spoke often at public

---

108. Martin Kent, "In Honor of the Holocaust Remembrance Day." Kent, a documentary filmmaker, reports that Friedman "was the first cousin of my mother's mother" (April 9, 2010), www.jpost.com/Magazine/Features/Years-later-we-would-remember.

109. One of these was the New York journal *Yidishe kultur*, edited by his cousin Nachman Meisel, whose editor's note for Blumental's first contribution (June 1945, p. 13) says, "Completed Warsaw University, his doctorate—a chapter of a fundamental work on [literary] creation in Polish." For this, and all subsequent articles, his byline reads "Dr. Nakhmen Blumental." However, Blumental's name bore no such title as late as 1939 in the *Literarishe bleter*, also edited by Meisel. This honorific "Dr." was also added by the editors of *yizkor* books, but it did not appear in any publication with which Blumental was directly associated.

110. "Prof. nakhmen blumental," *Lebns-fragn* 379–80 (November–December 1983): 21.

111. Noah Gris, "le-Ba'o shel hoker ha-Sho'ah D"r Yosef Kermish," *'Al ha-Mishmar* (June 14, 1950): 2. This long biographical article was also preceded by the short front-page announcement, "Dr. Joseph Kermish, the Jewish historian who was one of the founders and directors of the Central Jewish Historical Commission in Poland, author of a book on the Warsaw Ghetto Uprising and many other works of Jewish history—arrived in the country on the liner *Kommemiyut*." *'Al ha-Mishmar* (June 7, 1950): 1.

events in Paris, and their appearances were chronicled in the leading Yiddish literary journal.[112] On settling in New York, Friedman became one of the speakers at YIVO's forthcoming annual conference, in January 1949, at which he spoke on Jewish ethical and moral behavior during the Nazi era.[113] Attending his talk was the well-known poet Melech Ravitch, an acquaintance of Friedman's in Poland before the war and a founder of *Literarishe bleter* in Warsaw. Ravitch thereupon invited Friedman to deliver a six-day series of lectures in Montreal at the Jewish Public Library and *Folks-universitet*, of which he was the director.[114] In Montreal, Friedman's audience included Benjamin Orenstein, the lay historian who would become his earliest biographer and for whose Holocaust memoir Friedman had recently written the foreword.[115] Orenstein reports that Friedman was an "excellent and brilliant orator . . . possessed of supernatural strength. His listeners literally saw before their eyes the events of historical times, epochs and generations, which he masterfully related in a popular, clear, precise, and rich manner of speaking."[116]

Lest this enthusiastic reception imply an overly "popular" treatment, it should be recalled that Friedman was addressing the same "educated lay audience" that had been cultivated by Yiddish historians before the war. The version of his address that appeared in Yiddish indicates his opinion of the Yiddish-speaking audience, both as to comprehension and expectation.

---

112. See "Khronik," *Kiem* (May 1948): 349 (noting, separately, Friedman's imminent arrival from Munich and his heading the list of speakers at the celebration for Dworzecki's book on the Vilna Ghetto); (July–August 1948): 508 (Friedman and others speaking at a press conference for the Centre de documentation juive Contemporaine, at which Friedman was director of research); (April 1949): 954 (Dworzecki and others speaking at the opening of the Yiddish literary club, "Tłomackie 13"); (June 1949): 1081 (Dworzecki and others speaking at the Yiddish Writers and Journalists Union on the new Yiddish history of Zionism by Jacob Tsineman); and previously: (April 1948): 288 (noting, separately, publication of the journal coedited by Friedman in Munich and the speech at the Writers Union in Paris by Raphael Mahler on his return trip from Poland to America).

113. "Program of the Twenty-Third Annual Conference of the YIVO," *News of the YIVO* 30 (December 1948): 6*.

114. Melekh Ravitch, "D"r filip fridman," *Mayn leksikon* 4, no. 2 (Tel Aviv, 1982): 197.

115. Binyomin Orenshteyn, *Dos lebn un shafn fun d"r filip fridman* (Montreal, 1962) and *Khurbn chenstokhov* (Munich, 1948). The introduction to the latter was prepared by Friedman in his capacity as director of education for the American Joint Distribution Committee in the Displaced Persons camps of the US Zone of Germany.

116. Orenshteyn, *Dos lebn un shafn fun d"r filip fridman*, 47.

In the Labor Zionist *Idisher kemfer* (Jewish Fighter) of New York, his first paragraph announces that his discussion will be limited to "the social-ethical problematic that has developed with regard to our recent catastrophe," adding, "I will undertake only to lay out the problems. To analyze them in detail is a further work, for the future." In the sister publication, *Jewish Frontier*, the wording was revised to meet the author's or editor's assessment of English-language readers. Friedman's opening apologia was discarded, the overall text shortened and simplified, and references to Jewish historians, including Graetz and Dubnow, as well as Blumental, deleted.[117]

Each of the Yiddish historians followed the same tradition of presenting learned papers to audiences of educated laypersons. For the lecture series presented in 1952 by the Friends of YIVO in Israel, Trunk spoke on the state of Holocaust historiography and Kermish discussed sources for the study of the Holocaust period.[118] In the 1953 series, Trunk previewed his article, "Western European Jews in the Eastern European Ghettos," and, at an evening commemorating the tenth anniversary of the Warsaw Ghetto Uprising, Blumental spoke on the Ringelblum Archive and Kermish analyzed new documents on the uprising.[119] During Trunk's subsequent years in New York, he continued his public lectures at YIVO annual conferences as Friedman had done. A later example is his talk on tendencies in research on the Warsaw Ghetto Uprising on its thirtieth anniversary in 1973.[120]

In Israel, Dworzecki became a frequent speaker on Holocaust themes and achieved renown in both the Yiddish and Hebrew press.[121] He was the principal speaker at the joint commemoration of the ghettos presented

---

117. Friedman, "Etishe un sotsyale problemen fun unzer katastrofe in der natsi tkufe," *Idisher kemfer* (September 8, 1950, Rosh Hashanah): 54–58; "Jewish Reaction to Nazism," *Jewish Frontier* (September 1950): 20–24.

118. M. Ravitsky, "Gezelshaft 'fraynt fun yivo' in yisroel vert alt 2 yor," *Lebns-fragn* 12–13 (April–May 1952): 29; "Fun der tetikayt fun di yivo-fraynd in yisroel," *Yedies fun YIVO* 46 (September 1952): 3; English 5*. Among the other speakers were Mahler and Auerbach.

119. "Di geto-fayerungen in yisroel," *Lebns-fragn* 25 (May 1953): 7; "YIVO tetikayt in medines-yisroel," *Yedies fun YIVO* 50 (September 1953): 4; English 4*.

120. "Tsvey hoykhpunktn fun moderner yidisher geshikhte / Two Crises in Modern Jewish History [on Trunk's presentation about research on the Warsaw Ghetto Uprising at the YIVO Annual Meeting, May 6, 1973]," *Yedies fun YIVO* 126 (Summer 1973): 1–2; English 1*–2*.

121. In addition to items noted in the Yiddish press, of which a few samples are given in the text, an online search of the Hebrew press returns more than 400 results for

in a Tel Aviv movie theater in April 1961 by Yad Vashem, YIVO, and the Yiddish Writers Union. The Yiddish press reported that the theater had more than 1,900 seats, "which were completely filled," and that hundreds more listeners remained outside—"so strong is the desire for a Yiddish word in Israel."[122] Dworzecki also spoke on behalf of Yad Vashem at the dedication of a street in memory of the martyred Bundist activist Shmuel (Artur) Zygielbojm.[123] On a return visit to Paris in January 1967, a speech by Dworzecki was announced by his Yiddish publisher (Undzer kiem) with a page-wide headline, "Great 'Undzer kiem' evening with the participation of Dr. M. Dworzecki." On the same page appears the news of a "Literary Evening in Tel Aviv" that had recently celebrated Dworzecki's new Yiddish book, *Hirshke glik*, on the author of the partisan hymn in the Vilna Ghetto.[124]

In 1960, Dworzecki provided the foreword to the history of the Lodz Ghetto written by lay historian A. Wolf Yasni, a former member of the CJHC in Poland.[125] In Yasni's preface, he thanks Dworzecki for "encouraging and stimulating" his work, and he honors his former colleagues at the CJHC: "With deep respect and pain at his premature death, I recall my friend and teacher, the famous Jewish historian Dr. Philip Friedman, who brought me into the [CJHC] after the war," and "wishing them long years: Dr. Joseph Kermish . . . and Mgr. Nachman Blumental," both of whom he thanks for assistance with archival research.[126] The publication of his book was marked with a public symposium presented by Dworzecki, Blumental, the author, and Bund president Artuski at Zygielbojm Hall, the Bund headquarters in Tel Aviv.[127]

Dworzecki, of which three quarters appear in *Davar*, the official Labor-Zionist daily with which he was most aligned politically.

122. "Fun organizatsyoneln lebn," *Lebns-fragn* 115–16 (May–June 1961): 22.

123. "Derefent di gas u. n. fun artur ziglboym," *Lebns-fragn* 138–139 (June–July 1963): 10.

124. "Groyser 'undzer kiem'-ovent mit der bateylikung fun dr. m. dvorzshetski," *Undzer kiem* (February 4, 1967); "Literarisher ovent in tel-aviv tsum dershaynen fun bukh 'hirshke glik,'" *Undzer kiem* (January 1967); both on inside front cover.

125. Dworzecki, foreword to A. Volf Yasni, *Di geshikhte fun di yidn in lodzsh in di yorn fun der daytscher yidn-oysrotung*, vol. 1 (Tel Aviv, 1960), 7–11.

126. Ibid., 2. See also A. Volf Yasni, "Tsvantsik yor 'yidisher historisher institut' in poyln," *Lebns-fragn* 154 (March 1965): 6–7.

127. "Fun organizatsyoneln lebn," 23.

The Yiddish historians also became known to the public through electronic media. Blumental was among the first, appearing in evening "prime time" on a Yiddish radio program in Israel titled "Voice of Zion for the Diaspora" in 1952. He had recently contributed two chapters to the *yizkor* book of the city of Lublin, and he spoke about the Jewish history of Lublin for a series of talks subtitled "Holy Communities of Israel."[128] An unusual contribution to public education was Blumental's preparation in 1958 of "liner notes" for a long-play vinyl phonograph record of a Yiddish drama by actor Shammai Rosenblum, intended to give public exposure to the story of the Jews of the Lodz Ghetto.[129]

In New York, YIVO conducted a Yiddish radio program from 1963 to 1976, on which Trunk appeared at least three times as the featured speaker, and Blumental once. Trunk spoke in 1964 about the progress of his research at YIVO and Yad Vashem on the Jewish Councils, in preparation for his forthcoming book, *Judenrat* (during which he quoted only one other researcher in the field, Blumental);[130] in 1965, about Jewish resistance to the Nazis (commencing with a quote from Dworzecki);[131] and in 1968, about his recent conference paper at Yad Vashem on the varied attitudes of Jewish Councils toward armed resistance.[132] Blumental's appearance coincided with his visit to YIVO in 1967 for its Judenrat Colloquium (at which Trunk also appeared), and he spoke on Jewish conduct during the Holocaust.[133]

---

128. "Kehilot Lublin be-'Kol Tzion la-Golah,'" *'Al ha-Mishmar* (September 11, 1952): 3. Giving the radio program a Diaspora-oriented title may have been in part a deliberate misdirection (during the early, anti-Yiddish period of the state), as it was publicized and broadcast within Israel.

129. Liner notes to vinyl LP recording, *"Yizkor": In Memory of the Victims of the European Jewish Catastrophe 1940–1945: Play by Shammai Rosenblum, Recitator and Actor* [Hebrew, English, Yiddish] (Tel Aviv, 1958, produced by Yad Vashem and World Jewish Congress).

130. Web page: https://yivo.org/isaiah-trunk-on-the-lodz-ghetto-1964; sound recording: https://yivo.org/cimages/14yivo-wevd-podcast12201964.mp3. (The URL and web page are misleading; Trunk's topic was not his previous research and book on the Lodz Ghetto.).

131. Web page: https://yivo.org/interview-with-isaiah-trunk-on-anti-nazi-jewish-resistance-1965; sound recording: https://yivo.org/cimages/39yivo-wevd-podcast11211965.mp3.

132. Web page: https://yivo.org/Historian-Isaiah-Trunk-on-Holocaust-Research; sound recording: www.yivo.org/cimages/69yivowevdpodcast691968.mp3.

133. Web page: https://yivo.org/The-Role-of-Jewish-Police-in-the-Ghettos-1967; sound recording: https://yivo.org/cimages/47-yivo-wevd-podcast12171967.mp3. (The URL and web page are misleading; Blumental's topic was not the Jewish Police and the Judenrat.).

Previously, in 1963, Trunk appeared in a Yiddish radio program to publicize the major exhibition he had cocurated at YIVO on "Life, Struggle, and Uprising in the Warsaw Ghetto."[134] One of the very last media appearances by a Yiddish historian was a pair of talks given in April 1986 by Kermish on the evening Hebrew-language "Open University" television program of Israel Channel 1: "Nazi Germany during the Shoah" and "Jewish documentation created during the Shoah and its fate."[135] A number of interviews of Kermish also appeared in the Hebrew press, featuring his work.

These efforts by the Yiddish historians in the dual areas of historical research and public remembrance were rewarded with public honors. Kermish, for example, received several awards in the later years of his career: in 1984, the award of the World Federation of Polish Jews; in 1985, the prize in memory of Yiddish-Hebrew writer Itzhak Nimtzovich; and, in 1987, his premier award, the Ka-Tsetnik Prize at Yad Vashem, which he shared with British Holocaust historian Martin Gilbert. On this final occasion, one of the Yiddish journals to which he contributed, the *Yerusholayimer almanakh*, congratulated both recipients, "Dr. Martin Gilbert of England ... and our *heymisher* Dr. Joseph Kermish of Jerusalem," saying, "We greet heartily the awardees, and especially—our colleague, the beloved Joseph Kermish."[136]

Dworzecki became the only Yiddish historian to receive a state honor for his scholarly work when he was awarded the first Israel Prize in social science in 1953 in recognition of the Hebrew translation of his Vilna Ghetto history. A decade later, he received the prize of the Académie Nationale de Médecine in France for an article on the treatment of

---

134. "Haynt radyo-simpozyum vegn geto-oyfshtand," *Forverts* (June 9, 1963): 12. See also the exhibition catalog, *Oysshtelung: lebn kamf un oyfshtand in varshever geto / Exhibition: Life Struggle and Uprising in the Warsaw Ghetto* (New York, 1963).

135. "ha-Ti'ud ha-Germani-Natzi mi-yeme ha-Sho'ah" and "ha-Ti'ud ha-Yehudi she-notzar ba-Sho'ah ve-goralo" (television lectures, Open University, Channel 1), "Modi'in [current day television schedule]," *Ma'ariv* (April 7, 1986): 14; (April 14, 1986): 14.

136. "D"r yosef kermish un prof. martin gilbert—laureatn fun k. tsetnik-prayz," *Yerusholaymer almanakh* 18 (1988): 228. The Ka-Tsetnik Prize continues to be well known, but I have located no additional information on the other two awards; this award information comes from the unpublished autobiographical sketch of Kermish provided by Dov-Ber Kerler, whose father, Joseph Kerler, was editor and publisher of the Y.A. at the time.

post–concentration camp pathologies.[137] This latter award provided the occasion for a Yiddish feature article in Paris, headlined, "Dr. M. Dworzecki—Laureate of the Medical Academy in France."[138] Three other awards of his career illustrate the geographic range of his reputation and readership: the Leyb-Hoffer Prize established by the Argentine branch of the World Congress for Jewish Culture and presented at a banquet in his honor in Paris in 1949,[139] the 1957 Tzvi Kessel Prize in Mexico for Jewish Literature,[140] and the Holocaust literature prize established in New York in memory of Yiddish actress Diana Blumenfeld, a survivor of the Warsaw Ghetto.[141] Such awards remain little known outside the world of Yiddish letters but within that world were its principal honors. On the first anniversary of Dworzecki's death, a prize in Holocaust literature was created in his memory at the Yiddish Writers and Journalists Union in Israel, and the first recipient was Rachel Auerbach.[142] In 1981, the sixth Dworzecki prize was awarded to Blumental.[143]

In New York, Trunk received both Jewish and non-Jewish honors. Twice, he received the National Jewish Book Award—in 1967 as coeditor of the final volume of the Yiddish encyclopedia (on topics in Holocaust history), and in 1975 for his magnum opus, *Judenrat*, on the Jewish

---

137. Louis S. Copelman and Marc Dvorjetski, "Le traitement des asthénies et des anxiétés, séquelles de la pathologie concentrationnaire et post-concentrationnaire." See *Archives et manuscrits de la Bibliothèque de l'Académie nationale de médecine*, http://ccfr.bnf.fr/portailccfr/jsp/ccfr/sitemap/ead_sitemap_view.jsp?record=eadcalames%3AEADC%3ACalames-2012614126343078.

138. Yisroel Korn, "Dr. m. dvorzshetski—laurat fun der meditsin-akademye in frankraykh," *Undzer kiem* 34 (January 1964): 12–13.

139. "Khronik," *Kiem* (September–October 1949): 1244. The prize was for the original Yiddish version of his *Yerusholayim d'lite*.

140. The prize was for the Hebrew translation of the same. "Three Authors Win Prizes for Best Works of Jewish Literature in 1957," *Jewish Telegraphic Agency* (December 27, 1957), www.jta.org/1957/12/27/archive/three-authors-win-prizes-for-best-works-of-jewish-literature-in-1957.

141. It is possible that Dworzecki received the only award of this prize. One of the few outside references to it is the account of its creation by a memorial committee formed after her death in 1961 in Zalmen Zilbertsvayg, "Diana Blumenfeld-Turkov," *Leksikon fun yidishn teater*, vol. 4 (New York, 1963), 3188.

142. "Tikun toes," *Lebns-fragn* 107–8 (November–December 1977): 19. The prize was established in 1976 by his friend and fellow survivor from Vilna, the Yiddish memoirist Leyzer Engelshtern.

143. "Kultur-khronik," *Lebns-fragn* 349–50 (May–June 1981): 24.

Councils, written in Yiddish but published in English translation.[144] His signal honor was the receipt of a National Book Award from the National Book Foundation in 1973 for *Judenrat*, a unique achievement for a nonfiction work translated from Yiddish. This process of translation, in the linguistic and also cultural sense, is among the themes discussed in chapter 6.

As it happened, the only Yiddish historian to receive no awards or prizes was their acknowledged leader, Philip Friedman, whose death at the age of fifty-nine rendered his postwar career of fifteen years less than half the lengh of any of his colleagues' productive periods but left a published output of nearly equal quantity and widely praised quality. The statement by Salo Baron in his introduction to the posthumous collection of Friedman's works that "Friedman has been called 'the father of Holocaust history'" has itself been much quoted yet appears to derive from Baron's own wish to honor his friend with such a title. Of greater interest and specificity is another statement by Baron, published by him in two different versions twenty years apart. Immediately after Friedman's death in 1960, Baron described Friedman in his memorial address to the Academy for Jewish Research as "one of the founders of what is rapidly becoming almost a new discipline within Jewish studies."[145] The address was reprinted in 1980 as his introduction to Friedman's collected works. With twenty years' additional assessment of the field and of Friedman's place within it, Baron declares Friedman to be, simply, "the chief founder of a new discipline of Jewish studies."[146]

---

144. "Jewish Book Council Announces Awards for Five Books Published in 1966," *Jewish Telegraphic Agency Daily News Bulletin* XXXIV, no. 98 (19 May 1967): 4. As an indication of the place still held by Yiddish letters in American life, the president of the Jewish Book Council at the time was Hyman Bass, one of the best known and most prolific American Yiddish educators, authors, and editors.

145. Salo Wittmayer Baron, "Philip Friedman," *Proceedings of the American Academy for Jewish Research* 29 (1960–61): 1.

146. Salo Wittmayer Baron, Introduction to Philip Friedman, *Roads to Extinction*, ed. Ada June Friedman (New York, 1980), 1.

2

BECOMING YIDDISH HISTORIANS OF THE HOLOCAUST

Among the "surviving remnant" of East European Jews who endured the Nazi period, a remnant of intellectual leaders also survived—and, among these, a few who would become the professional historians of the Yiddish-speaking community of survivors. Their seemingly natural turn to writing Holocaust history was not inevitable. How did it happen that they, and not others, pioneered the study of the Jewish history of the Holocaust? What led them to develop an approach to Holocaust history that did not focus on the martyrdom of the victims or on exceptional cases of Jewish heroism—but on the everyday life (and not death) of the Jews under Nazi occupation? The explanation lies in a convergence of three historical circumstances.

First, Yiddish historiography had developed during the interwar period as an *anti-lachrymose* approach to Jewish social and cultural history, which proved unexpectedly suitable for the study of Jewish life under Nazi domination. Second, the survivors who became Yiddish historians of the Holocaust retained a constancy of personal attitudes, affinities, and interests that was not predictable from the discontinuities of their wartime experience. Third, by accident of fate, they, and not others, were present in Poland at the start of the war, and they emerged with the determination to study and convey to their fellow survivors the Jewish history of the Nazi period. These are the topics of the present chapter.

The Study of Jewish Life under the Nazis

In their occasional reflective writings on the Holocaust as a field of study, the Yiddish historians applied familiar methods to a new historical period. Their "historiosophy" (to use Philip Friedman's term) rarely extended to considering the effects of the Holocaust on the future of historical writing. Such themes as "rupture" and "discontinuity," so often applied to the Holocaust and its consequences, do not appear in their writings. It is only in their rare excursions to places of personal memory—as, for instance, in revisiting their prewar towns to find them devoid of Jews—that they describe, without naming it, the phenomenon of rupture. Where the Holocaust is proclaimed by John McCumber to be the "master rupture" that generates the secondary ruptures studied by postmodern historians and philosophers,[1] the Yiddish historians remained positivist seekers of continuities and proximate causes. The much-quoted statement by Jürgen Habermas that "Auschwitz has changed the basis for the continuity of the conditions of life within history"[2] is not anticipated in their works. Dan Diner's concept of a "rupture in civilization," arising from the Jewish encounter with unprecedented evil, is touched on only as one of various explanations for Jewish action or inaction.[3] The Yiddish historians found in the lives of Jews during the Holocaust not an interruption, but the intensified continuation of earlier trends and processes in Jewish history. Their unspoken task was to document the streams of pre-Holocaust Jewish life that continued to flow within the Nazi abyss.

How, then, is it possible to reconcile the Yiddish historians' focus on the Jewish history of the Holocaust with the relative absence from the field of most other Jewish historians during the early postwar years? A key is the Yiddish historians' non-martyrological approach to the study of

---

1. John McCumber, "The Holocaust as Master Rupture: Foucault, Fackenheim, and Postmodernity," in *Postmodernism and the Holocaust*, ed. Alan Milchman and Alan Rosenberg (Amsterdam-Atlanta, 1998), 247.
2. Jürgen Habermas, *Eine Art Schadensabwicklung* (Frankfurt a. M., 1987), 163.
3. See generally, Dan Diner, "'Rupture in Civilization,' On the Genesis and Meaning of Concept in Understanding," in *On Germans and Jews under the Nazi Regime*, ed. Moshe Zimmermann (Jerusalem, 2006), 33–48.

Jewish life under Nazi occupation in contrast to the usual conceptions of early Holocaust study as necessarily and exclusively concerned with the tragic outcome. Michael Marrus notes that early "historical discussion of the Jews under Nazism was primarily concerned with martyrology," as typified by the tragic personal accounts published in the *yizkor* books, and he contends that study of the victims was avoided because it was "perhaps seen as professionally inappropriate."[4] Lucy Dawidowicz contends that the "shock of the Holocaust probably accounts for the paucity of historical research" by early scholars and suggests that the best hope for Holocaust research lay (in 1969) with young Israeli historians, who have the "ability to face death—its idea and its reality."[5] David Engel provides an academic variant of Dawidowicz's tragic conception of the field with the argument that students of Salo Baron avoided Holocaust studies through an exaggerated allegiance to Baron's anti-lachrymose conception of Jewish history (discussed further below).[6]

Each of these historians cites Philip Friedman and one or more of the other Yiddish historians as the exceptions that *prove* the rule of early disinterest in Jewish Holocaust studies. Arguing the contrary point, historians of a later generation—such as Natalia Aleksiun, Boaz Cohen, and Laura Jockusch—cite Friedman and his colleagues as the exceptions who *disprove* the rule of early disinterest. Friedman is also cited by Hasia Diner as evidence against the "Myth of Silence" among Jewish historians in America.[7] Implicit in each argument is the assumption that Holocaust research was a natural imperative for survivor-historians and that their approach to the field differed from that of other Jewish historians, for whom the tragic nature of the subject was presumably a disincentive.

And yet, perhaps surprisingly, it was the Yiddish historians' anti-lachrymose approach to Jewish history that made possible their study of

---

4. Michael R. Marrus, *The Holocaust in History* (Hanover, 1987), 112 and 201.

5. Lucy S. Dawidowicz, *The Holocaust and the Historians* (Cambridge, 1981), 139 and 56.

6. David Engel, *Historians of the Jews and the Holocaust* (Stanford, 2010), 42ff. Although Engel does not mention the existence of a Jewishly centered trend of Holocaust historiography in the early postwar years, inclusion of the Yiddish historians in his narrative would not have undermined, but rather validated, his thesis.

7. Hasia R. Diner, *We Remember with Reverence and Love: American Jews and the Myth of Silence after the Holocaust, 1945–1962* (New York, 2009), 121.

the Holocaust. The notable characteristic of their works is a focus on Jewish life under Nazi occupation, and the struggle to sustain it, rather than on the forces that sought to extinguish it. Isaiah Trunk argues that "until the moment of final destruction, the ghetto *existed* for 2–3 years.... For us the question of how the ghetto lived is no less important than the question of how it was murdered."[8] Friedman similarly emphasizes that "within a Jewish life existed! Whatever it was, the ghetto teemed with activities, there were constant changes and developments in its life ... sudden metamorphoses and developments in the social and economic fabric."[9] Joseph Kermish reports that the work of the Central Jewish Historical Commission (CJHC), like Ringelblum's Oyneg Shabes project before it, "was already not confined to accounts of physical suffering and murder, but concentrated on the life of the Jews in conditions of danger and destruction."[10] Nachman Blumental analyzes the motifs of ghetto literature and concludes: "First of all, we are struck, to our great amazement, that despair—in emotion or thought—is found in so small a number of poems,"[11] and Friedman thereafter quotes Blumental to the same effect.[12] Blumental also rebuts the critical view of Holocaust literature later formulated by Theodor Adorno, who declared the writing of poetry after Auschwitz to be barbaric and argued that "turning suffering into images" wrongly supplants horror with something that "contains, however remotely, the power to elicit enjoyment."[13] Instead, in his preface to the first Yiddish book printed in Poland after the

---

8. Trunk, "Sotsyale antagonizmen in geto un di rol fun di yudenratn," *Yidishe shriftn* 6, no. 26 (June 1949): 6 (emphasis his).

9. Friedman, "Preliminary and Methodological Problems of the Research on the Jewish Catastrophe in the Nazi Period," *Yad Vashem Studies* II (1958): 96.

10. Kermish, "D"r filip fridman—der historiker fun khurbn," *Di tsukunft* (April 1975): 152. First published in Hebrew and English in *Yedi'ot Yad va-Shem* 23–24 (May 1960): 4–6 and *Yad Vashem Bulletin* 6–7 (June 1960): 4–6; see bibliography.

11. Blumental, "Di yidishe literatur unter der daytshisher okupatsye," *Yidishe kultur* 8, no. 1 (January 1946): 10.

12. Friedman, "Etishe un sotsyale problemen fun unzer katastrofe in der natsi tkufe," *Idisher kemfer* (September 8, 1950, Rosh Hashanah): 54; omitted from the English translation (see bibliography).

13. Theodor W. Adorno, "Commitment," in *Aesthetics and Politics*, ed. Ernst Bloch et al. (London, 1977), 189. The leading literary historian and critic Shmuel Niger argues, contrary to Adorno, that it is often necessary to add literary artistry to Holocaust accounts to render them more readable and thereby further the goal of educating the public: Shmuel Niger, ed., *Kidush hashem* (New York, 1948), 10.

war—a book of Holocaust-themed poetry—Blumental finds "a beginning of the renewal of Jewish life in Poland."[14]

Friedman endorses the anti-lachrymose approach to Jewish history in reviewing the first new volume of the Yiddish encyclopedia to appear after the Holocaust. He quotes from the introduction the statement, "'In order to *spin further the historical thread* . . . it is necessary, first of all, to know precisely what the past created and which of its elements can become valuable building blocks for the future,'" and he responds: "The editors, in the midst of the Holocaust, faced directly toward continuity and not death." Anchoring this sentiment in Jewish tradition, he appends the phrase, *le-hayim velo le-mavet* (for life and not for death—taken from the twice-yearly Jewish prayer for rain), concluding, "When the future historian of that period, in darkness, doubt, and loss, seeks a stream of light, he also needs to think of this introduction."[15]

For at least a generation before Salo Baron's first public formulation of the anti-lachrymose conception in 1928, an anti-lachrymose approach to Jewish history had been practiced, if not articulated, by the leading Jewish historians of Eastern Europe. Baron's well-known essay, "Ghetto and Emancipation," called on Jews to "break with the lachrymose theory of pre-Revolutionary woe" that painted the medieval period uniformly dark and the post-Enlightenment period equally bright.[16] He later extended this corrective to Jewish history as a whole, and his view achieved broad acceptance among other Jewish historians. In the case of the Yiddish historians, however, it may be more accurate to suggest that the anti-lachrymose view—set forth by Baron shortly after he arrived in America—had arisen within the same forward-looking cultural milieu that gave rise to the writing of Jewish history in Yiddish. As discussed in the introduction, a turn to the internal social and economic history of the Jews had emerged first among Jewish historians in late Imperial Russia and then in newly independent Poland. These historians set a new course

---

14. Blumental, foreword to Mendl Man, *Di shtilkeyt mont: lider un baladn* (Lodz, 1945), 4.

15. Friedman, "Di yidishe entsiklopedye—a kapitl kultur-geshikhte fun undzer dor," *Di tsukunft* (March 1951): 130 (emphasis his).

16. Salo W. Baron, "Ghetto and Emancipation: Shall We Revise the Traditional View?," *Menorah Journal* 14 (June 1928): 526.

for the historiography of Eastern European Jewry that was both national and optimistic, in reaction to the *Geistes- und Leidensgeschichte* (history of scholarship and suffering) identified with the earlier *Wissenschaft des Judentums* school of German Jewry.

This anti-lachrymose approach to Jewish history prevailed as Yiddish scholarship came to maturity between the world wars. A rare instance to the contrary, which appeared in Raphael Mahler's 1933 history of early Warsaw Jewry, received a rebuke from future Holocaust historian Isaiah Trunk: "In handling the question of the legal situation of the Jews of Mazovia [central Poland] in the fifteenth century, the author accents too little the *positive* aspects and makes too much use of the *negative*."[17]

Reflecting a generally positive view of Jewish history, the works of the interwar Yiddish historians reveal their interest in the internal history of East European Jewry, from late medieval to modern times. They focus particularly on social and economic relations; communal autonomy; Yiddish theater, press, and literature; Jewish guilds and occupations; *Haskalah* and Hasidism; legal, medical and educational systems; and—in a "material turn" that was intended to normalize Jewish history with respect to that of territorial peoples—Jewish art, architecture, antiquities, urban quarters, clothing, and foods.[18]

Within these rubrics, each of the future Yiddish historians of the Holocaust developed his own areas of specialization. Trunk produced synthetic local histories of towns in his home region near Lodz, emphasizing social and economic relations. Blumental gathered materials for a history of his hometown in Galicia before the war, and he published articles on Jewish folklore and Yiddish literature.[19] Dworzecki wrote on the Yiddishist and

---

17. Trunk, review of Emanuel Ringelblum, *Żydzi w Warszawie* (Warsaw, 1932), *YIVO bleter* V (1933): 62 (emphases his).

18. The material turn was a significant element of interwar Yiddish historiography. Methodologically, it was marked by collecting and preserving Jewish archival sources, first inspired by Dubnow's well-known appeal of 1891 to collect Jewish documents, undertaken institutionally by YIVO after 1925. The importance of the archival initiative increased after the Holocaust, when a primary activity of the CJHC, Yad Vashem, and YIVO was the recovery and preservation of materials from the Nazi period. However, regarding the fate of the material turn after the Holocaust, see the latter part of chapter 4.

19. He indicates in the *yizkor* book of his hometown that this was an unpublished history, destroyed during the Holocaust. See Blumental, *Sefer borshtshiv* (Tel Aviv, 1960), 8.

Hebraist school systems in Vilna (prior to his adopting history as a profession after the war). Kermish examined Jewish-Polish political relations from the time of the First Partition to the contemporary period. Friedman, whose interests were broadest, studied the Jewish encounter with modernity in his native Galicia, as well as economic and cultural aspects of Jewish life in Lodz, emancipation, and the Jewish Enlightenment, among other topics.

In sum, not one of the future Yiddish historians of the Holocaust produced a work during the interwar period devoted primarily to Jewish calamity or misfortune. The other Yiddish historians who were active during this period also rarely touched on lachrymose topics. The exception was Elias Tcherikower, whose works on the Ukrainian pogroms of World War I are discussed below, but who addressed this topic almost exclusively from the perspective of the "perpetrator."

The ironic consequence is that the Yiddish historians of the Holocaust could turn to virtually no prewar precedent in Yiddish for the scholarly treatment of Jewish catastrophe *as Jewish history*. They were confronted, both before and after the Holocaust, with a choice between the competing models of historiography and martyrology. The former cultivated an attitude of objectivity (as understood by the historians of the time), emphasizing the skeptical assessment of sources and the search for interrelations among events, while the latter projected an expectation of catastrophe onto the historian's choice of sources and events. Both had significant adherents among contemporary Jewish historians. It was far from certain that the Yiddish historians of the Holocaust would employ the attitudes and methods of secular historical-critical history in their research, and it was also far from certain that they would choose the internal aspects of Jewish life under Nazi domination for their research agenda in preference to the lachrymose paradigm resisted by Baron.

Not only did the Yiddish historians choose to represent the many aspects of Jewish life, but they also did so to the virtual exclusion of its extermination. The great majority of their writings are concerned with Jewish existence in the ghettos—including resistance in all its forms, social structure, communal organization and leadership, medical aid, cultural and political activity, and the daily struggle for existence and its momentary successes—but rarely with the tragic ends met by their protagonists.[20]

Lest this seeming contradiction between the historians' anti-lachrymose representation of events and the tragic outcome of such events suggest a pathology of denial, it should be recalled that the Yiddish historians were not conveying "news" of the Holocaust to a non-Jewish audience, but were exploring all-too-familiar themes for an audience of fellow survivors. The underlying assumption shared by the historians and their readers was an awareness of the ultimate catastrophe. The context of foreboding or imminent disaster that later readers might discern at times only between the lines was, for their intended readers, the dark cloud that was ever present in the historians' works. Thus, it would be misleading and reductionist to equate simplistically the Yiddish historians' anti-lachrymose approach with Baron's proposed corrective to the lachrymose bias. Baron did not propose, nor did the Yiddish historians attempt, to ignore the tragic consequences of Nazism. The demand by Baron that instances of anti-Jewish hatred be considered exceptional and not obscure long periods of tranquility and normal relations with non-Jews was intended to restore emotional balance to perceptions of earlier Jewish history. By contrast, the anti-lachrymose approach of the postwar Yiddish historians was intended to emphasize the positive force of Jewish agency during the Nazi period, while recognizing that it was set against the foregone conclusion of final destruction.

For the present discussion of Holocaust studies by Jewish historians, I propose a distinction between "lachrymosity" and its subset, "martyrology." It may be seen that the lachrymose impulse, turned outward, leads to perpetrator studies, such as those by Léon Poliakov, Gerald Reitlinger, and Raul Hilberg. These are most often "intentionalist" in orientation and lack nuance in their treatment of the Germans, seeing an early intent by Hitler to exterminate the Jews and a widespread willingness of

---

20. Exceptions are occasional articles on public figures, such as Blumental's "Der kidush-hashem fun radziner rebbe," in *Varshever yidn: yubiley-bukh: 1949–1959* (Buenos Aires, 1959), 120–25; and Dworzecki's "Der letster veg fun hirshke glik," *Undzer kiem* 47 (April 1965): 3–5; also, each of the historians' contributions to *yizkor* books on the Holocaust period in specific locales, and chapters of Trunk's *Lodzsher geto* (New York, 1962) and Friedman's *Oshvyentshim* (Buenos Aires, 1950).

Germans to assist. They tend to overlook the "righteous gentiles" among the Germans and the rivalries among Nazi officials that Jewish leaders attempted to exploit. Turned inward, the lachrymose impulse leads to martyrology—the portrayal of individual or group suffering and death, exemplified by the many memorial books that record the names of murdered Jews. Largely omitted from these works is the everyday struggle for survival on which the Yiddish historians based their internal Jewish historiography of the Holocaust.

As an approach to memory, martyrology erases the boundaries of time. It seeks, and finds, an inevitability of catastrophe that allows the motif of Jewish suffering to unite unrelated eras. Surprisingly, the historian most representative of the martyrological view during the early interwar period was Dubnow, despite his pioneering work in the secularizing of Jewish historiography and the related material turn. He was regarded as a spiritual father by most East European Jewish historians, including those who worked in Yiddish, but he did not adopt the optimistic orientation of most Yiddish historians. In the immediate prerevolutionary period, nearly all of Dubnow's many contributions to his own historical journal, *Evreiskaia Starina* (Jewish Heritage), deal with ritual murder accusations, anti-Jewish movements, expulsions, cantonists (the forced child soldiers in nineteenth-century Russia), protective passes, massacres, and the destruction of Hebrew books.[21]

It is not, therefore, unexpected that Dubnow's writings about the post–World War I pogroms would at times adopt the martyrological view. His introduction to Elias Tcherikower's pogrom history of 1923 begins with an invocation of the "thousand-year Jewish martyrology" and ends with a condemnation of "all the Pharaohs of Egypt and the past Hamans up to the collective Hamans of the recent periods."[22] He reiterates this atemporal view with specific reference to the three periods of Ukrainian pogroms in his article for YIVO's *Historishe shriftn* (edited by Tcherikower),

---

21. See Abraham G. Duker's listing of the journal's complete contents, "'Evreiskaia Starina': A Bibliography of the Russian-Jewish Historical Periodical," *Hebrew Union College Annual* VIII–IX (1931–32): 525–603.

22. Shimen Dubnov, "Di drite haydmatshine: historishe hagdome," in E. Cherikover, *Antisemitizm un pogromen in ukrayine 1917–1918: tsu der geshikhte fun ukrayinish-yidishe batsyungen* (Berlin, 1923), 9–15.

in which he claims that "one sees in all of them the exact same picture."²³ Regarding the latter claim, Steven Zipperstein observes that "European Jewry's leading advocate of historicism" has "used his scholarly platform to minimize the importance of social, economic, or political considerations" in analyzing the Ukrainian pogroms.²⁴

By contrast, Tcherikower does choose to emphasize the importance of such considerations, but largely in relation to the perpetrators' actions: "It would have been a serious mistake to see the whole explanation in the [Ukrainians'] historical inheritance and in the mystical formula 'Israel among the nations.' The direct causes of the events lie in the social-economic conditions in the Ukraine of that time."²⁵ As perpetrator history, his studies have been praised for their comprehensive and balanced evaluation of the various pogrom protagonists.²⁶ As Jewish history, his coverage of the victims continues the genre of the Jewish Crusades Chronicles, expanding the number of locations and witnesses, but preserving an immediacy that highlights individual events at the expense of structured narrative. It is, to borrow Ada Rapoport-Albert's phrase, martyrology "with footnotes."

Among the hundreds of works published by Yiddish historians during the interwar period, it would be difficult to identify a half dozen, apart from Tcherikower's pogrom studies, that are devoted to lachrymose topics in whole or in part. The rare occurrences of such topics in the writings of Yiddish historians during the interwar period occur at varying points along the spectrum between historiography and martyrology, further complicating the issue of precedents for Holocaust studies. There are three principal instances, which illustrate the range of such exceptions, as follows.

---

23. Shimen Dubnov, "Der tsveyter khurbn fun ukrayine (1768)," *Historishe shriftn* I (1929): 28.

24. Steven J. Zipperstein, "Ashkenazic Jewry and Catastrophe: A Review Essay," *Polin* 1 (2004): 327.

25. Eliyohu Cherikover, *Di ukrayiner pogromen in yor 1919* (New York, 1965), 12.

26. Elias Schulman, review of Tcherikower, "The Pogroms in the Ukraine in 1919," *Jewish Quarterly Review* 57, no. 2 (October 1966): 159–66; Henry Abramson, "Historiography on the Jews and the Ukrainian Revolution," *Journal of Ukrainian Studies* 15, no. 2 (1990): 33–45.

Closest to the pole of historiography is Isaiah Trunk, who avoids depiction of martyrology in his prewar studies. In his 1934 history of the Jews of Kutno in the eighteenth century, he emphasizes the contemporaneous causes of their political and economic distress.[27] In his 1936 monograph on the Jews of Płock, he devotes a section to the five pogroms that occurred between 1534 and 1656, but, as if in dialogue with Baron's "Ghetto and Emancipation" (not mentioned by any of the prewar Yiddish historians in Europe), he specifically disavows the lachrymose conception: "It would be one-sided and false if we remained silent regarding those, truth be told, small number of facts that give evidence . . . regarding peaceful coexistence and mutual trust."[28] This point was noted with approval in the review of Trunk's work by Mahler, which praises the inclusion of "evidence of peaceful cooperation between Jews and Christians."[29] Trunk also declares that official reports of wounds suffered by Christian attackers reveal that "Jews were well able to defend themselves."[30] This theme of Jewish physical courage is given expanded treatment in an article by Saul Ginsburg, "Daring Jewish Youths and Robbers of Former Times," written to dispel the myth that Russian Jews were cowards, "afraid of a blow and unable to deliver a blow."[31] The only Yiddish historian to discuss Baron's writings before the war was Friedman, who did not comment on Baron's now much-cited argument against "viewing the destinies of the Jews in the Diaspora as a sheer succession of miseries and persecutions."[32]

Tending toward the martyrological pole, Ginsburg appears again, this time with his studies of the cantonists, published from 1924 to 1939. These works are based on Russian archival sources to which Ginsburg gained access after the 1917 revolution and on testimony and eyewitness accounts by former cantonists. His discussion of the actions taken

---

27. Trunk, "A yidishe kehile in poyln baym sof fun XVIII yorhundert: kutno," *Bleter far geshikhte* 1 *("yunger historiker num. 3")* (1934): 87–140.

28. Trunk, *Shtudyes in yidisher geshikhte in poyln* (Buenos Aires, 1963), 62.

29. Rafoel Mahler, review of Trunk's *Di geshikhte fun yidn in plotsk 1237–1657* (Warsaw, 1939), *Jewish Social Studies* III, no. 3 (July 1941): 341.

30. Trunk, *Shtudyes*, 53.

31. Shoyl Ginzburg, "Amolike idishe khvatske yungen un gazlonim," *Historishe verk*, vol. I (New York, 1937), 266 (first portion published in *Forverts*, April 19, 1931, 8).

32. Friedman, review of Salo W. Baron, *Social and Religious History of the Jews* (New York, 1937, vol. 2, 31), *Gilyonot* VII, no. 3 (1939): 241–45.

by Russian officials is judicious, and his description of the fate suffered by the child soldiers is impassioned. Like Tcherikower's pogrom studies, these works provide a combination of outwardly focused historiography and inwardly focused martyrology. In his largely laudatory review of Ginsburg's three-volume collected works, the volume devoted to lachrymose topics receives the least attention by Friedman, and he expresses discontent with Ginsburg's treatment of the cantonists: "To be sure, the subject is not exhausted in this work; actually, only juvenile martyrdom and forcible baptism are described in detail,"[33] suggesting that Ginsburg's coverage of the most painful aspects of the cantonists' history did not suffice as a comprehensive investigation of their lives during the course of their years of conscription.

Thirdly, a simultaneous attraction to both the historiographical and martyrological approaches is illustrated by Friedman's review of the work by Jacob Shatzky on Natan Note Hannover, the chronicler of the Chmielnicki Uprising in 1648. In 1938, YIVO published a Yiddish translation of Hannover's Hebrew chronicle, *Yeven Metzulah* (Deep Mire), with a "historical-critical introduction" by Shatzky. In his review, Friedman praises Shatzky for using the latest Russian, Ukrainian, and Polish sources and for investigating the "causes, course, and consequences" of the Cossack uprising, but he detects a dissonance between the treatment and the subject: "Are they not two works from an entirely different world view? Children of two entirely foreign worlds that do not harmonize with each other?" In this instance, Friedman is unwilling to relegate the emotive martyrological voice to the closed canon and asks, "Would it not have been more fitting to give the *Yeven Metzulah* also an introduction (perhaps a more literary one), that would lead in with the mood and spirit of Nathan Hannover's composition?"[34]

Apart from these isolated examples, Tcherikower's life and work demonstrate that a Yiddish historian might himself oscillate between the historical and martyrological impulses over the course of his career. His writings exhibit an underlying state of historical optimism punctuated by

---

33. Friedman, review of Ginsburg's *Historishe verk* (New York, 1937–38), *Jewish Social Studies* III, no. 1 (January 1941): 97.

34. Friedman, "Gzeyres takh," *Literarishe bleter* (August 19, 1938): 745.

two cataclysmic disruptions—the pogroms of the First World War and the early successes of the Nazis a generation later.

This second disruption led to Tcherikower's pivotal address of January 1941 on "Jewish Catastrophes in Jewish History-Writing" (published as "Jewish Martyrology and Jewish Historiography").[35] Having fled from France in the fall of 1940 during the Nazi invasion, he spoke as the founding head of YIVO's Historical Section to the delegates at YIVO's first annual conference in New York, following the transformation of YIVO's New York branch into its headquarters by Max Weinreich. The address was an expansion of Tcherikower's survey article, "Jewish Historiography," which appeared in 1939 in the Yiddish encyclopedia.[36] In both, he presages Yosef Hayim Yerushalmi's observations on the absence of historical consciousness among Jews in the long interval between ancient and modern times. But in the 1941 version, he presages, further, Yerushalmi's perception of the inability of modern scholarship to provide a satisfying substitute for Jewish collective memory. Tcherikower's remedy is to reintroduce collective memory into the historical narrative by validating traditional Jewish accounts of martyrology, declaring, "without the old historical primitives we should never fully understand the Jewish past and the innermost experiences of the Jewish people, and would soon lose our historical bearings."[37] As Joshua Karlip has noted, it is "the conflict between meaninglessness and redemptive memory" that animates Tcherikower's attempted reorientation of modern historiography toward traditional martyrology.[38]

The paradox of the address is that it offers a tentative, but not further developed, statement of Tcherikower's views on the representation

---

35. E. Cherikover, "Yidishe martirologye un yidishe historiografye," *YIVO bleter* XVII, no. 2 (March–April 1941): 97–112; "Jewish Martyrology and Jewish Historiography," *YIVO Annual of Jewish Social Science* I (1946): 9–23. This work was apparently a late substitute for an intended article on "French Jews, Napoleon, and Jewish Orthodoxy," announced in *YIVO bleter* XVI, no. 2 (November–December 1940): 206.

36. E. Cherikover, "Yidishe historiografye," *Algemeyne entsiklopedye*, vol. Yidn I (Paris, 1939), 283–304.

37. Cherikover, "Jewish Martyrology and Jewish Historiography," 23.

38. Joshua M. Karlip, "Between Martyrology and Historiography: Elias Tcherikower and the making of a pogrom historian," *East European Jewish Affairs* 38, no. 3 (December 2008): 260.

of Jewish catastrophe. Tcherikower reviews past chronicles of Jewish catastrophe, particularly those published in Yiddish, but stops short of discussing his own pogrom studies. His disparaging critique of "our modern scientific study of history" reflects the disillusion he had expressed toward the benefits of Jewish emancipation in his latest European writings—turned now to disillusion with modern scholarship as a means for representing Jewish catastrophe. Taken together, this critique and the omission of his own pogrom studies appear to argue against the use of his pogrom studies as a template for histories of the current catastrophe. However, the momentum of his argument extends only to pointing out the traditional appeal of martyrology in contrast with the work of professional historians. It stops short of attempting a new resolution or synthesis, and Tcherikower offers no further guide for his fellow historians. In his remaining works, he does not return to the dilemma of attempting to craft a martyrological approach to modern catastrophe, nor does he undertake to write Holocaust history itself. Other recent refugees from Nazi Europe, such as the Yiddish lay historians Shlomo Mendelsohn and Leyb Shpizman,[39] began to publish studies of Jews under Nazi occupation as early as 1942, but Tcherikower turned instead to completing his collective history of French Jewry and to commencing his collective history of the American Jewish labor movement before his sudden death in 1943.[40] The sole reference to the Holocaust occurs in his introduction to the work on France, in which he indicates that it is now possible to study the complete history of Jewish emancipation in France from its inception to its liquidation.[41]

By the end of the pre-Holocaust period, the landscape of Yiddish historiography held few guideposts for the treatment of lachrymose topics, and those few gave conflicting direction toward the opposite poles of modern historical scholarship and latent martyrology. Reinforcing

---

39. Shloyme Mendelson, "Vi azoy lebn poylishe yidn in di getos," *YIVO bleter* XIX, no. 1 (January–February 1942): 1–27, and offprints in Yiddish and English. Leyb Shpizman, "Yidn in zaglembye beys der itstiker milkhome," *YIVO bleter* XIX, no. 2 (March–April 1942): 221–31, and *Di yidn in natsi-poyln* (New York, 1942).

40. E. Cherikover, ed., *Yidn in frankraykh*, 2 vols. (New York, 1942); *Geshikhte fun der yidisher arbeter-bavegung in di fareynikte shtatn*, 2 vols. (New York, 1943, 1945).

41. Cherikover, *Yidn in frankraykh*, I:7.

the attraction of the latter was Tcherikower's incipient call for revival of the martyrological approach, which was the sole discussion—however oblique—by a Yiddish historian of possible approaches to catastrophe prior to the development of Holocaust historiography.

It should be noted that two practical considerations may also have deterred the interwar Yiddish historians from researching the events of Jewish catastrophe nearest to them in time and geography, namely, the pogroms of the World War I period. First, they may have considered the anti-Jewish violence of that period in the Ukraine, Galicia, and Vilna to have received sufficient coverage in Tcherikower's pogrom studies and An-sky's much-published travel reports,[42] as well as Zalmen Rejzen's well-known anthology of 1922.[43] Second, censorship (and self-censorship) in interwar Poland may have constrained research on the anti-Jewish violence committed by the Polish army in Lwów in November 1918 and in Vilna in April 1919. Thus, Friedman refers only obliquely to the "heavy losses that the Jews suffered during the most heated battles in Lwów and . . . Vilna" in his review of Polish-Jewish history that appeared in the thirty-year jubilee volume published by the Warsaw daily *Haynt* (Today).[44] His article was later praised by editor Chaim Finkelstein for having "well executed the delicate task" of discussing the anti-Jewish policies of the Polish regime throughout the interwar period in such a manner that the volume "should not be confiscated" but, instead, "appeared without difficulty."[45]

Turning to the immediate postwar period, one finds that the trauma of the unprecedented tragedy redirected the world of Yiddish *literary* creation decisively toward the pole of martyrology. Ruth Wisse has observed

---

42. Sh. An-ski, *Khurbn galitsye: der yidisher khurbn fun poyln, galitsye un bukovina fun tog-bukh 1914–1917* in his *Gezamlte shriftn*, vols. 4–6 (Vilna-Warsaw-New York, 1921–22). This work, which commences with several articles about the wartime period, appeared immediately before the consolidation of Polish rule in Vilna.

43. Z. Reyzen, ed., *Pinkes far der geshikhte fun vilne in di yorn fun milkhome okupatsye* (Vilna, 1922).

44. Friedman, "Di nayeste geshikhte fun iden in poyln," *Haynt yoyvl-bukh* (Warsaw, 1938), 128. Referring to the events of 21 November 1918 in Lwów, Friedman inadvertently gives the date as 21 September.

45. Khaim Finkelshteyn, *"Haynt"—a tsayung bay yidn 1908–1939* (Tel Aviv, 1978), 239.

that Yiddish literature became the vehicle for Jewish mourning after the Holocaust and that "Yiddish traded places with Hebrew, becoming the language of the past, of sacral and historical memory."[46] The transfer to secular Yiddish writing of a task hitherto encompassed by Hebrew chronicles is reflected in the process of anthologizing the lachrymose literary canons of the respective languages: the classic anthologies of pre-Holocaust catastrophe end with the Hebrew works by Shimon Bernfeld of 1923–26 and A. M. Habermann of 1945,[47] and the major anthologies of Holocaust remembrance begin with Shmuel Niger's Yiddish anthology of 1948.[48]

The semi-liturgical use of medieval texts by modern Hebrew anthologists to induce "an emotional bond between the pre-modern sources presented and the modern reader" is discussed by David Myers in his "Crusade Memories and Modern Jewish Martyrologies."[49] Two of the principal strategies noted by Myers in Bernfeld's and Habermann's writings reappear in Niger's Yiddish collection, namely, the joining of historical periods to form an eternally lachrymose inheritance and the conflating of such periods with the present to induce a vicarious response by the modern reader.

As to the first, Myers quotes the statement by Bernfeld that "in our days, we see, unfortunately, that tragedy has not come to an end, but continues. Every historical period is one of the links in this long chain that has no end"[50]—a theme Niger then assumes in referring to the "unend-

---

46. Ruth R. Wisse, *The Modern Jewish Canon: A Journey Through Language and Culture* (New York, 2000), 204.

47. Shimon Bernfeld, ed., *Sefer ha-Dema'ot: me'ora'ot ha-gezerot veha-redifot vehashmadot*, 3 vols. (Berlin, 1923–26); A. M. Habermann, ed., *Gezerot Ashkenaz ve-Tzarfat* (Jerusalem, 1945). During Bernfeld's brief Yiddish phase of 1904–5, his only treatment of an extended period of Jewish history was a little-known essay published by Ginsburg, titled, "Slavery and Liberation of the Jewish People," which epitomizes the black-and-white view of medieval and modern times later rejected by Baron: "Knekhtshaft un bafrayung fun yidishn folk: a historish bild," *Dos leben* (April 1905): 4–17; (May 1905): 59–74. Further, Ismar Schorsch suggests that it was Bernfeld's *Sefer ha-Dema'ot* which inspired Baron's rejection of the lachrymose conception. See "The Lachrymose Conception of Jewish History," in Schorsch, *From Text to Context: The Turn to History in Modern Judaism* (Hanover, 1994), 379–80.

48. Shmuel Niger, ed., *Kidush hashem* (New York, 1948).

49. David N. Myers, "'Mehabevin et ha-Tsarot': Crusade Memories and Modern Jewish Martyrologies," *Jewish History* 13, no. 2 (Fall 1999): 51.

50. Myers, *Mehabevin*, 58.

ing scroll of our people's martyrology."⁵¹ As to the second, Myers quotes Habermann's exclamation, "'We never thought that the Middle Ages would repeat themselves'" and his plea that, in the Crusades materials, "'we will hear an echo of what befell our generation. We will also draw from them strength to bear the pain and offer a bit of consolation in order to continue.'"⁵² Myers posits a "therapeutic" desire "to construct a mythic community of historical fate between past and present"—a desire replicated by Niger in his preface to Sholem Asch's novel of 1919 on Jewish martyrdom in Chmielnicki's time: "What is the meaning of that holy and dreadful page of Jewish history? Never have we so desired to know, as now, when those dark and bitter times have returned . . . ."⁵³

From the literary perspective, David Roskies cites Niger's anthology as evidence that, for postwar anthologists, the "demarcation of time was the first thing to go. In an effort to work through the collective trauma, the surviving Yiddishists blurred the distinction between the culture that was irrevocably lost and the response to that destruction from afar."⁵⁴ Myers, too, is mindful of the role of tragedy in Jewish history and the necessity of memory to a healthy psychology, but he contends to the contrary, that "when the annals of Jewish history are reduced to a martyrology, both historical integrity and a font of creative cultural energy are lost."⁵⁵

As early as 1949, Baron had challenged the martyrological approach to Holocaust study. He rejected the de-historicizing of recent events, claiming, "Too many of us, both scholars and laymen alike, have come to believe that this tragedy was only the final link in a long chain of similar Jewish tragedies."⁵⁶ He similarly rejected the conjoining of historical periods, saying, "It is indeed our duty to examine, as rigorously as possible,

---

51. Niger, *Kidush hashem*, 8.
52. Quoted in Myers, *Mehabevin*, 59–60.
53. Niger, *Kidush hashem*, 865.
54. David Roskies, "The Holocaust According to Its Anthologists," *Prooftexts* 17, no. 1 (January 1997): 99.
55. Myers, *Mehabevin*, 61.
56. Salo W. Baron, "Opening Remarks [at conference on 'Problems of Research in the Study of the Jewish Catastrophe 1939–1945,' New York, April 3, 1949]," *Jewish Social Studies* XII, no. 1 (January 1950): 14.

the dissimilarities as well as the similarities which have existed between the great tragedy and the many lesser tragedies which preceded it."[57]

The question therefore arises: Would Yiddish historiography adopt the martyrological course prefigured by Bernfeld and followed by postwar Yiddish literature generally, or, as it had done in the interwar period, follow a course parallel to (and, in fact, preceding) Baron's anti-lachrymose approach?

Momentarily, in Friedman's first public statement as director of the Central Jewish Historical Commission, published in Lodz in the first issue of *Dos naye lebn* in April 1945, he veered toward the cathartic vision of martyrology offered by the Hebrew anthologists. He declared that each Jewish catastrophe of the past had been followed by retellings of the event that have "helped to bind the past to the future, to pump the fresh breath of life into the dry bones of the tormented people." Later that year, he issued an appeal for information about the lives of murdered Jewish intellectuals for inclusion in a lexicon (a series of *martyrologies* in the classical sense of the term) that would serve as "a book of lamentation for all Jews for all generations."[58] But with this, Friedman's brief excursion into martyrology ran its course, and all of his subsequent writings return to the anti-lachrymose approach of his prewar period.

Friedman later explains that the material available in the early days of Holocaust research "consisted mainly of one kind, *viz.* of descriptions of the suffering inflicted and the atrocities committed by the Nazis. Thus, we were reverting again to the historiographical system of *Leidensgeschichte* which had become obsolete a long time ago."[59] He further excuses this lapse by including Tcherikower:

May I be permitted to say that even a man of Eliahu Tcherikover's calibre, who was *certainly* a long way from the school of thought

---

57. Ibid., 16.
58. Friedman, "Vendung fun der Ts.Yy.H.K.," *Dos naye lebn* (December 1, 1945). A newspaper clipping of the article, saved and hand-dated by Friedman, is among his papers in the YIVO archives.
59. Friedman, "Problems of Research on the European Jewish Catastrophe," *Yad Vashem Studies* III (1959): 31 (Second World Congress of Jewish Studies, Jerusalem, August 4, 1957).

of Zunz and Graetz, opened by giving prominence to the martyrological idea as the central *leitmotiv* in laying down the fundamental points of reference for a study of the Catastrophe.[60]

Had Friedman and his colleagues continued to pursue a martyrological course, they would have joined the very different trajectory proposed by Laura Jockusch in her survey of modern Jewish precedents for Holocaust research. She traces the succession of early pogrom studies, including those by Tcherikower, with their emphasis on "documenting anti-Jewish violence and persecution" and "documentation of Jewish suffering,"[61] as precursors to the Jewish historical commissions created by survivors after World War II. In all of the instances she cites, the emphasis is notably on *documentation*, rather than critical or interpretative history. If this approach to Holocaust study had prevailed among the Yiddish historians, certain secondary aspects of their research agendas might have emerged as their principal concerns: documentation of German crimes, in which they were engaged briefly during the first postwar years and occasionally thereafter (as discussed in chapter 4); collection and publication of eyewitness accounts, in which all were engaged to some degree (as discussed in chapter 3) but which none considered an end in itself; and documentation of Jewish losses of life and property, as pursued by

---

60. Ibid., 31–32. Emphases and spelling per the original. Quoted from Friedman's 1957 address rather than the posthumous version in *Roads*, in which the editing depersonalizes the oral remarks and also directs them to a more general audience. Apart from this oblique reference, Friedman's only direct mention of Tcherikower's article on historiography and martyrology came in his "Fun antihistoritsizm tsum superhistoritsizm," *Kiem* (March 1948): 28–32, in which he argues, without engaging Tcherikower's interest in martyrology, that the recent flood of personal accounts by survivors had reversed the Jews' lack of interest in history. For Friedman's positive prewar assessment of Tcherikower, see his review of YIVO's *Historishe shriftn* III (Vilna-Paris, 1939), which declares Tcherikower's lead article on Russian-Jewish revolutionaries of the 1860s and 1870s "the most significant monographic contribution" to the volume: Friedman, "Di yidishe sotsyalistishe bavegung biz der grindung fun 'bund,'" *Literarishe bleter* (February 21, 1939): 66.

61. Laura K. Jockusch, "Chroniclers of Catastrophe: History Writing as a Jewish Response to Persecution before and after the Holocaust," in *Holocaust Historiography in Context: Emergence, Challenges, Polemics and Achievements*, ed. David Bankier and Dan Michman (Jerusalem, 2008), 136, 145.

Tcherikower's surviving colleague, Jacob Lestschinsky,[62] but which rarely figured in the Yiddish historians' works. Such a documentary enterprise would indeed have accorded with the Talmudic expression, "they cherished their troubles," which Myers cites as an epigram for the lachrymose conception of the Jewish historical experience and its various written manifestations.[63]

Yet the Yiddish historians remained virtually immune to the attraction of martyrology and, in particular, avoided its most pronounced manifestations. Out of more than 500 postwar works published by these historians, it appears that only two short essays depart from the path of critical history to seek metaphysical affinities between events or persons, in pursuit of the "mythic community of historical fate" posited by Myers. These essays, by Dworzecki and Blumental (the only two not originally trained as historians), do so by invoking their authors' personal connections to traditional touchstones of popular Jewish memory, and merit a brief look as examples of the course otherwise not taken.

In a discussion by Dworzecki of H. Leivick's 1949 dramatic poem, *Di khasene in fernvald* (The Wedding in Föhrenwald), Dworzecki identifies with the persona of the "Chronicler" who opens and closes the work. The Chronicler reveals himself to be a descendant of Natan Note Hannover. In the end, he is the one to witness an imagined reconciliation of the "community of the dead" with that of the living at a wedding of survivors in the Föhrenwald D.P. Camp, located on the site of the former extermination camp. With apparent reference to his own experience as a survivor-historian, he describes the Chronicler's role in witnessing the

---

62. Jacob Lestschinsky's *Crisis, Catastrophe, and Survival: A Jewish Balance Sheet, 1914–1948* (New York, 1948) is his best-known work in English and is the post–World War II continuation of his pogrom studies, "Der shrek fun tsiferen (pogrom statistik)," *Di tsukunft* (September–October 1922): 528–32; (September 1923): 546–50, republished in his *Tsvishn lebn un toyt* (Vilna, 1930), 19–53. That the 1948 work, written almost entirely from the lachrymose perspective, was not considered a substitute—or point of departure—for a general Jewish history during the period of the world wars is found in the announcement the following year (by the same sponsoring organization, the World Jewish Congress) of an international competition for "a textbook on Jewish history covering the period of 1914–19[4]8," for which the judges were to be Baron, Blumental, and Dinaburg, among others; see "Competition for Textbook," *The Palestine Post* (May 27, 1949): 6.

63. Myers, *Mehabevin*, 49–50.

symbolic joining of the past and present, declaring, "Not everyone is destined to see it. And not everyone had the privilege of doing so."[64]

Blumental writes of books he recovered from the remains of the Lodz Ghetto or that were brought to him at the CJHC by Polish peasants, in which messages had been left by their owners and for which he finds antecedents in the "Worms, Speyer or Mainz" of 1348 (the year of the Black Death and accompanying pogroms). He cites the Hebrew inscription from Bernfeld's *Sefer ha-Dema'ot* (Book of Tears) that was also cited by Tcherikower in his 1941 address—"I am the sole survivor [of the community]"—and quotes a recent Yiddish inscription by a Jew in hiding: "We are the few remaining Jews in all Poland." Blumental concludes, "that which happened yesterday in such-and-such Holy Community could recur tomorrow or the next day in another place, located nearby or thousands of kilometers away."[65]

Such examples illustrate that martyrology is limiting as a historiographical strategy. It tends to treat events as isolated episodes and to reduce them to familiar patterns, guided by fate rather than contemporaneous cause and effect. As Trunk observed in his final major work, *Jewish Responses to Nazi Persecution* (1979), the *yizkor* books and other popular Jewish treatments reflect "the dimension of *martyrology*, which naturally dominates the field and embodies the obligation to preserve and memorialize the tragic events of the war, if only in their bare detail, in their heartrending repetitiveness."[66] Trunk chooses instead to explore the varieties of active and passive responses to Nazi domination by Holocaust survivors of disparate backgrounds and outlooks—to the specific events of the Nazi period.

The predominance of the non-martyrological approach among the Yiddish historians is evident not only in works by the established historians but also in the writings of Dworzecki, the historian-to-be. During

---

64. Dworzecki, "Hamtze menuhah l'sheyres hapleyte," *Di tsukunft* (December 1955): 498.

65. Blumental, "Oyfshriftn oyf vent, ksovim un bikher," *Lebns-fragn* 145 (January 1964): 10; 146 (February 1964): 7–8. Blumental's wording indicates that he quoted directly from Bernfeld, not from Tcherikower's paraphrase. See Bernfeld, *Sefer ha-Dema'ot*, vol. II (Berlin, 1923), 89.

66. Trunk, *Shtudyes in yidisher geshikhte in poyln* (Buenos Aires, 1963), ix (emphasis his).

his early postwar period in Paris, he was familiar with the publications of the CJHC and became acquainted with Friedman immediately after the latter's departure from Poland. In accord with his own apparent inclination, and possibly reinforced by the example of the Yiddish historians, Dworzecki, too, adopted the non-martyrological approach. One may contrast his early history of the Vilna Ghetto, with the only comparable work, *Khurbn vilne*, by the poet Shmerke Kaczerginski,[67] his friend and fellow ghetto survivor. Dworzecki's is a sociological study of the institutions of collective resistance in the Vilna Ghetto (including lyrics by Kaczerginski to songs of protest), while Kaczerginski's is a collection of first-person martyrologies, many provided by the CJHC, preceded (in the words of Max Weinreich's foreword) by a "chronicle of death" at the Ponar massacre site,[68] followed by a "community *yizkor* lexicon" that lists prominent Vilna Jews who were murdered by the Nazis (including Dworzecki's wife). The same contrast may be observed between the scholarly chapters of Holocaust history contributed to *yizkor* books by all of the Yiddish historians and the chapters of popular memory and martyrology they often precede.

It was this determination by the Yiddish historians—whether by training or inclination—to apply the anti-lachrymose approach of prewar Yiddish historiography to the Holocaust period that made possible their concentration on the Jewish struggle for existence rather than the memory or inevitability of martyrdom.

The Unbroken Chain

The decision by each of the Yiddish historians to undertake the writing of Jewish historiography of the Holocaust was itself dependent on a continuity of personal sensibilities not predictable from their wartime experiences. Collectively, the Yiddish historians endured nearly all of the spatial and familial ruptures encountered by their fellow East European Jews during the Nazi era.

---

67. Sh. Katsherginski, *Khurbn vilne: umkum fun di yidn in vilne un vilner gegnt . . .* (New York, 1947).

68. M. Vaynraykh, introduction to Sh. Katsherginski, *Khurbn vilne* (New York, 1947), X.

Friedman survived in hiding "on the Aryan side" of his hometown, Lwów, with the aid of the philo-Semitic Christian Talmudist, Tadeusz Zaderecki. Blumental fled to the Soviet Union and found refuge in the capital of the Bashkir Autonomous Soviet Socialist Republic. Dworzecki, a doctor in the Polish army at the start of the war, was captured by the Germans, escaped, and returned to his home in Vilna, where he survived the Vilna Ghetto and a series of concentration camps. Trunk and Kermish followed the call of radio broadcasts for military-aged men to flee eastward to form a Polish army of resistance (later described by Trunk as a "bluff" to fool the Nazis).[69] Trunk fled to Białystok in Soviet-occupied Poland, but he was forced to work as a slave laborer in the Soviet Far East, clearing forests in the Komi Autonomous Soviet Socialist Republic. Kermish served as an agent of the Jewish underground, also in the Soviet zone of Poland, and, like Friedman, was hidden by a sympathetic Christian.[70]

In common with most survivors of the Holocaust, all of the Yiddish historians lost their immediate families to the Nazis. Blumental dedicated one of his first postwar writings, "A Voice from the Valley of Lament," to his murdered wife and son.[71] Dworzecki dedicated his history of the Vilna Ghetto to the memory of his father, mother, wife, and two sisters, "and all the other family members, colleagues, and youthful friends murdered in Ponar near Vilna, in the ghettos, in the concentration camps, and in the forests,"[72] and in his testimony at the Eichmann trial he relates having to choose between his wife and mother in using his allotted "passes." Salo Baron recounts that Friedman, "In his personal reticence . . . rarely spoke of this great ordeal in which he lost a wife and a daughter," as well

---

69. Trunk, "The Historian of the Holocaust at YIVO," in *Creators and Disturbers: Reminiscences by Jewish Intellectuals of New York / Drawn from conversations with Bernard Rosenberg and Ernest Goldstein* (New York, 1982), 63–64.

70. Kermish's unpublished biographical statement (see chapter 1 and bibliography) indicates that he was hidden by Franciszek Kamiński, a former fellow teacher at the municipal gymnasium in the Podolian town of Husiatyn (today Gusyatin, Ukraine), then in the Soviet zone of Poland, where Kermish was employed as a teacher of history and later principal, during the period 1939–41. The name is common in Polish, and this rescuer should not be confused with the Polish general or others of the same name.

71. Blumental, "A shtime fun yomer-tol," *Yidishe kultur* 7, no. 6 (June 1945): 13.

72. Dworzecki, *Yerusholayim d'lite in kamf un umkum* (Paris, 1948), 5.

as his mother, a brother, and a sister, "and himself was hounded from one underground location to another."⁷³ Trunk dedicated his history of his hometown to the memory of his mother, sisters, niece, and brothers-in-law who were killed in the Warsaw Ghetto and to his brother, who died soon after his release from a Soviet labor camp.⁷⁴

Despite their early optimism for the rebuilding of Jewish life in postwar Poland, they responded to the resurgent antisemitism and creeping Stalinism of the late 1940s by joining the majority of Polish Jews in their exodus from Poland. None remained after 1950. Friedman left in May 1946 to convey evidence for the Nuremberg Trials and settled in New York in 1948 after periods in Germany and France. Kermish, Blumental, and Trunk left for Israel in 1950, where Kermish and Blumental remained, while Trunk relocated to New York in 1954 following a year of waiting in Calgary. Dworzecki did not return to Poland, but lived in Paris from 1945 until moving to Israel in November 1949. All found new wives among the survivors, and all but Friedman raised new families in their new countries.

Dworzecki, who discussed problems of survivors' reintegration into civil society, offered the comparison that non-Jews returned to their *families*, but Jews "returned only to their people."⁷⁵ The Yiddish historians, too, "returned only to their people," and they did so not only through the writing of Jewish history but through fidelity to their prewar identities as self-reflective Jewish professionals. That fidelity may be observed during the Yiddish historians' postwar careers in the recurrence of their prewar attitudes, affinities, and interests.

It should also be noted that the "Jewish history" of the Holocaust that the Yiddish historians sought to write was of the Jewish world most familiar to them—Poland, broadly construed. Among the Yiddish historians of the Holocaust, only Trunk was born in central Poland, with all of the others originating in the border areas colonized by the medieval Polish-Lithuanian Commonwealth and located outside of present-day Poland. Their definition of Polish-Jewish history embraced nearly all of

---

73. Salo Wittmayer Baron, Introduction to *Roads*, 4.
74. Gabriel Trunk, email to the author, July 24, 2008, including information on Trunk's brother, Israel Trank (Srul-Shiye Trunk).
75. Dworzecki, *Almanakh fun di yidishe shrayber in yisroel* (Tel Aviv, 1962), 343.

the historical Pale of Settlement, including much of present-day Poland, Lithuania, Belarus, and Ukraine, and this territory became the primary locus of their research. Thus, their Jewish history of the Holocaust largely coincides with the Yiddish-speaking heartland of Eastern Europe, where the great majority of Jewish victims of Nazism lived before the war (but generally excluding the experience of Jews in Russia proper, the Balkans, the northern Baltic, and all lands farther west).

Within the geographic limit of the Polish-Lithuanian Commonwealth, the Yiddish historians of the Holocaust sought to extend the historiography of Ashkenazi Jewry as deeply as possible into the years of Nazi occupation. Not surprisingly, their postwar work suggests that the writing of Jewish history after the Holocaust also served to further their personal reintegration across the years of destruction. The following discussion examines the ways in which continuities of prewar political affiliations and personal attributes informed the Yiddish historians' postwar lives and work.

Political Continuities

Before World War II, the future Yiddish historians of the Holocaust were committed to various forms of Jewish nationalism in Poland. More interestingly, each historian's Holocaust writings retained the primary political orientation of his prewar years. Those orientations occupied differing places within the three-part complex of competing Jewish nationalisms in prewar Poland. Although seen in retrospect as the discrete movements known as Polish-Jewish nationalism, Diaspora nationalism, and Zionism, they were not mutually exclusive to any but their most theoretically minded adherents. The religious–secular divide, right-to-left spectrum, and language preferences were overlays that gave additional variation to each form of nationalism. The Yiddish historians represented several of these variations.

In its "pure" form, Polish-Jewish nationalism envisioned a joining of Polish and Jewish national heritages to create a distinctly Polish-Jewish identity; Diaspora nationalism projected a future in which the stateless Jewish nation would enjoy independent cultural development within and beyond the borders of any one country; and Zionism foresaw the restoration of a Jewish national homeland in the Land of Israel. The first tended toward moderate conservatism and the Polish language, the second toward the left and Yiddish, and the third toward every political direction and, in principle, the Hebrew language, but—in accordance with the practical "work in the present" policy adopted at the Helsingfors Zionist conference of 1906—also Yiddish.

Among the Yiddish historians discussed here, Kermish may be described as a Polish-Jewish nationalist with a trace of Zionism; Trunk and Blumental as Diaspora nationalists with elements of Polish-Jewish nationalism; and Friedman and Dworzecki as Zionists with strong tendencies toward Diaspora nationalism and secondary leanings toward Polish-Jewish nationalism. It is not surprising that in prewar output Kermish appeared only in Polish; Trunk and Blumental almost exclusively in Yiddish; and Friedman at times in Hebrew or German but otherwise in Polish and Yiddish. Dworzecki's limited prewar writing was equally in Yiddish and Hebrew. As discussed in the introduction, the choice to write in Yiddish during the interwar period represented a deliberate political statement in support of Yiddish culture, if not an exclusive commitment to Diaspora nationalism. All were secular in professional outlook, but the writings of Friedman, Trunk, and Dworzecki include allusions and metaphors that echo a traditional religious education. None identified with the nineteenth-century trend among Polish-Jewish historians toward assimilation nor with leanings by some of their contemporaries toward Communist internationalism.

Friedman was the most politically diverse of the Yiddish historians. Formally, he was aligned with center-left Zionism. From the completion of his doctorate in 1925 until the start of World War II, he was a teacher of history at the first of the so-called Braude Schools established by the liberal rabbi Markus Braude (prior to the founding of the Tarbut system in 1922), intended to prepare young Jews for eventual immigration to the Land of Israel and, in the interim, to increase national consciousness among Jews in Poland. Nearly all of Friedman's prewar works pertain to the history of Polish Jewry without engaging the cause of Zionism. But to the considerable extent that his historical writing appeared in politically aligned publications, he demonstrated allegiance to the Zionist movement by contributing almost exclusively to the leading Polish, Yiddish, and Hebrew Zionist publications of Lodz, Lwów, and Warsaw, and not to Bundist or Communist outlets.[76] On his arrival in New York, he resumed his connection to the Zionist press with articles in the Labor Zionist monthly, *Idisher kemfer*, and again eschewed other party presses. His sole appearance in the *American Historical Review* was in a positive review of new works favorable to Zionism and Israel.[77]

Friedman's scholarly and civic pursuits in prewar Poland were, however, largely associated with other forms of Jewish nationalism in Poland that contradicted a principal tenet of political Zionism—negation of the Diaspora—and exceeded the scope of practical "work in the present" envisioned by the Helsingfors Program. The spirit of Diaspora nationalism animates the majority of his prewar historical writings, as seen in his optimistic focus on progress in emancipation, economic and social structure, occupational distribution, and educational trends among Jews in Poland. The continuing trajectories of these topics during the Nazi period define many of his postwar writings. Practical support, too, for the project of Diaspora nationalism is found in his efforts to promote the development of scholarly work and institutions in Yiddish, notably through the Vilna YIVO. He contributed significant works to YIVO-sponsored journals before the war, and he returned as an author (and occasional coeditor) after the war. As mentioned in chapter 1, his lectureship in Jewish history at the YIVO *aspirantur* (post-graduate program) in Vilna was one of his few opportunities for university-level teaching before the war, and he continued at YIVO in New York after the war as head of its Historians' Circle.

The third nationalist trend to which Friedman was drawn, Polish-Jewish nationalism, is reflected in his commitment to Jewish regionalism within Poland. As a leader of the *Landkentnish* (Knowing the Land) movement, which promoted Jewish tourism and attachment to the land and its physical monuments, Friedman supported regionalism as both an

---

76. Most frequently, he contributed articles in Yiddish to the *Lodzsher togblat* of Lodz; in Hebrew to *Ofakim* of Warsaw; and in Polish to *Nasza Opinia* (Our Opinion) of Lwów and to *Nasz Przegląd* (Our View) and *Miesięcznik Żydowski* (Jewish Monthly) of Warsaw.

77. Friedman, "Reviews of Books," *American Historical Review* 58, no. 4 (July 1953): 880–82.

approach to Jewish history and a patriotic civic pursuit (also discussed in chapter 1).

Friedman expressed his multivalent political sympathies by extending undifferentiated recognition to all Jewish political trends, in both his prewar and postwar works. A prewar example is his coverage of Jewish politics in the 1938 survey of modern Polish-Jewish history commissioned by the Zionist Yiddish daily, *Haynt*.[78] A postwar example is his review of the Stanislav *yizkor* book of 1952, in which he argues that non-Zionist movements "are treated too superficially, particularly as regards the Bund, the workers movement, and the cultural movement in Yiddish language."[79]

Friedman did not, however, have sympathy for historical materialism or Ber Borochov's Marxist approach to Zionism that was adopted by Ringelblum and Mahler. In Ringelblum's 1929 review of Friedman's dissertation (on the struggle by Galician Jews for emancipation), Ringelblum claims that Friedman is "not one hair removed from the bourgeois historians of the old generation" in overlooking economic-materialist explanations for Jewish survival and emancipation.[80] At the International Congress of Historians held in Warsaw in 1933, Friedman was among the majority in the Jewish section who rejected the demand by Mahler (supported only by Ringelblum) that future Jewish historiography be written from the standpoint of historical materialism.[81] Friedman continued the conversation beyond the war years, arguing in his 1955 review of Ringelblum's early works that "Ringelblum 'galloped' to another extreme [than bourgeois history]" and ornamented the Jewish past with "proletarian

---

78. Friedman, "Di nayeste geshikhte," 132–34.
79. Friedman, "Yisker-bikher un regyonale literatur," *Di tsukunft* (April 1955): 180.
80. Emanuel Ringelblum, "A solide geshikhte-arbet," *Literarishe bleter* (September 27, 1929): 758. The review is unsigned, but Friedman identifies Ringelblum as the author in his own bibliography, as does Jacob Shatzky in his bibliography of Ringelblum's works in Emanuel Ringelblum, *Kapitlen geshikhte fun amolikn yidishn lebn in poyln* (Buenos Aires, 1953), LI.
81. Emanuel Ringelblum, "Der internatsyonaler kongres fun historishe visnshaft in varshe un di yidishe visnshaft," in *Kapitlen geshikhte fun amolikn yidishn lebn in poyln*, ed. Yankev Shatski (Buenos Aires, 1953), 476–77 (first published in *Di tsukunft*, April 1934, 223–28). Friedman conducted the same debate with Mahler, who published a materialist critique of Friedman's history of the Jews of Lodz, *Dzieje Żydów w Łodzi* (Lodz, 1935), *YIVO bleter* XI, no. 1 (1937): 71–79, to which Friedman replied that Mahler worked from an a priori theory that took precedence over facts: "Notitsn," *Lodzsher visnshaftlekhe shriftn* I (1938): 280.

masses, toiling Jewish poverty, economic isolation, social declassification and pauperization" to support his Marxist thesis.[82]

It is therefore more than surprising that Friedman's first public statement as director of the CJHC in 1945 should include a declaration that the study of Jewish history be conducted henceforth "with the razor-sharp method of dialectical-Marxist analysis."[83] It is one of the occasional statements by a Yiddish historian that requires cautious reading. Its inclusion, with or without his approval, provides an early indication of the pressures that would lead to his departure from Poland. By 1948, he had settled in New York, and in the following year reflected in a Yiddish essay on the state of world Jewry, comparing the consequences for the Jews of Communism and Nazism: "Left totalitarianism protected and defended the biological existence of the Jewish individual; however, it atomized and pulverized the Jewish national community and its Jewish culture." From this, Friedman concludes, "Both totalitarianisms together—so different in their goals and methods—put an end to Jewish cultural life in almost all of Europe."[84] He reiterates this theme in English in 1954, arguing that, "while the final solution in Nazi style meant total physical destruction, in the Communist fashion it stood for 'voluntary' total assimilation and disintegration."[85] His antipathy to Soviet Communism took the form of vigilance against Communist-inspired revisionism of Holocaust history. For example, his 1954 review titled "A Brand-New Interpretation of the Warsaw Ghetto Uprising" criticizes the successive editions of Ber Mark's histories of the uprising for, at first, recognizing the place of all political factions in the uprising, then foregrounding only the Communists and, during Stalin's last years, eliminating the non-Communists.[86]

The pan-Jewish nationalism practiced by Friedman and his avoidance of explicit political orientation contrast with Trunk's choice of a specific

---

82. Friedman, "Dos ringelblum bukh," *Di tsukunft* (October 1955): 384.
83. Friedman, "Unzer historishe oyfgabe," *Dos naye lebn* (April 10, 1945): 6.
84. Friedman, "Der kultur krizis in idishn lebn," *Idisher kemfer* (September 23, 1949, Rosh Hashanah): 49.
85. Friedman, review of Peter Meyer et al., *Jews in the Soviet Satellites* (Syracuse, 1953), *Political Science Quarterly* LXIX, no. 2 (June 1954): 289.
86. Friedman, "A shpogl naye oystaytshung fun varshever geto-oyfshtand," *Di tsukunft* (April 1954): 162–67.

political allegiance. Trunk had been a Zionist at an early age, but was later drawn to the Bund, the social-democratic General Union of Jewish Workers in Poland.[87] His prewar and postwar writings evince the alignment of his primary research interests with the program of Diaspora nationalism adopted by the Bund in Poland after World War I. Best known is its concept of *doikayt* (hereness) that sought to improve conditions for Jews in their land of residence, in opposition to the perceived surrender in Zionism's call for emigration. Trunk's interest in the history of Jewish self-government, likely suggested by his teacher, Balaban, and Balaban's prior monographs in the field, was reinforced by the Bund's advocacy for Jewish national cultural autonomy in independent Poland. As discussed in chapter 4, Trunk's studies of Jewish autonomy can be traced from his early histories to his best-known postwar work, *Judenrat*. Where the influence of the Bund differed from that of Balaban, Trunk followed Bundist ideology and sought instances of historical class conflict that contradicted his teacher's more unitary view of Jewish nationhood. The tendency toward socialist analysis appeared in each of the postwar Yiddish historians' writings but was especially prominent in Trunk's examinations of social conflict in the Nazi-imposed ghettos.

An indication of Trunk's continuing fidelity to his prewar identity is the specific recognition given to the Bund in his Holocaust writings. His 1955 review of Friedman's popular *Martyrs and Fighters* praises the inclusion of voices from all political streams but claims that Friedman neglected early rescue efforts by Bundist leader Shmuel Zygielbojm of the Polish National Council.[88] In Trunk's history of his hometown, Kutno, he notes that the impetus to found a school in the Kutno Ghetto came at the initiative of the Bund, "which had a fine tradition in that respect," having constructed a large brick school building in Kutno before the war.[89] In his Holocaust history of Piotrków-Trybunalski, he devotes a separate chapter to the Bund. He explains that the Bund's majority on the elected prewar community council led the Nazis to appoint Bundists to head the Ältstenrat

---

87. Trunk, "The Historian of the Holocaust at YIVO," 61–62.

88. Trunk, "A mekoyrim-antologye vegn varshever geto," *Unzer tsayt* (January 1955): 43–44.

89. Trunk, "Untergang fun der yidisher kutne," in *Sefer Kutnah veha-sevivah*, ed. David Shtokfish (Tel Aviv, 1968), 346.

(Council of Elders). He writes with evident pride that the Bund-led council provided "social assistance in all areas of food-provisioning, medical assistance, housing systems, child protection, refugee assistance, etc.,"[90] in unstated contrast to towns with councils led by other Jewish parties.

Trunk retained his ties to the Bund in the early postwar years, despite the permanent disruption of its political program. During his brief Israeli period, his first Yiddish publishing venue was the Bundist periodical, *Lebns-fragn* (Life Questions). In America, his articles appeared in the Bund's journal, *Unzer tsayt* (Our Time), and the nonpartisan *Di tsukunft* (The Future), but not in the Zionist or Communist Yiddish journals.[91] His major service to the Bund came with the publication in 1960 of the comprehensive history of the Bund, to which Trunk contributed the opening chapter on the Bund's origins and early history.[92]

Trunk's practical commitment to the cause of Diaspora nationalism took the form of institutional loyalty to YIVO, the movement's scholarly center before the war and its chief conservator after the war. Trunk had been the executive secretary of the YIVO-affiliated *Yunger historiker krayz* and also of YIVO's Historical Section in interwar Poland. He is credited by Kermish with compiling and analyzing the data for the Historical Section's well-known survey of Jewish communal records.[93] All of Trunk's principal prewar works had appeared in YIVO-sponsored publications, and he continued to contribute important works to the *YIVO bleter* and *YIVO Annual* after the war. While in Israel, he had twice presented research papers to the "Friends of YIVO" (as mentioned in chapter 1), and his chief postwar career began with his invitation to join YIVO professionally in 1954. At YIVO in New York, Trunk held the positions of chief

---

90. Trunk, "Der 'bund' in pyetrkov," in *Pyetrkov tribunalski un umgegnt / Pyetrkov Tribunalski veha-sevivah*, ed. Yankev Malts and Naftoli Lau (Tel Aviv, 1965), 467–68.

91. The single exception is his 1981 review of Friedman's posthumous *Roads to Extinction*, which appeared in the Labor Zionist *New Frontier*, a venue appropriate to his subject and one at which his son and translator, Gabriel Trunk, was then employed.

92. Trunk, "Di onheybn fun der yidisher arbeter-baveygung," in *Di geshikhte fun bund*, vol. 1, ed. G. Aronson et al. (New York, 1960), 11–106.

93. "Barikht fun der pinkeysim-aktsye" [unsigned] *Yedies fun YIVO* 83–84 (March–April 1939): 6–10. See Kermish, "Yeshaye trunk z"l," in Trunk, *Geshtaltn un gesheenishn [naye serye]* (Tel Aviv, 1983), 15 (Yiddish); Trunk, *Łódź Ghetto: A History*, trans. and ed. Robert Moses Shapiro (Bloomington, 2006), xxvii (English).

archivist and senior research associate and was also a member of the directorate. On Friedman's death, Trunk succeeded him as head of the Historians' Circle. With his article on "YIVO and Jewish Historical Science" in the volume of *YIVO bleter* dedicated to YIVO's fiftieth anniversary,[94] Trunk became the Yiddish historians' final expositor of YIVO's contributions to Diaspora nationalist historiography.

Traces of an opposing tendency toward Polish-Jewish nationalism are also found in Trunk's prewar and postwar works. These arise in his preference for local monographs, another likely influence of his teacher, Balaban, and in his concentration on the cities and regions of Congress Poland to the exclusion of the more ethnically diverse regions from which the other Yiddish historians of the Holocaust had come. Trunk's principal prewar works were histories of the Jews in his hometown of Kutno and the nearby city of Płock. On his return to Poland after the war, he resumed his work in form as well as content with monographs on the Jews in the labor camps and ghettos of the Warthegau region (Yiddish, *Varteland*), including Kutno, which had been annexed by Nazi Germany during the war.

The other Diaspora nationalist among the Yiddish historians of the Holocaust was Blumental, whose nonpartisan support for Yiddish culture contrasted with Trunk's specific loyalty to the Bund. During his years in prewar Lublin, the Bund-aligned *Lubliner togblat* had supported him during the controversy arising from his clandestine promotion of Yiddish culture among his gymnasium students, and the Bund's own *Lubliner shtime* had published his articles on Yiddish literature. But Blumental aligned himself with no party program. Many of his articles were also published by the well-known opponent of the Bund, his cousin Nachman Meisel, editor of the nonpartisan *Literarishe bleter* of Warsaw (in which Friedman and Trunk also appeared). Once in Israel, he contributed regularly to the Bund's official organ, *Lebns-fragn*, but on one occasion declared in its pages, "I am not a Bundist,"[95] and on another, "I belong to no

---

94. Trunk, "YIVO un di yidishe historishe visnshaft," *YIVO bleter* XLVI (1980): 342–54.

95. Blumental, "Yo geven, tsi nisht geven?," *Lebns-fragn* 282–83 (September–October 1975): 12.

party."⁹⁶ During the postwar period, articles by Blumental often appeared in New York in the ideologically opposed, pro-Soviet *Yidishe kultur*, of which Meisel had become the editor shortly before the war.

Blumental's prewar career as a teacher of Polish language and literature at the humanistic Polish-Jewish gymnasium in Lublin might suggest an inclination toward Polish-Jewish nationalism. However, Blumental regarded the teaching of Polish culture to his students not as fostering a desirable Polish-Jewish identity but as regrettably facilitating their assimilation. His own extracurricular writings and activities were devoted almost entirely to publicizing Yiddish literature, folklore, and literary history within the context of an autonomous Jewish Diaspora culture. In Blumental's works, that culture transcends the various political tendencies it embraced, and accordingly, political parties and affiliations are virtually absent from his writings both before and after the war.

In 1963, Blumental reviewed a proposal by the Israel teachers' union, part of the official Histadrut Labor Federation, to establish a program that would "immortalize the activity of 'Tarbut' [the Hebrew-Zionist school movement] and its co-workers in Poland." He comments approvingly, "May the work of their hands be blessed," but he objects to the exclusion of the similar, Hebrew-oriented schools of the Braude system not affiliated with Tarbut. He argued for inclusion of the Yiddish-oriented national schools of the TsYShO movement, followed by the religious Beys Yaakov schools, those of the folkist *Shul-kult* movement, and even those of the anti-Zionists. "The history of our people comprises the history of all tendencies of the Jewish people," he contended. "Everything that Jews created in the course of long generations, all of the true and false Torahs, is our possession."⁹⁷ The treatment of political movements in his Holocaust writings is characterized by this spirit of inclusiveness.

Kermish's prewar work prefigures a Jewish political pluralism that differs from Blumental's *klal-yisroel* (whole Jewish people) approach by focusing equally, but individually, on the various Jewish political movements. In his 1938 article on Jewish members of the Warsaw City Council,

---

96. Blumental, "Nokh der fayerung '60 yor bund,'" *Lebns-fragn* 77 (January 1958): 7.

97. Blumental, "Vegn an ongeveytiktn problem," *Lebns-fragn* 141–42 (September–October 1963): 10–11.

he lists the electoral standings of each of the Jewish political parties and discusses the members elected on the Zionist, Socialist, Bundist, Orthodox, or other party lists. His 1946 history of the Warsaw Ghetto Uprising and subsequent articles on the ghetto's underground press give similar recognition to each party's individual efforts. Like Friedman, Kermish rejects claims by Ber Mark and others at the JHI during its Stalinist period that only Jewish Communists and their pro-Soviet allies assisted the uprising or resistance; however, his emphasis is not on exposing Communist revisionism, like Friedman, but on supplying information to correct the record. His article on the role of women in the ghetto uprising (itself an innovation) counters Mark obliquely by citing the varied party affiliations of his heroines.[98] Finally, his 1959 article "Who Organized the Revolt?" identifies each of the Labor Zionist, Revisionist, Bundist, and Communist Party youth organizations from which the revolt's leaders emerged.[99]

Kermish himself avoided political affiliation by writing for nonpartisan literary and historical journals before and after the war, but he may be identified as a Polish-Jewish nationalist from his early life and work. He was unusual among Jewish historians of his generation for working in both the fields of Polish and Jewish history and for focusing his Jewish historical writing on the engagement of Jews with non-Jewish society. One example is his article on Jewish participation in the Warsaw City Council,[100] and another is his discussion of an "unknown patriotic letter" from the rabbi of Ludmir (Włodzimierz, Poland) to Polish leader Tadeusz Kościuszko,[101] both written in Polish. He was also unusual for receiving support from both Polish and Jewish sources. Publication of his

---

98. Kermish, "Di yidishe froy in varshever geto-oyfshtand," *Der poylisher yid* 8–9 (1958): 34–39. A somewhat earlier date may be appropriate for this article as an abridged Hebrew version had appeared in 1954 (see bibliography). Kermish did not otherwise appear in this or other pro-Soviet journals, and articles in this journal in Rio de Janeiro were often reprints. The lack of identifying information about Kermish or his article suggests that it may have been reprinted without his knowledge.

99. Kermish, "Di emese organizatorn fun geto-oyfshtand," *Yerusholayimer almanakh* 4 (1975): 11–22.

100. Kermish, "Reprezentacja Żydowska w Radzie Miejskiej M. St. Warszawy (1919–1938)," *Głos Gminy Żydowskiej* II, nos. 10–11 (October–November 1938): 318–22.

101. Kermish, "Nieznany list patriotyczny rabina do Kościszki z rozu 1792," *Głos Gminy Żydowskiej* I, no. 4 (October 1937): 87–88.

dissertation on the history of Lublin was financed by the City of Lublin. In addition to preparing a bibliography on the history of Warsaw Jewry for the Warsaw Jewish Community as a young historian, he was engaged by the (non-Jewish) Society of Friends of History in Warsaw to prepare a bibliography on the history of Warsaw.

After the war, Kermish became disillusioned with the possibility of Jewish progress in prewar Poland but continued his focus on Polish-Jewish relations. For example, the 1970 Yiddish version of his 1938 article on the Warsaw City Council was expanded to include the inability of Jewish Council members to obtain funding for municipal services or city employment for their constituents.[102] Although each of the Yiddish historians touched occasionally on Jewish relations with non-Jews during the Holocaust, they discussed non-Jews primarily as the contextual variable affecting options for resistance or rescue. One such work by Kermish is his short study "Arms Used by the Warsaw Ghetto Fighters," which provides one of the first synthetic accounts of the Jewish fighters' attempts to negotiate weapons purchases from Polish underground forces.[103] But only Kermish exhibits the breadth of interest in Polish-Jewish relations associated with Ringelblum. Over the course of his postwar career, he published a series of studies on the varying attitudes of Christian Poles toward Jews under Nazi occupation, concluding with his critical edition of Ringelblum's *Polish-Jewish Relations During the Second World War* of 1974.

Kermish's prewar attitude toward Zionism is not discernible from his writings, but his facility in Hebrew on arriving in Israel and the lack of religious allusions in his work suggest a secular Zionist education. His Hebrew publishing venue of choice for short articles was the Labor-Zionist daily *Davar* (Word), which also published features on him and his work. Of particular note is that he became the only Yiddish historian, and the only historian at Yad Vashem, to explore Israel-related themes of the Holocaust with his 1963 article, "The Land of Israel in the Life of the Ghetto as

---

102. Kermish, "Di yidishe reprezentants in varshever shtotrat," in *Sefer ha-Shanah / Yorbukh / Yearbook* III, ed. Aryeh Tartakower (Tel Aviv, 1970), new material on 292–93.

103. Kermish, "Di kley-zin fun di oyfshtendler in varshever geto," *Yedies fun yad vashem* 3 (September 1958): 4–6.

Reflected in the Illegal Warsaw Ghetto Press."[104] Of his eventual, comprehensive publication of the underground press in the Warsaw Ghetto, only the Zionist-oriented press was given advance coverage, both in this article and in a separate work on the Gordoniah youth movement in the ghetto.[105]

Turning last to Dworzecki, we find political affiliations similar to Friedman's but with opposite degrees of ideological and practical commitment to Zionism and Diaspora nationalism. His lifelong engagement with Yiddish language and culture proved secondary to his ideological commitment to political Zionism, which continued to animate his personal and professional life after the war. He recounted that he was a graduate of the Vilna Hebrew gymnasium, which he described as "the first Hebrew gymnasium in the Jewish Diaspora," and which became an early affiliate of the Tarbut Zionist school system.[106] As discussed in chapter 1, he became a partisan for Zionist-oriented education in the *kulturkamf* that divided much of secular interwar Jewry between supporters of the Hebrew national revival and Yiddish-oriented Diaspora nationalism. In his 1929 article, "The Bundist School System in the Dock," he quotes the testimony of expert "witnesses" who argue that the Bund schools opposed Judaism, Hebrew, and the Land of Israel and that the Bund claimed to support Jewish workers but, in contrast to the Tarbut agricultural schools, had failed to establish a single vocational school.[107] He followed up with an account of the four-day alumni conference of the Tarbut Hebrew Teachers' Seminary in Vilna, calling its graduates "an exceptionally important cultural factor in the Vilna province."[108] (As historical irony,

---

104. Kermish, "The Land of Israel in the Life of the Ghetto as Reflected in the Illegal Warsaw Ghetto Press," *Yad Vashem Studies* V (1963): 105–31.

105. Kermish, "ha-'Itonut ha-makhteretit shel 'Gordoniah' bi-me ha-Sho'ah be-Polin," in *'Itonut "Gordoniah" be-makhteret Geto Varshah*, ed. Arieh Avnon (Tel Aviv, 1966), 13–38.

106. Dworzecki, *Yerusholayim d'lite*, 267. The gymnasium was also known as a "real" gymnasium for its inclusion of physical and life sciences and contemporary European languages. It had been named in memory of its principal cofounder, the physician Josef Epsztajn, referred to by Dworzecki as Shabtai Epsztajn. Ibid.

107. Dworzecki, "Dos bundishe shul-vezn oyf der bashuldikungs-bank: groyse gezelshaftlekher mishpet iber di tsysho-shuln in vilne (a briv fun vilne)," *Haynt* (November 19, 1929): 4.

108. Dworzecki, "Di ershte absolventn-konferents fun hebreyishn 'tarbut'-seminar in vilne," *Haynt* (January 22, 1930): 4.

one may note that the papers of the Tarbut seminary were preserved at YIVO and were processed after the war by Trunk in New York.[109]) As with Trunk's allegiance to the Bund, Dworzecki took care to acknowledge the Tarbut movement in his post-Holocaust writing. His 1963 history of the Jews of Ludmir directs special attention to the Tarbut primary and agricultural schools that operated during the interwar years. Discussing the Nazi-Soviet division of Poland in September 1939, he praises the perseverance of the Tarbut teachers who maintained Hebrew as the language of instruction for several months under Soviet rule until forced to yield to Yiddish, the only language sanctioned by the USSR for use in Jewish institutions.[110]

Writing of his own activities in the Vilna Ghetto, Dworzecki recounts that on the third day of the ghetto's creation, he effected the unification of the Right Poale Zion and Hitahdut Zionist parties and later initiated creation of the Zionist *dakh* (roof), or Committee of Seven, of which he was one.[111] Although his history of the ghetto strives for balanced coverage of the ghetto's Zionist and non-Zionist political groups, the section on "*kultur-kamf* in the Ghetto" reports that the Zionist *dakh* struggled in the school system against the Bund, which had become more influential by having a supporter in the cultural section of the Judenrat.[112]

Within a month of his escape from the Germans in April 1945, Dworzecki had established himself in Paris and was publishing accounts of his ghetto experiences in the Yiddish newspaper of the Right Poale Zion, *Unzer vort* (Our Word). By September, his articles were carried in the Socialist Zionist *Idisher kemfer* (Jewish Fighter) of New York and, a month later, in the semiofficial Labor Zionist *Davar* of Tel Aviv. Like Kermish, he favored *Davar* for his short articles in Hebrew and, like Friedman, he did not appear in Bundist or Communist venues.

In prewar Poland, Dworzecki had displayed practical, if not theoretical, support for the cause of dual "Polish-Jewish" identity by such diverse

---

109. "Guide to the Records of Tarbut Hebrew Teachers Seminary, Vilna: 1920–1940," YIVO archives RG 23 (1979).

110. Dworzecki, "Di yidn in ludmir in loyf fun der geshikhte," *Pinkas Ludmir: Sefer-zikaron li-kehilat Ludmir* (Tel Aviv, 1962), 80–83.

111. Dworzecki, *Yerusholayim d'lite*, 358, 372.

112. Ibid., 224.

acts as promoting Jewish participation in the official Northern Trade Fair, held annually in Vilna,[113] and joining the (decidedly non-Jewish) Society of History and Antiquities of Krakow.[114] But he was the only Yiddish historian of the Holocaust not to return to Poland after the war. As early as September 1945, he held that pogroms in postwar Poland outweighed the new government's call to return. With a trace of the lachrymose attitude that he otherwise eschewed, he argued that Jews in Poland would become *shuts-yidn* (protected Jewish subjects), dependent on the government to reeducate a populace "who for generations was poisoned with bloody Jew-hatred," and that the "new proud Jewish race" should return only to its own homeland.[115] Contemplating the Jewish future simultaneously with his own, Dworzecki announced his transformation from political Zionist to immigrant-in-waiting a few months later. Anticipating the "crisis of the covenant" later articulated by Irving Greenberg,[116] he declares, "I no longer believe in a historical-political fate that will in all circumstances preserve the existence of our people." He announces, instead, that Jewish security is to be found only in the new society then emerging in the Land of Israel, "where every Jew is psychically and physically prepared to defend his wife, child, parents, and entire community."[117]

The relevance of the Yiddish historians' political inclinations in the postwar period is seen in their continuing presence in the historians' lives and work. Except for determined ideological partisans for Yiddish, Jewish emigrants from Eastern Europe, both before or after the Holocaust, almost universally discarded their Old World political allegiances and

---

113. Dworzecki, "A idisher prese-albom baym tsofn-yarid in poyln," *Unzer ekspres* (August 15, 1930): 16; *Haynt* (August 20, 1930): 6.

114. See photo, "Dr. Mark Dworzecki and other members of the Art and History Lovers of Krakow Antiquities standing in the courtyard of the Wawel Royal Castle" (date and provenance unknown; more correctly, "Society of History and Antiquities of Krakow/ Towarzystwo Miłośników Historii i Zabytków Krakowa"), www.eilatgordinlevitan.com/ krakow/krkw_pix/art/012608_47_b.gif and www.eilatgordinlevitan.com/radoshkovichi/ r_images/archives/121508_34_b.gif.

115. Dworzecki, "Kh'vil kontrolirn mayn gefil tsu poyln," *Idisher kemfer* (September 28, 1945): 7.

116. Irving Greenberg, "Voluntary Covenant," in *Perspectives* (pamphlet, New York, October 1982).

117. Dworzecki, "Vegn unzer farfirerishn optimizm," *Idisher kemfer* (March 8, 1946): 12.

adopted those common to their new home, whether in Israel or the Diaspora. The Yiddish historians, by contrast, clung to political orientations and parties that were marginal or would become irrelevant in their new homes, but which kept alive their ties to the prewar world.

Personal Continuities

In addition to retaining their prewar political orientations, the Yiddish historians of the Holocaust retained the personal characteristics of their earlier professional careers. Like their more deliberate political affiliations, each historian's personal inclinations and affinities remained largely constant despite the many discontinuities imposed by the Holocaust period.

The defining characteristic of Friedman's career as a Jewish historian—interrupted but not altered by his wartime experiences—was his ambition to give organization to the field of Jewish historical scholarship. Twice during the 1930s, he had proposed the creation of a worldwide union of Jewish historians (as described in chapter 1) and, on his own initiative, realized a version of this organizational plan in his adopted city of Lodz. Having transformed the academic group of the local *Landkentnish* society into the Academic Circle of the Society of Friends of YIVO in 1936, he proceeded to organize its scholarly work.[118] A preparatory period of archival research, collection of materials, and consultative sessions resulted in the publication in 1938 of a first volume of *Lodzsher visnshaftleke shriftn* (Lodz Scholarly Writings) with academic papers by Friedman and others on Jewish history and economics in Lodz—and a statement that future volumes need not be restricted to the region of Lodz.

Seven years later, Friedman returned to the liberated city of Lodz as director of the CJHC with a renewed opportunity to organize the study of Jewish history, but on the scale of all Poland and with the subject of the Nazi Holocaust. Kermish later recalled that Friedman excelled not only in scholarship but also in executive ability.[119] Under Friedman's leadership,

---

118. Friedman, Introduction to *Lodzsher visnshaftlekhe shriftn* I (1938): III–IV.
119. Kermish, "D"r filip fridman—der historiker fun khurbn," *Di tsukunft* (April 1975): 154. Baron also praised Friedman's "excellent organizational abilities" in his introduction to *Roads to Extinction*, 4.

Kermish, Blumental, and others prepared the questionnaires for eyewitnesses; Kermish established the commission's archives and library; and Rachel Auerbach organized the taking of testimonies. The first publications of wartime documents, testimonies, and synthetic histories were issued, including Friedman's first study of Auschwitz. Friedman convened two conferences in Lodz in 1945: a general meeting in August for members of the regional historical commissions,[120] and an academic conference in September at which he and his colleagues presented papers.[121] Intending to place the CJHC at the center of Holocaust research, Friedman drafted the agenda in April 1946 for a world conference of Jewish historians to be convened in Warsaw in September 1946.[122]

Yet it was the fate of Friedman's career that the preeminent role for which he had unknowingly prepared before the war was not to remain his. Recurring demands by the Soviet-dominated Central Committee of Polish Jews that the CJHC sever its ties to foreign sources of support and conform its research to Communist ideology led to Friedman's departure from Poland in May 1946. The consequence was the dispersion of his organizational energies into a variety of venues for the remainder of his life. As educational director for the American Joint Distribution Committee in the Displaced Persons camps of the US Zone of occupied Germany, he supervised publication activities by survivors from 1946 to 1948. As research director of the Centre de documentation Juive Contemporaine in Paris during the same period, he helped to organize the First European Conference of Jewish Historical Commissions and Documentation Centers, held in December 1947. As the pioneering writer on Jewish Holocaust historiosophy, as he put it, Friedman produced a series of prolegomena for the study of the Holocaust in 1948;[123] assessments of the state of European and American Holocaust study in

---

120. E. Shedletsky, "Baratung in der tsentraler yidisher historisher komisye," *Dos naye lebn* (August 20, 1945): 6.

121. E. Shedletsky, "Tsveyte visnshaftlekhe baratung fun der tsen. yidisher historisher komisye in poyln [September 19–20, 1945, Lodz]," *Dos naye lebn* (October 13, 1945): 5.

122. The conference was not held, no doubt in part because of Friedman's emigration and perhaps to avoid international publicity at a time of rising antisemitic violence in Poland.

123. Friedman, "Di forshung fun unzer khurbn," *Kiem* (January 1948): 47–54; "Fun antihistoritsizm tsum superhistoritsizm," *Kiem* (March 1948): 28–32; and "Di elementn

1949 and 1950;[124] and his pathbreaking programmatic outline for Holocaust research in 1950.[125] His ambition to coordinate and centralize the project of Holocaust research, in the manner of his earlier plan to organize the study of Jewish history in general, came nearest to realization with the transformation of his personal collection of 30,000 bibliographic references into the decades-long joint bibliographic project undertaken by YIVO and Yad Vashem, to which he contributed the first three volumes before his early death in 1960. Best known is the *Guide to Jewish History under Nazi Impact*,[126] which outlines the topics and sources for Holocaust study from the Jewish perspective.

Trunk, in the memorial essay by his colleague Kermish, is described as "one who excelled in modesty in all his actions" and as "a model of intellectual honesty." The combined effect was that Trunk's genre of choice in both his pre- and postwar writing was the synthetic monograph, founded on verifiable archival sources. In comparison with other Yiddish historians, he participated least in the personal or peripheral genres, producing few opinion pieces and no bibliographies or forewords to others' works. He was also more often the engagé historian, seeking in his prewar works to prove the antiquity and economic benefit of the Jewish presence in Poland. But his instrumentalism was rarely overt. The modesty to which Kermish referred appears in Trunk's preference—articulated early in his career and unchanged by his wartime experience—for understatement or indirection. In his first known work, a 1931 review of the anthology of medieval texts prepared by Mahler and Ringelblum for use in Yiddish schools, Trunk objected to the statement, "Jews were not the only moneylenders in the Middle Ages," arguing that such conclusions should be

---

fun undzer khurbn-forshung," *Hemshekh* 1 (April 1948): 4–10; continued as "Di memuaristik," *Hemshekh* 2 (1949): 26–34.

124. Friedman, "The European Jewish Research on the Recent Jewish Catastrophe in 1939–1945," *Proceedings of the American Academy for Jewish Research* 18 (1948–49): 179–211 (annual conference, December 12, 1948); and "Research and Literature on the Recent Jewish Tragedy," *Jewish Social Studies* XII, no. 1 (January 1950): 17–26.

125. See Friedman, "Outline of Program for Holocaust Research," in *Roads*, 571–76.

126. Friedman and Jacob Robinson, *Guide to Jewish History under Nazi Impact* (New York, 1960); Friedman, *Bibliyografiyah shel ha-sefarim ha-'Ivriyim 'al ha-Sho'ah ve-'al ha-gevurah* (Jerusalem, 1960); and Friedman and Joseph Gar, *Biblyografye fun yidishe bikher vegn khurbn un gvure* (New York, 1962).

left to the student to derive from the texts presented.[127] After the war, in a review of Ringelblum's prewar writings, he objected to a claim by Ringelblum about the political utility of Trunk's own history of Płock,[128] saying: "It is not hard to detect in these lines the apologetic undertone."[129] His comment anticipates the restrained tenor of his later *Judenrat*, which served as an indirect response to Hannah Arendt's criticisms of Jewish leadership and comportment under the Nazis. His last major work, *Jewish Responses to Nazi Persecution*, offers a further example of his understated approach: Trunk commences by setting forth typologies of Jewish responses to earlier catastrophes to demonstrate that the repetition of these responses should be considered heroic rather than inadequate in the unprecedented context of Nazi occupation, but he leaves to the reader the joining of these comparisons across time.

Another form of consistency between prewar and postwar approaches to Jewish scholarship is found in the commitment by Blumental to popular diffusion of Jewish knowledge, a commitment that instigated the major crises of both his prewar and postwar careers. His work at the humanistic gymnasium in Lublin before the war embraced his official career as a teacher of philosophy, Polish language, and Polish literature as well as an unofficial career in teaching Jewish studies. He recounted that his gymnasium's annual accreditation by capricious, antisemitic inspectors could be withheld if they detected Jewish accents in the students' Polish pronunciation or inadequate demonstrations of "Polish patriotism," however defined. School officials determined that both hazards could be avoided by forbidding the use of Yiddish by teachers and students. Blumental therefore resolved to provide extracurricular instruction in Yiddish language and literature—as compensation, he later wrote, for his "sin" of teaching only in Polish and for advancing his students' linguistic

---

127. Trunk, review of Rafoel Mahler and Emanuel Ringelblum, eds., *Geklibene mekoyrim tsu der geshikhte fun di yidn in poyln un mizrekh-eyrope: mitlalter (biz tsum yor 1506)*, 2 vols. (Warsaw, 1930), *YIVO bleter* II, nos. 1–2 (September 1931): 157.

128. Emanuel Ringelblum, introduction to Trunk, *Di geshikhte fun yidn in plotsk, 1237–1657* (Warsaw, 1939), V–VI, unsigned but credited to Ringelblum by Trunk in his "Emanuel ringelblum—der historiker 1900-1944," *Di tsukunft* (April 1965): 156.

129. Trunk, "Emanuel ringelblum—der historiker 1900-1944," *Di tsukunft* (April 1965): 156–57.

assimilation.¹³⁰ (Ironically, of course, it was this assimilation that enabled certain Jews to survive in hiding on the "Aryan side" of the ghetto walls during the Nazi occupation of Warsaw and other cities.)

In his youth, he had been active in the library association of his hometown, Borszczów, through which he offered Saturday morning lectures titled *Visnshaftlekhe shmuesn* (scholarly chats).¹³¹ He also became a *zamler* (collector) of folklore for YIVO and in 1929 published an appeal in the *Literarishe bleter* for public participation.¹³² On his arrival in Lublin, he was drawn to the work of the local *folks-universitet*, operated by the union of skilled trades workers, and delivered public lectures on Friday evenings in Yiddish. He reports that the audience consisted of students and alumni of the local Yiddish *folks-shul* (of the TsYShO network) and that students from his own gymnasium, though forbidden to attend, did so and participated in the discussion. He also organized a secret "seventh hour" class at his gymnasium in which his students "gradually became acquainted with Mendele and Peretz,"¹³³ the founders of modern Yiddish literature. A former student recalls that "he took on himself voluntarily the duty of teaching Yiddish and Yiddish literature ... without any pay," and that he popularized the work of YIVO among his students.¹³⁴ The same former student reported that Blumental's populist activities were "not to the liking of the director, who wanted to be rid of the liberal teacher," and that "a great number of graduates" organized a successful protest action. The protest was publicized by the editor of the *Lubliner togblat*, and Blumental was retained in his position.¹³⁵ As is well known in the history of Yad Vashem, a similar commitment to the popular exposition of Holocaust history, including Jewish literature and folklore—at the alleged expense

---

130. Blumental, "'Lubliner shtime' (a bintl zikhroynes)," *Lebns-fragn* 83 (July 1958): 9.

131. Shlomo Reibel, "ha-Hayim ha-hevratiyim veha-tarbutiyim be-Vorshtsov ben shete milhamot ha-'olam," in *Sefer borshtshiv*, ed. Blumental (Tel Aviv, 1960), 167.

132. Blumental, "Vos iz azoyns yidishe etnografye: bamerkungen fun a zamler," *Literarishe bleter* (July 12, 1929): 549.

133. Blumental, "Di yidish-poylishe gimnazye in lublin," in *Dos bukh fun lublin: zikhroynes, gvyes-eydes un materyaln iber lebn, kamf un martirertum fun lubliner yidishn yishev*, ed. M. Litvin and M. Lerman (Paris, 1952), 262.

134. Ruzshke Fishman-Shnaydman, *Mayn lublin: bilder funem lebns-shteyger fun yidn in farmilkhomedikn poyln* (Tel Aviv, 1982), 171.

135. Ibid., 171–72. She does not give the date of these events.

of more serious research—led to the dismissal of Blumental (and Rachel Auerbach) from Yad Vashem in 1958 and to their subsequent reinstatement under pressure from the press and survivor public.

When Kermish joined Friedman in liberated Poland, his previous inclination toward the documentary aspects of historical practice became the basis for his appointment as founding director of the CJHC's archives. In Israel, he repeated his archival initiative, first at Ghetto Fighters' House, and again at Yad Vashem, where he served as founding director of the archives from 1954 to 1979 and became primarily a documentary historian. Many of his lesser articles, and all of his major works, consist of annotated editions of Holocaust texts prefaced by discussions of historical context. The latter include his critical editions of writings by Ringelblum, Shimon Huberband, and Adam Czerniaków, and his compilations from the Oyneg Shabes archive and the underground press in the Warsaw Ghetto.

Dworzecki, the medical doctor–turned–historian, demonstrated the continuity of his prewar, wartime, and postwar interests through his medical work, which gave rise to a specific segment of his Holocaust studies. At the time of the German invasion in September 1939, Dworzecki was an officer and medical doctor in the Polish army and took part in the battle for the defense of Lwów. He relates that he was captured by the Germans near Krakow and escaped to Vilna, where he assisted the underground in the Vilna Ghetto and attempted without success to reach the partisans in the forests. Yitzhak Zuckerman, a surviving hero of the Warsaw Ghetto Uprising, later recounted that he had sent secret correspondence to the Vilna Ghetto by way of Dworzecki, whom he knew to be "a respected and well-known man."[136] Dworzecki came to describe his own work in the ghetto as "medical resistance," including the multiple tasks of practicing medicine in the hospital clinic, supervising the hygiene and treatment of school-age children as director of the Center for Medicine in the Schools, delivering popular lectures and publishing articles on epidemic prevention and other public health matters in the underground periodical, *Folksgezunt*, and, as a member

---

136. Yitzhak Zuckerman ("Antek"), *A Surplus of Memory: Chronicle of the Warsaw Ghetto Uprising*, trans. and ed. Barbara Harshav (Berkeley, 1993), 148.

of the "Yehiel" fighting group, training nurse-partisans in the first-aid treatment of wounded fighters.[137]

Dworzecki's first book, *The Fight for Health in the Vilna Ghetto*, published in 1946,[138] brought pioneering recognition to the medical field as an area of anti-Nazi resistance. He had commenced this work in the Vilna Ghetto and had thought the manuscript lost until a portion was discovered in the ruins of the ghetto by fellow survivor Avrom Sutzkever, who returned it to him in Paris (later, in Israel, Dworzecki would become a longtime contributor to Sutzkever's journal, *Di goldene keyt*).[139] His subsequent Holocaust works on the medical-historical theme followed three related paths: *victim* studies of Jews in the ghettos, camps, forests, and "Aryan side," which posit the creation by Jewish doctors under Nazi rule of a "new science" of "the pathology of the concentrationary universe";[140] *survivor* studies on such topics as the "health protection of the survivors";[141] and *perpetrator* studies of Nazi medical crimes. This last commenced with his motion on behalf of the Jewish Medical Association of Palestine for "anathema against the murderer-doctors" at the founding congress of the World Medical Association in Paris in 1947,[142] and it culminated in his 1958 book, *Europe Without*

---

137. Dworzecki, *Yerusholayim d'lite*, 396.
138. Dworzecki, *Kamf farn gezunt in geto-vilne* (Paris, 1946).
139. Yisroel Korn, "Dr. m. dvorzshetski—laurat fun der meditsin-akademye in frankraykh," *Undzer kiem* 34 (January 1964): 12.
140. Dworzecki, "La Pathologie de la déportation et les séquelles pathologiques des rescapés [3rd World Congress of Jewish Physicians, Haifa, August 11, 1955]," *Revue d'Histoire de la Médecine hebraïque* 30 (March 1956): 33; see Michael Dorland, *Cadaverland: Inventing a Pathology of Catastrophe for Holocaust Survival* (Waltham, 2009), 110–13, which credits Dworzecki with presenting "an entire research program" for a new field of study.
141. Dworzecki, "Gezunt-shuts fun der sheyres hapleyte," *Idisher kemfer* (February 15, 1946): 9–10. See also, among others, "Adjustment of Detainees to Camp and Ghetto Life and Their Subsequent Re-adjustment to Normal Society," *Yad Vashem Studies* V (1963): 193–219; "Neshome-problemen fun der sheyres-hapleyte," *Almanakh fun di yidishe shrayber in yisroel* (Tel Aviv, 1962), 334–45.
142. For a description of the proceedings, biographical sketch of Dworzecki, and annotated text of the motion, see Etienne Lepicard, "Jewish Medical Association of Palestine. Motion to the World Medical Association ([September, 16–21] 1947)," in *Silence, Scapegoats, Self-Reflection: The Shadow of Nazi Medical Crimes on Medicine and Bioethics*, ed. Volker Roelcke et al. (Göttingen, 2014), 315–26; Dworzecki, "Di daytshe meditsinishe farbrekhns farn mishpet fun ershtn internatsyonaln kongres fun doktoyrim

Children, on the Nazi plan for the biological subjugation of all non-Aryan peoples in Europe.[143]

Dworzecki's turn from medicine to the writing of Jewish history followed a familiar precedent in Vilna. Unlike other Jewish centers such as St. Petersburg, where historical writing often originated with lawyers (who began by chronicling the history of Jewish legal rights and disabilities), the first historians of modern Jewish history in Vilna were communal leaders who were also prominent physicians. Thus, for example, the opening chapters of the 1922 communal anthology on the history of Jewish Vilna during World War I were contributed by the physician-historians Cemach Szabad, Jacob Wygodski, and Abraham Wirszubski.[144] Dworzecki's Holocaust-era writing is uncannily prefigured in Wirszubski's article on World War I, "Popular Health and Medical Lifestyle in Vilna during the German Occupation,"[145] and Dworzecki would later recount Wygodski's death in the Vilna Ghetto.[146] As discussed in chapter 5, Dworzecki's own participation in "medical resistance" and his postwar writings on the subject did not limit his Holocaust research to the field of medicine but may well have facilitated his pivotal role in developing the historiography of other forms of unarmed resistance.

---

in pariz [September 1947 congress]," *Shriftn* 87–88 (August–September 1949): 93–102; original typescript of the motion, "Let us throw the anathema against the murderer-doctors" (misdated "9/30/1947"), Records of the World Jewish Congress, Jacob Rader Marcus Center of the American Jewish Archives, www.trumanlibrary.org/whistlestop/study_collections/nuremberg/documents/index.php?documentdate=1947-09-30&documentid=C194-3-1&studycollectionid=&pagenumber=1.

143. Dworzecki, *Eyrope on kinder* (Jerusalem, 1961).

144. On this anthology in particular, and community-building in Vilna during World War I in general, see Andrew N. Koss, "World War I and the Remaking of Jewish Vilna, 1914–1918" (PhD diss., Stanford University, 2010).

145. A. Virshubski, "Dos folksgezunt un der meditsinisher lebnssteyger in vilne beys der daytsher okupatsye (18 september 1915—1 yanuar 1919)," in *Pinkes far der geshikhte fun vilne in di yorn fun milkhome okupatsye*, ed. Z. Reyzen (Vilna, 1922), 81–108. The medical-historical tradition continued after the Holocaust with Dr. Mendl Sudarsky's leading role in preparing the two-volume collective history of Lithuanian Jewry, *Lite*, vol. 1 (New York, 1951), to which Philip Friedman contributed the bibliographic essay, and vol. 2 (Tel Aviv, 1965).

146. Dworzecki, "Der toyt fun d"r yankev vigodski," *Ilustrirte folks-bleter* (April 1946): 20–21.

Reintegration across the Divide

It may be said that the Yiddish historians cherished not "their troubles" but the reconstructed fragments of their pasts with which their postwar lives could be reunited. All chose to commemorate their prewar lives through the writing of historical chapters for *yizkor* books on their home cities or regions. None distanced himself from his prewar career or experiences, and none changed his name after the war.

In contrast to the well-known case of the Israeli author Ka-Tsetnik (pseudonym of Yehiel De-Nur, né Feiner), who disowned his earlier writings and is said to have destroyed library copies of his prewar Yiddish poetry and prose, Friedman drew together, across the Nazi divide, his own pre- and postwar intellectual efforts. He cherished the continuity of his historical output through the preparation of a bibliography of his works, published privately in 1955, that serves as his intellectual autobiography. Extant copies bear witness to his ongoing connection to his prewar work through dozens of handwritten emendations.[147]

Trunk, too, cherished the continuity of his efforts. He joined together the pre- and postwar studies of his home region to form the complementary halves of his 1963 book of collected Yiddish works, *Studies in Jewish History in Poland*.[148] He soon applied this joining of past and current work to his own city of Kutno. To supplement his prewar study on the history of the eighteenth-century city, he added chapters that continued his coverage to the First World War, the interwar period and, ultimately, the Holocaust period, followed by a reminiscence of his visit after the war.[149]

The several periods of Blumental's life are unified by his personal reminiscences. His late work, *Tsurikblikn* (Backward Glances),[150] offers sketches of personalities in his hometown from the preceding century and the period of his childhood that augment the more formal history of

---

147. See bibliography.
148. Trunk, *Shtudyes in yidisher geshikhte in poyln* (Buenos Aires, 1963).
149. Trunk, "A yidishe kehile in poyln baym sof fun XVIII yorhundert: kutno," *Bleter far geshikhte* 1 *("yunger historiker num. 3")* (1934): 87–140; "Geshikhte fun der yidisher kehile in kutne," in *Sefer Kutnah veha-sevivah*, ed. David Shtokfish (Tel Aviv, 1968), 29–53 (Hebrew 11–28); "Untergang fun der yidisher kutne," 340–53 (Hebrew 331–39); and "In mayn heymshtot," 419–21.
150. Blumental, *Tsurikblikn* (Tel Aviv, 1973).

his *yizkor* book. His memoirs of interwar and postwar life in Lublin, published in the Lublin *yizkor* book of 1952, serve to link these periods across the Nazi era. His more than sixty feuilleton-style pieces that appeared in Yiddish in Israel from 1958 to 1980 are enriched by personal asides that touch on events from his teaching career in prewar Lublin, persons he recognizes in a newly published roman à clef about prewar Lodz, and rare encounters with his former students from prewar Poland.

The Holocaust history of Kermish's adopted prewar home, the city of Warsaw, is the theme that unites all of Kermish's major postwar works with his prewar life. "Jewish Warsaw, the largest of all communities in Europe by number of souls, which before the Second World War was the center of Jewish literary creativity"—commences Kermish's introduction to Ringelblum's *Notes*—"this Jewish Warsaw was also the most important center for Jewish creativity in the ghetto years,"[151] and it became the site for the documentary histories of the wartime period that occupied the remainder of Kermish's career.

Dworzecki became a well-known personality among the survivor intelligentsia in Tel Aviv. Rachel Auerbach, the director of Yad Vashem's personal histories program, and Melech Ravitch, the poet and postwar memoirist, each remarked on Dworzecki's multiple careers and energetic schedule. Both recall that he continued his prewar profession as a medical doctor at Kupat Holim (the national health service of Israel), practicing medicine from early morning to early evening, while writing Holocaust history at home during the night. They recount that it was possible to visit him only in the late evening when he and his (second) wife would stroll near Dizengoff Square.[152] Dworzecki, too, recalls the couples he encountered strolling near Dizengoff, happily pushing a baby carriage and smiling at their "little Sabra." Reflecting on the fusion of his prewar and postwar lives, he observes, "you walk in pairs, man and woman, hand in hand, appearing to be two, and in truth, four, because each accompanies

---

151. Kermish, introduction to Emanuel Ringelblum, *Ksovim fun geto*, 2 vols. (Tel Aviv, 1985), vol. 1: *Togbukh* (1939–42), 5.

152. Rokhl Oyerbakh, "Tikun khatses," *Di goldene keyt* 27 (1957): 283; Melekh Ravitch, "Dr. mark dvorzshetski," *Mayn leksikon*, vol. 3 (Montreal, 1958), 152; also Yisroel Korn, "Dr. m. dvorzshetski—laurat fun der meditsin-akademye in frankraykh," *Undzer kiem* 34 (January 1964): 13.

his spouse who is no more . . . each of you seems to be one; and in his subconscious—he is two."[153]

A New Field of Jewish Historiography

The creation of an early Jewish historiography of the Holocaust by the Yiddish historians resulted not only from their adherence to an anti-lachrymose historical tradition and the persistence of their ideological and personal affinities across the prewar and postwar periods. Additional—and apparently decisive—impetus was given by the accident of their presence in Poland at the start of the war. Of the two dozen or so prewar Yiddish historians, not one who left Europe before the war turned to Holocaust historiography, whereas all of the future Yiddish historians of the Holocaust were survivors of the Nazi invasion. Virtually every *established*, or *emerging*, or *latent*, or *lay*, Jewish historian who survived the war years in Eastern Europe turned to writing Jewish history of the Holocaust and, in significant part, in Yiddish. Apart from the principal historians presented here as the Yiddish historians of the Holocaust, the outstanding example within each of the four categories named above is, respectively, Artur Eisenbach, Ber Mark, Szymon Datner, and A. Wolf Yasni, all of whom were associated with the CJHC.

Lest it be imagined, however, that Holocaust historiography was the natural or inevitable continuation of prewar historical work in Yiddish, it should be emphasized that the later careers of Yiddish historians who emigrated during the interwar period did not include studies of the Holocaust. Such historians as Raphael Mahler, Jacob Shatzky, Mark and Rachel Wischnitzer, Abraham Menes, and Nathan Michael Gelber had published significant works in Yiddish before the war and continued to write Jewish history in America or Israel (and in Yiddish to varying degrees), but with attention only to earlier periods of Jewish history or to locations outside of Europe.[154]

---

153. Dworzecki, "Tsu aykh, brider fun payn un fun vunder," *Di goldene keyt* 24 (1956): 133.

154. As noted previously, their contributions toward Holocaust studies consisted of Shatzky's reviews of *yizkor* books, Mahler's editing of two *yizkor* books, and Gelber's chapters of pre-Holocaust history for a number of *yizkor* books.

It may, of course, be suggested that more than historical accident underlay the decision to emigrate or remain in Europe, and that such decisions revealed a lesser or greater fealty to East European Jewish culture, and hence, to the fate and history of Polish Jews during the Holocaust, but any attempt to generalize is frustrated by living examples. Neither Mahler, who left for New York in 1937 and published an apologia on his shift from Yiddish to Hebrew in 1947 (before settling in Israel in 1951 where he continued to teach Jewish history),[155] nor Shatzky, who left for America in 1922 but remained the most committed to Yiddish culture of all Yiddish historians (to his eventual regret), turned to the writing of Holocaust history. Conversely, Kermish, who had been the least exclusive in his commitment to Jewish history of any future Yiddish historian, oriented his postwar career entirely toward the Jewish history of the Holocaust.

That the advancement of Jewish Holocaust studies in the early postwar period depended on the presence of scholars who had survived the war in Europe is illustrated by the course of events in both America and Israel. Between the cessation of Yiddish publishing at the Vilna YIVO in 1940 and the advent of the CJHC's *Bleter far geshikhte* (Pages for History) in 1948, only four scholarly journals appeared in Yiddish worldwide.[156] Of these, the *Argentiner YIVO shriftn* covered solely Argentine Jewish history. YIVO's *Yidishe shprakh* (Yiddish Language), written by linguists and not historians, offered a present-tense view of Yiddish linguistics and the dialects of former communities in Europe while tacitly ignoring the Holocaust until Blumental's lexicon of the Nazi period was serialized from 1956 to 1963. The bilingual journal, *Gedank un lebn / The Jewish Review*—published by the Jewish Teachers' Seminary and People's

---

155. Rafoel Mahler, "Yidish un hebreyish in likht fun der hayntiker virklekhkayt," *Yidishe kultur* 9, no. 6 (June 1947): 12–20.

156. In the Soviet Union, the Jewish Anti-Fascist Committee attempted to give public exposure to the Holocaust through publication of the ultimately suppressed, "Black Book" (see Kermish, "Tsu der geshikhte fun shvartsn bukh," *Di goldene keyt* 102 [1980]: 121–29). Friedman's invitation to the committee to attend his 1947 conference in Paris, carefully written with Soviet Yiddish orthography, was apparently not answered (YIVO Archive, RG 1258, F 396). The only Yiddish historian remaining alive in Soviet Russia, who would yet return to writing Jewish history in Yiddish, Hillel Aleksandrov, was not released and rehabilitated until 1956, and he did not write on the Holocaust.

University in New York from 1943 to 1948 and edited by Bernard Weinryb, Friedman's predecessor as dean—focused on all areas of Jewish history other than the Holocaust.[157]

Specific attention to the Holocaust is found only in the *YIVO bleter* of the New York YIVO, edited by Max Weinreich with the apparent intention that the Holocaust not eclipse YIVO's ongoing areas of scholarship. From 1940 to 1946, the journal's coverage of Jewish life in Nazi Europe was limited to three articles by the surviving lay historians Shlomo Mendelsohn and Leyb Shpizman; Ringelblum's now-famous letter on "Jewish cultural work in the ghettos of Poland"; and a martyrology of murdered YIVO staff members—plus Elias Tcherikower's article on historiography and martyrology. Thereafter, greater coverage of the Holocaust by the *YIVO bleter* demonstrated, first, that the Holocaust would receive increasing attention and, second, that Holocaust historiography would become increasingly professionalized within the existing framework of Yiddish scholarship. The volumes of 1947 and 1953 were each devoted wholly to Holocaust topics, with the distinction that the former consisted largely of first-person accounts by survivors (including Dworzecki) and the latter of research-based studies by surviving scholars (including Friedman, Trunk, and Kermish).

The dependence of early Jewish Holocaust studies on the presence of survivor scholars is further demonstrated by the activities of the YIVO Historians' Circle, chaired by Mark Wischnitzer from 1945 to 1949.[158] His reports for the period indicate that, out of twenty-six scholarly presentations by circle members, the only Holocaust topic was a discussion of the French-Jewish Council by Tcherikower's disciple, the surviving lay

---

157. Baron was a member of its editorial board, as was Mahler. Chapters of Mahler's major wartime project—a history of the early Karaites—were previewed in the Yiddish section. However, the single article in the Yiddish section to deal with Jews in Nazi Europe was an analysis of demographic changes in the East European ghettos that cites works by Kermish, Eisenbach, and Friedman: Abraham Melezin (later professor at City College, New York), "Demografishe farheltnishn in di getos in poyln," *Gedank un lebn* V, nos. 1–4 (January–December 1948): 86–100 (condensed from a Polish version published by the CJHC in 1946).

158. Mark Vishnitser, "Der historiker-krayz baym YIVO," *YIVO bleter* XXVII, no. 2 (Summer 1946): 371–79; XXIX, no. 2 (Summer 1947): 273–82; XXXIII (1949): 225–34.

historian Zosa Szajkowski.[159] With the reorganization and "renewal" of the Historians' Circle under Friedman's leadership in 1954,[160] the Holocaust became one of the principal areas of specialization proposed for the members' work, which Friedman listed as "bibliography, Holocaust research [*khurbn-forshung*], American Jewish history, cultural history, East European Jewish history, economic and social problems, and so forth."[161] Notably, the first two areas represent the start of the YIVO–Yad Vashem joint Bibliographical Series project, directed by Friedman, in which all of the Yiddish historians participated. Non-Holocaust historians at YIVO were also drawn to the project of commemorating the Jewish communities of Eastern Europe through their participation in Yad Vashem's *Pinkas ha-Kehilot* (Encyclopedia of Jewish Communities) project, for which they provided research and writing.[162]

Although, by contrast to YIVO, Yad Vashem had been established in 1953 expressly for Holocaust-related purposes, qualified personnel were not yet available from the Israeli academy to undertake the research aspect of Yad Vashem's mission, and survivor scholars were recruited for the staff. By 1958, the survivors and their eventual veteran-Israeli colleagues, who were products of the German academic tradition of the Hebrew University, came into public conflict. One of the causes was the collision between the survivors' emphasis on immediate research of the Jewish Holocaust experience and the perceived preference of Israeli academics for prolonged and wide-ranging study of historical context, including German antisemitism and Jewish-gentile relations in the Diaspora. The conflict is commonly said to have arisen between the established Israeli

---

159. Meeting of March 1, 1947. Szajkowski also discussed his firsthand observations about Holocaust studies in Europe at the meeting of December 21, 1947, summarizing his article, "Yidn in eyrope forshn zeyer umkum 1939–1946," *YIVO bleter* XXX, no. 1 (Fall 1947): 94–106.

160. "Historians' Circle Renews Activities," *News of the YIVO* 53 (June 1954): 4 (Yiddish) and 4* (English).

161. *Protokol fun der zitsung fun historiker-krayz opgehaltn dinstik, dem 5tn okt., 1954*, YIVO Archives, Trunk Collection, RG 483, F 54.

162. See, for example, the minutes of the Historians' Circle for October 5, 1954, ibid., and ongoing reports in the *News of the YIVO*. The *Pinkas* project, financed by the Conference on Jewish Material Claims Against Germany, also became an important source of outside revenue for YIVO and its staff members during the late 1950s and the 1960s.

historians (led by Yad Vashem's founding director, Ben-Zion Dinur) and the survivors (for this purpose, including Rachel Auerbach). However, a more apt demarcation of the fault line may be said to lie between those of Hebrew versus Yiddish orientation, who favored, respectively, research on the perpetrators versus the victims.[163] That the survivor scholars prevailed in this conflict led to Dinur's forced resignation in early 1959 and, as Dan Michman has pointed out, to the departure of the young scholars Dinur had brought to Yad Vashem from the Hebrew University. Thereafter, "Yad Vashem was abandoned to the Holocaust-survivor historians,"[164] and they were unable to train successors within the academy.

In America, the only scholarly publication in English to give early prominence to Holocaust studies was *Jewish Social Studies*, edited by Salo Baron, in which articles on Holocaust topics were largely the contribution of survivor scholars, including Friedman. Baron's support for Holocaust studies in this journal (and for Friedman's presentation at the 1948 conference of the American Academy for Jewish Research) did not, however, lead American Jewish historians to incorporate the Holocaust into their research agendas.[165] Conversely, Friedman's and Trunk's lectureships in Jewish history at Columbia University did not gain these historians prominence in the broader field of Jewish history. Thus, in America as in Israel, the survivor scholars remained both institutionally and intellectually separate from the mainstream of Jewish historical study.

---

163. The case in point is Natan Eck, a coworker of the survivor-historians and a survivor of the Warsaw Ghetto who had been active in Hebrew, but not Yiddish, cultural work in the ghetto. After the war, he published personal accounts of his wartime experiences in Yiddish, and edited his colleagues' Yiddish periodical at Yad Vashem (*Yedies fun yad vashem*), but virtually all of his scholarly work appeared in Hebrew. He joined the established Israeli historians in writing almost exclusively perpetrator, not Jewish, history of the Holocaust, and held views similar to Dinur's in seeking the "lesson" of the Holocaust. See Natan Eck, "Matarot ha-hoker ha-histori shel Yad va-Shem," *Yedi'ot Yad va-Shem* 4/5 (June 1955): 10.

164. Dan Michman, "Is There an 'Israeli School' of Holocaust Research?" in *Holocaust Historiography in Context: Emergence, Challenges, Polemics and Achievements*, ed. David Bankier and Dan Michman (Jerusalem, 2008), 42–44.

165. See David Engel, *Historians of the Jews and the Holocaust* (Stanford, 2010), 68–69. Hasia Diner centers her argument for the early emergence of Holocaust historiography in America on Friedman, but lists only Koppel Pinson, Uriel Weinreich, and Dagobert Runes in naming contemporary scholars who touched on Holocaust history at American institutions; *We Remember with Reverence and Love: American Jews and the Myth of Silence after the Holocaust, 1945–1962* (New York, 2009), 121–24.

Yet the estrangement was not reciprocal. The Yiddish historians of the Holocaust envisioned their work as being *within*, and not apart from, the practice of Jewish history. Each continued to write general Jewish history alongside Holocaust history,[166] and more importantly, all wrote Holocaust history from the perspective of Jewish historiography. In one of his programmatic essays of 1948, Friedman declared that "today, research on the recent *khurbn* has already grown to become a separate branch of our historiography" and that it deserved recognition, "just as there is a specialization in ancient history (Eastern period), in the Babylonian period (after the destruction of the Second Temple), in the Middle Ages, in the Dark Ages, and the like."[167] The following year, Kermish described the holdings of the library at the JHI and offered a similarly inclusive view of the new field: "During recent years, this literature has grown steadily to such a scope that one can boldly claim that study of the 1939–1945 period in the present day already constitutes a distinct branch of Jewish historiography."[168] The Yiddish historians of the Holocaust would become the practitioners of that new branch of Jewish historiography—in partnership with the survivor public, as discussed in the following chapter.

---

166. A few examples are: Friedman, "Der onhoyb fun dem idishn yishev in mizrekh-eyrope," *Idisher kemfer* (April 20, 1951, Pesach): 35–42; Trunk, "Di ershte tsaytshrift oyf yidish in rusland," *Unzer tsayt* (December 1962): 23–24; Dworzecki, "Di yidn in ludmir in loyf fun der geshikhte," *Pinkas Ludmir: Sefer-zikaron li-kehilat Ludmir* (Tel Aviv, 1962), 45–90; Kermish's expanded postwar version of his "Di yidishe reprezentants in varshever shtotrat" in *Sefer ha-Shanah / Yorbukh / Yearbook* III, ed. Aryeh Tartakower (Tel Aviv, 1970), 279–93; and chapters by Blumental on prewar periods of Jewish history in the *yizkor* books he edited on Baranów Sandomierz, Jezierna, and Miechów, and others, as well as several reviews by Friedman and Trunk of works by other historians on earlier periods of Jewish history.

167. Friedman, "Di forshung fun unzer khurbn," *Kiem* (January 1948): 49.

168. Kermish, "Vegn a biblyografye tsu der geshikhte fun poylishn yidntum in der tkufe fun der natsyonaler katastrofe (1939–1945)," *Bleter far geshikhte* II, nos. 1–4 (January–December 1949): 226.

3

NO SILENCE IN YIDDISH

The works of the Yiddish historians arose as part of the struggle by Jews under Nazi occupation to transmit a record of their experiences to their fellow Jews—an impulse for self-expression that continued to animate the surviving remnant. In their earliest writings, the Yiddish historians recognized "an urge to record for eternal memory" among the Jews in captivity and a "mighty folk movement" for self-expression among the survivors.[1]

They also recognized an imperative for public exposure in the writings that were hidden by Jews in the ghettos and camps and in the memoirs and testimonies of the survivors. The historians became, in a sense, the literary executors of the murdered authors, and they created a form of "lay–professional partnership" with their fellow survivors, replicating the prewar tradition of Yiddish scholarship that regarded the educated lay public as both informants and recipients of historical knowledge.

The Yiddish historians assumed the interrelated functions of documenting the popular urge for self-expression, giving exposure to the testaments of those who had perished, supporting commemorative efforts by survivors, incorporating the voices of both survivors and victims into their works, and making available the results of their research to the Yiddish-reading public. Their immersion in such materials led to reflections on the emotive aspect of survivor accounts and the relation between the survivor's and historian's voices within their own works.

They described the victims' and survivors' works of self-expression as links in the continuing "golden chain" of Jewish literary creativity, and they

---

1. Introductory quotations appear in full below, with citations.

undertook to "extend further the golden chain" by transmitting the essential content of these works to future generations through their historical writing. The intent of the present chapter is to provide an additional act of exposure by conveying to a new and wider audience the nature and scope of the Yiddish historians' engagement with the works of the victims and survivors.

Against the "Myth of Silence"

A recurring motif in the early writings of the Yiddish historians is the discovery of the literary productivity of their fellow survivors. They remarked that countless individuals within the internationally dispersed community of Yiddish-speaking survivors had undertaken a project of historical commemoration parallel to their own.

The later widespread belief that Holocaust survivors were largely silent until moved to speak during the early 1960s by the Eichmann trial or by accusations of passivity and complicity in Hannah Arendt's coverage of the trial and in Raul Hilberg's *Destruction of the European Jews* neglects the robust conversation of the Yiddish-speaking survivors. Scholarship on the emergence of Holocaust awareness in the early postwar period has focused primarily on the broad public sphere of American Jewry, not on the survivors' own cultural context.[2] To the extent that such research has considered the role of survivors, it has been to assess or explain their relative absence from that sphere.[3]

But for the worldwide community of Yiddish-speaking survivors, there was no "silence" and no "Myth of Silence." Yiddish-speaking survivors exhibited a striving for self-expression that was realized within their own public sphere. Their internal dialogue, conducted almost entirely in Yiddish, has been preserved for examination today in the books

---

2. Typical of the public focus is Deborah E. Lipstadt, "America and the Memory of the Holocaust, 1950–1965," *Modern Judaism* 16, no. 3 (October 1996): 195–214; for the detailed contrary argument, see Hasia R. Diner, *We Remember with Reverence and Love: American Jews and the Myth of Silence after the Holocaust, 1945–1962* (New York, 2009), which refers to Yiddish-language representation at 45–50; chapter 2 passim; and 207ff.

3. Beth Cohen, "The Myth of Silence: Survivors tell a different story," in *After the Holocaust: Challenging the Myth of Silence*, ed. David Cesarani and Eric J. Sundquist (London, 2011), 181–91, particularly 181–82 on the discouragement of survivor speech by American Jews.

and articles they published throughout their postwar dispersion. Confirmation of their vigorous "non-silence" is now also provided by recent research in related fields, such as studies of publishing in the Displaced Persons camps,[4] the literature of postwar Poland,[5] and the writings of specific populations such as child survivors.[6]

But the most direct evidence is the contemporaneous commentary provided by the survivors' own historians, who were simultaneously observers of, and participants in, the internal conversation of the Yiddish-speaking survivors. This commentary decisively negates any claim of a "Myth of Silence" among Yiddish-speaking survivors in the early postwar period.[7]

One of the first to recognize the survivors' urge for self-expression was Philip Friedman. During the early months of 1948, when Friedman awaited permission to immigrate to the United States, he published a series of Yiddish essays on the writing of Holocaust historiography that summarize the formative, European phase of his thinking. The posthumous collection of his Holocaust essays, *Roads to Extinction* (1980), is diminished by the omission of these fundamental articles. They reveal not only the early maturity of his thinking but also the immediacy of his responses to recent events.

One of these essays, "From Anti-Historicism to Super-Historicism," expands on the 1941 address by Elias Tcherikower, "Jewish catastrophe in the writing of Jewish History"[8] (discussed in chapter 2). Tcherikower had escaped from Paris a step ahead of the Nazis, and he addressed the

---

4. Tamar Lewinsky, "Dangling Root? Yiddish Language and Culture in the German Diaspora," in *"We Are Here": New Approaches to Jewish Displaced Persons in Postwar Germany*, ed. Avinoam J. Patt and Michael J. Berkowitz (Detroit, 2010), 308–34.

5. Joanna Nalewajko-Kulikov, "The Last Yiddish Books Printed in Poland," in *Under the Red Banner*, ed. Elvira Grözinger and Magdalena Ruta (Wiesbaden, 2008), 111–34.

6. Boaz Cohen, "Representing the Experiences of Children in the Holocaust," in Patt and Berkowitz, 74–97.

7. A portion of this chapter, directed specifically at refuting the myth of silence in the Yiddish-speaking world, appeared as Mark L. Smith, "No Silence in Yiddish: Popular and Scholarly Writing about the Holocaust in the Early Postwar Years," in *After the Holocaust: Challenging the Myth of Silence*, ed. David Cesarani and Eric J. Sundquist (London, 2011), 55–66.

8. Friedman, "Fun antihistoritsizm tsum superhistoritsizm," *Kiem* (March 1948): 30–31. He cites the conference title of Tcherikower's address ("Yidishe katastrofes in der yidisher geshikhte-shraybung") and the dates of the conference (January 3–5, 1941), neither of which appear in the *YIVO bleter*, instead of the published title and specific date of the address (January 3), suggesting that he had received a prepublication version of

first annual meeting of YIVO in New York on the unpreparedness of Jewish historiography, in comparison with Jewish martyrology, to record catastrophe. Tcherikower's address prefigures Yerushalmi's 1982 *Zakhor* in noting the disregard for historical writing that had prevailed in Jewish intellectual life from late antiquity until the emergence of Jewish historians in the nineteenth century, while recounting the many martyrological chronicles that were written (or popularized) in Yiddish.

Friedman builds on Tcherikower's analysis of Jewish "anti-historicism" to claim that the popularization of Jewish history by Heinreich Graetz in the second half of the nineteenth century awakened the Jewish masses to the importance of historical writing. As a result, Friedman continues, Jews were moved "to repay the great debt of silence that covered our history for two thousand years" with a new "super-historicism," and that, "particularly after the latest catastrophe, this tendency was still further intensified." Friedman declares that every major event of recent centuries inspired "a great deal of memoir writing," but that it would be a mistake to dismiss the recent flood of Holocaust memoirs as mere "graphomania" (a favored term from his, and also Blumental's, prewar writings). He argues instead that they represent a "mighty folk movement by which the folk-instinct seeks to eternalize the most severe catastrophe to befall us in 2,000 years." He declares that the urge to record by "hundreds of ordinary people who never in their lives dreamed of becoming writers" is "a healthy instinct of a people."[9] And the writers whom he counts as hundreds in this 1948 essay become "thousands" in the expanded version he published in 1950. There, Friedman acknowledges, "Even before the hands of the historian could touch the heated matter, the people themselves had created the history of their suffering."[10] He reports on the publication of more than 10,000 books and articles, which "is already a whole literature," and (referring to the Hebrew prophet Ezekiel) he declares: "All have become prophets, all have encountered God's burning fire and have brought speech to their mute lips."[11]

Tcherikover's "Yidishe martirologye un yidishe historiografye," *YIVO bleter* XVII, no. 2 (March–April 1941): 97–112.
    9. Friedman, "Fun antihistoritsizm tsum superhistoritsizm," 30–31.
    10. Friedman, "Unzer khurbn-literatur," *Idisher kemfer* (March 31, 1950, Pesach): 88.
    11. Ibid., 87 (Ezekiel 33:22).

Each of the Yiddish historians echoed Friedman's recognition of the survivors' urgency for self-expression. Joseph Kermish, for example, who served as founding archivist of the CJHC and assistant director after Friedman's departure, assessed the archives' holdings in 1949 and stressed the need for a comprehensive bibliography "to orient oneself in the sea" of memorial materials. He notes the existence, in every postwar place of Jewish residence, of "tens of books, hundreds of brochures, articles and memoirs . . . which attempt to reconstruct a world that has disappeared, and to erect a headstone over the scattered remains of the Jewish martyrs."[12]

The general memorial impulse that inspired survivors to speak also served as a catalyst for the Yiddish historians' own work. Kermish observes that "the great cataclysm penetrated deeply into the mood and feeling of our people," and it "impels us to record, to describe, to revivify that which so tragically disappeared."[13] Isaiah Trunk's turn to Holocaust history is explained by his son, Gabriel, who says that "in the absence of his mother and sisters in their Treblinka fate, he owed it to them and all the others to eternalize what had happened in the writing of that sacrosanct historiographic epic he was capable of and trained for."[14]

Nachman Blumental tells of returning from his wartime refuge in the Soviet Union to his town of Borszczów in Eastern Galicia to find that fewer than 100 of the town's 2,000 Jews had survived. "Day and night we sat together, listening to tales of the last three years. Everyone had an endless story to tell about his personal experiences, and no one ever tired of hearing it." He continues, "we passed from house to house, inquiring into the fate of former residents"—which led to surveys of surrounding towns—and the reader may observe that here commenced Blumental's commitment to Holocaust research.[15]

---

12. Kermish, "Vegn a biblyografye tsu der geshikhte fun poylishn yidntum in der tkufe fun der natsyonaler katastrofe (1939–1945)," *Bleter far geshikhte* II, nos. 1–4 (1949): 227.

13. Kermish, preface to *Ta'arukhat Sifre-Zikaron li-kehilot Yisra'el sheharvu* (Tel Aviv, 1961), 5 (Yiddish).

14. Email to the author, July 26, 2008.

15. Blumental, "Spinka, the Shabbes-Goy," *Yad Vashem Bulletin* 18 (April 1966): 31 (Yiddish original not located). In 1958, Blumental complained that the survivors' eagerness to speak during the early postwar years had turned to silence in Israel as their lives

Within a month of his escape from the Nazis in the spring of 1945, Mark Dworzecki arrived in Paris and began to publish a series of articles that document his transformation from survivor to historian. Relating the events of his own survival and liberation caused him to consider basic issues of Holocaust historiography. In June, he published an article titled "Remain Silent—or Tell the Whole Truth?," in which he concludes that every detail of the Jewish experience under the Nazis, both uplifting and degrading, must be told.[16] By September, he resolves to dedicate his "second life, the one after the camps, the one that is a gift of fate," to the mission of recounting that truth.[17]

Quantitative evidence for the "non-silence" of the Yiddish-speaking survivors and also for the predominance of Yiddish as the survivors' language of internal discourse is found in Friedman's contemporaneous accounts. In mid-1948, Friedman reviewed the publishing activities of the Displaced Persons camps in the US Zone of Germany, where he served as Educational Director for the American Joint Distribution Committee. He reported that Hebrew was the language of instruction for youth in preparation for their future lives in the Land of Israel but that Yiddish was the language of the adult survivors.

Specifically, he noted that 68 out of 83 textbooks published in the US Zone appeared in Hebrew, while 68 out of 84 newspapers appeared in Yiddish.[18] A decade later, he recounted that the joint YIVO–Yad Vashem

---

moved on or they felt a lack of public interest. He appears to refer to the survivors' reaction to the broader Jewish public sphere in Israel (as in America), not those who "feel themselves to be in the presence of a close and sympathetic friend." Blumental, "Vegn forshn di geshikhte fun 'bund,'" *Lebns-fragn* 82 (June 1958): 6. See also his "Nisht shvaygn un nisht lozn fargesn!," *Lebns-fragn* 84 (October 1958): 11. Also in 1958, Friedman refers to a waning and recent rebirth of interest in the Holocaust in his review, for an English-speaking Jewish audience, of five new Holocaust books in English. In no instance, however, does any of the Yiddish historians suggest that the survivor public had tired of Holocaust memory, despite occasional complaints in letters to the Yiddish press (apparently by prewar immigrant readers) that enough attention had been given to the Holocaust.

16. Dworzecki, "Farshvaygn—oder dertseyln dem gantsn emes?" *Unzer vort* (June 22, 1945): 3.

17. Dworzecki, "Oyf fir vegn veln mir fanandergeyn," *Unzer vort* (September 21, 1945): 2.

18. Friedman, "Dos gedrukte yidishe vort bay der sheyres hapleyte in daytshland," *Di tsukunft* (March 1949): 153; continued from February 1949 issue, 94–97. The article was written in the spring of 1948.

Bibliographical Series, which he directed from its formation in 1954 (and to which all of the Yiddish historians contributed), had identified 310 periodicals worldwide as richest in Holocaust materials as of January 1955, and that of these, 170 were in Yiddish and 35 in Hebrew.[19] The volumes of this series are each devoted to published writings in a given language—Hebrew, Hungarian, Yiddish, and English—but are sufficiently disparate in their coverage of genres, publication types, and time periods that they frustrate quantitative comparisons across languages. Nevertheless, close examination suggests that a graph of the data would find the continually ascending curve of Hebrew publications crossing the ultimately descending curve of Yiddish publications in the mid-1960s, confirming the numerical dominance of Yiddish during the first postwar decades.

An example of the growth and reception of Holocaust writing in Yiddish is the *Dos poylishe yidntum* series of books published by the Central Union of Polish Jews in Argentina.[20] The series published 175 titles on predominantly Holocaust themes from 1946 to 1966,[21] including one from each of the Yiddish historians except Dworzecki. Among the first was Kermish's early history of the Warsaw Ghetto Uprising, published jointly with the Jewish Historical Institute in Warsaw,[22] and the last was Blumental's collection of essays on Yiddish literature under Nazi occupation.[23] These bracketed Friedman's monograph on Auschwitz, for which Friedman listed twenty-seven reviews from the worldwide Yiddish press in his

---

19. Friedman, "A fertl-yorhundert 'khurbn-literatur,'" *Di tsukunft* (September 1959): 358.

20. For an overview, see Jan Schwarz, "A Library of Hope and Destruction: The Yiddish Book Series *Dos poylishe yidntum*, 1946–1966," *Polin* 20 (2007), 173–96; *Survivors and Exiles: Yiddish Culture after the Holocaust* (Detroit, 2015), 92–117.

21. The 175 volumes comprise 158 distinct titles, including 17 volumes with double or triple volume numbers.

22. Kermish, *Der oyfshtand in varshever geto: 19ter April–16ter mai 1943* (Buenos Aires, 1948; vol. 30). It was first published in Polish by the CJHC in 1946, and the JHI provided the Yiddish translation. See bibliography.

23. Blumental, *Shmuesn vegn der yidisher literatur unter der daytsher okupatsye* (Buenos Aires, 1966; vol. 175). It appeared as a final revival of the series following a two-year hiatus and was funded by a unique subvention by the Memorial Foundation for Jewish Culture.

bibliography,[24] and Trunk's first book of selected historical articles, which marked the start of his most active period of publishing.[25]

The public celebration of the twenty-fifth volume of the series in Buenos Aires in 1947 was greeted in the government-sanctioned Yiddish press in Poland with the statement that the series "has called forth great recognition and very warm appraisals from the whole world of Yiddish culture."[26] Friedman noted the value of the series for the study of Polish-Jewish history, commencing with "a certain number of historical monographs and collections," and he urged financial support by North American Jews rather than creation of a redundant publishing project.[27] The series became a historical treasure house that included books by other historians on earlier periods, local Holocaust histories by lay historians, memoirs by survivors, and literary works that together memorialized the Jews of Poland. In its first four years, 100,000 copies of volumes 1–65 were reported sold.[28] With the publication of volume 75 just one year later, the publisher, Abraham Mitelberg, reported 200,000 copies in circulation and a press run of 2,000 to 5,000 per title. The publisher then singled out Mordecai Strigler, Chaim Grade, and Friedman as examples of authors without whose works the publishing house would have no justifiable existence.[29]

The Continuity of Jewish Self-Expression

The desire for self-expression among those who experienced the Holocaust did not begin with the survivors but with those who lived in the ghettos and camps under Nazi occupation. Friedman writes that Emanuel

---

24. Friedman, *Oshvyentshim* (Buenos Aires, 1950; vol. 59). The reviews are listed in Friedman's bibliography of 1955.
25. Trunk, *Geshtaltn un gesheenishn* (Buenos Aires, 1962; vol. 165).
26. [B. Mark], "25 bikher 'dos poylishe yidntum,'" *Dos naye lebn* (December 14, 1947): 4 (unsigned; see bibliography).
27. Friedman, "Geshikhtlekhe forshungen vegn poylishn yidntum," *Idisher kemfer* (July 13, 1951): 12.
28. "Argentina," *American Jewish Yearbook 1951* (New York, 1952), 221–22. The article misstates as "three years" the period between volume 1 (March 15, 1946) and volume 64–65 (April 14, 1950).
29. A. Mitelberg, "Bikher-monument," *Oyfn shvel* (January 1952): 15.

Ringelblum had already noted in his diary in February 1941 that "the urge to write memoirs is so great that even in the labor camps young people wrote memoirs." Friedman himself declares that for some, "the urge to record for eternal memory was literally as strong as the instinct to save one's life,"[30] to which Kermish adds that postwar writing "is no doubt a continuation of that urge to record."[31] Dworzecki informs the readers of his history of the Vilna Ghetto that he had written and lost two diaries in the ghetto and that his new work was begun on April 28, 1945, in the German town of Saulgau near Württemberg, on the first day of his liberation.[32]

The continuity of Jewish expression was at times evoked through the metaphor of the "golden chain" traditionally applied to Yiddish literature. Blumental notes that the "golden chain of Jewish literary creativity was not interrupted in the Lodz Ghetto, even in the worst living conditions,"[33] and Friedman asserts in one of his first public statements as director of the CJHC that one of the great historic tasks of the CJHC is "to extend further the golden chain, to extend the chain between our past and our new future: to fulfill the Jewish commandment, 'And you shall tell your son' [Exodus 13:8]."[34] It should be noted that biblical allusions such as this, and the paraphrase of Ezekiel above, are rare among the generally secular Yiddish historians and occur only in their most impassioned statements.

Before the extent of literary creativity in the Warsaw Ghetto was revealed through recovery of the first portion of the Ringelblum Archive in September 1946, the CJHC had already retrieved hundreds of written materials from the ruins of the Lodz Ghetto. In the debris of the Chełmno extermination camp, Blumental had personally discovered a Yiddish verse cycle of ironic protest by an accomplished, anonymous poet, which he reconstructed and published.[35] Blumental declared that "in no epoch did there arise such a great number of works, and such a great number

---

30. Friedman, "Unzer khurbn-literatur," 87.
31. Kermish, *Ta'aruhat*, 5 (Yiddish).
32. Dworzecki, *Yerusholayim d'lite in kamf un umkum* (Paris, 1948), 20.
33. Blumental, foreword to S. Shayevitsh, *Lekh-lekho* (Lodz, 1946), 12.
34. Friedman, "Unzer historishe oyfgabe," *Dos naye lebn* (April 10, 1945): 6.
35. Blumental, "Vegn a literarisher shafung beys der daytsher okupatsye," *Kiem* (February 1948): 45–49.

of writers!"[36] On behalf of the CJHC, Friedman announced in the spring of 1946 that the commission had assembled "hundreds of songs of the ghettos, of partisan life, of the forests, of the camps" and "folk-sayings, folk-stories, fables," as well as sculptural works in all media.[37]

In their respective writings, Blumental and Dworzecki both remarked on the striving by Jews under Nazi occupation for internal communication. Blumental reported on messages of farewell and vengeance that were written hastily in the margins of books and on the walls of homes.[38] In "Ghettos and Concentration Camps Seek Contacts," Dworzecki recounts the sending of "news" between concentration camps by writing the names of murdered Jews on the walls of trains and on shipments of raw lumber. He describes the ghettos as "Jewish islands in a Nazi Ocean" (in early 1949, at the very time of the Berlin Airlift, when Berliners called themselves "islanders"), and he provides one of the earliest appreciations of the emissaries, mostly women, who risked their lives to smuggle messages and calls to revolt along a network of secret routes in Poland.[39] Dworzecki writes that these courageous emissaries, among them a few non-Jews, were the lifelines of news and morale for the Jews in forced isolation.

Not surprisingly, the efforts by captive Jews to record and communicate their struggles found responses among the Yiddish historians according to their own experiences and interests. Dworzecki, who had been acquainted in the Vilna Ghetto with Hirsh Glik, the author of the *Partizaner lid* (Partisan Hymn), thereafter prepared a monograph on Glik's life and work.[40] A 1953 essay by Dworzecki in appreciation of the poet and dramatist Yitskhok Katzenelson was inspired by his stay, on his last night in France before leaving for Israel, at the same Hotel Providence in Vittel in which Katzenelson had written his well-known "Song of the Murdered

---

36. Blumental, "Yidishe literatur unter der daytsher okupatsye," *Dos naye lebn* (September 14, 1945): 5.

37. Friedman, "Di yidishe historishe komisye in poyln," *Eynikeyt* (June 1946): 11.

38. Blumental, "Oyfshriftn oyf vent, ksovim un bikher," *Lebns-fragn* 145 (January 1964): 10; 146 (February 1964): 7–8.

39. Dworzecki, "Getos un kontsentratsye-lagern zukhn kontaktn," *Kiem* (April 1949): 899.

40. Dworzecki, *Hirshke glik: der mekhaber fun partizaner-himn* (Paris, 1966).

Jewish People" while interned by the Nazis.⁴¹ (The regard accorded both Dworzecki and his subject is reflected in the essay's placement as the lead article in the first issue of a new literary magazine in Buenos Aires.)

The recollection by Trunk of the dedicated folklorist Shmuel Lehman, and of Lehman's efforts in the Warsaw Ghetto to collect songs and stories from arriving refugees, was founded on his prewar acquaintance with Lehman and the public support that he and other leading Yiddish intellectuals had given to Lehman's work.⁴² In a similarly personal manner, Trunk's eulogy of Shmuel (Artur) Zygielbojm, the leader of the Polish Bund, who committed suicide in London in 1943 to protest his inability to mobilize Allied opposition to the Nazi murder of Polish Jews, derived from Trunk's lifelong allegiance to the Bund and his admiration for Zygielbojm.⁴³

Blumental, who had specialized in Jewish literary history before the war, devoted his postwar Yiddish work primarily to literary expression during the Holocaust. At the early date of September 19–20, 1945, the CJHC held its *second* academic conference in Lodz,⁴⁴ and Blumental presented his "Introduction to the History of Literary Creativity in Yiddish at the Time of the German Occupation."⁴⁵ He reported that the desire to "eternalize the most frightful act of violence in the world," as well as "to capture the everyday," had inspired Jews of every class and occupation. He discussed the literary salons and theaters of the Warsaw Ghetto and, by contrast, the spoken literature of street singers and news criers.⁴⁶

---

41. Dworzecki, "Dort vu s'iz geshribn gevorn 'dos lid fun oysghargetn yidishn folk,'" *Ilustrirte literarishe bleter* (September 1953): 3, 12, 16.

42. Trunk, "Shmuel lehman, z"l: der lamed-vovnik fun yidishn folklor," *Lebns-fragn* 10 (February 1952): 6. See "Tsu der yidisher gezelshaft!" *Literarishe bleter* (February 5, 1932): 99 (signed by Trunk, Weinreich, Ringelblum, and Schiper, among others).

43. Trunk, "Shmuel zigelboym," in his *Geshtaltn un gesheenishn* (Buenos Aires, 1962), 51–55.

44. The first, August 12, 1945, was devoted primarily to the work of the regional commissions.

45. Shedletsky, "Tsveyte visnshaftlekhe baratung," *Dos naye lebn* (October 13, 1945): 5. See *Protokol fun tsveytn visnshaftlekher baratung fun der Ts.Y.H.K. in lodzsh* [*Minutes of the second academic conference of the CJHC in Lodz*] *dem 19-tn un 20-tn september 1945*, 11–13. Archive of the Jewish Historical Institute, Warsaw, AZIH/CKZP/CŻKH/303/XX12.

46. Blumental, "Di yidishe literatur unter der daytshisher okupatsye," *Yidishe kultur* 8, no. 1 (January 1946): 10.

When Dworzecki questions whether the survivors have the right or obligation to reveal the experiences of the victims, he translates the victims' desire that their ordeal be remembered into a commandment for the living. In an article titled, "O, Help Me to Tell What I Saw . . . (a word about the mission of witnesses)," he proclaims, "Those who disappeared have commanded us: Tell!" and he urges, "Let each survivor . . . always tell only what is true; what he knows and how he knows it; and let all be told for the generations to come."[47]

The Imperative to Publish

The Yiddish historians' recognition of the many forms of "non-silence" among the victims soon led to their shared imperative to publish wartime materials. At first, Friedman proposed a measured pace for the publishing activity of the CJHC, outlining a two-year plan for collecting and publishing at the September 1945 conference. However, the consensus of those assembled was that "it is already high time to display the fruits of our efforts so far" and to publish as quickly as possible.[48] Friedman later ascribed this difference to conflicting scholarly-versus-publicistic views between the central and regional historical commissions,[49] but in his final report on the work of the CJHC, he concludes, "Seeking out and imparting to our people these creative works is one of the most important tasks" of the CJHC.[50] Under his successor, Blumental, the JHI emphasized that in addition to preserving materials for use by researchers its obligation was to "make them available for the widest mass readership."[51]

---

47. Dworzecki, "O, helf mir dertseyln vos ikh hob gezen . . . (a vort vegn der shlikhes fun eydes)," *Kiem* 9–10 (September–October 1948): 530–34. The English translation, "What I Saw," in *The Way We Think: A Collection of Essays from the Yiddish*, ed. Joseph Leftwich, vol. 2 (South Brunswick, 1969), 420–24, is apparently unauthorized or unsupervised; Dworzecki's name is misspelled "Dworzevsky," his birth year and year of *aliya* are incorrect, and he is credited only as a physician, not a historian.
48. Shedletsky, "Tsveyte visnshaftlekhe baratung," 5.
49. Friedman, "The European Jewish Research on the Recent Jewish Catastrophe in 1939–1945," *Proceedings of the American Academy for Jewish Research* XVIII (1949): 197.
50. Friedman, "Di yidishe historishe komisye in poyln," *Eynikeyt* (June 1946): 21.
51. *Prospekt fun di oysgabn fun der tsentraler yidisher historisher komisye in poyln* (Warsaw-Lodz-Krakow, 1947), 7.

Of first importance was the Oyneg Shabes archive, which Ringelblum had intended to publish as soon as possible after the war, and within it, Ringelblum's own *Notes*. Yet the publishing of wartime Yiddish documents in Poland was delayed, in the early years, by a shortage of funds and of Yiddish type,[52] and under the Soviet domination that became complete in mid-1949, by the emigration of leading historians and the imposition of ideological constraints on those who remained. The portions of Ringelblum's *Notes* that did appear in Warsaw in 1952 were criticized by Kermish and Blumental as tendentious selections, edited to claim undue and exclusive credit for the Communist partisans.[53] As late as 1965, Trunk lamented that "twenty years after the death of our historian-martyr, the materials from the Ringelblum Archive lie in the cupboards of the Jewish Historical Institute in Warsaw, and no redeemer for them has yet been found."[54]

To varying degrees, all of the Yiddish historians participated in publishing wartime Jewish writings. Dworzecki, for example, discovered and published excerpts from the Vilna Ghetto diary of his first Hebrew teacher, Moshe Olitski, whom he names as the founder of the first Tarbut Hebrew high school in the Diaspora and, later, founder of the school system in the Vilna Ghetto.[55] He notes that, despite the diary's Hebrew title (*Yeven Metzulah—Book 2*, intended as a parallel to Hannover's well-known pogrom chronicle of 1653), it was written in Yiddish, as were six of the eight surviving Vilna Ghetto diaries listed by Dworzecki. He was also an advocate for publication of such materials, urging that the wartime writings of Yosef Zilberman from the Sokołów Podlaski Ghetto, and his many articles of literary criticism in the Yiddish press of the Displaced

---

52. Blumental, foreword to S. Shayevitsh, *Lekh-lekho* (Lodz, 1946); he says that "the Germans destroyed all Jewish print shops, Yiddish type, etc." The same is reported by Mauritsi Horn, "Visnshaftlekhe un editorishe tetikayt fun der tsentraler yidisher historisher komisye baym TsKY"P un funem yidishn historishn institut in poyln in di yorn 1945–1950," *Bleter far geshikhte* XXIV (1986): 146.
53. Kermish, "In varshever geto," *YIVO bleter* XXXVII (1953): 282–96; Blumental, "Di yerushe fun emanuel ringelblum," *Di goldene keyt* 15 (1953): 235–42.
54. Trunk, "Emanuel ringelblum—der historiker 1900–1944," *Di tsukunft* (April 1965): 161.
55. Dworzecki, "Dos togbukh fun lerer moyshe olitski," in *Vilner zamlbukh / Me'asef Vilnah*, ed. Yisrael Rudnitsky (Tel Aviv, 1974), 96–105.

Persons camps, "which are scattered throughout the press of the D.P. camps, should be collected and published here in this country."[56]

The Yiddish historian most dedicated to "redeeming" the materials of Jewish self-expression was Kermish, who specialized in Jewish documentary history. It is characteristic that one of his earliest prewar articles (in Polish, 1937) brought to light an "Unknown Patriotic Letter from a Rabbi to Kościuszko in 1792,"[57] and that one of his latest (in Yiddish, 1983) did the same for "Unknown Letters from Zelig Kalmanovitch, of the Vilna Ghetto."[58] Most of his larger works are critical editions in Hebrew or English of materials from the Ringelblum Archive, while his essays are often discussions in Yiddish of those materials. An early project that follows the typical trajectory of his works is "The Testament of the Warsaw Ghetto," in which he analyzes the answers of leading intellectuals to an Oyneg Shabes questionnaire on the Jewish present and future after two-and-a-half years in the Warsaw Ghetto. A comprehensive Yiddish essay by Kermish appeared in 1951. This was excerpted in English in 1951, and condensed for Yiddish, Hebrew, and English versions in 1956–57.[59] The original Oyneg Shabes questionnaire and answers by three respondents appeared in Yiddish in 1948,[60] but complete publication of the extant responses occurred only with their inclusion in his 1986 English-language anthology of documents from the Warsaw Ghetto.[61]

As director of the Yad Vashem archives, Kermish declared in 1954, on the front page of the Hebrew edition of *News of Yad Vashem*, that it was

---

56. Dworzecki, "D"r yosef zilberberg," in *Sefer ha-zikaron Sokolov-Podliask*, ed. M. Gelbart (Tel Aviv, 1962), 658–59 (article date: 1952; original publication not located).

57. Kermish, "Nieznany list patriotyczny rabina do Kościszki z rozu 1792," *Głos Gminy Żydowskiej* I, no. 4 (October 1937): 87–88. Friedman and Balaban also contributed to this journal, as did Adam Czerniaków, the future leader of the Warsaw Judenrat, whose ghetto diary Kermish later edited for publication.

58. Kermish, "Umbakante briv fun zelig kalmanovitsh, fun vilner geto, tsu itsik giterman, in varshever geto," *Di goldene keyt* 110–11 (1983): 17–30.

59. Kermish, "Di tsavoa fun varshever geto," *Di goldene keyt* 9 (1951): 134–62. See bibliography for publication history.

60. Kermish [anon.], "Ankete fun 'oyneg shabes,'" *Bleter far geshikhte* I, nos. 3–4 (August–December 1948): 186ff.

61. Kermish, ed., *To Live with Honor, To Die with Honor!...: Selected Documents from the Warsaw Ghetto Underground Archives "O.S." ["Oneg Shabbath"]* (Jerusalem, 1986), 717–63 (section on "Ideas on destiny and Existence" with introductory essay by Kermish).

the institution's "obligation to publish source-materials from the ghetto archives,"[62] a position that figured in the internal conflict of 1958–60 between the East European immigrants and established Israelis (as described in chapter 2). His ultimate success may be credited to longevity and perseverance. He gives highest priority to three works, each of which he published in critical editions during the succeeding four decades—the Jewish underground press in the Warsaw Ghetto, Ringelblum's complete *Notes*,[63] and the writings of Ringelblum's historian colleague, Rabbi Shimon Huberband.[64]

His most sustained effort was devoted to the dozens of underground periodicals that served as the chief vehicle for political, and also literary, expression in the Warsaw Ghetto. Many were distributed by secret emissaries to the surrounding towns, and some continued to appear until the eve of the uprising. Each clandestine publication was affiliated with a given political or youth movement and provided its own perspective on events in the ghetto. Kermish's correspondence with Trunk, his archivist counterpart at YIVO in New York, reveals the drama of his efforts to compile and edit a Hebrew translation of the hundreds of extant issues. Kermish had already informed Friedman in 1954 that his bibliography of forty-two different Yiddish, Polish, and Hebrew publications was nearly complete.[65] In Yiddish letters that span from 1955 to 1978, Kermish assures Trunk that publication of the collection is imminent, while informing him of each new delay.[66] In 1955, he says, "I have pro-

---

62. Kermish, "Hovat pirsum mekorot me'arkhyone ha-geta'ot," *Yedi'ot Yad va-Shem* 3 (December 1954): 1; English summary, "Publication of Source-Material of Ghetto Archives Obligatory," 16.

63. Emanuel Ringelblum, *Ksovim fun geto*, 2 vols. (Tel Aviv, 1985), with introductory essay and supplementary materials by Kermish.

64. Blumental and Kermish, eds., Shimon Huberband, *Kiddush Ha-Shem—Ketavim mi-yeme ha-Sho'ah* (Tel Aviv, 1969); English translation by David E. Fishman in *Rabbi Shimon Huberband, Kiddush Hashem: Jewish Religious and Cultural Life in Poland During the Holocaust*, ed. Jeffrey S. Gsurock and Robert S. Hirt (New York, 1987), with introduction by Blumental and Kermish (xii–xxx), and preface by Gideon Hausner, praising the "relentless efforts" and "inspiring guidance of Dr. Kermish," xi.

65. Kermish to Friedman, report: "Tetikayt-barikht fun biblyografishn opteyl," October 1954, YIVO Archives, RG 1258, F 116, 2.

66. Letters between Kermish and Trunk, YIVO Archives, RG 483, F 29.

posed to publish it in 2–3 large volumes," including "photocopies with translations."[67]

Fifteen years later, he tells Trunk that the work of translation "is finally nearing completion."[68] In the intervening years, he had published a series of articles on the underground press, and their topics now constitute the proposed outline he shares with Trunk. These include such themes as the periodicals' party orientation and depiction of social conditions in the ghetto,[69] the Land of Israel in the life of the ghetto,[70] and the role of the press in preparing for armed resistance.[71] He also appointed Trunk to a newly formed editorial committee of party experts as the Bund representative, and in 1977–78 he obtained Trunk's intercession to gain access to materials from the Bund archive in New York. The complete work, with annotated translations organized chronologically over the period of the ghetto's existence, finally appeared in six volumes from 1979 to 1997.[72]

The imperative to publish was based on two perceived obligations. The first, as noted, was to the demand inherent in the victims' writings that they be known to posterity. The second was the obligation to the survivors that they be included in the process of historical assessment.

The Lay–Professional Partnership

At the YIVO conference of 1935, at which Dubnow praised the YIVO scholars for choosing an educated lay readership as the intended audience for their works (as noted in the introduction), Friedman spoke of the need to "popularize Jewish history" by publishing "historical books

---

67. Kermish to Trunk, November 3, 1955.
68. Kermish to Trunk, August 18, 1970.
69. Kermish, "Vegn der untererdisher prese fun varshever geto," *Di goldene keyt* 27 (1957): 243–57.
70. Kermish, "The Land of Israel in the Life of the Ghetto as Reflected in the Illegal Warsaw Ghetto Press," *Yad Vashem Studies* V (1963): 105–31 (also in Hebrew edition).
71. Kermish, "Di rol fun der untergrunt-prese in varshever geto in der tsugreytung fun bodn far a bavofntn kamf," *Unzer kiem* 49–50–51 (October 1965): 14–19. See bibliography for publication history.
72. Kermish, ed., *'Itonut-ha-makhteret ha-Yehudit be-Varshah* (Jerusalem, 1979, 1979, 1984, 1989, 1992). All volumes but the sixth (1997) bear Kermish's name as editor.

for the people."⁷³ Friedman's last prewar publication was a review of the collected works of Saul Ginsburg, in which he notes with approval that "most of the articles combine research based on primary sources with a popular form and a remarkable literary style."⁷⁴ After the war, he praised Leo Schwarz, in whose "cabinet" he had served in Munich, for presenting his 1953 account of the Displaced Persons camps, *The Redeemers*, as a "people's book capable of penetrating the masses."⁷⁵

By their choice of publishing venues, all of the Yiddish historians demonstrated their concurrence with Friedman's emphasis on popular scholarship. Each published one or more books in Yiddish for an educated lay audience. They contributed hundreds of articles to the leading Zionist, socialist, Bundist, Communist, literary, and general Yiddish periodicals in Europe, the United States, and Israel from 1945 to 1988 (usually, but not always, in accordance with their political allegiances, as indicated by the table in chapter 1).⁷⁶ The two Yiddish academic journals in which they appeared also had a largely nonacademic circulation: the *Bleter far geshikhte* of the JHI in Warsaw was tolerated by the regime "simply because they had a very limited audience (they were distributed mainly within a closed circle of Jewish readers).⁷⁷ Such readers were necessarily nonacademics, as the only remaining Yiddish-speaking historians in postwar Poland were the journal's authors, although the journal did reach a limited number of scholars abroad. Similarly, the *YIVO bleter* of New York was distributed chiefly to the dues-paying members of YIVO, whose copies would often arrive with an inserted slip of blue paper reading in Yiddish and English, "The enclosed publication is sent to you AS A GIFT."

---

73. Friedman, "Di oyfgabes fun undzer historisher visnshaft un vi azoy zey tsu realizirn," *YIVO bleter* XIII, nos. 3–4 (1938): 310.

74. Friedman, review of Ginsburg's *Historishe verk* (New York, 1937–38), *Jewish Social Studies* III, no. 1 (January 1941): 95.

75. Friedman, "Di sheyres hapleyte un yisker-literatur," *Di tsukunft* (April 1956): 168.

76. All of the Yiddish historians outside Poland were non- or anti-Communist, with the notable exception of Raphael Mahler who was a lifelong Marxist, but not pro-Soviet.

77. Feliks Tych, "The Emergence of Holocaust Research in Poland: The Jewish Historical Commission and the Jewish Historical Institute (ŻIH), 1944–1989," in *Holocaust Historiography in Context: Emergence, Challenges, Polemics and Achievements*, ed. David Bankier and Dan Michman (Jerusalem, 2008), 241.

All of the Yiddish historians were also frequent speakers on Holocaust topics to lay audiences both in person and via electronic media, as discussed in chapter 1.

The Yiddish historians' relationship with their survivor public may be described as a "lay–professional partnership" that developed from their recognition of the survivors' and victims' strong desire to communicate. They encouraged, promoted, and then drew upon, the survivors' works of self-expression. The historians addressed these works at two levels of authorship—the personal author and the *yizkor* book published by the memorial society of a given town. At both levels, they found the opportunity to discuss their own particular areas of interest in Holocaust history.

Works by survivors at the personal level of authorship—memoirs, poetry, fiction, and drama—were encouraged by the Yiddish historians through their contribution of "forewords" that would lend their imprimatur to the efforts of lesser-known authors. Such support accorded with YIVO's pre- and postwar practice of sponsoring autobiography contests to encourage Jewish self-expression in Yiddish.[78] As Max Weinreich, then research director at YIVO, wrote in his foreword to a wartime autobiography sponsored by YIVO, "The future historian will surely be gratified that the YIVO established among us Jews this new method: letting the ordinary person come to the podium and teach the meaning of his life."[79]

Blumental and Kermish, for example, each provided supportive forewords to the account of the Vilna Ghetto by Mendel Balberyszski, in which Blumental describes the author's personality, and Kermish focuses on the value of his quotations from ghetto documents that were later destroyed.[80] Most prolific in this regard was Blumental, who contributed not fewer than eighteen forewords to Yiddish books of memoirs, poetry, and historical fiction by lay authors, commencing with the first Yiddish

---

78. See Jeffrey Shandler, ed., *Awakening Lives: Autobiographies of Jewish Youth in Poland Before the Holocaust* (New Haven, 2002).

79. Max Weinreich, foreword to Ezriel Presman, *Der durkhgegangener veg* (New York, 1950), iii–iv.

80. Blumental and Kermish, forewords to M. Balberishki, *Shtarker fun ayzn* (Tel Aviv, 1967), 12–19.

book printed in postwar Poland, in 1945.[81] In each foreword, Blumental gave further development to the author's treatment of a topic that coincided with his own particular interests, such as the dilemma of choosing whether to flee during the German invasion or to remain and hope to obey and survive;[82] the dangers of life on the "Aryan side," especially for orphaned children;[83] the inner life and language of the Warsaw Ghetto;[84] and wartime events in Lublin, where Blumental had been a gymnasium teacher before the war.[85] Among the last is his foreword to the 1982 memoirs of a former student in Lublin whose reminiscence of Blumental appears to be the only such treatment of a Yiddish historian by a prewar acquaintance.[86]

Although the majority of such forewords appeared in Yiddish publications, they were in fact a continuation of the early practice among CJHC leaders of introducing each others' works, nearly all published in Polish in the first postwar years.[87] Two of these are Friedman's foreword to the monograph on the Białystok Ghetto by historian Szymon Datner, [88] and Kermish's foreword to the study of Żółkiew (today Zhovlva, Ukraine) by Gerszon Taffet, a prewar teacher of Jewish history who became director of the CJHC photographic section.[89] The language shift continued in Israel, where Blumental also contributed to the Hebrew translations of Yiddish wartime diaries, including those of a soldier in

---

81. Blumental, foreword to Mendl Man, *Di shtilkeyt mont: lider un baladn* (Lodz, 1945), 3–4.

82. Blumental, foreword to Yisroel Tabakman, *Mayne iberlebungen (unter natsishe okupatsye in belgye)* (Tel Aviv, 1957), ix–xvi.

83. Blumental, foreword to Yosef Zshemian, *Di papirosn-hendler fun plats dray kraytsn* (Tel Aviv, 1964), 9–11.

84. Blumental, foreword to Yerakhmiel Briks, *Di papirene kroyn* (New York, 1969), 5–7.

85. Blumental, foreword to D. Zakalik, *Gerangl* (Tel Aviv, 1958), 7–10.

86. Blumental, foreword to Ruzshke Fishman-Shnaydman, *Mayn lublin: bilder funem lebns-shteyger fun yidn in farmilkhomedikn poyln* (Tel Aviv, 1982), 5–6; see also 171 on Blumental.

87. For a complete list, see the CJHC's 1947 *Prospekt*.

88. Friedman, foreword to Szymon Datner, *Walka i zagłada białostockiego ghetta* (Lodz, 1946), 5–8.

89. Kermish, foreword to Gerszon Taffet, *Zagłada Żydów Żółkiewskich* (Lodz, 1946), 5–7.

the Polish People's Army,[90] a survivor of the Lodz Ghetto,[91] a partisan in the White Russian forests,[92] and an organizer of the resistance in the Warsaw Ghetto.[93]

A specific type of author encouraged by the Yiddish historians may be termed the "lay historian." A small number of such authors drew on materials from multiple sources to write general accounts of Jewish life under the Nazis that were not limited to personal experience. Friedman expressed support for the works of three lay historians in 1948. He provided laudatory forewords to the books by Joseph Gar and Benjamin Orenstein on Kovne (Kaunas)[94] and Częstochowa,[95] respectively, that were prepared in the Displaced Persons camps of the US Zone in Germany during his tenure as director of education. Friedman's multiple reviews of Dworzecki's first book praised it as the "best and most comprehensive work" on the Vilna Ghetto.[96] The same work was praised by another lay historian, Moyshe Kaganovitsh (known for his 1948 history of the partisan movement), who declared, "If all the books written about the Vilna Ghetto were to vanish in a cataclysm, and only Dworzecki's book remained, it would be sufficient for the future historian," and in Warsaw, Ber Mark pronounced it "the very best and most comprehensive" work on the Vilna Ghetto.[97] When Dworzecki later transitioned

---

90. Blumental, foreword to Shaul Kartchever, *Im ha-divizyah ha-shelishit 'al shem Tra'ugut: yomano shel hayal Yehudi ba-tzava ha-Poloni ha-amami* (Jerusalem, 1962), 5–6.

91. Blumental, foreword to Sara Selver-Urbach, *Mi-ba'ad le-halon beti: zikhronot mi-geto Lodz'* (Jerusalem, 1964), 7–9.

92. Blumental, foreword to Mordechaj Zajczyk, *Mi-yomano shel partizan nitzol ha-sho'ah* (Tel Aviv, 1971), 5–8.

93. Blumental, biographical sketch of the author in Batiah Temkin-Berman, *Yoman ba-mahteret* (Tel Aviv, 1956), 233–37.

94. Friedman, foreword to Yosef Gar, *Umkum fun der yidisher kovne* (Munich, 1948), 9–11.

95. Friedman, foreword to Binyomin Orenshteyn, *Khurbn chenstokhov* (Munich, 1948), 8–9.

96. Friedman, "Some Books on the Jewish Catastrophe," *Jewish Social Studies* XII, no. 1 (1950): 86. See also Friedman, review of *Yerusholayim d'lite*, *Kiem* (June 1948): 406–7; and "100 bikher in yidish vegn khurbn un gvure," *Jewish Book Annual* (5710/1949–1950) 8 (1950): 131 (Hebrew numbering).

97. M. Kaganovitsh, "'Yerusholayim d'lite in kamf un umkum' fun d"r m. dvorzshetski," *Farn folk* 25 (June 11, 1948): 13; and Ber Mark, "Biblyografishe notitsn," *Dos naye lebn* (April 9, 1948): 5.

from lay to academic historian, he in turn provided approving forewords for such works by others.[98]

The largest, and perhaps least known, contribution by the Yiddish historians to the public sphere of the Yiddish-speaking survivors is their work on behalf of the *yizkor* books, the memorial volumes published by survivors of destroyed communities. The contribution of the Yiddish historians includes both recognition and participation. All of the historians published discussions of the *yizkor*-book phenomenon. It was described by Kermish as a "far-reaching folk movement,"[99] by Friedman as a "new distinct genre,"[100] and by Blumental as a "new literary form"[101] (that exceeded in number and scope the earlier Jewish tradition of preparing memorial books of destroyed communities). Blumental suggests that "if each survivor—except the small number who 'want to forget'—had had the means to do so, he would have published a book" of his own experiences, but lacking the means "he joins as a 'partner' in a *yizkor* book." By the end of the 1950s, Friedman counts 270 such books, with 160 in Yiddish;[102] Blumental finds 200 in Yiddish and 90 in Hebrew[103]—and declares that he has read them all.[104]

In their reviews of *yizkor* books, the Yiddish historians regard most highly the books with the greatest concern for historical development,

---

98. Examples are his forewords to A. Volf Yasni (formerly of the CJHC), *Di geshikhte fun di yidn in lodzsh in di yorn fun der daytsher yidn-oysrotung* (Tel Aviv, 1960), 7–11; and Toni Solomon-Ma'aravi, *Teg fun tsorn* (Tel Aviv, 1968), Yiddish 8; English v–vi.

99. Kermish, *Ta'aruhat*, 5 (Yiddish).

100. Friedman, "Khurbn hosht," *Kultur un dertsyung* (October 1958): 19.

101. Blumental, "A nayer literarisher min—yisker-bikher," *Lebns-fragn* 99 (January 1960): 7.

102. Friedman, "A fertl-yorhundert 'khurbn-literatur,'" 361. A typical preponderance of Yiddish works is found in microcosm in Friedman's bibliography of postwar books and articles on the city of Częstochowa (1958), for which he cites seventy in Yiddish and six in Hebrew (see bibliography). In the early years, a small number of *yizkor* books were bilingual (some with duplicate chapters, others with materials unique to each language). As the transition to Hebrew progressed, bilingual, and then solely Hebrew, *yizkor* books came to predominate. A significant number of Yiddish volumes were also republished in Hebrew, for example, the book on Chełm (to which Friedman contributed a Jewish history of the town) that appeared in Yiddish in 1956 and in Hebrew in 1980.

103. Blumental, "A nayer literarisher min—yisker-bikher," *Lebns-fragn* 99 (January 1960): 7.

104. Blumental, "Pro Domo Non Sua," *Lebns-fragn* 110 (December 1960): 7.

but their own participation in *yizkor* books has received little recognition. Kugelmass and Boyarin, for example, note that some books "contain substantial essays by Jewish academic historians," but they do not elaborate.[105] It is true that a great number of *yizkor* books have been thought by historians, including the Yiddish historians, to provide no more than raw materials for future researchers, but this is due to a combined shortage of documentary materials and historians. Friedman explains that personal accounts prevail in the *yizkor* books because "all archival sources, both official and communal, were destroyed or are located behind an 'iron curtain.'"[106] He assesses the many tasks of the survivor-historians, declaring, "The work is huge; the best and brightest of our historians were murdered." To the famous dictum of Rabbi Tarfon—"The day is short, the work is great"—he adds, "and the workers . . . few [ellipsis his]."[107]

Nevertheless, each of the Yiddish historians did, in fact, contribute articles to *yizkor* books, including a Holocaust history of his own ancestral town or region. There are at least forty such books to which they contributed not less than seventy signed articles, most often substantial histories of a given town and occasionally brief personal accounts.[108] In several instances, separate periods are covered by different historians, as in the books for Vitebsk (1956) and Chmielnik (1960), for which Trunk provided prewar histories, while Friedman and Kermish, respectively, wrote histories of the Holocaust period. Blumental alone edited or contributed to approximately twenty *yizkor* books. Dworzecki appears to have written articles for only two, Ludmir (Volodymyr Volyns'kyi, Ukraine, 1962) and

---

105. Jack Kugelmass and Jonathan Boyarin, *From a Ruined Garden*, 2nd ed. (Bloomington, 1998), 40.

106. Friedman, "Di landsmanshaftn-literatur in the fareynikte shtatn far di letste 10 yor," *Jewish Book Annual (5712/1951–52)* 10 (1952): 82 (Hebrew numbering).

107. Friedman, "Fun antihistoritsizm tsum superhistoritsizm," *Kiem* (March 1948): 32.

108. For the purpose of this discussion, the category "*yizkor* book" includes the *Encyclopaedia of the Jewish Diaspora* [*Entsiklopediyah shel Galuyot*], of which the individual volumes (several in Yiddish) were sponsored by survivor organizations and contain signed monographs based on original research, but not the *Chronicle of Communities* [*Pinkas ha-Kehilot*] series published by Yad Vashem (to which the Yiddish historians also contributed), which consists almost exclusively of shorter, unsigned articles, compiled from secondary sources.

Map of Contributions to *Yizkor* Books by Yiddish Historians

Initial letters indicate the historian's last name; see accompanying legend.

		Yizkor Book (Jewish name)	Location (present day)
Friedman	F1	Lvov [Lemberg] (Jerusalem, 1956)	Lwów, Poland (Lviv, Ukraine)
	F2	Ratne (Buenos Aires, 1954)	Ratno, Poland (Ratne, Ukraine)
	F3	Chelm (Johannesburg, 1954)	Chelm, Poland
	F4	Chenstokhova (New York, 1958)	Częstochowa, Poland
	F5	Belchatov (Buenos Aires, 1951)	Bełchatów, Poland
	F6	Vitebsk (New York, 1956; Tel Aviv, 1957)	Viciebsk, Belarus
	F7	Rakishok (Johannesburg, 1952)	Rokiškis, Lithuania
	F8	Lite [Lithuania] (New York, 1951)	Lithuania
Trunk	T1	Kutno (Tel Aviv, 1968)	Kutno, Poland
	T2	Plotsk (Tel Aviv, 1967)	Płock, Poland
	T3	Vlotslavek (Tel Aviv, 1967)	Włocławek, Poland
	T4	Sokhachev (Jerusalem, 1962)	Sochaczew, Poland
	T5	Pyotrkov Tribunalski (Tel Aviv, 1965)	Piotrków Trybunalski, Poland
	T6	Lublin (Paris, 1952; Jerusalem, 1957)	Lublin, Poland
	T7	Chmielnik (Tel Aviv, 1960)	Chmielnik, Poland
	T8	Vitebsk (New York, 1956; Tel Aviv, 1957)	Viciebsk, Belarus
Dworzecki	D1	Maytshet [Molchadz] (Tel Aviv, 1973)	Mołczadź, Poland (Moŭčadź, Belarus)
	D2	Ludmir (Tel Aviv, 1962)	Włodzimierz Wołyński, Poland (Volodymyr Volyns'kyi, Ukraine)
Blumental	B1	Borshtshiv (Tel Aviv, 1960)	Borszczów, Poland (Borshchiv, Ukraine)
	B2	Budzanov (Haifa, 1970)	Budzanów, Poland (Budaniv, Ukraine)
	B3	Podhayts (Tel Aviv, 1972)	Podhajce, Poland (Pidhaitsi, Ukraine)
	B4	Yezyerne (Haifa, 1971)	Jezierna, Poland (Ozerna, Ukraine)
	B5	Bisk (Haifa, 1965)	Busk, Poland (Bus'k, Ukraine)
	B6	Rava Ruska (Tel Aviv, 1973)	Rawa Ruska, Poland (Rava-Rus'ka, Ukraine)
	B7	Sokal (Tel Aviv, 1968)	Sokal, Poland (Sokal, Ukraine)
	B8	Sarni (Jerusalem, 1961)	Sarny, Poland (Sarny, Ukraine)
	B9	Yanow 'al-yad Pinsk (Jerusalem, 1969)	Janów Poleski, Poland (Ivanava, Belarus)
	B10	Hrubieshov [Rubishov] (Tel Aviv, 1962)	Hrubieszów, Poland
	B11	Lublin (Paris, 1952; Jerusalem, 1957)	Lublin, Poland
	B12	Kozshenits (Tel Aviv, 1969)	Kozienice, Poland
	B13	Varshe [Warzaw] (Jerusalem, 1953)	Warszawa, Poland
	B14	Sokhachev (Jerusalem, 1962)	Sochaczew, Poland
	B15	Aleksander 'al-yad Lodz (Tel Aviv, 1968)	Aleksandrów Łódzki, Poland
	B16	Zaglembia [region] (Tel Aviv, 1972)	Zagłębie Region, Poland
	B17	Myekhov (Tel Aviv, 1971)	Miechów, Poland
	B18	Baranov (Jerusalem, 1964)	Baranów Sandomierz, Poland
	B19	Rozvadov (Jerusalem, 1968)	Rozwadów, Poland
	B20	Mir (Jerusalem, 1962)	Mir, Belarus
Kermish	K1	Galitsye [region] (Buenos Aires, 1968)	Galicja, Poland (Halychyna, Ukraine)
	K2	Kolomey (Tel Aviv, 1972)	Kołomyja, Poland (Kolomyya, Ukraine)
	K3	Kalushin (Tel Aviv, 1961)	Kałuszyn, Poland
	K4	Varshe [Warzaw] (Jerusalem, 1973)	Warszawa, Poland
	K5	Plotsk (Tel Aviv, 1967)	Płock, Poland
	K6	Pyotrkov Tribunalski (Tel Aviv, 1965)	Piotrków Trybunalski, Poland
	K7	Skarzysko-Kamienna (Tel Aviv, 1973)	Skarżysko-Kamienna, Poland
	K8	Chmielnik (Tel Aviv, 1960)	Chmielnik, Poland

Molchadz (Moŭčadź, Belarus, 1973),[109] but his full-page poem, "Remember the Jewish Catastrophe," was reprinted from his 1948 history of the Vilna Ghetto in at least eleven Yiddish and Hebrew *yizkor* books between 1952 and 1975.[110]

The map and legend on the preceding pages illustrate the geographic distribution of the Yiddish historians' contributions to the *yizkor* books. As may be seen, most of Blumental's many works are devoted to locales lying on a virtually straight path from Warsaw to his hometown of Borszczów in southeastern Galicia (today, western Ukraine), and several of Trunk's works are devoted to communities clustered around his hometown of Kutno to the west of Warsaw, both of which suggest a continuing attachment to their home region and its survivors. By contrast, the nearly random distribution of Friedman's and Kermish's cities reflects Friedman's breadth of interests and Kermish's more specific focus on the history of the Warsaw Ghetto.

The respect accorded the historians' contributions is evident from their frequent placement at the start of a book or section. The desire of editors for works by professional historians is also found in the occasional reprinting of works posthumously or without permission. The former occurred in the reuse of two of Friedman's articles about the Holocaust in eastern Galicia by a 1961 Buenos Aires *yizkor* book on Galicia.[111] A curious instance of the latter is found in the back translation from English into Yiddish of Blumental's essay on the legendary self-sacrifice of the Radziner Rebbe by a 1959 Buenos Aires *yizkor* book on Warsaw.[112] The

---

109. A single-page essay was reprinted in *Sefer ha-zikaron Sokolov-Podliask*, ed. M. Gelbart (Tel Aviv, 1962), 658–59 (article date: 1952; original publication not located).

110. See Dworzecki, "Gedenk di katastrofe fun yisroel" (1945) in the bibliography.

111. Friedman's "Der umkum fun di yidn in mizrekh-galitsye," *Fun letstn khurbn* 4 (March 1947): 1–13, and his review, "Kolomey—di hoyptshtot fun pokutye un ire yidn," *Di tsukunft* (September 1958): 354–55, were reprinted in *Yerlekher gedenk-bukh* 1 (Buenos Aires, 1961), 274–81 and 67–70. Neither reprint is listed in the posthumous continuation of Friedman's bibliography, nor is the original Kolomey review (leaving uncertain whether the reprint was authorized by Friedman or known to his widow).

112. Blumental's "Yitzhak Katznelson's Poem of the Radziner Rebbe," in *Extermination and Resistance: Historical Records and Source Material*, vol. 1, ed. Zvi Szner (Haifa, 1958), 20–27, was published first in English translation by Kibutz Lohame ha-Geta'ot (at which Blumental and Kermish had established the historical research center in 1950) in its first English-language anthology, after Blumental and Kermish's departure in 1953 for

wish to include professional historians is further indicated by the reuse of prewar and wartime Yiddish writings on various towns by the deceased historians Ringelblum, Huberband, Balaban, Mandelsberg, Dubnow, Ginsburg, Schiper, and Zinberg in dozens of volumes.

Yizkor books were also the facet of Holocaust historiography to which the surviving Yiddish historians who did not otherwise engage in Holocaust research did contribute. Among the *yizkor* books praised for editorial excellence by both Friedman and Trunk are those edited by Raphael Mahler on Częstochowa (1947) and Jacob Shatzky on Mława (1950).[113] Both Mahler and Shatzky also provided chapters of prewar history for these or other books, and Shatzky contributed to the genre by reviewing dozens of *yizkor* books.[114] I. M. Biderman, student and eventual biographer of Balaban, also edited several books.[115] The well-known historian of Eastern European Jewry, N. M. Gelber, wrote prewar histories for the *yizkor* books of at least twenty towns, for which he was praised in Trunk's memorial essay as "one of the few [non-Holocaust] Jewish historians who participated with their comprehensive historical monographs in a great number of *yizkor* books."[116]

The Yiddish historians recognized that the *yizkor* books were not universally well regarded. Blumental, for example, reports hearing directly from "a respected historian" that "the yizkor books have no value for Jewish history, and not only must one not help publish them, but to the contrary ... [final ellipsis his]."[117] He also acknowledges the many "factual errors"—generally of prewar history—pointed out by Shatzky's reviews, but he responds that the value of the books lies in their being the memories

---

Yad Vashem, and it appeared as "Der kidush-hashem fun radziner rebbe," in *Varshever yidn: yubiley-bukh: 1949–1959* (Buenos Aires, 1959), 120–25, where the note, "Yidish: Avrom Plotkin," indicates that Blumental was not the source of the Yiddish text.

113. Friedman, "A fertl-yorhundert," 360; Trunk, "A bukh vegn shedlets," *YIVO bleter* XLI (1957): 359.

114. See, among others, Yankev Shatski, "Referatn un retsenzyes: yisker-bikher," *YIVO bleter* XXXVII (1953): 264–82; and XXXIX (1955): 339–55.

115. Gostynin (1960); his hometown, Włocławek (1969); and Kolbuszowa (1971).

116. Trunk, "Nosn mikhl gelber—der letster fun a dor," in his *Geshtaltn un gesheenishn [naye serye]* (Tel Aviv, 1983), 70.

117. Blumental, "Vegn yisker-bikher," *Lebns-fragn* 102–3 (April–May 1960): 16 (continuation of "A nayer literarisher min").

of recent events written by laymen.¹¹⁸ Trunk also defends the books, saying, "There are exceptions—*yizkor* books that devote much space to the history of a given community."¹¹⁹ Kugelmass and Boyarin note in their later appraisal of the "historical veracity" of *yizkor* books that they "can indeed serve as a great resource for those who want to study Jewish life in twentieth-century Poland," particularly by providing the historian with "local details on general phenomena." They cite two examples of such uses: Trunk's *Judenrat* and Blumental's study of Holocaust folklore.¹²⁰ The importance of the *yizkor* books to the Yiddish historians and their survivor public has been validated in the twenty-first century by the ongoing process of online translation into English of hundreds of such volumes, by which these have become the most widely accessible of all sources of local Holocaust history.¹²¹

The Reciprocal Relationship

Not only did the Yiddish historians include their fellow survivors among their intended audience; they also actively sought the participation of survivors in their historical research. The "lay–professional partnership" continued the prewar YIVO tradition of soliciting documents, memoirs, and answers to questionnaires from the Jewish public. Historian Zosa Szajkowski credits the "training of a young generation of dedicated collectors" for making possible "the holy work" of "collecting documents in the face of death."¹²² Both he and Friedman describe the plan by a group of young prisoners at Auschwitz to bury a collection of personal accounts for future delivery to YIVO.¹²³ In commencing their postwar

---

118. Blumental, "Di literatur fun di landsmanshaftn," *Yedies fun yad vashem* 3 (September 1958): 27.
119. Trunk, "A bukh vegn shedlets," 359.
120. Jack Kugelmass and Jonathan Boyarin, "*Yizker Bikher* and the Problem of Historical Veracity: An Anthropological Approach," in *The Jews of Poland Between Two World Wars*, ed. Yisrael Gutman et al. (Hanover, 1989), 532.
121. See "Yizkor Book Project," www.jewishgen.org/yizkor.
122. Z. Shaykovski, "Yidn in eyrope forshn zeyer umkum, 1939–1946," *YIVO bleter* XXX, no. 1 (Fall 1947): 99.
123. Friedman, *Oshvyentshim*, 190. He refers to the plan as having been executed, but he presumably means the unfulfilled plan described by Abraham Levite in his Yiddish

research, the Yiddish historians resumed the practice familiar to East European Jewish historians of appealing to the Jewish public for historical materials.

When Friedman returned to Lodz in March 1945 as director of the CJHC, he published the notice (quoted in the introduction): "Dr. Philip Friedman has returned. Persons who possess memoirs, documents, photographs, or other materials about the Jewish destruction, are invited to come"—followed by his address and hours.[124] One month later, in his first public report as director of the CJHC, he concludes with the appeal, "Every Jew is obligated to fulfill his historic duty: some by bearing witness, others by bringing documents or photographs, or by indicating where historical materials are located," and he stresses, "Therefore, without waiting until later, but immediately after reading this article, you, Jewish reader, join with us and help us with our great, responsible work! We are waiting!"[125] Blumental recounts that a survivor of the Lodz Ghetto "came running to the CJHC ... with the happy news: 'I found my notes that I hid in a hole in the Ghetto.'"[126] By the end of May 1945, archivist Kermish declares that the collections "were constantly enriched by ever new materials on the part of Jews who understand the national-political and scholarly meaning of our work."[127]

Friedman and his colleagues at the CJHC also published instructions and sample questionnaires (in both Polish and Yiddish) for conducting oral interviews, and they trained a cadre of interviewers. In December of 1947, Kermish's report on the first three years of work by the (renamed) Jewish Historical Institute announced that more than 3,000 eyewitness

---

introduction to the proposed collection (dated January 3, 1945, two weeks before the camp's evacuation) that concludes, "May a few pages remain for the YIVO, for the Jewish archive of pain; may our free brothers who survive us read it, and perhaps they will also learn something." First published as "Dos zamlbukh *Oyshvits*," *YIVO bleter* XXVII, no. 1 (Spring 1946): 194–97; see also David Suchoff, "A Yiddish Text from Auschwitz: Critical History and the Anthological Imagination," *Prooftexts* 19, no. 1 (January 1999): 59–69.

124. Rokhl Oyerbakh, "D"r filip fridman z"l (dermonung un gezegenung)," *Di goldene keyt* 38 (1960): 178.

125. Friedman, "Unzer historishe oyfgabe," 6.

126. Blumental, foreword to Shloyme Frank, *Togbukh fun lodzsher geto* (Buenos Aires, 1958; Tel Aviv, 1958), 5.

127. Kermish, "Di arbet fun yidish-historishn arkhiv," *Dos naye lebn* (May 5, 1945): 5.

accounts had been collected.[128] The prescience of the Yiddish historians in their use of eyewitness accounts is one of several adumbrations of later methods and interests to be found in their work—a theme to be discussed in chapter 6.

The reciprocal aspect of the "lay–professional partnership" is the use by Yiddish historians of survivor accounts in their own works, made necessary by the absence of adequate German or Jewish documentary sources from the Nazi period. In Blumental's foreword to the Sarny *yizkor* book of 1961, he notes that, because of the destruction of Jewish documents, the book brings forth "a great quantity of facts and information that only those who were there know and remember."[129] "Kermish summarizes a view shared by all of the Yiddish historians in declaring that survivor accounts are the only means of "filling many voids in our historical research," without which "we would know almost nothing about the history and lifestyle of many communities" and "it would never be possible to reconstruct the entire scope of the destruction and robbery, persecution and murder."[130] A rare instance of such a void is related by Friedman in the Vitebsk *yizkor* book of 1956, in which he discusses the difficulty of writing the Holocaust history of a city for which there was no surviving Jewish eyewitness, and only one non-Jew who "could have no deep insight into the inner life of the ghetto."[131]

The use of eyewitness accounts was also credited by the Yiddish historians with a variety of positive virtues unrelated to the lack of documents. Before the war, in the spring of 1939, Friedman had reviewed a newly published lexicon of Warsaw Jewry and had reflected on the question, "How then does one encompass everything, to create a true, broad picture of the life of a large community in a given period?" He stresses, in praise of the author's method, that one "must have access to their papers,

---

128. Kermish, "3 yor tetikayt fun Ts.Y.H.K. un yidishn historishn institut baym Ts.K. fun yidn in poyln," *Dos naye lebn* (March 5, 1948): 6.

129. Blumental, preface to *Sefer yizkor li-kehilat Sarni*, ed. Yosef Kariv (Jerusalem, 1961), 11; Hebrew, 9.

130. Kermish, *Ta'aruhat*, 6–7 (Yiddish).

131. Friedman, "Umkum fun vitebsker yidn," in *Vitebsk amol: geshikhte, zikhroynes, khurbn*, ed. Grigori Aronson et al. (New York, 1956), 603–26; Hebrew edition, "Hashmadat yehude vitebsk," *Sefer Vitebsk* (Tel Aviv, 1957), 439–52.

minutes, community record books [*pinkeysim*], to their Written Law and—this is also *very* important—to their Oral Law."[132] He repeats nearly the same formulation, but with a new emphasis, in one of his early essays on Holocaust historiography in January 1948: "Apart from official sources (archives), there are—and these are the very most important—living sources, spirited reality with traces of the 'historical process' on their bodies and in their hearts."[133]

Blumental, as editor of his own town's *yizkor* book, relates that he had prepared the materials for a monograph on the history of the town during his student days, but that all was lost in the destruction. In the *yizkor* book, he gives priority to personal memory, explaining, "Our goal was not the history of our city on the basis of documents (this one can also do later), but the history of our city as we knew it."[134] Kermish emphasizes in his foreword to another *yizkor* book that "the popular tone and language and popular sayings of the people," are an "essential part of the book."[135] In his *Jewish Responses to Nazi Persecution*, Trunk assesses the value of eyewitness accounts in illuminating Holocaust phenomena that are beyond the scope of ordinary documentary sources. He lists such intangibles as "the psychological extremes caused in the victims . . . and the indelible scars left upon their psyches," and the "psychic shift . . . that led to the armed Jewish uprisings."[136]

As director of the CJHC, Friedman was a member of the official Polish investigating commission that visited Auschwitz in 1945, and one of the earliest uses of eyewitness accounts was his incorporation of testimony gathered during this visit into his monograph on Auschwitz.[137] He then

---

132. Friedman, "'Der idisher gezelshaftlekher leksikon,' [review of Ruben Feldshuh, *Yidisher gezelshaftlekher leksikon* (Warsaw, 1939)]," *Haynt* (April 7, 1939): 8 (emphasis his).

133. Friedman, "Di forshung fun unzer khurbn," *Kiem* (January 1948): 49 (using the traditional Yiddish-Hebrew for Torah and Talmud, *toyre shebiksav* and *toyre shebalpe*).

134. Blumental, *Sefer borshtshiv* (Tel Aviv, 1960), 8.

135. Kermish, foreword in English to *Sefer Zikaron li-kehilat Skarz'isko Kamiennah* (Tel Aviv, 1973), 260 (substantially a translation of his foreword to *Ta'aruhat* of 1962).

136. Trunk, *Jewish Responses to Nazi Persecution: Collective and Individual Behavior in Extremis* (New York, 1979), 61–62.

137. Friedman, *Oshvyentshim* (Buenos Aires, 1950), expanded from the Yiddish original of *This was Oswiecim* (London, 1946).

emphasizes the importance of survivor accounts in one of his seminal Yiddish essays of 1948, "The Elements of *Khurbn* Research," which devotes the majority of its coverage to this form of primary source material.[138] Friedman was also concerned that survivor accounts should be published in their unmediated accuracy. In more than one venue, he praises the scope and quality of the leading historical journal in the Displaced Persons camps, *Fun letstn khurbn* ("From the Last Extermination"), and the articles by its editor, Israel Kaplan (a trained historian, and later a leading Israeli author of Holocaust fiction), but criticizes Kaplan's "serious error" of "correcting" eyewitness accounts rather than printing them "in their original form and language and maintaining their documentary character and stylistic individuality."[139] In his own popular anthology of eyewitness accounts from the Warsaw Ghetto, Friedman emphasizes that he has preserved the "genuine style and other linguistic particularities" of the quoted materials (the largest number of which come from Yiddish sources).[140]

Trunk and Dworzecki both made increasing use of survivor accounts over the course of their careers, but arrived at this preference from disparate origins. Trunk's first postwar research was an investigation of the "Jewish Labor-Camps in the 'Varteland'" (his home region, near Lodz; in German, the *Warthegau*), which he indicates is based on German documents, Polish criminal investigations, and eyewitness accounts by survivors.[141] For a historian whose prewar works had dealt with earlier periods, often working from official Polish court records written in Latin, and which could not have included accounts by living persons, this commenced a departure from his established habits of research. In his 1949 essay on the Jewish Councils, he cites information from recently published memoir-histories on Częstochowa (by Orenstein) and Lodz (by

---

138. Friedman, "Di elementn fun undzer khurbn-forshung," *Hemshekh* 1 (April 1948): 4–10; continued as "Di memuaristik," *Hemshekh* 2 (1949): 26–34.

139. Friedman, "Dos gedrukte yidishe vort bay der sheyres hapleyte in daytshland," *Di tsukunft* [2nd part] (March 1949): 151.

140. Friedman, *Martyrs and Fighters: The Epic of the Warsaw Ghetto* (New York, 1954), 13.

141. Trunk, "Yidishe arbet-lagern in 'varteland,'" *Bleter far geshikhte* I, no. 1 (January–March 1948): 116.

Israel Tabaksblat),[142] but not from unpublished survivor accounts. In his *Lodzsher geto* of 1962, the unusual abundance of official German and Jewish documents required only slight reliance on survivor accounts. Conversely, in his *Judenrat* of 1972, Trunk found it necessary to overcome the scarcity of wartime or postwar accounts by members of Jewish Councils. Few had dared to keep contemporaneous records, and only a handful of Judenrat members survived. His research notes reveal the array of supporting materials from *yizkor* books, personal accounts, and questionnaires that lie behind the sources he discusses in his preface to *Judenrat*. In all, he collected materials on the Jewish Councils of 405 Jewish locations. His major research tool was a confidential questionnaire of ghetto survivors on the backgrounds and behavior of Judenrat members and ghetto policemen, resulting in 927 completed forms (which remain sealed in the YIVO archives). Finally, his last major work, *Jewish Responses to Nazi Persecution*, is constructed entirely of sixty-two eyewitness accounts from the YIVO archives (primarily in Yiddish), which Trunk reports have been translated with fidelity to the original idioms of the speakers.[143]

Dworzecki's first major work, his 1948 *Yerusholayim d'lite in kamf un umkum* (Jerusalem of Lithuania in Struggle and Extermination), which has itself become one of the most often cited sources of historical information on the Vilna Ghetto, is based almost entirely on personal recollection. It cites relatively few documentary sources, but relies on the author's breadth of observation and memory to reconstruct events and conversations. In his progression toward greater use of survivor accounts, his 1966 monograph on the well-known poet Hirsh Glik is based on his own conversations with Glik in the Vilna Ghetto, augmented by the available documents and his interviews of survivors. He indicates that those interviews draw on the 120 interviews he had already assembled for his forthcoming history of the Nazi camps in Estonia, to which he and most Vilna Ghetto residents were deported.[144] His last major work, the history of the Estonian camps (for which he received his PhD

---

142. Trunk, "Sotsyale antagonizmen in geto un di rol fun di yudenratn," *Yidishe shriftn* 6, no. 26 (June 1949): 6.

143. Trunk, *Jewish Responses*, 74.

144. Dworzecki, *Hirshke glik* (Paris, 1966), 79.

from the Sorbonne in 1967), is notable for its reliance on an eventual 174 eyewitness testimonies—26 conducted by Dworzecki himself—and dozens of published accounts by survivors.[145] In his introduction, he offers the explanation that, because he had experienced the camps himself, he "used the utmost caution in order to recount the events, not according to his own recollection, but on the basis of as many eyewitness accounts as possible."[146]

The Yiddish historians were nonetheless aware of the difficulties of relying on survivor accounts, and they often acknowledge the issues of inaccuracy or exaggeration. Kermish refers to the "inexactitude of human memory and the subjective observations of those involved."[147] Friedman discusses the errors made by eyewitnesses, as well as their limited perspective of events, and argues that special training is required for interviewers "to be objective (but not passive)" and to avoid projecting their own tendencies onto the witness.[148] Trunk anticipates the issues raised forty years later by Christopher Browning in assessing the effects of time and emotion on eyewitnesses' recollections, noting their "reliability as to the event itself" despite frequent errors in names, dates, and numbers.[149] Blumental suggests that historians should act as counselors to editors of *yizkor* books, advising them on such matters as mediating conflicts between eyewitnesses to a given event.[150] In the case of the Kołomyja *yizkor* book of 1957, Friedman praises the editor, Yiddish literary critic and essayist Shlomo Bickel, for "taking upon himself the heavy task of analyzing the contradictory reports" of the leader of the

---

145. Dworzecki, *Vayse nekht un shvartse teg (yidn-lagern in estonye)* (Tel Aviv, 1970), 28.

146. Ibid., 30.

147. Kermish, "Historical Sources Relating to the Warsaw Ghetto Uprising," in Blumental and Kermish, *ha-Meri veha-mered be-geto Varshah / Resistance and Revolt in the Warsaw Ghetto* (Jerusalem, 1965), xxxii.

148. Friedman, "Di element fun undzer khurbn-forshung," 8–9.

149. Trunk, *Judenrat: The Jewish Councils in Eastern Europe under Nazi Occupation* (New York, 1972), xxvi. See Christopher R. Browning, *Remembering Survival: Inside a Nazi Slave-Labor Camp* (New York, 2010).

150. Blumental, "Di literatur fun di landsmanshaftn," *Yedies fun yad vashem* 3 (September 1958): 26–28; translated as, "Writings on the Disaster Period," *Yad Vashem Bulletin* 3 (July 1958): 24–27.

town's Judenrat.[151] In Dworzecki's history of the Nazi camps in Estonia, he stresses that he "strove always to 'confront' the testimonies, one with another" and with the available published documents and archival materials, "with the purpose of approaching, to the extent possible, the historical truth."[152]

A concluding example of the "lay–professional partnership" that encompasses all of its aspects is Blumental's final book, a collection of words and expressions used by Jews under Nazi rule. Blumental relates that he began to gather material immediately after returning to Poland in 1944 because he "almost could not understand" the Yiddish of the survivors he met, although "every one of them very willingly recounted [his story], as if to be rid of the heavy load that weighed on him."[153] Blumental drew first on conversations, and then primarily on the published accounts of living and deceased writers to preserve thousands of elements of Jewish speech from the Nazi era. From 1956 to 1963, he serialized the entries for the first seven letters of the alphabet in the YIVO journal *Yidishe shprakh*. In his introduction to the series, he explains that the language of the time "provides a key to the folk-spirit. It helps us understand the life of our martyrs. Each expression is saturated with blood. Each word is literally a symbol, an entire world."[154] Blumental's collection became a lifelong project, and he continued to gather material until the completed book was published in 1981.[155]

The Voices of the Yiddish Historians

Two voices may be heard in the writings of the Yiddish historians—the voice of the professional historian who presents historical materials and that of the same historian who comments from the survivor perspective.

---

151. Friedman, "Kolomey—di hoyptshtot fun pokutye un ire yidn," *Di tsukunft* (September 1958): 355.
152. Dworzecki, *Vayse nekht un shvartse teg*, 30.
153. Blumental, *Verter un vertlekh fun der khurbn-tkufe* (Tel Aviv, 1981), 7.
154. Blumental, "Verter un vertlekh fun der khurbn-tkufe," *Yidishe shprakh* (January–March 1956): 25–26.
155. Gabriel Trunk, son of Isaiah Trunk, recalls that on a visit to Blumental in 1970, he observed the kitchen cabinets of Blumental's apartment stacked high with the card files of this work in progress. Telephone conversation with the author, May 4, 2009.

The dynamic between these voices, the seemingly "objective" and "subjective" aspects of the historians' own responses to the Holocaust, was an early historiographic issue for Friedman and other Yiddish historians. Friedman wrote that the subjectivity of eyewitness accounts "is often the best guarantee of their authenticity and sincerity" and that it is "only the historian in using these sources who needs to be objective." Yet the simple division of labor implied by these statements is complicated by his awareness that the historians are themselves survivors and that both the "objective" and "subjective" aspects of their works are part of the larger project of survivor self-expression.

As research director of the Centre de documentation Juive Contemporaine in Paris (concurrently with his service in Munich for the American Joint Distribution Committee), Friedman assisted its president, Isaac Schneersohn, in organizing the "First European Conference of Jewish Historical Commissions and Documentation Centers," held in Paris, December 1–10, 1947. Kermish represented the CJHC of Poland, and Blumental also contributed a paper.[156] Among the other delegates were Léon Poliakov, Alfred Werner, and Simon Wiesenthal.

Friedman reported that the great majority of delegates considered it too early to attempt synthetic historical works on the Holocaust and favored only the collecting and publishing of documents.[157] In his own address, which became one of his Yiddish essays of 1948, he attributes this view chiefly to the conviction that the historical distance needed for unemotional, objective research was still lacking. He acknowledges the difficulty of remaining strictly objective, "when emotional motives like love, hate, reverence toward the martyrs, feelings of revenge and anger, cannot be completely eliminated."[158] But he disputes the possibility of strict ob-

---

156. The CJHC was the only non-French institution with two contributors, presumably at Friedman's invitation.

157. Friedman ["Dr. Philipp Friedmann"], "Die Parisder Konferz der jüdischen Historiker," *Die Neue Welt* (Jewish newspaper in Munich) 2, no. 5 (January 29, 1948). Clipping with Friedman's handwritten notation of newspaper name, date, and issue in his collected papers, YIVO Archives, RG 1258, F 534.

158. Friedman, "Di forshung fun undzer khurbn," 49. The Yiddish essay is a slightly expanded version of his conference address, published as "Les problèmes de recherche scientifique sur notre dernière catastrophe," in *Les Juifs en Europe (1939–1945)* (Paris, 1949), 72–80.

jectivity in any historical work, arguing that every historian "adapts the events about which he writes into a synthetic whole according to his conception of the world, whether it be materialist, idealist, or positivist," and that "through whatever school of thought he chooses for his synthesis, he becomes subjective." In this way, Friedman refuses to allow himself and the other survivor-historians to be uniquely disqualified, as a class, from the task of Holocaust representation. This corresponds with the position taken forty years later by Saul Friedländer in his well-known exchange of letters with Martin Broszat, in which he argued against the latter's assertion that Jewish (but not German) historians were too emotionally committed to their subject to treat Holocaust history with the requisite detachment.[159]

It should not be inferred, however, from Friedman's remarks on subjectivity that he and the other Yiddish historians were proto-deconstructionists who considered historical truth unfathomable and its representation largely a matter of rhetoric. They were workaday positivist historians, influenced during their formative years by then-current approaches to broadly descriptive social history, who saw their task as recovering the truth of historical events within living memory. Friedman was content to pursue an objectivity he defined as "being true to the sources, analyzing events without ulterior motives, and not allowing oneself to be misled by personal sympathies or antipathies."[160] Trunk reaches a similar conclusion about the potential for objective research in a 1952 address to the Friends of YIVO in Israel. He dismisses the views then current among many survivors (likely in his audience) that only those who had experienced a given terror of the Holocaust had the ability or right to discuss it. He argues instead that "a painful, responsible caution in ascertaining and verifying the facts" is one of the obligations of Holocaust research.[161]

---

159. "Martin Broszat and Saul Friedländer: A Controversy about the Historicization of National Socialism," *Yad Vashem Studies* 19 (1988): 1–47.
160. Friedman, "Di forshung fun undzer khurbn," 51.
161. Trunk, "Vegn khurbn-forshung," in his *Geshtaltn un gesheenishn* (Buenos Aires, 1962), 127–28. This is likely an updated version of Trunk's address on "tendencies in the historiography of the recent catastrophe" reported in *Yedies fun YIVO* 46 (September 1952): 3; English 5*.

Both Friedman and Trunk state that "objectivity" requires an empathic response from the Holocaust historian. Friedman concludes his 1948 essay with advice to the Yiddish reader not included in the official French version of his conference paper. He declares that it is impossible for the (Jewish) historian to "lock his heart and mind to the pain of his people," that being objective does not mean "being without a heart," and that the suffering caused by the murder of families "is engraved in the heart of every Jew, without distinction whether he is a historian, a judge, or an ordinary Jew."[162] Trunk states that accurate Holocaust research requires "a deep—to the point of identification—intimacy with the object of study" and "a deep-reaching knowledge of the psychology of individuals and groups in extreme life situations."[163] Both anticipate the view by Friedländer that "self-awareness of the historian of the Nazi epoch or the Shoah is essential" in the form of critically identifiable commentary: "Whether this commentary is built into the narrative structure of a history or developed as a separate, superimposed text is a matter of choice, but the voice of the commentator must be clearly heard."[164]

According to Friedman, "the experienced historian will find the right way to express what he feels," without disturbing the objectivity that inspires trust among his readers. "Most often," he says, "the subjective is given voice by the author in his preface or in his conclusions, and also at times in certain stylistic turns and asides,"[165] here also prefiguring the observation many decades later by Robert Rozett that "[o]nly a handful of survivors who have become professional historians have proven their capability to be both historians and witnesses, and they usually take great care to delineate between their two voices."[166] An example is found in one of the works prepared by a lay historian under Friedman's supervision in Germany during the period of Friedman's 1948 essays. In his

---

162. Friedman, "Di forshung fun undzer khurbn," 52.
163. Trunk, "Vegn khurbn-forshung," 128.
164. Saul Friedländer, "Trauma, Transference and 'Working Through,'" *History and Memory* 4, no. 1 (1992): 53.
165. Friedman, "Di forshung fun unzer khurbn," 52.
166. Robert Rozett, *Approaching the Holocaust: Texts and Contexts* (London, 2005), 19.

foreword to Joseph Gar's history of Kovne under the Nazis, Friedman praises Gar's decision to separate the book into a first, "dynamic" part that gives a chronological account of the Jews' sufferings, and a second, "static" part that provides a "systematic overview of the social structure of the ghetto." He concludes that the book "can serve—in its serious, scholarly approach—as an example for many authors" who have otherwise vulgarized the history of the Holocaust.[167]

Special praise is given by Friedman to Dworzecki's history of the Vilna Ghetto. In his review of June 1948, Friedman describes it as "a complicated literary genre" that comprises both a memoir and a "historical-sociological study." He says that offering expression to each of these two voices is an accomplishment that gives the book "freshness, suspense, and colorfulness from one side," and "specificity, exactness, and detailed exhaustiveness from the other"—an evaluation repeated in his subsequent Yiddish and English reviews.[168]

In the few works that relate to their own personal experiences, the Yiddish historians present a complete separation of voices, which is otherwise exceptional in their writings. Friedman's monographic article, "The Destruction of the Jews of Lwów," discusses at length the Jews who hid on "the Aryan side" of the city, but leaves for his first endnote the statement which begins, "The author of this article lived in Lwów during the entire period of the Nazi occupation . . . ."[169] Trunk announces in a 1948 footnote to his study of labor camps that he has completed a manuscript on "the history of the destruction of the Jewish community of Kutno," and only the knowing reader would discern that he is referring to his own hometown.[170] In the *yizkor* book of Kutno, which carries histories by Trunk of the Jews in prewar and wartime Kutno, he adds two personal articles, separate from the main text. One is a biography of his father, the last rabbi of Kutno, Yitskhok Yehuda Trunk; the other is an account of his postwar visit in 1946, in which he describes the town as both familiar and

---

167. Friedman, foreword to Yosef Gar, *Umkum*, 10–11.
168. Friedman, review of *Yerusholayim d'lite*, *Kiem* (June 1948): 406–7.
169. Friedman, "Hurban Yehude Lvov," in *Entsiklopediyah shel Galuyot: Lvov*, ed. N. M. Gelber (Jerusalem, 1956), 731.
170. Trunk, "Yidishe arbet-lagern in 'varteland,'" 116n6.

foreign in the absence of Jewish residents and landmarks.[171] For the early period, he reuses his own 1934 history of Kutno but without comment deletes his original opening sentence: "The 18th century was one of the worst periods in the history of the Polish Jews."[172]

Blumental, Dworzecki, and Kermish take the same approach to separating the personal from the historical in writing of their own locales. Blumental served as editor and coauthor of the *yizkor* book for his hometown of Borszczów, yet aside from his editor's preface, he is virtually absent from the narrative, although twenty Blumental family members appear in the list of the town's murdered residents. Only later did he publish a separate article in which he, too, describes the experience of his first postwar return and his reaction to the erasure of "every vestige of the Jewish past" from his hometown.[173] Dworzecki provides two articles for the 1973 *yizkor* book of his own hometown, Molchadz (or Maytshet). One is a historian's account of the partisans and forest fighters of the town, and, separately, a chronicle of the recent generations of his family that includes the fates of his nearest relatives and the careers of his children in Israel.[174] By contrast, Kermish does not figure at all in the history of his home region, "Galician Jewry during the Hitler Occupation," which he contributed to the *Sefer galitsye* of 1968.[175] It appears that his only self-reflective words about the Nazi period are to be found in a brief unpublished autobiographical sketch that describes his experiences of wartime flight and return.[176]

---

171. Trunk, in *Sefer Kutnah veha-sevivah* (Tel Aviv, 1968): "Geshikhte fun der yidisher kehile in kutne," 28–53; "Untergang fun der yidisher kutne," 340–53; "ha-Rav Yitskhok Yehuda Trunk," 243–46; "In mayn heymshtot," 419–24.

172. Trunk's account of prewar Kutno is expanded from his "A yidishe kehile in poyln baym sof fun XVIII yorhundert: kutno," *Bleter far geshikhte* 1 *("yunger historiker num. 3")* (1934): 87–140.

173. Blumental, "Spinka, the Shabbes-Goy," *Yad Vashem Bulletin* 18 (April 1966): 30.

174. Dworzecki, "Mishpahat Dvorz'etski" and "Partizanim ve-Yehude-ha-'ayarot be-'ayarot Meytshet," in *Sefer-zikaron li-kehilat Meytshet*, ed. Ben-Tzion H. Ayalon (Tel Aviv, 1973), 211–17 and 346–66 (English translation online; see bibliography).

175. Kermish, "Dos galitsishe yidntum beys der hitler-okupatsye," *Sefer galitsye: gedenk bukh* (Buenos Aires, 1968), 9–40.

176. "Di byografye fun d"r yosef kermish" (see see "Writings about Kermish" in the bibliography).

More normative in the case of the Yiddish historians—and of Yiddish-speaking survivors generally—is a joining of the emotive and dispassionate voices not commonly found in English and other Western languages but which creates in Yiddish the potential for integration of the two voices. By the end of the war, a shared language of internal discourse about the Holocaust had developed in Yiddish, based on traditional usages, which the Yiddish historians also adopted. To do otherwise would have been to write in an artificial and un-Yiddish manner, and it would have separated private memory and public history in a way inauthentic in Yiddish. As a result, the nearly ubiquitous complaint outside of Yiddish circles regarding the "inadequacy of language" for the task of Holocaust representation is not to be found in their works, nor do they search for new forms of expression.

The Yiddish historians use the common idioms of the Yiddish-speaking survivors, and not merely in their most "emotive" passages, but, more importantly, in their most "objective" passages as well. They share the survivors' anger—with such expressions as *Natsi rotskhim* (Nazi murderers) or *Natsi talyen* (hangman) and *Hitlers treyfen'm moyl* (un-kosher mouth) that are widespread in Yiddish writing generally, but infrequent in their own otherwise unemotional works. They share the survivors' expressions of irony or scorn—as in Blumental's statement that German officials were carrying out their *rebens toyre* ("rebbe's Torah"), to indicate "Hitler's commands."[177] They give new meaning to metaphors from the shared tradition—as in Friedman's use of the term *toyre shebalpe* (the traditional term for the religious "Oral Law") to give honor to the new phenomenon of oral testimony.[178] And they also identify with their readers—as in Trunk's self-introduction, "I consider myself to be a Jew, who for a few years has . . . ,"[179] where the word "Jew" (*yid*) connotes in Yiddish simply a "person," a Jew among Jews.

The use of shared emotive expressions was inherent in the survivors' linguistic milieu, and it diminished only slightly with time. Trunk, for example, uses the metaphor "those who experienced the seven levels of

---

177. Blumental, "A shtime fun yomer-tol," *Yidishe kultur* 7, no. 6 (June 1945): 16.
178. Friedman, "Di forshung fun undzer khurbn," 49.
179. Trunk, "Sotsyale antagonizmen," 6.

Gehenna" (a traditional Jewish term for hell, or place of eternal punishment) at the start of his 1952 address, and he returns to the same metaphor in the preface to his last major work, *Jewish Responses to Nazi Persecution* of 1979. There, he refers to the survivors whom he quotes in the book as those "who lead us in an abysmal descent through the 'seven levels of Gehenna.'"[180]

The existence of such an internal discourse, and also its seeming unsuitability for use by those outside of its natural sphere, is demonstrated by the treatment by English translators of the Yiddish historians' more florid words and phrases (although generally retained by Hebrew translators). Trunk's "Gehenna" metaphor survived translation in part because his son was a co-translator of this late work. Such expressions are found among all of the Yiddish historians, but examples from those who lacked the proficiency to participate in translating their works into English are most informative about the perceptions of outsiders. Kermish's inclusion of himself in the shared historical narrative is undone by the translator, who converts "so that future generations will know what the Nazis did to our people" (in both Yiddish and Hebrew) into "so that future generations should hear of them" (in English).[181] Kermish's use of shared hyperbole, as in "the greatest crime in history," is reduced to merely "the Nazi crimes."[182] Each instance occurs in the declaratory opening sentence of an article. Blumental's first essay on the *yizkor* book phenomenon has, as a section heading, the expression *Papirene matseves* ("Paper Headstones"), which the translator at Yad Vashem converts to "Memorial books a 'fashion.'"[183] Total excision of such shared references is found in the treatment

---

180. Trunk, *Jewish Responses*, xii.
181. Kermish, "Makoyres vegn di khinukh problemen in geto," *Yerusholayimer almanakh* 23 (1974): 179; "Origins of [more correctly, 'Sources Regarding'] the Education Problem in the Ghetto," *Yad Vashem Bulletin* 12 (December 1962): 28; "Mekorot li-be'ayot ha-hinuh ba-geto," in *ha-Yeled veha-no'ar ba-Sho'ah veha-gevurah*, ed. Aryeh Bauminger, Nahman Blumental, and Yosef Kermish (Jerusalem, 1965), 11.
182. Kermish, "Di tsavoa fun varshever geto," *Di goldene keyt* 9 (1951): 134; "The Testament of the Warsaw Ghetto," *Jewish Frontier* (September 1951): 9. The original introductory section does not appear in the condensed Yiddish, Hebrew, and English versions of 1956–57.
183. Blumental, "Di literatur fun di landsmanshaftn," *Yedies fun yad vashem* 3 (September 1958): 26; "Writings on the Disaster Period: Memorial books by survivors of

of Blumental's phrase, "stained with innocent blood all of our holy days" (referring to the timing of German *Aktions* to coincide with Jewish holy days) in the Yiddish and Hebrew versions, which the translator omits from the English version.[184]

None of the Yiddish historians reflected consciously on the ability of this shared language of internal discourse to bridge the gap between private memory and public history. But the concluding theme of Friedman's expanded essay of 1950 on the writing of Holocaust literature is his unwillingness to concede the permanent divergence of the popular and scholarly voices, even in the work of historians. He predicts the ultimate waning of interest in the "emotional" voice (as being of primary interest to the survivors themselves), and the limited but "with time ever-increasing" appeal of the "intellectual" voice, while suggesting a third form of expression that is a "sublimation" of the two. He asserts that the average person will not read thousands of original historical documents or learned articles but that the "whole immensely great documentary literature, the whole generations-long diligent work of scholars, enters the marrow of the folk first though this means of artistic-esthetic distillation."[185] Friedman presages Yerushalmi's well-known statement about the public preference for literary over historical representation of the Holocaust ("I have no doubt that its image is being shaped, not at the historian's anvil, but at the novelist's crucible"[186]) in naming Tolstoy, Feuchtwanger, and the

---

communities," *Yad Washem Bulletin* 3 (July 1958): 24; no section heading appears in "Sifre ha-zikaron shel saride ha-kehilot," *Yedi'ot Yad va-Shem* 15–16 (April 1958): 23.

184. Blumental, "Yidn hobn gekemft—aleyn: gedankn vegn dem oyfshtand in varshe," *Yedies fun yad vashem* 8–9 (September 1959): 3; "ha-Yehudim lahmu livadam . . . ," *Yedi'ot Yad va-Shem* 19–20 (May 1959): 5; "The Jews Fought Alone . . . ," *Yad Vashem Bulletin* 4–5 (October 1959): 2.

185. Friedman, "Unzer khurbn-literatur," *Idisher kemfer* (March 31, 1950, Pesach): 91. On the value of literary works as sources of historical knowledge, see the latter part of chapter 4 below.

186. Yosef Hayim Yerushalmi, *Zakhor* (Seattle, 1982), 98. The dynamic to which Yerushalmi ascribes the public's greater interest in literary representation, namely, the transformation of historical events into popular legends, is treated by Friedman three years later, in his statement, "With a sure instinct, the people lifts a certain historical event out of its actual historical boundaries and raises it up in the pantheon of its history [referring to events of the Warsaw Ghetto Uprising]." See Friedman, "Varshever oyfshtand," *Di tsukunft* (April 1953): 195.

Yiddish historical novelist Joseph Opatoshu as purveyors of popular historical knowledge. He argues that historical research provides the "mortar and bricks" for the creation of "poetry, prose, and historical synthesis," and he asserts parenthetically (but most significantly) that "the historian-synthesizer must always be an artist." As the exemplar of his desired approach, he cites the most widely read of Jewish historians, Heinreich Graetz, who "makes old and distant periods new and vivid for the reader, and the reader need not feel that these lively pictures emerge from a filter that sifts thousands of documents and historical works."[187]

Friedman prescribes this artistic blending of voices for his own work. The preface to his history of Auschwitz, also written in Munich in 1948, expresses the wish that his book will be "simultaneously systematic, objective, scientifically supported, and from the other side—rich in color and steeped in the pain of millions."[188] The review of Friedman's book by Samuel Gringauz, former president of the Congress of Liberated Jews in the US Zone of Germany, notes Friedman's status as both scholar and survivor and declares that the book is "a fortunate combination of thorough investigation, scientific systematization and responsive emotional approach."[189] (Revealingly, the reviewer—himself a Yiddish-speaking survivor—questions Friedman's use of emotional asides, but is unaware that he makes use of same engaged idiom in doing so: "Despite some objections which could be raised concerning the advisability of intermittent emotional digressions, the book is to be regarded as one of the most outstanding contributions to the everlasting record of this horrible period of Jewish and human history.")

In Friedman's foreword to Benjamin Orenstein's personal history of the destruction of Częstochowa, written during the same early postwar period, Friedman praises the author for having "analyzed all aspects of Jewish life" under Nazi rule but adds that, for the more traumatic events, "a dispassionate objectivity is nearly impossible" and "psychological truth is often more important than the historical." Friedman here declares that

---

187. Friedman, "Unzer khurbn-literatur," 91.
188. Friedman, *Oshvyentshim* (Buenos Aires, 1950), 9.
189. Samuel Gringauz, review of Friedman's *Oshvyentshim*, *Jewish Social Studies* XIV, no. 4 (October 1952): 377.

the best and most faithful description is often one "which conveys the atmosphere and emotional tension of those events made holy by the blood and suffering of martyrs, and not only a chronological, indifferent, and uninvolved compiling of dry facts and figures."[190] Here he coincides with the later assertion by Friedländer that the historian must confront "a field dominated by political decisions and administrative decrees which neutralize the concreteness of despair and death," and which "loses its historical weight when merely taken as data."[191] The works of the Yiddish historians, however structured, are thus marked by a responsibility to uphold their authors' simultaneous roles as historical observers and engaged commentators, both contributing to the internal dialogue of their fellow survivors.

The Final Link in the Chain

The intense engagement of the Yiddish historians in the survivors' project of Holocaust representation required the functioning of an intact cultural system that would include informants, recorders, consumers, and the agency of a Yiddish publishing industry. The seeming wonder of a creative spark that could produce a shared literature of remembrance on all six inhabited continents was, owing to its very dispersion, increasingly susceptible to linguistic assimilation. The high period of Yiddish Holocaust historiography did not end with Friedman's premature death in 1960, but it had passed its apogee at the time of Dworzecki's death in 1975.

By the mid-1980s, when the last major Yiddish works of the surviving historians were published, these works had acquired the character of a summing-up for the record. The appearance in 1981 of Blumental's Nazi-era Jewish lexicon completed thirty-five years of work. The 1983

---

190. Friedman, foreword to Binyomin Orenshteyn, *Khurbn chenstokhov* (Munich, 1948), 8–9. This work also testifies to the desire to publish in Yiddish despite a shortage of Yiddish type for printing; it is one of the exceptionally rare works published entirely in Yiddish but transliterated into Latin letters (in Polish phonetic orthography, not German or English).

191. Saul Friedländer, "Trauma, Memory and Transference," in *Holocaust Remembrance: The Shapes of Memory*, ed. Geoffrey H. Hartman (Oxford, 1994), 53–54.

collection of Trunk's later writings,[192] published after his sudden death in 1981, preserved for history the Yiddish original of his opening essay in *Jewish Responses to Nazi Persecution*. In addition to his memorial articles on leading Yiddish scholars, the book included Kermish's own biographical tribute to Trunk. The publication in 1985 of the authoritative Yiddish edition of Ringelblum's *Notes*, with an introductory essay by Kermish,[193] completed the project begun in Warsaw by the now-deceased Blumental, who had written in 1949, "To me has come the fate to prepare Ringelblum's [*Notes*] for publication."[194]

In the early postwar years, the worldwide market for Yiddish publications had supported the establishment or expansion of Yiddish publishing venues throughout the Yiddish diaspora. By the early 1980s, Yiddish publishing had largely retreated to the earlier Jewish practice of advance subvention. To continue to publish in Yiddish required an uneconomic commitment to Yiddish and its remaining readers.[195] Blumental's 1981 lexicon was published by a committee of six organizations, including Yad Vashem, Ghetto Fighters' House, the Yiddish Writers Union, and the Society of Lublin Survivors, with financing from seven foundations and two dozen individuals. The works by Trunk and Kermish required support from similar, if shorter, lists of institutions and individuals. Trunk says in the foreword to his final book of collected writings that it could not be published in Argentina like the previous volume: "The Yiddish cultural life there, which had once shone with its achievements in Yiddish, lies today in ruins. Fortunately, the State of Israel continues the ruptured genealogical chain of publishing books in Yiddish."[196]

The "lay–professional partnership" had become more than a later observer's theoretical construct. The urge to "extend further the golden chain" of Jewish self-expression in the language of the survivors continued

---

192. Trunk, *Geshtaltn un gesheenishn [naye serye]* (Tel Aviv, 1983).

193. Kermish, introduction to Emanuel Ringelblum, *Ksovim fun geto*, 2 vols. (Tel Aviv, 1985), vol. 1: *Togbukh (1939–1942)*, 5–48 (Hebrew numbering).

194. Blumental, "Di arbet iber ringelblums ksav-yad," *Yedies: byuletin fun yidishn historishn institut in poyln* [1] (November 1949): 4.

195. The later and posthumous works by Friedman and Dworzecki had already appeared in English and Hebrew, respectively. Trunk's later works appeared first in English translation, and those of Blumental and Kermish, variously, in English and Hebrew.

196. Trunk, *Geshtaltn un gesheenishn [naye serye]* (Tel Aviv, 1983), 17.

to give impetus to the works of the surviving historians, but their final Yiddish works had themselves become the object of a new "imperative to publish" on the part of their remaining survivor public. This was the final phase of a reciprocal enterprise by which the Yiddish historians simultaneously drew on, and contributed to, the survivors' internal discourse to create a scholarly record of Jewish Holocaust experience for the Yiddish-speaking public. The content of that record is the subject of the following chapters.

4

HOLOCAUST HISTORY AS JEWISH HISTORY

Accounts of early Holocaust scholarship necessarily commence with the Central Jewish Historical Commission (CJHC) in postwar Poland. For several months in late 1944 and early 1945, as Soviet forces gradually reversed the German occupation of Poland, it appeared that it might be possible for the surviving Jewish remnant to rebuild a Jewish communal life in Poland. Moreover, it appeared that the state-supported national autonomy promised to the Jews at the end of World War I, and largely denied by the interwar Polish republic, would at last be attained. The newly formed Central Committee of Polish Jews presided over the revival of the Association of Writers, Journalists and Artists and over the creation of schools affiliated with each of the pre-war Jewish political movements, as well as a state Yiddish theater, and, not least, the CJHC.

Among the research centers founded in the first postwar years, the CJHC was unique for having among its leaders recognized prewar scholars, a staff that grew to nearly one hundred members, and the status of a quasi-governmental agency. Jonas Turkov, the founding president of the Writers Association which had sponsored the creation of the CJHC in late 1944, described the CJHC as holding "the place of honor in the cultural life of Lodz," when that city served as the temporary capital of newly liberated Poland.[1] The visiting head of the American Jewish Labor

---

1. Yonas Turkov, *Nokh der bafrayung (zikhroyes)* (Buenos Aires, 1959), 221.

Committee, Jacob Pat, declared, "The address [of the CJHC] in Lodz will forever become a part of Jewish history."[2]

The story of the CJHC is the foundation story of Jewish Holocaust research in Eastern Europe (and of the revival of East European Jewish scholarship generally), and it also holds a significant place in the foundation story of renewed Jewish communal life in Poland. Like the subjects of many foundation stories, the history of the CJHC has been put to the service of competing agendas. Conflicts that were present within the CJHC, and between it and its regional branches and the Central Committee of Polish Jews, appear both explicitly and covertly in the accounts left by contemporary observers and memoirists. Not surprisingly, these conflicts are reflected in the differing observations of more recent historians and complicate the present-day search for the Yiddish historians' scholarly intentions.

Further complicating an examination of the Yiddish historians' intentions is the political context in which they attempted to work, which at first enabled and then suppressed independent Jewish scholarship in postwar Poland. At its creation in 1944, the CJHC was the beneficiary of the latest and perhaps most successful realization of the project of Diaspora nationalism. By the time of the final Stalinist takeover of Poland in mid-1949, the CJHC had fallen victim to one of the briefest and most ruinous instances of the "royal alliance" in modern Jewish history. The intervening five years had witnessed the combined reenactment in Poland of two earlier Jewish calamities—the pogroms after World War I that forced Jews in the Ukraine to seek the protection of the invading Red Army, further intensifying the antisemitic attacks studied by Elias Tcherikower,[3] and the destruction by the Soviet government during the 1930s of the Jewish cultural institutions it had sponsored in the 1920s as a means of gaining Jewish allegiance to the Soviet cause. In postwar Poland, pogroms and murders led to a similar Jewish dependence on the unpopular but officially egalitarian Communist regime, and late-Stalinist

---

2. Jacob Pat, *Ash un fayer* (Buenos Aires, 1946), 82.
3. See chapter 2. On this aspect of postwar Jewish history in Poland, see Natalia Aleksiun, "The Vicious Circle: Jews in Communist Poland, 1944–1956," *Studies in Contemporary Jewry* XIX (2003): 157–80.

antisemitism sought to eradicate Jewish nationalism and particularism in both the Soviet Union and Poland during the late 1940s.

On the occasion of Philip Friedman's death in 1960, Rachel Auerbach reflected on the achievements of the CJHC. She noted particularly the works "which to this day are among the most fundamental items of Holocaust literature," published by the CJHC during the years 1945 to 1947: "The tragedy therein is that these publications . . . , which in those years we regarded very critically, considering them nothing more than a beginning and a temporary phase—appear to us now . . . like the fruits of a still-unsurpassed 'golden age.'"[4] Accordingly, the foundation story of early postwar Holocaust research has acquired the added character of an Eden myth, to which veterans of the CJHC and later historians have turned to examine the intentions of its protagonists before their dispersal.

It is not self-evident that the Yiddish historians intended to study the Holocaust primarily from the perspective of Jewish experience—and that they intended to do so from the start of their postwar careers. With the exception of Mark Dworzecki, who lived in Paris until 1949 and openly pursued a national-Jewish approach to Holocaust history, the Yiddish historians who remained in Europe were prevented by political constraints in Poland from freely stating or pursuing their intended program of research. It should be recognized that the directions taken by their early writings and activities derive only in part from conviction, but often from near compulsion, and occasionally from happenstance.

The first section of this chapter seeks to establish that the focus of the Yiddish historians was specifically on the Jewish aspects of Holocaust history and that this focus originated in the earliest period of their work despite pressure to the contrary.

The second section examines their use of Nazi documents and testimony as sources of Jewish historical information, their transition from German to Jewish sources, and their eventual public call for a Jewish orientation to Holocaust study as a corrective to widespread reliance on German sources.

---

4. Rokhl Oyerbakh, "D"r filip fridman z"l (dermonung un gezegenung)," *Di goldene keyt* 38 (1960): 178, 181.

The third section discusses the Yiddish historians' principal approaches to the Jewish history of the Holocaust, all grounded in forms of historicization that have at times been considered unacceptable in German-oriented history of the Nazi era but which are vital to writing Holocaust history from the Jewish perspective.

The Early Struggle for a Jewish Orientation

It is tempting to imagine that the founders of the CJHC had in mind the creation of a "comprehensive historical reconstruction of the Holocaust on the Polish land," as Feliks Tych, director of the successor Jewish Historical Institute, suggests in his 2008 history of the CJHC and the JHI. Tych states that the instructions for oral history interviewers prepared in 1945 by Joseph Kermish and Nachman Blumental under Philip Friedman's leadership "indicate how modern and advanced the project truly was." He supports this claim by observing that their sample questions encompassed "all the actors playing on the stage of history: *perpetrators*, with their instruments, methods and helpers; *victims*, with the whole palette of their responses, . . . and finally, . . . the complete panorama of attitudes of the *local population*."[5]

Evidence of this "comprehensive" approach may be found in the participation by the Yiddish historians in an arguably new method of historical research. As director of the CJHC, Friedman was a member of the Polish High Commission to Investigate the German Crimes in Poland, and he visited Auschwitz as part of an official commission of inquiry in April and May 1945. His notes on the physical conditions observed by the commission and on testimonies by Jewish and non-Jewish survivors, as well as official German documents collected by the CJHC, formed the basis for his well-known early history of Auschwitz.[6] Similarly, the site of the Chełmno extermination camp was visited by Friedman, Blumental, and Kermish as part of an official

---

5. All quotations are from Feliks Tych (director of the JHI, 1995–2007), "The Emergence of Holocaust Research in Poland: The Jewish Historical Commission and the Jewish Historical Institute (ŻIH), 1944–1989," in *Holocaust Historiography in Context: Emergence, Challenges, Polemics and Achievements*, ed. David Bankier and Dan Michman (Jerusalem, 2008), 231 (emphases his).

6. Friedman, *This was Osweicim: The Story Of A Murder Camp* (London, 1946); *Oshvyentshim* (Buenos Aires, 1950).

delegation in May 1945,[7] and Treblinka was visited twice by Kermish, in 1945 and 1947,[8] with such investigations leading to extensive reportage if not scholarly monographs.[9] A novel aspect of this seemingly comprehensive approach was the initiation by Kermish of the idea of interviewing a leading Nazi war criminal as a method of Jewish historical research.

One might easily conclude that the Yiddish historians' nearly exclusive turn to "victim" studies, which occurred only on leaving Poland, was occasioned by their separation from indigenous resources for "perpetrator" and "bystander" research, augmented by their subsequent close connection to Jewish research institutes and survivor circles. But such a conclusion would be superficial and inaccurate. Nearly all of the Yiddish historian's works pertaining to "perpetrator" or "bystander" topics date from the period after they left Europe, including the essays by Kermish and Trunk on Polish-Jewish relations and Friedman's seminal work on the righteous gentiles, *Their Brothers' Keepers*.[10] As for a "comprehensive" approach, Friedman's article on the Jewish badge, which details the introduction of distinctive marks by the Germans in each occupied country, together with the range of responses by both the Jews and their non-Jewish neighbors, also dates from this post-European period.[11] Most importantly, with this article by Friedman, the evidentiary trail runs cold: among all of the Yiddish historians' works, this article alone strives to present a "comprehensive" treatment of the type suggested by Tych.

A more nuanced understanding may come from the wide-ranging topical outline that Friedman prepared in 1950 for the new field of Holocaust research.[12] In this outline, he attempts to provide an exhaustive list of the Holocaust-related topics that require investigation. Virtually all of the works of the Yiddish historians, and of most other Holocaust historians

---

7. Blumental and Kermish, "Khelmno," *Dos naye lebn* (June 10, 1945): 3.

8. Kermish, "Tsum tsveytn mol in treblinke," *Dos naye lebn* (June 4, 1947): 4, 6.

9. Articles by Rachel Auerbach, who was also a member of the official delegation to Treblinka, appeared often in *Dos naye lebn* and were published in book form by the CJHC as *Oyf di felder fun treblinke* (Warsaw-Lodz, 1947).

10. Friedman, *Their Brothers' Keepers* (New York, 1957).

11. Friedman, "The Jewish Badge and the Yellow Star in the Nazi Era," *Historia Judaica* XVII, no. 1 (April 1955): 41–70.

12. Friedman, "Outline of Program for Holocaust Research," in *Roads to Extinction: Essays on the Holocaust*, ed. Ada June Friedman (New York, 1980), 571–76.

as well, could find their places within this outline. But Friedman does not suggest that the outline as a whole should be adopted as the research agenda of any one historian or group of historians, nor does he propose relationships or interconnections among its various parts to suggest an integrated work plan. The outline may more properly be regarded as the call for a *multifaceted* rather than *comprehensive* approach to Holocaust research. And it is for their multifaceted approach to the Jewish history of the Holocaust that the Yiddish historians should also be recognized.

Less easily dispelled is the dualist view that finds in the activities of the CJHC an equal emphasis on the study of perpetrators and victims. This view is typically based on contemporaneous statements by leaders of the CJHC. Thus, historian Shlomo Netzer cites a 1946 report by Noe Gruss, a leading member of the CJHC, stating that the commission's chief goals were "memorializing the murdered and aiding in the pursuit of Nazi criminals in order to bring them to trial."[13] Friedman's debut article of 1945 in *Dos naye lebn* was cited in 1986 by Maurycy Horn, then director of the JHI in his history of the CJHC, to indicate that Friedman's principal objectives for the CJHC were "collecting documents about the crimes committed by the Hitlerites against the Jewish people, as well as searching for sources on the Jewish resistance movement."[14] Most recently, Natalia Aleksiun cites another early statement by Friedman in support of the two-part claim that "collecting documentation of the Nazi crimes and of the fate of Jewish communities became a personal and national duty" for members of the JCHC.[15]

As to the "perpetrator" aspect of this dual agenda, it is undoubted that the Yiddish historians willingly assisted in the prosecution of Nazi criminals. Friedman's service as a member of the Polish High Commission to Investigate the German Crimes in Poland culminated in his contribution of the "Jewish" chapter to the official publication, *German Crimes*

---

13. Shlomo Netzer, "The Holocaust of Polish Jewry in Jewish Historiography," in *The Historiography of the Holocaust Period: Proceedings of the Fifth Yad Vashem International Historical Conference* [Jerusalem, March 1983], ed. Yisrael Gutman and Gideon Greif (Jerusalem, 1988), 138.

14. Mauritsi Horn, "Visnshaftlekhe un editorishe tetikayt fun der tsentraler yidisher historisher komisye baym TsKY"P un funem yidishn historishn institut in poyln in di yorn 1945–1950," *Bleter far geshikhte* XXIV (1986): 145.

15. Natalia Aleksiun, "The Central Jewish Historical Commission in Poland 1944–1947," *Polin* 20 (2007): 77.

in Poland.¹⁶ His departure from Poland in May 1946 was for the purpose of providing materials for the Nuremberg Trials. While in Nuremburg, he was credited by Joseph Wulf, a former colleague at the CJHC, with identifying Amon Göth, the commandant of the Kraków-Płaszów concentration camp then disguised as an ordinary SS member, and initiating his return to Poland for trial.¹⁷ The Yiddish journalist Shmuel-Leyb Shnayderman also met with Friedman in Nuremberg, where Friedman "came to study documents with a connection to the murder of Polish Jewry," and recounts that they attended the trial then in progress of "the 'masters' of the Jewish martyrology in Poland: Goering, Streicher, Frank, Kaltenbrunner, Jodl."¹⁸ The Yiddish historians who remained in Poland after Friedman's departure represented the CJHC as expert witnesses at the Polish trials of Nazi criminals: Blumental, who was Friedman's successor as director, testified at the trials of both Rudolf Höss, commandant of Auschwitz, and Josef Bühler, deputy governor-general of the General Government.¹⁹ Kermish, as assistant director of the CJHC, testified against Ludwik Fischer, the Nazi governor of Warsaw.²⁰ CJHC historian Isaiah Trunk testified against Eilert Hesemeyer, a Nazi official in occupied Włocławek; Józef Górniewicz of the Lithuanian Waffen-SS in Baranowicz; and Ludwik Korn in the Warsaw Ghetto.²¹ (Much later, in 1961,

---

16. Friedman, "Extermination of the Polish Jews in the Years 1939–1945," in *German Crimes in Poland* (Warsaw, 1946), 125–67.

17. Yosef Vulf, "Talyen fun krokever yidn farn gerikht," *Dos naye lebn* (August 30, 1946): 2.

18. Sh. L. Shnayderman, *Tsvishn shrek un hofenung (a rayze iber dem nayem poyln)* (Buenos Aires, 1947), 214–15.

19. See "Dos yidishe folk bashuldikt: di ekspertize fun mgr. nakhmen blumental oyfn protses fun rudolf hes," *Dos naye lebn* (March 27, 1947): 1–2; and "Di 'regirung' fun der general-gubernye un ir oysrotung-politik legabe di yidn: ekspertize fun direktor fun yid. hist. institut mgr. nakhmen blumental oyfn biler- [Büler] protses in kroke," *Dos naye lebn* (June 30, 1948): 4.

20. See Yitskhok Barshteyn, "Dray yidishe expertn bashuldikn . . . ," *Dos naye lebn* (February 6, 1947): 3.

21. See "Ekspertize fun mgr y. trunk," *Dos naye lebn* (September 6, 1948): 6, 8. For the latter two trials, see Véronique Mickisch, "Jewish Historiography between Socialism and Nationalism: A Portrait of Historian Isaiah Trunk (1905–1981)" (MA thesis, Free University of Berlin, 2017). Artur Eisenbach, not included here as one of the "Yiddish historians," testified on behalf of the CJHC at the trial of Hans Biebow, administrator of the Lodz Ghetto; see "Ekspertize fun mgr. arn ayzenbakh: der umkum fun di yidn in 'varte-land' un di rol fun lodzsher talyen hans bibov," *Dos naye lebn* (April 28, 1947): 3.

Mark Dworzecki was a witness at the Eichmann trial in Jerusalem, and the video of his testimony has been made available online.[22])

For each of these trials, the historians conducted original research on the Nazi program of extermination in general and on matters relevant to the given trial. Trunk, for example, set forth a proto-"functionalist" theory of individual criminal responsibility on the part of Nazi officials by explaining that anti-Jewish actions in the field often preceded the order from higher up that would "legalize" the thefts of Jewish property or murders that had taken place. Accordingly, he identified the first known instance of the imposition of the Jewish badge in occupied Poland—in Włocławek—a month prior to its promulgation by the General Government.[23]

An already-advanced perspective on the Final Solution is found in Friedman's chapter in *German Crimes in Poland*, which was published by the Polish government in English in 1946 to promote the prosecution of Nazi criminals. Here, Friedman identifies the process of forced relocation of Polish Jews, first to local ghettos, then to regional urban ghettos, and finally to concentration camps, and assigns approximate numbers to the victims. At this early date, he also concludes, "The idea of totally annihilating the Jews most probably crystallized in the spring of 1941"[24]—a position closer to those of more recent historians, but which countered the earier dates commonly asserted at that time by proto-"intentionalists."

Had the Yiddish historians chosen to proceed from the preparation of war crimes materials into the general field of perpetrator studies, they might well have made significant contributions to this field as well. However, nearly all of their early perpetrator research was directed toward the limited topic of German criminality. One such work, with a foreword by Friedman, was a six-language, large-format album of wartime photographs, titled *Extermination of Polish Jews*, selected to illustrate "the

---

22. See https://youtu.be/9MfBeMc3ksc?t=216.

23. "Ekspertize fun mgr y. trunk." Trunk indicates that the Jewish badge was instituted in Włocławek on October 24, 1939, prior to its general promulgation on November 23. This point was overlooked by Léon Poliakov in his well-known study of the Jewish Star, *L'étoile jaun* (Paris, 1949), 18; *Di gele late* (Paris, 1952), 18; but was noted by Friedman in "The Jewish Badge and the Yellow Star in the Nazi Era," *Roads to Extinction*, 12, 28n3.

24. Friedman, *Roads to Extinction*, 223; original version: "The idea of the extirpation of the Jews probably took shape in the spring of 1941 . . . ," Friedman, "Extermination of the Polish Jews" (1946), 146.

crimes committed by the occupier against the Jewish population."²⁵ The public face of the CJHC in the Zionist press in Poland consisted largely of articles written by Kermish under the rubric, "From the Gallery: German War Crimes,"²⁶ plus news stories in which he was featured under such headings as "The Criminal Hitlerites Will Answer"²⁷ and "Preparing the Indictment Against Gen. Stroop."²⁸

Friedman's early history of Auschwitz grew from notes he commenced during visits to Auschwitz as a member of the official commission of inquiry. His chapter on German medical crimes served almost immediately as the basis for the corresponding section in Max Weinreich's 1946 indictment of Nazi intellectuals, *Hitler's Professors: The Part of Scholarship in Germany's Crimes Against the Jewish People*, published simultaneously in Yiddish and English.²⁹ During the same period—in Paris—Dworzecki addressed the founding congress of the World Medical Association with his demand of "anathema" for "the murderer-doctors" (as noted in chapter 2).

And yet the Yiddish historians at the CJHC did not cross the threshold from studies of Nazi criminality to the field of perpetrator studies. Simply put, they considered their participation in war crimes trials a civic activity, separate from their professional pursuits. In Friedman's words, "Besides the scholarly objective, we also have an emotional and voluntaristic approach."³⁰ Kermish noted the same separation of motives,

---

25. Friedman, foreword to Gerszon Taffet, *Zagłada Żydostwa Polskiego: Album Zdjęć* (Lodz, 1945), unpaginated.

26. Kermish, "Z galerii: Niemieckich przestów wojennych," *Mosty* 2, no. 53 (August 19, 1947): 3; 2, no. 54 (August 22, 1947): 3–4; and "Z galerii: Niemieckich przestów wojennych: Franz Konrad (na podstawie nicopublikowanych materiałów)," *Mosty* 2, no. 62 (September 23, 1947): 3.

27. "Za aniszcznie stolicy i zagładę Żydów: odpowiadać będą przestępcy hitlerowscy," *Mosty* 3, no. 133 (November 18, 1948): 4.

28. "Byli uczestnicy powstania w getcie warszawskim: przygotowuią gen. Stgroopowi," *Mosty* 4, no. 67 (June 9, 1949): 3.

29. M. Vaynraykh, "Hitlers profesorn," *YIVO bleter* XXVII, no. 2 (Summer 1946): 262–67; Max Weinreich, *Hitler's Professors: The Part of Scholarship in Germany's Crimes Against the Jewish People* (New York, 1946), 196–201; both citing Friedman's 1946 Polish edition.

30. *Barikht fun der organizir farzamlung fun der "gezelshaft fraynd fun der Ts.Y.H.K."* [Minutes of the organizing meeting of the Society of Friends of the CJHC], October 9, 1945, at the quarters of the CJHC, Lodz, 2. Archive of the Jewish Historical Institute, Warsaw, CŻKH/303/XX folder 405.

reporting, "From the very start of its work, the Commission also undertook practical tasks apart from its scholarly research work and made contact with the agencies that were occupied with the activity of meting out the appropriate punishment to the German criminals."[31]

Merely to say, however, that the Yiddish historians engaged in civic as well as professional tasks is to suggest a parallel with the multiple roles typically required of scholars in institutional settings—a parallel that obscures the drama of the Yiddish historians' situation in postwar Poland.

Friedman's exclamation to his future wife, historian Ada Eber, soon after their liberation in August 1944, "I have found a way to get even with Hitler and his criminal regime . . . I have already started to collect eyewitness reports . . . ,"[32] is far from issuing a call for historians to prepare indictments for war crimes trials. At the time of his statement, war crimes trials were not yet a practical reality in either the American or Polish public spheres. Had such trials not been instituted (they began at the local level in Poland in November 1944), his statement would doubtless appear to be an independent utterance of Ringelblum's demand that Jews write their own history lest the Germans be given the last word. Instead, his statement has been joined with later statements and events to suggest that investigation into Nazi crimes—and hence, perpetrator research—was inherent in his vision of the Jewish historian's task.

The outside observer with the closest knowledge of the Yiddish historians in postwar Poland, Raphael Mahler, was not misled. As codirector with Ringelblum of the prewar *Yunger historiker krayz* (Young Historians Circle) in Warsaw, he had known and worked with at least three of these historians before the war: Friedman, Trunk, and Kermish. He published

---

31. Kermish, "3 yor tetikayt fun Ts.Y.H.K. un yidishn historishn institut baym Ts.K. fun yidn in poyln," *Dos naye lebn* (March 5, 1948): 6. In this report, and in his memorial essay on Friedman, Kermish reports with apparent satisfaction the CJHC's contributions to prosecuting Nazi war criminals, which served both the public interest and the historians' own sense of justice, but he separates this civic duty of the commission from the research agenda of its historians. See Kermish, "D"r filip fridman—der historiker fun khurbn," *Di tsukunft* (April 1975): 153; "The Founder of the Jewish Historical Commission in Poland after the Second World War," *Yad Vashem Bulletin* 6–7 (June 1960): 5–6.

32. Natalia Aleksiun, "The Central Jewish Historical Commission," 78; and Aleksiun, "Philip Friedman and the Emergence of Holocaust Scholarship: A Reappraisal," *Simon Dubnow Institute Yearbook* 11 (2012): 336.

two substantial articles on the activities of the CJHC and JHI that appeared as cover stories in the New York journal *Yidishe kultur* before undertaking a teaching visit to Poland in the fall of 1947.[33] It may be seen from the content of these articles that he had read, and drew upon, the writings by Friedman and others that described the seemingly dual mission of the CJHC. But in his first article, Mahler states the mission solely in terms of Jewish historiography: "The commission set for itself the task of studying exhaustively and comprehensively the martyr-history of the Jews in Poland under Nazi occupation."[34] In the second article, he writes with modest pride that the JHI's new scholarly journal, *Bleter far geshikhte*, has styled itself as the renewal of the journal of the same name that he and Ringelblum had edited before the war. He notes that its principal contributors "were all active members of the *Historiker-krayz* before the war."[35] In both articles, he refers only to the rebirth of Jewish history-writing in postwar Poland, and in neither does he count among the professional obligations of his historian colleagues the study of German crimes or the pursuit of war criminals.

This understanding of the historians' mission is corroborated by A. Wolf Yasni, a close collaborator of the historians at the CJHC who had been a journalist before the war and would become an active lay historian of the Holocaust in Israel. In 1965, he published a reminiscence of their early period ("consecrated to the memory of my teacher, Dr. Philip Friedman"). He states that the survivor-historians "collected archival materials and eyewitness accounts" in order to carry out the tasks they felt obligated to pursue: "to bring before the world the acts of horror the Germans carried out against millions of Jews, also to document Jewish resistance, the struggle to maintain humanity ['the image of God' in man] during the

---

33. Regarding Mahler's teaching visit to Poland, see "Hartsike oyfname far d"r rafoel mahler in vlotslav: derefenung fun kurs fun yidisher geshikhte," *Dos naye lebn* (September 28, 1947): 5.

34. Rafoel Mahler, "A groyse natyonale oyfgabe: di tsentrale yidishe historishe komisye in poyln," *Yidishe kultur* 8, no. 2 (February 1946): 2.

35. Rafoel Mahler, "Di forshung fun der letster yidisher martirologye oyf naye vegn," *Yidishe kultur* 11, no. 2 (February 1949): 2. Here, Mahler lists Blumental among his former *Yunger historiker krayz* members; however, Blumental does not appear in the final lexicon of members in Mahler's *Historiker un vegvayzer* (Tel Aviv, 1967), 302–15.

barbarity of the German-Hitler period."[36] Not included among the activities he recounts are the pursuit of Nazi criminals or the study of the Final Solution as a subject separate from its effect on its victims.

The extent and nature of participation by historians in the civic project of punishing Nazi criminals was the principal area of conflict among the leaders of the CJHC. More specifically, the drive to punish Nazi criminals in Poland became linked with the successful attempt by pro-Communist forces to absorb the democratic Left on the one hand, and suppress the anti-Soviet, antisemitic, nationalist Right on the other. This linkage was expressed in terms of a continuing fight against "fascism" and "the reaction" (the term used at the time for Polish political forces that resisted the Soviet takeover). Just as the American-led denazification campaign in the western zones of Germany diminished with the growing need for German allies in the Cold War, the corresponding campaign in Poland intensified with the drive to eliminate opposition to Soviet domination of Eastern Europe.

An example within the Jewish sphere is the January 1946 front-page editorial in *Dos naye lebn* by the editor, Mikhl Mirsky, who was also director of the Central Committee of Polish Jews. It declares that recent friction between the United States and the Soviet Union "nourished all the reactionary forces in the world . . . . As usual, our domestic reactionary forces used this favorable atmosphere to bring unrest, uncertainty into the political situation in Poland in order to erode our friendly relations with the Soviet Union."[37] Then, with the final Soviet takeover of Poland in late 1949, Secretary-General Joel Lazebnik exhorted delegates at the committee's November conference, "We must publicize widely among the Jewish working-class population the interest we share with German democracy [the new German Democratic Republic ("East Germany")] in eradicating all vestiges of Nazism and fascism"—as if such movements remained to be combated in Poland.[38]

---

36. A. Volf Yasni, "Tsvantsik yor 'yidisher historisher institut' in poyln," *Lebns-fragn* 159 (March 1965): 6.
37. M. Mirski, "Moskve," *Dos naye lebn* (January 3, 1946): 1.
38. "Farshartkn unzer onteyl in der sotsyalistisher boyung: barikht-referat fun y. lazebnik," *Dos naye lebn* (November 21, 1949): 6.

At the Central Jewish Historical Commission, it was Friedman who contended with the early stages of Soviet encroachment, in which Jewish institutions were supported and yet manipulated by the ruling hierarchy. In his initial public message as director in April 1945, he declared that the murdered victims cry out, "Be not silent, take vengeance!"—a demand consistent with the early statement recalled by his wife. But he comes to a new conclusion: "[W]e are preparing the great indictment for world public opinion that will, in a solid juridical and historical form, present a summation of the shameful and barbaric Hitlerite acts of extermination and demand a proper judgment for the criminals." Lest his statement be taken at face value—and any statement published under Communist hegemony requires multiple levels of interpretation—it should be remembered that these words appear in the same essay as Friedman's assertion that Jewish historical research must henceforth be conducted "with the knife-sharp method of dialectical-materialist analysis."[39] Turning then to Friedman's final statement as director, published in June 1946, there appears a still further alignment with official policy: "We must forge the weapon against fascism . . . . We have built our fighting positions and drawn up our artillery ready to shoot; we will attack our enemy with the heavy shots of our '*materyaln un dokumentn*'" (referring to the three volumes of documentary materials published by the CJHC).[40]

How does it happen that a historian was drawn so deeply into partisan posturing? A first answer is found in the reports by Jacob Pat, director of the American Jewish Labor Committee, who visited Friedman and the CJHC in January 1946. Like the many prominent American Jews (generally left-leaning) who visited postwar Poland,[41] he considered the CJHC an essential destination and discussed his encounters there. Most other visitors provide a tourist's glimpses: the painting in the lobby (variously Lodz Ghetto dictator Rumkowski[42] or an old traditional Jew in

---

39. Friedman, "Unzer historishe oyfgabe," *Dos naye lebn* (April 10, 1945): 6.
40. Friedman, "Di yidishe historishe komisye in poyln," *Eynikeyt* (June 1946): 11.
41. For example: "Twice I was in Lodz . . . . And twice I was in the Historical Commission." P. Novik, *Eyrope—tsvishn milkhome un sholem: rayze-bilder, batrakhtungen* (New York, 1948), 160.
42. Ibid.

beard and *peyes*[43]), rooms filled with Nazi documents and materials from the Ringelblum Archive,[44] and the taking of eyewitness accounts from survivors.[45] Some, like the well-known Yiddish travel journalist Chaim Shoshkes, offered praise: "Thanks to Dr. Friedman, the energetic and methodical director of the Jewish Historical Commission in Poland, from fragments, stories and eyewitness accounts the whole tragic history of the Hitler years in Poland have been restored and ascertained."[46]

But it happens that, uniquely, Pat published two reports of his visit that are self-consciously divergent, one in 1946 while Friedman and his colleagues were still in Poland, and a second on the occasion of Friedman's death in 1960. In the first, he relates that, according to Friedman, "They were at that time governed by one main feeling—revenge for our holy martyrs, gathering the complete documentary accusation-material."[47] Both of Pat's accounts describe the CJHC's growing collections of German and Jewish documentary materials and Friedman's urgent wish to secure funding to search for the Oyneg Shabes archive buried by Ringelblum and his associates under the now-vacant area of the Warsaw Ghetto. However, in the second account, Pat declares only that Friedman's overriding concern was for locating the Ringelblum Archive and "beginning immediately to publish in books the ghetto-materials already assembled."

In this second account Pat provides an uninhibited portrayal of the situation he observed, saying, "people spoke with me in disguised speech, half-sentences. . . . The fear of communism hung in the air. At each table were Jewish Communists—as far as I recall—Mirsky, [Shimon] Zachariasz, [Dovid] Sfard, who were later the imposed masters over the survivors

---

43. Dora Taytlboym, *Mitn ponem tsum lebn: rayze-ayndrukn* (Paris, 1952), 192.
44. Ibid., 192–97.
45. Y. Hirshhoyt, "Dr. filip fridman—der historiker fun undzer khurbn," *Di tsukunft* (August 1965): 283; and Hirshhoyt, "Dr. filip fridman—der historiker fun undzer khurbn," *In gang fun der geshikhte* (Tel Aviv, 1984), 326. (These two accounts, both written after Friedman's death, are similar in their treatment of the Polish period; the second was occasioned by the 1980 publication of Friedman's *Roads to Extinction*.) See also Samuel Wohl, *Mayn rayze keyn varshe* (New York, 1947), 21, recounting a meeting of the Jewish Literary Society in Lodz at which Ber Mark presided and presenters included Avrom Sutzkever, Chaim Grade, Shmerke Kaczerginski, and "Blumental, director of the Historical Commission."
46. Khaym Shoshkes, *Poyln—1946 (Ayndrukn fun a rayze)* (Buenos Aires, 1946), 140.
47. Yankev Pat, *Ash un fayer: iber di khurves fun poyln* (New York, 1946), 77.

Second Academic Conference of the Central Jewish Historical Commission, September 19–20, 1945, Lodz. At the head of the table, Friedman sits with his back to the wall, Blumental is standing, and Kermish is in uniform. Rachel Auerbach is on the right (facing the camera). Yad Vashem Photo Archive, Jerusalem. 1427/223.

of Polish Jewry." Pat discloses that Friedman came to him in his hotel room with a detailed plan and budget for locating and excavating the Ringelblum Archive which, he quotes Friedman as saying, "the martyrs hid, before their departure, for the coming generations." At a time when harm could no longer come to Friedman or his colleagues, Pat writes, "Dr. Ph. Friedman said to me that one must not delay . . . '—It should not become too late.' "[48]

As for the events that took place within the four walls of the CJHC, when Mirsky and his fellow overseers were "at each table," the internal disputes of the commission's leaders were preserved for posterity in the minutes of their meetings. The minutes of the CJHC's Second Academic Conference, held September 19–20, 1945 in Lodz, provide the views of the two principal camps that were in continual conflict at the CJHC.

---

48. Yankev Pat, "Dr. filip fridman—a por shtrikhn," *Di tsukunft* (March 1960): 107–8.

The conference was not a public event, but took place in a well-appointed conference room in the building of the Central Committee. The minutes and photographs indicate the presence of about twenty-five scholars and political leaders. Photos taken in the evening show the windows opened wide. Despite the apparent late-summer heat, the participants honor the event with their best business attire. Vases of flowers decorate the conference table. On the wall at the head of the table is a propaganda poster that invokes the Jewish religious symbols of a holy book and menorah and declares in Yiddish, "May historical TRUTH be the GRAVE of FASCISM!"

Revealed in the minutes is a clash of intentions for the CJHC, with the scholars of the central branch on one side, and the political leadership and members of the leftist Krakow branch on the other. The purpose of the event was for the scholars to present their work in the format of a traditional academic conference—remarkable in itself less than five months after the defeat of Nazi Germany. Friedman spoke on the overall goals and achievements of the CJHC, Kermish on the holdings of its archives, Blumental on Yiddish literature of the occupation period, and others on fields ranging from Jewish partisan movements to the psychology of Jewish child survivors. Mirsky, a prewar member of the Communist Party who remained an apologist for the Communist regime until his death in 1993, interjected his views on at least three occasions to exhort or excoriate the presenters. Early on, he declared that the commission "ought to be an institution that fights against fascism and the reaction which starts once again to raise its head."[49] At another point, he warned that the commission "must not limit itself to the problems of the occupation and avoid current issues . . . . The Germans were beaten but the fight with fascism endures," adding that "there should not be any thick volumes" but rather "short and valuable contributions."[50] Near the end, he spoke again to demand that the CJHC "not become similar to YIVO, locked in itself." Whereas Friedman had opened the conference asserting, "Our task must be strictly scholarly

---

49. *Protokol fun tsveytn visnshaftlekher baratung fun der Ts.Y.H.K. in lodzsh* [Minutes of the second academic conference of the CJHC in Lodz] *dem 19-tn un 20-tn september 1945*, 8. Archive of the Jewish Historical Institute, Warsaw, AZIH/CKZP/CŻKH/303/XX12.

50. Ibid., 10.

[*visnshaftlekh*]," this was countered by Mirsky who argued that the CJHC "dare not be a purely *visnshaftlekh* institution, but must step out in public and take an active part in the fight against reaction."[51]

Several of the presenters attempted to confront, or else mollify, Mirsky. Mendel Balberyszki, a partisan from Vilna (for whose autobiography Blumental and Kermish would later both write introductions), attacked directly: "Mirsky's line is political and the historical commission cannot occupy itself with political matters."[52] Friedman sidestepped by pleading lack of personnel, funding, and technical facilities.[53] Blumental replied subtly that the "uprisings in Treblinka and Sobibór were not only episodes in the fight against the reaction in a certain period of history, but events that . . . found their response in Jewish literature," thereby lending present-day relevance to the study of that "anti-fascist" literature.[54] The only specific support for Mirsky's position came from Nella Rost of the leftist Krakow branch who announced that the "historical commission in Krakow has realized the postulates" set forth by Mirsky through its propaganda work.[55]

In the end, Friedman presented a report on the CJHC's proposed activities that included ten categories of future research and publishing on the Jewish experience of Nazi rule—and which concluded conspicuously last and least with the statement, "We are also preparing materials for indictments in trials against the Hitlerian criminals for various judicial bodies."[56] This was the sole reference in his opening or closing remarks to the subject of Nazi trials, and he did not mention the "fight against fascism."

Two weeks later, Friedman had been made to conform. In a public meeting of the Society of Friends of the CJHC, Friedman announced in his opening remarks, "We must be a fighting instrument against fascism and antisemitism."[57] The identical phrase was repeated by Friedman's successor, Blumental, when he represented the JHI at the first conference of

---

51. Ibid., 23.
52. Ibid., 11.
53. Ibid., 9.
54. Ibid., 12.
55. Ibid., 9.
56. Ibid., 22.
57. *Barikht fun der organizir farzamlung*, 2.

Yad Vashem in Jerusalem two years later: "In addition to the scholarly work, we are doing what we call applied history. There is no room here for pure history. Everything we do is a weapon in the war against fascism and anti-Semitism."[58] At the Society of Friends meeting, Friedman concluded by saying that the CJHC had good relations with various official bodies and had received valuable documents for its work. He declares that it is, therefore, "our obligation to give evidence of Hitlerian crimes"—to which he adds the justification, "and from the second side, it is also a form of fighting against antisemitism."[59]

Yet the historians did resist the politicizing of their scholarly work. Blumental, for example, previewed his expert testimony against Höss for his colleagues and members of the Central Committee in March 1947. He was urged by some to act as "an accuser in the name of all the Jews who were killed," and by Mirsky to be less scientific, saying, "For scholarly purposes, accuracy is necessary. However, this trial pursues political goals." Blumental responded that he would testify not "as an accuser but as an expert."[60] Nevertheless, the banner headline that appeared across the front page of *Dos naye lebn* on the day following his testimony reads, "The Jewish People Accuses."[61]

In this struggle over the proper function of the historian, Friedman similarly disavowed a political role and redoubled his commitment to objectivity. Despite his early insistence on "vengeance" through historical work, the theoretical articles on Holocaust study which he published shortly after leaving Poland insist that legal punishment "is a matter for the judge and prosecutor who compile the indictment according to *their* methods, making use of historical materials." He emphasized that "the

---

58. July 14–15, 1947; Yad Vashem Archives, AM/237. Quoted in Boaz Cohen, "Holocaust Research at Yad Vashem in the 1950s," in *Holocaust Historiography in Context: Emergence, Challenges, Polemics and Achievements*, ed. Bankier and Michman (Jerusalem, 2008), 261n16.

59. *Barikht*, 4.

60. See Laura Jockusch, "'Collect and Record! Help to Write the History of the Latest Destruction!' Jewish Historical Commissions in Europe, 1943–1953" (PhD diss., New York University, 2007), 225–28; and slightly condensed version in her *Collect and Record! Jewish Holocaust Documentation in Early Postwar Europe* (New York, 2012), 114–16.

61. Blumental, "Dos yidishe folk bashuldikt: di ekspertize fun mgr. nakhmen blumental oyfn protses fun rudolf hes," *Dos naye lebn* (March 27, 1947): 1.

accusatory tendency" and the school of thought which holds that world history is the court of Last Judgment (*veltgerikht*) are superfluous because "the Jews do not need convincing and the nations of the world would be better convinced through substantive, objective work than emotional phraseology."[62]

Participation in war crimes research and trials was not a civic obligation of the CJHC that complemented the historians' own scholarship on the Jewish experience of the Holocaust. An increasing research emphasis on Nazi crimes would threaten to displace the historians' Jewish-oriented approach to Holocaust studies in favor of perpetrator studies. Three other government policies also militated against the Jewish orientation of their work as Soviet control of Poland grew more secure: the regime became increasingly opposed to 1) Jewish particularism, in the form of Jewish schools, languages, newspapers, and cultural organizations; 2) political pluralism, including non-Communist Jewish political movements; and 3) Western interference, including foreign aid for Jewish organizations. In the spring of 1946, on the third anniversary of the Warsaw Ghetto Uprising, Ber Mark, editor of the government-sanctioned Yiddish newspaper *Dos naye lebn*, found it necessary to universalize Jewish heroism with the claim that the Jewish fighters' "bloody self-sacrifice was part of the great fight of freedom-loving humanity against Hitlerism," before declaring specifically that it was "their own independent heroic Jewish chapter in the recent war of liberation."[63] By late 1950, he was reduced to asserting that the first key to understanding the Warsaw Ghetto Uprising was "the politics of Anglo-Saxon finance capital and its connection with German imperialism."[64] Where the 1947 edition of his history of the uprising states

---

62. Friedman, "Di forshung fun unzer khurbn," *Kiem* (January 1948): 52. Here Friedman uses *veltgerikht* to indicate Schiller's (and later, Hegel's) "Die Weltgeschichte ist das Weltgericht," which he quotes in full on the previous page. There, he argues that Jewish historians formerly "sat upon the judge's chair and pronounced sentence for good or ill" over such figures as Nebuchadnezzar, Titus, Frederick the Great, Joseph II, and Napoleon "without considering that, from the world-historical standpoint and *especially* in the history of their own people, they were evaluated altogether differently" (all emphases his).

63. "Rede fun b. mark oyf der geto-akademye in varshe," *Dos naye lebn* (May 3, 1946): 6.

64. B. Mark, "Problemen fun der forshung fun di vidershtand-bavegungen in di getos," *Yedies: byuletin fun yidishn historishn institut in poyln* [2] (November 1950): 2.

that the chief forces of the underground in the ghetto were the Zionists, Bundists, and Communists (in that order),[65] the 1953 edition claims that the "reactionary leaders of the Zionists and of the 'Bund' refused to join" the "anti-fascist bloc" in the ghetto, which was headed by members of the Polish Workers Party (the Communists)—and that the Zionists and Bundists cooperated with the American Joint Distribution Committee, "which was a partner of the traitorous Judenrat."[66]

Once the Soviet takeover of Poland had been completed in late 1949, all of the independent Jewish schools had been nationalized, non-Communist political parties outlawed, and foreign Jewish relief organizations banned (notably the "Joint" and ORT). The Communist Jewish leadership joined the offensive by projecting the regime's anti-nationalist, anti-pluralist, and anti-Western positions in a Jewish idiom. The address by Secretary-General Lazebnik to the delegates at the Central Committee conference in November 1949 accordingly urged vigilance against the "speculative-capitalistic, nationalistic, Zionist-Bundist and Trotskyite elements" still active in the country.[67]

At the Jewish Historical Institute, the historians who would soon emigrate from Poland retreated to areas of political safety—in the first edition of the JHI's new information bulletin, published in November 1949, Trunk writes on the holdings of the JHI's library, Kermish on the displays in its new museum, and Blumental on preservation work for materials in the Ringelblum Archive.[68] By the end of the year, all three had left for Israel, and soon the JHI's *Bleter far geshikhte* would carry lead articles by and about Stalin, with an appropriate front-page

---

65. B. Mark, *Dos bukh fun gvure: oyfshtand fun varshever geto* (Lodz, 1947), 76. The prior, 1947 Moscow edition does not include this statement but does refer to the importance of the underground publishing activities of all three groups (44–45).

66. B. Mark, *Dokumentn un materyaln vegn oyfshtand in varshever geto* (Warsaw, 1953), 31.

67. "Farshtarkn unzer onteyl in der sotsyalistisher boyung: barikht-referat fun y. lazebnik," *Dos naye lebn* (November 21, 1949): 6. In Friedman's papers at YIVO, this article appears with his handwritten date and notation highlighting the section devoted to the reorganization of the JHI. RG 1258, F 475.

68. Trunk, "Di shtudir-biblyotek baym yidishn historishn institut," *Yedies: byuletin fun yidishn historishn institut in poyln* [1] (November 1949): 7; Kermish, "Der muzey fun poylishn yidntum," 8; and Blumental, "Di arbet iber ringelblums ksav-yad," 4–6.

portrait. As Blumental later remarked, historical scholarship under Soviet hegemony was forced to take the lead in altering the Soviet role in World War II from co-conqueror of Poland with Nazi Germany to that of "liberator of the enslaved world." The alternative, he said, was to be named "a reactionary, a falsifier . . . and an enemy of mankind [ellipsis his]." He concluded, "No one wanted to be a fascist, or a 'social-fascist,' and so on."[69]

After their departure, and that of several other researchers, the report by the JHI on the tenth anniversary of the CJHC's founding would dismiss "the exodus of some Zionist archivists and historians in 1949," claiming that it did not diminish the JHI at all and that the early progress of the CJHC had come *despite* its "nationalist elements." The same report would reiterate official claims that "those who were sitting on their suitcases" had shown "inadequate adherence to the only creative scientific method, the method of dialectical materialism," and it announced that a subsequent turn to Marxist methodology "had made it possible" for the JHI to be absorbed by the Polish Academy of Sciences.[70] In the inverted rhetoric of the time, the takeover of the JHI was explained by Hersh Smoliar, a high-ranking Jewish Communist official, as a means "to secure the full independence" of the JHI.[71]

German versus Jewish Historical Sources

Despite official pressures, the Yiddish historians resisted engagement in perpetrator studies during their time at the CJHC and JHI, as indicated by their nearly total avoidance of voluntary perpetrator research beyond the imposed task of documenting German crimes. Of the twenty-six publications listed in the prospectus issued by the CJHC in 1947, only

---

69. Blumental, "Geshikhtlekher emes—tsi partey-'geshikhte'?: arum vidershtand-fragn unter der daytsher okupatsye," *Lebns-fragn* 288–89 (March–April 1976): 8.

70. "Tsen yor zaml-, forshung-, un farlag-arbet vegn geshikhte fun yidn in poyln," *Bleter far geshikhte* VII, nos. 2–3 (April–August 1954): 8, 9, 11, 13, 18. Although anonymous, it is in the writing style of Ber Mark and appeared during his directorship of the JHI.

71. Hersh Smolyar, *Oyf der letster pozitsye mit der letster hofenung* (Tel Aviv, 1982), 184.

three have an exclusively German focus and no more than four a mixed German and Jewish focus.[72] Of the nineteen subject areas proposed by Kermish for a bibliography of the JHI's holdings, no more than four represent the perpetrators' perspective.[73] The list of each Yiddish historian's own publications in the bibliography indicates a similar predominance of Jewish over German subjects.

Nevertheless, the Yiddish historians embraced the long-established tradition of using non-Jewish documents as sources of Jewish historical information in the absence of Jewish sources. As a stateless people through all of its prior period of European history, the Jews lacked one of the central institutions of a state, namely, a depository or archive for documents of national importance. In Eastern Europe, the only form of Jewish archive was the *pinkas* (record book) kept by each local Jewish community, which was often not well preserved over the course of centuries. Seeking Jewish historical information in non-Jewish archives was a practice to which Jewish historians had been accustomed before the war and against which Dubnow had protested in his well-known appeal of 1891 for the collecting of Jewish historical sources as a national obligation (a task undertaken by YIVO between the world wars). Trunk's prewar monographs on the history of early Jewish settlements in Kutno and Płock, for example, rely almost entirely on his drawing of Jewish information from Latin documents in Polish municipal, royal, and judicial archives. It is not surprising that his first major postwar work, "Jewish Labor Camps in the Warthegau" of 1948, is "based chiefly on German documents, which we found in the archive of the Lodz Ghetto administration." However, the body of this study, after a brief introduction to the German administration, is devoted to the details of Jewish existence in

---

72. *Prospekt fun di oysgabn fun der tsentraler yidisher historisher komisye in poyln* (Warsaw-Lodz-Krakow, 1947). The list covers works published by the Central branch of the CJHC. Publications of the regional branches (primarily Krakow) are almost exclusively Jewish in nature, as indicted by the full-page list of thirty-five works offered for sale under the heading, "Tsentrale yidishe historishe komisye," in the *yoyvel numer* (jubilee issue) of *Dos naye lebn* (apparently early 1947; without page numbers).

73. Kermish, "Vegn a biblyografye tsu der geshikhte fun poylishn yidntum in der tkufe fun der natsyonaler katastrofe (1939–1945)," *Bleter far geshikhte* II, nos. 1–4 (January–December 1949): 231–32.

the camps: living conditions, food, work, regulations, pay, clothing, intra-camp movements, and punishments.[74]

As to the credibility of German sources, Trunk is careful to state that "Nazi duplicity and deception" often render such sources unreliable but that he has found it possible to use German documents in two circumstances: "when the statements contained in them were made without awareness of their significance (which occurred surprisingly often among the arrogant but dull Nazi bureaucrats) and when they present their subject in a frankly unfavorable light"[75]—a position he continued to hold and repeated nearly verbatim in his 1962 history of the Lodz Ghetto.[76] In 1963, he added a third category: top-secret reports of actual events, as opposed to anti-Jewish propaganda which commonly exaggerated attacks by Jewish partisans to justify harsh reprisals.[77] Friedman similarly dismisses the usual run of German documents, arguing that they so disguise Nazi atrocities with lies and euphemisms as to be without use, but he goes on to specify a few "rare exceptions" that correspond with Trunk's criteria for acceptance.[78] Friedman argues, moreover, that select German sources could be used to clarify important questions, citing, on the one hand, German anti-Jewish policies, and on the other, "the legal, economic, and social situation of the Jews" and "questions of Jewish self-government."[79]

Two of the German sources Friedman considered exceptional were the secret reports by Jürgen Stroop and Friedrich Katzmann, the generals who commanded, respectively, the destruction of the Warsaw Ghetto and the Jewish labor camps in Lwów and elsewhere in Eastern Galicia. Both were placed in evidence by the prosecution at the Nuremberg Trials. The report

---

74. Trunk, "Yidishe arbet-lagern in 'varteland,'" *Bleter far geshikhte* I, no. 1 (January–March 1948): 116–17. With an anger not displayed in his later works, he defines his terms parenthetically here, for example: food ("frightful hunger"), work ("suffering"), pay ("a bitter joke").

75. Ibid., 117.

76. Trunk, *Lodzsher geto* (New York, 1962), xiii; quoted from *Łódź Ghetto: A History*, trans. and ed. Robert Moses Shapiro (Bloomington, 2006), 5.

77. Trunk, "Nokh amol vegn yidishn vidershtand kegn di natsis," *Di tsukunft* (April 1963): 152–53.

78. Friedman, "Di elementn fun undzer khurbn-forshung," *Hemshekh* 1 (April 1948): 6.

79. Ibid., 5.

by Stroop served as the principal source for Kermish's 1946 history of the Warsaw Ghetto Uprising.[80] Kermish emphasized the importance of Stroop's report in the absence of adequate Jewish accounts, saying, "Contrary to his intention, the German general has given with his report a mostly reliable testimony of Jewish heroism."[81] He notes, for example, that only from Stroop's report does one learn that on the second day of the uprising the Jewish fighters disabled a German tank.[82] As Blumental later commented, when the report "is divested of its party phraseology, of its 'conventional lies' (if Max Nordau's term may be used in this context) . . . the real truth will remain: the heroism of the Ghetto fighters."[83] The report by Katzmann was likewise cited by their colleague Artur Eisenbach as a unique source of information on Jewish resistance in Galicia. In a 1949 study, Eisenbach cites the value of Katzmann's report for making it known that Jewish fighters bought weapons from Italian soldiers in Galicia and built bunkers in the city of Rohatyn that measured thirty meters in length and were equipped with electric lights, radio, and two-story sleeping bunks.[84]

The various merits of German documents were enumerated by Blumental, who noted their general truthfulness in assessing Jewish fighting capabilities[85] and their accuracy in reporting the appropriation of "ownerless" Jewish property.[86] He quotes from German sources, on at least three occasions from 1962 to 1978, the exclamation by German officials: "The Jews are shooting!"[87] From New York on the fifteenth anniversary

---

80. Kermish, *Der oyfshtand in varshever geto: 19ter April–16ter Mai 1943* (Buenos Aires, 1948).

81. Kermish, "An epos fun heldntum: di raportn fun general stroop vegn geto-oyfshtand," *Dos naye lebn* (April 23, 1946): unnumbered page.

82. Kermish, "Tsu der forshung vegn geto-oyfshtand," *Di goldene keyt* 15 (1953): 145.

83. Blumental, "Strops barikht vi a historisher makor," *Lebns-fragn* 136–37 (April–May 1963): 8.

84. A. Ayzenbakh, "A vikhtiker historisher dokument tsu der geshikhte fun yid. vidershtand bavegung in galitsye," *Dos naye lebn* (March 11, 1949): 4.

85. Blumental, "German Document on the Bialystok Ghetto Revolt," *Yad Vashem Bulletin* 14 (March 1964): 22. See also, "Tenu'at ha-partizanim le'or mismakhim germaniyim," translated from the Yiddish by M. Halmish, in *Sefer ha-partizanim ha-Yehudim*, vol. 2 (Merhavyah, 1958), 631–61.

86. Blumental, "Der yidisher khurbn in daytshe dokumentn," in *Pinkes Zaglembye*, ed. Y. Rapaport (Melbourne, 1972), 294.

87. Blumental, "Der varshever geto-oyfshtand in der geshikhte fun tsveytn velt-krig," *Lebns-fragn* 123–24 (March–April 1962): 9; "Fun yanuar biz april 1943," *Lebns-fragn*

of the Warsaw Ghetto Uprising, Trunk reports that, with the continuing scarcity of Jewish accounts of the uprising, "the report of the oppressor and hangman" (Stroop) remained "the most detailed document on the course of the uprising."[88]

Nevertheless, Kermish's book on the Warsaw Ghetto Uprising—the event most central to collective Jewish memory of resistance—was criticized by his colleagues at the CJHC for lacking specifics about the Jewish defenders.[89] When Stroop was brought to Warsaw for trial by the Polish court, Kermish proposed a remedy he considered innovative. He obtained permission on behalf of the JHI to interview Stroop in prison in March 1948 and then to revisit him the following year for interviews with Rachel Auerbach and ghetto fighters Marek Edelman and Stefan Grayek. Kermish later claimed success for the "experiment in gathering new historical material in this way" in his book, *The Warsaw Ghetto Uprising in the Eyes of the Enemy*.[90] In response to the request by Kermish for his view of Jewish defense preparations and fighting abilities, Stroop replied that the Germans had expected "not the least resistance" but found that "the defenders of the ghetto had prepared themselves for several months' defense," and he provided details of the infrastructure and provisioning of their bunkers as well as the types of weapons and tactics used by the Jewish fighters.[91]

Throughout their careers, the Yiddish historians confronted the necessity of relying on German sources for Jewish historical information. Until the fall of 1946, German documents abandoned in Lodz by the

---

160–61 (April–May 1965): 3; and "Erev pesakh TaShaG—19 april 1943," *Lebns-fragn* 311–12 (April–May 1978): 4.

88. Trunk, "19ter april 1943–1958," *Unzer tsayt* (April–May 1958): 20. Trunk also reported on the German mayor of Podembitz, Poland (fired for his pro-Jewish and pro-Polish sympathies), whose diary "is so far the only known source" of information on Jewish living conditions, relations between residents and newly arrived exiles, and the Jews' fear of the Nazis. "Shtelung fun daytshn tsu der hitleristisher oysrotung-politik," *Di tsukunft* (April 1962): 148.

89. "Visnshaftlekhe zitsungen fun der tsentr. yid. historisher komisye," *Dos naye lebn* (November 1, 1946): 9.

90. Kermish, ed., *Mered Geto Varshah be-'ene ha-oyev: ha-dohot shel ha-General Yurgen Shtrop / The Warsaw Ghetto Revolt as Seen by the Enemy* (Jerusalem, 1966), LI.

91. Kermish, "Shtroops tshuves oyf an ankete" (unsigned introduction and text), *Bleter far geshikhte* I, nos. 3–4 (August–December 1948): 166–85.

fleeing German occupiers predominated in the holdings of the CJHC. With the recovery of the first portion of the Ringelblum Archive in September 1946, Blumental wrote, "If our materials [so far] consist chiefly of German documents, . . . the Ringelblum Archive is above all a collection of Jewish materials."[92] In 1948, the discovery of "unknown Jewish documents on the period of the April uprising" in the Warsaw Ghetto was celebrated by Kermish with an article by that name in the Polish-Jewish press.[93]

Once established at Yad Vashem in the mid-1950s, Blumental and Kermish expanded their concern for securing Jewish sources. Blumental spoke in 1955 on the proposed work program at Yad Vashem, saying, "Everything connected to the life and death of the Jews in Europe must be collected by us." He argued that press and radio appeals to the public must be supplemented by organized "groups of friends" who would convince their acquaintances to donate documents to Yad Vashem.[94] On occasion, Kermish published announcements about new Jewish sources on the Warsaw Ghetto Uprising.[95] Nevertheless, Blumental would write in 1960 that the failure to mount a general expedition in search of Jewish source materials had become "our great guilt." He referred to the Jewish magnates who had funded the visit to Kishinev by the Hebrew national poet Chaim Nachman Bialik after the pogrom of 1903 (resulting in his famous epic poem, "In the City of Slaughter") and the visit to Galicia and Bukovina by the Jewish ethnographer and writer S. An-sky to investigate the pogroms during World War I (resulting in his well-known reportage, published in English as *The Enemy at his Pleasure*), lamenting that "we stand even lower" than those victims of the Nazis who risked everything to preserve their documents for the future. The blame he ascribes, in part, to the quantity of documents left behind by the Germans, "measured

---

92. Blumental, "Vos shtelt mit zikh for der ringelblum arkhiv?" *Dos naye lebn* (November 1, 1946): 9.

93. Kermish, "Nieznane dokumenty żydiwskie z okresu powstania kwiestniowego," *Mosty* 3, no. 46 (April 19, 1948): 6, 35.

94. Blumental, "Vegn a program fun togteglekher arbet far der yad-vashem-forshung," *Yedi'ot Yad va-Shem* 4–5 (June 1955): 23 (complete in Yiddish, but incomplete in the English section).

95. Kermish, "New Jewish Sources for the History of the Warsaw Ghetto Uprising," *Yad Vashem Bulletin* 15 (August 1964): 27–33.

today in tons . . . which had so intoxicated the world—particularly the historian—that he forgot what was missing . . . and what one must begin seeking!"[96]

The Yiddish historians also recognized a dialectic between the uses of German and Jewish sources that supported the use of each: Kermish announced in 1956 that, because "the literature on Jewish resistance [outside of Warsaw] has until now made use primarily of Jewish sources," a well-rounded picture requires the use of "documents from unfriendly sources."[97] Two decades later, in his memorial essay on Rachel Auerbach, he reflects on the importance of her life's work in collecting Jewish testimonies and concludes that the need for such collecting would not be reduced "by the discovery of whole archives of official documents" but, on the contrary, "is increased because it must serve as a counterweight to the documentation from hostile and foreign sources—in order to comment correctly and fill with Jewish content" the framework of memory.[98] Blumental adds to the "pro-German" side of the scale still another view of this dialectic relationship, "If we had come to the world with only our evidence regarding the Warsaw Ghetto Uprising, it is doubtful that we would have had such a moral success as that achieved for us by the Nazi murderer."[99]

The conflict between the study of Nazi criminality and of Jewish Holocaust experience is exemplified by Blumental's lexicon of words and phrases from the Nazi period. In recounting Blumental's arrival at the CJHC, Friedman described Blumental as a folklorist,[100] and, although he succeeded Friedman as director of the CJHC and wrote much Holocaust history, it was to his love of Jewish folk creativity that Blumental remained the most committed. The archive of more than 200,000 German

---

96. Blumental, "Undzer groyser shuld," *Yidishe kultur* 22, no. 2 (February 1960): 16. The term *shuld* can be translated variously as debt or responsibility, but he refers here to a moral failing, in the sense of "guilt."

97. Kermish, "Mekorot ha-'oyev misparim 'al gevurah Yehudit," *Yedi'ot Yad va-Shem* 6–7 (January 1956): 5.

98. Kermish, "Rokhl Oyerbakh—di grinderin funem eydes-verk 'yad vashem,'" in Rohkl Oyerbakh, *Baym letstn veg* (Tel Aviv, 1977), 313.

99. Blumental, "Vi halt es mitn forshn di hitler-tkufe?" *Lebns-fragn* 193 (May 1966): 7.

100. Friedman, "Polish Jewish Historiography between the Two World Wars (1918–1939)," *Jewish Social Studies* XI (October 1949): 407.

and Jewish documents that he assembled was acquired in 2019 by YIVO, which announced plans to digitize them for public access.[101] His final book, *Verter un vertlekh* of 1981,[102] is rightly seen as the culmination of the series of articles he began to publish in 1956 in YIVO's journal of linguistics, *Yidishe shprakh*,[103] but it has at times been traced erroneously to the book he published in Poland in 1947 under the title, *Innocent Words*, on the reuse of prewar German terms by the Nazis.[104] This earlier work detailed the linguistic camouflage of Nazi crimes, but from the German perspective. Although portions of the earlier work were serialized in Yiddish in 1945,[105] it sets forth only German words and expressions, illustrated by examples from German usage. Where an entry in the earlier work coincides with one in the later work—for example, *Juden-Aktion* (an anti-Jewish atrocity), *Musselman* (a living corpse in the camps), or *Erzatz* (a replacement for "relocated" Jewish slave labor)—the description has been replaced in the later work with examples from Jewish sources and usage. Moreover, the entries have shifted in origin from German to Yiddish (with some in Polish and Hebrew). Although Yad Vashem announced in 1955 that Blumental was being given "lengthy leave" to finish the originally intended work,[106] and portions were published by Yad Vashem in 1957, 1960 and 1967,[107] the book did not appear.[108] Instead, Blumental devoted himself to compiling a work that would serve not as

---

101. Gal Beckerman, "The Holocaust Survivor Who Deciphered Nazi Doublespeak," *New York Times* (June 24, 2019), www.nytimes.com/2019/06/24/books/holocaust-nazi-archive.html.

102. Blumental, *Verter un vertlekh fun der khurbn-tkufe* (Tel Aviv, 1981).

103. Blumental, "Verter un vertlekh fun der khurbn-tkufe," *Yidishe shprakh* XVI, no. 1 (January–March 1956): 22–28; serialized from "alef" to "zayin" (April–May 1963).

104. Blumental, *Słowa Niewinne* (Krakow-Lodz-Warsaw, 1947).

105. Blumental, "Historisher verter-bukh," *Dos naye lebn* (May 20, 1945): 4; (June 20): 4; (December 15): 4.

106. "A Book about Nazi Terminology," *Yedi'ot Yad va-Shem* 4–5 (June 1955): 26.

107. Blumental, "On the Nazi Vocabulary," *Yad Washem Studies* I (1957): 49–66; "'Aktion,'" *Yad Washem Studies* IV (1960): 57–96; and "From the Nazi Vocabulary," *Yad Vashem Studies* VI (1967): 69–82. With the first installment, the editor, Shaul Esh, indicated that Blumental was preparing his manuscript in Yiddish and that it would be translated into Hebrew for publication (182).

108. A notice of the impending book also appeared in the semi-official Hebrew daily *Davar* in 1961: Eli Nisan, "Milon le-munakhim natziyim yotz'e 'al-yede 'Yad va-Shem,'" *Davar* (February 1, 1961): 2.

an indictment of German crimes, as others had done,[109] but as a testament to Jewish resilience. A representative entry reads: "One old Jew says to the other, 'None of us will survive to the end of the war.' The other responds, 'Don't worry, it's true that not you, not I, will survive; but *we* will survive.'"[110]

Arguing against the Tide

During the first decade of their work, the Yiddish historians considered the centrality of Jewish experience to be the normative basis for Holocaust research. Thus, Friedman's review of the first, pathbreaking attempt at a synthetic history of the Holocaust—Léon Poliakov's 1951 *Harvest of Hate*—attributes the scant coverage of Jewish experience to lack of familiarity with Jewish sources. He argues that "the inner problems of ghetto life, the social and ethical conflicts, the catastrophic economic decline are handled superficially," which he ascribes to "the fact that Poliakov made little use of the rich *khurbn*-literature in Yiddish, in part also in Polish and Hebrew."[111]

By the second decade, Friedman and the other Yiddish historians had come to realize that the practitioners of Holocaust research outside their own circle had largely chosen to ignore the subject of Jewish experience. In Friedman's 1954 review of *The Final Solution* by Gerald Reitlinger, he points out that Reitlinger "did not intend to study the complicated inner developments of Jewish life and the persecutions' impact on the Jewish

---

109. Examples are Heinz Pächter et al., *Nazi-Deutsch: A Glossary of Contemporary German Usage* (New York, 1944) and Cornelia Berning, *Vom "Abstammungnachweis" zum "Zuchtwart": Vokabular des Nationalsozialismus* (Berlin, 1964).

110. "Iberlebn" (to survive) in *Verter un vertlekh*, 24 (emphasis his). The prevalence of this statement was such that Friedman had also reported it as early as 1950, quoting it in Yiddish as, "We, European Jews, may disappear, but not the Jewish people," and in his English version as, ". . . , but the Jewish people as such, will survive." "Etishe un sotsyale problemen fun unzer katastrofe in der natsi tkufe," *Idisher kemfer* (September 8, 1950, Rosh Hashanah): 55; "Jewish Reaction to Nazism," *Jewish Frontier* (September 1950): 21.

111. Friedman, "Bikher vegn hayntsaytiker yidisher geshikhte," *Kultur un dertsyung* (October 1951): 17. Friedman translates Poliakov's original French title, *Breviaire de la haine*, as "Dos bentsherl fun sine" (using the Yiddish diminutive for the small book of daily prayers said after meals: "the little prayer book"—"of hate").

community,"[112] and in his 1955 review of Poliakov and Wulf's *Das Dritte Reich und die Juden* observes that "while the vicious image of the Nazi evil doers has been widely circulated, the human side of their victims has been neglected."[113]

Hannah Arendt's *Eichmann in Jerusalem* provoked a similar response from Trunk. Within weeks of its publication in *The New Yorker*, he repeated in Yiddish one of the assertions most quoted from her writing: "Wherever Jews lived, there were recognized Jewish leaders and this leadership, almost without exception, cooperated in one way or another, for one reason or another, with the Nazis."[114] Trunk crafts a two-pronged response, contrasting the forced cooperation of Jewish leaders with the outright collaboration to be found in most European countries on the one hand—and naming outstanding Jewish figures who died opposing the Nazis on the other. As to the latter, he points to the problem of sources: "Only a complete ignorance of Jewish sources on the history of the Holocaust could have led her to such a sort of 'statement.'"[115]

The second decade of Holocaust research saw the Yiddish historians expand their work from internally directed initiatives to providing a deliberate corrective to the work of others. A few months before Raul Hilberg set down the words that have continued to resonate from the preface of his magnum opus—"This is not a book about the Jews. It is a book about the people who destroyed the Jews"—Trunk in New York and Blumental in Israel issued separate calls to the contrary. In an essay on the internal life of the ghettos, Trunk argued, "It is high time that our Holocaust research turn its attention away from the Nazi side . . . to interest in

---

112. Friedman, review of Gerald Reitlinger, *The Final Solution* (1953), *Jewish Social Studies* XVI, no. 2 (April 1954): 189.

113. Friedman, review of Léon Poliakov and Josef Wulf, *Das Dritte Reich und die Juden* (Berlin, 1955), *Jewish Social Studies* XIX, nos. 1–2 (January–April 1957): 92.

114. Hannah Arendt, *Eichmann in Jerusalem. A Report on the Banality of Evil* (New York, 1963), 125.

115. Trunk, "Nokh amol vegn yidishn vidershtand kegn di natsis," *Di tsukunft* (April 1963): 155–56n13. The placement of this discussion in a lengthy final footnote suggests a late addition to an article ready for publication. The word "statement" is transliterated from English. One of the best-known responses to Arendt's work, *And the Crooked Shall be Made Straight* (New York, 1965), was written by Jacob Robinson, Friedman's close collaborator in the joint YIVO–Yad Vashem bibliography project, who thereafter sponsored and wrote the introduction to Trunk's 1962 *Lodzsher geto*, from which Robinson quotes several times.

the Jewish side, to its life up to the time of the murder."[116] Blumental wrote similarly in an essay on Jewish comportment under Nazi occupation, "We omit from our present consideration the German factor, to which much attention has been devoted.... Here we will dwell on the second side, the object."[117]

A poetic formulation of this corrective is set out by Dworzecki in his essay on Leivik's dramatic poem, "Di khasene in fernvald." Dworzecki recites the question that his alter ego, the all-seeing "Chronicler," poses to the prophet Elijah ("who calls to life the surviving remnant"): "Will not the impurity of the murderers' wickedness also drown the holiness of the victim?," to which Elijah replies, "Do not occupy yourself too much, my son, with the evil of the persecutors. Occupy yourself with the persecuted."[118]

The best-known call for a Jewish orientation in Holocaust studies is the statement by Friedman that may well be the most widely quoted from his body of work. In the summer of 1957, he undertook his only visit to Israel, where he delivered three lectures on Holocaust historiography. He spoke in the seeming knowledge that he and his colleagues had already lost the fight for victim studies to be the normative form of Holocaust study among Jewish historians in Europe and America. At this time, Yad Vashem had not yet published a journal or other significant works of original scholarship (itself a cause of contention between survivors in Israel and the Yad Vashem leadership), and he apparently hoped to influence the direction of work at Yad Vashem (which would soon become the subject of open conflict between his survivor colleagues and the directorate, dominated by established Israelis).

116. Trunk, "Problemen fun ineveynikstn geto-lebn," *Di tsukunft* (April 1960): 150; reprinted in his *Geshtaltn un gesheenishn* (Buenos Aires, 1962), 130.

117. Blumental, "Tsum problem vi di yidn hobn zikh farhaltn unter der daytsher okupatsye," in *YKUF almanakh*, ed. Nakhmen Mayzil (New York, 1961) [article dated July 1960], 359. At the 1972 YIVO conference on the Judenrat, Blumental objected that another of the presenters had "made use exclusively of German documents, and the documents created by the so-called [Jewish] representation, ... but the underground operated outside these documents," and that the presenter had "not taken into account the sources in Yiddish or Hebrew." Blumental, "Der yudenrat un di yidishe politsey," *Aroyfgetsvungene yidishe reprezentantsn unter der natsisher memshole: kolokvyum fun yivo, detsember 2–5, 1967* (New York, 1972), Yiddish 57; English 82*.

118. Dworzecki, "Hamtze menuhah l'sheyres hapleyte," *Di tsukunft* (December 1955): 494.

Friedman commenced his first lecture with the observation that authors of Holocaust histories published so far (Reitlinger, Poliakov, Joseph Tenenbaum, and others) "view the problem, as it were, from the outside. They see what their oppressors did to the Jews; what the Jews suffered. But they have not looked within . . . And within a Jewish life existed!"[119] And, in his final lecture, he called for "a radical change in the field of research relating to the Catastrophe," arguing that neither the study of persecutions nor uprisings was sufficient. Rather, "What we need is a history of the Jewish people during the period of Nazi rule in which the central role is to be played by *the Jewish people*. . . . In short: our approach must be definitely 'Judeo-centric' as opposed to 'Nazi-centric.'"[120]

Jewish Approaches to Holocaust History

Writing Holocaust history from the Jewish perspective evokes responses to ethical dilemmas of Holocaust historiography that are mirror images of those evoked by works arising from non-Jewish perspectives. To cite a well-known example: the use of data obtained through medical experiments by Nazi doctors has been widely condemned, whereas publication of research on "starvation disease" by doctors in the Warsaw Ghetto has been considered a moral imperative—and was undertaken in Warsaw immediately after the war by the American Joint Distribution Committee.[121] A similar asymmetry of moral attitudes is found in the area of historical research. Paradoxically, each of the means of historicizing the Holocaust that were set forth by certain nationalist and apologist West German historians during the *Historikerstreit* (historians' debate) of the 1980s—and which served to diminish or marginalize the murder of the Jews—had

---

119. Friedman, "Preliminary and Methodological Problems of the Research on the Jewish Catastrophe in the Nazi Period," *Yad Vashem Studies* II (1958): 96.

120. Friedman, "Problems of Research on the European Jewish Catastrophe," *Yad Vashem Studies* III (1959) [Second World Congress of Jewish Studies, Jerusalem, August 4, 1957]: 33 (emphasis his). Friedman did, however, support perpetrator research in principle, serving on Hilberg's doctoral committee at Columbia University and recommending his dissertation to Yad Vashem (also in 1957), which refused to publish it because of its attitude toward the Jews.

121. See Emil Apfelbaum, *Maladie de famine: Recherches cliniques sur la famine exécutées dans le ghetto de Varsovie en 1942* (Warsaw, 1946).

already become, in the hands of the Yiddish historians, necessary elements of the Jewish approach to Holocaust study.

Three such avenues taken by these German historians during the 1970s and 1980s that led toward the perceived sin of diminishing the Holocaust find their redemptive opposites in Jewish-centered Holocaust study:

1. The wish to contextualize the Nazis' destruction of the Jews through comparison with other genocides or national calamities (including German losses in World War II)[122]—which threatens the "unique" status of the Holocaust—had already provided the basis for the Yiddish historians' scholarly approach to Holocaust study;
2. The desire to restore historical context to the Nazi era by tracing longer-term trends through earlier or later periods[123]—which threatens to divert attention from a pervasively criminal regime to innocuous trends of longer duration—is the approach that had already enabled the Yiddish historians to situate the Jews' experience of Nazi domination within the continuity of Jewish historical experience; and
3. The impetus for the writing of *Alltagsgeschichte* (history of everyday life) that emerged in the 1980s in West Germany as a new form of historical research[124]—which, when applied to the period of Nazi Germany, risks a shift in focus from the role of ordinary

---

122. The exemplars of the new nationalist and apologist trend in postwar West German historiography that ignited the *Historikerstreit* were Andreas Hillgruber, author of *Zweierlei Untergang* (1986), and Ernst Nolte, author of *Der europäische Bürgerkrieg, 1917–1945: Nationalsozialismus und Bolschewismus* (1987). The former implied equivalence between the Nazi Holocaust and the expulsion of ethnic Germans from the eastern territories lost at the end of the war. The latter suggested equivalence (and cause and effect) in the Bolshevik and Nazi murders of specific groups—and weighed the severity of the Nazi Holocaust against the Armenian Genocide and Pol Pot murders in Cambodia.

123. Most often cited is Martin Broszat's proposal that Nazi-era social insurance plans be considered in the context of contemporaneous European, and subsequent West German, plans. See his "A Plea for the Historicization of National Socialism," in *Reworking the Past: Hitler, the Holocaust, and the Historians' Debate*, ed. Peter Baldwin (Boston, 1990), 86.

124. Regarding Broszat's "Bavaria Project" of 1977–83, a regional example of an *Alltagsgeschichte* of the Nazi period, Saul Friedländer expressed the apprehension that such studies, while honorable in themselves, could help to legitimize truly apologist works. See his "Some Reflections on the Historicization of National Socialism," in *Hitler, the Holocaust, and the Historians' Debate*, ed. Peter Baldwin (Boston, 1990), 88–102.

Germans in the apparatus of genocide to the "normal" occurrences of daily life—had already brought to the Yiddish historians' writing of Jewish history a means of restoring voice and agency to the victims.

Each of these approaches is discussed below with reference to the work of the Yiddish historians.

The Holocaust and Prior Catastrophes

As to the first point, the concept of "uniqueness," it may be argued that this is a perpetrator category of discourse that is most productive for studying the means and motives of German crimes but is not instructive for the study of Jewish history. The Yiddish historians may well have considered the Holocaust to be without precedent or parallel, when viewed from the perspective of other crimes against humanity, but they did not find the issue relevant to their study of Jewish responses. As Elly Dlin put it, "The uniqueness of the Holocaust is not connected to anything that the Jews did or did not do; it is rooted within the Nazis and their accomplices."[125] Insistence on the uniqueness of the Holocaust is not, therefore, an element of the Yiddish historians' studies of the Jews.

On the contrary, the Yiddish historians contextualized both the content of the Holocaust period and the writing of its history. In a 1948 essay, Friedman compares the latest catastrophe to the destruction of the First and Second Temples, saying, "The Jewish people survived many similar and more serious catastrophes." He indicates that although the Jews lost 35 percent of their global population in the Holocaust, the contrast with earlier catastrophes is more than quantitative: "In our history, there were catastrophes in which more than 35 percent of our people were murdered." However, he continues, "In the qualitative aspect indeed lies the difference between the latest catastrophe and the earlier catastrophes. Destroyed were such fresh and creative branches of our folk-organism as Polish and Lithuanian Jewry."[126] Friedman also contends that the

---

125. Elly [Elliott] Dlin, "Meanings of the Holocaust: Lecture 1: Is the Holocaust Unique?" (July 7, 2008), www.jewishagency.org/meanings/content/24039.
126. Friedman, "Di forshung fun unzer khurbn," *Kiem* (January 1948): 47.

unprecedented geographic range of the Holocaust requires new approaches for its investigation. "Unlike earlier catastrophes in Jewish History, which for the most part were confined to one country, . . . [t]he international character of the destruction is of tremendous importance both for the scope of scientific study, its methods and scholarly apparatus."[127] Tacitly contesting the concept of Jewish Holocaust exclusivity is Friedman's essay on the "remarkable partnership of fate" of the Gypsies and Jews. He draws comparisons, and occasional contrasts, between the Nazis' treatment of the two peoples, arguing that the extermination of the Gypsies was pursued only slightly less effectively than that of the Jews.[128]

Following Friedman's premature death in 1960, the role of Holocaust "historiosopher" was assumed by Trunk, his close colleague in New York, who directly disputed the thesis of uniqueness. Trunk argued that if the Holocaust were regarded as unassailably unique, and therefore ineffable and unfathomable, it would elude the tools of historical inquiry. In his essay, "On *khurbn-research*," he recounts the many unique characteristics of the Nazi genocide, "heretofore unknown in our historical experience—the coldly planned, premeditatively executed, murderously calculated extermination of millions of people." He nevertheless concludes, "The Nazi period was different, but not totally different in nature from other great catastrophes in human history that historical science has researched and continues to research." He claims that "the primary task of every historical study—which is, according to the classic formulation of Ranke, to ascertain 'how it actually was'—can also be achieved to a great degree with regard to study of the Holocaust." Comparing, in addition, the extant sources of information, he reports that "no national Jewish catastrophe left behind a documentation so rich in quantity as our recent *khurbn*."[129]

---

127. Friedman, "The European Jewish Research on the Recent Jewish Catastrophe in 1939–1945," *Proceedings of the American Academy for Jewish Research* 18 (1948–1949) [annual conference, December 12, 1948]: 179.

128. Friedman, "A merkvirdike goyrldike shutfes," *Kiem* (August–September 1950): 1661–67; translated as "The Extermination of the Gypsies: A Nazi Genocide Operation Against an 'Aryan People,'" *Jewish Frontier* (January 1951): 11–14.

129. Trunk, "Vegn khurbn-forshung," in his *Geshtaltn un gesheenishn* (Buenos Aires, 1962), 128.

The imperative that the Holocaust should receive more adequate study than prior Jewish catastrophes had been the subject of an early speech by Kermish at the inaugural meeting of the Society of Friends of the CJHC in October 1945. Exhorting his audience that study of the latest catastrophe should not suffer from the shortcomings of research on prior catastrophes, he invokes Dubnow's view that "Jewish history is the chain that unites all generations, that he who does not know history is not a Jew." He builds his argument, saying, "In Jewish history, we are missing an important array of sources"—naming the Crusades, the Spanish Inquisition, and post–World War I pogroms as catastrophes for which specifics on Jewish losses were inadequate. He gives recognition to previous pogrom studies, but expresses regret that such projects were not fully executed or published. Included were the investigations by Leon Motzkin of the 1905–6 Ukrainian pogroms and their precursors,[130] the first-person account by An-sky of the pogroms in Galicia during World War I,[131] and most particularly the research by Elias Tcherikower and his colleagues on the Ukrainian pogroms after World War I.[132] Kermish's historical review was, in fact, a paraphrase of recent comments by Jacob Lestschinsky, the remaining member of Tcherikower's team, on the achievements and inadequacies of past research on Jewish catastrophes. Lestschinsky's comments prefaced a 1944 book of proposed questionnaires for the study of the Nazi Holocaust that appears to be the only link between Tcherikower's group and the historians at the CJHC.[133] (In the CJHC's own book of proposed questionnaires, Friedman acknowledges Lestschinsky's "exhaustive work" but declares that, unfortunately, it is not suited to the task because the author could not yet have known the extent of the catastrophe and that so few scholars, only amateurs, would remain to work as interviewers.[134]) On the basis of this overview, Kermish urges his listeners to

130. *Die Judenpogrome in Russland*, 2 vols. (Cologne-Leipzig, 1910).
131. Sh. An-ski, *Khurbn galitsye: der yidisher khurbn fun poyln, galitsye un bukovina fun tog-bukh 1914–1917* in his *Gezamlte shriftn*, vols. 4–6 (Vilna, 1921–22).
132. See chapter 2.
133. Yankev Leshtshinski, *Di yidishe katastrofe: di metodn fun ir forshung* (New York, 1944), 31.
134. Unsigned preface to *Metodologishe onvayzungen tsum oysforshn dem khurbn fun poylishn yidntum* (Lodz, 1945), [iii–iv], prepared "under the direction of Dr. Philip Friedman," and listed in Friedman's own bibliography as a publication edited by him.

support the work of the CJHC, claiming that the existence of the CJHC is "a demonstration that Polish Jewry understands its historic task"—in contrast with Jewish responses to past catastrophes.[135]

The Continuity of Jewish History

It will not surprise the student of Jewish history that Friedman's essay, "The Fate of the Jewish Book [under the Nazis],"[136] begins with a capsule history of the burning of Jewish books as the precursor to the burning of Jews. He recounts the burning of Torah scrolls in ancient times and of the Talmud and Kabbalah during the Christian Middle Ages and thereafter. The student of Jewish history need not be informed that Jewish books were considered by antisemites to be both the source and embodiment of Jewish otherness. But one finds that his seemingly natural placement of the Nazi campaign to destroy Jewish books within the context of historical antisemitism is a perspective unique to the writing of Jewish history. Where Friedman traces the "auto-da-fé" of book burning that the Nazis commenced in 1933 solely to precedents in Jewish history, historians of Nazi book burning—as a German rather than anti-Jewish phenomenon— find precedents in the separate heritage of German book burning, from Luther's destruction of the papal bulls to the burning of the Treaty of Versailles by Nazi students in 1929.[137]

Thus, the second point—historicizing the Nazi period by reference to earlier or later periods—is a process that begins with the historian's choice of context. Situating the Nazi period within the long-term processes of German history marginalizes the Holocaust, whereas situating

---

135. *Barikht fun der organizir farzamlung fun der "gezelshaft fraynd fun der Ts.Y.H.K."* [*Minutes of the organizing meeting of the Society of Friends of the CJHC*], October 9, 1945, at the quarters of the CJHC, Lodz, p. 6. Archive of the Jewish Historical Institute, Warsaw, CŻKH/303/XX folder 405.

136. Friedman, "The Fate of the Jewish Book in the Nazi Era," *Jewish Book Annual* 15 (1957–1958): 3–13.

137. See, for example, Leonidas E. Hill, "The Nazi Attack on un-German Literature," in *The Holocaust and the Book: Destruction and Preservation*, ed. Jonathan Rose (Amherst, 2001), 14; Gerhard Sauder, *Die Bücherverbrennung: Zum 10. Mai 1933* (Munich, 1983), 9–19; and, similarly, Albrecht Schöne, *Göttinger Bücherverbrennung 1933: Rede am 10. Mai 1983 zur Erinnerung an die "Aktion wider den undeutschen Geist"* (Göttingen, 1983), 14, 24–26.

the Jewish responses to Nazi domination within the continuum of *Jewish* history enables the Yiddish historians to find meaning or precedent, rather than randomness or novelty, in those responses.

An early instance from within the Vilna Ghetto itself is the article by Dworzecki, "Medicine and Medical Workers among Jews in the Medieval Ghettos," which appeared in the final issue of the underground public health journal *Folksgezunt* in August 1943.[138] This article continued his prewar interest in the Jewish-historical aspects of medical practice, as indicated by his lecture, "The Jewish Role in the Creation of Medical Ethics," at the 1937 conference of Jewish doctors in Vilna.[139] A similar desire to historicize the position of the Jews in Nazi-imposed ghettos, and perhaps also "normalize" and give momentary reassurance regarding their apparently unprecedented situation, is found in the talk that Meyer Balaban delivered in the Warsaw Ghetto at the opening of the clandestine medical school in 1941, titled, "Social Help and the Hospital System in the Jewish Quarters of Old-Time Poland."[140]

Although Trunk would later write that "the Nazi-German imposed ghetto had nothing in common with the so-called medieval ghetto"[141] (and Baron would say, "To repeat the cliché of the 1930s that the Nazis have brought back the Dark Ages, is tantamount to maligning the

---

138. Dworzecki, "Meditsin un meditsiner bay yidn in der tekufe fun mitlalterlekhe getos," *Folksgezunt* 18 (August 1943). This journal continued the prewar journal of the same name. Unfortunately, it has not been possible to locate a copy of this issue, which Dworzecki cites in his *Yerusholayim d'lite*, 215–16. Other issues are in the YIVO archives. Dworzecki was likely familiar with the series of articles by Ringelblum on the history of Jewish doctors in Poland that had appeared in the sister publication *Sotsyale meditsin* from 1931 to 1938. These are listed and reprinted in Emanuel Ringelblum, *Kapitlen geshikhte fun amolikn yidishn lebn in poyln*, ed. Yankev Shatski (Buenos Aires, 1953). However, Ringelblum's articles cover periods later than the medieval ghettos and could not have served as source material for Dworzecki's article.

139. "1-ter tsuzamenfor fun yidishe doktoyrim fun vilner un navaredker kant" [May 16–17, 1937], bilingual Yiddish–Polish program booklet, YIVO Archives, RG 29, F 143.1, http://polishjews.yivoarchives.org/archive/?p=digitallibrary/digitalcontent&id=2134#.

140. See Trunk, "Meir balaban—der forsher fun der ko'olisher organizatsye un oytonomye in amolikn poyln (30 yor nokh zayn toyt in varshever geto)," *YIVO bleter* XLIV (1973): 205; and Barbara Engelking-Boni and Jacek Leociak, *The Warsaw Ghetto: A Guide to the Perished City* (New Haven, 2009), 251 (citing the underground newspaper *Gazeta Żydowska* 59, July 16, 1941).

141. Trunk, *Lodzsher geto*, 1; quoted from *Łódź Ghetto: A History*, 9.

medieval civilization"[142]), Blumental perceived a medieval parallel in the field of popular culture. His early works on Yiddish literature under the German occupation refer to the "return to the Middle Ages" forced upon the Jews by the "wave of reaction" that characterized German policy both inside and outside of Germany. He declared that "certain problems of the deep Middle Ages that were distant from us, very distant—became suddenly, thanks to Hitlerism, very near."

One change observed by Blumental was that literary creativity in the ghettos "was brought to the public in the spoken language." He said this was true in the ghettos of Lodz and Warsaw for both the intelligentsia who attended readings of new works by well-known writers and for the common folk who received their literature in the street. He indicates that "street-singers" ("as they were called in the Lodz Ghetto") attracted large groups of emotion-filled listeners who were also moved to protect the singers from the ghetto police. Blumental quotes a letter by the poet Simkhe Bunim Shayevitsh, written in the Lodz Ghetto in 1942, in which Shayevitsh says there is no alternative "but to imitate the old-time troubadours, minnesingers and our Jewish Broder-singers." Blumental carries the analogy further with the assertion that "the same troubadour—just as in the Middle Ages . . . fulfills a *social function*. His task is to inform, alert the people, convey the latest news—a form of living newspaper," who offers "a song, a parody, a scene, a joke, a saying" after each alarming new event in the ghetto. Blumental asserts that "even the rhyme, the style has a popular [*folksstimlekh*] medieval sound."[143]

Historical analogies are also sought by Blumental outside of Jewish history for the cultural conditions arising from the dictatorial form of "self-government" imposed by the Germans. He likens the writing to be found in the official "Ghetto Newspaper" of the Lodz Ghetto to the "court literature" that flourished in "every absolute monarchy." He finds that in the Lodz Ghetto, "just as formerly with Louis XIV, they also celebrated the Jewish king (as Rumkowski was indeed called in the Lodz Ghetto)."[144]

---

142. Salo Baron, "Opening Remarks," *Jewish Social Studies* XII, no. 1 (January 1950): 16.
143. Blumental, "Di yidishe literatur unter der daytshisher okupatsye," *Yidishe kultur* 8, no. 1 (January 1946): 9–10 (emphasis his).
144. Blumental, preface to S. Shayevitsh, *Lekh-lekho* (Lodz, 1946), 10.

Far from regarding the Holocaust period as beyond comparison, Kermish, too, seeks benchmarks outside the ghetto and calls forth Jewish, as well as non-Jewish, points of reference in both the past and present. Regarding one of his favored fields of study, the underground press of the Warsaw Ghetto, he declares, "In content, the newspapers published in the Ghetto were not of a lower standard than those issued prior to the outbreak of war."[145] In several of his articles from the 1950s, he uses the underground press as a primary source of information on social and economic conditions in the ghetto. On the basis of published financial statements of the Warsaw Judenrat, Kermish concludes, "The tax policy of the Judenrat was without parallel in the history of the repression of Jews by Jews."[146] Because neither the rich nor poor had significant income, and the rich would not consent to a tax on assets, the chief source of revenue for the Judenrat was a tax on consumption. The burden of taxes therefore fell disproportionately on the poor through their purchases of food and medicine. On at least three occasions—in 1951 in Yiddish, and again in 1957 and 1986 in English—he quotes the underground Bundist newspaper *Der veker* (The Awakener) on the contentious problem of taxation in the Warsaw Ghetto, saying, "there is no government in Europe that would not be ashamed to construct its budget on the basis of consumption taxes."[147]

Kermish further contextualized the Holocaust period of history in arguing that the "psychological readiness for revolt" among the various political groups in the ghettos could be traced to each group's prewar structure. At the Yad Vashem conference on Jewish resistance in 1968, he contended that "the potential defense forces that appeared and developed in the conditions of the German occupation were continuations of the public and political forces that had crystallized in the two decades

---

145. Kermish, "Vegn der untererdisher prese fun varshever geto," *Di goldene keyt* 27 (1957): 100.

146. Ibid., 117.

147. Kermish, "Di tsavoa fun varshever geto," *Di goldene keyt* 9 (1951): 155; "Vegn der untererdisher prese fun varshever geto," *Di goldene keyt* 27 (1957): 118; and *To Live with Honor, To Die with Honor! . . . : Selected Documents from the Warsaw Ghetto Underground Archives "O.S." ["Oneg Shabbath"]* (Jerusalem, 1986), 291.

between the two World Wars,"[148] and that these forces shaped each political group's underground publications in the Ghetto.

In only this area of "psychological readiness" did the Yiddish historians allow their historicizing impulse to backshadow the Holocaust onto prior events. The Yiddish historians did not otherwise allow their writings on earlier periods to be influenced by the knowledge of the destruction to come. Friedman cautioned about the danger posed by pseudo-historicism, in the form of backshadowing.[149] In his 1951 review of Jacob Shatzky's history of Warsaw Jewry in prior centuries, he contends that "Shatzky was strongly influenced by the spirit of his own times, particularly the romanticism of Jewish martyrology revived in our literature after the tragic experiences of the years 1939–1945." Friedman concludes with a charitable but firmly anti-lachrymose critique: "Thus, oversensitive and compassionate as he is, the author is prone to see examples of Jewish martyrology, pogroms, persecutions and expulsion even where there are only slight hints of such events."[150]

The subject of "psychological readiness" was prefigured during the 1930s by Max Weinreich, sociologist and YIVO leader. Weinreich had studied the subject of resistance and self-help on the part of disfavored minority populations, finding parallels between the situations of Polish Jews and African Americans and concluding that such groups needed "weapons for the weak." In the words of historian Leila Zenderland, Weinreich reoriented YIVO's prewar social science work to be "a tool of survival, a way for individuals to protect themselves in a hostile environment" and to serve in "strengthening both the cultural and the personal resources of a stateless population increasingly under siege."[151] She points to the connection between the prewar activities shaped by Weinreich at YIVO

---

148. Kermish, "Di rol fun di geto-oyfshtandn in kamf kegn di natsis," in *Tsuzamen: zamlbukh far literatur, kunst, yidishe problemen un dokumentatsye*, ed. Sh. L. Shnayderman (Tel Aviv, 1974), 306.

149. On this subject in general, with particular emphasis on the Holocaust, see Michael André Bernstein, *Foregone Conclusions: Against Apocalyptic History* (Berkeley, 1994).

150. Friedman, review of Yankev Shatski, *Geshikhte fun yidn in varshe*, vols. 1, 2 (New York, 1947, 1948), *Jewish Social Studies* XIII, no. 4 (October 1951): 361.

151. Leila Zenderland, "Social Science as a 'Weapon of the Weak': Max Weinreich, the Yiddish Scientific Institute, and the Study of Culture, Personality, and Prejudice," *Isis* 104 (2013): 764 and 772.

and the similar types of work undertaken by Ringelblum's Oyneg Shabes project in the Warsaw Ghetto: "Jews had begun to use cultural activities of all kinds, from music to art to writing, as survival techniques—their versions of the 'weapons of the weak.'" After the Holocaust, Weinreich himself transformed his prewar concept into a broader theory of ongoing resistance. His student, the prominent sociolinguist Joshua Fishman, indicates that shortly before his death in 1969 Weinreich had proposed a project for YIVO "that would reveal the constant creative resistance of Polish Jewry throughout the two very difficult decades between the world wars." Fishman contends that the resistance demonstrated by the Jews in the Warsaw Ghetto was "not alien to the psyche of Polish Jewry, because the entire Jewish history of the interwar period was a history of resistance: cultural, social, economic, political, even physical." Fishman concludes, "The resistance in the Warsaw Ghetto must be seen as the culmination of the entire prior resistance."[152] The resulting volume of research papers published in 1974 opens with a hundred-page article by Trunk on "Economic Antisemitism in Poland Between the Two World Wars," in which he discusses the increasingly militant stand taken by Jewish groups (particularly the Bund) for Jewish economic survival.[153]

Trunk did not find the Nazi period of Jewish history to be so incomparable with prior periods as to be immune to the usual tools of historical comparison. For example, he contrasts prewar and wartime conditions in two articles on the Jews of Lublin that appeared in the Lublin *yizkor* book of 1952. Here one finds a relatively rare instance of quantitative historiography among the postwar Yiddish historians. In the first of two articles, a historical survey of prewar Lublin, he provides statistical tables of population growth from 1550 to 1939.[154] In his companion article, "Sanitary Conditions and Mortality in the Ghetto" during the Holocaust period,

---

152. Joshua A. (Shikl) Fishman, ed., *Shtudyes vegn yidn in poyln 1919–1939/Studies on Polish Jewry 1919–1939: The interplay of social, economic, and political factors in the struggle of a minority for its existence* (New York, 1974), v–vi (English v*–vi*).

153. Trunk, "Der ekonomisher antisemitizm in poyln tsvishn di tsvey velt-milkhomes," ibid. (Fishman), 3–98.

154. Trunk, "Bletlekh fun der fargangenhayt (tsu der geshikhte fun yidishn yishev in lublin fun di eltste tsaytn biz sof fun 18tn y"h)," in *Dos bukh fun lublin: zikhroynes, gvyes-eydes un materyaln iber lebn, kamf un martirertum fun lubliner yidishn yishev*, ed. M. Litvin and M. Lerman (Paris, 1952), 27.

he provides data comparing the monthly prewar mortality rate (1.1 per 1,000) with that of the Nazi era (a peak of 12.4 per 1,000 in early 1942).[155] These studies were followed immediately by his paper on "Epidemics and Mortality in the Warsaw Ghetto, 1939–1942,"[156] and a decade later by the chapter on "Diseases and Mortality" in his book on the Lodz Ghetto.[157] In each of these works, Trunk integrates the Nazi period with the prewar period through a historicizing maneuver to be condoned only in Jewish historiography of the Holocaust: he presents the annual mortality rates among Jews during the prewar and Nazi periods in tables of data organized according to the Jews' principal causes of death from medical ailments, leaving the sudden change in living conditions to be inferred from the data.

It is Trunk who provides the most sustained example of a historian's commitment to following a thread of Jewish history to its culmination during the Nazi era. The subject—the Judenrat or imposed governing Jewish Council—is a central topic of discourse and contention among historians as well as laypersons concerned with Jewish responses to Nazi persecution. For Trunk, research on the Judenrat represented the final stage of his lifelong interest in the subject of Jewish autonomy, a political objective he shared with Dubnow (perhaps more so than other Bundists) and a research objective learned from his mentor, Balaban.[158]

Trunk produced a remarkable pair of papers on the subject of Jewish Councils in 1956 at a turning point in his approach to the topic. In one,[159] he notes the "oligarchic character"[160] of a Jewish Council and cites the

---

155. Trunk, "Sanitare farheltenishn un shtarbikayt in geto," ibid. (Litvin/Lerman), 361–62.

156. Trunk, "Milkhome kegn yidn durkhn farshpreytn krankeytn," *YIVO bleter* XXXVII (1953): 58–100.

157. Trunk, *Lodzsher geto* (New York, 1962); *Łódź Ghetto* (Bloomington, 2006), chapter V.

158. See Trunk, "Shimen dubnov un di yidishe mizrekh-eyropeyishe historyografye," *Di tsukunft* (December 1960): 465–71; and "Meir balaban—der forsher fun der ko'olisher organizatsye un oytonomye in amolikn poyln (30 yor nokh zayn toyt in varshever geto)," *YIVO bleter* XLIV (1973): 198–206.

159. Trunk, "Der va'ad medinat rusyah (raysn)," *YIVO bleter* XL (1956): 63–85; "The Council of the Province of White Russia," *YIVO Annual of Jewish Social Science* XI (1956/1957), 188–210.

160. Ibid., Yiddish 63; English 188.

council's various abuses: that the "burden of taxes became unbearable" and crushed the masses of Jews, "who with the greatest efforts barely eked out a meager living";[161] that those in the highest economic positions constituted the group most represented on the council and "attempted to avoid payment of income, property, and other communal taxes";[162] that, in one instance, a "meat tax, which had originally been an extraordinary levy, designed to meet an emergency, soon turned into a regular communal indirect form of tax";[163] and that the leader of a certain council arranged for soldiers to compel payment from "those who protested against the unjust levy of taxes,"[164] while another council threatened to do so.[165]

Yet this was a research paper on the Jewish Council of White Russia in the seventeenth and eighteenth centuries. It is Trunk's other paper that discusses the phenomenon of the Judenrat. This second work commences with a similar discussion of the favoritism shown by Jewish Councils to the more propertied classes, with which they were more closely linked, and the use of the ghetto police to enforce the councils' demands, proceeding to the evolution of the Judenrat's role as *decisor* of matters of life and death.[166] Both were written shortly after the Kastner Affair of 1954–55 in Israel, in which Rudolf Kastner, a leader of the Aid and Rescue Committee in Budapest, was accused of collaborating with Adolf Eichmann to obtain safe passage for a select group of Hungarian Jews while concealing his knowledge that hundreds of thousands of others would be sent to their deaths.

Despite a certain sympathy for members of the various *Judenräte*, most of whom he indicates were compelled to serve and acted with the best of intentions, Trunk nevertheless argues that a "Judenrat ideology"

---

161. Ibid., Yiddish 78; English 203.
162. Ibid., Yiddish 75; English 200.
163. Ibid., Yiddish 79; English 204.
164. Ibid., Yiddish 71; English 196.
165. Ibid., Yiddish 73; English 198.
166. Trunk, "Der fal rudolf kastner in likht fun der yudenratlisher ideologye," *Unzer tsayt* (April–May 1956): 23–27. The traditional Jewish term *decisor* is applicable because the leaders of the councils discussed the ruling by Maimonides prohibiting the sacrifice of certain community members to save others and requested opinions from leading rabbis on its applicability to their circumstance as part of their own debates on the question.

of differential treatment governed their conduct. He points out that only under the Nazis, after "an interruption of hundreds of years (since the Middle Ages), has a Jewish representative institution received so many economic and juridical-administrative functions with regard to the Jewish population."[167] He implies that their ideology of differential treatment arose from the same personal and institutional impulses that guided the Jewish Councils of the past. His thesis is that this ideology led, first, to the Judenrat strategy of "salvation [of the fittest] through work" and, ultimately, to its members' acquiescence in the role of choosing which Jews would be delivered for "resettlement" in labor and death camps—under the illusion that they could succeed in saving the most valuable portion of the ghetto's population. He asserts that the Kastner trial "was not and must not be" only a judgment of the person, "who may have had the best of intentions," but of the entire way of thinking "that was in those tragic years a 'rescue'-program of certain circles in Jewish society."[168]

Parenthetically, it should be noted that the Kastner Affair became the Israeli cause célèbre of the mid-1950s and that it led to the only apparent instance of censorship of a Yiddish historian outside the Soviet bloc. In Israel, Kastner had risen to the post of spokesman for the Ministry of Trade in the *Mapai*-led government of Moshe Sharrett. Once accusations against him appeared in print, a libel suit was brought on his behalf by the government, and his actions (and those of the Jewish Councils generally) became identified with the ruling Labor Party coalition. The court verdict against him in 1955 led to the fall of the coalition. In 1957, Kermish published an article on the underground press in the Warsaw Ghetto. It was printed in full by Yad Vashem in both Hebrew and English. However, the Yiddish version, which appeared in *Di goldene keyt* (funded by the ruling Labor Party) omitted the many passages that quoted negative views of the Judenrat.[169]

---

167. Ibid., 23–24.
168. Ibid, 27.
169. Compare the Yiddish version of "Vegn der untererdisher prese fun varshever geto," *Di goldene keyt* 27 (1957): 243–57, with the complete English and Hebrew versions in *Yad Washem Studies* I (1957): 85–123 (Heb. 69–92). Much of the excised material had appeared there prior to the Kastner Affair in his "Di tsavoa fun varshever geto," *Di goldene keyt* 9 (1951): 134–62.

The two papers on Jewish Councils published by Trunk in 1956 are remarkable for the second reason that they were outgrowths of a similar pair he published in the late 1940s. The first was his "Problems of Jewish Existence in Light of Our History," his only work to appear outside of Poland before his departure. Here, he discusses without political constraint a long-favored topic of Jewish historiography: explanations for Jewish survival over the ages. Rejecting the economic-utility theory and others, he praises "autonomism," claiming that it "extends like a red thread through the entire two-and-a-half-thousand-year history." He prefigures his study of the Jewish Council of White Russia, writing that the Jewish Council of the past often "degenerated into an instrument of heavy economic exploitation of the broad folk masses, transforming itself into an oligarchic clique of powerful community leaders and tax farmers." However, he argues that "it was a tragic historical mistake of the emancipation movement to enter into combat not against the obsolete and old-fashioned structure of Jewish self-rule but with the very principle of Jewish internal autonomy in general."[170] (In the *yizkor* book of his hometown, he wrote with evident pride that his father, the last rabbi of Kutno, had initiated the reestablishment of the old-time "District Council [*Va'ad ha-Galil*]" in their region of Poland before the war.[171]) The other early paper, on social antagonisms in the ghettos,[172] turns this lifelong interest in Jewish autonomy toward its most recent example, the Judenrat, providing the basic text for his article on "Judenrat ideology" during the Kastner Affair, to which he then added new conclusions on the moral and ethical dilemmas again being debated.

One of the chief controversies addressed by Trunk in his later writings on the Judenrat was the issue of whether the Nazi-imposed governing bodies should be considered a "Jewish leadership." This was also one of the rare instances of disagreement among Yiddish historians. Dworzecki is

---

170. Trunk, "Yidishe kiem-problemen in likht fun undzer geshikhte," *Oyfn sheydveg: hayntsaytike problemen fun yidishn natsyonaln kiem: ershter zamlheft* (Munich, 1948), 54–55.

171. Blumental, "ha-Rav Yitskhok Yehuda Trunk," in *Sefer Kutnah veha-sevivah*, ed. David Shtokfish (Tel Aviv, 1968), 245.

172. Trunk, "Sotsyale antagonizmen in geto un di rol fun di yudenratn," *Yidishe shriftn* 6, no. 26 (June 1949): 6–7.

quoted by Israel Gutman as saying that many in the Vilna Ghetto thought of Judenrat members "as having gone astray and having led others astray. But no one thought of the *Judenrat* people as the Jewish leadership!"[173] Similarly, Blumental asserted at the YIVO Colloquium on the Judenrat in 1967 that "we approach this institution as if it were a Jewish one, while in truth it was an official German institution, although formally occupied by Jews and pseudo-Jews [converts]."[174]

Despite such objections, the long view of Jewish autonomy taken by Trunk led him to incorporate the Nazi-era councils into the narrative of Jewish history. On the eve of publication of his exhaustive study of the Judenrat, he offered a preview of his conclusions at the 1971 conference of the American Historical Association: "The argument that the Councils were a German institution because they were established on German orders is not valid at all. All of the community representatives for hundreds of years in the history of the Diaspora had been established by orders of various governments. They did not fail to be Jewish institutions for all of that." Recounting instances in which prior Jewish leaderships "were collectively responsible for the collection of taxes, and for the delivery of recruits to the army *(cantonists)* in the reign of Czar Nicholas I," he asserts that "serving the interests of the State was not a new task for the Jewish Councils" under the Nazis.

Trunk calls explicitly for a historicizing approach. He argues that "the phenomenon of the Councils should be discussed within the framework of Jewish history and not as a unique and peculiar episode." He declares that the historian "is not free from seeking historical analogies," and he concludes by asserting that "a historical comparison between the role of the *Kehila* during the *Cantonist* era . . . [and the *Judenräte*] may prevent us from considering the Councils as a singular phenomenon without any parallel in Jewish history."[175]

---

173. Yisrael Gutman, "The Judenrat as a Leadership," in *On Germans and Jews under the Nazi Regime*, ed. Moshe Zimmermann (Jerusalem, 2006), 313.

174. Blumental, "Der yudenrat un di yidishe politsey," 90.

175. Trunk, "The Jewish Councils in Eastern Europe under Nazi Rule (An Attempt at a Synthesis)" [American Historical Association Conference, December 29, 1971], *Societas—A Review of Social History* (Summer 1972): 238–39.

Against what was Trunk arguing? First, it should be noted that the early dates of his prior works on Jewish autonomy and the wartime Jewish Councils negate the common assumption that his *Judenrat* arose in response to disparagement of Jewish leadership under the Nazis by Raul Hilberg or Hannah Arendt in the early 1960s. Further, the project for a history of the Jewish Councils had been commenced by Friedman before his death in 1960, and Trunk became his successor. Nevertheless, the need for a clarifying study of the councils was intensified by Hilberg's contention, first expressed in his pioneering 1961 history of the Holocaust,[176] that the councils served to facilitate the death of the Jews—followed by Arendt's reportage on the 1961 trial of Adolf Eichmann that implied a fatal meekness on the part of the victims.[177] Trunk, therefore, also intended his work to counter the view, which he attributed to both Hilberg and Arendt, that "the weak or even complete absence of physical resistance in the ghettos . . . or the collaborationism of the Jewish Councils" was "a peculiarly Jewish manifestation, conditioned by 2,000 years of Jewish submissiveness." He denounced this contention as "a false and ignorant interpretation of Jewish history."[178]

Trunk's purpose for insisting on the necessity of historical analogies becomes apparent in his *Judenrat*, where he challenges the suggestion of Jewish submissiveness as the precursor to Nazi-era Jewish behavior. He cites the late historian Saul Ginsburg and the then-president of Israel Zalman Shazar as calling for an empathic approach to Jewish leaders in tsarist Russia,[179] who, with obvious parallels to Judenrat members, were forced to seek a course between accommodation to intractable power and an attempt to protect, selectively, the members of the community deemed most necessary for its survival. He challenges directly the accusation of a Jewish historical conditioning for passivity: "Having lived in hostile environments, and having been oppressed by inimical

---

176. Raul Hilberg, *The Destruction of the European Jews* (Chicago, 1961).

177. Hannah Arendt, "Eichmann in Jerusalem—I," *The New Yorker* (February 16, 1963).

178. Trunk, "Nokh amol vegn yidishn vidershtand kegn di natsis," *Di tsukunft* (April 1963): 155–56.

179. Trunk, *Judenrat: The Jewish Councils in Eastern Europe under Nazi Occupation* (New York, 1972), 436.

authorities, the Jews throughout the ages had not accepted persecution without attempting to find remedies."[180] He then reviews the historically tested modes of "intervention and bribery" that Judenrat members tried to reenact during the Nazi period—with temporary and occasional successes, but with an ultimate futility that could not have been foreseen from historical experience.

This desire to contextualize and thereby lend realistic expectation to the range of Jewish responses possible under Nazi domination is found in the works of each of the Yiddish historians. The ability of such contextualizing to offer a measure of relief from the perceived shame of Jewish powerlessness is one of the themes to be explored in chapter 5.

The Study of Everyday Life

The third path toward historicizing the Nazi period is that of *Alltagsgeschichte*, the history of everyday life. As Saul Friedländer writes, "The *Alltagsgeschichte* of German society has its necessary shadow: the *Alltagsgeschichte* of its victims."[181] Here, as in other forms of Holocaust historicization, the Jewish perspective is the mirror image of the perpetrator perspective. The emergence of "ever-more minute research into various aspects of everyday life and social change during the Nazi era," Friedländer observes, "understates the 'already well-known' facts of mass extermination and atrocity."[182] Yet the study of everyday Jewish life under German occupation reveals the experience of that genocide by its victims. The history of the everyday is the primary historical method of the Yiddish historians, and the great majority of their works are devoted to writing Jewish *Alltagsgeschichte* (to use a later term,[183] broadly defined), commencing in the earliest period of their activity.

---

180. Ibid., 388.
181. Saul Friedländer, "Trauma, Transference and 'Working Through,'" *History and Memory* 4, no. 1 (1992): 53.
182. Ibid., 47.
183. It is, of course, anachronistic to identify the Yiddish historians with an approach that did not arise as a formal discipline until the 1980s (and in West Germany), as is a more general identification of their work with the parent field of microhistory (a development of the 1960s), but both terms are nevertheless appropriate to much of their work. Nearly all of their research is engaged in "asking large questions in small places," as Charles Joyner said of microhistory in *Shared Traditions: Southern History and Folk*

The Yiddish historians' research comprises many of the subject areas of interest to the historian or social scientist. At times, their emphasis on daily life was explicit, as in Trunk's articles on "Problems of Internal Ghetto Life"[184] and in his doctoral dissertation of 1969 on "Internal Conditions in the Ghettos in Eastern Europe under Nazi Rule."[185] More often, this emphasis was inherent in the topics examined. A few of the topic areas that recur most frequently are the following five:

Jewish Councils: their composition; degree of continuity with prior leaderships; extent of popular legitimacy; untenable role as both servant and master; strategies for survival or lack thereof; humility or messianic aspirations of their leaders.

Political groups: continuity of prewar parties; underground political activity and publications; cooperation and conflict among parties; shifts in balance of power between young activists and official leaderships under changing conditions; moral preparation for resistance.

Social differentiation and class conflict: continuities and ruptures in prewar class structure; rapidly changing lines of definition; declassification, pauperization, pseudo-proletarianization, rise of a criminal class of "lumpen-bourgeoisie"; effects on chances for survival; differential treatment by official bodies.

Armed resistance: internal and external factors assisting or preventing armed uprisings; acquisition of weapons; preparations for defense; relations with non-Jewish groups; evidence of resistance in unknown locales.

Unarmed resistance (also, "passive" or "spiritual" resistance): cooperation for self-help and social welfare; organized cultural and educational programs; economic resistance; overt and clandestine medical work; creative works by individuals.

A representative example of the multifaceted nature of the Yiddish historians' research agenda may be drawn from their works on the subject

---

Culture (Urbana, 1999), 1. However, it is the "everyday" aspect of *Alltagsgeschichte* that should be stressed here, rather than the bottom-up approach usually associated with it.

184. Trunk, "Problemen fun ineveynikstn geto-lebn," *Di tsukunft* (April 1960): 150–55.

185. Trunk, "Ineveynikste farheltenishn in di getos in mizrekh-eyrope unter natsisher hershaft" (PhD diss., Jewish Teachers' Seminary and People's University, May 1969), English and Yiddish tables of contents: YIVO Archives, RG 483, F 52.

of food. The multiple valences of this subject with other areas of research, which illustrate the general problem of interconnection, include, among others: the duty of a Judenrat to ensure provisioning of the ghetto, and the effect on relations with independent self-help organizations; taxes on food, and the broader issue of inequity in the sharing of economic burdens; the problem of starvation as a pervasive factor in daily life, also leading to a new field for medical research (by Jewish doctors in the Warsaw Ghetto); the imperative for smuggling food from outside the ghettos, manifested as personal heroism and resistance especially among mothers and children, or among other individuals as a source of profiteering and speculation; the status of food-sufficiency or -insufficiency as the new, and perhaps sole, determinant of economic class in the ghettos; and the starvation rations allotted in the camps, combated at times by the forming of cooperative groups to guard and prepare the results of illicit scavenging—all of which are the subjects of various studies by the Yiddish historians.

In attempting to examine the details of daily life in the ghettos and camps, the Yiddish historians fulfilled both of the principal intentions usually attributed to Ranke's dictum, *wie es eigentlich gewesen*. The more realist interpretation is found in Trunk's translation, "how it actually was" (*vi iz es eygentlekh geven*), which accompanies his assertion: "It would be no exaggeration to say that the history of the Lodz Ghetto, for example, can be written by a chronological method, day by day, for the course of more than four years."[186] But, Trunk continues, "We know astonishingly little today [1960] about the day-in, day-out struggle of the ghettos for their physical and spiritual existence; about the far-reaching changes in the physical and psychic make-up of the ghetto Jew." The question of how the Jews were able "to prolong their existence for a much longer period than anticipated in the Nazi strategy of extermination through starvation and plague" is among the issues of daily life that he says require investigation.[187] A similarly realist instance of the phrase was used

---

186. Trunk, "Vegn khurbn-forshung," in his *Geshtaltn un gesheenishn* (Buenos Aires, 1962), 129.

187. Ibid., 130; first published in "Problemen fun ineveynikstn geto-lebn," *Di tsukunft* (April 1960): 150.

by Kermish, in praising Ringelblum's "sense of responsibility for the truth as it really was" in describing his work on the history of Polish-Jewish relations during World War II.[188]

This realist approach was also applied by Yiddish historians to the study of creative writing in the ghettos. For example, in the compendium of ghetto literature published by Ber Mark in 1955, he asserts that the works he presented "serve as a reliable illustration of the various stages of the 'living' and the passing away of the Warsaw Ghetto."[189] Blumental expresses surprise at the degree of factual knowledge to be gleaned from the writing of Yitskhok Katzenelson, the martyred poet of the Warsaw Ghetto. He writes, for example, that Katzenelson recorded the name of General Stroop when it was unknown to the leaders of the Warsaw Ghetto Uprising and to the world at large prior to the Nuremberg Trials. He also notes that Katzenelson referred by name to "Operation Reinhard," the Nazis' plan to murder the Jews of the General Government of Poland, while it was still top secret.[190]

As one might expect, the study of creative writing also invoked the second approach, the non-realist, or ideal, approach implied by Ranke's dictum. The "essences" of daily life (as in Peter Novick's well-known interpretation of Ranke: "how it essentially was"[191]) are sought in literature on the ghettos. In one instance, Blumental refers to the famed survivor of the Lodz Ghetto, author Isaiah Spiegel, contending, "A historian can give you precise statistics on the mortality in the ghetto caused by starvation" but that Spiegel attains "what no historian can achieve. He does not limit himself to facts, but conveys the atmosphere, I would say: life itself."[192] Dworzecki offers the same point in his review of a novel by Leyb Kurland: "Documentary literature conveys the chronicle of events, but a novel," he says, can convey "what the chronicle, the document, the historical

---

188. Kermish, introduction to Emanuel Ringelblum, *Polish-Jewish Relations During the Second World War* (Jerusalem, 1974), xxxiv.

189. Ber Mark, *Tsvishn lebn un toyt* (Warsaw, 1966), 9.

190. Blumental, "Yitskhok katsenelson—vi a historiker fun der umkum-tkufe," *Yidishe kultur* 16, no. 6 (June 1954): 19.

191. Peter Novick, *That Noble Dream* (Cambridge, 1988), 28.

192. Blumental, "A literarishe geshikhte fun lodzsher-geto," *Di goldene keyt* 17 (1953): 244–45.

treatment cannot convey, namely, the atmosphere of those days and the spiritual climate of the people during those events."[193]

The Topics Not Covered

Despite the multifaceted interests of the Yiddish historians in aspects of daily life under Nazi occupation, the question arises—what is omitted? Not surprisingly, the chief omissions occur in the areas outside of their personal research interests, and the topics omitted are also, not coincidentally, at the borders of typical political, economic, or social history, namely: the spiritual and material aspects of Jewish life.

That the Yiddish historians were secular Jews (albeit with varying degrees of religious education) helps to explain the relative scarcity of religious topics in their works. Yiddish historical writing in post-Emancipation times has largely focused on nonreligious aspects of Jewish life. The choice of Yiddish as a medium for modern historical scholarship is an innovation that rarely penetrated the Orthodox or *haredi* ("ultra-Orthodox") worlds. For example, the pioneering Orthodox historians of Jewish history in the late nineteenth and early twentieth centuries, Isaac Hirsch Weiss and Ze'ev Yavetz (Jawitz), published their works in Hebrew. A century later, the leading *haredi* lay historians continued to write their principal works in Hebrew but had adopted the chief characteristics of Yiddish historical research—collecting eyewitness accounts, organizing public *zamlers* to gather historical materials, focusing on the internal aspects of Jewish history, and writing for an educated lay audience.[194]

---

193. Dworzecki, "Di vos zeyer haynt iz bashotnt mitn nekhtn," *Di goldene keyt* 68 (1970): 219.

194. Works by two leading figures are Menahem Getz, *Yerushalayim shel ma'lah* (Jerusalem, 1973), a history of *haredi* Jerusalem (and its struggle against secular and liberal Jewish encroachments); expanded Yiddish translation Menakhem Mendil Gerlits, *Di himldige shtot: yerusholayim shel male*, 3 vols. (Jerusalem, 1979–80); and Sh. Y. Gelbman, *Sefer Moshi'an shel Yisra'el: toldot rabenu ha-kadosh Ba'al Divre Yo'el mi-Satmar*, 9 vols. (Kiryas Yo'el, 1987–); about Gelbman, see David N. Myers, "Remembering the Satmar Movement's Chronicler," *Tablet Magazine* (April 3, 2015), http://tabletmag.com/scroll/190062/remembering-the-satmar-movements-chronicler, Yiddish translation, "Der historiker un arkhivist fun satmar," *Der yid* (April 15, 2015).

Religious Jews and their lives under Nazi domination were treated with respect and sympathy by each of the Yiddish historians, but they were not the principal topic of any of these historians' writings. To the extent that religious topics arise, they are to be found chiefly in broader studies that survey a variety of cultural and social issues. Thematic studies include Trunk's 1969 article on "Religious, Educational and Cultural Problems," which examines religious issues from the institutional perspective,[195] and his *Jewish Responses to Nazi Persecution*, which includes a group of eyewitness accounts by religiously observant Jews.[196] Site-specific studies include Dworzecki's history of the Vilna Ghetto,[197] and Kermish's anthology of documents from the Warsaw Ghetto,[198] each of which has a brief section devoted to religious Jewry. A notable exception is the Yiddish anthology edited by lay historian Menashe Unger on spiritual resistance among religious Jews, which includes citations from Blumental, Dworzecki, Friedman, and Trunk (among many others).[199]

The Holocaust historian destined to be the "Yiddish historian of religious life" was Rabbi Shimon Huberband, Ringelblum's principal historian colleague in the Oyneg Shabes project in the Warsaw Ghetto. The struggle by traditional Jews to maintain religious observance in the Nazi-imposed ghettos and the specific abuses they endured were frequent subjects of his works. Had Huberband survived, the religious component of the Yiddish historians' writings would have been augmented by his continued work and perhaps furthered by his influence. When Friedman learned of the manuscripts by Huberband that were found in the first portion of the Ringelblum Archive to be recovered, he recommended their publication as a book of their own.[200] Twenty years later, the annotated volume

---

195. Trunk, "Religious, Educational and Cultural Problems in the Eastern European Ghettos under German Occupation," *YIVO Annual of Jewish Social Studies* XIV (1969): 160–68 (later incorporated into his *Judenrat*).

196. Trunk, *Jewish Responses to Nazi Persecution* (New York, 1979), 21–25; "Yidishe reaktsye tsu natsi redifes," *Geshtaltn un gesheenishn [naye serye]* (Tel Aviv, 1983), 297–300.

197. Dworzecki, *Yerusholayim d'lite in kamf un umkum* (Paris, 1948), 288–94.

198. Kermish, *To Live with Honor, To Die with Honor!*, 410–30.

199. Menashe Unger, *Der gaystiker vidershtand fun yidn in getos un lagern* (Tel Aviv, 1970).

200. Friedman, "Forshungen fun letstn khurbn," *YIVO bleter* 34 (1950): 234.

of Huberband's works, deciphered, translated, and edited by Blumental and Kermish, would become the sole project of a predominantly religious character by postwar Yiddish historians.[201]

The area of material culture is a similar lacuna in the Yiddish historians' Holocaust works. By historical accident, the topic areas of the "material turn" that arose before the war (as noted in chapter 2) were of marginal interest to the particular historians who would become historians of the Holocaust. It is possible that the only specific prewar reference to material culture per se by one of these historians is a brief mention of "Jewish architecture" by Blumental that begins, "Speaking of material culture."[202] More typical is Trunk's article on the Jewish quarter of Płock that discusses its changing location, legality, and conflicts of ownership, rather than physical appearance.[203] Material culture itself was studied principally by historians who did not survive or had emigrated before the war. The former include Balaban,[204] Schiper,[205] and Ringelblum,[206] who had been active in

---

201. Blumental and Kermish, eds., Shimon Huberband, *Kiddush Ha-Shem—Ketavim mi-yeme ha-Sho'ah* (Tel Aviv, 1969) [English, 1986; see bibliography].

202. Blumental, "Vos iz azoyns yidishe etnografye: bamerkungen fun a zamler," *Literarishe bleter* (July 12, 1929): 549. A singular instance of "materiality" by a future Holocaust historian is Friedman's study of headstones in the old Jewsih Cemetery in Lodz, "Matsevot bet ha-kevarot ha-yashan be-Lodz," *Stary Cmentarz Żydowski w Łodzi* (Lodz, 1938), Hebrew section 5–115.

203. Trunk, "Der yidisher kvartal in plotsk in XVI un XVII y.h.," *Landkentnish* 9, no. 4 (December 1937): 1–4; 10, no.1 (April 1938): 7–8.

204. Mayer Balaban, *Die Judenstadt von Lublin* (Berlin, 1919) [Yiddish: *Di yidn-shtot lublin* (Buenos Aires, 1947)] describes the history and appearance of Jewish landmarks. Many of his works on Jewish art, architecture, and crafts are listed in the bibliography to Israel M. Biderman, *Mayer Balaban: Historian of Polish Jewry* (New York, 1976). In Yiddish, see particularly Balaban's *Yidn in poyln* (Vilna, 1930). Not listed, but of importance for the Yiddish-reading public is his "Unzere kunst—un kultur—oytseres," *Literarishe bleter* (October 18, 1929): 818–20; (October 25): 839–40; (November 1): 860–61; (November 15): 903–4; (November 22): 913–15, a Yiddish translation of chapter 2 of his *Zabytki Historyczne Żydów w Polsce* (Warsaw, 1929).

205. Yitskhok Shiper, *Geshikhte fun yidisher teater-kunst un drame* (Warsaw, 1927), for example, describes the physical appearance and stage sets for Jewish theater performances of prior centuries: chapter 8 of vol. 1 (and portions of others).

206. On Jewish antiquities in Poland, see Emanuel Ringelblum, "Vegn yidishe altertimlekhkaytn in poyln," *Literarishe bleter* 7, no. 33 (August 15, 1933), 615–16; on clothing of past times, "Yidishe malbushim in poyln sof 18 y"h," *Fun noentn over* I, no. V (1938): 17–20.

the Jewish Antiquities Commission in Warsaw[207] and wrote on material aspects of Jewish history. The latter include Shatzky, who devoted several works to the history of Yiddish publishing, and Rachel Wischnitzer, whose articles on Jewish art and architecture gradually turned from Europe to America, and from Yiddish to English, after the war.

The Yiddish historians of the Holocaust continued their prewar focus on social, economic, and intellectual issues to the near exclusion of material culture, thereby separating Yiddish Holocaust historiography from the prewar material turn. Seeming exceptions will be found most often to focus not on the *object* but on the *process* by which objects were destroyed or stolen by the Nazis and recovered by the Allies.[208] Although Trunk and Kermish both became directors of archives, and Blumental created his own archive of manuscripts—while Friedman and Dworzecki each dealt with bibliographies—the Yiddish historians' works rarely treat documents as historical artifacts. They are concerned exclusively with the content and not the provenance or condition of the primary sources they cite, and they are indifferent to whether such documents are originals or microfilmed copies. Trunk describes with satisfaction the extensive holdings of YIVO in New York and the project undertaken before his arrival to retrieve YIVO's prewar European archives,[209] but none of the Yiddish historians actively participated in the larger goal of rescuing the documentary heritage of European Jewry (taken to such excess

---

207. Lucjan Dobroszycki offers a brief description of the *Komisye tsu forshn yidishe altertimlekhkaytn* of the Warsaw Historical Commission of the Historical Section of YIVO in 1929, in his "YIVO in Interwar Poland: Work in the Historical Sciences," in *The Jews of Poland Between Two World Wars*, ed. Yisrael Gutman et al. (Hanover, 1989), 501–3.

208. Examples are Friedman's "The Fate of the Jewish Book," *Jewish Book Annual* 15 (1957–1958): 3–13; and Trunk's "Opgeratevete yidishe kultur-oytseres nokh der milkhome [Rescued Jewish Cultural Treasures after the War]" in his *Geshtaltn un gesheenishn* (Buenos Aires, 1962), 262–67. Rare exceptions are survey works such as those on Vilna, Lodz, and Auschwitz by Dworzecki, Trunk, and Friedman, respectively, that mention various aspects of the manmade environment. A notable example of the reverse case, in which objects that were recovered are the subject of study, is Mordechai V. Bernstein's book, *Nisht derbrente shaytn* [*Unburnt Embers*], published by the Argentine branch of YIVO in 1956.

209. Trunk, "The Historian of the Holocaust at YIVO," in *Creators and Disturbers: Reminiscences by Jewish Intellectuals of New York / Drawn from conversations with Bernard Rosenberg and Ernest Goldstein* (New York, 1982), 67–70.

by their YIVO colleague Zosa Szajkowski[210]). Despite the several references by Friedman and Kermish in their early reports on the CJHC and JHI to the large number of paintings and sculptures in their museum, they produced no works on art in the ghettos or camps. And despite the continuing relationship of Blumental and Kermish with their first home in Israel, the Ghetto Fighters' House (for whose journal they continued to write), with its well-known collection of Holocaust artwork, it was not to art but to their own most treasured subjects of folklore and the Ringelblum Archive that each returned with determination in old age.[211] The only use of wartime materials as historical objects among the Yiddish historians appears to have been a unique traveling exhibition cocurated by Kermish for Yad Vashem in 1979 titled "Jewish Creativity in the Holocaust."[212]

From the General to the Specific

The remaining omission to be noted in the works of the Yiddish historians is not a topic but rather the absence of a synthetic history of the Holocaust. In this connection, it is worth noting again that the research outline prepared by Friedman in 1950 was for a comprehensive *description* that would encompass all Holocaust research,[213] not an agenda to be undertaken by any one historian or group of historians. The only synthetic account of the Holocaust by a Yiddish historian was a survey article by Trunk that appeared in the Yiddish encyclopedia in 1966, which gave equal attention to perpetrator and victim history and to a variety of

---

210. See Lisa Moses Leff, "Rescue or Theft? Zosa Szajkowski and the Salvaging of French Jewish History," *Jewish Social Studies* 18, no. 2 (Winter 2012): 1–39.

211. It was instead their early colleague at the Ghetto Fighters' House, Miriam Novitch, whose culminating project was the album of concentration camp art, *Spiritual Resistance: Art from Concentration Camps—With Essays by Miriam Novitch, Lucy Dawidowicz, and Tom L. Freudenheim* (Philadelphia, 1981).

212. Kermish and Yechiel Szeintuch, eds., *Jewish Creativity in the Holocaust: Exhibition of Jewish Creativity in the Ghettoes and Camps under Nazi Rule (1939–1945)* (Jerusalem: 1979; exhibition catalog in Hebrew, Yiddish, English). One might also cite Blumental's brief coverage of the album of artwork created in the ghetto of his hometown by a younger Blumental, presumably his cousin, in his *Sefer borshtshiv* (Tel Aviv, 1960), 219–21.

213. See Friedman, *Roads to Extinction* (New York, 1980), 571–76.

geographic locations.²¹⁴ Had one or more of the Yiddish historians produced a synthetic history of Jewish life under Nazi rule in Eastern Europe, it would likely have resembled the chapters in part 2 of Lucy Dawidowicz's *The War Against the Jews* of 1990, which rely heavily on works by Trunk, Dworzecki, Friedman, Blumental, and Kermish (in roughly that order of prominence) and on the published sources most cited in their writings. By contrast, the works of the Yiddish historians consist almost exclusively of original research from archival sources and deal with specific locations, persons, institutions, or processes—which is only partly anticipated by the prominence of regional studies and monographs in the works of prewar Yiddish historians.

After the war, Friedman renewed his early advocacy for a regional approach to Jewish history (as discussed in chapter 1) but, in the early 1950s, revealed a surprising reversal in his assessment of the relative places of regional and synthetic studies. His first call for Jewish regionalism in 1933 had stressed that the new historical practice of regionalism by European historians "did not mean merely research of a given place, which was nothing new," but rather "a specific system of historical research which will deepen our knowledge of the Jewish folk masses," and "which can lead to new general results and even to revision of opinions which have a central importance for our scholarship."²¹⁵ Here he echoed the limited endorsement of regionalism by the well-known French-Jewish historian Marc Bloch, a leader of the Annales school in Paris, who had argued that "a good study of local history could, no doubt be defined as follows: a question of general interest posed to the documents furnished by a particular region."²¹⁶ As an example, Friedman cited the widely held view that Jewish economic activity in Poland had become increasingly "productivized" (engaged in labor or craft rather than trade) during the

---

214. Trunk, "Der farnikhtungs-protses fun eyropeyishn yidntum in der natsi-tkufe," *Algemeyne entsiklopedye*, vol. Yidn VII (New York, 1966), 1–15.

215. Friedman, "Di oyfgabes fun undzer historisher visnshaft un vi azoy zey tsu realizirn," *YIVO bleter* XIII, nos. 3–4 (1938): 309 (first presented in Polish at the 1933 International Historical Congress in Warsaw, then in Yiddish at the 1935 YIVO conference in Vilna).

216. Quoted from Susan W. Friedman, *Marc Bloch, Sociology and Geography: Encountering Changing Disciplines* (Cambridge, 1996), 79.

nineteenth century—leading to predictions of continued "normalization" of Jewish occupational structures in twentieth-century Poland—but which had been recently disproved on the basis of regional studies by Trunk, Mahler, Schiper, and Friedman himself.[217] In his major essay on regionalism of 1937, he stresses (as a paragraph of its own), "One dare not forget that the place of honor in scholarship must be occupied by large problems and synthetic tasks," with the explanation: "Regionalism helps us penetrate deeper by excavating the concrete building blocks of scholarly synthesis. . . . This is the meaning of regionalism and its contribution to the 'larger,' general scholarly research."[218] After the war, in 1951, he reprinted this essay in the leading New York journal *Di tsukunft* with a new conclusion that expanded his view of Jewish regionalism to include the emerging phenomenon of Holocaust *yizkor* books, while maintaining his insistence on the primacy of synthesis.[219]

Friedman, as well as his postwar colleague Trunk, pointed to Meyer Balaban as the exemplar of this regional-to-general aspiration. Friedman's seventieth birthday tribute to Balaban in 1937 honored him as the founder and most active practitioner of modern Jewish history in Poland. He referred to Balaban's regional monographs on Lemberg (Lwów), Krakow, and Lublin as his "very most important works," and concluded with the hope: "The crowning of his creation should be a synthetic work that would encompass the entire Jewish history of Poland—in all periods and in all aspects of Jewish life."[220] Late in life, Trunk memorialized his teacher, Balaban, in an essay that also cites Balaban's regional monographs and praises him as the stimulus for a generation of students' studies in the field of Polish-Jewish regional history. Trunk then laments the loss during the Nazi occupation of Balaban's manuscript for "a synthetic history of the [Jewish] community in Poland from oldest times to the outbreak of the Second World War."[221]

---

217. Friedman, "Di oyfgabes," 309.
218. Friedman, "Regyonalizm," *Landkentnish* (July 1937): 1.
219. Friedman, "Der regyonalistishe geshikhte-shraybung un di romantik fun der alter heym," *Di tsukunft* (December 1951): 464–69.
220. Friedman, "Prof. meir balaban," *Literarishe bleter* (March 12, 1937): 169–70.
221. Trunk, "Meir balaban—der forsher fun der koolisher organizatsye un oytonomye in amolikn poyln (30 yor nokh zayn toyt in varshever geto)," *YIVO bleter* XLIV (1973): 204.

Unseen, no doubt, by nearly all of Friedman's usual readers was his last, most comprehensive, and most surprising discussion of regionalism, which appeared in 1952 in the *yizkor* book of a small Lithuanian town published in Johannesburg (in which he does not touch on the town's history but apparently wishes to support its memorial project with his contribution of an essay).[222] He commences with the brief acknowledgment: "Modern Jewish historiography traces its lineage to two great Jewish scholars," Marcus Jost and Heinreinch Graetz, "whose works were grand synthetic compositions that encompassed the whole history of the Jewish people in all times and all countries,"[223] but he does not refer again to this impliedly outmoded form (nor to its later practitioners, Dubnow and Baron, on whom he had written before the war). Instead, he devotes his essay to tracing the rise and development of the monographic approach to local Jewish history that had already come to guide the work of most Jewish historians of his own and later generations.

Friedman's observations, apart from their prescience regarding the direction of Jewish historical writing, reflect the changing state of Jewish Holocaust studies. In his first postwar works, he had continued to seek those broader syntheses that might be derived from disparate local studies but found his work impeded by a scarcity of material. Before the war, Friedman had taken to task the Yiddish historian Jacob Shatzky for drawing a general conclusion about Jewish-gentile relations during the Chmielnicki massacres of 1648 from a single example, declaring, "deductions do not proceed from the specific to the general" (thus inverting a contrary rule of rabbinical hermeneutics and restating it in Hebrew to emphasize his modernizing departure).[224] Yet in several of his early Holocaust writings, he resorted to the same device in the absence of wider sources. His foreword to Joseph Gar's 1948 history of the Holocaust in

---

222. In his review of this *yizkor* book, Friedman would say that "townsfolk from a small community have succeeded with very modest means in erecting a great monument." See "Yisker-bikher un regyonale literatur," *Di tsukunft* (April 1955): 180.

223. Friedman, "Monografyes fun yidishe kehiles un shtet in der yidisher geshikhte shraybung," in *Yisker-bukh fun rakishok un umgegnt*, ed. Melekh Bakaltshuk-Felin (Johannesburg, 1952), 439.

224. Friedman, "Gzeyres takh," *Literarishe bleter* (August 19, 1938): 568 (in his words, "Ein lomdim min ha-perat 'al ha-kelal").

Kovne, for example, argues that "a natural scientist who wants to identify the taste of seawater need not study the entire quantity of water in the ocean" (and that "from the microcosm he may discern the macrocosm"), so that, from Gar's description of the destruction of the Jews of Kovne, "we can suppose how it proceeded in the 'macrocosm,' everywhere" in Lithuania.[225]

The unexpected turn to be found in Friedman's Johannesburg essay of 1952 is that he abandons his repeated insistence on synthesis as the theoretical basis for regional studies and finds in regionalism its own inherent justification. He responds to the growing popular literature of the Holocaust, and its nearly exclusive focus on specific sites of Jewish memory, with the observation that "since the great catastrophe of European Jewry, the scholarly interest has been joined by a second, very strong emotional element . . . which brought more force and inner warmth to our regional literature." He indicates that "since about 1940, our regional history-writing has been simultaneously a *yizkor* literature," and he declares that the collective project of creating *yizkor* books, particularly those with well-developed historical sections, is the successor to the writing of local monographs that had prevailed among individual historians before the war.[226]

Trunk similarly describes the *yizkor* books as "the monographs of the shtetl," and in reviewing one that he judged to have the requisite historical depth, he pronounces it "a contribution to our regional literature."[227] By contrast, Friedman and Trunk's fellow Yiddish historian Shatzky argued that the *yizkor* book phenomenon had ended the scholarly pursuit of regional history. Shatzky contended that the nearness in time of the Holocaust had displaced public interest in the detailed history of earlier periods (a concern shared by both Friedman and Trunk[228]). "This psychological impediment makes regional studies more and more difficult

---

225. Friedman, foreword to Yosef Gar, *Umkum fun der yidisher kovne* (Munich, 1948), 10.
226. Friedman, "Monografyes," 448.
227. Trunk, "A bukh vegn shedlets," *YIVO bleter* XLI (1957): 359, 364.
228. Friedman, "Yisker-bikher un regyonale literatur," *Di tsukunft* (April 1955): 179; Trunk, "A bukh vegn shedlets," 359.

in general . . . and the events of the permanent drama known as Jewish history, which at times endured for generations, are pushed into a place of unimportance."[229] Shatzky concludes that "at the present moment, regional history is an academic anachronism."[230]

Far from concurring with Shatzky that the scholarly pursuit of regionalism had become obsolete, Trunk sought a means for its renewal. Soon after Friedman's premature death in 1960, he published his first major essay on historical practice, "How Should One Study the History of the Destroyed Jewish Communities in Poland?," which addresses the study of prewar history but hints at his future attitude toward regionalism in Holocaust history. He notes that the form of regionalism practiced before the war had become unrealistic at a time when archives in Soviet-controlled Poland were inaccessible and young historians had yet to be trained for detailed work. For each destroyed city or town, he proposes instead a "short synthetic history" (or "condensed community monograph") that will construct "the portrait of the community" by seeking "less the factual history and more the basic outline of its social-economic and cultural development, the place it occupies in the general cultural-historical picture of Polish Jewry."[231] Of note is that his proposal signals a reversal in his expectations of local Jewish history, away from creating the building blocks of synthesis and toward the elevation of individual essences in the study of Jewish historical sites.

Finally, in Trunk's magnum opus, *Judenrat*, he formally dispenses with the goal of synthesis. On the contrary, he says that, while "it is possible to find common features in the general pattern of the activities of the Councils— . . . I am, however, of the opinion that the entire Council phenomenon cannot be analyzed in general terms." He then cautions that the varying local conditions, personalities, attitudes, "internal, demographic, and economic structures," and dissimilar history, traditions, and

---

229. Yankev Shatski, "Referatn un retsenzyes: yisker-bikher," *YIVO bleter* XXXVII (1953): 266.

230. Yankev Shatski, "Problemen fun yidisher historyografye," *Di tsukunft* (March 1955): 126.

231. Trunk, "Vi azoy forsht men di geshikhte fun di khorev gevorene kehiles in poyln?," in *Almanakh yidish*, ed. Yankev Pat et al. (New York, 1961), 279–80, 285.

geographic position of each community require the researcher to "beware of the temptation to simplify or generalize."[232]

I would suggest a further explanation for this turn from the general to the specific. One senses from the Yiddish historians' body of Holocaust works that a project of grand synthesis that would encompass the perpetrator, victim, and bystander perspectives, and also draw generalizing trends from multiple locations, was not undertaken for the reason that it might have proved unrewarding. Through their choice of sources, both archival and living—and in this way only—the Yiddish historians may be said to have "cherished their troubles," as the Crusades chroniclers before them had done. The satisfaction gained from their work, and the solace attained for their own losses, appear to have come in part from the historians' ability to draw close to the presence of their murdered fellow Jews and the surviving remnant—and to give them voice.[233]

If in any sense it may be said that their works were responses to the demands of the survivors (including their own demands as survivors), answers to the urgent questions posed by the experience of the Holocaust lay not in the writing of general histories but in addressing specific issues. One of these—the question, "How could this have happened to us?"—appears as a recurring subtext of the Yiddish historians' works. It is the theme of the following chapter.

---

232. Trunk, *Judenrat: The Jewish Councils in Eastern Europe under Nazi Occupation* (New York, 1972), xxix–xxx. Note that Trunk's essay, "The Jewish Councils in Eastern Europe under Nazi Rule (An Attempt at a Synthesis)," *Societas—A Review of Social History* (Summer 1972): 221–39 is a conference-paper *summary* of his book, not a *synthetic* treatment of his research.

233. A related sentiment is expressed by Blumental in assessing the seeming reluctance of certain *yizkor*-book committees to complete their volumes—that to end the work is "to tear away from that past that is so dear to us. One wants still to live in that former world, with *those* people, with *those* problems. And with . . . *oneself from that time*" (emphases and ellipsis his). Blumental, "Etlekhe sakh-hakhlen [from his series on *yizkor* books]," *Lebns-fragn* 113–14 (March–April, 1961): 8.

5

THE SEARCH FOR ANSWERS

The Yiddish historians of the Holocaust inherited a tradition of engaged scholarship that had prevailed in Eastern Europe before World War II.[1] In addition to strengthening Jewish national consciousness, a goal of the prewar Yiddish historians was to provide arguments that could be used to counter Polish antisemitism. These historians' works emphasized the historical support of Jews for Polish independence, their contributions to the Polish economy, and their centuries of residence in a given location.

As might be expected, the engaged practice of historical writing resumed after the Holocaust in the conditions of postwar Poland among the Yiddish historians of the Central Jewish Historical Commission (CJHC). The renewal of Jewish life in liberated Poland depended on the support and protection of a largely unpopular Communist regime, with the hope of gaining the sympathy of non-Jewish Poles. In 1946, for example, Joseph Kermish republished his prewar Polish article on the patriotism and loyalty of Polish Jews during Kościuszko's revolt of 1794,[2] with obvious relevance to Jewish aspirations of the day. Indeed, the work of the Yiddish historians and the CJHC in early postwar Poland may be seen as an extended exercise in political engagement. The CJHC and its personnel attained a semiofficial status unimaginable for Jewish intellectuals in prewar Poland. The historians of the CJHC served on official government commissions of inquiry and as expert witnesses in war crimes trials.

---

1. See discussion in the introduction.
2. Kermish, "Nieznany list patriotyczny rabina do Kościszki z rozu 1792," *Głos Gminy Żydowskiej* I, no. 4 (October 1937): 87–88; reprinted in *Opinia* 2, no. 5 (25 September 1946): 18.

Philip Friedman was appointed to teach Jewish history at the University of Lodz, the first academic position awarded to any Yiddish historian in Poland.[3] Kermish, who had become a captain in the Soviet-led Polish People's Army and taught history during the war at the officer training school near Zhytomyr, remained in uniform and was promoted to the rank of major during his time at the CJHC, where he was often described as "Dr.-Major Kermish." At the end of the war, he was awarded the Order of Polonia Restituta for his service as a partisan fighter and in the Polish army—and presumably for services yet to come.[4]

Their semiofficial status afforded the Yiddish historians a degree of access to the non-Jewish media that would also have been unimaginable before the war. Apart from scholarly articles written in Yiddish, most of the books published by the CJHC appeared in Polish, including accounts by Polish-Christian witnesses to the Holocaust. A shortage of Yiddish type after the war is often mentioned as the cause, but a desire to reach the non-Jewish public must be considered once the first Yiddish books were published in 1946. Favorable reviews of Polish works by the CJHC appeared in non-Jewish Polish publications, ranging in orientation from socialist and Communist to Catholic and nationalist, and were publicized by the CJHC in Yiddish translation.[5]

Yet with increasing Soviet domination of Poland and continuing acts of antisemitic violence, the Yiddish historians despaired of reconstituting Jewish communal life in postwar Poland. In contrast to Kermish's 1946 reprint on Polish Jews during Kościuszko's revolt, the only new research on prewar Jewish history by a Yiddish historian of the Holocaust was an article published in 1948 by Isaiah Trunk on Jewish attitudes toward the

---

3. "D"r f. fridman—lektor in lodzsher universitet," *Dos naye lebn* (December 23, 1945): 1.

4. "[D"r. Yosef Kermish]." *Amerikaner* (September 14, 1945): 5.

5. The retrospective "prospectus" of publications by the CJHC, issued at the time of its dissolution in fall 1947, *Prospekt fun di oysgabes fun der tsentraler yidisher historisher komisye in poyln* (Warsaw-Lodz-Krakow, 1947), quotes favorable reviews for each of its publications. Of a total of twenty-five reviews, eleven are from eight non-Jewish Polish-language periodicals, including one on a work by Blumental in *Głos Ludu* (Czechoslovak Communist) and one on a work by Friedman in *Przegląd Zachodni* (Polish-nationalist and Catholic). The remaining reviews are from Yiddish periodicals in Poland, the US, and Argentina.

November Uprising of 1830. This article demonstrates the subtlety of which he was capable in the changed circumstances of the time: commencing with a diversionary analysis of the socioeconomic situation of the Jews in Congress Poland, likely designed to satisfy the Communist overseers, he contends that the attitude of the masses of Polish Jews to the revolt of 1830 "could not have been other than indifference"—in light of the refusal by the new Polish leaders to grant equal civic rights to the Jews.[6] Trunk finds, instead, that Jewish support came only from the select few who were likely to benefit from their connections to the revolutionary leaders, a situation recurring as he wrote.

By the time this article appeared, Friedman had already settled in the West, and Trunk, Kermish, and Nachman Blumental had determined to leave Poland, while Mark Dworzecki had resolved not to return from Paris.[7] The mass exodus of a quarter million Polish Jews in the first years of the Soviet takeover equaled in number the influx of survivors who had returned to Poland after the war. Those who remained were the relatively few who chose, or found themselves compelled, to live in accordance with the ruling ideology that suppressed both national and religious Jewish communal life.

The last possibility for the realization of the Diaspora nationalist vision in Europe had been extinguished—and with it the prewar practice of historical engagement that had developed to advance this vision. Once the Yiddish historians of the Holocaust arrived in America and Israel, between 1948 and 1950, the most urgent postwar Jewish problems that might have spurred engaged historical research on the Holocaust had been resolved: a Jewish national home had been established in the State of Israel, and most of the Jews in the Displaced Persons camps of Europe had been resettled.

---

6. Trunk, "Di yidn un der november-oyfshtand fun 1831 [sic; 1830]," *Dos naye lebn* (December 1, 1948): 4; (December 6, 1948): 4 (see second part). Jewish attitudes toward the various Polish uprisings were a favorite subject of Polish-Jewish historians. For example, Friedman stated views similar to Trunk's regarding the limited proportion of Jews favorable to the November Uprising in his critique of Schiper's contrary assertion of wide support: "Dr. y. shiper—poylishe yidn besn november-oyfshtand," *Literarishe bleter* (March 16, 1934): 172.

7. Dworzecki, "Oyf fir vegn veln mir fanandergeyn," *Unzer vort* (September 21, 1945): 2.

In the absence of a contemporary "Jewish Question," it appeared that the Yiddish historians might concentrate on writing the Jewish history of the Holocaust without political engagement. Specifically, they chose not to embrace the other instrumental uses that their work on the Holocaust might have engendered:

They had been among the first to discuss the theft of Jewish property by German fighters, and the concealing of such crimes as a motive for mass murder,[8] but they did not participate in preparing the documentation for reparations claims. Moreover, two of the Yiddish historians, Dworzecki and Blumental, were outspoken in opposing the 1952 reparations agreement between West Germany and Israel (which nevertheless provided much of the funding for Yad Vashem and YIVO during the 1950s and 1960s).

Moreover, they did not seek redress by becoming "Nazi hunters." As discussed in chapter 4, they rejected the role of accuser, and they resisted diversion of their scholarship into perpetrator studies. They did not follow the example of Elias Tcherikower, the future founder of YIVO's Historical Section, who created a documentation center to collect evidence of crimes against Jews during the post–World War I Ukrainian pogroms. Neither did they choose to conduct research for the documentation centers established after the Holocaust by Simon Wiesenthal in Vienna and Tuviah Friedman in Haifa.

Further, the Yiddish historians did not join the cause of preparing evidence for cases in Jewish "honor courts" against surviving members of Jewish Councils who were accused of collaborating with the Nazis.[9] With the Communist takeover of the Jewish Historical Institute in Warsaw in 1949, this work became one of its stated aims. This new stance was applauded by Gerald Reitlinger, the author of the first prominent general history of the Holocaust, who wrote, "It is rather sad to recall how little of this spirit [of investigating Jewish Council members] there was in the

---

8. See, e.g., "Ekspertize fun mgr y. trunk," *Dos naye lebn* (September 6, 1948): 6, 8.

9. For example, the Yiddish historians do not figure in Laura Jockusch and Gabriel N. Finder, *Jewish Honor Courts: Revenge, Retribution, and Reconciliation in Europe and Israel after the Holocaust* (Detroit, 2015), with the exception of a few references to notes prepared by Blumental and Kermish for use in Polish civil courts in the course of their work at the CJHC (271).

first post-war researches of the Central Jewish Historical Commission of Poland,"[10] at the time it was led by the Yiddish historians.

They also resisted the temptation to apply the practice of Holocaust historiography to the more popular pursuit of Holocaust memory. They understood that commemoration of "martyrs and heroes"—the stated aim of most Holocaust memorials, including Yad Vashem—would engender a return to the lachrymose vision of Jewish history and its seeming antidote, the search for cases of exceptional Jewish heroism, both of which obscure the Jews' everyday struggle for existence under Nazi occupation.[11]

Perhaps most significantly, they did not seek "the lesson" of the Holocaust as it was understood by the founding director of Yad Vashem, Ben-Zion Dinur—who held that the destruction of European Jewry confirmed the Zionist doctrine of *shelilat ha-galut* (negation of the exile), so that, in Dinur's words, "'Diaspora' and 'destruction' are not two separate categories; rather, 'Diaspora' includes 'destruction.'"[12] The singular statement by Kermish in 1954—"[W]e must draw national conclusions for future generations. We have a sacred obligation to learn the lessons of the trials of this generation"[13]—requires the same careful reading as Friedman's supposed conversion to "dialectical-Marxist analysis" in 1945 Poland (as discussed in chapter 2). It is the only such statement by a Yiddish historian, and it appears only once, and only in Hebrew, in the first article published by Kermish under Dinur's leadership at Yad Vashem. To the contrary, as discussed in chapter 6, the works of the Yiddish historians tend toward implicit validation of Jewish life in the Diaspora.

---

10. Gerald Reitlinger, *The Final Solution: The Attempt to Exterminate the Jews of Europe: 1939–1945* (New York, 1953), 66.

11. Friedman's *Martyrs and Fighters* (New York, 1954) is, despite its popularizing title, a sociological study of everyday life among the Jews in Warsaw, from the time of the German invasion to the Polish uprising of 1944, constructed of quotations from primary sources edited by Friedman into a continuous narrative.

12. Quoted in Boaz Cohen, "Setting the Agenda of Holocaust Research: Discord at Yad Vashem in the 1950s," in *Holocaust Historiography in Context: Emergence, Challenges, Polemics and Achievements*, eds. David Bankier and Dan Michman (Jerusalem, 2008), 260, from Arielle Rein, "Historian as Nation-Builder: Ben-Zion Dinur's Evolution and Enterprise (1884–1948)" (PhD diss., Hebrew University of Jerusalem, 2000), 2.

13. Kermish, "la-Matsav be-heker ha-Sho'ah," *Yedi'ot Yad va-Shem* 1 (April 30, 1954): 10.

Had no other public cause more convincingly demanded the Yiddish historians' scholarly attention, they might have avoided the instrumental use of Holocaust research. But they encountered the single issue that would occupy their collective consciences for the remainder of their careers, and which would become the final subject of engaged historical research by Yiddish historians—the accusation that the Jewish victims of the Holocaust had allowed themselves to be murdered without resisting.

This chapter will discuss the Yiddish historians' engaged response to the accusation of passivity, an accusation that became the principal issue of Holocaust history among the community of survivors to which they, too, belonged. The Yiddish historians crafted both an apologetic defense and a dynamic offense. The first portion of this chapter deals with the Yiddish historians' repeated and comprehensive refutations of the claim that Jews could have resisted more effectively. The second discusses their development of a new concept of unarmed resistance that gained increasing acceptance in the field of Holocaust studies and which offered a measure of redemption to the memories of those accused of "going as sheep to the slaughter."

The Question of Questions

For the Yiddish historians, the problem of resistance and passivity was the Question of Questions. In the 1945 article that may well be Blumental's first postwar writing, he voices the feeling of many survivors, saying that "when you consider the problem of defense, . . . you burn with the hellfire of the feeling of shame, why did the Jews themselves not mount a defense but let themselves be led to their deaths like cowardly sheep!"[14]

The tenth anniversary of the Warsaw Ghetto Uprising brought forth the first articles—in April 1953, by Friedman and Trunk—wholly devoted to the subject of resistance. Each commences with this question.

---

14. Blumental, "A shtime fun yomer-tol," *Yidishe kultur* 7, no. 6 (June 1945): 14. At this early date, Dworzecki also quoted (and rejected) the same accusation, saying, "It is doubtful that [Jewish demographer] Jacob Lestschinsky was correct in his questioning outcry . . . , 'How was it that [the Jewish victim] let himself be led to the slaughter?,'" "Ir zayt ale gerekht . . . ," *Idisher kemfer* (August 17, 1945): 9.

Friedman asks, "Why did the Warsaw Ghetto Uprising come only in April 1943, when more than 350,000 Jews in Warsaw had already been murdered?" And he follows with a dozen similar questions about the lateness of organizing partisan groups, escaping to the forests, or preparing for armed uprisings, and about the acquiescence of Jews from every country in being transported to the camps.[15] Trunk summarizes the issue, saying, "The question can be formulated briefly thus: why did resistance come so late and therefore so weak, and why did the Jewish masses go so passively to their deaths?"[16] In the same year, Blumental writes, "For all of us there is a baffling problem that disturbs us a great deal: why were there among the Jews so few expressions of active opposition to the German monster," which he says is the question that "arises among everyone who reflects on the events of that time."[17] In the *yizkor* book of his hometown, Borshtshiv (Borszczów, Poland; today Borshchiv, Ukraine), Blumental relates that he himself would ask survivors, "Why did you let yourselves be slaughtered like lambs, why did you not put up any resistance?"[18]

In his article, "On the Problem of How Jews Conducted Themselves Under German Occupation," written in 1960, Blumental reflected on the question posed by Ringelblum in the Warsaw Ghetto, "'Why are the Jews dying quietly,'" adding: "in other words, why did the ordinary Jew let himself be taken to the *akedah* [the biblical binding of Isaac] without any active resistance?"[19] Then, in 1968, Kermish deciphered additional pages of Ringelblum's *Notes* and, in the first report of his findings, quotes the now-familiar lament recorded by Ringelblum: "How much longer will we

---

15. Friedman, "Der idisher vidershtand kegn der natsi-hershaft," *Idisher kemfer* (April 3, 1953, Pesach): 89.

16. Trunk raised the question for the first time in his "Yidisher umkum un vidershtand (tsu der kharakteristik fun unzer khurbn)," *Lebns-fragn* 24 (April 1953): 3; a month later he restated it more fully (as quoted here) in "Di problem vidershtand in undzer khurbn-literatur," *Di tsukunft* (May–June 1953): 253.

17. Blumental, "A literarishe geshikhte fun lodzsher-geto," *Di goldene keyt* 17 (1953): 237.

18. Blumental, *Sefer borshtshiv* (Tel Aviv, 1960), 235.

19. Blumental, "Tsum problem vi di yidn hobn zikh farhaltn unter der daytsher okupatsye" [dated July 1960], in *YKUF almanakh*, ed. Nakhmen Mayzil (New York, 1961), 360. This article is a generalized examination of the subject in his similarly titled chapter in *Sefer borshtshiv*, 231–38.

go 'as sheep to the slaughter? . . . Why is there no call to escape to the forests? No call to resist?' This question torments all of us."[20]

Indeed, Blumental would respond at least four times to the much-quoted accusation of "going as sheep to the slaughter" by deflecting it onto the perpetrators. In 1945, he declared that even if true, the fact of Jewish passivity (and the guilt or indifference of others) "dare not relieve even a hair of responsibility for these events from the German people."[21] In 1961, he demands to know, "Do even sheep on their own, of their own will, go to their slaughter?"[22] Three years later, he asks, "Are sheep not a symbol of purity and innocence!? And when slaughterers lead the sheep into the slaughterhouse, are the slaughterers or the sheep guilty!?"[23] And then, at the 1968 Yad Vashem conference on Jewish resistance, he reiterates, "But even if the majority did go 'as sheep,' what of it? Who bears the guilt—the sheep or the slaughterer!"[24] The poet Abba Kovner, a partisan leader in the Vilna Ghetto, said later of his authorship of the phrase, "Let us not be taken like sheep to the slaughter" (in December 1941), that it was intended to inspire rebellion, not condemnation, and that even "during the fighting when there might have been sheep . . . I have never thought that the sheep had anything to be ashamed of."[25]

During the first decades after the Holocaust, public discussion of the accusation of Jewish passivity by public figures among the survivors

---

20. Kermish, "Emmanuel Ringelblum's Notes hitherto Unpublished," *Yad Vashem Studies* VII (1968): 178 (quoting from Ringelblum's note of June 17, 1942). For the Yiddish original, prepared for publication by Kermish, see Emanuel Ringelblum, *Ksovim fun geto*, vol. 2 (Tel Aviv, 1985), 409–10.

21. Blumental, "A shtime fun yomer-tol," 15.

22. Blumental, foreword to Yeshaye Zandberg, *Der soyne in di moyern* (Tel Aviv, 1963), 10.

23. Blumental, "Apikursishe gedanken: tsum yortog fun geto-oyfshtand," *Lebns-fragn* 147 (March 1964): 5.

24. Blumental, "Sources for the Study of Jewish Resistance," *Jewish Resistance During the Holocaust: Proceedings of the Conference on Manifestations of Jewish Resistance, Jerusalem, April 7–11, 1968* (Jerusalem, 1971), 70.

25. Abba Kovner, "Discussion," in *The Holocaust as Historical Experience*, eds. Yehuda Bauer and Nathan Rotenstreich (New York, 1980), 252. For a general discussion of the term and its history, see Yael S. Feldman, "'Not as Sheep Led to Slaughter'?: On Trauma, Selective Memory, and the Making of Historical Consciousness," *Jewish Social Studies* 19, no. 3 (2013): 139–69.

most often consisted of denials. Two examples that were well known and much circulated in their time, translated from Yiddish into English, are Hersh Smoliar's "The Lambs were Legend . . ." (1955) and Israel Efroykin's "The Myth of Jewish Cowardice" (1959),[26] which took, respectively, the opposing approaches of avowing widespread Jewish heroism on the one hand and Jewish self-sacrifice on the other. In rare instances, such a denial would come from a Yiddish historian. Writing in America, and well before the Eichmann trial engendered widespread public interest in the Holocaust, Trunk argues that the claim of Jewish passivity was a misconception traceable to lack of interest in learning the details of Jewish life during the Holocaust. He contends that "Jewish resistance in the Nazi period was a phenomenon far more widespread than usually recognized," and as a corrective he cites several examples of Jewish armed resistance.[27] In another instance, Friedman responds to his own question about the lateness of Jewish resistance with the argument, "Despite Jewish resistance coming so *late*, it came *much sooner* than that of other oppressed peoples."[28] However, these occasional indirect responses were the exception among the Yiddish historians.

The principal defense by the Yiddish historians to the accusation of Jewish passivity was to explain the obstacles that prevented armed resistance. At a time when the dominant tropes of Jewish public discourse on the Holocaust were "destruction and heroism" (as stated in the official name of Yad Vashem), they avoided discussion of martyrs and heroes and favored, instead, the study of everyday life. Included in their study of the daily struggle for existence under Nazi domination were the conditions that enabled or prevented effective resistance.

---

26. Hersh Smoliar, "The Lambs Were Legend—The Wolves Were Real: A new look at the charge of Jewish passivity in the Ghettoes," *Jewish Currents* (April 1959): 7–11 (translated from 1958 Yiddish original); and Israel Yefroikin (Efroykin), "The Lie of Jewish Cowardice," *The Jewish Digest* (March 1957): 17–20 (condensed translation of his 1948 "Kedushe un gvure . . . ," discussed below). The best-known early example from the more conservative wing of American Jewish publications (and written in English, not Yiddish) is Oscar Handlin, "Jewish Resistance to the Nazis," *Commentary* 34 (1962): 398–405 (responding to both Bettleheim and Hillberg).

27. Trunk, "Tsum 14tn yortog fun oyfshtand in varshever geto: vegn yidishn vidershtand in der natsi tkufe," *Unzer tsayt* (April–May 1957): 16.

28. Friedman, "Der idisher vidershtand," 89 (emphasis his).

Other historians of the time touched on these conditions only in passing. For example, Gerald Reitlinger, in his pioneering history of the Holocaust which also appeared in the tenth anniversary year of 1953, devotes significant discussion to the Warsaw Ghetto Uprising. Yet he refers briefly to just one of its impediments, the deceptive German tactic of granting temporary exemptions from deportation, which "anaesthetised the will to resist, for the individual strove to acquire and keep his scrap of paper as if it had some permanent value."[29] In succeeding decades, it continued to be customary for one or a few such issues to be raised in the course of tracing the rise of Jewish resistance, but not as a subject of its own, by most other Jewish scholars, including Raul Hilberg (1961), Shaul Esh (1962), Yehuda Bauer (1973), Lucy Dawidowicz (1975), and Martin Gilbert (1985).[30]

By contrast, explanations for the absence or lateness of armed resistance are the specific subject of all or a significant part of many works by the Yiddish historians over the course of their careers. The articles by Friedman and Trunk that appeared on the occasion of the tenth anniversary of the Warsaw Ghetto Uprising were not the start of their research, but its first summation. Their articles of April 1953 were devoted entirely to setting forth, categorizing, and explaining the effects of various obstacles to the mounting of armed Jewish resistance. Friedman's thoughts were further refined and condensed in an English version of 1959 that achieved renown in the posthumous collection of his writings published in 1980. The article by Trunk was the final work of his early Israeli period, and a companion piece the following month was his first to appear in New

---

29. Gerald Reitlinger, *The Final Solution: The Attempt to Exterminate the Jews of Europe: 1939–1945* (New York, 1953), 260.

30. Raul Hilberg, *The Destruction of the European Jews* (Chicago, 1961), 1030–31 (on collective responsibility); Shaul Esh, "The Dignity of the Destroyed: Towards a Definition of the Period of the Holocaust," *Judaism* 2, no. 11 (1962): 99–111; reprinted in *The Catastrophe of European Jewry*, ed. Yisrael Gutman and Livia Rothkirchen (Jerusalem, 1976), 360 (on Nazi deceptions); Yehuda Bauer, *They Chose Life: Jewish Resistance in the Holocaust* (New York, 1973), 32 (on lack of arms and outside help; confidence in Allied victory) and 36 (on Nazi deception); Lucy S. Dawidowicz, *The War Against the Jews, 1933–1945* (New York, 1975), 321 (on isolation of the Lodz Ghetto); and Martin Gilbert, *The Holocaust: A History of the Jews of Europe during the Second World War* (New York, 1985), 484 (on family responsibility, in a single quotation).

York. This second article was devoted entirely to contrasting the opinions that had already been expressed by leading Jewish historians and public figures, prominent among them Dworzecki and Blumental.[31] Trunk reiterated and expanded these thoughts in his overview of Holocaust history for the Yiddish encyclopedia in 1966, concluding: "The wonder is not why the Jewish population, in conditions without precedent in human history, did not resist" but that "they found in themselves the physical strength and moral heroism to go out and fight against the largest and most savage military machine in modern history."[32] The importance of this issue for Trunk may be seen in his having selected only one portion of his Yiddish history of the Lodz Ghetto for separate publication in English during his lifetime—the chapter on the conditions that prevented armed resistance.[33]

The many other thoughts by Yiddish historians on this theme appear in articles and book chapters ranging in date from 1945 to 1981. However, these arose in two distinct waves. The first, commencing in 1945 and cresting by 1953, consists largely of the Yiddish historians' attempts to respond to the internal dialogue of the survivor community and its anguished question: How could this happen—*to us*? The second wave came in response to the revelations of Jewish victimhood that were given wider public currency during the televised trial of Adolf Eichmann (April to August 1961) and the subsequent publication of Hannah Arendt's trial dispatches in which she attacked "the submissive meekness with which Jews went to their death" (notwithstanding her assertion that the Jews had resisted no less than other peoples under Nazi occupation).[34] In the early 1960s, Arendt's accusations, together with those of Bruno Bettleheim, who claimed that the "Jews

---

31. Trunk quotes from Dworzecki's article, "Un efsher vet geshen a nes? . . . ," *Kiem* (January 1948): 77–78, as it was incorporated into *Yerusholayim d'lite* (Paris, 1948), 85–88. I have been unable to identify the unnamed work by Blumental from which Trunk quotes at length (and praises Blumental's "penetrating analysis") and so have quoted it from this article by Trunk.

32. Trunk, "Der farnikhtungs-protses fun eyropeyishn yidntum in der natsi-tkufe," *Algemeyne entsiklopedye,* vol. Yidn VII (New York, 1966), 15.

33. Trunk, "Note: Why Was There No Armed Resistance Against the Nazis in the Lodz Ghetto?" *Jewish Social Studies* XLIII, nos. 3-4 (Summer–Autumn 1981): 329–34; translation of chapter VIII of *Lodzsher geto* (1962).

34. Hannah Arendt, "Eichmann in Jerusalem—I," *The New Yorker* (February 16, 1963): 42.

marched themselves into death,"[35] and Raul Hilberg, who argued that the Jews had "unlearned the art of resistance,"[36] formed a trio in condemnation of the alleged complicity of the Jews in their own destruction. This second wave of responses, whether in Yiddish or other venues, bears at times the more didactic tone of informing an audience outside the community of survivors about the details of Jewish existence under Nazi rule.

In more recent decades, it has become routine to commence discussions of Jewish resistance with a recital of the many impediments to its success. A prominent example is Nechama Tec's 1997 discussion of "facts, omissions, and distortions" in the study of Jewish resistance (republished in 2014). Notably, the section titled, "What Conditions Promote Resistance? Which of These Conditions Were Available to East European Jewry?" relies almost exclusively on the 1959 article by Friedman, quoted from the posthumous collection of his writings.[37] Most recently, in 2015, an anthology whose title conveys the specific theme—*How Was it Possible?*—includes a chapter reprinted from Trunk's *Judenrat*.[38] Whether or not the trend may be traceable to a gradual transference of the Yiddish historians' works to the English-speaking world, it appears that their desired result has been realized to a degree. Patrick Henry, for example, in the introduction to his 2014 anthology on Jewish resistance, declares that "the myth of Jewish passivity during the Holocaust has been thoroughly discredited in the scholarly world" (if not yet "in the popular mentality"), a point he supports but without directly citing any of the Yiddish historians.[39]

It remains the case that few of the Yiddish historians' writings about the impediments to armed resistance are available in English. For this

---

35. Bruno Bettelheim, *The Informed Heart: Autonomy in a Mass Age* (New York, 1960), 300.

36. Raul Hilberg, *The Destruction of the European Jews* (Chicago, 1961), 667.

37. Nechama Tec, *Jewish Resistance: Facts, Omissions, and Distortions* (Miles Lerman Center for the Study of Jewish Resistance, United States Holocaust Memorial Museum, 1997). See notes 54, 55, 56, 58, and 63. (The article also cites works by Blumental, Dworzecki, Kermish, and Trunk.) Republished in *Jewish Resistance Against the Nazis*, ed. Patrick Henry (Washington, DC, 2014), 40–70.

38. Trunk, ["Indirect Rule"] reprint of chapter 4 of *Judenrat* in Peter Hayes, *How Was It Possible? A Holocaust Reader* (Lincoln, 2015), 336–48.

39. Patrick Henry, "Introduction," *Jewish Resistance Against the Nazis* (Washington, DC, 2014), xiii.

reason, I have selected their chief responses to the "Question of Questions" for the following thematic summary. One purpose is to demonstrate the early origin, topical breadth, and persistence of their efforts to combat an accusation they considered shameful and false. Of perhaps greater interest to Jewish historiography is that these writers speak from the joint perspectives of historian and survivor in choosing the topics and materials to be shared. When dealing with such seemingly objective matters as the indispensability of arms for the mounting of armed resistance, they provide an internal view of Jewish concerns and reactions that is often available to historians only through the assimilation of otherwise less accessible personal accounts. I have tended toward their more revealing passages. To convey their thoughts in unmediated form—while also making available related statements by the same or other historians—I have quoted directly from a representative sampling and then cited similar instances in the footnotes. The themes are organized into three categories: German Actions, Surrounding Conditions, and Jewish Responses.

I. German Actions. Whereas German-oriented historians might be expected to investigate the measures taken to prevent Jewish resistance through reference to reports of German intelligence or of decisions taken in the field, the Yiddish historians, in their wish to write Holocaust history from the Jewish perspective, directed their attention to the ways in which the Jews in Nazi-imposed ghettos experienced the various tactics of repression.

Collective Responsibility: Kermish indicates that "the Nazis applied the principle of collective responsibility in all cases of resistance," declaring: "Those in favor of active resistance were faced with a tragic dilemma: did they have the right to expose to certain death people who would otherwise survive?"[40] Writing immediately after the Eichmann trial, and

---

40. Kermish, "Der khurbn," in *Pyetrkov tribunalski un umgegnt / Pyetrkov Tribunalski veha-sevivah*, ed. Yankev Malts and Naftoli Lau (Tel Aviv, 1965), Yiddish 772; Hebrew 4; "The Destruction of the Jewish Community of Piotrków by the Nazis during World War II," trans. P. Wollman (Tel Aviv, 1965; see bibliography), reprinted in *A Tale of One City: Piotrków Trybunalski*, ed. Ben Giladi (New York, 1991), 352. Kermish quotes Ringelblum in his "Emmanuel Ringelblum's Notes hitherto Unpublished," 178, 180; as does Blumental in his "Sixteen Years after the Ghetto Rising," *Yad Vashem Bulletin* 6–7 (June 1960): 13. See also Trunk, "Di problem vidershtand," 180 (note).

the appearance of Hilberg's and Arendt's accusations of 2,000 years of ingrained Jewish passivity, Blumental finds not a failure of self-defense but fulfillment of a moral obligation: "In the course of long generations the sense of responsibility was implanted in the hearts of Jewish children.... It was because of this sense of responsibility, to a very considerable extent, that events took the course they did." He then cites a rare example of active resistance in which he says the young people from the town of Lenin (near Pinsk) were ready to revolt or escape, but "continued to suffer for many months until they finally heard that the Jews of their town had been massacred.... Three hundred of them successfully reached the forest."[41]

Debilitation: Trunk observes that the Jews were "'prepared' through hunger, terror, and demoralization to willingly let be done with them what the Germans demanded."[42] He quotes Blumental's observations that the changed demographic structure in the ghettos had reduced the number of men capable of fighting, that the inhabitants were physically weakened by hunger and sickness, and that they had a lessened "psychological capability for resistance as a result of both the physical and spiritual situations created by the Germans in the ghettos."[43] Trunk, too, addresses the claims by Hilberg and Arendt: "Frankly, I do not believe that one can interpret the lack of resistance, or its inadequacy or its brevity, as a specifically Jewish phenomenon conditioned by 2,000 years of Jewish compliance and passivity," but rather, that Jewish behavior mirrored that of civilian populations in the occupied countries and "was the result of a deliberate policy carried out by the Nazis—and which they achieved with considerable success—to paralyze the subjugated peoples' will to resist."[44]

---

41. Blumental. "Accepted Ideas—and Active Resistance to the Nazi Regime," *Yad Vashem Bulletin* 12 (December 1962): 42 and 44; abbreviated Yiddish version, "Di traditsyonele dertsyung un der kamf kegn natsizm," *Lebns-fragn* 196–97 (July–August 1968): 13. See also Trunk, "Letters from Readers: Jewish Resistance," *Commentary* (August 1962): 160; and Ringelblum quoted by Blumental, "Sixteen Years after the Ghetto Rising," 13.

42. Trunk, "Yidisher umkum un vidershtand," 3.

43. Trunk, "Di problem vidershtand," 256.

44. Trunk, "Letters from Readers," 161. See also Trunk, "Note: Why Was There No Armed Resistance," 330 (on the removal of the young, healthy male population from the Lodz Ghetto); and Blumental, "Introduction to Individual Chapters." in *ha-Meri vehamered be-geto Varshah/Resistance and Revolt in the Warsaw Ghetto: A Documentary History*, ed. Blumental and Kermish (Jerusalem, 1965), xlv.

Deception: Trunk writes of the German tactic of forcing Jews who were newly deported from ghettos to "labor camps" to write encouraging letters to those who remained in the ghetto to inform them that families were together and were provided with good food. "These letters naturally evoked an optimistic attitude among many. Being condemned to destruction, they still could not accept the idea of the unavoidable end and they latched onto the least illusion."[45] Discussing the early period of the Jewish Councils, Blumental says "the slogan 'Jewish autonomy'—a status for which enlightened Jews had long fought—was able to deceive and lead many astray,"[46] not least the leader of the Warsaw Ghetto, Adam Czerniaków, who until the last moment "received reassuring replies to his questions from the German authorities: they had no information about deportation plans."[47]

Disorientation: Kermish describes the Jews in the ghettos as living in "a constant state of siege,"[48] subject to the "lightning-quick tempo of German actions."[49] According to Trunk, "No day was like another. Varied, disorienting, and stunning German orders in a short timeframe continually rained down on the heads of the ghetto residents and made it impossible to formulate a plan of action."[50]

Divide and Rule: As early as 1945, Friedman analyzes the internal social dynamics of the ghettos and concludes, "The principle of 'divide and rule' [teyl un hersh] was implemented to cause conflict between the various groups of the Jewish population, bestowing a certain immunity on

---

45. Trunk, *Lodzsher geto* (New York, 1962), 468; quoted from *Łódź Ghetto: A History*, trans. and ed. Robert Moses Shapiro (Bloomington, 2006), 397.

46. Blumental, "Tsum 15-tn yortog fun varshever geto-oyfshtand," *Lebns-fragn* 80–81 (April–May 1958): 5. See similarly his "Shuldik tsi nisht shuldik? Tsu der frage vegn der rol fun di yuden-ratn in der hitler-tkufe," *Folk un velt* (March 1968): 7. On other deceptions, see Friedman, "Vi s'halt mit di yidn in poyln," *Eynikeyt* (September 1945): 11; Blumental, "Vos hobn mir gelernt?" *Lebns-fragn* 323–24 (March–April 1979): 6; and Kermish, "Di emese organizatorn fun geto-oyfshtand," *Yerusholayimer almanakh* 4 (1975): 11; "Meholele ha-Mered," *Yedi'ot Yad va-Shem* 19–20 (May 1959): 4.

47. Blumental, "A Martyr or a Hero? Reflections on the Diary of Adam Czerniaków," *Yad Vashem Studies* VII (1968): 166.

48. Kermish, "Der khurbn [in Piotrków Trybunalski]," 772 [English 352].

49. Kermish, "Di emese organizatorn," 11; "Meholele ha-Mered," 4.

50. Trunk, "Di problem vidershtand," 256. See also Blumental, "Tsum problem vi di yidn hobn zikh farhaltn," 361.

'privileged' Jewish groups (skilled workers, artisans, professionals, Jewish police, Judenrat) who were later, like everyone, cynically and brutally murdered."[51] Trunk adds that, in a situation "where saving oneself temporarily could *only* come at the expense of others," the Nazis "deliberately strove to intensify the antagonisms and social conflicts in the ghettos. This was one of the means of disarming the ghetto populace, weakening the feeling of national solidarity in order to deal with divided, mutually antagonistic groups."[52]

II. Surrounding Conditions. The Yiddish historians coincide with later Holocaust historians in general in identifying two principal factors that limited the potential for active Jewish resistance: the lack of arms and the difficulty of obtaining them.

Lack of Arms: Trunk reports that, leading up to the first revolt in the Warsaw Ghetto in January 1943, the Jewish fighters had been able to obtain only ten old pistols on the Polish black market to smuggle into the ghetto.[53] Blumental writes of their "uncountable disappointments" in seeking weapons and that "in a time of highly developed technology," the shortage of weapons "psychologically defeated the Jews."[54] Kermish describes the difficult process of obtaining arms from the Polish underground and, not surprisingly, indicates that the "problem of supplying arms to the ghetto was one of the major concerns of the leaders of the revolt as well as its rank and file."[55] Dworzecki argues, "one underestimates the importance of possessing weapons. One can say: weapons call forth the fighting spirit."[56]

Lack of Sources: Friedman indicates that, although Jews were at times able to buy small arms on the Polish black market, including "rusty revolvers and rifles from Polish peasants who had buried them," in general,

---

51. Friedman, "Vi s'halt mit di yidn in poyln," 11.
52. Trunk, "Yidisher umkum un vidershtand," 4 (emphasis his).
53. Trunk, "Di problem vidershtand," 255. On the same, see Friedman, "Der idisher vidershtand," 91–92.
54. Blumental, "Tsum problem vi di yidn hobn zikh farhaltn," 365.
55. Kermish, "Arms Used by the Warsaw Ghetto Fighters," *Yad Washem Bulletin* 3 (July 1958): 5–9.
56. Dworzecki, "Vos mir hobn di kinder nit gelernt . . . ," *Idisher kemfer* (November 23, 1945): 12–13.

"there was considerable difficulty in obtaining arms."[57] He notes that the Polish countryside (with its large forests) was better suited to Jewish resistance than Western Europe, "but unfortunately not the surrounding people,"[58] whom he claims had adopted the new "jungle morality" introduced by the Germans.[59] Friedman also observes that the official Polish resistance had at times rejected Jewish partisans, while the more favorable left-wing groups "were still very weak during the years of 1941 to 1943, when they were most needed."[60] More pointedly, Trunk writes of the "vicious attitude on the part of the surrounding population (with the exception of certain left-democratic circles, some sectors of the intelligentsia, and Catholic spiritual leaders),"[61] which he contends was aggravated by German prewar and wartime propaganda and by permitting Poles to acquire the possessions left behind when Jews were forced into ghettos.[62] Dworzecki describes the impossibility of resistance in the Vilna Ghetto, "surrounded by a population of Lithuanians and Poles—who would not help in the fight—and who would even hand over the fighters to the enemy."[63] Trunk, Friedman, and Blumental concur that the least favorable location for resistance was the Lodz Ghetto (in the western portion of Poland annexed by Germany), where the Germans had expelled and replaced the local Polish population with ethnic Germans from other regions.[64] In Lodz, they were able to seal the ghetto most effectively—leading Trunk to conclude, "There could, therefore, be no talk of bringing weapons in from the outside."[65]

III. Jewish Responses. Recognizing that the accusation of Jewish passivity focused specifically on Jewish behavior, the Yiddish historians'

---

57. Friedman, "Der idisher vidershtand," 92.
58. Friedman, "In vald un feld," *Idisher kemfer* (May 15, 1953): 12.
59. Friedman, "Parshes varshe," *Di tsukunft* (April 1950): 181.
60. Friedman, "Der idisher vidershtand," 93. On the difficulties faced by Jewish partisans, see also Trunk, "Yidisher umkum un vidershtand," 4.
61. Trunk, "Di problem vidershtand," 255.
62. Trunk, "Yidisher umkum un vidershtand," 3.
63. Dworzecki, "Un efsher vet geshen a nes? . . . ," *Kiem* (January 1948): 78.
64. Trunk, *Lodzsher geto*, 464–65; *Łódź Ghetto*, 394–95. Blumental, "A literarishe geshikhte fun lodzsher-geto," 238 (quoting the surviving ghetto author Isaiah Spiegel).
65. Ibid. (Trunk), Yiddish 465, English 395. On the importance of Jewish contacts outside the ghetto, see Blumental, "20 yor nokhn geto-oyfshtand in byalistok," *Lebns-fragn* 140 (August 1963): 8.

search for explanations for the absence or lateness of armed resistance led to their more penetrating (and at times subjective and personal) observations of internal Jewish issues, ranging from the practical to the psychological.

Lack of Leaders: Commencing with the first day of the German invasion, Polish Jews were faced with a loss (and not a failure) of leadership, as the Yiddish historians would emphasize. As for the Jewish men who would have the military skills for armed resistance, Friedman points out, "The trained Jewish military men were mobilized in part in 1939 (Polish-German war), partly in 1941 by the Soviet government, and were mostly away with the military or captured." (An example among the Yiddish historians themselves was Dworzecki, who was mobilized as a military doctor, captured by the Germans near Lwów, and then escaped and returned home to find himself in the Vilna Ghetto.) Regarding Jewish civic leaders, Friedman writes that some fled in 1939, others were arrested and expelled during the Soviet occupation of Eastern Poland (1939–41), and that "everywhere that the Germans entered they began with an extermination action against Jewish intellectuals and the remaining political leadership" (whose names they had often assembled prior to the invasion). As a result, Friedman concludes, "in most cases, leadership passed to new, untrained, young elements."[66] And, of course, it is well known that the resistance leaders were invariably the new, young leaders of the Jewish political movements. Blumental put forth the theory that many Jews chose not to step into positions of leadership in the belief that the Germans would target only leaders and that safety lay in being among the masses, as no one had ever tried to exterminate an entire people.[67]

Loyalty to Laws: "As strange as it may sound," Friedman writes, "there was a large number of people among the Jewish population for whom respect for governmental order was so strong they could not free themselves from a certain feeling of duty and loyalty, even to the evil Nazi regime." He indicates that many saw in the Judenrat and the Jewish police

---

66. Friedman, "Der idisher vidershtand," 92. On the flight of Jewish leaders from the Nazis, see also Blumental, foreword to Israel Tabakman, *Mayne iberlebungen (unter natsishe okupatsye in belgye)* (Tel Aviv, 1957), ix–xvi.

67. Blumental, "Tsum problem vi di yidn hobn zikh farhaltn," 364.

"the embodiment of a legitimate order."[68] Trunk presents the same line of argument, saying, "Apart from those trained for active resistance by party youth groups," most Jews had "a tradition of loyalty to laws and governments," to which he adds, "as their only means of opposition they used the [traditional] method of intercession [*shtadlones*], and brought up their children in this spirit"[69] (here portraying as a civic virtue the behavior condemned by Arendt as an ingrained habit of accommodation). As Blumental says of the imposed Jewish leadership, "Simply, the Judenrat began its work in a world that it knew from before the war and with means well tested in that world."[70] He continues, "In fact, the only ones who obeyed the Hitler-laws were the Judenräte and the Jews who believed in the Judenräte . . . ," while the laws "were only a pretense, under which the Jews were in fact outside of every law!"[71]

Jewish Illusions: The Yiddish historians repeatedly touched on three illusions that delayed the Jews' turn from credulity to resistance: the belief in German civilization, in German rationality, and in world opinion. In his first article on Jewish resistance, Trunk writes that it was "impossible to believe that a civilized state in the heart of Europe would apply this system of physical annihilation to a peaceful innocent population," adding: "No one wanted to believe this dreadful secret, despite all the warning sounds that passed from ghetto to ghetto." He quotes Blumental's further assertion that "the Jews could not believe . . . that the civilized world would look upon it with indifference."[72] In writing about "the development of the idea of self-defense," Blumental says, "there were people among the intelligentsia (especially the jurists) who hoped that so far as the civilian population in the occupied country was concerned, the Germans would have to observe international obligations and consider world opinion." He explains, "This belief, widespread in Poland and in the other

---

68. Friedman, "Parshes varshe," 181.
69. Trunk, "Di problem vidershtand," 257.
70. Blumental, "Der lubliner yudenrat," *Kol Lublin—Lubliner shtime* 2 (November 22, 1964): 11.
71. Blumental, "Shuldik tsi nisht shuldik?," 10.
72. Trunk, "Yidisher umkum un vidershtand," 3; his quote of Blumental appears in Trunk, "Di problem vidershtand," 256, and he reiterates this point in his "Letters from Readers," 160.

occupied countries, was gradually dispelled," but he argues, it "can explain to a large extent the tardiness of Jewish reaction, which came only after the majority of the Jewish population had been exterminated by the Nazis and the strength of the Jewish resistance had been weakened."[73] Within the closed world of the ghettos, the Jews and their leaders encountered the further illusion of "rescue through work,"[74] which arose from their experience of German officials who preferred to profit from Jewish labor than allow Jews to be deported. As Trunk describes it, the Judenräte "with good or evil intentions" also spread the illusion that "one could save oneself by working for the German war-machine."[75] And he offers the general conclusion that "Jewish psychological readiness for armed resistance" was paralyzed by "faith and illusions that prevailed among broad circles, in almost all ghettos."[76]

"Treacherous Optimism": The Yiddish historians speak of two related forms of unwarranted optimism that worked against the possibility of armed resistance. One was personal, the other general. In his 1946 essay, "On our Treacherous Optimism," and again in his 1948 essay, "And Perhaps a Miracle Will Occur" (using the traditional Jewish term *nes* for "miracle"), Dworzecki writes about "the fatal belief in a miracle" that led individuals to believe that even in the face of death, "the miracle could still happen to you personally." He enumerates: "They won't catch *you*," or, "Even on the way to Ponar, *you* might still be able to run away," and once at the graveside, "could still experience the miracle of not being shot." He concludes that, "if there were so many chances for each one to personally rescue himself from death—why then should he think of resistance?," when resistance "in the eyes of most ghetto dwellers" meant "resignation from life, going certainly and openly to face death."[77] More generally, the historians write of the certainty of German defeat. Blumental says,

---

73. Blumental, *ha-Meri veha-mered be-geto Varshah*, xxxvii.
74. On Mordechai Rumkowski of the Lodz Ghetto, see Friedman, *Roads to Extinction* (New York, 1980), 343; and Trunk, *Lodzsher geto*, 359–75; *Łódź Ghetto*, 313–23.
75. Trunk, "Yidisher umkum un vidershtand," 4.
76. Trunk, "Di problem vidershtand," 255.
77. Dworzecki, "Vegn unzer farfirerishn optimizm," *Idisher kemfer* (March 8, 1946): 10; "Un efsher vet geshen a nes? . . . ," 77–78 (emphases his). The same hope for a miracle is noted by Blumental, *Sefer borshtshiv* (Tel Aviv, 1960), 233. On Dworzecki's last point, see also his, "Un efsher vet geshen a nes? . . . ," 78.

"people were convinced that World War II would end after the large-scale offensive of the Western armies in the Spring of 1940," and then again after the Soviet Union entered the war in June 1941.[78] He writes, further, that "everyone without exception was convinced the Hitler regime was a passing phenomenon, that ultimately it would be beaten and ousted, that 'salvation is indeed near.'"[79] Dworzecki relates, "the end of the war was imminent—so believed every Jew, and so he solemnly believed from the first day of the war," and then, once the Soviet Union had entered the war, it was only a matter of "a few weeks (perhaps four weeks? Perhaps six?)." And that any day, word might come of "a revolution in Germany," or "a coup by the general staff," or that "Hitler died suddenly or was murdered."[80] Friedman touches on the same illusion, saying, "The Jewish conviction that justice was bound to triumph and that the root of evil would vanish, remained indestructible . . . . This optimism did not stem from reality."[81] Trunk argues that, to the end, the same illusion prevailed, but that by July and August 1944 German reverses led to the certainty of German defeat and to a new "hope to hold on and survive," such that it would have been "psychologically impossible to motivate a mass that was caught up by such feelings to enter into a hopeless struggle that in the given circumstances could conclude in only one fashion—destruction with a heroic death."[82]

Unpreparedness: In a single respect only, two of the Yiddish historians take on themselves, and the Jews generally, acknowledgment of the claim that they entered the Nazi period peculiarly unprepared. In his 1945 essay, "What We did not Teach Our Children," Dworzecki writes that the children, wives, and old people in the ghettos knew that their fathers (or husbands or sons) "would not protect them" because they "were not prepared to fight, did not have anything to fight with, and did not know how to fight with an armed enemy."[83] Blumental speaks more broadly,

---

78. Blumental, *ha-Meri veha-mered be-geto Varshah*, xxxvii–xxxviii.
79. Blumental, "Shuldik tsi nisht shuldik?," 10.
80. Dworzecki, "Un efsher vet geshen a nes? . . . ," 77.
81. Friedman, "Etishe un sotsyale problemen fun unzer katastrofe in der natsi tkufe," *Idisher kemfer* (September 8, 1950, Rosh Hashanah): 54.
82. Trunk, *Lodzsher geto*, 466; quoted from *Łódź Ghetto*, 395.
83. Dworzecki, "Vos mir hobn di kinder nit gelernt," 12.

saying that the Germans prepared by stages for years, but not the Jews: "We Jews, throughout the entire world," were unprepared, "and this unpreparedness cost us unnecessary blood."[84] On two occasions, Blumental speaks of himself alone. In 1958, he writes, "How could I, just a few years before our great catastrophe, write and teach our masses such things as what constitutes a 'beautiful sound' [in Polish pronunciation] . . . instead of shouting at the top of my lungs: Jews, a misfortune is about to befall you!"[85] A decade later, he writes, "I feel guilty for them, my former students . . . for the *crime* that we—teachers and educators—committed against them in not preparing them for life, for what awaited them . . . immediately after the vacation of 1939," and adopting the form of the traditional Jewish prayer of atonement, he concludes, "And for that sin [*het*], I beg you—forgiveness!"[86]

The Response

In parallel with this defensive campaign to explain the impediments to Jewish resistance, there was also an offensive campaign to redefine "resistance" in the realistic context of Jewish life under Nazi occupation. Unlike the defensive campaign, which arose spontaneously among all of the Yiddish historians, this more daring initiative appears to have originated largely with a single historian, Dworzecki. As will be seen, this effort, too, experienced an earlier phase arising within the internal discourse of the survivor community and a later, post-Eichmann phase oriented in part toward the wider Jewish and non-Jewish worlds.

As a general concept, "resistance" to the Nazis was—and often still is—considered only in terms of armed or physical acts of resistance, whether carried out by Jews or others. Dworzecki understood that physical violence was generally impossible for the Jews but that other forms of countering the Nazis were the means by which some Jews were able to prolong their lives and, without which there would have been virtually

---

84. Blumental, foreword to Israel Tabakman, x; and "Der zin fun varshever geto-oyfshtand," *Lebns-fragn* 148–49 (April–May 1964): 4.

85. Blumental, "'Lubliner shtime' (a bintl zikhroynes)," *Lebns-fragn* 83 (July 1958): 10.

86. Blumental, "Der takhles fun lernen . . . ," *Lebns-fragn* 210–11 (September–October 1969): 10–11 (emphasis his).

no survivors of the Holocaust. Dworzecki's innovation was to redefine resistance to include the everyday actions by which most Jews attempted to thwart the Nazis' murderous intent.

In redefining Jewish "resistance," Dworzecki used the German and French concepts of "spiritual resistance" (*geistiger Widerstand* and *Résistance spirituelle*), which he expanded in scope from the individual to the collective, from the potential to the actual, and from the religious to the secular. Simultaneously, he transformed the nascent Jewish concept of "the sanctification of life" (*Kidush ha-Hayim*, articulated in the Warsaw Ghetto) from the theological to the practical. Both of these he joined to create a new concept of Jewish resistance that would come to be known as *Amidah* ("standing up against"), encompassing every form of Jewish resistance against the Nazis. He published the first statement of his argument at the early date of June 1946.

Dworzecki's redefinition of resistance is important for its content and for its timing. His all-encompassing view has become increasingly normative in the study of Jewish resistance, and he has received increasing recognition for his contribution to the field. However, such recognition invariably points to the paper he presented at the 1968 Yad Vashem Conference on Manifestations of Jewish Resistance, which first appeared in English in 1971 under the title, "The Day-To-Day Stand [*Amidah*] of the Jews."[87] The conference's focus on resistance in all its forms may rightly be seen as a reaction to the Eichmann trial (at which Dworzecki also testified) and to the accusations of Arendt, Hilberg, or Bettleheim.

Although Dworzecki's conference paper is often cited as an early example of the study of nonviolent forms of Jewish resistance, it represents the culmination of his thoughts on unarmed resistance. The actual timeline of Dworzecki's contribution is that his first, seminal article that urged recognition of all forms of unarmed Jewish resistance, "*Farshidn zenen geven di vegn*" (Varied were the Ways) appeared in Yiddish in June 1946

---

87. Dworzecki, "The Day-To-Day Stand of the Jews," in *Jewish Resistance During the Holocaust: Proceedings of the Conference on Manifestations of Jewish Resistance, Jerusalem, April 7–11, 1968* (Jerusalem, 1971), 152–81 (Hebrew version, 1970; see bibliography for publishing history, at 1968).

in the Zionist journals *Unzer vort* in Paris and *Idisher kemfer* in New York. This was followed in 1948 by an extended excerpt in Shmuel Niger's Yiddish anthology, *Kidush hashem*, and a verbatim Hebrew translation in Simon Rawidowicz's journal *Metsudah*—with a final appearance in his own 1956 book of collected Yiddish essays in Hebrew translation.[88] Therefore, his article should be read in the context of the early internal dialogue of the survivor community, of which it was a part and to whom it was addressed—and not as a reaction to later events.

The article is written in the style of a prose poem, slightly more than 2,000 words in length. Dworzecki sets forth his argument by acknowledging the "stories of active Jewish fighting" that have come to constitute the "epic of Jewish resistance in the ghettos, forests, and fronts—the epic that blinds with its tragic beauty," followed by a short list of the impediments to active resistance. He then introduces the central theme of his article: "Do we not commit a great wrong against our murdered fathers and mothers, brothers and wives, when we speak only of the active, armed fight in the ghettos—and we do not recount the other means of Jewish struggle?" The substance of the work is thereafter devoted to the "varied" forms of unarmed resistance observed by him in the Vilna Ghetto, presented in six "stanzas":

The building of a "Jewish underground city" of bunkers and tunnels in which Jews hid or attempted to escape;

The life-threatening task of smuggling food into the ghetto by "abandoned children," "lone mothers," and the "thousands of brother Jews" (who worked for German industries outside the ghetto);

The inventiveness by which skilled individuals converted ordinary materials into such necessities as heaters, clothing, tools, cleanser, and medical instruments—to make "endurable this unbearable life";

The "Jewish doctors, nurses and sanitary workers" who, virtually without implements or medications, prevented or stopped the spread of epidemics under conditions of ghetto life;

---

88. Dworzecki, "Farshidn zenen geven di vegn," *Unzer vort* (June 21, 1946): unnumbered third page; see bibliography for publication history. In the 1956 version, the final portion was shortened to omit references to Jewish weakness and calls for future strength that may have seemed anachronistic after the establishment of the State of Israel.

The teachers who created schools and devoted themselves to their children, the writers who recorded events "so the time of barbarism will not be forgotten," and the poets, artists, actors, and choral singers who "produced cultural resistance against the German intent to break them spiritually before their murder"; and

The rabbis who struggled to continue religious observance and "created moral resistance against the German intent to break the Jewish spirit."

With respect to each of these forms of resistance, Dworzecki invokes the judgment of history. He asks whether the future historian will regard the building of bunkers as "how the Jews ran away from the fight"; whether in smuggling food, "the Jews in the time of their fateful murder risked their lives for bread and not for their honor"; and whether "it is madness to write poems, and put on theater, and teach children facing death." To each of these he imagines a "quiet request to the Jewish writer of history" from all of those who struggled: "On the day when you seal the book of Jewish resistance, ask yourself whether in our deeds there also lies resistance to the Germans' murderous intent."

The article is a preview of the principal section of Dworzecki's forthcoming history of the Vilna Ghetto. This section is titled "Varied were the Ways of Struggle," and toward the end of it, he concludes: "Varied were the ways of Jewish resistance in the ghetto: it found expression in cultural, moral, religious, economic, sanitary, and political struggle; and it was later more clearly revealed in the partisan fighting movement in the ghetto."[89]

Dworzecki attempted to create an academic curriculum for the study of Jewish resistance in accordance with this conception in his 1949 proposal for the establishment of a research institute in Holocaust studies at the Hebrew University. His proposal contains only two substantive sections, one devoted to Jewish resistance and the other to German crimes. Mirroring his recent writings, the topics listed for study in the section titled "Manifestations of the Jewish Struggle" are spiritual, medical, and political struggle, followed by armed struggle, and ending with "Life in the bunkers and outside the ghettos."[90] By comparison, Friedman's

---

89. Dworzecki, *Yerusholayim d'lite*, 401.
90. See appendix in Boaz Cohen, *Israeli Holocaust Research: Birth and Evolution*, trans. Agnes Vazsonyi (Abingdon, 2013), 279–81.

contemporaneous "Outline of Program for Holocaust Research" (begun in 1945 and completed in 1950) includes all of the aspects except for the medical aspect, but forms of unarmed resistance occupy only a small portion of his much broader research agenda.[91]

Before proceeding, it should be noted that several terms commonly used in connection with Jewish unarmed resistance—including "spiritual," "passive," and "nonviolent," as well as the phrase "the sanctification of life"—have had and retain distinct meanings in this and other contexts of resistance. In much scholarly writing on the Holocaust, particularly in Israel, such words have yielded to the all-encompassing term, *Amidah*. However, Dworzecki's innovation was conceptual, not terminological, and none of these terms appears in his 1946 article. Apart from *Amidah*, the expression that has come to be most associated with Dworzecki and his broad view of resistance is "spiritual resistance," and it is the evolving meaning of this term that has special relevance for Dworzecki's thought.

"Spiritual resistance" was the principal, if not exclusive, description for unarmed opposition to Nazi domination in use by Jews (and non-Jews) before and during World War II. It connoted the perceived possibilities and, perhaps more importantly, the perceived limitations of unarmed resistance to the Nazis. What, then, was the semantic setting into which Dworzecki stepped when he commenced to redefine the scope of spiritual resistance? Let us consider a few of the better-known examples, all arising in the context of the German expression *geistiger Widerstand* and, to a lesser extent, the French term *Résistance spirituelle*.

A precursor was the June 1933 lecture at the University of Basel by the non-Jewish German philologist Harold Fuchs, titled, "Spiritual Resistance against Rome in the Ancient World." He discusses the resistance of Greek and other writers of the ancient world, including the rabbis, to the intellectual hegemony of Rome through works that preserved their own religious worldviews and predicted the end of Roman rule. He indicates that even after the Roman destruction of Jerusalem and the Temple, the Jews' "faith in their own election [by God] and the confident expectation that Rome would ultimately meet its own downfall gave to their

---

91. Friedman, "Outline of Program for Holocaust Research," in *Roads to Extinction*, 571–76.

[spiritual] resistance a scarcely ever waning strength."[92] It is, of course, difficult to imagine the reading aloud of this and similar passages in June 1933 without an eye toward current affairs (during the third month of increasing anti-Jewish restrictions in Germany). The phrase "spiritual resistance" does not occur in the text of the lecture, but only in the title, suggesting its possible late addition (perhaps as late as the first publication in 1938) with an intended double meaning. The resistance portrayed by Fuchs is an expectation of deliverance, grounded in faith.

During World War II, Thomas Mann delivered a series of anti-Nazi lectures from his exile in America that were broadcast to Germany by the British Broadcasting Company, addressed to "German listeners!" (*Deutsche Hörer!*). In August 1941, he informs his listeners that "a kind of spiritual, mental or intellectual sabotage 'of the bloody and abysmal adventure that Hitler has plunged you Germans into,' had already begun . . . by the simple act of tuning in a forbidden frequency to hear a forbidden and exiled writer." He declares in January 1942 that he was " 'not one who calls for bloody deeds.' " Instead, this talk has been described as an attempt "to educate his countrymen toward the day when Germans would arise as one and go out into the streets shouting 'down with the war and destruction of peoples.' " Mann concludes, " 'In the moment you decide to be free, you are free.' "[93] In Mann's spiritual resistance, too, one finds a resistance of the mind, predicated here on individual moral conviction (if not religious faith)—in preparation for action, and manifest in the expectation of action.

Ernst (Akiba) Simon, the renowned scholar of Jewish thought at the Hebrew University, who assisted Martin Buber in creating the centralized

---

92. Harald Fuchs, *Der Geistige Widerstand Gegen Rom in der Antiken Welt* (1938), reprint (Berlin, 1964), 21.

93. All quotations from Alan F. Keele, "Six Authors in Search of a Character: The importance of Helmuth Hübener in post-war German literature," Guest Faculty Essay in *Perspectives–Student Journal of Germanic and Slavic Languages* 12 (Winter 2004), formerly online at http://germslav.byu.edu/perspectives/w2004.php. The author exaggerates slightly in crediting Mann with coining the term "geistiger Widerstand." On Mann's radio broadcasts in general, see Martina Hoffschulte, "*Deutsche Hörer!": Thomas Manns Rundfunkreden (1940 bis 1945) im Werkkontext* (Münster, 2004). For texts of Mann's early addresses see Thomas Mann, *Listen, Germany!: Twenty-Five Radio Messages to the German People Over BBC* (New York, 1943).

adult education program for German Jewry in the early Nazi period, discussed the program's goals after the war in his essay "Jewish Adult Education in Nazi Germany as Spiritual Resistance." He recounts that their focus was on the future, that they "hoped and believed" enough German Jews would survive the regime. He explains: "These survivors were to be prepared for that day, however near or however far off it might be, that they might witness it in their human and Jewish dignity and from then on begin a new life." Simon likens the situation of the Jews under Nazism to the "two historical levels" seen by the biblical prophets: "the imminent catastrophe and the restoration that follows it." He explains, "This was the deepest source from which was derived the spiritual and the religious resistance of some leading German Jews. It could hardly be said that they succeeded, or that they could succeed, in imbuing the masses of their followers with this conviction."[94] In this passage, one finds again a resistance of expectant waiting, but one confined to individuals capable of receiving inspiration from the example of the prophets.[95]

In the French context, a growing literature on the subject of *Résistance spirituelle* focuses on the series of clandestine wartime pamphlets titled *Cahiers du Témoignage crétien* (Booklets of Christian Witness), published by liberal Catholic theologians.[96] It "disseminated reliable information about the occupation of France and the Nazi genocide elsewhere, encouraged and exhorted French Christians to conscientious witness, and provided accurate versions of papal pronouncements,"[97] under the slogan "France, beware of losing your soul." Historians and later theologians ascribe to the *Cahiers* varying attitudes toward active

---

94. Ernst Simon, "Jewish Adult Education in Nazi Germany as Spiritual Resistance," *Leo Baeck Institute Yearbook* I (1956): 89–90. This essay previewed Simon's fuller treatment, *Aufbau im Untergang. Jüdische Erwachsenenbildung im nationalsozialistischen Deutschland als geistiger Widerstand* (Tübingen, 1959).

95. Simon was also, with Buber and Judah Magnus, a leader of the small bi-national group "Brit Shalom" in prestate Israel, which advocated accommodation rather than confrontation with the Arabs, and the question inevitably arises of possible links between their political views and their conception of spiritual resistance in contrast with those of Dworzecki, who was and remained a statist, socialist Labor Zionist.

96. For the texts, see François and Renée Bédarida, *La Résistance spirituelle 1941–1944: Les Cahiers clandestins du Témoignage chrétien* (Paris, 2001).

97. David Grumet, "Yves de Montcheuil: Action, Justice, and the Kingdom in Spiritual Resistance to Nazism," *Theological Studies* 68, no. 3 (2007): 626.

resistance (and its practitioners on the left and right and the ethics of their methods).[98] But the "spiritual resistance" associated with it is the religiously oriented mentality from which the publication flowed and which it strove to inculcate, as distinct from the practical outcomes to which it might lead.

With these examples as background, a final contrast to Dworzecki's views is found in the writings of Auschwitz survivor Viktor Frankl, the Viennese psychotherapist. Frankl is described by Lawrence Langer as having "almost single-handedly invented the idea of spiritual resistance in *Man's Search for Meaning*," Frankl's memoir of Auschwitz, first published in German in 1946.[99] One of the lines most often quoted is his description of those inmates, presumably including himself, who summoned the inner resources for survival while in Auschwitz: "Sensitive people who were used to a rich intellectual life may have suffered much pain . . . but the damage to their inner selves was less. They were able to retreat from their terrible surroundings to a life of inner riches and spiritual freedom."[100] Aside from his controversial implication that survival in Auschwitz depended largely on resolve or state of mind, one finds here, too, a spiritual resistance that is decidedly individual (and select), deriving from unspecified inner resources, and existing independently of any action that it might or might not precipitate.

Dworzecki's first writings on unarmed resistance reveal his struggle to arrive at an all-inclusive concept. He commenced writing his history of the Vilna Ghetto in late spring 1945 and completed it in November 1946,[101] during which time he prepublished several short essays and two larger chapters. By January 1946, he had completed the first major selection to be previewed. It covered the topic most personal to him, the "fight for health in the Vilna Ghetto" conducted by himself and his fellow

---

98. Ibid.; and Monique Gruber, "La Résistance spirituelle, fondement et soutien de la Résistance active. L'exemple des Cahiers clandestins du Témoignage chrétien (1941–1944)," *Revue des Sciences Religieuses* 78, no. 4 (2004): 486.

99. Lawrence L. Langer, *Admitting the Holocaust: Collected essays* (New York, 1996), 181.

100. Viktor Frankl, *Man's Search for Meaning: An Introduction to Logotherapy* (New York, 1963), 56.

101. Dworzecki, *Yerusholayim d'lite*, 20.

doctors and nurses.¹⁰² In his foreword, he devotes a paragraph to each of the forms of resistance he observed in the ghetto—including "political," "economic," "cultural," "moral," and "armed" resistance—as preface to his present topic, "medical-sanitary resistance." In his apparent search for a unifying approach, he arrives at one conclusion that would come to characterize all of his writings on Jewish resistance: "These acts of resistance acquired clearly collective forms." However, each type of resistance remained an independent expression of some as-yet unnamed larger process.

By April 1946, Dworzecki's first writing on the subject of unarmed resistance indicates his further confrontation of the problem of conceptualizing the new forms of resistance he had witnessed during the war. The second major selection of his Vilna Ghetto history to be previewed was the opening portion of his chapter, "The Cultural System in the Vilna Ghetto," which appeared in March 1946 in the journal *Parizer shriftn* (Parisian Writings; of which he was a founding coeditor). The complete chapter would include all manifestations of cultural activity: the school systems (secular, religious, technical, and musical); organized athletics; literature, art, and music (each with competitions and public presentations); scholarship and scientific work; the "House of Culture" with its library, reading room, archive, and statistical section; Sunday lecture series for working adults; theater in Yiddish and Hebrew; and the press. His opening sentence reads, "One of the most illustrious chapters in the Jewish life of the Vilna Ghetto, of Jewish spiritual resistance-activity, was the cultural system in the ghetto." At the conclusion of this introduction, he invites other surviving witnesses to "complete the testimony of the tragedy of the Vilna Ghetto in general, and of the illustrious chapter of Jewish spiritual resistance-activity in particular."¹⁰³ His repetition of the

---

102. Dworzecki, *Kamf farn gezunt in geto-vilne* (Geneva-Paris, 1946). This booklet of seventy-eight pages was, in fact, the unabridged version, published in condensed form in his *Yerusholayim d'lite*, 187–221. He later widened his discussion from the Vilna Ghetto to all of occupied Europe, summarized in "Jewish Medical resistance During the Catastrophe," in *Extermination and Resistance: Historical Records and Source Material*, vol. 1, ed. Zvi Szner (Haifa, 1958), 117–20.

103. Dworzecki, "Dos kultur-vezn in vilner geto," *Parizer shriftn* 2-3 (March 1946): 28.

awkward neologism, "spiritual resistance-activity" (*gaystiker vidershtand-tetikayt*), indicates both his deliberate construction of the term and his difficulty in confronting a concept of unarmed resistance, commonly considered static in nature, with the vision of intense activity he retained from his experience of the ghetto—hence, the joining of "activity" with "spiritual resistance."

Dworzecki resolved the seeming incongruity between his own perceptions and the prevailing view of spiritual resistance in favor of his own vision. The final version of the chapter on cultural activity reads, "If in the course of years the Vilna Jewish community bore the name *Jerusalem of Lithuania*, the Vilna Ghetto is worthy, in the cultural sense, of bearing the name *Jerusalem of the ghettos*, as a symbol of Jewish spiritual resistance under the Nazi regime."[104] In the interval of a few months, he had claimed and redefined the term "spiritual resistance" as both the name and intellectual construct of his broad view of unarmed resistance in the area of culture—consisting of *collective* as well as individual efforts; *active* engagement in addition to private moral steadfastness; and a *variety* of cultural activities extending well beyond (though including) demonstrations of religious faith and ethical standards.

To these forms of cultural or spiritual resistance, Dworzecki added the other types of unarmed resistance recognized by his article, "Varied were the Ways," to create his all-encompassing concept of Jewish unarmed resistance. The additional group includes such activities as building bunkers and smuggling food. These constructive, practical efforts he later assigned to the category of *Kidush ha-Hayim*, "the sanctification of life,"[105] introduced by Natan Eck. As is customary, Dworzecki ascribed the concept of *Kidush ha-Hayim* to Eck's account of Rabbi Isaac Nissenbaum who is said to have declared in the Warsaw Ghetto, "Once Jews practiced *Kiddush Hashem* ["the sanctification of the Holy Name" in choosing death over apostasy]; today, Jews must practice *Kiddush Hahayim*." The term and the concept of *Kidush ha-Hayim*

---

104. Dworzecki, *Yerusholayim d'lite*, 222 (emphasis his). This statement was quoted verbatim by Trunk (and attributed to "a historian and eyewitness from the Vilna Ghetto") in "Dos kultur lebn in getos" in his *Geshtaltn un gesheenishn* (Buenos Aires, 1962), 207.

105. Dworzecki, "The Day-To-Day Stand of the Jews," 379.

were popularized by Shaul Esh's well-known article, "The Dignity of the Destroyed," of 1962.[106] Like Dworzecki's "Varied were the Ways," Eck's ideas are those of a survivor in the mid-1940s. Indeed, the article in which they appear was first published—not in Hebrew in 1960 as universally stated,[107] and not in 1954 as asserted by Shaul Esh[108]—but rather in Yiddish in April 1945 on the second anniversary of the Warsaw Ghetto Uprising in the Paris journal *Unzer vort*,[109] coedited by Eck, some days before Dworzecki's liberation and a month before he would commence to publish in the same journal.

Whether Dworzecki had read or heard the idea of *Kidush ha-Hayim* directly from Eck in Paris is not apparent. Eck had introduced the idea of *Kidush ha-Hayim* with the words, "Against Hitler's will to destroy was set the Jewish will—to live." He contends, as Dworzecki would soon also, that there was a great deal to celebrate about the armed uprising of the Warsaw Ghetto, "but why *only* about the final battle and its fighters, why *only* about the armed uprising?" However, Eck proceeds to argue that "not only the heroes of April 19 died with honor, but all of our martyrs also brought us no dishonor" and that "those who seek heroes" have the duty "to speak out about our murdered masses who, after a hard, stubborn struggle, fell on the field of the world's dishonor in that bitter Jewish war"—a turn to the opposite extreme of indiscriminate sanctification with which Dworzecki would not have concurred. Two months later, Dworzecki published his essay, "Remain silent, or tell the whole truth?," regarding the positive and also negative aspects of Jewish conduct under the Nazis,[110] and many years later, he would say of Jewish conduct under the Nazis, "The duty of the historian is to reveal the historical truth . . . .

---

106. Shaul Esh, "The Dignity of the Destroyed: Towards a Definition of the Period of the Holocaust" *Judaism* 2, no. 11 (Spring 1962): 106–7.

107. The usual citation is to Eck's collection of essays (the majority translated from Yiddish originals), *ha-Toʻim be-darkhe ha-mavet* (Jerusalem, 1960), 343–47.

108. Shaul Esh, "The Dignity of the Destroyed." In endnote 16, Esh states that Eck first published on the subject of *Kiddush Hahayim* in 1954, and he speculates that this may have prompted Simon Rawidowicz's use of the term that same year.

109. Nosn Ek, "Di gefalene in yidishn krig," *Unzer vort* (April 19, 1945): 1. A singular exception appears to be Boaz Cohen in his *Israeli Holocaust Research*, 212–13.

110. See for example, Dworzecki, "Farshvaygn—oder dertseyln dem gantsn emes?" *Unzer vort* (June 22, 1945): 3.

He should not fear to be an accuser and not recoil from being a defender."[111] With regard to the concept of *Kidush ha-Hayim*, it may be said that Eck framed the problem and Dworzecki supplied the solution: Eck praised the Jews' "silent, stubborn passive resistance" but offered no details of its means or forms. Dworzecki converted the underlying lesson of Rabbi Nissenbaum's nonspecific exhortation to preserve Jewish life into a conviction that the activities which did so were forms of unarmed resistance worthy of the historian's specific attention.

Two questions arise:

First, did Dworzecki's recognition of a broad range of cultural and practical activities as forms of unarmed resistance reflect an attitude prevalent in Yiddishist or survivor discourse or among other Yiddish historians? The evidence suggests that it did not. Unarmed activities were not recognized as forms of resistance in Kermish's 1946 history of the Warsaw Ghetto Uprising, nor in Trunk's 1948 study of the Jews in slave-labor camps and 1949 study of the Jews in the Warthegau region, nor in Friedman's history of Auschwitz, written in 1948.[112] In the early postwar years, cultural and educational activity was more often valued as the seedbed,[113] or else the camouflage,[114] for armed resistance. In the 1948 article by Blumental, "The Yiddish Language and the Struggle against the Nazi Regime," he argues that unarmed activities are worthy of attention because they "reflect the origin and growth of the resistance movement, the factors that led to fighting."[115] This instrumental view of unarmed resistance is confirmed by actual participants. The partisan Chaika Grossman, for example—writing in the first issue of the Yiddish publication produced

---

111. Dworzecki, "Reply," in *Jewish Resistance During the Holocaust: Proceedings of the Conference on Manifestations of Jewish Resistance, Jerusalem, April 7–11, 1968* (Jerusalem, 1971), 187.

112. Although published in 1950, Friedman's foreword indicates that the book was completed in 1948.

113. Kermish, *Der oyfshtand in varshever geto: 19ter April–16ter Mai 1943* (Buenos Aires, 1948), 21.

114. Trunk, "Shtudye tsu der geshikhte fun yidn in 'varteland' in der tkufe fun umkum (1939–1944)," *Bleter far geshikhte* II, nos. 1–4 (January–December 1949), quoted here from his *Shtudyes in yiddisher geshikhte in poyln* (Buenos Aires, 1963), 229.

115. "Di yidishe shprakh un der kamf kegn natsi-rezshim," *Bleter far geshikhte* I, nos. 3–4 (August–December 1948): 106.

by the survivor-historians at Yad Vashem—responds to the complaint by Mordechai Anielevitch, a leader of the Warsaw Ghetto Uprising, that three years had been wasted on cultural activity, rather than learning to fight, with the justification: "Wasn't the cultural and educational activity unconditionally necessary in the first period of extermination? Didn't it perhaps show the way for youth to Jewish revolt?"[116] According to Samuel Kassow, Ringelblum had responded to the same complaint by Anielewicz with an "unmistakable note of self-reproach and regret" that his own generation had failed to lead the armed fight and was more concerned with surviving than with an "'honorable death.'"[117] Kassow notes, however: "Others, like Mark Dworzhetsky who survived the Vilna Ghetto, stressed how important theater and cultural activities were in warding off depression and apathy."[118]

Second, did Dworzecki's view of spiritual resistance as a collective, active, and multifaceted phenomenon—so different from the prevailing German and French concepts of *geistiger Widerstand* and *Résistance spirituelle*—emerge from a dissident view that was common in Yiddishist circles during or after the war? The two principal postwar Yiddish works on the subject of spiritual resistance suggest, rather, that Dworzecki's conception was his own.

One of these works was published in 1949 by Israel Efroykin, a public intellectual and community figure who had collaborated with Elias Tcherikower and Zelig Kalmanovitch in publishing the journal *Oyfn sheydveg* (At the Crossroads) in Paris immediately before World War II. Returning to Paris from his wartime refuge in Uruguay, he founded and edited the new Yiddish journal *Kiem* (Existence), commencing in January 1948, in which he published essays on current issues, including a number of articles by Dworzecki. In the late interwar period, Efroykin had been preoccupied with the consequences for Jewish tradition of the

---

116. Khayke Grosman, "Di geshikhte fun a bavegung," *Yedies fun yad vashem* 1 (April 1957): 22. The complaint was voiced to, and recorded by, Ringelblum. Kermish refers to it, too, but without comment in his "New Jewish Sources for the History of the Warsaw Ghetto Uprising," *Yad Vashem Bulletin* 15 (August 1964): 31.

117. Samuel D. Kassow, *Who Will Write Our History? Emanuel Ringelblum, the Warsaw Ghetto, and the Oyneg Shabes Archive* (Bloomington, 2007), 370–1.

118. Ibid., 474n161, citing Dworzecki, *Yerusholayim d'lite*, 248.

assimilation of Enlightenment values that resulted from Jewish emancipation, and then, of the sudden reversal of Jewish emancipation in most of Europe.[119] The postwar continuation of this concern was manifest in his analysis of Jewish responses to Nazism, particularly the assimilation of non-Jewish values of heroism and armed resistance. In April of 1948, he published the essay that would provide the title and first chapter of his 1949 book, *Kedushe un gvure bay yidn amol un haynt* (Jewish Holiness and Heroism in the Past and Today), which appeared in English as "The Myth of Jewish Cowardice."[120] He argues, "Is not our entire Diaspora existence a through-and-through unceasing act of resistance?"—in his view, one consisting of Jewish religious and moral steadfastness in preserving Jewish peoplehood and faith rather than non-Jewish values of physical might. "Only when Jews lost these concepts of heroism and took on foreign ones, only then did it 'turn out' that we were cowardly and fearful. Jews didn't lose their courageousness, but the gauge with which one began to measure it."[121]

Efroykin indicates his familiarity with Dworzecki's writing. For example, "as Dr. Mark Dworzecki so excellently characterized, in his splendid and richly documented work on the destruction of Vilna," from which Efroykin quotes, "the mood of the Vilna Ghetto" was that resisting meant unnecessary death, while one had yet to travel to Treblinka.[122] Yet he retains his own, traditional concept of spiritual resistance. He refers to an idealized Jewish victim of Nazism: "Did these troubles break only his body, weaken only his physical strength, or also diminish his human sensibility and befoul his soul? Here, and only here, lies the correct criterion with which to evaluate the moral steadfastness of people and their capacity for spiritual resistance."[123] Immediately after Efroykin's death in 1954, Dworzecki published a detailed appreciation of Efroykin's

---

119. See, generally, Joshua M. Karlip, *The Tragedy of a Generation: The Rise and Fall of Jewish Nationalism in Eastern Europe* (Cambridge, 2013).
120. Y. Efroykin, "Kedushe un gvure bay yidn amol un haynt," *Kiem* 4 (April 1948): 257–65 (continued in May and July–August issues).
121. Y. Efroykin, *Kedushe un gvure bay yidn amol un haynt: gezeyres tash–tashah* (New York, 1949), 8; 11–12.
122. Ibid., 93.
123. Ibid., 97.

major works, including *Kedushe un gvure*, in which, perhaps tellingly, he omits mention of the term "spiritual resistance," used so differently by Efroykin.[124]

A year later in 1950, the novelist and essayist Abraham Ajzen—who, like Dworzecki, was a Vilna Ghetto and labor camp survivor—published his well-known work, *Dos gaystike ponem fun geto* (The Spiritual Face of the Ghetto). The chapter titled "Gaystiker vidershtand" is devoted largely to the theme of those who willingly and silently went to their deaths in deliberate preference to living in a world defined by Nazi values—a theme also much discussed by Efroykin—and concludes with seeming praise for those "many, many" who committed suicide in the Vilna Ghetto, recognizing that their lives had already ended with the German invasion.[125] Conversely, Dworzecki says, "Suicides in the ghetto were an extremely rare occurrence," and he names the three of which he was aware.[126] Ajzen refers to the "cultural activities, the wonderful web of spiritual works," that were "symbols of the unbending, spiritual stubbornness" of the Jewish people,[127] but he does not recognize in them an active expression of unarmed resistance. Like others who held the instrumental view of cultural activity, he stresses that the "psychological function" of their cultural work was in "strengthening their weakened 'I' and courage and preparing them for an active zealous and physical resistance,"[128] thus, a more abstract spiritualized concept of resistance, in contrast with the textured quotidian resistance envisioned by Dworzecki. If the writings of Efroykin and Ajzen may be taken to represent the view then predominant in Yiddish letters, it may then be said that Dworzecki's work was neither influenced by, nor a reflection of, a divergent Yiddishist conception of spiritual resistance.

---

124. Dworzecki, "Yisroel efroykin," *Di goldene keyt* 20 (1954): 207.

125. A. Ayzen, *Dos gaystike ponem fun geto* (Mexico [City], 1950), 124–31.

126. Dworzecki, *Yerusholayim d'lite*, 188. The same point is made with regard to the Warsaw Ghetto by Kermish in his "Di tsavoa fun varshever geto," *Di goldene keyt* 9 (1951): 140. These contrasting views by and Ayzen and Efroykin (on despair, apathy, and resignation) and Dworzecki (on hope and faith in deliverance) were also later noted by Trunk in "Der farnikhtungs-protses fun eyropeyishn yidntum," *Algemeyne entsiklopedye*, vol. Yidn VII (New York, 1966), 13.

127. Ayzen, *Dos gaystike ponem fun geto*, 127.

128. Ibid., 86.

The reception of Dworzecki's earliest writings in Yiddish-language circles was uniformly enthusiastic. All reviewers pronounced his history of the Vilna Ghetto to be the one indispensable and comprehensive work on the subject. A distinction emerges, however, between the reviews by literary critics and by historians. On the one hand, literary critics readily assimilated Dworzecki's concept of unarmed resistance. For example, Jacob Glatstein's review of Dworzecki's history of the Vilna Ghetto, *Yerusholayim d'lite*, refers to the "second portion of the book, which analyzes the ways of struggle" (the section titled, "Varied were the Ways") and declares: "The future world will appreciate the uprising of the spirit and exult in the perseverance that prevailed in the Jewish hell."[129] Similarly, Jacob Mestel quotes with approval from Dworzecki's foreword to *Kamf farn gezunt in geto-vilne* (Fight for Health in the Vilna Ghetto) his references to political, economic, cultural, and medical resistance and concludes, "the proudest poem could not instill in you as much confidence and faith, as this small booklet—with the confidence and firm faith that the nation of Israel lives."[130]

On the other hand, the historians pursued their own agendas, as seen in their reviews of *Yerusholayim d'lite*. In Warsaw, Ber Mark praises Dworzecki's exhaustive description of life in the Vilna Ghetto, but is silent on the subject of unarmed resistance and, predictably, expresses regret at the lack of Marxist attention to class conflict.[131] In Rome, Moshe Kaganovitsh, the lay historian of the partisan movement, declares the book alone sufficient for the future historian's re-creation of the Vilna Ghetto, but is similarly silent about unarmed resistance and, from his perspective, wishes for greater detail about the partisan movement.[132] Still in Paris with Dworzecki, and writing in the same journal, Friedman praises the historian's craft—the structure of the work by which the "static"

---

129. Yankev Glatshteyn, "*Yerusholayim d'lite*" [review], *In tokh genumen*, vol. I (Buenos Aires, 1960), 176–81 (reprinted from his column in *Idisher kemfer*, 1949).

130. Yankev Mestl, "'Kamf farn gezunt in vilner geto,'" *Yidishe kultur* 9, no. 2 (February 1947): 63.

131. Ber Mark [anon.], "Biblyografishe notitsn," *Dos naye lebn* (April 9, 1948): 5.

132. M. Kaganovitsh, "'*Yerusholayim d'lite in kamf un umkum*' fun d"r m. dvorzshetski," *Farn folk* 25 (June 11, 1948): 13.

(sociological) portions of the work are bracketed by the "dynamic" (personal) accounts at the front and back, and the stance taken by Dworzecki, in contrast to many other writers, by which he "never allows himself to don the prayer shawl [*tales*] of a martyr or a hero."[133] And shortly thereafter, Friedman praises Dworzecki for providing "an all-around and systematic description of all aspects of ghetto life in Vilna—economic, hygienic, cultural, political and party movements, resistance and partisan activities, labor camps, German terror and Jewish suffering,"[134] but without noting Dworzecki's assertion that these many activities constituted forms of unarmed resistance.

The principal element of change to be observed in the Yiddish historians' writings, commencing in the 1950s, is their adoption of Dworzecki's argument that the everyday, unarmed efforts by Jews to survive under Nazi rule should be recognized as forms of resistance—to be followed in later decades by its adoption in broader historical circles as a normative view of Jewish unarmed resistance.

Trunk's early articles of 1953 on Jewish resistance distinguish between commentators who held a "narrow" view that recognized only armed revolt and those with a "broad" view that included all forms of resistance. Of the latter he says: "Dr. M. Dworzecki, for example, writes, 'Varied were the ways of resistance in the ghetto. It found expression in cultural, moral, religious, financial-economic, and political struggle,'"[135] here quoting directly the all-inclusive statement in Dworzecki's *Yerusholayim d'lite*. By 1959, however, Trunk had adopted Dworzecki's view as his own. In his article, "Armed and Unarmed Resistance in the Warsaw Ghetto," Trunk echoes Dworzecki's original 1946 article nearly verbatim, arguing that the heroism and self-sacrifice of the Warsaw Ghetto Uprising "must not, with its blinding glory, overshadow for us the fact

---

133. Friedman, review of Dworzecki, *Yerusholayim d'lite, Kiem* (June 1948): 407.

134. Friedman, "Some Books on the Jewish Catastrophe," *Jewish Social Studies* XII, no. 1 (January 1950): 86; condensed in "100 bikher in yidish vegn khurbn un gvure," *Jewish Book Annual* 8 (5710/1949–50): 131.

135. Trunk, "Di problem vidershtand," 254 (quoting from *Yerusholayim d'lite* [Paris, 1948]), 401; the same was paraphrased without Dworzecki's name in Trunk's briefer article of the prior month in Israel, "Yidisher umkum un vidershtand," 4.

that in the course of the whole period of the sinister Nazi occupation there took place a permanent, stubborn resistance" against the Nazis "that expressed itself in the most varied forms—in the economic, political, cultural, and religious fields." Searching for terminology, he declares that these forms "are unjustly termed 'passive'—but they demand a stronger, *active* force that often extends to self-sacrifice."[136] He soon turns to the term used by Dworzecki for collective, active, and wideranging forms of unarmed resistance. His article of the following year, "Problems of Internal Life in the Ghettos," concentrates on political and cultural life in the ghettos, concluding that cultural activity "bore the clear indication of spiritual resistance."[137] Trunk repeats this same identification of cultural activity with spiritual resistance in his 1966 Yiddish encyclopedia article on the Holocaust but extends his view to align in a further respect with Dworzecki's, announcing: "A clear expression of spiritual resistance was the political life which manifested itself in a number of large and small ghettos."[138] In this latter category he includes the underground newspapers published by the various political parties (the favorite topic of his fellow historian Kermish) and the organized groups of multilingual "radio listeners" who risked their lives to own or build forbidden radios and report on the news of German defeats in the war. In addition to these forms of "spiritual resistance," Trunk sets forth here the other types of unarmed resistance that constitute an "attitude of self-defense," such as the underground economy (including connections to Polish commerce, underground manufacturing, and smuggling food) and social self-help organizations—effectively completing his adoption of the "varied" conception of resistance set forth twenty years earlier by Dworzecki. Explicit evidence of Trunk's regard for Dworzecki's concept is found in his 1965 radio interview for YIVO in New York on the subject of Jewish resistance, in which he recites in full the same quotation from

---

136. Trunk, "Der bavofnter un nisht-bavofnter vidershtand fun varshever geto," *Unzer tsayt* (April–May 1959): 31 (emphasis his).

137. Trunk, "Problemen fun ineveynikstn geto-lebn," *Di tsukunft* (April 1960): 155. The same was repeated in his "Der farnikhtungs-protses," 9.

138. Trunk, "Der farnikhtungs-protses," 10.

Dworzecki's "Varied were the Ways" found in his articles of 1953.[139] And finally, late in life, Trunk would reiterate:

> [I]n the broader meaning of the notion, "resistance," including cultural, religious, economic, sanitary, and political resistance, Jews in the ghettos, and to some extent in the camps, were defying and resisting the oppressors almost constantly. As the late Mark Dvorzhetsky put it: the sole fact of staying alive longer than the German calculations predicted was an act of resistance.[140]

The first intimation by Friedman of a recognition of the importance of unarmed resistance is found in his 1950 article on the Warsaw Ghetto. He reflects on the hundreds of thousands who went to their deaths before the great uprising, saying, "We will never discover how much quiet personal heroism lay in each individual tragedy. I mean the daily heroism of each and every day, which is at times more difficult than the one-time heroism of the battlefield," including that of the Jewish women, mothers, and child smugglers, "which had to be born anew each day."[141] His 1951 history of the Jews of Bełchatów reports that smuggling was a "form of economic struggle [*virtshaftlekhn kamf*] against the occupier and sabotage of his policy of robbery."[142] In tandem with Trunk's 1953 articles on Jewish resistance, his second article on the Warsaw Ghetto Uprising asks, "[W]hat is heroism overall? Is it only physical heroism

---

139. "Interview with Isaiah Trunk on Jewish Anti-Nazi Resistance" (November 21, 1965), https://yivo.org/interview-with-isaiah-trunk-on-anti-nazi-jewish-resistance-1965 (Web page); https://yivo.org/cimages/39yivo-wevd-podcast11211965.mp3 (sound recording). Like the rabbis of Jewish tradition, he preserves for posterity the views of others with whom he disagrees (quoting, e.g., the ideas of Abraham Ajzen on a supposed Jewish preference for death over life in a Nazi-ruled world, as discussed above) but endorses Dworzecki's view by posing a condition that only it would satisfy: "It is clear that all of Jewish life under the Nazis would not have been possible without an attitude of resistance."

140. Trunk, "Closing Statement," in *The Holocaust as Historical Experience*, ed. Yehuda Bauer and Nathan Rotenstreich (New York, 1980), 270.

141. Friedman, "Parshes varshe," *Di tsukunft* (April 1950): 183–84.

142. Friedman "Di geshikhte fun di yidn in belkhatov," in *Belkhatov yisker-bukh*, ed. Mark Turkov (Buenos Aires, 1951), 47.

based on the strength of the body?" He asks further, "Is then spiritual and moral resistance of the Jewish masses, of Jewish women, men and children, of the aged, of writers, thinkers, rabbis, teachers, yeshiva students, Hasidim, not heroism?"[143] Yet he continues to adhere to the traditional definition of spiritual resistance that he ascribes to Efroykin's writings on *Kidush ha-Shem* (self-sacrifice),[144] as Trunk had done at this same time.

In the years immediately following, Friedman too would come to adopt Dworzecki's concept of spiritual and other forms of unarmed resistance. Friedman's lectures at Yad Vashem in 1957 on the subject of Holocaust research address, first, his call for the re-centering of Holocaust studies on the neglected aspect of Jewish experience (as discussed in chapter 4) and, second, the study of Jewish resistance in all its forms. In this latter portion, he announces, "First of all I wish to discuss forms of unarmed resistance . . . ," and it is to this topic that he devotes the largest measure of his remarks. He commences his discussion of "spiritual or moral resistance" with the traditional Jewish practice of *Kidush ha-Shem* (self-sacrifice), and then broadens the concept to include those who "listened to Allied radio broadcasts" or engaged in open satire against the Nazis (a theme much stressed by Blumental, as discussed in chapter 6). To these he adds, in the manner of Dworzecki, a cultural element: "Similarly every form of clandestine education of children was a form of Spiritual Resistance." He continues his survey with the recognition that another "form of Resistance was economic in character," in which he includes both sabotage of factory work and smuggling.[145] A later version of this address, for a conference in Belgium in 1958, includes a further form of resistance (here labeled "passive") which was "the building of various, sometimes very ingenuous, dugouts, usually called 'bunkers' . . .

---

143. Friedman, "Varshever oyfshtand—der brenendiker dorn," *Di tsukunft* (April 1953): 195.

144. Friedman, "Der idisher vidershtand kegn der natsi-hershaft," *Idisher kemfer* (April 3, 1953, Pesach): 89.

145. Friedman, "Preliminary and Methodological Problems of the Research on the Jewish Catastrophe in the Nazi Period," *Yad Vashem Studies* II (1958): 115–18.

which the Germans sometimes had great difficulties discovering and 'conquering.'"[146]

Kermish, by contrast with Trunk and Friedman, did not reflect on the public discourse regarding resistance but wrote directly from his own research. His 1946 history of the Warsaw Ghetto Uprising lacked attention to unarmed resistance, no doubt because of it was based largely on German sources. The impetus for his embrace of the subject a short time later was his study of Ringelblum's 1942 survey of the intellectual elite of the Warsaw Ghetto, titled, "Two and a Half Years of War." Kermish had published the questionnaire and extant responses in 1948 while still in Poland and, once settled in Israel, reported his findings in the 1951 article, "The Testament of the Warsaw Ghetto." At this early date, he ascribes aspects of unarmed resistance to categories he has already named "economic resistance" (including smuggling, establishing commercial ties with Christian merchants, and creating raw materials for underground manufacturing), "passive resistance" (encompassing the sabotage of factory output as well as defiance of German orders), and "cultural resistance" (which he found was "embodied in building a network of cultural institutions, schools, and theaters"). In a later article on "cultural work and other forms of resistance," he quotes statements by Dworzecki in *Yerusholayim d'lite* asserting the psychological maturity of schoolchildren and their eagerness to join in the daily struggle for existence.[147]

These forms of unarmed resistance reappear in each of the historical articles written by Kermish for *yizkor* books of Jewish communities during the 1960s. Commencing with the town of Chmielnik in 1960, he developed a template for writing wartime history that consisted of three parts—life during the early period of Nazi occupation, the extermination process, and Jewish resistance. In each instance, he begins the third part with the various forms of unarmed resistance. In Chmielnik, these

---

146. Friedman, "Jewish Resistance to Nazism: Its Various Forms and Aspects," in *European Resistance Movements 1939–1945: First International Conference on the History of the Resistance Movements Held at Liège-Bruxelles-Breendonk 14–17 September 1958* (Oxford, 1960), 204.

147. Kermish, "Mekoyres vegn di khinukh problemen in geto," *Yerusholaymer almanakh* 2–3 (1974): 182; "Origins of [more correctly, 'Sources Regarding'] the Education Problem in the Ghetto," *Yad Vashem Bulletin* 12 (December 1962): 30.

included economic resistance in all its forms; passive resistance to German decrees; and cultural, political, and educational activities.[148] His history of Kałuszyn (1961) augments the category of "passive resistance" to include social self-help activities, hiding Jews from the Warsaw Ghetto who had escaped from transports to Treblinka, and the flight of other residents into the woods.[149] An enlarged discussion for the town of Piotrków Trybunalski (1965) includes the passive resistance of religious Jews who dared to pray in public and who rescued Torah scrolls from the Germans as well as by others who created literary works, illegal libraries, and an illegal gymnasium and lyceum.[150] In the book on Płock (1967), he gives special attention to townsmen who took refuge elsewhere, most notably Herman Kruk, who helped to rescue the cultural treasures of YIVO in the Vilna Ghetto and there wrote his own well-known diary.[151] His historical chapter for the *yizkor* book of the Galicia region (1968) discusses literary works and "literary evenings" as "an important act of psychological self-defense against the methods of 'dehumanization' that the Germans methodically employed against the ghetto captives."[152]

After Dworzecki, Blumental had been the first to argue for recognition of unarmed forms of resistance, "which reflect the rise and growth of the resistance movement, the factors that led to fighting—and occupied a greater time-period as well as wider territory than the fight itself." In his 1948 article on the Yiddish language and the fight against the Nazis, Blumental argues that "Nazism killed Jews first through language, before doing so in reality" and that the Jews under Nazi rule strengthened morale by ridiculing the enemy, telling jokes in which Jews outsmarted Nazis,

---

148. Kermish, "Khmilniker yidn untern natsi-rezshim," in *Pinkes khmyelnik: yiskerbukh nokh der khorev-gevorener yidisher kehile*, ed. Efrayim Shedletski (Tel Aviv, 1960), 678–81.

149. Kermish, "Martirologye, vidershtand un umkum fun der yidisher kehile in kalushin," in *Sefer kalushin*, ed. Aryeh Shamri et al. (Tel Aviv, 1961), 338–41.

150. Kermish, "Der khurbn," in *Pyetrkov tribunalski un umgegnt/Pyetrkov Tribunalski veha-sevivah*, ed. Yankev Malts and Naftoli Lau (Tel Aviv, 1965), 765–66; "The Destruction of the Jewish Community of Piotrkow by the Nazis during World War II," trans. P. Wollman (1965), in *A Tale of One City: Piotrków Trybunalski*, ed. Ben Giladi (New York, 1991), 348–49.

151. Kermish, "Di plotsker yidn untern natsi-rezshim," in *Plotsk: toldot kehilah 'atikat-yomin be-Polin*, ed. Eliyahu Eisenberg (Tel Aviv, 1967), 497.

152. Kermish, "Dos galitsishe yidntum beys der hitler-okupatsye" in *Sefer galitsye: gedenk bukh*, ed. Yosef Okrutni (Buenos Aires, 1968), 30.

and by spreading warnings in coded Yiddish. He argues that historically such uses of language "maintain human worth and prevent the human being from declining in his own self-consciousness, teach the vanquished not to be influenced by the stronger, [and] fortify faith in his own strength which will ultimately bring redemption." With time, he did not limit himself to this utilitarian view of unarmed resistance (as having value only for promoting armed resistance) but, like Kermish, wrote chapters for *yizkor* books that include recognition of unarmed resistance as a positive force in itself. He devotes a section to economic resistance in his 1953 article on the Warsaw Ghetto,[153] and he discusses aspects of passive resistance, cultural work, building bunkers, occupational resilience, secret schools for children, and fleeing to the forests in the *yizkor* books of his own town of Borszczów (1960)[154] and of Hrubieszów (1962),[155] Busk (1965),[156] and Miechów (1971).[157]

Blumental sets forth the logic of the Yiddish historians' insistence on the value of unarmed resistance in his 1967 essay "The Fight of the Jews Against the Nazi Regime." Adopting Dworzecki's tone, he contends, "The fight against the oppressor includes the most varied forms," and he elaborates:

> The enemy would starve the Jews in the ghettos and camps, so the Jews smuggled products from the Aryan side; the enemy would drown the Jews in filth and sickness, so the Jews created health commissions and secret places of healing; the enemy would deprive the Jews of education, especially the youth, that they should

---

153. Blumental, "Geto Varshah ve-hurbano," in *Entsiklopediyah shel Galuyot*, vol. I: Warsaw, ed. Yitshak Gruenbaum (Jerusalem, 1953), 618–21.

154. Blumental, *Sefer borshtshiv* (Tel Aviv, 1960), 219–24 (cultural work), 233 (passive resistance).

155. Blumental, "Dos yidishe hrubieshov in di yorn 1939–1945," in *Pinkes hrubieshov: tsum 20-tn yortog nokh der groyzamer khurbn fun unzer gevezener heym*, ed. Borukh Kaplinski (Tel Aviv, 1962), 110–11 (education, communal prayer).

156. Blumental, "Dos yidishe bisk: shtrikhn tsu zayn geshikhte," in *Sefer Busk*, ed. Abraham Shayari (Haifa, 1965), 57–58 (bunkers).

157. Blumental, "Le-toldot Yehude Maikhov," in *Sefer yizkor Maikhov, Kharshnitsah, u-Kshoinz*, ed. Blumental and Ben-Azar (Tel Aviv, 1971), 51 (education).

not even know of their Jewishness, so the Jews created secret schools, secret lectures—and under the nose of the occupier there arose a rich and multifaceted Yiddish literature, of which the very fact of its existence was anti-Hitlerish.[158]

For the Yiddish historians, the value of unarmed resistance was not that "resistance" defined in such innocuous terms as "spiritual," "passive," "economic," or "cultural" might injure or deter the Germans, but rather that it was the only means of resistance in which the great mass of Jews could, and did, engage and which might reduce the threat of their immediate or eventual murder—outcomes the historians associated, respectively, with direct confrontation or absolute passivity. These historians might have argued (but did not, perhaps because it was to them self-evident) that the small number of Jews who survived the years of Nazi occupation could not have done so without these varied means of self-preservation.

An extended example of such forms of resistance is found in Dworzecki's history of the Jewish camps in Estonia, completed in 1967 as his doctoral dissertation at the Sorbonne, and published in 1970.[159] The chapter titled "Spiritual Resistance and the Camp Inmate (the *Amidah*)" emphasizes the collective nature of such resistance, in contrast with the "retreat . . . to a life of inner riches and spiritual freedom" lauded by Viktor Frankl. On the basis of eyewitness accounts, Dworzecki recounts the prevalence of mutual aid and self-sacrifice in sharing food, protecting the less able, teaching in secret, and giving medical aid. He also indicates that in the camps "there arose spontaneously a specific type of mutual aid," by which fellow inmates "would join in a 'collective' to help each other . . . to 'organize' together, cook a soup together, put to the common good all that might be 'taken,' in order to withstand the suffering in the camp together."[160] He relates separately, in

---

158. Blumental, "Der kamf fun di yidn kegn natsi-rezshim," *Lebns-fragn* 184–85 (April–May 1967): 2.

159. Dworzecki indicates that he prepared it simultaneously in French, Yiddish, and Hebrew (*Mahanot ha-Yehudim be-Estoniyah*, Jerusalem, 1970).

160. Dworzecki, *Vayse nekht un shvartse teg (yidn lagern in estonye)* (Jerusalem, 1970), 294. He had written similarly about collective mutual aid among concentration camps inmates in his "Adjustment of Detainees to Camp and Ghetto Life and Their Subsequent Re-adjustment to Normal Society," *Yad Vashem Studies* V (1963): 205.

the following chapter, the many forms of cultural activity among the camp inmates, including "'secret cultural evenings' during which they would sing folksongs, chiefly ghetto-songs, and recite ('declaim') from memory poems from famous Yiddish poets."[161] Spiritual resistance in the form of collective mutual aid remained a recurring theme in Dworzecki's work. In one of the last works to be published before his sudden death in 1975, he provided annotations for the Vilna Ghetto diary of his own "first teacher of Hebrew in Vilna," Moshe Olitski. He offers the concluding statement that the diary "is an exalted document that bears witness to the spiritual resistance in the Vilna Ghetto, which was also expressed, in this case, in the area of schooling, in the concern for teachers and children."[162]

The culminating moment for this validation of unarmed resistance was the 1968 Yad Vashem Conference on Manifestations of Jewish Resistance (in the Hebrew title, *Amidah*), of which he was a principal organizer. Dworzecki's address, "The Day-to-Day Stand [*Amidah*] of the Jews," has been published repeatedly in both Hebrew and English and has become the generally cited source for the recognition of unarmed resistance in all its forms.[163] It sets forth his definition of *Amidah*:

> The concept "stand" is a comprehensive name for all expressions of Jewish "non-conformism" and for all the forms of resistance and all acts by Jews aimed at thwarting the evil design of the Nazis—a design to destroy the Jews, to deprive them of their humanity, and to reduce them to dregs before snuffing out their lives.[164]

---

161. Dworzecki, *Vayse nekht un shvartse teg*, 301.

162. Dworzecki, "Dos togbukh fun lerer moyshe olitski," in *Vilner zamlbukh/Measef Vilnah*, ed. Yisrael Rudnitski (Tel Aviv, 1974), 105.

163. Dworzecki had presented substantially the same material in his paper at the Twelfth International Congress of Historical Sciences in Vienna in 1965, but it was printed only in mimeographed form in French and then as a pamphlet in Spanish translation in Buenos Aires by the World Jewish Congress: Dworzecki, *Historia de la resistencia antinazi judía, 1933–1945: problemática y metodología* (Buenos Aires, 1970).

164. Dworzecki, "The Day-To-Day Stand of the Jews," in *Jewish Resistance During the Holocaust: Proceedings of the Conference on Manifestations of Jewish Resistance, Jerusalem, April 7–11, 1968* (Jerusalem, 1971), 153.

By the time of the 1968 conference, Dworzecki's wish to extend to the Jewish victims of Nazism the recognition he believed was owed for their widespread unarmed resistance had become the shared agenda of the Yiddish historians. In the writings of each of these historians, evidence of such resistance had already provided the redemptive answer to the troubling claim of Jewish passivity. Blumental's and Kermish's own addresses at the 1968 conference concur with the definition advocated by Dworzecki (while, on this occasion, Trunk discussed *armed* resistance). Blumental defines resistance as "opposition to every hostile act of the enemy, . . . not only physical acts, but also the spiritual and moral resistance."[165] Kermish declares, "The Jewish resistance movement is a wide concept," and he enumerates each type of unarmed activity so far reported in his various works.[166] Looking ahead two decades, it may be noted that the section devoted to cultural, economic, political, and related activities in Kermish's 1986 anthology of the Oyneg Shabes project is headed, in the style of Dworzecki, "Resistance in its Several Forms."

Yet it may be asked how directly the adoption of this broad and positive concept of unarmed resistance by the other Yiddish historians may be traced to Dworzecki's influence. Among these historians, all of whom were acquainted with Dworzecki and his writings, only Trunk specifically credits this concept to Dworzecki, and he does so repeatedly. Yet the record of Dworzecki's role as an innovator is not entirely blank. In 1953, Blumental wrote specifically about Dworzecki's capacity for originating influential ideas. Referring to a widely held view on a different subject that he attributed to Dworzecki, Blumental relates that Dworzecki had "once in a conversation, expressed altogether simply and openheartedly, in his way, that it was one of the 'golden ideas' he created after the war and which were immediately projected by everyone back onto the past."[167] Whether Dworzecki's

---

165. Blumental, "Sources for the Study of Jewish Resistance," in *Jewish Resistance During the Holocaust: Proceedings*, 46–47.
166. Kermish, "The Place of the Ghetto Revolts in the Struggle Against the Occupier," in *Jewish Resistance During the Holocaust: Proceedings*, 308.
167. Blumental, "Nisht keyn gvure un nisht keyn gayst!," *Arbeter vort* (April 30, 1953): 3. The subject was the designation of Zelig Kalmanovitch as "the *novi* [prophet] of the Vilna Ghetto," with which Blumental disagreed but traced to Dworzecki.

recognition of varied forms of unarmed resistance was one of those "golden ideas" accepted by his contemporaries may perhaps be judged from comments published by Rachel Auerbach in 1957. In the leading Israeli Yiddish journal, *Di goldene keyt*, she reviewed the collected Hebrew translation of Dworzecki's early writings. Here, she indicates that Dworzecki's first book, *Yerusholayim d'lite*, "had already laid specific stress on the instances of not only active—armed—resistance, but also of passive resistance," and she specifies each of the forms of unarmed resistance recognized by him. She contends that before the accusation of "going as sheep to the slaughter" had become widespread, Dworzecki "had already prepared the answer." She says further that Dworzecki had provided the answer that "one ought to give to the young generation, by which they will understand that 'varied were the ways of struggle,'" in this way repeating the title of his 1946 Yiddish article then newly available in Hebrew translation.[168]

The rapid acceptance and adoption of Dworzecki's view of unarmed resistance by Yiddish-speaking intellectuals during his lifetime were not matched by historians outside this circle. To whatever extent unarmed resistance had gained recognition among "outsiders" prior to the 1968 Yad Vashem conference, such recognition referred chiefly to the nonspecific ideal of *Kidush ha-Hayim* as reported by Eck and popularized by Esh. A principal aim of the 1968 Yad Vashem conference was to contest the claims of Jewish passivity that emerged during the early 1960s with new research on both armed and, especially, unarmed resistance. The presentations by Dworzecki and others were intended to introduce to the wider scholarly world a practical program of Holocaust historiography centered on unarmed resistance. Yet the influence of the 1968 conference was not immediate, and two trends may be seen in the external reception of Dworzecki's concept of unarmed resistance—neglect, followed by acknowledgment and acceptance.

The first trend appears in Yehuda Bauer's well-known 1973 pamphlet *They Chose Life: Jewish Resistance in the Holocaust*. The section titled "Quiet Resistance" quotes the statement on *Kidush ha-Hayim* attributed by Eck to Rabbi Nissenbaum. The body of this section then discusses the

---

168. Rokhl Oyerbakh, "Tikun khatses," *Di goldene keyt* 27 (1957): 279–80, 282.

varied forms of unarmed resistance and their importance to sustaining Jewish life that would have been familiar to readers of works by Dworzecki and the other Yiddish historians. Curiously, Bauer writes, "Details regarding the cultural life of Vilna are found, for instance, in Mark Dworzecki's *Yerushalayim de'Lite*"—without indicating that the details he cites are but a single example from the book's central portion devoted to the broader goal of recognizing the many forms of unarmed resistance.[169] Bauer repeats the same material in his "Jewish Emergence from Powerlessness" of 1979, without any attribution, and then offers a condensed version as his definition of *Amidah* in 2001 and again 2004.[170] Not surprisingly, this first trend sustains its own trajectory. Michael Marrus, to cite one example of many, in 1998 quotes the particulars of Bauer's 1973 and 1979 discussions of unarmed resistance and points to Bauer as their apparent origin: "Yehuda Bauer argues for an inclusive approach, one that declares 'keeping body and soul together' under circumstances of unimaginable privation and misery as one way of resisting the Nazis."[171]

Others preferred to credit Esh: Israel Gutman declares in his 1984 article "Kiddush ha-Shem and Kiddush ha-Hayim" that Esh "popularized kiddush ha-Hayim as expressing the Jewish response to the Holocaust. He defined it as the revelation of a strong will to live, of a struggle for survival. . . . I believe that [E]sh's view is generally correct."[172] Dan Michman writes in 1998 about changes in Holocaust research during the 1960s, saying that "'the resistance branch' of literature also underwent a change. A new concept evolved, that of *amidah*. . . . Shaul Esh, one of the first to take this path of thought instead used the term *Kiddush ha-Hayim*."[173]

---

169. Yehuda Bauer, *They Chose Life: Jewish Resistance in the Holocaust* (New York, 1973), 32–37, 60 (notes, for chapter V).

170. Yehuda Bauer, *The Jewish Emergence from Powerlessness* (Toronto, 1979), 34–45; *Rethinking the Holocaust* (New Haven, 2001); and "The Problem of Non-Armed Jewish Reactions to Nazi Rule in Eastern Europe" in *New Currents in Holocaust Research*, ed. Jeffry M. Diefendorf (Evanston, 2004), 57.

171. Michael R. Marrus, *The Holocaust in History* (Hanover, 1987), 136–37.

172. Yisrael Gutman, "Kiddush ha-Shem and Kiddush ha-Hayim," *Simon Wiesenthal Center Annual* 1 (1984): 185–202.

173. Dan Michman, "Research on the Holocaust in Belgium and in General: History and Context," in *Belgium and the Holocaust: Jews, Belgians, Germans*, ed. Dan Michman (Jerusalem, 1998), 11–12.

That it remains possible indefinitely, through lack of acquaintance with the Yiddish historians' body of work on unarmed resistance, to attribute the origin of the idea to other and later sources is seen in the chapter titled "Resistance?" in Tom Lawson's 2010 *Debates on the Holocaust*. He discovers the concept of *Amidah* in the context of the 1968 Yad Vashem conference. In a passage attributed to Dan Michman's analysis, rather than primary sources, he asserts that the term *Amidah* "was used from the end of the 1960s to conceptualise this wider definition of resistance, most notably employed by Yehuda Bauer and Shaul Esh."[174] Not mentioned are the Yiddish historians' contributions to the topic in general, as well as the fine point that the term *Amidah* was used as early as 1951 by Eck in the journal *Dapim*, edited by Blumental.[175]

A turning point toward acknowledgment of the Yiddish historians' works—and, more importantly, toward the use of their works for later research—was the book by Rabbi Joseph Rudavsky on spiritual resistance that appeared in 1987. It was first prepared in 1978 as his doctoral dissertation on *Kidush ha-Hayim* and was then published under the title *To Live with Hope, To Die with Dignity: Spiritual resistance in the ghettos and camps*.[176] It is the first major work to assimilate the collective output of Dworzecki and his colleagues (and like-minded others) in the area of spiritual resistance. Accordingly, its central argument is that Jews in Nazi captivity "would strive to educate their children, to continue their Jewish studies, to observe their religion, and even to carry on the Zionist struggle for the Jewish Homeland as if the ghetto were just a transient episode," and that scholars of Jewish law, poets, composers, and writers

---

174. Tom Lawson, *Debates on the Holocaust* (Manchester-New York, 2010), 252.

175. I am myself indebted to a secondary source for this observation. Boaz Cohen, in his *Israeli Holocaust Research*, 212, points out that Eck initiated the use of the term *'Amidah* in his brief note in *Dapim* (January–April 1951): 208. Considering Blumental's statement that most of *Dapim*, which he edited, was written in Yiddish and translated into Hebrew by the publisher (see chapter 1), the question arises as to whether the Hebrew term was first used by Eck or a translator.

176. Joseph Rudavsky, *To Live with Hope, To Die with Dignity: Spiritual Resistance in the Ghettos and Camps* (Mahwah, 1987). Rudavsky quotes Esh on the meaning of *Kidush ha-Hayim* and devotes his first chapter to tracing the origins of the concept through the centuries of rabbinic writings.

would continue their manifold activities.[177] Rudavsky's sources include interviews with Dworzecki, Trunk, Kermish, and Blumental (as well as Auerbach and others),[178] and his endnotes are dense with citations of their works, most conspicuously Dworzecki's.

The change heralded by Rudavsky finds recognition in the article, "Spiritual Resistance in the Ghettos and Concentration Camps," newly written for the 2007 edition of the *Encyclopaedia Judaica* by Adina Dreksler and Michael Berenbaum, which summarizes the state of the field in the early twenty-first century.[179] In the manner of the Yiddish historians, they define spiritual resistance as comprising "education and religion, underground publications, self-help kitchens, humor, cultural creativity, and efforts to create a historical record." The article's bibliography, which is neither alphabetical nor chronological, lists first among its primary sources Dworzecki's books on the Vilna Ghetto and Jewish labor camps in Estonia and first among its secondary sources Rudavsky's book on spiritual resistance. The article reflects the widespread adoption of Dworzecki's redefinition of spiritual resistance. Since the early years of the twenty-first century, for example, both Yad Vashem and the US Holocaust Memorial Museum have come to promote this definition on their websites,[180] and the Jewish State Museum in Vilnius has found it appropriate to use the categories set forth by

---

177. Ibid., 39–40. Rudavsky was founding director of the Center for Holocaust and Genocide Studies, Ramapo College of New Jersey, 1979–96, following a long career as a pulpit rabbi. The title of the book is a variant of Kermish's title for his anthology of Ringelblum's Oyneg Shabes project (published the prior year): "To Live with Honor and Die with Honor!" It illustrates the metamorphosis of meaning ascribed to "honor." The origin of the phrase is Ringelblum's famous public letter of March 1944, in which "honor" (or "dignity," depending on the translator) is applied to armed, no less than unarmed, resistance. Kermish used it for his anthology (in which the letter is reprinted), despite devoting barely 20 of its 800 pages to any form of armed resistance. Rudavsky then applied his variant title to a work devoted exclusively to unarmed resistance.

178. Regrettably, his interview notes were not preserved (private communications with the author, July 2015).

179. Adina Dreksler and Michael Berenbaum, "Spiritual Resistance in the Ghettos and Concentration Camps," in *Encyclopaedia Judaica*, 2nd ed., ed. Fred Skolnik and Michael Berenbaum, vol. 19 (Detroit, 2007), 360–65.

180. Yael Weinstock Mashbaum, "Spiritual Resistance During the Holocaust: 'What We Value,'" www.yadvashem.org/articles/general/spiritual-resistance-during-the-holocaust.html; US Holocaust Memorial Museum, "Spiritual Resistance in the Ghettos," *Holocaust Encyclopedia*, www.ushmm.org/wlc/en/article.php?ModuleId=10005416.

Dworzecki (including his specialty, medical resistance) as the framework for their 2002 book, "Spiritual Resistance in the Vilna Ghetto."[181]

The second trend emerged in the early years of the twenty-first century, as the treatment of spiritual and other forms of unarmed resistance (allowing for a certain fluidity of terminology) became increasingly marked by the pairing of two elements: a definition quoted from Dworzecki's writings and an acknowledgment and acceptance of his authority. For example, Robert Rozett quotes Dworzecki's definition of *Amidah*, followed by his own (as published in the 1990 *Encyclopedia of the Holocaust*) which he says "is not all that different from Dworzecki's."[182]

This trend is particularly marked among newer scholars who have turned directly to primary sources in preference to received commentaries. Three books illustrate the growth of this phase:

Michal Aharony's 2015 critique of Hannah Arendt traces Rozett's path in quoting Dworzecki's definition of *Amidah*, followed by Rozett's own from the *Encyclopedia of the Holocaust* (which Aharony, too, finds "very similar to that of Dworzecki"). She then quotes a "useful explanation" of *Amidah* by Bauer, but announces, "For the purposes of my work, I employ the wide definition of resistance as *amidah*, as given above by Dworzecki and in the *Encyclopedia of the Holocaust*." Elsewhere, she says simply, "Here I follow Marc Dwoezecki's [sic] definition of *amidah*."[183]

Gudrun Schroeter's 2007 study of cultural production in the Vilna Ghetto quotes the definitions of resistance offered by both Blumental and Dworzecki at the 1968 Yad Vashem conference. She devotes a central chapter to cultural resistance that opens with her own definition of spiritual resistance: "Spiritual resistance in the ghetto found expression in the multifaceted cultural, social, and religious institutions" pertaining to health, social welfare, secular and religious schools, Hebrew and Yiddish

---

181. Rachel Kostanian-Danzig, *Spiritual Resistance in the Vilna Ghetto* (Vilnius, 2002); see specifically the table of contents, the author's definition of spiritual resistance on page 21, and the many references to Dworzecki's *Yerusholayim d'lite*.

182. Robert Rozett, "Jewish Resistance," in *The Historiography of the Holocaust*, ed. Dan Stone (New York, 2004), 347.

183. Michal Aharony, *Hannah Arendt and the Limits of Total Domination: The Holocaust, Plurality, and Resistance* (New York, 2015), 130, 10n20.

choirs, symphony orchestra, "and much more."[184] She then quotes liberally from Dworzecki's *Yerusholayim d'lite* and other first-person accounts in describing each of these forms of resistance.

The most innovative work is Boaz Cohen's 2013 history of Holocaust research in Israel. In a chapter devoted to the 1968 conference, he quotes from both Blumental's and Dworzecki's definitions of *Amidah* and notes Dworzecki's role in conceiving the conference. But first, he turns to the earliest primary source to address specific forms of unarmed resistance: Dworzecki's 1946 article, "Varied were the Ways." Of this, Cohen writes, "When describing the activities of doctors and smugglers, teachers and children, [Dworzecki] uses the terminology of fighting—'revolt,' 'struggle,' and 'rebellion,' thus granting them legitimacy that seems to have been previously non-existent in the eyes of the public."[185]

Of course, as Cohen also notes, the promotion of *Amidah* as the vehicle to rehabilitate Jewish honor was not universally accepted. Lucy Dawidowicz, in particular, argued that "the meaning of resistance was strained beyond its usual meaning." Targeting Dworzecki's concept of *Amidah*, she says, "The most widely accepted definition of resistance that was postulated at the conference was not of resistance as an auxiliary form of warfare, but rather as a process familiar in medicine or physics."[186] Nevertheless, hers has become a minority position. Cohen's 2015 biographical article on Dworzecki indicates that "his concept of '*amidah* as the organizing concept for Jewish life in the ghettos is used in Israeli high school curricula and in educational discussions."[187] As Rozett points out, "by the beginning of the twenty-first century, the concept of *Amidah*, if not the word itself, had become an almost undisputed keystone for our understanding of Jewish resistance."[188]

Over the course of four, five, and six decades, the narrative that has come to predominate in countering the accusation of Jewish passivity is

---

184. Gudrun Schroeter, *Worte aus einer zerstörten Welt: Das Ghetto in Wilna* (St. Ingbert, 2007), 54–55, 287.
185. Boaz Cohen, *Israeli Holocaust Research*, 209–25, 213.
186. Lucy S. Dawidowicz, *The Holocaust and the Historians* (Cambridge, 1981), 133.
187. Boaz Cohen, "Dr Meir (Mark) Dworzecki: the historical mission of a survivor historian," *Holocaust Studies* 21, nos. 1–2 (2015): 34.
188. Robert Rozett, "Jewish Resistance," 347.

the two-pronged approach innovated by the Yiddish historians: a defense consisting of researching and making known the impediments to armed resistance, coupled with an offense aimed at reshaping the concept of resistance to embrace the Jews' everyday efforts to sustain life.

The eventual acceptance and adoption of this narrative parallels the gradual transference of the Yiddish historians' works to the wider world of Holocaust study. This process of transfer—or at times, anticipation—is the subject of chapter 6.

6

THE TRANSMISSION OF A CULTURE

In postwar Europe, the Yiddish historians of the Holocaust were among the small circle of intellectual leaders who formed the mainstream of a new historical endeavor. With their dispersal to Israel and America, they remained an intellectual elite, but of a minority culture with secondary status in both general and scholarly circles. Consequently, their works might have remained the largely inaccessible property of an insular community of survivors and fellow Yiddish-speakers, destined to become ever more esoteric as Yiddish literacy declined.

However, two complementary and opposite trends have emerged to lend their works continuing and broader attention. The first is translation. The second, which arose much later, after a period of transition, is a turn to scholarship in original languages.

Translation

Isaiah Trunk received two National Jewish Book Awards, apart from his National Book Award of 1973. These two awards are reminders of the multilingual Jewish culture that once prevailed, even in America, and of its gradual demise. At a time when these awards and the *Jewish Book Annual*, both created by the Jewish Book Council, recognized almost equal numbers of books in English, Yiddish, and Hebrew, Trunk shared a National Jewish Book Award in 1967 as coeditor of the final volume of the

Yiddish encyclopedia, which was devoted to Holocaust history.[1] During the 1970s, as awards for books in Yiddish became scarcer and for books in Hebrew all but ceased (in favor of works translated from these languages), Trunk received his second award—for a work in English translation. Having found that his comprehensive history of the Lodz Ghetto, published in Yiddish in 1962, remained unknown outside of Yiddish circles (remedied only by its posthumous publication in English in 2006), he entered the mainstream of American scholarship by publishing his second major work, *Judenrat*, only in English translation. The result was his second National Jewish Book Award, in 1975.[2]

Judenrat also became the first—and only—work of Yiddish scholarship to earn a National Book Award (as noted in chapter 1). In his acceptance speech, Trunk indicated his awareness of the act of cultural transference he had brought about. He shared his "understanding that the award is not to me but to the subject, which has finally gained entry into American historiography, not as a purely Jewish subject, but as one that reflects the general human condition."[3] Immediately before the publication of *Judenrat*, historian Gerd Korman speculated about the many reasons for the absence of Holocaust history from American historical writing.[4] And then soon after, he remarked on the recent availability of two works in English, one by Henri Michel, the leading French historian of resistance,[5] and the other by Trunk, saying, "Isaiah Trunk has given us a monumental study which can teach anybody who can read English, the realities of Jewish life in the Ghetto"—concluding that "the world of scholarship now has books in English with which a historian

---

1. "Hyman G. Bass [prominent Yiddish educator and editor], president of the Jewish Book Council, said the $500 Leon Jolson Award for the best book on the Nazi holocaust will go to Abraham Kiln, posthumously, Dr. Mordecai Kosover and Isaiah Trunk, co-editors of the 'Algemeine entsiklopedia: Yidn 7' of the Central Yiddish Cultural Organization," in "Jewish Book Council Announces Awards for Five Books Published in 1966," *Jewish Telegraphic Agency Daily News Bulletin* (May 19, 1967): 4.

2. Again, the Leon Jolson Award, given this time to Trunk alone. See the complete list of recipients, www.jewishbookcouncil.org/awards/njba-list.

3. "Isaiah Trunk Honored," *Congress Bi-Weekly* 40, no. 8 (May 18, 1973): 26.

4. Gerd Korman, "The Holocaust in American Historical Writing," *Societas* 2 (1972): 251–70.

5. Presumably Michel's *The Shadow War; European Resistance, 1939–1945*, trans. Richard Barry (New York, 1972).

who has yet to discover the Holocaust phenomenon can find the keys for understanding."⁶

Trunk's last major work, *Jewish Responses to Nazi Persecution* (1979), was also first published in English translation.⁷ Thirty years later, Jürgen Matthäus and Mark Roseman, the editors of the first volume of the *Jewish Responses to Persecution* series published by the US Holocaust Memorial Museum, recognized Trunk's book as "the first English-language source compilation" of eyewitness testimony. Moreover, they describe it as the "pathbreaking volume from which this series borrows its title."⁸ The author of a later volume in the series confirms Trunk's continuing influence: "This chapter, moving along the path charted by Trunk, seeks to document the ways in which the radical and ever-increasing persecution affected familiar and well-established givens of life."⁹

Similarly, the works of each of the Yiddish historians to appear in English are those by which they first became well known outside of Yiddish-speaking circles. These include Philip Friedman's *Martyrs and Fighters* (on the Warsaw Ghetto, 1954) and *Their Brothers' Keepers* (on the Christian rescuers, 1957), followed by his articles in the much-cited posthumous collection, *Roads to Extinction* (1980); Nachman Blumental's and Mark Dworzecki's papers on resistance at the 1968 Yad Vashem conference (discussed in chapter 5); Dworzecki's final research paper, on the International Red Cross (1974);¹⁰ and Joseph Kermish's 1986 anthology of the Oyneg Shabes project.¹¹ Each of these is frequently cited by historians quoting from English-language sources. An analogous process occurred

---

6. Gerd Korman, "Warsaw Plus Thirty: Some Perceptions in the Sources and Written History of the Ghetto Uprising," *YIVO Annual of Jewish Social Science* XV (1974): 296.

7. Trunk, *Jewish Responses to Nazi Persecution* (New York, 1979); "Yidishe reaktsye tsu natsi redifes," *Geshtaltn un gesheenishn [naye serye]* (Tel Aviv, 1983), 274–314.

8. Jürgen Matthäus et al., "Introduction," in *Jewish Responses to Persecution (Vol. I) 1933–1938*, ed. Matthäus and Mark Roseman (Lanham, 2010), xvi and xxi.

9. Emil Kerenji, *Jewish Responses to Persecution (Vol. IV) 1942–1943* (Lanham, 2015), 406.

10. Dworzecki, "The International Red Cross and its Policy vis-à-vis the Jews in Ghettos and Concentration Camps in Nazi-Occupied Europe," in *Rescue Attempts During the Holocaust: Proceedings of the Second Yad Vashem International Historical Conference, Jerusalem. April 8–11, 1974* (Jerusalem, 1977), 71–122.

11. Kermish, ed., *To Live with Honor, To Die with Honor!...: Selected Documents from the Warsaw Ghetto Underground Archives "O.S." ["Oneg Shabbath"]* (Jerusalem, 1986).

in the reception of these historians' works within the Hebrew-language sphere.[12]

The late arrival of works by the Yiddish historians in the dominant languages of Jewish Holocaust research has led to predictable observations by other historians that appear to overlook (or else, dismiss) the principal bodies of Holocaust research in Yiddish. Three examples are representative:

Yehuda Bauer writes in 2001 that, in the "beginning of Holocaust historiography," the first historians "dealt mainly with the perpetrators.... Later the first attempts were made to describe the way Jews reacted. The initial publication was probably Philip Friedman's *Their Brothers' Keepers* [presumably, he meant the earlier *Martyrs and Fighters*], but he was not followed until very much later, when Isaiah Trunk published his *Judenrat*"[13]—thereby neglecting the historians' many studies in Yiddish that preceded these English-language works.

Tim Cole offers two observations in 2004. The first: "After 1961, cultural developments within the ghettos were interpreted as acts of cultural resistance,"[14] which overlooks the accounts of cultural resistance published by Dworzecki and the other Yiddish historians in the 1940s and 1950s. And, second, on the difficult issue of social conflict in the ghettos, he reports that "evidence of social inequalities within the ghettos is ... one of the reasons why ghettos have been somewhat sidelined in historical literature on the Holocaust,"[15] thereby neglecting pioneering works by the Yiddish historians devoted specifically to social antagonisms in the ghettos,[16] as well as their Holocaust studies in general, of which the majority deal with the ghettos in one manner or another.

---

12. The most cited sources in Hebrew are Friedman's articles on the "failed messiahs" of the ghettos, Blumental's compilations on the Lublin and Białystok Jewish Councils, Blumental and Kermish's anthology of the Warsaw Ghetto Uprising, Kermish's six-volume critical edition of the underground press in the Warsaw Ghetto, and the Hebrew translation of Dworzecki's history of Vilna Ghetto (each cited in the bibliography).

13. Yehuda Bauer, *Rethinking the Holocaust* (New Haven, 2001), 68.

14. Tim Cole, "Ghettoization," in *The Historiography of the Holocaust*, ed. Dan Stone (Basingstoke-New York, 2004), 71.

15. Ibid., 72.

16. Some of these are: Dworzecki, "Sotsyale untersheydn in geto," *Di tsukunft* (March 1947): 168–72; Trunk, "Sotsyale antagonizmen in geto un di rol fun di yudenratn," *Yidishe*

Todd Endelman, writing in 1991, contends that the accusations by Bettleheim, Hilberg, and Arendt of the early 1960s occasioned a new direction in Holocaust studies: "One consequence of the debate was that historians of European Jewry began examining questions of Jewish behavior in Nazi-occupied Europe," and he lists as examples such long-standing topics of the Yiddish historians as armed resistance in the ghettos, partisan movements, the *Judenräte*, and the extent of Jewish information about the Nazis' intentions.

Transition: A Case Study

Endelman's article offers a case study in the process by which historians not in the circle of Yiddish scholarship encountered and appraised the seeming novelty of works outside their own areas of linguistic and textual familiarity. In the first decades following World War II, the attitude of Jewish historiography toward the legitimacy of Jewish life in the Diaspora is said by Endelman to have consisted of two phases. In the first phase, arising out of the immediate trauma of the Holocaust, the Jews' inability to prevent the catastrophe was often portrayed as a failure of Jewish leadership and, more broadly, as proof that continued existence in the Diaspora was untenable. In the second phase, reacting directly to the first, a new perspective reinterpreted the same historical experience in ways that permitted a validation of life in the Diaspora.

Such is the picture presented by Endelman in his 1991 essay, "Legitimization of the Diaspora Experience in Recent Jewish Historiography."[17] His chronology appears to draw heavily from a 1979 survey article on Holocaust historiography by Yehuda Bauer and Aharon Weiss, which sets forth the periodization that has remained constant in Bauer's writings.[18]

---

shriftn 6, no. 26 (June 1949): 6–7; Friedman, "Sotsyale konfliktn in geto," *Idisher kemfer* (Pesach 1954): 77–83; (April 30, 1954): 13–14 ["Social Conflict in the Ghetto," *Roads to Extinction*, 131–52]; Kermish, "Vegn der untererdisher prese fun varshever geto," *Di goldene keyt* 27 (1957): 243–57.

17. Todd M. Endelman, "The Legitimization of the Diaspora Experience in Recent Jewish Historiography," *Modern Judaism* 11 (1991): 195–209.

18. Yehuda Bauer and Aharon Weiss, "Historiography of the Holocaust," *Encyclopaedia Judaica 1977/78 Year Book*, ed. Pinchas Hacohen Peli (Jerusalem, 1979), 218–21.

Endelman's original contribution is to relate the perceived changes in attitude of these two phases explicitly to the issue of Diaspora legitimacy. As will be seen, however, the accepted chronology is not in fact adequate to establish causation, and the trend toward affirmation of the Diaspora may instead be traced to a different source.

The crucial point of Endelman's account occurs at the transition from the first to the second phase. He names Bettelheim, Hilberg, and Arendt as the principal scholars whom critics accused of "indicting European Jews for failing to resist their persecutors and even for actively cooperating in their own destruction" and thereby lending support to the Diaspora-negating view. Endelman presents as the antidote the rise of a new group of Diaspora-affirming scholars whose works he then cites.[19] It is important to note that the principal works of the earlier scholars date from the early 1960s,[20] and that those in the later group commence in the early 1970s.

First among the later works cited by Endelman is Trunk's *Judenrat* (1972), in which the detailed examination of Jewish self-governance and social organization caused it to be seen as a corrective to earlier polemics. In 1975, it was the subject of a symposium later published in Bauer and Rotenstreich's book, *The Holocaust as Historical Experience*. In this, Bauer characterizes Hilberg's *The Destruction of the European Jews* (1961) and Trunk's *Judenrat* as "the two great classics of Holocaust historiography."[21] Here also, Hilberg takes credit for recommending Trunk's book to his publisher.[22] The participants, including leading historians and other Jewish thinkers, voice only occasional points of agreement, but unite in appraising Trunk's work as a new direction in Holocaust studies.

What, however, was new? The depth of Trunk's research was unprecedented, but not his area of concentration. The roots of Trunk's *Judenrat* were twofold: Trunk had developed its major themes through a

---

19. Endelman, "The Legitimization of the Diaspora Experience," 198n10.
20. Bruno Bettelheim, *The Informed Heart* (Glencoe, 1960); Raul Hilberg, *The Destruction of the European Jews* (Chicago, 1961); Hannah Arendt, *Eichmann in Jerusalem* (New York, 1963).
21. Yehuda Bauer and Malcolm Lowe, "Introduction," in *The Holocaust as Historical Experience*, ed. Yehuda Bauer and Nathan Rotenstreich (New York, 1981), viii.
22. Ibid., 232.

succession of related works commencing in 1949.[23] All were published in Yiddish and devoted significant portions to Jewish "autonomy" and internal organization under Nazi rule. Second, Trunk relates in his memorial essay on Friedman, who died in 1960, that Friedman's great unfinished project was his work on the Judenrat and that the material Friedman had collected for many years, and published in small part,[24] would need to "await its redeemer"[25] (and an extended period of further research by Trunk). It is not trivial to reiterate that *Judenrat* was written entirely in Yiddish and then translated into English for publication. Trunk's history of the Lodz Ghetto was equally comprehensive, with a major section on Jewish "self-governance," but its audience was limited to readers of Yiddish. Endelman and others correctly observed the new path taken by Trunk's *Judenrat*, but it is possible that its newness lay less in its subject than in its audience.

The second category of "new" historiography for which Endelman cites an example is that of resistance, and for this he names Bauer's *They Chose Life: Jewish Resistance in the Holocaust* (1973). Its selection may best be explained by assuming that Endelman's attention was fixed on works published in English in the 1970s rather than on the much earlier works by Dworzecki and other Yiddish historians.

---

23. Trunk, "Shtudye tsu der geshikhte fun yidn in 'varteland' in der tkufe fun umkum (1939–1944), *Bleter far geshikhte* II, nos. 1–4 (January–December 1949): 64–166; "Sotsyale antagonizmen in geto un di rol fun di yudenratn," *Yidishe shriftn* 6, no. 26 (June 1949): 6–7; "Der fal rudolf kastner in likht fun der yudenratlisher ideologye," *Unzer tsayt* (April–May 1956): 23–27; "Problemen fun ineveynikstn geto-lebn," *Di tsukunft* (April 1960): 150–55; "Strategye un taktik fun di yudenratn in mizrekh-eyrope," in *Aroyfgetsvungene yidishe reprezentantsn unter der natsisher memshole: kolokvyum fun yivo, detsember 2–5, 1967* (New York, 1972), 76–88; "Di batsyung fun di yidnratn tsu der frage fun bavofntn vidershtand kegn di natsis," in *ha-'Amidah ha-Yehudit bi-tekufat ha-Sho'ah* (Jerusalem, 1970), 409–35.

24. Friedman, "ha-Tasbikh ha-meshihi shel takif be-geto ha-Natzi [on Merin in Sosnowicz]," *Bitzaron* XXVIII, no. 5 (April 1953): 29–40; "ha-Tasbikh ha-meshihi shel takife ha-geto [on Gens in Vilna]," *Bitzaron* XXXIX, no. 3 (1953): 151–58 and XXXIX, no. 4 (1954): 232–39; each published in English in *Roads* (1980); condensed jointly as "Two Saviors Who Failed," *Commentary* 26 (December 1958): 479–91; "Go'ale sheker be-geta'ot Polin [on Rumkowski in Lodz]," *Metsudah* VII (1954): 602–18; and "Problems of Research in Jewish 'Self-Government' ('Judenrat') in the Nazi Period," *Yad Vashem Studies* II (1958): 95–113.

25. Trunk, *Geshaltn un gesheenishn* (Buenos Aires, 1962), 45.

Endelman's next citation is Walter Lacquer's *The Terrible Secret: Suppression of the Truth about Hitler's "Final Solution"* (1980). However, the "suppression" to which Lacquer refers did not exist in Yiddish (as discussed in chapter 3) but had to be overcome in the dominant languages of wartime America and Europe.[26]

Endelman's final citation is Israel Gutman's *The Jews of Warsaw, 1939–1943: Ghetto, Underground, Revolt*, published in 1983. Of the many works that might have been chosen, the chief virtue of this work for Endelman's argument is its date. He might have cited Gutman's earlier work on the Warsaw Ghetto leader Mordechai Anielevitch,[27] published in Hebrew in 1963. Or more pertinently, the first major histories of the Warsaw Ghetto Uprising by Kermish and Ber Mark, which appeared in Poland in 1946 and 1947, respectively.[28]

Endelman's chronology poses two additional problems. First, an inconsistent treatment of scholars creates a deceptive causality—he charts the development of Arendt's works from the 1940s through the 1960s but omits the parallel chronology that would give similar precedent to Trunk's later work. Second, a genuine instance of cause and effect is dated in a manner that confounds chronology: Endelman, Bauer and Weiss, and others point to Bettelheim's 1960 work, *The Informed Heart*, as a chief cause of the reaction that marked the second phase of postwar writing. However, in the Yiddish-speaking world, this reaction did not begin in the 1960s. Bettelheim's 1943 article, "Individual and Mass Behavior in Extreme Situations,"[29] was reviewed in the *YIVO bleter* in 1947 by his-

---

26. Walter Lacquer, *The Terrible Secret: Suppression of the Truth about Hitler's "Final Solution"* (Boston, 1980). Chapter 5, "The Jews in Nazi-Occupied Europe: Denial and Acceptance," indicates the widespread (if delayed) transmission to the West of reports by Ringelblum, the Bund, and others.

27. Yisrael Gutman, *Mered ha-netsurim: Mordekhai Anilevitch u-milhemet Geto Varshah* (Merhavyah, 1963).

28. Kermish, *Powstanie w getcie warszawskim (19 kwietnia–16 maja 1943)* (Lodz, 1946), Yiddish trans., *Der oyfshtand in varshever geto: 19ter april–16ter mai 1943* (Buenos Aires, 1948); B. Mark, *Dos bukh fun gvure: oyfshtand fun varshever geto* (Lodz, 1947); expanded version of *Der oyfshtand in varshever geto* (Moscow, 1947).

29. Bruno Bettelheim, "Individual and Mass Behavior in Extreme Situations," *Journal of Abnormal and Social Psychology* XXXVIII (1943): 417–52. Hannah Arendt did not, however, find fault with this aspect of Bettelheim's analysis in her "Social Science Techniques and the Study of Concentration Camps," *Jewish Social Studies* XII (January 1950): 64.

torian Josef Guttmann, who argued against the disparaging attitude already present in Bettelheim's writing, saying that Bettelheim did not have the facts later found in many primary sources, and concluding with an impassioned defense of those who "fought stubbornly for their lives, for their human worth and for their ideals."[30]

Although the search for causation cannot be resolved by a chronology that posits two consecutive phases of postwar historiography, Endelman's observation of two opposing trends is not illusory. I would suggest that the trend he sees as legitimizing Jewish life in the Diaspora did not arise as a reaction to Bettelheim, Hilberg, Arendt, or other postwar historians, but can be traced to an unbroken chain of East European Jewish historians, commencing at the latest with Simon Dubnow and Saul Ginsburg, and continuing throughout the twentieth century to their heirs among the Yiddish historians of the Holocaust. That this trend emerged comparatively slowly into the Western "mainstream" may be explained by the scarcity of Yiddish historians after the war and the slow process of translation in transmitting their works to a wider audience. (For this purpose, "Western" encompasses both American scholarship and the institutional circles in Israel, particularly the Hebrew University, which adhered to the German academic model on which they were founded.)

The process of translation—in both its linguistic and literal sense of moving from one setting to another—was part of the more general process of cultural transmission that occurred in the area of Yiddish culture during the half-century following World War II. Its largest output was in the field of literature—in the many translations of Sholem Aleichem, Y. L. Peretz, Sholem Asch, S. An-sky, and others; and the anthologies of prose and poetry assembled by Joseph Leftwich (starting in 1939), Irving Howe, Eliezer Greenberg, and others. Of special importance for Yiddish historiography is the *YIVO Annual of Jewish Social Science*, which appeared in twenty-two volumes from 1946 to 1995 and became the first gateway for works by Yiddish historians to reach speakers of English. The initial volume brought Elias Tcherikower's "Jewish Martyrology and Jewish Historiography"; volume VIII (1953–54) included articles by

---

30. Yosef Gutman, "Referatn un retsenzyes," *YIVO bleter* XXX, no. 2 (1947): 291–96.

Friedman, Trunk, and Kermish (who cited Blumental); and works by Friedman continued to appear through the 1950s and by Trunk into the mid-1970s. The *YIVO Annual* has remained a source of otherwise inaccessible material for later scholars. An example is Trunk's "Epidemics and Mortality in the Warsaw Ghetto,"[31] on which Charles Roland and Jacob Jay Lindenthal each rely heavily in their studies of medicine in the Warsaw Ghetto.[32]

This transitional phase, in which selected works of Holocaust history entered the scholarly mainstream through translation, was a characteristic of Holocaust literature in general that began during the late 1960s and of which the Yiddish historians' works was a specific instance. Thus, Bauer and Weiss posit essentially the same schema as Endelman in discovering in the late 1960s a sudden emergence of responses to accusations arising earlier in the decade. They contend: "From objections to the books of Hilberg, Arendt, and Bettelheim there developed an apologetic literature which tried to defend the stand of the Jews: e.g. Y. Suhl, *They Fought Back* [and others]."[33] However, this line of argument also encounters a contradiction. Yuri Suhl's well-known book consists of English translations of works first published in Yiddish (or Polish or Russian) between the mid-1940s and mid-1950s, well before the trio of accusers' writings appeared in the early 1960s.[34] It is, rather, the act of translation that is new and which gives the subject of resistance an appearance of novelty.

One may discern an affirmative attitude toward continued Jewish life in the Diaspora not only from the Yiddish historians' writings on resistance but more crucially from their writings on the "righteous among the nations" who hid or aided Jews under Nazi occupation.

---

31. Trunk, "Epidemics and Mortality in the Warsaw Ghetto 1939–1942," *YIVO Annual of Jewish Social Science* VIII (1953): 82–122.

32. Charles G. Roland, *Courage Under Siege: Starvation, Disease, and Death in the Warsaw Ghetto* (Oxford, 1992); and Jacob Jay Lindenthal, "The Epidemiological Status and Health Care Administration of the Jews Before and During the Holocaust," in *Jewish Medical Resistance in the Holocaust*, ed. Michael A. Grodin (New York, 2014), 1–33.

33. Yehuda Bauer and Aharon Weiss, "Historiography of the Holocaust," 219.

34. Yuri Suhl, ed., *They Fought Back: The Story of Jewish Resistance in Nazi Europe* (New York, 1967). Included are historical accounts by Ber Mark and also his wife, Esther Mark.

Kermish and Friedman, who were each hidden by Christian colleagues, and Dworzecki, who observed acts of rescue by Christian Lithuanians, were the historians most drawn to this subject. As early as 1946, Kermish highlighted the actions of Polish-Christian rescuers in his foreword to Gerszon Taffet's memoir of the town of Żółkiew, and much later he treated the subject of organized Christian aid.[35] Dworzecki recorded the efforts to save Jews by Anton Schmidt, the "anti-Nazi Sergeant in the Vilna Ghetto," in both his *Yerusholayim d'lite* of 1948 and a separate account of 1958.[36]

Friedman's address at the YIVO Annual Conference of January 1955 was devoted to the Christian rescuers,[37] and its publication in Yiddish was his first specific work on the subject. In it he declares, "these events deserve to be treated in a separate book."[38] The result was *Their Brothers' Keepers* of 1957, which became widely known as the first English book on the subject of the "righteous gentiles." It provided detailed accounts of rescuers' actions in each country occupied by the Nazis. Here Friedman also reports: "Dr. Mark Dworzecki, chronicler of the Vilna ghetto, cites seventeen Lithuanian scholars and university professors who helped Jews in various ways."[39]

The book's afterlife has come in the work of Rabbi Harold Schulweis, founder of the Jewish Foundation for the Righteous, who writes: "Sifting through the ashes of the Shoah, searching for an ember of hope, I came upon Philip Friedman's *Their Brothers' Keepers*. This pioneer work opened a new world for me."[40] Moreover, he had first been drawn to the

---

35. Kermish, foreword to Gerszon Taffet, *Zagłada Żydów Żółkiewskich* (Lodz, 1946), 5–7; "The Activities of the Council for Aid to the Jews ('Zegota') in Occupied Poland" (Yad Vashem Conference, Jerusalem, April 8–11, 1974), in *Rescue Attempts During the Holocaust* (Jerusalem, 1977), 367–98.

36. Dworzecki, *Yerusholayim d'lite*, 332, 336, 340; see bibliography for the Yiddish, English, and Hebrew versions of his 1958 article, "Anton Schmidt . . . ," which also refers to Friedman's publication of related materials in 1955 (*YIVO bleter* XXXIX).

37. "YIVO Conference Highlights Wide Variety of Scholarly Topics," *News of the YIVO* 56 (March 1955): 2*.

38. Friedman, "Khsidey umos ho'oylem in natsi peryod," *Idisher kemfer* (April 8, 1955, Pesach): 57.

39. Friedman, *Their Brothers' Keepers* (New York, 1957), 138.

40. Harold M. Schulweis, "Globalism and the Jewish Conscience," in *Jews and Judaism in the 21st Century*, ed. Edward Feinstein (Woodstock, 2007), 13.

subject by Friedman's original article in Yiddish.[41] Schulweis's influential lecture of 1963, published that year (and again in 1988) as "The Bias Against Man," was the culmination of his search for a new paradigm of post-Holocaust Jewish education that would not, in his words, "succumb to a view of history raised to the heights of metaphysical fatalism." His new approach was to formulate his own anti-lachrymose view of Jewish history (without reference to Salo Baron's writings) in which the history of the Holocaust could be taught without "a morale-breaking pessimism in rehearsing the tragic past alone." He contends, "It is not enough to quote biblical, rabbinic or Hassidic texts to sustain our faith in man. *Morality needs evidence*, hard data, facts in our time and in our place to nourish our faith in man's capacity for decency."[42] Friedman provided the facts. In an implicit endorsement of the future of Jewish life among the nations of the world, Schulweis concludes: "We are not cameras recording the past. We are children of prophets, creating conditions for a better future. We are not slaves of history. We use history to break the bonds of historic fatalism."[43]

It is indeed possible to infer from the Yiddish historians' works an affirmative attitude toward the possibility of a Jewish future in the Diaspora. But such convictions are also to be found as explicit statements in their own Yiddish works. As early as 1948, in Friedman's first programmatic essay on the study of the Holocaust, he argues that "some Jewish leaders may conclude: The European era of our history has ended," but he

---

41. In conversations with Rabbi Schulweis in July 2014, he told me he had first read Friedman's thoughts in the original Yiddish. He also found in Friedman a point of connection to my own work on the Yiddish historians, which he had encouraged over the preceding decade with the gift of the Yiddish books remaining from his father's library, notably the authoritative Yiddish edition of Dubnow's *Velt geshikhte fun yidishn folk*, 10 vols. (Buenos Aires, 1948–56). More could be written on the place of the righteous gentiles in Schulweis's conception of "predicate theology," which seeks godliness in human behavior; and on his call for support of the righteous gentiles, which exemplifies his "and therefore" interpretation of the ends of Jewish prayer.

42. Harold M. Schulweis, "The Bias Against Man," *Jewish Education* 34, no. 1 (1963): 9; reprinted in *Dimensions: A Journal of Holocaust Studies* 3, no. 3 (1988): 8 (emphasis his). Schulweis did, however, mention Baron in quoting the question posed to him by the defense counsel at the Eichmann trial, which implied that Eichmann was only the latest in a history of preordained persecutors of the Jews.

43. Ibid., 14.

says that such a conclusion "is too quick, so long as 25 percent of world Jewry is still in Europe." He contends: "In our history we have learned that dried-out branches can at times also blossom anew when their historical hour strikes. Jewish communities that are today far removed from creative Jewish life can, in changed circumstances, again return to us."[44] Once settled in New York as dean of the Yiddish-oriented Jewish Teachers' Seminary and Peoples University, Friedman reflected on the problem of assimilation: "The structural crisis cannot be completely resolved, except in one's own land, by the harmonious joint effect of 'Torah, language, and land' (Yehuda Halevy). But in the Diaspora, we will continue to be in a state of permanent struggle against the cultural crisis, and I see no reason to despair. Struggle is life; there is no life and development without continual struggle."[45]

Nor did the Yiddish historians who settled in Israel adopt the then-current Zionist stance of "negation of the Diaspora" (all, for example, retained their own family names, in contrast to many immigrants who adopted new Hebrew names). Blumental, in his multipart essay of 1961 on the phenomenon of the *yizkor* books, expressed unhappiness at the attitude of some Israelis toward these books, saying that he is speaking "not of the strange situation in which young people deliberately approach the *landsmanshaftn* books with a negative attitude: negation of the Diaspora, of Diaspora-types, etc. Regrettably, we see such cases in our present everyday life."[46] Only Dworzecki had insisted, while still in Paris, that Israel was the place for a secure Jewish future, but he nonetheless wrote respectfully of his fellow survivors who chose other destinations for their postwar lives.[47]

The final task that arises from Endelman's analysis is to discern the nature of the phenomenon he describes as the "legitimization of the Diaspora experience." Having noted that it is rooted in the Eastern European Jewish tradition of scholarship, one may also observe a more fundamental

---

44. Friedman, "Di forshung fun unzer khurbn," *Kiem* (January 1948): 47–54.

45. Friedman, "Der kultur krizis in idishn lebn," *Idisher kemfer* (September 23, 1949, Rosh Hashanah): 54.

46. Blumental, "Etlekhe sakh-hakhlen," *Lebns-fragn* 113–14 (March–April 1961): 8.

47. Dworzecki, "Oyf fir vegn veln mir fanandergeyn," *Unzer vort* (September 21, 1945): 2.

characteristic. The much-quoted call in Friedman's Jerusalem address of 1957 for a "Judeo-centric" approach to Holocaust history was echoed by Trunk in 1960 immediately after Friedman's death (both quoted in chapter 4). Trunk then reissued his statement in the 1962 book of his collected works, updated to include a reference to the Eichmann trial:

> It is already high time that our Holocaust research turn its attention from the Nazi side whose persecutions and murders are well enough documented (and it is difficult to add something new after the Nuremberg and Eichmann trials), and turn our attention to the Jewish side, to its life before the murders.[48]

Friedman's and Trunk's exhortations present the defining characteristic of the Yiddish historical tradition: an *internal* approach to Jewish history that necessarily leads to a positive attitude toward Jewish life. Israeli Holocaust historian Amos Goldberg specifically credits Friedman for setting the direction of Holocaust research in Israel: "The Israeli school of Holocaust research crystallized during the 1970s and 1980s, and . . . responds to a large extent to Philip Friedman's early appeal in 1957, during a lecture at the World Congress of Jewish Studies: 'What we need is a history of the Jewish People during the period of Nazi Rule.'"[49]

Remarkably, but not surprisingly, Hilberg states at the 1975 conference on Trunk's *Judenrat*: "Let me add in conclusion that the whole subject of Jewish life under the Nazis in the terminal hours of its existence is really just now surfacing as a field for study."[50] As with Endelman, Bauer, and others, Hilberg's reliance on the passive voice disguises the actors to whom his remarks properly refer, namely, those outside the language community of the Yiddish historians for whom their research agenda may indeed have been unknown until it began "surfacing" in English or Hebrew.

---

48. Quoted from Trunk, *Geshaltn un gesheenishn* (Buenos Aires, 1962), 130, which reiterates this statement from his "Problemen fun ineveynikstn geto-lebn," *Di tsukunft* (April 1960): 150.

49. Amos Goldberg, "The History of the Jews in the Ghettos: A Cultural Perspective," in *The Holocaust and Historical Methodology*, ed. Dan Stone (New York, 2012), 83.

50. "Discussion: The Judenrat and the Jewish Response," in *The Holocaust as Historical Experience*, 233.

It would be an oversimplification to reduce the unending struggle between internal and external approaches to Jewish history to a comparison of "Eastern" and "Western" practices. But it is important to note that the Diaspora-affirming attitude that has become increasingly prominent in the field of Holocaust studies is rooted in the internal approach to Jewish history, and that it is the influence of this approach—not the spontaneous emergence of a new approach—that Endelman has charted.

The Turn to Original Languages

The partial awareness of Yiddish-language scholarship that occurred through the medium of translation has led to a turn—not unlike the rediscovery of classical languages and texts in the early Renaissance—toward research in original languages, a process that began in the final decade of the twentieth century. So long as Yiddish remained the academic vernacular of the last generation of Yiddish-trained scholars educated in Europe before the Holocaust, Yiddish scholarship continued to be the nearly exclusive territory of these scholars. With their passing, Yiddish scholarship, too, entered the postvernacular period identified by Jeffrey Shandler as the general state of nonreligious Yiddish culture in the early twenty-first century.[51] In the area of scholarship, postvernacularity has continued to evolve beyond the phases of translation and re-contextualizing of Yiddish-within-English. A new generation of postvernacular scholars of Yiddish has claimed the language and its texts as their own cultural inheritance and have turned their scholarly energies toward reclaiming its authors and their works.

The turn to original languages (primarily Yiddish, but also other languages of Jewish culture in Eastern Europe) is most evident numerically among scholars of literature; its corollary is the growth of research by historians who have focused their work on the recovery of East European Jewish history from original Yiddish sources. A subset of this group consists of historians of Holocaust historiography whose subjects are the Yiddish historians, if not necessarily the Yiddish orientation of their

---

51. Jeffrey Shandler, *Adventures in Yiddishland: Postvernacular Language and Culture* (Berkeley, 2006).

works. Most notably, these include Natalia Aleksiun, Boaz Cohen, and Laura Jockusch. Still others, to be discussed below, are historians of the Holocaust itself who have turned in varying degrees to the works of their Yiddish-speaking forebears.

One stimulus for the turn to original languages is that many of the Yiddish historians' works continue to be accessible only in Yiddish, in particular their earlier writings which are often the most revealing of their intentions. It is with only slight exaggeration that a member of the newer generation of Yiddish-oriented historians, Jan Schwartz, observes: "Like most post-1945 Yiddish writing, the works of surviving Jewish historians and literary scholars from Eastern Europe—such as Nakhmen Blumenthal, Philip Friedman, Bernard Mark, Mark Dworzecki, and Joseph Kermish—who began collecting and systematically analyzing testimonies and artistic works immediately after the war, have been largely invisible in English."[52] Trunk's absence from Schwartz's list attests to the visibility of his English-language works—any future research on the Lodz Ghetto or the Jewish Councils must first engage the findings of his *Łódź Ghetto* or *Judenrat*. But what of the Yiddish historians' works that are available only in Yiddish?

Has the turn toward research in original Yiddish sources helped to integrate the Yiddish historians' works into the ongoing chain of historical scholarship on the Holocaust? The answer affects the history of Holocaust historiography in relation to two innovations the Yiddish historians brought to Holocaust research, one methodological, the other thematic. These are discussed in the remainder of this chapter.

The Yiddish historians renewed in their postwar historical work the prewar Yiddishist tradition of seeking out and incorporating the popular voice. As discussed in chapter 3, their works rely in large measure on contemporaneous wartime accounts and survivor memoirs and testimony. Trunk's 1979 English-language compilation of (primarily Yiddish) testimonies, mentioned above, is the final product of the long concentration on collecting witness testimonies organized by Friedman and his colleagues at the Central Jewish Historical Commission of Poland, commencing in 1944.

---

52. Jan Schwartz, *Survivors and Exiles: Yiddish Culture After the Holocaust* (Detroit, 2015), 4.

Contrary to the usual process of scholarly succession, most of the Yiddish historians of the Holocaust did not have intellectual heirs in academia. Friedman's early death cut short the teaching legacy he might have had at YIVO and at Columbia University, where he included the Holocaust period in his courses on modern Jewish history as early as 1952.[53] Trunk's longer career at YIVO and as a lecturer at Columbia included students who were future historians (see chapter 1), but few have become known in Holocaust studies. At the time of his sudden death in 1981, Trunk had recently made arrangements to settle in Israel and take up a university position in Holocaust history.[54] At Yad Vashem, Blumental and Kermish did not have (and perhaps did not seek) academic heirs. As Dan Michman points out, the success of the survivor-historians in their fight with the establishment figures at Yad Vashem in 1958 led to the departure of founding director Ben-Zion Dinur and the severing of institutional relations with the Hebrew University. "Yad Vashem lost overnight any possible role it might have had in the development of Holocaust research in Israel for many years to come,"[55] he writes.

Dworzecki was the only survivor-historian associated with Yad Vashem to have a university appointment, and he regarded his mission to be one of public education, not the training of academic successors. On the fourth anniversary of his installation in the world's first chair in Holocaust studies (at Bar-Ilan University in 1959), he reported on his aims and accomplishments in the pages of the Paris journal *Undzer kiem* (Our Existence). He explained that his principal purpose was to train future teachers of Jewish history in the area of Holocaust studies, which, he was proud to announce, was a graduation requirement of the university. He reported that, at the rate of fifty students per year, two hundred students

---

53. "Announcement of the Center of Israeli Studies for the Winter and Spring Sessions, 1952–1953," *Columbia University Bulletin of Information* 52, no. 23 (June 21, 1952): 7 (History 155A, "Jews in Europe since 1914," which includes "World War II and extermination of Jews in Nazi-occupied countries").

54. Personal communications to the author from his son, Gabriel Trunk.

55. Dan Michman, "Is There an 'Israeli' School of Holocaust Research," in *Holocaust Historiography in Context: Emergence, Challenges, Polemics and Achievements*, ed. David Bankier and Dan Michman (Jerusalem, 2008), 44.

had already completed work under the auspices of the Holocaust chair.[56] He had earlier explained that most of his students would go on to become teachers of Jewish history and that his curriculum gave much attention to the ghettos and camps and to resistance in its moral, spiritual, religious, economic, sanitary, political, and armed forms, with an overall aim of teaching his students "to identify with the Jews in the Nazi abyss, to feel their situation of being without escape, to understand the Jewish voices and deeds in a 'world without mercy.'"[57]

Yet Dworzecki's teaching did not find favor with Michman, who claims that Dworzecki "had little influence on the development of Holocaust research, nor did he have many disciples among the next generation—perhaps because of his teaching style, which relied on emotion and first-hand experience, which did not intellectually attract the younger generation of students."[58] At the seemingly late date of 2008 for such a contention, Michman explains the alleged deficiency of Dworzecki's approach: "Dworzecki required all students in his introductory survey course on the Holocaust to interview a Holocaust survivor. In this way, he continued the trend toward documentation that emerged among the survivor community but did not cultivate the methods of scholarly research."[59]

On the contrary, however, the collecting and judicious use of personal accounts has increasingly become a principal tool of Jewish-oriented Holocaust scholarship. It began as a defining element of the survivor-historians' method, first in Poland and then influencing the course taken by the Central Historical Commission in Munich,[60] followed by Yad

---

56. Dworzecki, "4 yor katedre fun khurbn un vidershtand in universitet bar-ilan, yisroel," *Undzer kiem* 28 (May 1963): 10.

57. Dworzecki, "Der khurbn-limud in yisroel," *Undzer kiem* 13 (December 1961): 5.

58. Michman, "Is There an 'Israeli' School," 43. He notes that "in the wake of a bitter personal disagreement, Jozeph Melkman-Michman [Micham's father, general director of Yad Vashem, 1957–60], the last of the 'Dinur gang,'—left the institution in 1960." Ibid.

59. Ibid., 44n12.

60. Moshe Feigenbaum, cofounder with Israel Kaplan of the commission in Munich (which published the journal of survivor testimonies *Fun letstn khurbn*) had worked with Friedman at the CJHC before arriving in Munich in December 1945 on his eventual way to prestate Israel. A. Wolf Yasni indicates that the Munich group adopted the agenda and methods set by Friedman's CJHC: "Tsvantsik yor 'yidisher historisher institut' in poyln," *Lebns-fragn* 154 (March 1965): 6–7.

Vashem and YIVO. Annette Wieviorka traces to Friedman and his colleagues at the Central Jewish Historical Commission (and in Munich) the genesis of the period she calls "the era of the witness."[61] The importance of gathering survivor accounts was the subject of Friedman's 1949 methodological essay, "Di memuaristik" [Memoir-writing],[62] and he continued to encourage this practice on his arrival in New York. His cousin, American filmmaker Martin Kent, recalls: "My mother told me that it was Dr. Friedman who urged her to go to Manhattan one day in 1953, and visit the YIVO Institute for Jewish Research, where she told the story of her family's Holocaust experiences," adding, "I marvel now at the vision of Dr. Friedman and others engaged in the same work; they knew how vital it was to record these testimonies."[63]

Reliance on eyewitness accounts—with the appropriate cautions noted by its advocates—has gained acceptance among historians far removed from the Yiddish historians' area of influence. As is well known, Christopher Browning's 2010 work on the Nazi slave-labor camp at Starachowice was prepared in large part to demonstrate the possibility of writing Holocaust history on the basis of personal accounts, in this case of the victims (while being mindful of the dangers as well).[64] Likely unknown to Browning was Trunk's 1948 monograph on the 173 Nazi slave-labor camps of the annexed Warthegau region of Poland (to the west of Starachowice), which made extensive use of questionnaire responses and eyewitness accounts, as well as contemporaneous documents from the Ringelblum Archive, particularly in the chapters on living conditions and punishments.[65]

Such reliance on the voice of the victim is the historical method for which Martin Gilbert's 1985 history of the Holocaust has been most widely praised. As Bloxham and Kushner note, "The centrality of victim

---

61. Annette Wieviorka, *The Era of the Witness*, trans. Jared Stark [from French, 1998] (Ithaca-London, 2006), ix–xi.

62. Friedman, "Di memuaristik," *Hemshekh* 2 (1949): 26–34.

63. Martin Kent, "In Honor of the Holocaust Remembrance Day" (April 9, 2010), www.jpost.com/Magazine/Features/Years-later-we-would-remember.

64. Christopher R. Browning, *Remembering Survival: Inside a Nazi Slave-Labor Camp* (New York, 2010).

65. Trunk, "Yidishe arbet-lagern in 'varteland,'" *Bleter far geshikhte* I, no. 1 (January–March 1948): 114–69; I, no. 2 (April–June 1948): 14–45.

testimony in its various forms marks this book as pathbreaking."[66] However, Gilbert's history is also pathbreaking for its unexpected, and unacknowledged, reliance on Yiddish sources. In the sections most concerned with Jewish life under Nazi occupation,[67] the reader may be surprised to discover the outsized prominence of a single Polish town, Piotrków Trybunalski—and the sixteen citations to Joseph Kermish's Holocaust history of this town in its *yizkor* book of 1965. Based almost entirely on personal accounts by victims and survivors, Kermish's history well serves Gilbert's purpose, but the status of Piotrków Trybunalski as the exemplar of general trends is unexplained. The apparent answer is that its *yizkor* book was the only one from which a historical chapter by a Yiddish historian had been translated into English at the time of Gilbert's writing. As noted in chapter 3 above, the much later online posting of English translations has made the *yizkor* books the most widely translated source of Holocaust information. Had Gilbert written at a later date, or been able to access the original Yiddish texts, the scope of his work might have included at least a dozen other towns researched by the Yiddish historians (to mention only these historians and their works in *yizkor* books). Gilbert also quotes the abbreviated account given by Dworzecki at the 1961 Eichmann trial of the first discovery in the Vilna Ghetto of the fate of those sent to the "labor camp" at Ponar, neglecting the much fuller description to be found in Dworzecki's 1948 *Yerusholayim d'lite*.[68] In all, Gilbert quotes from English translations of works by Blumental, Dworzecki, Friedman, Kermish, and Trunk (as well as Blumental's one book in Polish), but misses the many subjects covered only in their Yiddish writings.

Turning from the methodological to the thematic, it would be difficult to find an area of Jewish Holocaust research in which the Yiddish historians did not anticipate the agendas of later historians. Their concentration on the Jewish history of the Holocaust informed not only their method

---

66. Donald Bloxham and Tony Kushner, *The Holocaust: Critical Historical Approaches* (Manchester, 2005), 39.

67. Commencing with chapter 7 in Martin Gilbert, *The Holocaust: A History of the Jews of Europe during the Second World War* (New York, 1985); the nearly identical British edition of 1986 bears the title *The Holocaust: The Jewish Tragedy*.

68. Ibid., 194, 848n38. Dworzecki, *Yerusholayim d'lite*, 53–56.

of inquiry but also their choice of topics, so that subsequent Holocaust research has turned increasingly to areas in which the Yiddish historians pioneered. Until the end of the twentieth century, it was only the exceptional scholar who built historical narratives on the Yiddish historians' Yiddish works. One example is Solon Beinfeld, whose articles on life in the ghettos, particularly the Vilna Ghetto and on medical resistance in Vilna, quote liberally from Dworzecki's *Yerusholayim d'lite* and Trunk's *Lodzsher geto*.[69]

By contrast, Holocaust historians who came of age academically in the early twenty-first century have turned to the Yiddish historians' original Yiddish works in larger numbers and with, one might say, greater enthusiasm than the sum total of prior generations of non-Yiddish historians. Theirs is the generation of the turn to original languages. A few examples reveal a larger process:

Nachman Blumental, who was perhaps less appreciated in his lifetime than the other Yiddish historians—his training was not formally in history and his favored subjects were Yiddish literature and folklore—has gained new regard at a time of increased interest in the place of language in cultural history. Amos Goldberg, for example, writes in 2012 that language "possesses an unconscious independence which embodies the truth of the speaker, of the era, and of the culture in which it is spoken." He relates that, while some postwar Jewish intellectuals investigated the Nazi use of language, "Blumenthal, however, went even further and thoroughly examined the changes that Yiddish underwent in his fascinating and comprehensive work titled *Verter un vertlekh fun der khurbn-tkufe* [Words and Sayings of the Holocaust Period]."[70] David Roskies had previously declared the same work to be one of two "standard reference works" on Jewish language during the Holocaust.[71]

---

69. Solon Beinfeld, "Life in the Ghettos of Eastern Europe," in *Genocide: Critical Issues of the Holocaust*, ed. Alex Grobman and Daniel Landes (West Orange, 1983), 173–89; "The Cultural Life of the Vilna Ghetto," *Simon Wiesenthal Center Annual* 1 (1984): 5–25; "Health Care in the Vilna Ghetto," *Holocaust and Genocide Studies* 12, no. 1 (1998): 88–98.

70. Amos Goldberg, "The History of the Jews in the Ghettos," (PhD diss., Hebrew University, 2004), 93–94.

71. David Roskies, "What Is Holocaust Literature?," in *Jews, Catholics, and the Burden of History*, ed. Eli Lederhendler (Oxford, 2005), 205 endnote 31. The other was Yisroel Kaplan, *Dos folks-moyl in natsi-klem: reydenishn in geto un katset* (Munich, 1949).

Blumental's 1966 book of writings on "Yiddish literature under the German occupation"[72] is the subject of a 2014 article by the young French specialist in Yiddish literature, Fleur Kuhn-Kennedy.[73] The same book is one of the principal works discussed by Holocaust historian Miryam Trinh in her 2011 article on the state of research on Holocaust poetry.[74] Her dissertation supervisor, Yehiel Sheintuch of the Hebrew University (formerly a young colleague of both Blumental and Kermish) reported in the Yiddish *Forverts* in 2012 that Blumental's son had given Trinh access to Blumental's personal collection, which Sheintuch describes as "today, the largest remaining private collection" of Holocaust literature, with "about 1,000 works of poetry," some of which served as the basis for Blumental's own research. (Sheintuch recounts that, "with a pistol in his pocket," Blumental went from one city to another in postwar Poland and "singlehandedly assembled valuable documentation that remained after the Holocaust years."[75])

The 2007 published dissertation by Gudrun Schroeter on written culture in the Vilna Ghetto quotes repeatedly from both Dworzecki's *Yerusholayim d'lite* and Trunk's *Lodzsher geto*;[76] the 2007 published dissertation by Ingo Loose, on the role of German credit banks in the destruction and economic exploitation of Poles and Jews in occupied Poland, cites Trunk's history of the Nazi slave-labor camps in the Warthegau and his *Lodzsher geto*;[77] and the 2012 article by Katarzyna Person of the Jewish Histori-

---

72. Blumental, *Shmuesn vegn der yidisher literatur unter der daytsher okupatsye* (Buenos Aires, 1966). The principal material cited by these authors is found in Blumental's first two chapters—his first major work on the subject, which became available online via this book; see "Di yidishe literatur unter der daytshisher okupatsye," *Yidishe kultur* 8, no. 1 (January 1946): 6–10.

73. Fleur Kuhn-Kennedy (PhD, Université Sorbonne Nouvelle—Paris 3, 2013), "Autour de Nakhmen Blumental: réfléchir aux écritures de la Catastrophe dans l'après-guerre," *Lire une collection en yiddish Histoire et mémoire d'un monde disparu au lendemain de la catastrophe* (February 19, 2014), http://poly.hypotheses.org/250.

74. Miryam Trinh (PhD, Hebrew University, 2013), "L'écriture poétique durant la Shoah," *Yod* 16 (December 6, 2011), http://yod.revues.org/292. DOI: 10.4000/yod.292.

75. Yekhiel Shayntukh, "Fun khurbn biz tsum vider-oyfboy: naye bikher un forshungen in yerusholayim," *Forverts* (May 11, 2012).

76. Gudrun Schroeter (PhD, Freie Universität Berlin, 2006), *Worte aus einer zerstörten Welt: Das Ghetto in Wilna* (St. Ingbert, 2007).

77. Ingo Loose (PhD, Humboldt-Universität zu Berlin, 2005), *Kredite für NS-Verbrechen: Die deutschen Kreditinstitute in Polen und die Ausroubung der polnischen und judischen*

cal Institute in Warsaw on aspects of the Ringelblum Archive cites early Yiddish articles by both Kermish and Blumental.[78]

More than chance has dictated each author's choices of Yiddish sources. One may speculate that a sense of impending cultural loss among the first generation of scholars of the new millennium motivated their turn to Yiddish and the retrieval of Yiddish sources, but the extent of their ability to do so reflects a more mundane circumstance. Nearly all of the sources cited by these authors had recently been made available through the online archive of the Yiddish Book Center in Amherst, Massachusetts (or in a few cases were available in hard copy at the home institution of the author).[79] The books posted online by the center reflect a process of selection that began at the start of the digital age of Yiddish books. In 2004, Zachary Baker, the well-known Judaica bibliographer and librarian, compiled a list of 1,000 "essential Yiddish books" from those scanned for preservation in the center's holdings. He indicates that "limiting this bibliography to the universe of *belles lettres* and criticism would have resulted in a skewed perspective of Yiddish cultural expression and the modern Jewish experience alike," leading to his addition of works from other fields, including history.[80] Each of the Yiddish historians of

---

Bevölkerung 1939–1945 (Munich, 2007), 16n396; Loose also quotes from Trunk's "Arbetlagern" in his "Die Bateiligung deutscher Kreditinstitute an der Vernichtung der ökonomischen Existenz der Juden in Polen 1939–1945," in *Die Commerzbank und die Juden, 1933–1945*, ed. Ludolf Herbst and Thomas Weihe (Munich, 2004), 223–71. Loose's focus on German rather than Jewish acts may explain the absence of Trunk's 1949 history of Jewish life in the occupied Warthegau from Loose's "Wartheland," in *The Greater German Reich and the Jews: Nazi Persecution Policies in the Annexed Territories 1939–1945*, ed. Wolf Gruner and Jorg Osterloh, trans. Bernard Heise [from German, 2010] (New York, 2015), 189–218.

78. Katarzyna Person (PhD, University of London, 2010), "The Initial Reception and First Publications from the Ringelblum Archive in Poland, 1946–1952," *Gal-Ed: On the History and Culture of Polish Jewry* 23 (2012): 59–76; see n23: Kermish, "Gen. Stroops [tshuves] oyf an ankete mit anareynfirvort fun dir. Kermish," *Bleter far Geshikhte* 1, nos. 3–4 (1948): 166–85; n41: Blumental, "Di arbet iber Ringelblums ksavyadn," *Yedies: byuletin fun yidishn historishn Institut* [1] (November 1949): 3–6; and n72: Blumental, "Di yerushe fun emanuel ringelblum," *Di goldene keyt* 15 (1953): 240.

79. By 2004, thousands of books had been made available by the center in the form of digital reprints, and approximately 11,000 were posted online in 2009 and shortly thereafter.

80. Zachary M. Baker, *Essential Yiddish Books: 1000 Great Works from the Collection of the National Yiddish Book Center: Introduction* (N.p., n.p., text indicates 2004), www.yiddishbookcenter.org/collections/digital-yiddish-library/1000-essential-yiddish-books.

the Holocaust is represented by one or more titles,[81] as are each of the other principal authors of Yiddish historiography in general.[82] Thus, the turn to Yiddish sources by scholars of the new millennium was facilitated by a concurrent turn toward the promotion of these sources by those who had come to value and preserve them.

Yet it must be noted that the great majority of the Yiddish historians' writings are to be found only in journals and other periodicals and not in book-length monographs. The current account must therefore pivot from the past to the evolving present to ask: What has been the fate, or influence, of writings by Yiddish historians that are available only to researchers with the foresight or good fortune to find them on paper or microfilm? So far, only a few of the periodicals in which their works appear are available online, although that number is gradually increasing, and it is those works that remain to be discovered by later historians of the Holocaust.

The Yiddish historians' less accessible Yiddish works, which have neither been translated nor yet become available online, adumbrate the research agendas of later generations:

Blumental had urged as early as 1948 that humor and ridicule be considered forms of unarmed resistance,[83] and he repeated his contention

---

81. These include Blumental's *Shmuesn*, Dworzecki's *Yerusholayim d'lite* and *Hirshke glik*, Friedman's *Oshvyentshim*, Kermish's *Oyfshtand*, and Trunk's *Geshtaltn un gesheenishn* (1983) and *Lodzsher geto*.

82. The list includes books in Yiddish by historians Mayer Bałaban, Elias Cherikover, Simon Dubnow, Saul Ginsburg, Raphael Mahler, Emanuel Ringelblum, and Jacob Shatzky; literary historians Elias Schulman, Meir Wiener, and Israel Zinberg; and lay historians Julian Hirshaut, A. Wolf Yasni, and Moshe Kahanovitsh (spelling per Baker's list).

83. Blumental, "Di yidishe shprakh un der kamf kegn natsi-rezshim," *Bleter far geshikhte* I, nos. 3–4 (August–December 1948): 106–24. Blumental's thesis was implicitly endorsed by Friedman in his review ("Forshungen fun letstn khurbn," *YIVO bleter* XXXIV [1950]: 231–39), notwithstanding errors Friedman alleges in the origins of certain examples (see 237–38). This review appears to be the only instance of intemperate or ad hominem remarks by Friedman or any other Yiddish historian, perhaps motivated by some discontent or conflict with Blumental who had been appointed to succeed him as director of the CJHC after his departure. He says, for example, that "Blumental, who was in Russia during the German occupation" (while he himself was in hiding in German-occupied Lwów), was unfamiliar with relevant events. It seems prudent to maintain a balanced view of his criticisms. Friedman later returned to favorable mentions of Blumental's work.

at the 1968 Yad Vashem conference (as discussed in chapter 5).[84] The objection by Lucy Dawidowicz that the conference theme improperly expanded "resistance" to encompass "whatever Jews did to thwart" the Nazis, was aimed most directly at Blumental: "Probably the most strained presentation was one which claimed that telling jokes against Hitler was a form of resistance."[85] In later decades, Blumental's view gained adherents. In his 1997 essay, "Humor in the Holocaust," philosopher of humor John Morreall argues that "humor focused attention on what was wrong and sparked resistance to it."[86] In 2003, historian Louis Kaplan retraced (in a more structured manner than Blumental) the corpus of anti-Nazi humor that Blumental had engaged in 1948. He recounts not less than a dozen anti-Nazi barbs, including one told by Blumental (e.g., that, at the start of 1942, Jews in the Ghetto would say the new year should be called "1941A" because Hitler had promised to win the war in 1941).[87] Yet Kaplan limits himself almost entirely to material from a single source (Jacob Sloan's 1953 English translation of Ringelblum's *Notes*), rather than the materials quoted by Blumental from the much broader sources already collected by the Jewish Historical Institute in Warsaw.

Kaplan's observation—"The primacy of the Jewish joke in the service of resistance against the Nazi oppressor also helps to account for the fact that Ringelblum's *Notes* contain only one joke that is completely self-directed in character"[88]—supports Blumental's thesis about the place of humor in Jewish resistance, but it also points to the relevance of Blumental's article for future research. Inexplicably, the study published in 2014 by Chava Ostrower, *It Kept Us Alive: Humor in the Holocaust*, based on interviews of Holocaust survivors, reports findings contrary to Kaplan's

---

84. Blumental, "Sources for the Study of Jewish Resistance," *Jewish Resistance During the Holocaust: Proceedings of the Conference on Manifestations of Jewish Resistance, Jerusalem, April 7–11, 1968* (Jerusalem, 1971), 50–51.

85. Lucy S. Dawidowicz, *The Holocaust and the Historians* (Cambridge, 1981), 133–34.

86. John Morreall, "Humor in the Holocaust: Its Critical, Cohesive, and Coping Functions," Holocaust Teacher Research Center (November 11, 2001), www.holocaust-trc.org/humor-in-the-holocaust.

87. Louis Kaplan, "'It Will Get a Terrific Laugh': On the Problematic Pleasures of Politics of Holocaust Humor," in *Hop on Pop: The Politics and Pleasures of Popular Culture*, ed. Henry Jenkins et al. (Durham, 2002), 348; and Blumental, "Di yidishe shprakh," 114.

88. Ibid.

statement.[89] Her respondents recall a minimum of anti-Nazi humor and, instead, primarily those forms she describes as defense mechanisms and gallows humor. Had Ostrower compared her findings with Blumental's, it might have prompted a check of further variables, such as age (her respondents were all teenagers during the war), the memory value of personal versus political humor, or divergent experiences peculiar to the minority who survived—and the many other possibilities suggested by Blumental's article.

On the subject of Jewish women and resistance, Lenore Weitzman has suggested that the relative neglect of the role of women reflects the often-secret nature of their activities.[90] Her well-known article of 2004, "Women of Courage," focuses on the Jewish women who "smuggled underground newspapers, forged identity cards, secret documents, money, food, medical supplies, guns, ammunition—and other Jews—in and out of the ghettos of Poland, Lithuania, and parts of Russia." Weitzman quotes particularly the prediction by Ringelblum in the Warsaw Ghetto, "'The story of the Jewish women will be a glorious page in the history of Jewry during the present war,'" but finds to the contrary: "Instead of being recognized, as Ringelblum predicted, as 'leading figures,' they have typically been ignored."[91] Early attention to the works of the Yiddish historians might have prevented the neglect to which Weitzman refers. In at least

---

89. Chaya Ostrower, *It Kept Us Alive: Humor in the Holocaust* (Jerusalem, 2014). For an overview of her research, see Ostrower's "Humor as a Defense Mechanism in the Holocaust," www.academia.edu/554260/Humor_as_a_Defense_Mechanism_in_the_Holocaust. One may note that Blumental said in his foreword to one of Rachmil Bryk's novels of the Lodz Ghetto that the story "also possesses humor—folk humor"; see Yerakhmiel Briks, *Di papirene kroyn* (New York, 1969), 7. Four decades later, Bryk's daughter writes: "I translated fragments of my father Rachmil Bryks's writings from Yiddish to English from his book, 'Di Papirene Kroyn' . . . for Chaya's book [on humor] . . . . The text relates to the life of Yankele, der Folkzinger (Yankele Hershkowitz) in the Lodz Ghetto. Pages 276, 370n.20, 372, 378 n.32, 379." See Bella Bryks-Klein and Chaya Ostrower, Academia: Beit Berl Academic College, https://beitberl.academia.edu/Departments/Psychology/Documents.

90. Lenore J. Weitzman, "Living on the Aryan Side in Poland: Gender, Passing, and the Nature of Resistance," in *Women in the Holocaust*, ed. Dalia Ofer and Lenore J. Weitzman (New Haven, 1998), 217.

91. Lenore J. Weitzman, "Women of Courage: The *Kashariyot* (Couriers) in the Jewish Resistance During the Holocaust," in *New Currents in Holocaust Research*, ed. Jeffry M. Diefendorf (Evanston, 2004), 112–13.

three articles during the 1940s, Dworzecki praises the indispensable role of the messengers, almost all of whom were women, referring specifically to the "holy heroism" of the "female messengers."[92] He declares, "The historical researcher will record the fact of the mighty, active participation of the Jewish woman in the resistance movement."[93] In an article published in 1971, Dworzecki declares that "the women demonstrated more initiative, endurance, energy, ability to work, than the men, and were better able to cope," and that "in missions from ghetto to ghetto, in slipping across borders, in smuggling weapons and communiques—the young Jewish women were the first in each difficult task."[94]

On the subject of gender as "a relative newcomer in the field of Holocaust studies," Lisa Pine argues that the "the era of 'second-wave feminism' in the 1970s" and the concurrent "proliferation of survivors' memoirs" inspired and enabled the rise of women's studies within Holocaust research. "Pioneering articles published by Joan Ringelheim and Sybil Milton in 1984" are credited by Pine as the foundation for later research. She contends that prior to this "questions pertaining to gender simply were not asked."[95] Yet, anticipating these much later research interests, a lesser-known chapter of Dworzecki's 1948 *Yerusholayim d'lite*, "The Ghetto Person: Man, Woman, Child, Youths, the Aged," discusses specifically the altered roles of men and women in the ghettos and the unprecedented burdens assumed by women, in whom he observed "a new psychological stance, which I would call a *catastrophe dynamism*."[96]

Separately, Kermish, the specialist on the Warsaw Ghetto, writes during the 1950s on the topic of "The Jewish Woman in the Warsaw Ghetto Uprising": "The Jewish woman played an extremely important role in the resistance movement of the Warsaw Ghetto as the distributor

---

92. Dworzecki, "Farshvaygn—oder dertseyln dem gantsn emes?" *Unzer vort* (June 22, 1945): 3. See also "Di untererdishe shlikhim fun geto tsu geto," *Idisher kemfer* (April 16, 1948): 3–4 (chapter 18 of *Yerusholayim d'lite*); and "Getos un kontsentratsye-lagern zukhn kontaktn," *Kiem* (April 1949): 899 (expanded version of the previous).

93. Dworzecki, *Yerusholayim d'lite*, 299.

94. Dworzecki, "Der mentsh in thom (draysik yor zint vilner geto)," *Di goldene keyt* 74 (1971): 73–82 (condensed and augmented version of *Yerusholayim d'lite*, chapter 12).

95. Lisa Pine, "Gender and Family," in *The Historiography of the Holocaust*, ed. Dan Stone (New York, 2004), 364.

96. Dworzecki, *Yerusholayim d'lite*, 299 (emphasis his).

of the illegal press, and especially as the contact between the ghetto and the Aryan side and among the ghettos in the hinterland and in Warsaw."[97] He continues with a discussion of the period of the uprising itself and the "indescribable heroism" of the "fighting Jewish young women" whom he names from each political arm of the uprising, together with their particular actions. While hardly presaging the field of gender studies, this article places Kermish ahead of other Holocaust historians in recognizing specific roles for women in the resistance. And again, in one of his last Yiddish articles, published in 1983, Kermish repeats his reference to the "secret messengers of the Jewish underground in Warsaw and in Vilna, particularly the heroic young Jewish women."[98]

An increased acquaintance with the Yiddish historians' own words, found only in Yiddish periodicals, might have consequences for additional fields: recognition of the phenomenon of escape from trains as a form of resistance (as, for example, in Tanja von Fransecky's important book of 2014[99]) might be read against Dworzecki's 1966 discussion of "those who fled from the trains."[100] The role of Holocaust historian Joseph Wulf (who is said to have "failed utterly" in his own time by Nicolas Berg in a 2008 article subtitled, "A Forgotten Outsider Among Holocaust Scholars"[101]), might be contextualized more broadly by Blumental's 1969 essay in praise

---

97. Kermish, "Di yidishe froy in varshever geto-oyfshtand," *Der poylisher yid* 8–9 (1958): 34. It is likely that the original Yiddish version first appeared at an earlier date in a publication I have not located. An abridged version of this article appeared in Hebrew as "ha-Lohemet ha-Yehudit be-mered Geto Varshah," *Davar* (April 29, 1954): 2.

98. Kermish, "Umbakante briv fun zelig kalmanovitsh, fun vilner geto, tsu itsik giterman, in varshever geto," *Di goldene keyt* 110–11 (1983): 25.

99. Tanja von Fransecky, *Flucht von Juden aus Deportationszügen in Frankreich, Belgien und den Niederlanden* (Berlin, 2014).

100. Dworzecki, "Vilner vos zenen gelofn: fun ponar—fun di deportatsye-banen—fun di estishe katsetn," *Di goldene keyt* 57 (1966): 198–211. For a still earlier recognition by Kermish (in Polish) of "the 'jumpers' who leaped out of speeding railway cars," see his foreword to Gerszon Taffet, *Zagłada Żydów Żółkiewskich* (Lodz, 1946), 6.

101. Nicolas Berg, "Joseph Wulf, A Forgotten Outsider Among Holocaust Scholars," in *Holocaust Historiography in Context: Emergence, Challenges, Polemics and Achievements*, ed. David Bankier and Dan Michman (Jerusalem, 2008), 167–206 (listing comprehensively, but exclusively, the treatments of Wulf to be found in German, and not Wulf's earliest Holocaust writings in Yiddish from 1945 to 1952). Wulf's early postwar work is given due coverage in Klaus Kempter's "'Objective, Not Neutral': Joseph Wulf, a Documentary Historian," *Holocaust Studies* 21, nos. 1–2 (October 2015): 38–52, but again without reference to writings in Yiddish by or about Wulf.

of his former colleague[102]—who has been recognized most recently as the subject of an international conference in Paris in 2018.[103] The latter-day interest in German thefts from ordinary Jews in the course of murderous actions (discussed by Jonathan Petropoulos in 2006 and Dieter Pohl in 2007,[104] among others)—as opposed to the better-known taking of property and artworks—might be augmented by the expert testimonies by Kermish and Trunk on this subject at Polish war crimes trials, which appeared in the Yiddish press in Lodz in the 1940s.[105] The potential influence of the Yiddish historians' writings on these and similar topics awaits the wider availability of the Yiddish periodicals in which they appear.

The answer to the question posed above is therefore a partial yes. The turn toward research in original Yiddish sources has led to specific instances of integrating the Yiddish historians' works into the ongoing chain of historical scholarship on the Holocaust, particularly in regard to their eyewitness approach to Holocaust history and increasingly, though far from completely, in topic areas foreshadowed by their shared research agenda.

Yet one may also ask, if indeed the Yiddish historians had no academic heirs, are such instances of foreshadowing truly noteworthy? I would suggest that, first, such recognition is a matter of simple justice. Withholding recognition of the early survivor-historians' research on a given topic in Holocaust history differs only in degree from erasing the testimony of the victims or survivors whose voices they preserved. And, more practically, I would suggest that later research should not necessarily be seen

---

102. Blumental, "Der oyftu fun yosef vulf," *Di goldene keyt* 65 (1969): 200–206.

103. See Mark L. Smith, "Joseph Wulf—The Path Not Taken: His early career in Yiddish Holocaust studies," invited conference paper for "Joseph Wulf: A Polish-Jewish Historian in Western Germany," joint project of Zentrum für Literatur- und Kulturforschung (Berlin) and Centre de Recherches Historiques, École des Hautes Études en Sciences Sociales (Paris); Polish Academy of Sciences, Paris (February 16, 2018), https://savoirs-inclassables.ehess.fr.

104. Jonathan Petropoulos, "The Nazi Kleptocracy: Reflections on Avarice and the Holocaust," in *The Holocaust in International Perspective*, ed. Dagmar Herzog (Evanston, 2006), 29–38; and Dieter Pohl, "The Robbery of Jewish Property in Eastern Europe Under Nazi Occupation, 1939–1942," in *Robbery and Restitution: The Conflict Over Jewish Property in Europe*, ed. Martin Dean et al. (New York, 2007), 68–80.

105. Kermish, "Der talyen fun lodzsher yidntum—hans bibov," *Dos naye lebn* (March 13, 1946): 5, 7; and Trunk, "Ekspertize fun mgr y. trunk," *Dos naye lebn* (September 6, 1948): 6, 8.

as superseding in depth or comprehension the work of those historians most directly connected with their subject. Rather, when historians conduct a "literature search" at the initial stage of research on a given subject, their search should be considered incomplete if it is limited to works in the major languages of Holocaust study without considering works written in Yiddish (and other languages) by the original scholars in the field.

In the Field of Yiddish Studies

The cultural transmission of the Yiddish historians' works from the world of the Yiddish-speaking survivors to that of ongoing scholarship and public accessibility suggests a further area of integration: the transference of their works beyond the limited sphere of historical writing to their inclusion in the field of Yiddish studies in general.

The omission of the Yiddish historians' works from the present-day study of Yiddish letters accords with Western categories of thought that run counter to the origin and development of Yiddish scholarship.[106] When Elias Tcherikower sought to recount the long history of historical chronicles in Yiddish in his "Jewish Martyrology and Jewish Historiography" of 1941,[107] he might well have consulted the two standard histories of Yiddish literature then recently published to identify the principal works of history he wished to discuss: Israel Zinberg's history of Jewish literature devotes a chapter to the writings he describes as "the third branch of Old Yiddish prose—historiography."[108] Max Erik's history of Yiddish literature similarly offers a chapter on works of history, commencing with the

---

106. Ber Borochov, generally considered the founder of the national approach to Yiddish philology, included in his seminal bibliography a listing (item no. 356) for Moritz Steinschneider's *Die geschichtsliteratur der Juden in druckwerken und handschriften* of 1905, in which Steinschneider comments on the principal historical chronicles in Yiddish and in Yiddish translation. See "Di biblyoteyk fun'm yidishn filolog: firhundert yor yidishe shprakhforshung," in *Der pinkes: yor-bukh far der geshikhte fun der yidisher literature un shprakh, far folklor, kritik un biblyografye*, ed. Sh. Niger (Vilna, [1913]), separate pp. 1–66.

107. E. Cherikover, "Yidishe martirologye un yidishe historiografye," *YIVO bleter* XVII, no. 2 (March–April 1941): 97–112.

108. Following traditional storybooks (*mayse-bikher*) and morality books (*musersforim*): Yisroel Tsinberg, *Di geshikhte fun literatur bay yidn*, vol. VI: *Alt-yidishe literatur fun di eltste tsaytn biz der haskole-tkufe* (Vilna, 1935), 259; (Buenos Aires, 1967), 208.

statement, "Historical literature in Yiddish has developed since the 16th century, and it belongs—both according to the number of writings and to their execution and historical value—to the most important fields of Old Yiddish literature."[109]

This inclusion of historical works in the ongoing formation of the canon of Yiddish letters continued after the Nazi invasion of Poland. For example, one of the first books published secretly in 1940 during the Nazi occupation of Warsaw—in Yiddish, by the Dror Labor-Zionist movement—was titled, "Suffering and Heroism in the Jewish Past in Light of the Present." Together with essays and fiction by well-known authors, it includes excerpts from historical works by Dubnow, Graetz, Bernfeld, Zinberg, and, most pertinently, from Tcherikower's history of the Ukrainian pogroms of 1917–18.[110] That the organic growth of the Yiddish prose canon continued even after World War II may be observed in the anthology *The Yiddish Essay* published in New York in 1946 by Yiddish literary critic and essayist Shlomo Bickel "as a teaching-book for the higher classes in the Yiddish secular high schools in America" and also "as a reading-book for adults, which will acquaint them with well-selected exemplars of the essay genre."[111] Here, among nonfiction works of all genres, appear writings by the Yiddish historians Erik, Ginsburg, Shatzky, Schiper, Mahler, Menes, Tcherikower, and Zinberg. As late as 1991, the Union of Yiddish Writers and Journalists in Israel selected both Kermish and Dworzecki to be among the local Yiddish writers (nearly all of fiction and verse) whose works are included in their anthology, *Yiddish Literature in the State of Israel*.[112]

The field of Yiddish letters has traditionally been a self-reflective one, and it has also been sufficiently active (and compact) to inspire a century-long series of authoritative "lexicons" of Yiddish writers. The

---

109. Max Erik, *Di geshikhte fun der yidisher literatur fun di eltste tsaytn biz der haskole-tkufe, fertsenter-akhtsenter yorhundert* (Warsaw, 1928), 373.

110. *Payn un gvure in der yidisher over in likht fun der kegnvart* (Warsaw, July–August 1940; 3rd. ed. Munich, 1947), also discussed in Kermish, 'Itonut-ha-mahteret ha-Yehudit be-Varshah, vol. 1: May 1940–January 1941 (Jerusalem, 1979), 44–52.

111. Shloyme Bikl, ed., *Di yidishe esey: a zamlung* (New York, 1946), 7.

112. See *Yidish-literatur in medines-yisroel: antologye* (Tel Aviv, 1991); Dworzecki, "'Zog nit keyn mol az du geyst dem letstn veg!,'" vol. 1, 256–60, and Kermish, "Nisht bloyz kortshak aleyn . . . ," vol. 2, 330–34 (each with a photo and brief biography).

first such work, a single volume by Zalmen Rejzen that appeared in Warsaw in 1914, did not take note of the new field of Yiddish historical writing,[113] but his subsequent four-volume edition of 1926–29 included multipage biographies of Erik, Ginsburg, Ringelblum, Shatzky, Schiper, Tcherikower, and Zinberg, among others.[114] After World War II, the series was renewed by the Congress for Jewish Culture in New York with its eight-volume *Biographical Dictionary of Modern Yiddish Literature* of 1956–81, funded by the Conference on Material Claims Against Germany.[115] It includes all of the Yiddish historians of the Holocaust as well as their non-historian colleagues and lay historians. Only Dworzecki, who had opposed the 1952 West German reparations agreement with Israel and refused to benefit personally from reparations payments, presumably (like Isaac Bashevis Singer) declined to participate, is represented with a token entry—an omission later rectified by Berl Kagan's supplementary volume of 1986.[116] Most recently, the tradition of including historians within the overall category of Yiddish writers was confirmed by Chaim Beider's lexicon of Soviet Yiddish writers, published by the Congress for Jewish Culture in 2011.[117]

This inclusive view of historical writing has not been limited to scholars of Yiddish literature such as Zinberg and Erik, or compilers of Yiddish lexicons, but existed broadly before World War II as an integrated approach to Jewish culture. The leading example is Meyer Waxman, whose magnum opus, *A History of Jewish Literature*, included the writings of Jewish historians—in all languages.[118] However, there does not appear to be any postwar academic treatment that places Yiddish historians within

---

113. Zalmen Reyzen, *Leksikon fun der yidisher literatur un prese* (Warsaw, 1914).

114. Zalmen Reyzen, *Leksikon fun der yidisher literatur, prese un filologye*, 4 vols. (Vilna, 1926–29).

115. [Various editors], *Leksikon fun der nayer yidisher literatur* (New York, 1956–81).

116. Berl Kahan, "Dvorzshetski, Mark," *Leksikon fun yidish-shraybers* (New York, 1986), 191–93.

117. Khaym Bayder, *Leksikon fun yidishe shrayber in ratn-farband*, ed. Boris Sandler and Gennady Estraikh (New York, 2011).

118. Meyer Waxman, *A History of Jewish Literature*, vol. 4; book VIII: Jewish Learning and Thought (1880–1935); chapter XI: History, Geography, Biography, and Autobiography (New York, 1941), 718–866.

the rubric of "Yiddish writers" or "Jewish literature" (whether of the prewar, wartime, or postwar period).

The issue is not an incidental question of classification but is fundamental to the process by which Yiddish historical writings were traditionally created and received. The great majority of the Yiddish historians' writings first appeared in publications other than scholarly journals—and these, as well as their articles in scholarly journals, were written for a general audience. The original readers of the Yiddish historians' works would expect to find them on pages adjoining political essays, poetry, and fiction. The unitary nature of Yiddish cultural consumption argues for removal of the barrier between history and other forms of writing erected by external categories of thought. I would argue that among the more than 500 Yiddish books, articles, essays, and *yizkor* book chapters quoted in the present work there are those that merit a return to the earlier tradition of including historical writing within the study of Yiddish literary production.

Like other Yiddish-speaking intellectuals of their time, the historians wrote an academic Yiddish that, on the one hand, met the challenge of adapting the folk vernacular to the needs of modern secular scholarship and, on the other, retained the varieties of dialect, idiom, and sources of allusion that their readers would recognize as authentic to *mame-loshen*, their Yiddish mother tongue. For example, the *Great Dictionary of the Yiddish Language*—which is organized in the style of the *Oxford English Dictionary*, with examples of word usage in sentences quoted from well-known authors—provides a number of quotations from the writings of two Yiddish historians, Trunk and Blumental, to illustrate Holocaust-related uses of Yiddish words.[119]

Concomitantly, the value to Yiddish studies of the Yiddish historians' works extends beyond their writings *on* the Holocaust to the many original writings *from* the Holocaust that are made available through their research. Thus, I would suggest that the Yiddish historians may properly be considered as both creators and transmitters of Yiddish literary creativity suitable for inclusion in the broader field of Yiddish studies.

---

119. Judah Joffe and Yudel Mark, *Groyser verterbukh fun der yidisher shprakh*, 4 vols. (New York, 1961–80). Trunk appears eleven times in vols. 2, 3 and 4; Blumental twice in vol. 4.

Transmission of their works from the world of the survivors to that of present-day scholarship should, therefore, also include the expansion of their audience to students of Yiddish culture in general. From the available evidence, that audience has come into existence, and it is only a knowledge of the sources that has yet to be acquired.

Had this chapter been written a decade earlier, it would have discussed the reception of the Yiddish historians' works almost entirely in retrospect and with regard to the writings available in translation. Instead, the ongoing rediscovery of their original Yiddish works by a new generation of scholars has required a turn to contemporary history. At the time of this writing, most of their book-length works are available online,[120] and their articles in periodicals have an increasing promise of becoming accessible though online sources (specifically, at the "Index to Yiddish Periodicals" and the "Historical Jewish Press").[121] One of the aims of the present work has been to recover the products of a decidedly closed period of Jewish historical writing for a new English-speaking audience. It is an unexpected development to discover the gradual emergence of a new readership in Yiddish. To promote the recovery of the Yiddish historians' works both in Yiddish and in other languages, I have prepared the bibliography to be found at the end, preceded by a few "Concluding Thoughts."

---

120. See the online archive of the Yiddish Book Center, www.yiddishbookcenter.org/books/search.

121. See "Index to Yiddish Periodicals" of the Hebrew University, http://yiddish-periodicals.huji.ac.il and the full-text postings of the "Historical Jewish Press" sponsored by the National Library of Israel and Tel Aviv University, http://web.nli.org.il/sites/JPress/English/Pages/default.aspx. For a complete run of *YIVO bleter*, see http://hebrewbooks.org/home.aspx.

CONCLUDING THOUGHTS

The Yiddish historians adopted all of the usual attributes of Western historical scholarship except one: virtually no article or chapter, and scarcely any book, ends with a statement of conclusions. In rare exceptions such as Isaiah Trunk's *Lodz Ghetto* and *Judenrat*, the final chapter offers more summary than conclusion. As to *Judenrat*, the complaint was voiced by Raul Hilberg at a conference devoted to this book that "an entire set of observations and conclusion is left buried in the text.... For a review of *Judenrat*, nothing is more important than a consolidation of these points in analytic form," which Hilberg then provided.[1]

More than mere happenstance has led to these divergent cultural habits and expectations. Just as Yiddish historical writing on the Holocaust inverts certain norms of its time—by focusing on Jews rather than Germans; on everyday life and not death; and on historical continuities rather than ruptures, among others—it also addresses its readers in a different manner. The advice given to authors of academic works—to craft a conclusion that answers the "so what?" question, or that makes the work relevant to the life of the reader, or offers a time-saving option to reading the entire work—are similarly inverted in Yiddish historical scholarship.

The author of an academic monograph in the Western tradition may aspire to write the rare "crossover" that draws a broad readership, but the opposite may be said here, too, of the Yiddish historians. No scholarly work in Yiddish could have been published for the few dozen scholars

---

1. Raul Hilberg, "The Ghetto as a Form of Government: An Analysis of Isaiah Trunk's *Judenrat*," in *The Holocaust as Historical Experience*, ed. Yehuda Bauer and Nathan Rotenstreich (New York, 1980), 156. One may note that Hilberg's analysis serves both to continue his earlier support of Trunk's scholarship and to mitigate the omission, much noted by critics of his own work, of research on the Jews' response to Nazis, which could now be remedied to some extent on the basis of Trunk's original research.

and libraries who might have purchased it. From the start, their works were intended to be "crossovers," and they were received as such by their readers. Both before and after the Holocaust, this audience could be presumed to read a work in its entirety, for its obvious relevance to their lives, and would have needed little assistance in drawing conclusions that accorded or conflicted with their prior convictions.

The Yiddish historians' original readers would, I believe, have prefaced the following thoughts with the common Yiddish expression, *es iz iberik tsu zogn*—"needless to say"—in other words, well-known and unsurprising. But the process of cultural transmission in the post-vernacular age of Yiddish requires a departure from the norms of Yiddish culture for a more explicit form of expression.

The principal aim of the Yiddish historians was to study the history of the Holocaust from the perspective of its Jewish victims. The traditions of Yiddish historical scholarship provided the means.

First, however, one must acknowledge that the foundation which led to the rise of "Yiddish historians" had ceased to exist after the early years of their careers as Holocaust historians. Where Jewish historians had turned to Yiddish during the interwar period as an act of political identification with a nascent secular national movement, those who wrote the final chapters of Yiddish historical work after the Holocaust could do so only for love of their language and loyalty to the victims and their fellow survivors. As Yiddish historian Jacob Shatzky (author of three volumes on the history of Warsaw Jewry) said shortly before the breakdown that preceded his early death in 1956, "My people is dead, my theme is a dead one, and I am also dead tired."[2] The political and intellectual project that gave rise to modern Yiddish historical writing had been diminished by Jewish assimilation before the Holocaust and nearly eliminated by Nazism and Communism before it was rendered irrelevant by the success of a Hebrew-speaking Jewish nation in Israel. One must acknowledge that the movement of Yiddishist Diaspora nationalism now exists only as a subject for historical research.

It is therefore tempting to treat the final works of its historians as either the late ruins of a lost culture or a monument to that culture. However, I

---

2. Recounted in Yosef Tenenboym, "D"r yankev shatski—polihistor un historiograf (an opshatsung)," in *Shatski-bukh*, ed. Y. Lifshits (New York, 1958), 31.

take the approach that I believe the Yiddish historians themselves would have preferred, as seen in their rejection of the similar poles of "destruction and heroism" in Holocaust studies. Theirs would have been a realistic *khezhbn hanefesh*, or spiritual account-taking, without undue emphasis on specific failures or achievements.

They used the historical methods familiar from prewar Yiddish historiography in drawing on the reservoir of popular experience. In the post-Holocaust period, this took the form of relying on testimonies, eyewitness accounts, and memoirs (in the absence of documentary sources), which has become a broadly accepted practice in the more recent Jewish study of the Holocaust. As their works continue to be read (and to be rediscovered in Yiddish), it is possible that their insistence on the use of personal accounts will also influence the future course of Jewish historical writing in general.

Most significantly, the Yiddish historians undertook the task of writing Holocaust history as the experience of a living people. By historical accident, it was they and no other school or generation of historians who survived the Nazi invasion. Scholars who might have written in the spirit of the medieval chroniclers would likely have focused on moments of ultimate tragedy and have recorded fateful dialogues for posterity. Yet such accounts, however reverential, would lack the historical context or detail needed to satisfy the survivors' demands for answers or modern scholarship's insistence on verifiable data. Had the Holocaust been studied solely by scholars writing from the "perpetrator" perspective, the available research would be limited to the Nazi machinery of destruction into which Jews entered in life and from which they exited in death—without knowledge of the life within.

Instead, the anti-lachrymose tradition of prewar Yiddish scholarship led these historians to study and preserve the details of everyday life in the ghettos and camps. This approach allowed the Yiddish historians to avoid backshadowing the inevitable outcome of nearly any inquiry onto their subjects' daily struggle for existence (as they also did not backshadow the Holocaust onto earlier periods of Jewish history). As a result, we receive from the Yiddish historians a non-martyrological history of the experience of Jewish catastrophe for perhaps the first time in the historiography of Jewish catastrophe—namely, a history focused on how Jews lived and not how they died. In fact, it might be said that the Yiddish historians' wish to hold fast to the evidence of Jewish life drew their attention more strongly toward the ghettos and away from the death camps—and toward researching specific aspects of ghetto life rather than attempting to write comprehensive histories of the Holocaust.

Within their preferred setting of the ghettos in Nazi-occupied Poland, the Yiddish historians continued to study the areas of interest they and other Yiddish historians had developed before the war. Chief among these were the areas in which the Yiddish historians contributed most significantly to knowledge about Jewish life in the ghettos: 1) the history of Jewish autonomy or self-government, reenacted by the Nazi-imposed Jewish Councils, 2) the continuing influence of prewar political affiliations in the ghettos, and 3) problems of social differentiation and class conflict. Added to these, in the unique circumstances of the Nazi occupation, was their research on armed resistance and most especially on forms of unarmed resistance.

This last topic—the redemption of Jewish honor through recognition of the many ways that Jews struggled to remain alive under Nazi domination—is the most innovative contribution by the Yiddish historians. Avoiding the one extreme of focusing too narrowly on Jewish martyrdom, they also avoided the opposite extreme of concentrating unduly on acts of armed revolt. They recognized that most of those who survived did so only because many Jews had engaged in a daily fight against conditions intended by the Nazis to hasten their deaths. The urging by Dworzecki and his fellow Yiddish historians for recognition of varied forms of unarmed resistance is the area in which they most prefigured and, to some degree, influenced the research agendas of nearly all subsequent scholars.

The chief contribution of the Yiddish historians to the development of Jewish historiography as a whole is a demonstration that the period of the Holocaust need not be sequestered from the preceding and succeeding periods. The contention that Holocaust historiography developed as an academic discipline separate from the study of Jewish history overlooks the alternative example of the Yiddish historians and their integrated practice of both Jewish and Holocaust history. In their own postwar careers, each would continue to write on earlier periods of Jewish history. In their Holocaust studies, they considered its *Jewish* history (if not its *Nazi* history) to be a continuation of earlier forces and processes that should be traced across the seeming divide of the Nazi period.

The customary separation of the three periods—"between the world wars," "during the years 1939–45," and "after the Holocaust"—is rendered less categorical by the Yiddish historians' works. Examples may be drawn from each area of the Jews' interactions during the Holocaust: In the area of internal relations, the Yiddish historians demonstrate the continuing role of prewar political affiliations in defining relations among Jews under Nazi occupation. Their research on Jewish life in the ghettos is pathbreaking in exploring the effects of competing loyalties among Zionists, Bundists, socialists, Communists, and others in organizing communal leadership, schools, self-help, and cultural events—in addition to the more commonly studied effects of political conflict on organizing armed resistance. As to the Jews' non-Jewish neighbors, their research on wartime contacts between Jews and non-Jews reveals the continuing influence of prewar Christian attitudes, as well as prewar relationships between Jews and gentiles, in determining the possibilities for rescue, smuggling, hiding, or obtaining arms during the Nazi occupation. Regarding Jewish attitudes toward the Nazis, they turned to historical parallels in the Jews' relations with earlier oppressive regimes to refute accusations by Hilberg and others of Jewish historical conditioning for passivity. Trunk, in particular, argued against a false understanding of both the Nazi period and earlier periods of Jewish history in contending that the Jews had attempted, not unrealistically, to reemploy with the Nazis the familiar and historically tested modes of intervention and inducement that had succeeded in the past.

Writ large, the edifying effect of the Yiddish historians' works on the writing of both Jewish and Holocaust history is that no aspect of prewar Jewish life should be considered to have ended or become unfathomable with the onset of Nazi domination, nor should any aspect of Jewish life or responses to Nazism during the Holocaust be considered absolutely lacking in illumination from earlier periods of Jewish history.

Reinserting the Yiddish historians of the Holocaust into the narrative of Holocaust historiography disturbs certain accepted truths. The nearly ubiquitous assertion that the earliest Holocaust research focused on the Nazi perpetrators, and that research on the victims commenced only in the early 1960s, must yield before the first fifteen years of the Yiddish historians' published output and its largely Jewish orientation. The assertion that research on Jewish leadership and Jewish comportment under Nazi domination arose only in the early 1960s in response to accusations of Jewish passivity and complicity is contested by the preparatory studies published by Isaiah Trunk and Philip Friedman in the 1940s and 1950s.

Thus, without the Yiddish historians, the most common misconceptions about early Holocaust research would be correct. We would believe that the first Jewish historians to study the Holocaust were drawn only to the necessary but demoralizing task of charting the course of murderous antisemitism. We would believe that they had been animated more by outrage or grief than by love for the victims or respect for the rescuers. Without the Yiddish historians, we would believe that the Jewish historical profession had abandoned the victims to their Nazi-imposed fate of silence. But, instead, we know from their works that these historians devoted themselves immediately after the Holocaust to studying the Jewish struggle to sustain life.

In closing, I return to the aims of the present work. My first objective has been to introduce the concept of the "Yiddish historians," a cohort of scholars whose works are united by virtue of their participation in the joint project of writing modern Jewish history in Yiddish. Second, I have attempted to demonstrate that the context of Yiddish historical scholarship lends cohesion to the lives and research agendas of a specific group of postwar Yiddish historians who undertook the study of the Holocaust. Third, and most importantly, I have argued for a new appreciation of the Yiddish historians' efforts and contributions toward the writing of a Jewish history of the Holocaust. In the modest phrasing of the metaphor most often used by Yiddish-language scholars of the past, it is my hope to have laid another *tsigl far dem binyen*—a brick for the edifice—of that appreciation.

BIBLIOGRAPHIES

Bibliography of Philip Friedman 325

Bibliography of Isaiah Trunk. 341

Bibliography of Nachman Blumental. 359

Bibliography of Joseph Kermish. 381

Bibliography of Mark Dworzecki 396

General Bibliography 416

In addition to the usual goal of documenting the sources consulted, the purpose of these bibliographies is to make known and encourage greater use of the Yiddish historians' works. I have attempted to recover as many as possible (including writings about the historians), with special emphasis on works in Yiddish. I have also annotated the publication and translation history of each work.

An English translation is provided for each foreign-language title except where the meaning is obvious or the translation history includes a similar title. All ellipses (. . .) are original to the published titles. Conference papers are listed under the year of the conference rather than the year of publication in one or another language.

As indicated in the front matter, all citations of online sources were re-accessed and verified on February 6, 2019. Because virtually all *yizkor* books are available online in the combined New York Public Library–Yiddish Book Center Yizkor Book Collection (www.yiddishbookcenter.org/collections/yizkor-books), I have not provided individual links to these books.

Archival Sources

Archive of the Jewish Historical Institute, Warsaw

Meeting minutes of the Central Jewish Historical Commision
Correpondence of historians with the institute

YIVO Archives, New York

Philip Friedman Collection, RG 1258
Isaiah Trunk Collection, RG 483

Periodicals

Yiddish

Amerikaner (New York)
Arbeter tsaytung (Warsaw)
Arbeter vort (Paris)
Baderekh (Rome)
Bafrayung (Lodz)
Bafrayung (Munich)
Bikher velt (Warsaw)
Bleter far geshikhte (Warsaw)
Bleter far yidisher dertsyung (New York)
Eynikeyt (New York)
Farn folk (Rome)
Filologishe shriftn (Vilna)
Folk un velt (New York)
Folk un tsyen (Jerusalem)
Folks-shtime (Warsaw)
Folksgezunt (Paris)
Folksgezunt (Vilna and Vilna Ghetto)
Forverts (New York)
Der fraynd (St. Petersburg)
Fun letstn khurbn (Munich)
Fun noentn over (Vilna)
Gedank un lebn (New York)
Di goldene keyt (Jerusalem)
Haynt (Warsaw)

Hayntike nayes (Tel Aviv)
Hemshekh (Munich)
Heymish (Tel Aviv)
Historishe shriftn (Warsaw, Vilna-Paris)
Ibergang (Munich)
Idisher kemfer (New York)
Ilustrirte folks-bleter (Paris)
Ilustrirte literarishe bleter (Buenos Aires)
In gang (Rome)
In gerangl (Brussels)
Inzl (Bucharest-Lodz-Warsaw-Białystok)
Kiem [Kiyum] (Paris)
Kultur un dertsyung (New York)
Landkentnish (Warsaw)
Landsberger lager-tsaytung (Landsberg)
Dos leben (St. Petersburg)
Lebns-fragn (Tel Aviv)
Letste nayes (Tel Aviv)
Literarishe bleter (Warsaw)
Lodzsher visnshaftlekhe shriftn (Lodz)
Lubliner shtime—Kol Lublin (Tel Aviv)
Morgn zshurnal (New York)
Dos naye lebn (Lodz)
Nyu-yorker vokhnblat (New York)
Os (Lodz)
Oyfn shvel (New York)
Pakn Treger (Amherst)
Parizer shriftn (Paris)
Pyonern-froy (New York)
Der poylisher yid (Rio de Janeiro)
Di prese (Buenos Aires)
Shriftn (Buenos Aires)
Shul-vegn (Warsaw)
Tealit [Teater-literatur] (New York)
Di tsukunft (New York)
Tsu hilf dem lerer (Paris)
Tsushtayer (Lwów) [Lemberg]
Undzer lodzsh (Buenos Aires)
Undzer veg (Munich)

Undzer veg (New York)
Unzer ekspres (Warsaw)
Unzer kiem [kiyum] (Paris)
Unzer tsayt (New York)
Unzer vort (Paris)
Vokhnshrift (Warsaw)
Vort (Munich)
Yedies: byuletin fun yidishn historishn institut in poyln (Warsaw)
Yedies fun yad vashem (Jerusalem)
Yedies fun Y.G.F.L. [Landkentnish] (Warsaw)
Yedies fun YIVO (New York)
Yerusholayimer almanakh (Jerusalem)
Der yid (New York)
Yidishe kultur (New York)
Yidishe shprakh (New York)
Yidishe shriftn (Lodz)
Yidishe tsaytung (Landsberg)
YIVO bleter (Vilna and New York)
Di yudishe [idishe] velt (Vilna)
Yugnt veker (Warsaw)
Yunger historiker (Warsaw)

English

American Historical Review (Chicago)
American Jewish Historical Quarterly (Waltham)
Commentary (New York)
Congress Bi-Weekly (New York)
Dimensions: A Journal of Holocaust Studies (New York)
East European Jewish Affairs (London)
European History Quarterly (London)
Hebrew Union College Annual (Cincinnati)
Historia Judaica (New York)
Holocaust and Genocide Studies (Oxford)
Holocaust Studies (Edgware)
Isis (Chicago)
Jewish Book Annual (New York)
Jewish Currents (New York)
The Jewish Digest (Bridgeport)

Jewish Education (New York)
Jewish Frontier (New York)
Jewish Quarterly Review (Philadelphia)
Jewish Social Studies (New York)
Jewish Spectator (New York)
Jewish Telegraphic Agency Daily News Bulletin (New York)
Journal of Abnormal and Social Psychology (Albany)
Journal of Ukrainian Studies (Toronto)
Judaism (New York)
Leo Baeck Institute Yearbook (London)
Modern Judaism (Baltimore)
Monatshefte (Madison)
Morningside Gardens News (New York)
New York Times (New York)
The New Yorker (New York)
News of the YIVO (New York)
Polin: Studies in Polish Jewry (Oxford)
Polish Review (New York)
Proceedings of the American Academy for Jewish Research (New York)
Prooftexts (New York)
The Reconstructionist (Philadelphia)
Science in Context (Cambridge)
Simon Dubnow Institute Yearbook (Göttingen)
Simon Wiesenthal Center Annual (Chappaqua)
Social Theory and Practice (Tallahassee)
Societas (Oshkosh)
Studies in Contemporary Jewry (Bloomington)
Theological Studies (Baltimore)
Yad Vashem Bulletin (Jerusalem)
Yad Vashem Quarterly Magazine (Jerusalem)
Yad Vashem Studies (Jerusalem)
Yiddish (Queens College, New York)
YIVO Annual of Jewish Social Science (New York)

Hebrew

'Al ha-Mishmar (Tel Aviv)
Bitzaron (New York)
Dapim le-heker ha-Sho'ah veha-mered (Tel Aviv)

Davar (Tel Aviv)
Gal-Ed (Tel Aviv)
Gilyonot (Tel Aviv)
Korot (Jerusalem)
Ma'ariv (Tel Aviv)
Masu'ah (Tel Aviv)
Metsudah (London)
ha-Tzefira (Warsaw)
Tzion (Jerusalem)
Yad Vashem Kovets Mehkarim (Jerusalem)
Yediot Bet Lohame ha-Geta'ot (Haifa)
Yedi'ot Yad va-Shem (Jerusalem)

Polish-Yiddish (bilingual)

Trybuna Akademicka (Warsaw)
Głos Gminy Żydowskiej [*Voice of the Jewish Community*] (Warsaw)

Polish

Mosty [*Bridges*]: *biuletyn "Haszomer Hacair"* (Warsaw)
Nowy Głos [*New Voice*] (Warsaw)
Opinia (Warsaw-Lodz)

French

Le Monde Juif (Paris)
Revue des Sciences Religieuses (Strasbourg)
Revue d'Histoire de la Médecine hebraïque (Paris)
Yod [Online] (Paris)

Spanish

Davar (Buenos Aires)

German

Die Neue Welt (Munich)

Bibliography of Philip Friedman

Scope: Prewar and postwar works consulted, and their publication history (in order by date of Yiddish publication), plus articles discovered to be missing from Friedman's own bibliography and posthumous continuation (see the booklet *Writings of Philip Friedman* below).

Books by Friedman

This was Oswiecim: The Story of a Murder Camp—Compiled from official records and evidence and eye-witness accounts. Translated from the Yiddish original by Joseph Leftwich. London: United Jewish Relief Appeal, 1946.

Oshvyentshim [*Auschwitz*]. Buenos Aires: Tsentral farband fun poylishe yidn in argentine, 1950. Spanish, *Auschwitz*. Translated by Elias Singer (Buenos Aires: Sociedad Hebraica Argentina, 1952).

Martyrs and Fighters: The Epic of the Warsaw Ghetto. New York: Frederick A. Praeger, 1954.

Writings of Philip Friedman: A Bibliography. New York: "privately printed," 1955. Mimeographed typescript available at many libraries (a copy with handwritten emendations and Friedman's home address and telephone number on the back cover held by UCLA Library); posthumous continuation (1955–61, presumably by his widow, Ada [June] Eber Friedman) in YIVO archives, RG 1258, F 538.

Their Brothers' Keepers. New York: Crown, 1957.

Bibliyografiyah shel ha-sefarim ha-'Ivriyim 'al ha-Sho'ah ve-'al ha-gevurah [English titlepage: *Bibliography of Books in Hebrew on the Jewish Catastrophe and Heroism in Europe*]. Jerusalem: Yad Washem and YIVO, 1960.

[with Jacob Robinson]. *Guide to Jewish History under Nazi Impact*. New York: Yad Washem and YIVO, 1960.

[with Yosef Gar]. *Biblyografye fun yidishe bikher vegn khurbn un gvure* [English titlepage: *Bibliography of Yiddish Books on the Catastrophe and Heroism*]. New York: Yad Washem and YIVO, 1962.

Roads to Extinction: Essays on the Holocaust. Edited by Ada June Friedman. New York: Conference on Jewish Social Studies / Jewish Publication Society of America, 1980.

[Editor]. *Lodzsher visnshaftlekhe shriftn* [*Lodz Scholarly Writings*] I (Lodz, 1938).

[Editor]. *Metodologishe onvayzungen tsum oysforshn dem khurbn fun poylishn yidntum* [*Methodological Instructions for Investigating the Destruction of Polish Jewry*] ("under the direction of Dr. Philip Friedman"). Lodz: Tsentraler yidisher historisher komisye, 1945.

[Editor with Ben-Zion Hibel]. *Shriftn far literatur, kunst un gezelshaftlekhe fragn* [*Writings for Literature, Art and Communal Questions*]. Munich: Shrayber-farband fun sheyres-hapleyte, 1948.

Articles by Friedman

1931

"A sotsyialer konflikt in lodzsh onheyb 19th y"h [A Social Conflict in Lodz at the Beginnning of the 19th Century]." *YIVO bleter* II, no. 1–2 (September 1931): 145–49.

1932

"Tsvey lodzsher yidn hobn oyfgeboyt balut [Two Lodz Jews Built Balut (the original industrial center of Lodz)]." *Lodzsher togblat* 64 (1932).

1934

"Dr. y. shiper—poylishe yidn besn november-oyfshtand [Dr. Y. Schipper—Polish Jewry During the November Uprising (of 1830–31)]." *Literarishe bleter* (March 16, 1934): 172.

1937

"Prof. meir balaban." *Literarishe bleter* (March 12, 1937): 169–70 (cover story).

"Regyonalizm [Regionalism]." *Landkentnish* (May 1937): 3–7; (July 1937): 1–3 (both not listed in Friedman's bibliography). See expanded version, "Der regyonalistisher geshikhte-shraybung ... ," 1951.

1938

"Der onteyl fun yidn in poylishn oyfshtand [The Participation of Jews in the Polish Uprising]." *Inzl* 4, no. 2 (February 1938): 1–2 (not listed in Friedman's bibliography).

"Di nayeste geshikhte fun iden in poylen [The Most Recent History of Jews in Poland]." In *Haynt yoyvl-bukh*, 123–39. Warsaw: Haynt, 1938.

"Di oyfgabes fun undzer historisher visnshaft un vi azoy zey tsu realizirn [The Tasks of Our Historical Scholarship and How to Realize Them]." *YIVO bleter* XIII, nos. 3–4 (1938): 301–12.

"Gzeyres takh [The (Evil) Decree of 1648–49; review of Jacob Shatzky's introduction to Nathan Hannover's *Yeven Metzulah* [*Deep Mire*] of 1653 (Vilna, 1938)]." *Literarishe bleter* (August 19, 1938): 567–68.

"Historishe literatur vegn yidn in der lodzsher voyvodshaft [Historical Literature on Jews in the Lodz District] (1918–1937)." *Lodzsher visnshaftlekhe shriftn* I (Lodz, 1938): 133–48.

"Matsevot bet ha-kevarot ha-yashan be-Lodz [Tombstones of the Old (Jewish) Cemetery in Lodz]." *Stary Cmentarz Żydowski w Łodzi* (Lodz: Nakł. Gminy Wyznaniowej Żydowskiej m. Łodzi, 1938): Hebrew section 5–115. Hebrew reprinted (Ashdod: Mekhon zikhron kedoshe Polin, 1998).

"Notitsn [Notices]." *Lodzsher visnshaftlekhe shriftn* I (Lodz, 1938): 277–82.

"Żydostwo austriackie jego dzieje i losy [Austrian Jewry, Its History and Destiny]." *Nowy Głos* [New Voice] (April 7, 1938): 5 (not listed in Friedman's bibliography).

Introduction to *Lodzsher visnshaftlekhe shriftn* I (Lodz, 1938): III–IV.

1939

"'Der idisher gezelshaftlikher leksikon' [The Jewish Community Lexicon; review of Ruben Feldshuh, *Yidisher gezelshaftlekher leksikon* (Warsaw, 1939)]." *Haynt* (April 7, 1939): 7.

"Di yidishe sotsyalistishe bavegung biz der grindung fun 'bund' [The Jewish Socialist Movement until the Founding of the 'Bund'; on YIVO's *Historishe shriftn* III, 1938]." *Literarishe bleter* (February 21, 1939): 65–66 (cover story).

Review of Salo M. Baron, *Social and religious history of the Jews* (New York, 1937). *Gilyonot* VII, no. 3 (1939): 241–45.

1941

Review of Saul M. Ginsburg, *Historishe verk* [*Historical Works*] (New York, 1937–38). *Jewish Social Studies* III, no. 1 (January 1941): 95–97.

1945

"Briv fun der bafrayter eyrope [A Letter from Liberated Europe]." *Yidishe kultur* (October 1945): 61 (not listed in Friedman's bibliography).

"Kinder in Oshvyentshim [Children in Auschwitz]." *Dos naye lebn* (June 20, 1945): 4. Verbatim preview of chapter 23, *Oshvyentshim*. English translation, chapter XI, *This was Oswiecim* (1946).

"Komisye zamlt materialn vegn der tragedye fun poylishe yidn [Commission Collects Materials about the Tragedy of Polish Jewry]." *Yidishe kultur* (August–September 1945): 72–73.

"Kontsentratsye-lager Oshvyentshim [Concentration Camp Auschwitz]." *Dos naye lebn* (May 20, 1945): 4, 6. Early version of chapter 6, *Oshvyentshim*. English translation, chapter II, *This was Oswiecim*.

"Unzer historishe oyfgabe [Our Historic Task]." *Dos naye lebn* (April 10, 1945): 6.

"Vendung fun der Ts.Yy.H.K. [Appeal from the Central Jewish Historical Commission]." *Dos naye lebn* (December 1, 1945) (not listed in Friedman's bibliography).

"Vi azoy Oshvyentshim hot mekabel-ponem geven zayne gest [How Auschwitz Welcomed its Guests]." *Dos naye lebn* (May 31, 1945): 5. Verbatim preview of chapter 7, *Oshvyentshim*. English translation, chapter III, *This was Oswiecim*.

"Vi s'halt mit di yidn in poyln [How it Goes with the Jews in Poland]." *Eynikayt* (September 1945): 11–13, 31.

Foreword to Gerszon Taffet, *Zagłada Żydostwa Polskiego: Album Zdjęć* [Extermination of Polish Jews: Album of Pictures], unpaginated. Lodz: Centralna Żydowska Komisja Historyczna w Polsce, 1945; six languages (not listed in Friedman's bibliography).

1946

"Di yidishe historishe komisye in poyln [The Jewish Historical Commission in Poland]." *Eynikeyt* (June 1946): 10–11, 21.

"Extermination of the Polish Jews in the Years 1939–1945." In *German Crimes in Poland*, 125–67. Warsaw: Central Commission for Investigation of German Crimes in Poland, 1946. Revised English translation, *Roads* (1980), 211–43.

Foreword to Szymon Datner, *Walka i zagłada białostockiego ghetta* [The Struggle and Extermination of the Białystok Ghetto], 5–8. Lodz: Centralna Żydowska komisja Historyczna, 1946.

1947

"Der umkum fun di yidn in mizrekh-galitsye [The Extermination of the Jews in Eastern Galicia]." *Fun letstn khurbn* 4 (March 1947): 1–13. Reprinted in *Yerlekher gedenk-bukh* 1, ed. Nechemias Zucker and Nachum Lindman

(Buenos Aires: Farlag galitsye, 1961), 67–70; and in *Sefer Monastrishch: Matsevat zikaron li-kehilah kedoshah*, ed. Meir Segal (Tel Aviv: Irgun yotz'e Monastrishch be-Yisrael, 1974), 83–89.

"Les problèmes de recherche scientifique sur notre dernière catastrophe [The Problems of Scholarly Research on our Recent Catastrophe]." In *Conférence européenne des commissions historiques et des centres de documentation juifs [1–10 December 1947, Paris]. Les Juifs en Europe (1939–1945): Rapports*, 72–80. Paris: Éditions du Centre [de documentation Juive Contemporaine], 1949.

1948

"'Daytshe visnshaft' in kontsentratsye-lager ['German Science' in the Concentration Camp]." *Bafrayung* 50–51 (12 and 19 March 1948). Verbatim preview of chapter 14, *Oshvyentshim*. English, chapter VI of *This was Oswiecim*. This and chapter 15 translated as "Crimes in the Name of 'Science,'" *Roads*, 322–32. Spanish, "Crimenes en nombre de la ciencia." *Davar* [Buenos Aires] 30 (September–October 1950): 75–79.

"Di elementn fun undzer khurbn-forshung [The Elements of our *Khurbn*-Research]." *Hemshekh* 1 (April 1948): 4–10; continuation, "Di memuaristik," *Hemshekh* 2 (1949): 26–34.

"Di forshung fun unzer khurbn [The Study of Our *Khurbn*]." *Kiem* (January 1948): 47–54. Reprinted in *Shriftn far literatur, kunst un gezelshaftlekhe fragn*, 75–86.

"Die Parisder Konferenz der jüdischen Historiker [The Paris Conference of Jewish Historians]." *Die Neue Welt* 2, no. 5 (January 29, 1948). Abbreviated (and de-depersonalized) German translation of Friedman's statement quoted in Hibel, "Konferentz" (1947).

"Fun antihistoritsizm tsum superhistoritsizm [From Anti-Historicism to Super-Historicism]." *Kiem* (March 1948): 28–32.

"Shul-vezn un dertsyung in der sheyres hapleyte in daytshland [The School System and Education among the Survivors in Germany]." *Kiem* (September–October 1948): 557–65.

"The European Jewish Research on the Recent Jewish Catastrophe in 1939–1945." *Proceedings of the American Academy for Jewish Research* 18 (1948–1949): 179–211 (annual conference, December 12, 1948). Revised version, "The European Research on the Holocaust," *Roads*, 500–524.

Foreword to Binyomin Orenshteyn, *Khurbn chenstokhov* [*The Destruction of Częstochowa*], 8–9. Munich: Central Farvaltung fun der Czenstochower landsmanshaftn in der amerikaner zone in daytshland, 1948.

Foreword to Yosef Gar, *Umkum fun der yidisher kovne* [*The Extermination of Jewish Kaunas*], 9–11. Munich: Farband fun litvishe yidn in der amerikaner zone in daytshland, 1948.

Review of Dwozecki, *Yerusholayim d'lite in kamf un umkum* [*Jerusalem of Lithuania in Struggle and Extermination*] (Paris, 1948). *Kiem* (June 1948): 406–7.

1949

"100 bikher in yidish vegn khurbn un gvure [100 Books in Yiddish on the Destruction and Heroism]." *Jewish Book Annual* 8 (5710/1949–50): 122–32; 9 (5711/1950–51): 80–92 (Hebrew page numbering).

"A. sh. hershbergs 'pinkes Byalistok' [review of A. Sh. Hershberg, *Chronicle of Białystok* (New York, 1950)]." *Byalistoker shtime* (March–April 1949): 29–31.

"Der kultur krizis in idishn lebn [The Cultural Crisis in Jewish Life]." *Idisher kemfer* (September 23, 1949, Rosh Hashanah): 49–55. Reprinted in *Shriftn* (June–July 1952): 28–32.

"Di memuaristik [Memoir-Writing; continuation of "Di elementn" (1948)]." *Hemshekh* 2 (1949): 26–34.

"Di tsiln un oyfgabes fun yidisher hekherer dertsyung in amerike baym hayntikn tog [The Goals and Tasks of Jewish Higher Education in Present-day America]." *Bleter far yidisher dertsyung* I, no. 1 (June–September 1949): 49–53.

"Dos gedrukte yidishe vort bay der sheyres hapleyte in daytshland [The Printed Yiddish Word among the Survivors in Germany]." *Di tsukunft* (February 1949): 94–97; (March 1949): 151–55.

"Polish Jewish Historiography between the Two World Wars (1918–1939)." *Jewish Social Studies* XI (October 1949): 373–408. Reprinted in *Roads*, 467–99.

1950

"A merkvirdike goyrldike shutfes [A Remarkable Partnership of Fate]." *Kiem* (August–September 1950): 1661–67. English, "The Extermination of the Gypsies: A Nazi Genocide Operation Against An 'Aryan People,'" *Jewish Frontier* (January 1951): 11–14. Reprinted in *Roads*, 381–86.

"Etishe un sotsyale problemen fun unzer katastrofe in der natsi tkufe [Ethical and Social Problems of Our Catastrophe in the Nazi Period]." *Idisher kemfer* (September 8, 1950, Rosh Hashanah): 54–58 (YIVO conference, January 1950). Abridged English translation, "Jewish Reaction to Nazism," *Jewish Frontier* (September 1950): 20–24.

"Forshungen fun letstn khurbn [Studies on the Recent Destruction; review of *Bleter far geshikhte* (*Pages for History*) I]." *YIVO bleter* XXXIV (1950): 231–39.

"Khurbn-varshe—in shpigl fun der literatur [The Destruction of Warsaw—as Reflected in Literature]." *Kultur un dertsyung* (April 1950): 9–12; (May): 61–63.

"Parshes varshe [The History of Warsaw]." *Di tsukunft* (April 1950): 179–84.

"Research and Literature on the Recent Jewish Tragedy." *Jewish Social Studies* XII, no. 1 (January 1950): 17–26. Revised and condensed version of "The European Research" (1949).

"Some Books on the Jewish Catastrophe." *Jewish Social Studies* XII, no. 1 (January 1950): 83–94.

"Unzer khurbn-literatur [Our *Khurbn*-Literature]." *Idisher kemfer* (March 31, 1950, Pesach issue): 87–91.

1951

"A monument far an umgekumener yidisher kehile [A Monument for a Murdered Jewish Community; review of Shatzky's *Pinkes mlave* (*Chronicle of Mlave*, 1950)]." *YIVO bleter* XXXV (1951): 272–75 (not listed in Friedman's bibliography).

"American Jewish Research and Literature on the Jewish Catastrophe of 1939–1945." *Jewish Social Studies* 13 (1951): 235–50. Hebrew, "Mehkar ve-sifrut ha-Sho'ah ba-Amerikah," *Dapim le-heker ha-Sho'ah vehamered* 2 (1st series, January–April 1951): 51–68 (not listed in Friedman's bibliography).

"Biblyografye fun der khurbn-literatur vegn lite [Bibliography of the *Khurbn*-Literature on Lithuania]." In *Lite*, vol. 1, edited by Mendel Sudarsky et al., 1923–40. New York: Kultur-gezelshaft fun litvishe yidn, 1951.

"Bikher vegn haynttsaytiker yidisher geshikhte [Books on Modern Jewish History]." *Kultur un dertsyung* (October 1951): 15–18.

"Der onhoyb fun dem idishn yishev in mizrekh-eyrope [The Beginning of the Jewish Community in Eastern Europe]." *Idisher kemfer* (April 20, 1951, Pesach): 35–42.

"Der regyonalistishe geshikhte-shraybung un di romantik fun der alter heym [Regional History-Writing and the Romantic Charm of the Old Home]." *Di tsukunft* (December 1951): 464–69.

"Der yidisher oyfshtand in varshe [The Jewish Uprising in Warsaw]." In *Mir zaynen do . . .*, 13–14. New York: Farband fun gevezene yidishe katsetler un partizaner, 1951.

"Di geshikhte fun di yidn in belkhatov." In *Belkhatov yisker-bukh*, edited by Mark Turkov, 19–60. Buenos Aires: Tsentral farband fun poylishe yidn in argentine, 1951. English, trans. by Hiller and Phyllis Bell, "The History of the Jewish People in Belchatow." www.jewishgen.org/yizkor/Belchatow/bel019.html.

"Di landsmanshaftn-literatur in the fareynikte shtatn far di letste 10 yor." *Jewish Book Annual* 10 (5712/1951–52): 81–96 (Hebrew numbering). English, "Landsmanshaftn Literature in the United States during the Past Ten Years," in *Memorial Books of Eastern European Jewry: Essays on the History and Meanings of Yizker Volumes*, ed. Rosemary Horowitz (Jefferson: McFarland, 2011), 43–53.

"Di yidishe entsiklopedye—a kapitl kultur-geshikhte fun undzer dor [The Yiddish Encyclopedia—A Chapter of Cultural History of Our Generation]." *Di tsukunft* (March 1951): 130–33.

"Geshikhtlekhe forshungen vegn poylishn yidntum [Historical Studies on Polish Jewry]." *Idisher kemfer* (July 13, 1951): 12–13.

Review of Yankev Shatski, *Geshikhte fun yidn in varshe* [History of the Jews in Warsaw], vols. 1, 2 (New York, 1947, 1948). *Jewish Social Studies* XIII, no. 4 (October 1951): 359–62.

1952

"Der idisher lerer seminar [The Jewish Teachers' Seminary]." *Idisher kemfer* (March 14, 1952): 11.

"Der kultur krizis in idishn lebn." *Shriftn* (June–July 1952): 28–32 (reprint from 1949).

"Monografyes fun yidishe kehiles un shtet in der yidisher geshikhte shraybung [Monographs on Jewish Communities and Cities in Jewish History-Writing]." In *Yisker-bukh fun rakishok un umgegnt*, edited by Melekh Bakaltshuk-Felin, 438–51. Johannesburg: Rakishker landsmanshaft in yohanesburg, durem afrike, 1952.

1953

"Der idisher vidershtand kegn der natsi-hershaft [Jewish Resistance against Nazi Rule]." *Idisher kemfer* (April 3, 1953, Pesach): 88–94; (May 8): 9–11; (May 15): 12–13; (May 22): 10–11, 14.

"Der ivo un zayn kultur-svive [YIVO and Its Cultural Setting]." *Idisher kemfer* (January 2, 1953): 5–6.

"ha-Tasbikh ha-meshihi shel takif be-geto ha-Natzi." *Bitzaron* XXVIII, no. 5 (April 1953): 29–40. English, "The Messianic Complex of a Nazi

Collaborator in a Ghetto: Moses Merin of Sosnowiec," *Roads*, 353–64. English condensation, "Two 'Saviors' Who Failed," *Commentary* 26, no. 6 (December 1, 1958): 479–91.

"ha-Tasbikh ha-meshihi shel takife ha-geto [The Messianic Complex of Nazi Collaborators]." *Bitzaron* XXXIX, no. 3 (1953): 151–58; XXXIX, no. 4 (1954): 232–39. English, "Jacob Gens: 'Commandant' of the Vilna Ghetto," *Roads*, 365–80. English condensation, "Two 'Saviors' Who Failed," *Commentary* 26, no. 6 (December 1, 1958): 479–91.

"Reviews of Books [by R. Learsi, A. Bein., G. de Gaury, H. Lehrman]." *American Historical Review* 58, no. 4 (July 1953): 880–82.

"Varshever oyfshtand—der brenendiker dorn [The Warsaw Uprising—The Burning Thorn]." *Di tsukunft* (April 1953): 194–95.

1954

"A shpogl naye oystaytshung fun varshever geto-oyfshtand [A Brand-New Interpretation of the Warsaw Ghetto Uprising; on Ber Mark]." *Di tsukunft* (April 1954): 162–67.

"Der lubliner rezervat un der madagaskar-plan." *YIVO bleter* XXXVII (1954): 5–36. English, "The Lublin Reservation and the Madagascar Plan," *YIVO Annual of Jewish Social Science* 8 (1953): 151–77. Reprinted in *Roads*, 34–58.

"Farshidene makoyres vegn ratne [Various Sources regarding Ratne]." In *Yisker-bukh ratne: dos lebn un der umkum fun a yidish shtetl in volin*, edited by Yankev Botoshanski and Yitskhok Yanosovich, 19–26. Buenos Aires: Ratner landslayt fareyn in argentine un nord-amerike, 1954.

"Go'ale sheker be-geta'ot Polin." *Metsudah* VII (1954): 602–18. English, "Pseudo-Saviors in the Polish Ghettos: Mordechai Chaim Rumkowski of Lodz," *Roads*, 333–52.

"Sotsyale konfliktn in geto." *Idisher kemfer* (Pesach 1954): 77–83; (April 30, 1954): 13–14. English, "Social Conflict in the Ghetto," *Roads*, 131–52.

"Tsu der geshikhte fun di yidn in khelm: der onheyb un di geshikhte fun a yidishn yishev [On the History of the Jews in Chełm: The Beginning and the History of a Jewish Community]." In *Yisker-bukh khelm*, edited by Melekh Bakaltshuk-Felin, 13–38. Johannesburg: Khelemer landsmanshaft in yohanesburg, durem-afrike, 1954. Hebrew, "Divre ha-yomim shel ha-Yehudim be-Helem," in *Sefer ha-zikaron li-kehilat Helem*, ed. Shimon Katz (Tel Aviv: Irgun yotz'e Helem be-Yisra'el uveha-aratsot ha-brit, Tel Aviv, 1980/81), 37–56. English trans. by Rae Meltzer, "The Beginning and the History of a Yiddish [sic] Community," www.jewishgen.org/yizkor/chelm/che013.html.

Review of Gerald Reitlinger, *The Final Solution* (London, 1953). *Jewish Social Studies* XVI, no. 2 (April 1954): 186–89.

Review of Peter Meyer et al., *Jews in the Soviet Satellites* (Syracuse, 1953). *Political Science Quarterly* LXIX, no. 2 (June 1954): 288–90.

1955

"Byalistok un di byalistoker yidn beys der tsveyter velt-milkhome [Białystok and the Białystok Jews during the Second World War (bibliography)]." *Byalishokter shtime* 35, nos. 273–74 (1955): 23–25 (not listed in Friedman's bibliography).

"Dos ringelblum bukh [The Ringelblum Book; review of *Kapitlen geshikhte fun amolikn yidishn lebn in poyln* (*Historical Chapters from Former Jewish Life in Poland*) by Emanuel Ringelblum, ed. Yankev Shatski (Buenos Aires, 1953)]." *Di tsukunft* (October 1955): 384–85.

"Khsidey umos ho'oylem in natsi period." *Idisher kemfer* (April 8, 1955, Pesach): 54–58 (YIVO conference, January 16, 1955). English, "'Righteous Gentiles' in the Nazi Era," *Roads*, 408–21.

"The Jewish Badge and the Yellow Star in the Nazi Era." *Historia Judaica* XVII, no. 1 (April 1955): 41–70. Reprinted in *Roads*, 11–33.

"Tsi iz in der natsitsayt geven an 'ander daytshland'?" *YIVO bleter* XXXIX (1955): 104–64. English, "Was there an 'Other Germany' during the Nazi Period?," *YIVO Annual of Jewish Social Science* X (1955): 82–127. Reprinted in *Roads*, 422–64. Reprinted in *East European Jews in Two Worlds: Studies from the YIVO Annual*, ed. Deborah Dash Moore (Evanston: Northwestern University Press and YIVO, 1990), 191–234.

"Yisker-bikher un regyonale literatur [*Yizkor* Books and Regional Literature]." *Di tsukunft* (April 1955): 178–81.

1956

"Di sheyres hapleyte un yisker-literatur [The Survivors and Memorial Literature]." *Di tsukunft* (April 1956): 165–69.

"Hurban Yehude Lvov." In *Entsiklopediyah shel Galuyot: Lvov*, ed. N. M. Gelber, 593–734. Jerusalem: Entsiklopediyah shel Galuyot, 1956. English, "The Destruction of the Jews of Lwów, 1941–1944," *Roads*, 244–321.

"Umkum fun vitebsker yidn [The Extermination of Vitebsk Jewry]." In *Vitebsk amol: geshikhte, zikhroynes, khurbn*, edited by Grigori Aronson et al., 603–26. New York: n.p., 1956. Hebrew, "Hashmadat Yehude Vitebsk," in *Sefer Vitebsk*, ed. Baruh Karu (Tel Aviv: Irgun yotz'e Vitebsk vehasevivah be-Yisra'el, 1957), 439–52.

1957

"Der historiker fun poylishn yidntum [The Historian of Polish Jewry]." In *Yankev shatski—tsum ondenk [Jacob Shatzky—In Memoriam]*, edited by Philip Friedman et al., 53–59. New York: Klub fun poylishe yidn, 1957, with English abstract (not listed in Friedman's posthumous bibliography). Incorporated as second half of "Yankev shatskis ort" (1958).

"Problems of Research on the European Jewish Catastrophe." *Yad Vashem Studies* III (1959): 25–39 (Second World Congress of Jewish Studies, Jerusalem, August 4, 1957). Reprinted in *Yad Vashem Studies on the European Jewish Catastrophe and Resistance* III (Jerusalem, 1959): 25–39; in *From Hatred to Extermination: Seven Lectures Delivered at the Second World Congress for Jewish Studies ... August 4, 1957* (Jerusalem, 1959), 25–39; in *The Catastrophe of European Jewry: Antecedents—History—Reflections: Selected Papers*, ed. Yisrael Gutman and Livia Rothkirchen (Jerusalem: Yad Vashem, 1976), 633–50; and in *Roads*, 554–67. Hebrew, "Heker ha-historiyah shel tekufat ha-Sho'ah uve-'ayoto," in Gutman and Rothkirchen, *Sho'at Yehude Eropah: Reka, Korot, Mashma'ut* (Jerusalem: Yad Vashem, 1973), 437–48.

"Sotsyale un politishe bavegungen [Social and Political Movements (in the US)]." In *Algemeyne entsiklopedye*, vol. Yidn V, 42–83. New York: Dubnov-fond un entsiklopedye komitet, 1957 (not listed in Friedman's posthumous bibliography).

"The Fate of the Jewish Book in the Nazi Era." *Jewish Book Annual* 15 (1957–58): 3–13. Reprinted in *Roads*, 88–99.

Ukraynish-yidishe batsyungen in der tsayt fun der natsisher okupatsye." *YIVO bleter* XLI and *Shmuel niger bukh* (1957–58): 230–63. English, "Ukrainian-Jewish Relations During the Nazi Occupation," *YIVO Annual of Jewish Social Science* XII (1958–59): 259–96. Reprinted in *Roads*, 176–208 (none listed in Friedman's posthumous bibliography).

Review of Léon Poliakov and Josef Wulf, *Das Dritte Reich und die Juden* (Berlin, 1955). *Jewish Social Studies* XIX, nos. 1–2 (January–April 1957): 91–92.

1958

"An oysbeserung fun historiker d"r filip fridman [A Correction from Historian Dr. Philip Friedman (letter to the editor)]." *Heymish* (December 5, 1958): 2.

"15 yor nokhn varshever geto-oyfshtand [15 Years after the Warsaw Ghetto Uprising]." *Folk un velt* (April 1958): 43–49 (not listed in Friedman's posthumous bibliography).

"Jewish Resistance to Nazism: Its Various Forms and Aspects." In *European Resistance Movements 1939–1945: First International Conference on the History of the Resistance Movements Held at Liège-Bruxelles-Breendonk 14–17 September 1958*, 195–214. Oxford: Pergamon Press, 1960. Expanded version in *Roads*, 387–408. Hebrew, "ha-Hitnagdut ha-Yehudit le-Natzizm—Hebetim ve-Tsurot," in *Sho'at Yehude Eropah: Reka, Korot, Mashma'ut*, ed. Yisrael Gutman and Livia Rothkirchen (Jerusalem: Yad Vashem, 1973), 361–73.

"Khurbn hosht [The Destruction of Hoshcha; review of *Sefer Hoshtsh* (*Memorial Book of Hoshcha*, New York, 1957)]." *Kultur un dertsyung* (October 1958): 19–20 (not listed in Friedman's posthumous bibliography).

"Kolomey—di hoyptshtot fun pokutye un ire yidn [Kołomyja—The Capital of Pokuttya and Its Jews]." *Di tsukunft* (September 1958): 354–55. Reprinted in *Yerlekher gedenk-bukh* 1, ed. Nechemias Zucker and Nachum Lindman (Buenos Aires: Farlag galitsye, 1961), 67–70 (both not listed in Friedman's posthumous bibliography).

"Preliminary and Methodological Problems of the Research on the Jewish Catastrophe in the Nazi Period." *Yad Vashem Studies* II (1958): 95–131. Part 1, "Problems of Research in Jewish 'self-government' ('Judenrat') in the Nazi Period," reprinted with emendations in *Roads*, 539–50. Partial revision of Part 2, "Jewish Resistance," incorporated in "Jewish Resistance to Nazism," *Roads*, 387–408.

"Umkum un vidershtand fun chenstokhover yidn in der tsayt fun der natsisher okupatsye (a biblyografisher iberblik) [Extermination and Resistance among Częstochowa Jews at the Time of the Nazi Occupation (A Bibliographic Survey)]." In *Chenstokhov: nayer tsugob-material tsum bukh "Chenstokhover yidn*, edited by Sh. D. Zinger, 68–76. New York: United Czenstochover Relief Committee and Ladies Auxiliary, 1958.

"Yankev shatzkis ort in der mizrekh-eyropeyisher yidisher geshikhte-shraybung [Jacob Shatzky's Place in Eastern European Jewish History-Writing; memorial essay]." In *Shatski-bukh: opshatsungen vegn d"r yankev shatski*, edited by Y. Lifshits, 11–27. New York: YIVO, 1958 (not listed in Friedman's posthumous bibliography). Second half reprints his "Der historiker fun poylishn yidntum" (1957).

1959

"A fertl-yorhundert 'khurbn-literatur' [A Quarter Century of 'Khurbn-Literature']." *Di tsukunft* (September 1959): 358–62. English, "The Literature of the Catastrophe," *The Reconstructionist* (April 1, 1960): 11–16.

1961

"Der umkum fun di yidn in mizrekh-galitsye." In *Yerlekher gedenk-bukh* 1, edited by Nechemias Zucker and Nachum Lindman, 67–70. Buenos Aires: Farlag galitsye, 1961 (reprint from 1947; not listed in Friedman's posthumous bibliography).

"Geshikhte fun di yidn in ukrayine: fun di eltste tsaytn biz tsu der untergang fun der poylisher melukhe (sof 18-tn y"h) [History of the Jews in Ukraine: From the Oldest Times to the Fall of the Polish Kingdom (End of the 18th Century)]." In *Yidn in ukrayine*, vol. 1, edited by Mendl Osherowitsh et al., 1–68 New York: Gezelshaft tsu fareybikn dem ondenk fun ukrayiner yidn, 1961.

"Kolomey—di hoyptshtot fun pokutye un ire yidn." In *Yerlekher gedenk-bukh* 1, edited by Nechemias Zucker and Nachum Lindman, 67–70. Buenos Aires: Farlag galitsye, 1961 (reprint from 1958; not listed in Friedman's posthumous bibliography).

Writings about Friedman

"Announcement of the Center of Israeli Studies for the Winter and Spring Sessions, 1952–1953." *Columbia University Bulletin of Information* 52, no. 23 (June 21, 1952).

"Azkarah le-D"r Filip Fridman [Memorial Service for Dr. Philip Friedman]." *Davar* (February 16, 1960): 3.

"D"r f. fridman—lektor in lodzsher universitet [Lecturer at Lodz University]." *Dos naye lebn* (December 23, 1945): 1.

"D"r filip fridman [obituary]." *Yedies fun YIVO* 74 (April 1960): 1, 7.

"Ershte zitsung fun banaytn historiker-krayz [First Meeting of Renewed Historians' Circle]." *Yedies fun YIVO* 53 (June 1954): 4; English, "Historians' Circle Renews Activities," 4*.

"Fun der idisher literatur: A nay bukh vegn der nayster idisher geshikhte [From Jewish Literature: A New Book on Modern Jewish History; review of Friedman's *Korot ha-Yehudim ba-tekufah ha-hadashah* (*History of the Jews in the Modern Period*, Warsaw, 1937)]." *Haynt* (March 2, 1934): 7 (not listed in Friedman's bibliography).

"Khronik [Chronicle]." *Kiem* (May 1948): 349; (July–August 1948): 508.

"Visnshafts-krayz tsu forshen dos idishe leben in lodzsher kant [Academic Circle to Study Jewish Life in the Lodz District]." *Haynt* (April 4, 1934): 4.

"YIVO Conference Highlights Wide Variety of Scholarly Topics." *News of the YIVO* 56 (March 1955): 2*.

Aleksiun, Natalia. "Philip Friedman and the Emergence of Holocaust Scholarship: A Reappraisal." *Simon Dubnow Institute Yearbook* XI (2012): 333–46.

———. "An Invisible Web: Philip Friedman and the Network of Holocaust Research." In *Als der Holocaust noch keinen Namen hatte / Before the Holocaust Had Its Name*, edited by Regina Fritz et al., 149–65. Vienna: New Academic Press, 2016.

Ayzenbakh, M. A. [Artur Eisenbach]. "Daytshe farbrekhns in poyln [German Crimes in Poland; review of Friedman's 'Extermination of the Polish Jews in the Years 1939–1945' (1946)]." *Eynikeyt* (December 1946): 14–15 (not listed in Friedman's bibliography).

Baron, Salo Wittmayer. "Philip Friedman." *Proceedings of the American Academy for Jewish Research* 29 (1960–61): 1–7.

———. Introduction to Philip Friedman, *Roads to Extinction*, edited by Ada June Friedman, 1–8. New York: Jewish Publication Society of America, 1980.

Eck, Natan. "To the Memory of a Friend." *Yad Vashem Bulletin* 6–7 (June 1960): 6–7.

Finkelshteyn, Khaim. *"Haynt"—a tsayung bay yidn 1908–1939* ("Today"—A Newspaper for Jews; on Friedman's contribution to the 1938 jubilee volume, 239). Tel Aviv: Y. L. Perets, 1978.

Fuks, Khaym Leyb. "Fridman, filip." In *Leksikon fun der nayer yidisher literatur*, vol. 7, 486–89. New York: Alveltlekhn yidishn kultur kongres, 1968.

Gelber, N. M. "The Late Dr. Philip Friedman." *Yad Vashem Bulletin* 6–7 (June 1960): 3–4.

Glatshteyn, Yankev. "Der farlag 'dos poylishe yidntum' [The Publishing House 'Polish Jewry'; review of Friedman's *Oshvyentshim (Auschwitz)*]." *Idisher kemfer* (July 7, 1950): 12–13 (in Glatshteyn's column, "In tokh genumen [In Essence])."

Gringauz, Samuel. Review of Friedman's *Oshvyentshim*. *Jewish Social Studies* XIV, no. 4 (October 1952): 376–77.

Hibel, Ben-Zion ["B. H–L."]. "Konferents far khurbn-forshung: a geshprekh mit d"r filip fridman [Conference for *Khurbn*-Research: A Conversation with Dr. Philip Friedman]." *Undzer veg* [Munich] (December 19, 1947):

8, 7. Abbreviated (and de-personalized) German translation reprinted under Friedman's byline, "Die Pariser Konferenz" (1947).

Hirshhoyt, Y [Julian Hirshaut]. "A sakh vegn hobn gefirt tsu der fartilikung [Many Roads Led to the Extermination; on Friedman's *Roads to Extermination* (1980)]." *Di tsukunft* 87, no. 9 (1981): 262–65. Reprinted as "Dr. filip fridman—der historiker fun undzer khurbn," in Y. Hirshhoyt, *In gang fun der geshikhte* (Tel Aviv: Y. L. Perets, 1984), 326–35.

———. "Dr. filip fridman—der historiker fun undzer khurbn [The Historian of Our *Khurbn*]." *Di tsukunft* (August 1965): 282–86 (not duplicated by the preceding).

Kahan [Kagan], Berl. "Fridman, filip." In *Leksikon fun yidish-shraybers*, 454. New York: Rayah Ilman-Kagan, 1986.

Kent, Martin. "In Honor of the Holocaust Remembrance Day [childhood recollection of his cousin, Friedman]" (April 9, 2010), www.jpost.com/Magazine/Features/Years-later-we-would-remember.

Kermish, Joseph. "D"r filip fridman—der historiker fun khurbn [the Historian of the *Khurbn*]." *Di tsukunft* (April 1975): 151–54. English, "The Founder of the Jewish Historical Commission in Poland after the Second World War," *Yad Vashem Bulletin* 6–7 (June 1960): 4–6. Hebrew, "M'yased ha-Vua'ad ha-Historit be-Polin ahar ha-Milhamah," *Yedi'ot Yad va-Shem* 23–24 (May 1960): 4–6.

Linder, Menakhem. "Historish-ekonomisher regyonalizm [Historical-Economic Regionalism]." *Literarishe bleter* (July 24, 1936): 1–2.

Mahler, Rafoel. "Oshvyentshim [review and summary of Friedman's *To jest Oświęcim* (1945)]." *Eynikeyt* (April 1946): 5, 29–30.

Mark, Yudel. "Philip Friedman." *Jewish Book Annual* 18 (1960–61): 76–80.

Orenshteyn, Binyomin. *Dos lebn un shafn fun d"r filip fridman* [*The Life and Work of Dr. Philip Friedman*]. Montreal: Yidisher kultur klub, 1962.

———. "Dr. filip fridman der lemberger [Dr. Philip Friedman of Lwów]." In *Sefer galitsye: gedenk bukh*, edited by Yosef Okrutni, 168–79. Buenos Aires: Farlag "Galitsye" baym tsentral farband fun galitsyaner yidn in buenos ayres, 1968 (revised and condensed version of the preceding).

Oyerbakh, Rokhl. "D"r filip fridman z"l (dermonung un gezegenung) [Dr. Friedman, of Blessed Memory (Hail and Farewell)]." *Di goldene keyt* 38 (1960): 178–84.

Pat, Yankev. "Dr. filip fridman—a por shtrikhn [A Few Lines]." *Di tsukunft* (March 1960): 107–8.

Ravitch, Melekh. "D"r filip fridman." In *Mayn leksikon*, vol. 4:2, 196–98. Tel Aviv: Y. L. Perets, 1982.

Ringelblum, Emanuel. "A solide geshikhte-arbet [A Solid Historical Work; review of Friedman's published dissertation, *Die galizischen Juden im Kampfe um ihre Gleichberechtigung* [*The Galician Jews in the Struggle for Their Equal Rights*] *(1848–1868)*]." *Literarishe bleter* (September 27, 1929): 758–59 (author anonymous but named in Friedman's bibliography and in Shatzky's Ringelblum compilation).

Schulweis, Harold M. "Globalism and the Jewish Conscience." In *Jews and Judaism in the 21st Century*, edited by Edward Feinstein, 7–19. Woodstock: Jewish Lights Publishing, 2007.

———. "The Bias Against Man." *Jewish Education* 34, no. 1 (1963): 6–14. Reprinted in *Dimensions: A Journal of Holocaust Studies* 3, no. 3 (1988): 4–8.

Shpizman, Leyb. "D"r filip fridman—der historiker fun khurbn [The Historian of the *Khurbn*]." *Geshtaltn*. Buenos Aires: Kiem, 1962, 278–84 (article date: April 1960; original publication not located).

Y. Sh. [Shvartzbart, Yitzkhok]. "A nay vikhtik bukh in english vegn dem varshever geto-oyfshtand [A New Important Book in English on the Warsaw Ghetto Uprising; review of Friedman's *Martyrs and Fighters* (1954)]." *Folk un velt* (April 1954): 31–32.

Stauber, Roni. *Laying the Foundations for Holocaust Research: The impact of the historian Philip Friedman*. Jerusalem: Yad Vashem, 2009.

Tepfer, Naomi Flax. "Dr. Ada Eber-Friedman." *Morningside Gardens News* (January 18, 1975): 3; (February 28, 1975): 3 (both formerly online).

Trunk, Isaiah. "A mekoyrim-antologye vegn varshever geto [An Anthology of Sources on the Warsaw Ghetto; review of Friedman's *Martyrs and Fighters* (1954)]." *Unzer tsayt* (January 1955): 42–44.

———. "Dr. filip fridman, der historiker [The Historian]." *Di tsukunft* (October 1961): 390–93. Reprinted in Trunk, *Geshtaltn un gesheenishn* (1962), 35–46.

———. "Perspective in Pain: Philip Friedman's Holocaust Studies [review of Friedman's *Roads to Extinction*]." *Jewish Frontier* (April 1981): 8–12.

———. "Poylisher Mantshester [Polish Manchester; review of Friedman's *Dzieje Żydów w Lodzi* [*History of the Jews in Lodz*] (1936)]." *Landkentnish* (January 1936): 2–7.

Vulf, Yosef [Joseph Wulf]. "Talyen fun krokever yidn farn gerikht [Hangman of Krakow Jews on Trial; on Friedman's role in bringing Amon Göth to trial in Poland]." *Dos naye lebn* (August 30, 1946): 2.

Weinbaum, Laurence. "Remembering a Forgotten Hero of Holocaust Historiography [review of Stauber, above]." *Jewish Political Studies Review* 243–44 (Fall 5773/2012): 132–36, http://jcpa.org/wp-content/uploads/2013/05/BR4.pdf.

Bibliography of Isaiah Trunk

Scope: All locatable prewar works and postwar Yiddish writings, plus works consulted in all languages, and their publication history (in order by date of Yiddish publication).

Books by Trunk

Di geshikhte fun yidn in plotsk [*The History of the Jews in Płock*], 1237–1657. Warsaw: YIVO, 1939. Condensed Hebrew version, "Le-toldot Yehude Plotsk bi-me ha-benayim uve-roshit ha-at ha-hadashah (1237–1657)," in *Plotsk: toldot kehilah 'atikat-yomin be-Polin*, ed. Eliyahu Eisenberg (Tel Aviv: ha-Menorah, 1967), 17–35.

Lernbukh fun yidisher geshikhe: sistematisher kurs: zekster klas [*Textbook for Jewish History: Systematic Course: Sixth Grade*]. Warsaw: Tsentral komitet fun di yidn in poyln, 1947.

Yidishe arbet-lagern in "Varteland" [*Jewish Labor Camps in the "Warthegau"* (district of Western Poland annexed by Nazi Germany)]. Warsaw: Yidisher Historisher Institut, 1948.

Geshtaltn un gesheenishn (historishe eseyen) [*Figures and Events (Historical Essays)*]. Buenos Aires: Tsentral farband fun poylishe yidn in argentine, 1962 (collected works, listed below).

Lodzsher geto. New York: YIVO and Yad Vashem, 1962. English, *Łódź Ghetto: A History*, trans. and ed. Robert Moses Shapiro (Bloomington: Indiana University Press, 2006). English trans. of chapter VIII of Yiddish original, "Note: Why Was There No Armed Resistance Against the Nazis in the Lodz Ghetto?" *Jewish Social Studies* (1981); reprinted in Marrus (1989).

Shtudyes in yidisher geshikhte in poyln [*Studies in Jewish History in Poland*]. Buenos Aires: Yidbukh, 1963 (collected works, listed below).

Judenrat: The Jewish Councils in Eastern Europe under Nazi Occupation. New York: Macmillan, 1972. Hebrew, *Yudnrat: ha-Mo'atsot ha-Yehudiyot be-Mizrah Eropah be-tekufat ha-Kibush ha-Natzi* (Jerusalem: Yad Vashem,

1979). Chapter 4 reprinted in *How Was it Possible? A Holocaust Reader*, ed. Peter Hayes (Lincoln: University of Nebraska Press / Jewish Foundation for the Righteous, 2015), 336–48.

Jewish Responses to Nazi Persecution: Collective and Individual Behavior in Extremis. New York: Stein and Day, 1979. Yiddish original of first section published in *Geshtaltn un gesheenishn [naye serye]* (1983), 274–314.

Geshtaltn un gesheenishn [naye serye] [*Figures and Events [New Series]*]. Tel Aviv: Y. L. Perets, 1983 (collected works, listed below).

[Editor with Mordecai Kosover]. *Algemeyne entsiklopedye*, vol. Yidn VII (devoted to Holocaust topics). New York: Dubnov-fond un entsiklopedye komitet, 1966.

Articles by Trunk

1931

Review of Rafoel Mahler and Emanuel Ringelblum, eds., *Geklibene mekoyrim tsu der geshikhte fun di yidn in poyln un mizrekh-eyrope: mitlalter (biz tsum yor 1506)* [*Collected Sources on the History of the Jews in Poland and Eastern Europe: Middle Ages (to the Year 1506)*], 2 vols. (Warsaw, 1930). *YIVO bleter* II, nos. 1–2 (September 1931): 155–57.

1932

"A yorgang 'YIVO-bleter' [A Year of 'YIVO bleter']." *Literarshe bleter* (February 12, 1932): 104–5.

"Tsu der yidisher gezelshaft! [To the Jewish Community!—appeal regarding folklorist Shmuel Lehman, signed by Trunk and others]." *Literarishe bleter* (February 5, 1932): 99.

1933

"Der 1-ter turistisher instruktorn-kurs in voronyenke (ayndrukn un baobakhtungen) [The 1st Course for Sightseeing Instructors in Woronienke (Impressions and Observations)]." *Yedies fun Y.G.F.L.* [*Landkentnish*] 4, no. 7 (November 1933): 14–15.

"Geshikhtlekhe tematik in der moderner yidisher literatur [Historical Themes in Modern Yiddish Literature]." *Vokhnshrift* 3, no. 44 (November 17, 1933): 3.

"Ven un vu hobn zikh yidn bazetst in mazovshe [When and Where Did Jews Settle in Mazovia (Mazowsze)]." *Landkentnish* 1 (1933): 47–60. Reprinted in *Shtudyes*, 11–24.

Review of Emanuel Ringelblum, *Żydzi w Warszawie* [Jews in Warsaw] (Warsaw, 1932). *YIVO bleter* V (1933): 61–66.

1934

"A yidishe kehile in poyln baym sof fun XVIII yorhundert: kutno [A Jewish Community in Poland at the End of the 18th Century: Kutno]." *Bleter far geshikhte* 1 *("yunger historiker num. 3")* (1934): 87–140. Reprinted in *Shtudyes* as "Di yidishe kehile in kutno baym sof 18tn yorhundert," 71–108.

"Badaytung fun sots. virtshaftlekhe badingungen far der dertsyung [Significance of Social-Economic Conditions for Education]." *Shul-vegn: khoydeshshrift fun der tsentraler yidisher shul-organizatsye in poyln* 2, nos. 1–2 (October 1934): 19–22.

"Der yidisher mehus fun der yidisher gez. far landkentnish [The Jewish Nature of the Jewish Society for Knowing the Land]." *Yedies fun Y.G.F.L.* [*Landkentnish*] 5, no. 1 (April 1934): 13–14.

"Individual-psikhologishe dertsyung [Individual-Psychological Education]." *Shul-vegn* 1 (March 1934): 12–14; 2 (April 1934): 45–50; 4 (May 1934): 116–20.

1936

"Poylisher mantshester [Polish Manchester; review of Friedman's *Dzieje Żydów w Lodzi* [History of Jews in Lodz] (1936)]." *Landkentnish* (January 1936): 2–7.

1937

"Der yidisher kvartal in plotsk in XVI un XVII y.h. [The Jewish Quarter in Płock in the 16th and 17th Century]." *Landkentnish* 9, no. 4 (December 1937): 1–4; 10, no. 1 (April 1938): 7–8. Preview from *Di geshikhte fun yidn in plotsk*.

"Tsu der geshikhte fun yidn in mazovye in 15-tn y"h [On the History of the Jews in Mazovia (Mazowsze) in the 15th Century]." *Historishe shriftn* II (1937): 206–22.

1938

"Bamerkungen tsum historishn opteyl fun der oysshtelung 'yidn in poyln' [Observations on the Historical Section in the Exhibition 'Jews in Poland']." *Shul-vegn: khoydeshshrift fun der tsentraler yidisher shul-organizatsye in poyln* 6, no. 1 (October 1938): 35–40.

"Di lere vegn mentsh [review of *Alfred adler, der mentsh un zayn lere* [Alfred Adler, the Man and His Teaching] by Trunk's brother, Israel Trank (pseud. of Srul-Shiye Trunk) (Warsaw, 1938)]." *Os* 2, no. 2 (February 1938): 43–46.

"Di rekhtlekhe lage fun di yidn in plotsk in XVI y"h (a fragment fun a historisher monografye vegn plotsker yidn) [The Legal Status of the Jews in Płock in the 16th Century (An Extract from a Historical Monograph on Płock Jewry)]." *Bleter far geshikhte* II (1938): 89–126. Excerpt from *Di geshikhte fun yidn in plotsk*. Reprinted in *Shtudyes* as "Di rekhtlekhe lage fun yidn in plotsk in 16tn un in der ershter helft 17tn y"h," 25–70.

1939

[anon.] "Barikht fun der pinkeysim-aktsye [Report on the Community Record Books Project]." *Yedies fun YIVO* 83–84 (March–April 1939): 6–10. Analysis and authorship ascribed to Trunk by Kermish in *Geshtaltn un gesheenishn* [*naye serye*] (1983), 8; *Łódź Ghetto* (2006), xxii.

"Tsu der diskusye vegn program fun geshikhte-limud in undzere shuln [On the Discussion Regarding the Program of History-Study in Our Schools; conference of history teachers, January 7–8, 1939, Vilna]." *Shul-vegn: khoydeshshrift fun der tsentraler yidisher shul-organizatsye in poyln* 6, nos. 3–4 (June 1939): 170–75.

1946

"Pinkes-poyln [Chronicle of (the Jews in) Poland; on the memorial book of that name proposed by the Central Jewish Historical Commission]." *Dos naye lebn* (November 28, 1946): 9.

1947

"'Grine felder' fun perets hirshbeyn in nider-shlezishn yidishn teater [*Green Fields* by Perets Hirshbeyn in the Yiddish Theater of Lower Silesia (the formerly German district planned for resettlement of Jewish survivors; review of theater performance)]." *Dos naye lebn* (March 31, 1947): 5.

"Kultur arbet in shotn fun toyt [Cultural Work in the Shadow of Death]." *Yugnt veker* 3, no. 4 (April 1947): 19.

1948

"Di yidn un der november-oyfshtand fun 1831 [The Jews in the November Uprising (of Poland against Russia) in 1831 (correctly, 1830)]." *Dos naye lebn* (December 1, 1948): 4; (December 6, 1948): 4.

"Ekspertize fun mgr y. trunk [Expertise of Magister Y. Trunk (at the war crimes trial of Eilert Hesemeyer)]." *Dos naye lebn* (September 6, 1948): 6, 8.

"Yehoshua rabinovitsh—fargesener bundisher tuer in varshever geto [Joshua Rabinovitsh—Forgotten Bund Activist in the Warsaw Ghetto]." In *Historisher zamlbukh. Materyaln un dokumentn tsushtayer tsu der geshikhte fun algemeynem yidishn arbter-bund*, 119. Warsaw: Ringen, 1948.

"Yidishe arbet-lagern in 'varteland.' [Jewish Labor Camps in the 'Warthegau' (district of Western Poland annexed by Nazi Germany)]." *Bleter far geshikhte* I, no. 1 (January–March 1948): 114–69; I, no. 2 (April–June 1948): 14–45. Offprint, *Yidishe arbet-lagern in "Varteland"* (Warsaw: Yidisher Historisher Institut, 1948).

"Yidishe kiem-problemen in likht fun undzer geshikhte [Problems of Jewish Existence in Light of Our History]." In *Oyfn sheydveg: haynttsaytike problemen fun yidishn natsyonaln kiem: ershter zamlheft*, 47–63. Munich: Fraye tribune, 1948.

1949

"Di shtudir-biblyotek baym yidishn historishn institute [The Research Library of the Jewish Historical Institute (in Warsaw)]." *Yedies: byuletin fun yidishn historishn institut in poyln* [1] (November 1949): 7.

"Shtudye tsu der geshikhte fun yidn in 'varteland' in der tkufe fun umkum [A Study of the History of the Jews in the "Warthegau" in the Period of the Extermination] (1939–1944)." *Bleter far geshikhte* II, nos. 1–4 (January–December 1949): 64–166. Reprinted in *Shtudyes*, 171–289.

"Sotsyale antagonizmen in geto un di rol fun di yudenratn [Social Antagonisms in the Ghettos and the Role of the Jewish Councils]." *Yidishe shriftn* 6, no. 26 (June 1949): 6–7.

1951

"Yidn in natsishe lagern [Jews in Nazi Camps]." In *Mir zaynen do . . .*, 5–7. New York: Farband fun gevezene yidishe katsetler un partizaner, 1951. Reprinted in *Shtudyes*, 290–97. Expanded and revised English version, "Uprising in the Camps," in *The Fighting Ghettos*, ed. and trans. Meyer Barkai (Philadelphia-New York: J. B. Lippincott, 1962), 283–91; translated from *Sefer Milhamot ha-Geta'ot*, ed. Itzhak Zuckerman and Moshe Basak (Tel Aviv: Bet Lohame ha-Geta'ot, 1954).

1952

"Bletlekh fun der fargangenhayt (tsu der geshikhte fun yidishn yishev in lublin fun di eltste tsaytn biz sof fun 18tn y"h) [On the History of the Jewish Community in Lublin from the Oldest Times to the End of the 18th

Century]." In *Dos bukh fun lublin: zikhroynes, gvyes-eydes un materyaln iber lebn, kamf un martirertum fun lubliner yidishn yishev*, edited by M. Litvin and M. Lerman, 26–58. Paris: Parizer komitet far shafn a monografye vegn yidishn yishev in lublin, 1952. Reprinted without first and last chapters in *Shtudyes*, 109–58 (dated 1949). Hebrew, with added first chapter, "Toldot Yehude Lublin," in *Entsiklopediyah shel Galuyot: Lublin*, ed. Nahman Blumental and Meir Korzen (Jerusalem: Entsiklopediyah shel Galuyot, 1957), 21–68.

"Sanitare farheltenishn un shtarbikayt in geto [Sanitary Conditions and Mortality in the (Lublin) Ghetto]." In *Dos bukh fun lublin: zikhroynes, gvyes-eydes un materyaln iber lebn, kamf un martirertum fun lubliner yidishn yishev*, edited by M. Litvin and M. Lerman, 357–62. Paris: Parizer komitet far shafn a monografye vegn yidishn yishev in lublin, 1952 (misattributed to his cousin, Y. Y. Trunk).

"Shmuel lehman, z"l: der lamed–vovnik fun yidishn folklore." *Lebns-fragn* 10 (February 1952): 6. Reprinted in *Pinkas Sokhatshev [Sochaczew]*, ed. A. Sh. Stein and Gavriel Weisman (Jerusalem: Irgun Sokhatshev be-Yisra'el, 1962), 271–73. Reprinted in *Geshtaltn un gesheenishn* (1962), 47–50. English trans. by Jerrold Landau, "Shmuel Lehman of blessed memory, the Lamed Vovnik of the Jewish People," www.jewishgen.org/yizkor/Sochaczew/so248.html.

"Tsum 10-tn yortog fun natsyonaln khurbn [On the 10th Anniversary of the National *Khurbn*]." *Lebns-fragn* 12–13 (April–May 1952): 6.

Review of L. Brener, *Vidershtand un umkum in chenstokhover geto* [*Resistance and Extermination in the Częstochowa Ghetto*]. *Dapim le-heker ha-Sho'ah veha-mered* 2 (first series, February 1952): 154–57.

1953

"Di problem vidershtand in undzer khurbn-literatur [The Problem of Resistance in Our *Khurbn*-Literature]." *Di tsukunft* (May–June 1953): 253–57. Reprinted in *Shtudyes*, 298–307 (not in table of contents).

"Mayrev-eyropeyishe yidn in di mizrekh-eyropeyishe getos [Western European Jews in the Eastern European Ghettos]." *Di goldene keyt* 15 (1953): 80–102.

"Milkhome kegn yidn durkhn farshpreytn krankeytn [The War against Jews by Spreading Illnesses]." *YIVO bleter* XXXVII (1953): 58–100. English, "Epidemics and Mortality in the Warsaw Ghetto, 1939–1942," *YIVO Annual of Jewish Social Science* VIII (1953): 82–122. Reprinted in *The Nazi Holocaust*, vol. 6: The Victims of the Holocaust; vol. 1, ed. Michael R. Marrus (Westport: Meckler, 1989), 3–43.

"Yidisher umkum un vidershtand (tsu der kharacteristik fun unzer khurbn) [Jewish Extermination and Resitance (on the Characteristics of our Khurbn)]." *Lebns-fragn* 24 (April 1953): 3–4.

1954

"Belkhatov yisker bukh—a vikhtiker baytrog [Bełchatów *Yizkor* Book—An Important Contribution]." *Di tsukunft* (July–August 1954): 290–91.

"Nisht fargebn di farbrekher, nisht farvishn di shpurn fun farnbrekhn! [Do not Forgive the Crimimals, Do not Wipe Away the Traces of the Crimes!]." *Unzer tsayt* (April–May 1954): 14–15.

1955

"A historisher reportazsh vegn khurbn ashkenaz [A Historical Reportage on the *Khurbn* in Germany; review of Mordechai Wolf Bernstein, *In labirintn fun tkufes* [*In Labyrinths of Ages*] (Buenos Aires, 1955)]." *Unzer tsayt* (November 1955): 43–45.

"A mekoyrim-antologye vegn varshever geto [An Anthology of Sources on the Warsaw Ghetto; review of Friedman's *Martyrs and Fighters* (1954)]." *Unzer tsayt* (January 1955): 42–44.

"Der monument fun dem yidishn folks-lerer [The Monument to the Jewish School Teachers; review of ed. Kh. Sh. Kazdan, *Lerer yisker bukh di umgekumene lerer fun tsysho shuln in poyln* [*Yizkor Book of the Murdered Teachers of the Central Yiddish School Organization in Poland*] (New York, 1954)]." *Unzer tsayt* (July 1955): 49–51.

"Farvos hobn di natsis umgebrakht zeks milyon yidn in eyrope? [Why Did the Nazis Murder Six Million Jews in Europe?]." *Di tsukunft* (April 1955): 147–50. Reprinted in *Shtudyes*, 161–70.

"Yidn in natsishe lagern [Jews in Nazi Camps]." In *Mir zaynen do . . .*, 5–7. New York: Farband fun gevezene yidishe katsetler un partizaner, 1951. Reprinted in *Shtudyes*, 290–97. Expanded and revised English version, "Uprising in the Camps," in *The Fighting Ghettos*, ed. and trans. Meyer Barkai (Philadelphia-New York: J. B. Lippincott, 1962), 283–91; translated from *Sefer Milhamot ha-Getaòt*, ed. Itzhak Zuckerman and Moshe Basak (Tel Aviv: Bet Lohame ha-Getaòt, 1954).

1956

"An umbakanter dokument vegn dem kamf in di kehiles fun lemberger svive [An Unknown Document on the Struggle in the Communities of the Lwów Region], 1735–1758." *YIVO bleter* XL (1956): 221–24.

"A pyonerish verk in unzer historish-pedagogisher literatur [A Pioneering Work in Our Historical-Pedagogical Literature]." *Unzer tsayt* (November–December 1956): 51–53.

"Der fal rudolf kastner in likht fun der yudenratlisher ideologye [The Case of Rudolf Kastner in Light of the Judenrat Ideology]." *Unzer tsayt* (April–May 1956): 23–27.

"Der va'ad medinat rusyah (raysn)." *YIVO bleter* XL (1956): 63–85. Reprinted in *Geshtaltn un gesheenishn* (1962), 59–82. English, "The Council of the Province of White Russia," *YIVO Annual of Jewish Social Science* XI (1956/1957): 188–210.

1957

"A bukh vegn shedlets [A Book about Siedlce; review of A. Volf Yasni, *Sefer yizkor li-kehilat Shedlets* [*Yizkor Book for the Community of Siedlce*] (Buenos Aires, 1956)]." *YIVO bleter* XLI (1957): 359–64.

"Mikhtavim mi-shanot ha-Sho'ah [Writings from the Years of the Shoah]." *Yediot Bet Lohame ha-Geta'ot* 18–19 (April 1957): 22–29. Reprinted in *Zakhor: Kobets ti'ude le-mesirot nefesh be-tekufat ha-Sho'ah* 12 (1991): 118–27.

"Tsum 14tn yortog fun oyfshtand in varshever geto: vegn yidishn vidershtand in der natsi tkufe [For the 14th Anniversary of the Uprising in the Warsaw Ghetto: On Jewish Resistance in the Nazi Period]." *Unzer tsayt* (April–May 1957): 16–18. Reprinted in *Shtudyes* as "Der farnem fun yidishn vidershtand," 308–12 (not in table of contents).

"Yankev shatskis tsushtayer tsu der geshikhte fun yidishn arbeter-klas un zayne politishe bavegungen [Jacob Shatzky's Contribution to the History of the Jewish Working Class and Its Political Movements]." In *Yankev shatski—tsum ondenk*, edited by Philip Friedman et al., 600–666 New York: Klub fun poylishe yidn, 1957, with English abstract. Adapted, together with "*Yankev shatskis tsushtayer*" (1957) for *Geshtaltn un gesheenishn* (1962), 29–34.

1958

"19ter april 1943–1958." *Unzer tsayt* (April–May 1958): 20–21.

1959

"A virdiker monument far a farshnitener yidisher kehile [A Worthy Monument for a Detroyed Jewish Community; review of *Pinkes Zamosc* (Buenos Aires, 1957)]." *Di tsukunft* (February 1959): 91–92.

"Chenstokhov—a 'mazldike' yidishe kehile [Częstochowa—A 'fortunate' Jewish Community (for having a worthy *yizkor* book); review of Sh. D.

Zinger, ed., *"Chenstokhover yidn"* (1958)]." *Di tsukunft* (July–August 1959): 320–22.

"Der bavofnter un nisht-bavofnter vidershtand fun varshever geto [Armed and Unarmed Resistance in the Warsaw Ghetto]." *Unzer tsayt* (April–May 1959): 31–33.

1960

"Der neo-natsizm un di konspiratsye fun farshvaygn [Neo-Nazism and the Conspiracy of Silence]." *Unzer tsayt* (March 1960): 16–18.

"Di onheybn fun der yidisher arbeter-bavegung [The Beginning of the Jewish Labor Movement]." In *Di geshikhte fun bund*, vol. 1, edited by G. Aronson et al., 11–106. New York: Unzer tsayt, 1960.

"Di yidishe kehile in khmielnik in 19-tn yorhundert (bafelkerung un ekonomik) [The Jewish Community in Chmielnik in the 19th Century (Population and Economics)]." In *Pinkes khmyelnik: yisker-bukh nokh der khorev-gevorener yidisher kehile*, edited by Efrayim Shedletski, 91–96. Tel Aviv: Irgun yotz'e Hmyelnik be-Yisra'el, 1960.

"Problemen fun ineveynikstn geto-lebn [Problems of Internal Ghetto Life]." *Di tsukunft* (April 1960): 150–55. Section "alef" reprinted in *Geshtaltn un gesheenishn* (1962), 129–31; section "gimel" reprinted in *Geshtaltn*, 132–39; section "dalet" expanded as "Dos kultur-lebn in di getos" in *Geshtaltn*, 173–239.

"Shimen Dubnov un di yidishe mizrekh-eyropeyishe historyografye [Simon Dubnow and East-European Jewish Historiography]." *Di tsukunft* (December 1960): 465–71. Reprinted in *Geshtaltn un gesheenishn* (1962), 9–28.

1961

"20 yor nokh hitlers onfal oyf sovet-rusland [20 Years after Hitler's Attack on Soviet Russia]." *Unzer tsayt* (July–August 1961): 20–21.

"Dr. filip fridman, der historiker [Dr. Philip Friedman, the Historian]." *Di tsukunft* (October 1961): 390–93. Reprinted in *Geshtaltn un gesheenishn* (1962), 35–46.

"Vi azoy forsht men di geshikhte fun di khorev gevorene kehiles in poyln? [How Should One Study the History of the Destroyed Jewish Communities in Poland?]." In *Almanakh yidish*, edited by Yankev Pat et al., 275–86 New York: Alveltlekhn yidishn kultur-kongres, 1961. Reprinted in *Geshtaltn un gesheenishn* (1962), 108–23.

1962

"Di ershte tsaytshrift oyf yidish in rusland [The First Yiddish Periodical in Russia]." *Unzer tsayt* (December 1962): 23–24.

"Di yidishe kehile in sokhachev fun di eltste tsaytn bizn 19tn y. h. [The Jewish Community in Sochaczew from the Oldest Times to the 19th Century]." In *Pinkas Sokhatshev*, edited by A. Sh. Stein and Gavriel Weisman, 11–28 (Hebrew 607–11). Jerusalem: Irgun Sokhatshev be-Yisra'el, 1962. Condensed English trans. by Jerrold Landau, "The History of a Community," www.jewishgen.org/yizkor/Sochaczew/so601.html#History.

"Dos kultur-lebn in di getos [Cultural Life in the Ghettos]." In *Geshtaltn un gesheenishn* (1962), 173–239. English trans., concluding section of "Religious, Educational and Cultural Problems in the Eastern European Ghettos under German Occupation," *YIVO Annual of Jewish Social Science* XIV (1969): 182–95. Reprinted in *East European Jews in Two Worlds: Studies from the YIVO Annual*, ed. Deborah Dash Moore (Evanston: Northwestern University Press and YIVO, 1990), 155–91.

"Ketubot be-'Ivrit-Yidish 'al mismakhim Polanim meha-me'ah ha-17 veha-18 [Marriage Contracts in 'Hebrew-Yiddish' in Polish Documents of the 17th and 18th Century]." In *Sefer ha-yovel mugash li-khevod Dr. N. M. Gelber, le-regel yovlo ha-shiv'im*, edited by Yisra'el Klausner et al., 79–84. Tel Aviv: 'Olamenu, 1962/1963.

"Letters from Readers: Jewish Resistance [on Raul Hilberg]." *Commentary* (August 1962): 159–62. Expanded Yiddish version, "Nokh amol vegn yidishn vidershtand [Again regarding Jewish Resistance]" (1963).

"Shmuel [Artur] Zigelboym." *Geshtaltn un gesheenishn* (1962), 51–55 (original publication not located).

"Shtelung fun daytshn tsu der hitleristisher oysrotung-politik [Attitude of Germans to the Hitlerian Policy of Extermination]." *Di tsukunft* (April 1962): 146–48.

"Vegn khurbn-forshung [On *Khurbn* Research]." *Geshtaltn un gesheenishn* (1962): 127–29.

"Yidish-rusishe historyografye." *Geshtaltn un gesheenishn* (1962), 83–107. English, "Historians of Russian Jewry," in *Russian Jewry (1860–1917)*, ed. Jacob Frumkin et al. (New York: Thomas Yoseloff, 1966), 454–71.

1963

"A nay verk vegn yidisher kultur-geshikhte in galitsye un poyln in der ershter helft fun 19tn yorhundert [A New Work on Jewish Cultural History in Galicia and Poland in the First Half of the 19th Century; review of Raphael Mahler, *ha-Hasidut veha-Haskalah* [*Hasidism and Haskalah*] (1961)]." *Di tsukunft* (November 1963): 443–45. Reprinted in *Geshtaltn un gesheenishn* [*naye serye*] (1983), 45–51.

"Nokh amol vegn yidishn vidershtand kegn di natsis [Again regarding Jewish Resistance against the Nazis]." *Di tsukunft* (April 1963): 152–56. Partial composite of "Tsum 14tn yortog" (1957) and "Letters from Readers" (1962).

1964

"Der lebnsveg fun a perzenlekhkayt [The Life's Journey of a Personality (on Dubnow)]." *Unzer tsayt* (June 1964): 42–44.

"Poylish-yidishe batsyungen in dem peryod fun der 2ter velt-milkhome [Polish-Jewish Relations in the Period of the Second World War]." *Di tsukunft* (April 1964): 151–57. Reprinted in *Shtudyes*, 315–32.

"Sources to the Warsaw Ghetto Uprising" (English trans. of paper delivered in Polish at the Polish Institute, New York, May 10, 1963). *Polish Review* IX, no. 1 (Winter 1964): 87–93.

Review of *The Martyrdom of Jewish Physicians in Poland: Studies by Leon Wulman and Joseph Tenenbaum* (New York, 1963). *American Jewish Historical Quarterly*, 54, no. 1 (September 1964): 94–98.

1965

"Der 'bund' in pyetrkov [The 'Bund' in Piotrków]." In *Pyetrkov tribunalski un umgegnt / Pyetrkov Tribunalski veha-sevivah*, edited by Yankev Malts and Naftoli Lau, 451–70. Tel Aviv: Redaktsye komitet fun der pyetrkover landsmanshaft in yisroel, 1965.

"Emanuel ringelblum—der historiker 1900–1944." *Di tsukunft* (April 1965): 155–61. Reprinted in *Shtudyes*, 52–65.

1966

"Der farnikhtungs-protses fun eyropeyishn yidntum in der natsi-tkufe [The Process of Destruction of European Jewry in the Nazi Period]." *Algemeyne entsiklopedye*, vol. Yidn VII, 1–15. New York: Dubnov-fond un entsiklopedye komitet, 1966.

1967

"'Amnezye' durkh der hintertir ['Amnesia' through the Back Door]." *Unzer tsayt* (October 1967): 27–29.

"Der letster fun a dor [The Last of a Generation; memorial essay on historian N. M. Gelber]." *Di tsukunft* (January 1967): 25–27.

"Fun der fargangenhayt fun der brisk-kuyaver kehile [From the Past of the Brześć Kujawski Jewish Community]." In *Vlotslavek un umgegnt / Vlotslavek veha-sevivah*, edited by Kathriel Tnursh and Meir Korzen, 777–80. Tel Aviv: Farband yotsey vlotslavek un umgegnt in yisroel un di fareynikte shtatn / Irgun yotze Vlotslavek be-Yisra'el veha-Aratsot ha-Berit, 1967.

"Geshikhte fun der yidisher kehile in plotsk." In *Plotsk: toldot kehilah 'atikat-yomin be-Polin*, edited by Eliyahu Eisenberg, 149–87 (Hebrew 36–65). Tel Aviv: ha-Menorah, 1967. Condensed English trans. by Ada Holtzman, "The History of the Jews of Plotzk from the 17th Century to World War I," www.jewishgen.org/Yizkor/plock/plo005.html#Page16.

"Geshikhte fun yidn in Vlotslavek biz dem ershtn velt-krig [The History of the Jews in Włocławek until the First World War] (1802–1914)." In *Vlotslavek un umgegnt / Vlotslavek veha-sevivah*, edited by Kathriel Tnursh and Meir Korzen, 47–86. Tel Aviv: Farband yotsey vlotslavek un umgegnt in yisroel un di fareynikte shtatn / Irgun yotze Vlotslavek be-Yisra'el veha-Aratsot ha-Berit, 1967.

"Le-toldot Yehude Plotsk bi-me ha-benayim uve-roshit ha-at ha-hadashah." In *Plotsk: toldot kehilah 'atikat-yomin be-Polin*, edited by Eliyahu Eisenberg, 17–35. Tel Aviv: ha-Menorah, 1967. Condensation of *Di geshikhte fun yidn in plotsk, 1237–1657* (Warsaw, 1939). Condensed English trans. by Ada Holtzman, "History of the Jews of Plotzk from the Middle Ages until the 17th Century (1237–1657)," www.jewishgen.org/Yizkor/plock/plo005.html#Page10.

"Strategye un taktik fun di yudenratn in mizrekh-eyrope [The Strategy and Tactics of the Jewish Councils in Eastern Europe]." *Aroyfgetsvungene yidishe reprezentantsn unter der natsisher memshole: kolokvyum fun yivo, detsember 2–5, 1967* (New York: YIVO, 1972), 76–88 (and discussion thereafter).

"Yankev shatski—der historiker (tsu zayn tsentn yortsayt) [Jacob Shatzky—the Historian (on the Tenth Anniversary of His Death)]." *Di goldene keyt* 58 (1967): 188–93. Adapted from "Yankev shatskis tsushtayer" (1957) and *Geshtaltn un gesheenishn* (1962), 29–34.

1968

"Di batsyung fun di yidnratn tsu der frage fun bavofntn vidershtand kegn di natsis." In *ha-'Amidah ha-Yehudit bi-tekufat ha-Sho'ah*, edited by Yisrael Gutman and Livia Rothkirchen, 409–35 (Hebrew 160–80). Jerusalem: Yad Vashem, 1970. English, "The Attitude of the Judenrats to the Problems of Armed Resistance against the Nazis," in *Jewish Resistance During the Holocaust: Proceedings of the Conference on Manifestations of*

Jewish Resistance, Jerusalem, April 7–11, 1968 (Jerusalem: Yad Vashem, 1971), 202–25. Reprinted in *The Catastrophe of European Jewry: Antecedents—History—Reflections: Selected Papers*, ed. Yisrael Gutman and Livia Rothkirchen (Jerusalem: Yad Vashem, 1976), 422–50. Hebrew, "ha-Yudenratim ve-yahasam le-be'ayot ha-meri ha-mezuyan neged ha-Natzim" in Gutman and Rothkirchen, *Sho'at Yehude Eropah: Reka, Korot, Mashma'ut* (Jerusalem: Yad Vashem, 1973), 309–33.

"Geshikhte fun der yidisher kehile in kutne." In *Sefer Kutnah veha-sevivah*, edited by David Shtokfish, 29–53 (Hebrew 11–28). Tel Aviv: Irgun yotz'e Kutnoh veha-sevivah be-Yisra'el uve-hutz-la-aretz, 1968. English trans. by Carole Turkeltaub Borowitz, "The History of the Jewish Community of Kutno," www.jewishgen.org/yizkor/kutno/kut011.html.

"ha-Rav Yitskhok Yehuda Trunk [Rabbi Isaac Judah Trunk (Isaiah Trunk's father)]." In *Sefer Kutnah veha-sevivah*, ed. Shtokfish, 243–46.

"In mayn heymshtot [In My Hometown]." In *Sefer Kutnah veha-sevivah*, ed. Shtokfish, 419–21.

"Untergang fun der yidisher kutne [The End of Jewish Kutno]." In *Sefer Kutnah veha-sevivah*, ed. Shtokfish, 340–53 (Hebrew 331–39).

"The Organizational Structure of the Jewish Councils in Eastern Europe." *Yad Vashem Studies* VII (1968): 147–64. Preview of chapter 4 of *Judenrat*. Hebrew, "Ha-Mivneh ha-irgune shel mo'atsot ha-Yehudim be-Mizrakh Eropah," *Yad Vashem Kovets Mehkarim* 7 (1968): 137–53.

"Vegn rafoel mahlers kontseptsye fun yidishn geshikhte [On Raphael Mahler's Conception of Jewish History]." *Di tsukunft* (October 1968): 462–66. Reprinted in *Geshtaltn un gesheenishn* [*naye serye*] (1983), 32–44.

1969

"Avrom menes a"sh—shrikhn tsu der kharakteristik fun dem mentsh un zayn verk [(Historian) Abraham Menes, of Blessed Memory—A few Lines on the Characteristics of the Man and His Work]." *Di tsukunft* (December 1969): 420–24.

"Religious, Educational and Cultural Problems in the Eastern European Ghettos under German Occupation." *YIVO Annual of Jewish Social Science* XIV (1969): 159–95. Reprinted in *The Nazi Holocaust*, vol. 6: The Victims of the Holocaust; vol. 1, ed. Michael R. Marrus (Westport: Meckler, 1989), 44–80.

1970

"Sikumav shel mishal 'al hevre ha-yudenratim [Summary of the Governance of the Members of the Jewish Councils]"; preview of *Judenrat*, Appendix I,

"Analysis of the Evaluation of the Behavior of the Members of the Jewish Councils in Our Poll and Some Eyewitness Accounts," *Dapim le-heker ha-Sho'ah veha-mered* 1 (2nd series, 1970): 119–35.

1972

"The Jewish Councils in Eastern Europe under Nazi Rule (An Attempt at a Synthesis [more accurately, a summary]) [American Historical Association Conference, December 29, 1971, cosponsored by the Conference Group for Social and Administrative History and YIVO]." *Societas—A Review of Social History* (Summer 1972): 221–39 (with introduction by Nathan Reich and comments by Herbert S. Levine).

1973

"Der kultur-aspekt fun der yidisher arbeter-bavegung in amerike [Sixth World Conference of Jewish Studies, Hebrew University, August 1973]." *Divre ha-Kongres ha-'olami ha-shishi le-mada'e ha-Yahadut*, vol. II. Jerusalem: ha-Igud ha-'olami le-mada'e ha-Yahadut, 1975, 257–64 (English summary, 429–30). Reprinted in *Geshtaltn un gesheenishn* [*naye serye*] (1983), 111–69. English, "The Cultural Dimension of the American Jewish Labor Movement," *YIVO Annual of Jewish Social Science* XVI (1976): 342–93.

"Di poylishe demokratye un der heymisher antisemitizm [Polish Democratic Circles and Domestic Antisemitism]." *Di tsukunft* (May 1973): 226–30.

"ha-Poli'arkhiyah ha-Natzit u-matsav ha-Yehudim be-shetahim ha-kibushim [Nazi Polyarchy and the Situation of the Jews in the Occupied Areas]." *Dapim le-heker ha-Sho'ah veha-mered* 2 (2nd series, 1973): 7–22.

"Isaiah Trunk Honored [acceptance remarks for 1972 National Book Award]." *Congress Bi-Weekly* 40, no. 8 (May 18, 1973): 26. Reprinted as "On Receiving the National Book Award," *Yiddish: A Quarterly Journal Devoted to Yiddish and Yiddish Literature* 1, no. 3 (1973–1974): 47–48.

"Meir balaban—der forsher fun der ko'olisher organizatsye un oytonomye in amolikn poyln (30 yor nokh zayn toyt in varshever geto) [Meir Balaban—the Researcher of Communal Organization and Autonomy in Old-Time Poland (30 Years after His Death in the Warsaw Ghetto)]." *YIVO bleter* XLIV (1973): 198–206. Reprinted in *Geshtaltn un gesheenishn* [*naye serye*] (1983), 19–31.

"Vegn a veynik bakantn 'sumaryush' (zamlung) fun privilegyes far di yidn fun der lubliner kehile [Regarding a Little-Known 'Sumariusz' (Archival Collection) of Privileges for the Jews of the Lublin Community], 1750."

YIVO bleter XLIV (1973): 256–58. Reprinted in *Kol Lublin—Lubliner shtime* 9 (November 1973): 29–30.

1974

"Der ekonomisher antisemitizm in poyln tsvishn di tsvey velt-milkhomes [Economic Anisemitism in Poland between the Two World Wars]." In *Shtudyes vegn yidn in poyln 1919–1939 / Studies on Polish Jewry 1919–1939*, edited by Joshua A. Fishman, 3–98. New York: YIVO, 1974, . Reprinted in *Geshtaltn un gesheenishn [naye serye]* (1983), 170–273.

1975

"A nayer forshung vegn yidishe biblyografye [A New Study on Jewish Bibliography; review of Berl Kahan [Kagan], *Sefer ha-prenumerantn: vegvayzer tsu prenumerirte hebreyishe sforim un zeyere khoysmim fun 8,767 kehiles in eyrope un tsofn-afrike* [Pre-subscribers: A Guide to Pre-subscribed Hebrew Religious Books and Their Subscribers from 8.767 Communities in Europe and North Africa] (New York, 1975)]." *YIVO bleter* XLV (1975): 147–50.

"Closing Statement." In *The Holocaust as Historical Experience*, edited by Yehuda Bauer and Nathan Rotenstreich (Conference: The Holocaust—A Generation After, New York, March 1975), 268–71. New York: Holmes & Meier, 1981.

"Der kultur-aspekt fun der yidisher arbeter-bavegung in amerike" (see 1973).

1976

"le-Toldot ha-historiografiyah ha-Yehudit-Polanit [On the History of Polish-Jewish Historiography]." *Gal-Ed* III (1976): 245–68.

1977

"The typology of the Judenräte in Eastern Europe." In *Patterns of Jewish Leadership in Nazi Europe, 1933–1945: proceedings of the Third Yad Vashem International Historical Conference, Jerusalem, April 4–7, 1977*, edited by Yisrael Gutman and Cynthia I. Haft, 17–30. Jerusalem: Yad Vashem, 1979. Hebrew, "Tipologiyah shel ha-yudenratim be-Mizrakh-Eropah," in *Demut ha-hanhagah ha-Yehudit be-aratsot ha-shelitah ha-Natzit, 1933–45*, ed. Yisrael Gutman (Jerusalem: Yad Vashem, 1979), 11–22.

1979

"Jewish response to Nazi persecution: collective and individual behavior in 'extremis.'" In *The Solomon Goldman Lectures: Perspectives in Jewish*

Learning, vol. 2, edited by Nathaniel Stampfer, 1–18. Chicago: The Spertus College of Judaica Press, 1979. Preview-summary of *Jewish Responses*, Part I.

1980

"Sh. Anski, der groyser humanist fun zayn dor (tsu zayn 60tn yortsayt) [Sh. An-sky, the Great Humanist of His Generation (on the 60th Anniversary of His Death)]." *Di tsukunft* (November 1980): 341–43.

"YIVO un di yidishe historishe visnshaft." *YIVO bleter* XLVI (1980): 242–54. Reprinted in *Geshtaltn un gesheenishn* [*naye serye*] (1983), 97–110. Condensation: "Der tsushtayer fun yivo tsu yidisher historiografye," *Yedies fun YIVO* 134 (July 1975): 5, 8; English, "YIVO and Jewish Historiography," *News of the YIVO* 134 (July 1975): 3*, 7*–8*.

1981

"Note: Why Was there No Armed Resistance Against the Nazis in the Lodz Ghetto?" *Jewish Social Studies* XLIII, nos. 3–4 (Summer–Autumn 1981): 329–34. Translation of chapter VIII of *Lodzsher geto*. Reprinted in *The Nazi Holocaust*, vol. 7: Jewish Resistance to the Holocaust, ed. Michael R. Marrus (Westport: Meckler, 1989), 185–90 (excerpt).

"Perspective in Pain: Philip Friedman's Holocaust Studies [review of Friedman's *Roads to Extinction*]." *Jewish Frontier* (April 1981): 8–12.

1982

"Homer bilti yadu'a shel 'mishlahat An-ski' be-shanim [Unknown Material from the 'An-sky Mission' in the Years] 1912–1916." *Gal-Ed* VI (1982): 229–45.

"The Historian of the Holocaust at YIVO [first-person account by Trunk]." In *Creators and Disturbers: Reminiscences by Jewish Intellectuals of New York / Drawn from conversations with Bernard Rosenberg and Ernest Goldstein*, 61–74. New York: Columbia University Press, 1982.

1983

"Nosn mikhl gelber—der letster fun a dor [Natan Mikhel Gelber—The Last of a Generation]." *Geshtaltn un gesheenishn* [*naye serye*] (1983), 66–72.

"Yidishe reaktsye tsu natsi redifes [Jewish Responses to Nazi Persecution]." *Geshtaltn un gesheenishn* [*naye serye*] (1983), 274–314. English, first portion of *Jewish Responses to Nazi Persecution* (1983).

Online Sound Recordings of Trunk (YIVO Radio Program, WEVD, New York)

Interview of Trunk on the progress of his research at YIVO and Yad Vashem on the Jewish Councils, in preparation for his forthcoming book, *Judenrat* (December 20, 1964). Web page: https://yivo.org/isaiah-trunk-on-the-lodz-ghetto-1964; sound recording: https://yivo.org/cimages/14yivo-wevd-podcast12201964.mp3. (The URL and web page are misleading; Trunk's topic was not his previous research and book on the Lodz Ghetto.).

Interview of Trunk on the subject of resistance (November 21, 1965). Web page: https://yivo.org/interview-with-isaiah-trunk-on-anti-nazi-jewish-resistance-1965; sound recording: https://yivo.org/cimages/39yivo-wevd-podcast11211965.mp3.

Interview of Trunk on his recent conference paper at Yad Vashem on the varied attitudes of Jewish Councils toward armed resistance (June 9, 1968). Web page: https://yivo.org/Historian-Isaiah-Trunk-on-Holocaust-Research; sound recording: www.yivo.org/cimages/69yivowevdpodcast691968.mp3.

Writings about Trunk

"Di geshikhte fun yidn in plotsk [The History of the Jews in Płock; YIVO Historical Section discussion of Trunk's book]." *Yedies fun YIVO* 1–2 (81–82) (January–February 1939): 16–17.

"Haynt radyo-simpozyum vegn geto-oyfshtand [Radio Symposium Today on Ghetto Uprising]." *Forverts* (June 9, 1963): 12.

"Isaiah Trunk (1905–1981) [obituary]." *Yedies fun YIVO* 156 (Spring 1981): 1–2; English 1*–2*.

"Isaiah Trunk, Author of a History of Jews During the Nazi Era [obituary]." *New York Times* (April 1, 1981): D22.

"Jewish Book Council Announces Awards for Five Books Published in 1966." *Jewish Telegraphic Agency Daily News Bulletin* XXXIV, no. 98 (May 19, 1967): 4.

Oysshtelung: lebn kamf un oyfshtand in varshever geto / Exhibition: Life Struggle and Uprising in the Warsaw Ghetto. New York: YIVO, 1963.

"Tsvey hoykhpunktn fun moderner yidisher geshikhte / Two Crises in Modern Jewish History [on Trunk's presentation about research on the Warsaw Ghetto Uprising at the YIVO Annual Meeting, May 6, 1973]." *Yedies fun YIVO* 126 (Summer 1973): 1–2; English 1*–2*.

A., "Yeshaye trunk [memorial essay]." *Unzer tsayt* (May 1981): 81–82.

Fuks, Khaym Leyb. "Trunk, Yeshaye." *Leksikon fun der nayer yidisher literatur*, vol. 4, 128–30. New York: Alveltlekhn yidishn kultur kongres, 1961.

Hirshhoyt, Y. Review of Trunk's *Lodzsher geto* (1962). *YIVO bleter* XLIII (1966): 318–23.

Kahan [Kagan], Berl. "Trunk, Yeshaye." *Leksikon fun yidish-shraybers*, 287–88. New York: Rayah Ilman-Kagan, 1986.

Kermish, Joseph. "Yeshaye trunk." *Di goldene keyt* 108 (1982): 149–56. Reprinted as "Yeshaye trunk z"l," in Trunk, *Geshtaltn un gesheenishn [naye serye]* (Tel Aviv: Y. L. Perets, 1983), 7–16. English, "Isaiah Trunk," in Trunk, *Łódź Ghetto: A History*, trans. and ed. Robert Moses Shapiro (Bloomington: Indiana University Press, 2006), xxi–xxviii. Condensation: English, "Isaiah Trunk (1905–1981): In Memoriam," *Yad Vashem Studies* XIV (1981): 335–40; Hebrew, "le-Zikaro shel Yeshayah Trunk (1905–1981)." *Yad Vashem Kovets Mehkarim* 14 (1982), 253–57.

Mahler, Raphael. Review of Trunk's *Geshikhte fun yidn in plotsk* [*The History of the Jews in Płock*] (1939). *Jewish Social Studies* III, no. 3 (July 1941): 339–41.

Mickisch, Véronique. "Jewish Historiography between Socialism and Nationalism: A Portrait of Historian Isaiah Trunk (1905–1981)" (MA thesis, Free University of Berlin, 2017).

Novik, Pesakh. "Yudenrat un vidershtand: di khurbn-literatur un y. trunks bukh 'Yudenrat' [Yudenrat and Resistance: The *Khurbn*-Literature in Y. Trunk's book, 'Judenrat']." *Yidishe kultur* 36, no. 4 (1974): 15–22.

Ringelblum, Emanuel. Introduction to Trunk, *Di geshikhte fun yidn in plotsk* [*The History of the Jews in Płock*], *1237–1657*, V–VI. Warsaw: YIVO, 1939, unsigned but credited to Ringelblum in Trunk's "Emanuel ringelblum— der historiker 1900–1944," *Di tsukunft* (April 1965): 156.

Smith, Mark L. "Trunk, Isaiah." *Encyclopaedia Judaica*, 2nd ed., edited by Fred Skolnik and Michael Berenbaum, vol. 20, 160–61. Detroit: Macmillan USA/Keter, 2007.

Valdman, A. "700 yohr idisher yishuv in poyln [review of Trunk's *Geshikhte fun yidn in Plotsk*]." *Haynt* (10 March 1939): 10.

Bibliography of Nachman Blumental

Scope: Relevant prewar works and all locatable postwar Yiddish writings, plus works consulted in all languages, and their publication history (in order by date of Yiddish publication).

Books by Blumental

Słowa Niewinne [*Innocent Words* (on the "Nazi-German" vocabulary)]. Krakow-Lodz-Warsaw: Centralna Żydowska Komisja Historyczna w Polsce, 1947.

Sefer borshtshiv [*Memorial Book of Borszczów*]. Tel Aviv: Y. L. Perets, 1960 (compiler and editor; author of all unsigned chapters). Historical and other sections by Blumental translated into English by Miriam Beckerman, www.jewishgen.org/Yizkor/borszczow/Borszczow.html#TOC.

Shmuesn vegn der yidisher literatur unter der daytsher okupatsye [*Chats on Yiddish Literature under German Occupation*]. Buenos Aires: Tsentralfarband fun poylishe yidn in argentine, 1966 (collected works, listed below).

Tsurikblikn [*Backward Glances*]. Tel Aviv: Hamenora, 1973.

Verter un vertlekh fun der khurbn-tkufe [*Words and Sayings from the Khurbn-Period*]. Tel Aviv: Y. L. Perets, 1981.

[Editor with Meir Korzen]. *Entsiklopediyah shel Galuyot* [*Encyclopedia of the Diaspora*], vol. V: Lublin. Jerusalem: Entsiklopediyah shel Galuyot, 1957.

[Editor with Kermish]. *Mul ha-oyev ha-Natzi: Lohamim mesaprim* [*Face to Face with the Nazi Enemy: Fighters Recount*] *1939–1945*, vol. 1, with joint introduction. Tel Aviv: Irgun Nekhe ha-milhamah ba-Natzim be-siyu'a Yad va-Shem, 1961. Consists almost entirely of Yiddish narratives.

[Editor]. *Darko shel Yudenrat: te'udot mi-geto Bialistok / Conduct and Actions of a Judenrat: Documents from the Bialystok Ghetto* (Hebrew). Jerusalem: Yad Vashem, 1962.

[Editor]. *Sefer Mir* [*Memorial Book of Mir*]. Jerusalem: Entsiklopediyah shel Galuyot, 1962.

[Editor]. *Sefer-yizkor Baranov* [*Yizkor Book of Baranów Sandomierz*]. Jerusalem: Yad Vashem, 1964.

[Editor]. *Mehkarim le-toldot Yehude Lublin* [*Studies on the History of Jews of Lublin*] by Bela Mandelsberg-Shildkroyt (collected translation of her prewar Yiddish historical articles). Tel Aviv: Hug mokire shemah shel B. Mandelsberg-Shildkroyt, 1965.

[Editor with Kermish]. *ha-Meri veha-mered be-geto Varshah / Resistance and Revolt in the Warsaw Ghetto: A Documentary History* (Hebrew). Jerusalem: Yad Vashem, 1965.

[Editor]. *Te'udot mi-geto Lublin: Yudenrat le-lo derekh / Documents from the Lublin Ghetto: Judenrat without Direction* (Hebrew). Jerusalem: Yad Vashem, 1967.

[Editor]. *Aleksander "a"y lodz"* [*Memorial Book of Aleksandrów Łódzki*]. Tel Aviv: Irgun yotz'e Aleksander, 1968.

[Editor]. *Sefer yisker rozvadov un umgegnt* [*Yizkor Book of Rozwadów and Vicinity*]. Jerusalem: Yad Vashem, 1968.

[Editor with Kermish, Natan Eck, and Arieh Tartakower]. *Yoman geto Varsha: 6.9.1939—23.7.1942*. Jerusalem: Yad Vashem, 1968. English [with Raul Hilberg and Stanislaw Staron], *The Warsaw Diary of Adam Czerniakow: Prelude to Doom* (New York: Stein and Day, 1979).

[Editor with Kermish]. *Kidush ha-Shem—Ketavim mi-yeme ha-Sho'ah* by Shimon Huberband. Tel Aviv: Zakhor, 1969. English, *Rabbi Shimon Huberband, Kiddush Hashem: Jewish Religious and Cultural Life in Poland During the Holocaust*, trans. David E. Fishman, ed. Jeffrey S. Gurock and Robert S. Hirt (Hoboken-New York: KTAV/Yeshiva University Press, 1987).

[Editor with Mordecai Nadav]. *Yanov 'al-yad Pinsk sefer zikaron* [*Memorial Book of Janów Poleski (Ivanava)*]. Jerusalem: Irgun yotz'e Yanov a"y Pinsk be-Yisrael, 1969.

[Editor with Avivah Ben-Azar]. *Sefer yizkor Maikhov, Kharshnitsah, u-Kshoinz* [*Memorial Book of Miechów, Charsznica, and Książ Wielki*]. Tel Aviv: Irgun yotz'e Maikhov, Kharshnitsah, u-Kshoinz, 1971.

Articles by Blumental

1929

"Der goyrl fun a yidisher shul in a galitsishn shtetl [The Fate of a Yiddish School in a Small Town in Galicia]." *Tsushtayer: dray-khadoshim shrift far literatur kunst un kultur* 1 (September 1929): 64.

"Vos iz azoyns yidishe etnografye: bamerkungen fun a zamler [What Exactly is Jewish Ethnography: Observations from a Collector]." *Literarishe bleter* (July 12, 1929): 549.

1938

"Tsveyter turnus aspirantur u. n. fun tsemakh shabad [The Second Session of the Aspirantur (Graduate-Level Program) Named for Zemach Szabad]." *Literarishe bleter* (January 27, 1938): 74–75; (February 3): 94–95.

"Videramol vegn rasizm [Again Regarding Racism]." *Literarishe bleter* (September 16, 1938): 607–8.

1939

"A glezl tey mit di lodzsher moler [A Glass of Tea with the Lodz Painters]." *Literarishe bleter* (February 3, 1939): 37–38 (signed: "N. B–L/Lodzsh").

1945

"A shtime fun yomer-tol [A Voice from the Valley of Lamentations]." *Yidishe kultur* 7, no. 6 (June 1945): 13–18. Second half reprinted as introduction to *Shmuesn*, 9–16.

"Historisher verter-bukh [Historical Dictionary; on Nazi terminology]." *Dos naye lebn* (May 20, 1945): 4; (June 20): 4; (December 15): 4. Partially incorporated into *Słova Niewinne* (1947).

[With Kermish]. "Khelmne [Chełmno; on the visit of the official Commission of Inquiry]." *Dos naye lebn* (June 10, 1945): 3–4.

"Yidishe literatur unter der daytsher okupatsye [Yiddish Literature under the German Occupation]." *Dos naye lebn* (September 14, 1945): 5.

Foreword to Mendl Man, *Di shtilkeyt mont: lider un baladn* [*The Stillness Calls: Poems and Ballads*], 3–4. Lodz: Borokhov-farlag, 1945.

1946

"Di migratsye fun yidishn folks-lid unter der daytsher okupatsye [The Migration of the Yiddish Folksong under the German Occupation]." *Yidishe kultur* 8, no. 7 (July 1946): 12–17. Reprinted in *Shmuesn*, chapter 1; and in *Folks-shtime* (September 25, 1982): 6.

"Di yidishe literatur unter der daytshisher okupatsye [Yiddish Literature under the German Occupation]." *Yidishe kultur* 8, no. 1 (January 1946): 6–10. Reprinted in *Historisher zamlbukh. Materyaln un dokumentn tsushtayer tsu der geshikhte fun algemeynem yidishn arbter-bund* (Warsaw: Ringen, 1948), 113–18. Reprinted as chapters 1 and 2 of *Shmuesn*.

"Lider gezungen in di getos un lagern fun poyln [Songs Sung in the Ghettos and Camps of Poland]." *Yidishe kultur* 8, no. 7 (July 1946): 12–17.

"Vos shtelt mit zikh for der ringelblum arkhiv? [What Constitutes the Ringelblum Archive?]" *Dos naye lebn* (November 1, 1946): 9.

Preface to S. Shayevitsh, *Lekh-lekho [Get Thee Out; poem from 1942 found in the ruins of the Lodz Ghetto]*, 5–16. Lodz: Tsentraler yidisher historisher komisye, 1946. Part 1 reprinted as "Dos literarishe lebn in litsmanshtat-geto," *Undzer lodzsh* 3 (September 1954): 85–87; part 2 as "S. Shayevitsh—der dikhter fun lodzsher geto," *Undzer lodzsh* 5 (October 1957): 60–61.

1947

"Aperçu sur les ghettos de Pologne sous l'occupation allemande [Overview of the Ghettos of Poland during the German Occupation]." In *Conférence européenne des commissions historiques et des centres de documentation juifs [1–10 December 1947, Paris]. Les Juifs en Europe (1939–1945): Rapports*, 199–204. Paris: Éditions du Centre (de documentation Juive Contemporaine), 1949.

"Di 'yad vashem'-konferents in yerusholayim: ayndrukn fun nakhmen blumental oyf a tsumentref mit yidishe shrayber [July 13–14, 1947: The Yad Vashem Conference in Jerusalem: Impressions by Nachman Blumental in a Meeting with Yiddish Writers]." *Dos naye lebn* (October 17, 1947): 6.

"Dos yidishe folk bashuldikt: di ekspertize fun mgr. nakhmen blumental oyfn protses fun rudolf hes [The Jewish People Accuses: The Expertise of Magister Nachman Blumental at the Trial of Rudolf Höss]." *Dos naye lebn* (March 27, 1947): 1–2.

1948

"Der groyser yidisher filolog [The Great Philologist]: b. borokhov." In *Yidishe shriftn: literarish zamlbukh*, edited by Leyb Olitski et al., 162–65. Lodz: Fareyn fun yidishe literatn un zshurnalistn in poyln, 1948.

"Der historiker: tsu der ferter yortsayt: D"r emanuel ringelblum vi a forsher fun der geshikhte fun yidn unter der daytsher okupatsye [The Historian: On the Fourth Anniversary of (his) Death: Dr. Emanuel Ringelblum as a Researcher of the History of the Jews under German Occupation]." *Arbeter tsaytung* 3 (January 1, 1948): 6–7.

"Di 'regirung' fun der general-gubernye un ir oysrotung-politik legabe di yidn: ekspertize fun direktor fun yid. hist. institut mgr. nakhmen blumental oyfn biler-protses in kroke [The 'Government' of the *Generalgouvernement* and Its Extermination Policy Toward the Jews: Expertise of

Director of Jewish Historical Institute Magister Nachman Blumental at the Büler Trial in Krakow]." *Dos naye lebn* (June 30, 1948): 4.

"Di yidishe literatur unter der natsi-okupatsye." In *Historisher zamlbukh. Materyaln un dokumentn tsushtayer tsu der geshikhte fun algemeynem yidishn arbter-bund*, 113–18. Warsaw: Ringen, 1948 (reprint from 1946).

"Di yidishe shprakh un der kamf kegn natsi-rezshim." *Bleter far geshikhte* I, nos. 3–4 (August–December 1948): 106–24. English summary, "Jewish language and struggle against fascist regime," VIII–IX.

"Dr. emanuel ringelblum." *Yidishe kultur* 10, no. 7 (July 1948): 48–50.

"Etlekhe bamerkungen vegn dem pronom vos bay mendelen [Some Observations on the Pronoun 'Vos' (What) as Used by Mendele]." *Yidishe shprakh* VIII, nos. 1–2 (1948): 16–20.

"Memoriał do Kongresu Intelektualistów: złożony przez delegatów żydowskich [Memorandum to the Congress of Intellectuals: Composed by the Jewish Delegates]." [with B. Mark], *Mosty* 3, no. 104 (September 2, 1948): 4.

"Mendele moykher sforim [one of the founders of modern Yiddish and Hebrew literature]." *Yidishe kultur* 10, no. 1 (January 1948): 5–9.

"Refleksje w związku z 5-ą rocznicą powstania w getcie warszawskim [Reflections on the 5th Anniversary of the Warsaw Ghetto Uprising]." *Mosty* 3, no. 46 (April 19, 1948): 12, 35.

"Vegn a literarisher shafung beys der daytsher okupatsye [On a Literary Creation during the German Occupation (a poem cycle found by Blumental in the ruins of the Chełmno Extermination Camp)]." *Kiem* (February 1948): 45–49. Reprinted in *Shmuesn*, 91–106.

1949

"Di arbet iber ringelblums ksav-yad [The Work on Ringelblum's Manuscript]." *Yedies: byuletin fun yidishn historishn institut in poyln* [1] (November 1949): 4–6.

"Di migratsye fun di poylishe yidn unter der daytsher okupatsye [The Migration of the Polish Jews under the German Occupation]." *Bleter far geshikhte* II, nos. 1–4 (January–December 1949): 167–74.

"Vegn lid 'zog nisht keynmol . . .' [On the Song, 'Never Say . . .']." *Yidishe shriftn* (April 1949): 11.

1951

"Shtamt take mendeles 'masoes' fun cervantes 'don kikhot'? [Does Mendele's 'Masoes' (Travels) Really Derive from Cervantes's 'Don Quixote'?]." *Yidishe kultur* 13, no. 11 (December 1951), 5–11.

1952

"Di yidish-poylishe gimnazye in lublin [The Jewish-Polish Gymnasium in Lublin (before the Second World War)]." In *Dos bukh fun lublin: zikhroynes, gvyes-eydes un materyaln iber lebn, kamf un martirertum fun lubliner yidishn yishev*, edited by M. Litvin and M. Lerman, 259–63. Paris: Parizer komitet far shafn a monografye vegn yidishn yishev in lublin, 1952.

"Lublin nokh der tsveyter velt-milkhome [Lublin after the Second World War]." In *Dos bukh fun lublin*, ed. Litvin and Lerman, 593–98.

Review of Binem Heler, *Dos lid iz geblibn* [*The Song Remained*] (Warsaw, 1951). *Yidishe kultur* 14, no. 8 (August–September 1952): 53–54.

1953

"A literarishe geshikhte fun lodzsher-geto [A Literary History of the Lodz Ghetto]." *Di goldene keyt* 17 (1953): 244–49.

"A monografye vegn y. l. perets [A Monograph on Y. L. Perets; on Shmuel Niger, *Yitskhok leybush perets 1852–1952* (Buenos Aires, 1952)]." *Di goldene keyt* 16 (1953): 227–31.

"Briv in redakstye [Letter to the Editor; on the journal *Dapim* and Yiddish]." *Lebns-fragn* 26 (June 1953): 15.

"Di yerushe fun emanuel ringelblum [The Legacy of Emanuel Ringelblum]." *Di goldene keyt* 15 (1953): 235–42.

"Geto Varshah ve-hurbano [The Warsaw Ghetto and Its Destruction]." In *Entsiklopediyah shel Galuyot*, vol. I: Warsaw, edited by Yitshak Gruenbaum, 601–32. Jerusalem: Entsiklopediyah shel Galuyot, 1953.

"ha-Yehudim ba-hitkomemut Varshah [The Jews in the Warsaw Uprising]." In *Entsiklopediyah shel Galuyot*, vol. I: Warsaw, edited by Yitshak Gruenbaum, 801–16. Jerusalem: Entsiklopediyah shel Galuyot, 1953.

"Nisht keyn gvure un nisht keyn gayst! [No Heroism and No Spirit; on Zelig Kalmanovitch]." *Arbeter vort* (March 6, 1953): 3; (March 20): 3; (April 3): 3; (April 17): 3–4; (April 30): 3–4.

1954

"Dos literarishe lebn in litsmanshtat-geto [Literary Life in Litzmannstadt (Lodz) Ghetto]." *Undzer lodzsh* 3 (September 1954): 85–87 (reprint of part 1 of preface to Shayevitsh, 1946).

"Dr. emanuel ringelblum der historiker fun der umkum-tkufe in der yidisher geshikhte [Dr. Emanuel Ringelblum the Historian of the Extermination Period in Jewish History]." *Undzer veg* [New York] (March 1954): 6–8.

"Lider un melodyes in getos un lagern [Songs and Melodies in Ghettos and Camps]." *Yedies fun yad vashem* 2 (July 29, 1954): 2–3. Hebrew, "Shirim u-manginot be-geta'ot u-mahanot," 2–3. Reprinted with slight abbreviation in *Yidishe kultur* 26, no. 4 (April 1964): 12.

"Mah ta'am ha-isuf shelanu?" *Yedi'ot Yad va-Shem* 3 (December 1954): 8–9. English, "Why are we Collecting . . . ?," 16.

"Yitskhok katsenelson—vi a historiker fun der umkum-tkufe [Itzhak Katzenelson (the poet)—as a Historian of the Extermination Period]." *Yidishe kultur* 16, no. 6 (June 1954): 18–21. Hebrew, "Yitshak Katsnelson ki-historyon shel tekufat ha-Sho'ah," *Yediot Bet Lohame ha-Geta'ot* 5–6 (1954): 4–6.

Review of Mendl Man, *Oyfgevakhte erd [Awakened Ground]* (Tel Aviv, 1953). *Di goldene keyt* 18 (1954): 202–5.

1955

"A Book about Nazi Terminology." *Yedi'ot Yad va-Shem* 4–5 (June 1955): 26.

"Iz shoyn, heyst es, shmerke nito? [Already, that is to Say, Shmerke is No More?]." In *Shmerke katsherginski ondenk-bukh*, 32–33. Buenos Aires: A komitet, 1955.

"Vegn a program fun togteglekher arbet far der yad-vashem-forshung." *Yedi'ot Yad va-Shem* 4–5 (June 1955): 23. English, "On a Programme of Day-to-Day Work for Yad Vashem Research," 23. Hebrew, "Al tokhnit yom-yomit lahkor ha-Sho'ah," 17; continued, 6–7 (January 1956): 8.

1956

"Verter un vertlekh fun der khurbn-tkufe [Words and Sayings of the *Khurbn*-Period]." *Yidishe shprakh* XVI, no. 1 (January–March 1956): 22–28. Serialized from "alef" to "zayin" (April–May 1963). Completed version: *Verter un vertlekh fun der khurbn-tkufe* (1981).

Foreword to Batyah Temkin-Berman, *Yoman ba-mahteret [Underground Diary]* (biographical sketch of the author), 233–37. Tel Aviv: Bet Lohame ha-Geta'ot, 1956. Reprinted in *Le-zikhrah shel lohemet: 'al Batyah Temkin-Berman le-yom ha-shanah ha-10 le-motah, 1953–1963* (Tel Aviv: ha-Va'adah ha-tsiburit le-hantsahat zikhrah shel Batyah Temkin-Berman, 1963), 21–26.

1957

"A rekvye nokh di lerer fun di yidishe shuln [A Requium for the Teachers of the Yiddish Schools; on Y. Pat, *Di lererin ester [The Teacher Esther]* (Buenos Aires, 1956)]." *Di goldene keyt* 27 (1957): 269–73.

"Der biterer goyrl fun yidishn partisan." *Yedies fun yad vashem* 1 (April 1957): 4–7. English, "The Plight of the Jewish Partisan," *Yad Washem Bulletin* 1 (April 1957): 4–7. Hebrew, "Mar goralo shel ha-partizan ha-Yehudi," *Yedi'ot Yad va-Shem* 12 (January 1957): 4–5, 7–8.

"Ikh entfer kegn mayn viln ... [I Answer against My Will ...]." *Yedies fun yad vashem* 2 (November 1957): 6. English, "An Unwilling Reply," *Yad Washem Bulletin* 2 (December 1957): 6. Hebrew, "Al korehi ani mashiv ...," *Yedi'ot Yad va-Shem* 13 (April 1957): 4.

"Le-korot ha-Sho'ah shel Lublin [On the History of the Shoah in Lublin]." In *Entsiklopediyah shel Galuyot*, vol. V: Lublin, edited by Blumental, 659–76. Jerusalem: Entsiklopediyah shel Galuyot, 1957.

"On the Nazi Vocabulary." *Yad Washem Studies* I (1957): 49–66. "Al tevah shel lashon ha-Natzim," in Hebrew edition (1957), 41–55; continued as "'Aktion'" and "From the Nazi Vocabulary."

"S. Shayevitsh—der dikhter fun lodzsher geto [The Poet of the Lodz Ghetto]." *Undzer lodzsh* 5 (October 1957): 60–61 (reprint of Part 2 of preface to Shayevitsh, 1946).

Foreword to Israel Tabakman, *Mayne iberlebungen (unter natsishe okupatsye in belgye)* [*My Experiences (under Nazi Occupation in Belgium)*], ix–xvi. Tel Aviv: Y. L. Perets, 1957.

1958

"A kleyne skitse—a groyse maysterverk [A Short Sketch—A Great Masterpiece; on Ka-Tsetnik]." *Heymish* (July 1, 1958): 2.

"Briv in redakstye [Letter to the Editor; on *Sefer Lublin* (*Memorial Book of Lublin*)]." *Lebns-fragn* 79 (March 1958): 18.

"Di literatur fun di landsmanshaftn [The Literature of the Hometown Associations]." *Yedies fun yad vashem* 3 (September 1958): 26–28. English, "Writings on the Nazi Period: Memorial books by survivors of communities," *Yad Washem Bulletin* 3 (July 1958): 24–27. Hebrew, "Sifre ha-zikaron shel saride ha-kehilot," *Yedi'ot Yad va-Shem* 15–16 (April 1958): 22–24.

"Groteske-'visnshaft' in der arbet fun 'yad vashem' [Grotesque 'Scholarship' in the Work of 'Yad Vashem'; on the editing of Eliezer Yerushalmi, *Pinkas Shavli: yoman mi-Geto Lita'i* (Jerusalem, 1958)]." *Letste nayes* (May 16, 1958); conclusion in *Hayntike nayes* (May 18, 1958).

"'Lubliner shtime' (a bintl zikhroynes) ['Voice of Lublin (newspaper)' (Some Memories)]." *Lebns-fragn* 83 (July 1958): 9–10.

"Nisht shvaygn un nisht lozn fargesn! [Do not be Silent and Do not Forget!]." *Lebns-fragn* 84 (October 1958): 11.

"Nokh der fayerung '60 yor bund' [After the Celebration '60 Years of the Bund']." *Lebns-fragn* 77 (January 1958): 7–8.

"Tenu'at ha-partizanim le'or mismakhim germaniyim [The Partisan Movement in Light of German Documents]." In *Sefer ha-partizanim ha-Yehudim*, vol. 2, translated from Yiddish by M. Halmish, 631–61. Merhavyah: Sifriyat Po'alim, 1958.

"Tsum 15-tn yortog fun varshever geto-oyfshtand [On the 15th Anniversary of the Warsaw Ghetto Uprising]." *Lebns-fragn* 80–81 (April–May 1958): 4–6.

"Vegn forshn di geshikhte fun 'bund' [On Researching the History of the 'Bund']." *Lebns-fragn* 82 (June 1958): 5–6.

Foreword to D. Zakalik, *Gerangl* [*Struggle*], 7–10. Tel Aviv: Y. L. Perets, 1958.

Foreword to Shloyme Frank, *Togbukh fun lodzsher geto* [*Diary from the Lodz Ghetto*]. Buenos Aires: Tsentral farband fun poylishe yidn in argentine, 1958, 5–7; 2nd ed. (Tel Aviv: Farlag Menorah, 1958).

Liner notes to vinyl LP record, *"Yizkor": In Memory of the Victims of the European Jewish Catastrophe 1940–1945: Play by Shammai Rosenblum, Recitator and Actor* (Hebrew, English, Yiddish). Tel Aviv: Yad Vashem and World Jewish Congress, 1958.

1959

"Ashre ha-ma'amin [Blessed Are the Faithful; on faith in humanity and in victory as leading to resistance]." *Lebns-fragn* 87 (January 1959): 6.

"Der kidush-hashem fun radziner rebbe [The Self-Sacrifice of the Radziner Rebbe]." In *Varshever yidn: yubiley-bukh: 1949–1959*, 120–25. Buenos Aires: Farband fun varshever un prager yidn, 1959. Back-translation from "Yitzhak Katznelson's Poem of the Radziner Rebbe," in *Extermination and Resistance: Historical Records and Source Material*, vol. 1, ed. Zvi Szner (Haifa: Ghetto Fighters' House, 1958), 20–27; also published in Hebrew as "ha-Shir 'al ha-Radzynai shel Yitshak Katsenelson," *Yediot Bet Lohame ha-Geta'ot* 8 (January 1955).

"Legende un virklekhkayt (tsum zekhtsntn yortog fun geto-oyfshtand) [Legend and Reality (On the Sixteenth Anniversary of the Ghetto Uprising)]." *Lebns-fragn* 90–91 (April–May 1959): 3–4.

"R I F [contesting the soap claim]." *Yidishe kultur* 21, no. 6 (June–July 1959): 35–40.

"Sholem aleykhem (tsum 100-stn geboyrn-tog) [Sholem Aleichem (On His 100th Birthday)]," *Lebns-fragn* 89 (March 1959): 7–8.

"Yidn hobn gekemft—aleyn: gedankn vegn dem geto-oyfshtand in varshe." *Yedies fun yad vashem* 8–9 (September 1959): 3–5. Hebrew, "ha-Yehudim lahmu livadam: harehorim ʻal mered Geto Varshah," *Yediʻot Yad va-Shem* 19–20 (May 1959): 4–6. English, "The Jews Fought Alone: Thoughts on the Warsaw Ghetto Revolt," *Yad Vashem Bulletin* 4–5 (October 1959): 2–4.

1960

"ʻAktion' [(on the German word) ʻAktion']." *Yad Washem Studies* IV (1960): 57–96. Hebrew edition (1960): 57–94.

"A nayer literarisher min—yisker-bikher [A New Literary Form—*Yizkor* Books]." *Lebns-fragn* 99 (January 1960): 7–8; continued in 100, 102–3, 105, 108–9, 110, 113–14, 117, and 119–20 with various titles. First portion reprinted as "Undzere yisker-bikher," *Yidishe kultur* 22, no. 4 (April 1960): 3–6; seventh portion reprinted as "Vegn di yisker-bikher (eynike sekhaklen)," *Yidishe kultur* 23, no. 6 (June–July 1961): 30.

"Dos drite oyshvits [The Third Auschwitz]." *Yidishe kultur* 22, no. 10 (December 1960): 39–43.

"Oyfn keyver fun a noentn fraynd [At the Grave of a Close Friend; on Motl Kushnir]." *Lebns-fragn* 104 (June 1960): 4.

"Sixteen Years after the Ghetto Rising." *Yad Vashem Bulletin* 6–7 (June 1960): 13–15. Hebrew, "Shesh esre shanim ahar mered Geto Varsha," *Yediʻot Yad va-Shem* 23–24 (May 1960): 10–12.

"Undzer groyser shuld [Our Great Guilt/Obligation; on the failure to search adequately for Jewish source materials on the Holocaust]." *Yidishe kultur* 22, no. 2 (February 1960): 16–20. Hebrew, "Meʻuvat shetzarikh tikun [A Wrong that Must be Righted; literally, "What is Crooked Must be Made Straight," paraphrasing Ecclesiastes 1:15]," *Yediot bet Lohame ha-Getaʻot* 21 (May 1959): 37–41.

Review of Natan Eck, *ha-Toʻim be-darkhe ha-mavet* [*Wandering on the Roads of Death*; personal memoir, largely translated from prior Yiddish articles] (Jerusalem, 1960). *Yidishe kultur* 22, no. 7 (August–September 1960): 39–42.

1961

"Di yidishe kamfs-organizatsye in dem poylishn oyfshtand [The Jewish Fighting Organization in the Polish Uprising]." In *Khalutsim in poyln: antologye fun der khalutsisher bavegung*, vol. 2, edited by Leyb Shpizman, 330–34. New York: forsh-institut fun der tsyenistisher arbeter-bavegung, 1961. Partial Yiddish version of "ha-Yehudim ba-hitkomemut Varshah" (1953).

"Exemplary Heroism [on Gusta Dawidson Draegner]." *Yad Vashem Bulletin* 8–9 (March 1961): 5–6, 19. Hebrew, "Gevurah lelo dugma," *Yediʻot Yad va-Shem* 25–26 (February 1961): 4–5.

"Tsu der geshikhte fun program un oysfirung fun der yidn-farntilikung." *Yedies fun yad vashem* 6 (March 1961): 6–10. English, "About the Concept and Implementation of Annihilation," *Yad Vashem Bulletin* 10 (April 1961): 9–11, 23. Hebrew, "Le-toldot ha-rayon shel hishmidat ha-Yehudim ve-bitsuaʻo," *Yediʻot Yad va-Shem* 27 (1961): 8.

"Tsum problem vi di yidn hobn zikh farhaltn unter der daytsher okupatsye [On the Problem of How the Jews Conducted Themselves under the German Occupation]." In *YKUF almanakh*, edited by Nakhman Mayzl, 359–67. New York: Yidisher kultur farband, 1961.

"Vegn di yisker-bikher (eynike sekhaklen) [On the *Yizkor* Books (Some Conclusions)]." *Yidishe kultur* 23, no. 6 (June–July 1961): 30 (reprint from 1960).

Foreword to Simkhe Polakevitsh, *In a fremder hoyt* [*In Someone Else's Skin*], 5–9. Tel Aviv: Y. L. Perets, 1961.

Preface to Yosef Kariv, *Sefer yizkor li-kehilat Sarni* [*Yizkor Book of the Community of Sarni*], 11–12. Jerusalem: Yad Vashem, 1961; Hebrew 9–10.

1962

"A tsendlik yorn rov in sokhachev." In *Pinkas Sokhatshev*, edited by A. Sh. Stein and Gavriel Weisman, 40–43. Jerusalem: Irgun Sokhatshev be-Yisraʻel, 1962. English trans. by Jerrold Landau, "A Score of [correctly, ten] Years as the Rabbi of Sochaczew (Rabbi Shmuel Yitzchak Landau of Blessed Memory)," www.jewishgen.org/yizkor/Sochaczew/so029.html#Page40.

"Arum psak-din in aykhman-protses [On the Judgment in the Eichmann Trial]." *Lebns-fragn* 121–22 (January–February 1962): 11–12. Reprinted as "Gnade-toyt (arum aykhman-protses)," *Yidishe kultur* 24, no. 4 (April 1962): 4–5.

"Der varshever geto-oyfshtand in der geshikhte fun tsveytn velt-krig [The Warsaw Ghetto Uprising in the History of the Second World War]." *Lebns-fragn* 123–24 (March–April 1962): 9–10.

"Di a"g arishe zayt [The So-Called Aryan Side]." *Lebns-fragn* 132 (December 1962): 7–8. Preview of foreword to Shloyme Shapiro, *Zikhroynes* (1963).

"Dos yidishe hrubieshov in di yorn [Jewish Hrubieszów in the Years] 1939–1945." In *Pinkes hrubieshov: tsum 20-tn yortog nokh der groyzamer khurbn fun unzer gevezener heym*, edited by Borukh Kaplinski, 91–114. Tel Aviv: Irgun yotsey hrubieshov in yisroel un di fareynikte shtatn, 1962.

"Eichmann Trial Throws New Light on History." *Yad Vashem Bulletin* 11 (April–May 1962): 2–9. Hebrew, "He'im hevi ha-mishpat hidushim lahkor ha-histori?" *Yedi'ot Yad va-Shem* 28 (December 1961): 2–7.

"'Nusakh lublin' [The (Jewish Cultural) Tradition of Lublin]" *Lubliner shtime—Kol Lublin* 1 (1962): 4–5 (reprinted in 1978).

"Oyflage fun bukh DU PREL [on Dr. Max Freiherr du Prel], *Das Deutsche General-Gouvernement Polen* (Krakow, 1940)." In *Pinkas Sokhatshev* [*Sochaczew*], edited by A. Sh. Stein and Gavriel Weisman, 544–45. Jerusalem: Irgun Sokhatshev be-Yisra'el, 1962. English trans. by Jerrold Landau, "The Publication of the Book Du Prel," www.jewishgen.org/yizkor/Sochaczew/so514.html#Page544.

"Undzer yugnt un di literatur vegn umkum un gvure [Our Youth and the Literature on Extermination and Heroism]." *Lebns-fragn* 125 (May 1962): 11–12.

Foreword to Nusia Szyfman, *Dos lebn nokh far mir . . . : briv fun geto un lager* [English titlepage: *My Whole Life Is Before Me . . . : Letters from the Ghetto and Camp*], 9–18. Jerusalem: Yad Vashem, 1962.

Foreword to Shaul Kartchever, *Im ha-divizyah ha-shelishit 'al shem Tra'ugut: yomano shel hayal Yehudi ba-tzava ha-Poloni ha-amami* [*With the Third Division, named Traugut: The Diary of a Jewish Soldier in the Polish People's Army* (Jerusalem, 1962)], 5–6. Jerusalem: Yad Vashem, 1962.

1963

"Der groyser verter-bukh fun der yidisher shprakh [The Great Dictionary of the Yiddish Language; review]." *Lebns-fragn* 135 (March 1963): 13–14.

"Magishe denken bay yidn in der natsi-tsayt." *Yidishe kultur* 25, no. 4 (January 1963): 13–17. English, "Magical Thinking Among the Jews During the Nazi Occupation," *Yad Vashem Studies* V (1963): 221–36.

"Strops barikht vi a historisher makor." *Lebns-fragn* 136–37 (April–May 1963): 7–8. English, "The Stroop Report—A Reliable Historical Source Despite its Distortions," *Yad Vashem Bulletin* 13 (October 1963): 21–24.

"20 yor nokhn geto-oyfshtand in byalystok [20 Years after the Ghetto Uprising in Białystok]." *Lebns-fragn* 140 (August 1963): 8–9.

"Vegn an ongeveytiktn problem [A Painful Problem; on memorializing the various prewar Jewish school movements]." *Lebns-fragn* 141–42 (September–October 1963): 10–11.

Foreword to Shloyme Shapiro, *Zikhroynes fun a maran in der tkufe fun der natsi-katastrofe* [*Memoirs of a Marrano in the Period of the Nazi*

Catastrophe], 7–13. Buenos Aires: Tsentral farband fun poylishe yidn in argentine, 1963.

Foreword to Yeshaye Zandberg, *Der soyne in di moyern* [*The Enemy within the Walls*], 9–12. Tel Aviv: Y. L. Perets, 1963.

1964

"Apikursishe gedanken: tsum yortog fun geto-oyfshtand [Heretical Thoughts: On the Anniversary of the Ghetto Uprising]." *Lebns-fragn* 147 (March 1964): 5.

"Baranov—shtrikhn tsu ir geshikhte [Baranów—Some Lines on Its History]." In *Sefer-yizkor Baranov*, edited by Blumental (1964), 29–35.

"Der lubliner yudenrat [The Lublin Judenrat]." *Kol Lublin—Lubliner shtime* 2 (November 22, 1964): 3, 11.

"Der zin fun varshever geto-oyfshtand [The Purpose of the Warsaw Ghetto Uprising; on the diary of Chaim Aron Kaplan]." *Lebns-fragn* 148–49 (April–May 1964): 4.

"German Document on the Bialystok Ghetto Revolt." *Yad Vashem Bulletin* 14 (March 1964): 19–25. Hebrew, "Mismak Germani 'al mered Geto Bialistok," *Yedi'ot Yad va-Shem* 31 (December 1963): 21–25.

"Lider un melodyes in getos un lagern." *Yidishe kultur* 26, no. 4 (April 1964): 12 (reprint from 1954).

"Oyfshriftn oyf vent, ksovim un bikher." *Lebns-fragn* 145 (January 1964): 10; and 146 (February 1964): 7–8. Reprinted in *Shmuesn*, 32–59.

"The Jewish Complex of Ludwik Landau." *Yad Vashem Bulletin* 15 (August 1964): 33–43. Hebrew, "ha-Tasbik ha-Yehudi shel Ludvik Landau," *Yedi'ot Yad va-Shem* 32 (March–April 1964): 26–35.

"Yo shuldik—nisht shuldik?! [Guilty—Not Guilty; on Rolf Hochhuth, *The Deputy* (1963)]." *Lebns-fragn* 150–51 (June–July 1964): 7; continued in 152, 153–54 ("Hot di 'habima' gedarft shteln dem 'shtelfartreter' [Should the 'Habima' (Theater) Stage *The Deputy*])," and 155–56.

Foreword to Sara Selver-Urbach, *Mi-ba'ad le-halon beti: zikhronot mi-geto Lodz'*, 7–9. Jerusalem: Yad Vashem, 1964. English translation in *Through the Window of My Home: Recollections from the Lodz Ghetto*, trans. Siona Bodansky (Jerusalem: Yad Vashem, 1986), 11–13.

Foreword to Yosef Zshemyan [Ziemian], *Di papirosn-hendler fun plats dray kraytsn* [*The Cigarette Dealer of plac Trzech Krzyży (Three Crosses Square, Krakow)*], 9–11. Tel Aviv: Hamenorah, 1964. Reprinted as "Vunderlekhe geshtaltn," *Yidishe kultur* 26, no. 10 (December 1964): 16.

1965

"A. a. robak—der kemfer far yidish [A. A. Roback—The Fighter for Yiddish]." *Lebns-fragn* 167 (November 1965): 7–8; 168 (December 1965): 7–8.

"Bela, she-hikartiyah ani [Bela, as I Knew Her; on historian Bela Mandelstam]." In *Mehkarim le-toldot Yehude Lublin*, edited by Blumental (1965), 15–28.

"Daytshe krigs-farbrekher farn gerikht . . . [German War Criminals in Court . . .]." *Lebns-fragn* 157 (January 1965): 6–7; (March): 8.

"Dos yidishe bisk: shtrikhn tsu zayn geshikhte [Jewish Busk; Some Lines on Its History]." In *Sefer Busk*, edited by Abraham Shayari, 30–60. Haifa: Irgun yotz'e Busk be-Yisra'el, 1965.

"Fun yanuar biz April [From January to April] 1943." *Lebns-fragn* 160–61 (April–May 1965): 3–4.

"Introduction to Individual Chapters." In *ha-Meri veha-mered be-geto Varshah / Resistance and Revolt in the Warsaw Ghetto: A Documentary History*, edited by Blumental and Kermish (1965), xxxvii–xlviii.

"The Nature of the Jewish Partisan Movement." In Yehiel Granatstein and Moshe Kahanovich, *Biographical Dictionary of Jewish Resistance / Leksikon ha-Gevurah*, vol. I, 12–16. Jerusalem: Yad Vashem, 1965.

"Vi azoy iz dos meglekh geven? [How Was It Possible?]" In *Sefer Busk*, ed. Shayari, 260–62.

1966

"A grus fun un far rumenye [A Greeting from and for Romania; on Emil Săculeț." *Yidishe folks-lider* (Bucharest, 1959)], *Lebns-fragn* 174–75 (June–July 1966): 9–10; (August–September): 9.

[With Kermish]. "Jews in the War Against the Nazis." In *Jewish Heroism in Modern Times: A Hanukah Anthology*, 49–88. Jerusalem: World Zionist Organization, 1966.

"Pro Domo Non Sua [Not for My Own Sake; on his book, *Shmuesn* (1966)]." *Lebns-fragn* 179–80 (November–December 1966): 14.

"Spinka, the Shabbes-Goy." *Yad Vashem Bulletin* 18 (April 1966): 30–33. Hebrew, "Spinka—'goy-shabbat,'" *Yedi'ot Yad va-Shem* 35 (November–December 1965): 21–23.

"The General Encyclopedia in Yiddish and the Holocaust." *Yad Vashem Bulletin* 18 (April 1966): 26–30. Hebrew, "Tekufat ha-Sho'ah lefi ha-Entsiklopediyah ha-Kelalit, sidrat 'Yidn,'" *Yedi'ot Yad va-Shem* 34 (April 1965): 47–51.

"Vi halt es mitn forshn di hitler-tkufe? [What is the State of Research on the Hitler Period?]." *Lebns-fragn* 193 (May 1966): 7–8.

Foreword to Ch. A. Kaplan, *Megilat yisurin: yoman Geto Varshah* [*Scroll of Agony: Warsaw Ghetto Diary*], 29 (Hebrew numbering). Jerusalem: Yad Vashem, [1966].

1967

"Amolik yidish vilne—andersh gezen [Former Jewish Vilna—Seen Differently; on Avrom Karpinovitsh]." *Lebns-fragn* 188–89 (November–December 1967): 21.

"Arum 'zog nisht keynmol . . .' [On 'Never Say . . .']." *Yidishe kultur* 29, no. 6 (June–July 1967): 37–43, 53.

"Concerning the Question: When Did the Idea of the 'Final Solution' Originate in Hitler's Germany?" *Yad Vashem Bulletin* 20 (April 1967): 6–10. Hebrew, *Yedi'ot Yad va-Shem* 37 (February 1967): 17–20.

"Der kamf fun di yidn kegn natsi-rezshim." *Lebns-fragn* 184–85 (April–May 1967): 2–3. Partial English version, "Jewish Resistance under the Nazis" (1968).

"Der yudenrat un di yidishe politsey [The Judenrat and the Jewish Police]." In *Aroyfgetsvungene yidishe reprezentantsn unter der natsisher memshole: kolokvyum fun yivo, detsember 2–5, 1967*, 89–103ff; 101*–2*. New York: YIVO, 1972 (discussion).

"'Di geshikhte fun yidn in lodzsh' ['The History of Jews in Lodz'; on A. Volf Yasni, *Di geshikhte fun di yidn in lodzsh in di yorn fun der daytscher yidn-oysrotung*, vol. 2 (Tel Aviv, 1966)]." *Lebns-fragn* 188–89 (November–December 1967): 13–14.

"From the Nazi Vocabulary." *Yad Vashem Studies* VI (1967): 69–82. Continuation of "On the Nazi Vocabulary" and "Aktion." Hebrew edition (1966): 59–71.

"Shmuesn vegn yudenrat [Chats on the Judenrat]." *Lebns-fragn* 181–82 (January–February 1967): 9–10.

Foreword to M. Balberishki [Mendel Balberyszski], *Shtarker fun ayzn*, 12–15. Tel Aviv: Hamenorah, 1967. English translation in Mendel Balberyszski, *Stronger than Iron: The Destruction of Vilna Jewry 1941–1945: an eyewitness account*, rev. and ed. by Theodore Balberyszski (Jerusalem: Gefen, 2010), xxvii–xxix.

1968

"Abisl statistic [Some Statistics]," "Di baron hirsh shule in rozvadov [The Baron Hirsch School in Rozwadów]" and "Idishe industri-unternemungen [Jewish Industrial Undertakings]." In *Sefer yisker rozvadov un umgegnt*, edited by Blumental (1968), 17–18, 90–92 (Hebrew 86–89), 148–49.

"Aleksander: shtrikhn tsu ir geshikhte [Aleksandrów Łódzki: Some Lines on Its History]." In *Aleksander "a"y Lodz*," edited by Blumental (1968), 28–34.

"A Martyr or a Hero? Reflections on the Diary of Adam Czerniaków." *Yad Vashem Studies* VII (1968): 165–71. Hebrew edition (1968), 155–60.

"Der goyrl fun tsvey yidishe kinder: miryam un shulamis [The Fate of Two Jewish Children: Miriam and Shulamit]." In *Sefer Sokal: Tartakov, ve-Ranz, Stoyanov veha-sevivah*, edited by Avraham Homet, 317–23. Tel Aviv: Irgun yotz'e Sokal veha-sevivah, 1968.

"Der kamf fun di yidn kegn hitler-rezshim." *Lebns-fragn* 192–93 (March–April 1968): 4–5. Partial English version, "Jewish Resistance under the Nazis," 1968.

"Der oyfshtand in der varshever geto [The Uprising in the Warsaw Ghetto]." In *Der oyfshtand in varshever geto: aroysgegbn tsum finf-un-tsvantsikstn yortog (1943–1968)*, 4–8. New York: Alveltlekhn yidishn kultur-kongres, 1968.

"Di traditsyonele dertsyung un der kamf kegn natsizm [Traditional Education and the Fight against Nazism]." *Lebns-fragn* 196–97 (July–August 1968): 13. Condensation of English version, "Accepted Ideas—and Active Resistance to the Nazi Regime," *Yad Vashem Bulletin* 12 (December 1962): 41–45.

"Jewish Resistance under the Nazis." *Yad Vashem Bulletin* 22 (May 1968): 8–13. Partial English composite of "Der kamf" (1947) and (1968). Hebrew, *Yedi'ot Yad va-Shem* 39 (May 1968): 5–9.

"Mendele moykher sforim—(tsu zayn 50stn yortsayt) [On the 50th Anniversary of His Death]." *Lebns-fragn* 190–91 (January–February 1968): 15–16.

"Shuldik tsi nisht shuldik? Tsu der frage vegn der rol fun di yuden-ratn in der hitler-tkufe [Guilty or Not Guilty? On the Question of the Role of the Jewish Councils in the Hitler Period]." *Folk un velt* (March 1968): 6–11. See also "Le Judenrat" (1969).

"Sources for the Study of Jewish Resistance." *Jewish Resistance During the Holocaust: Proceedings of the Conference on Manifestations of Jewish Resistance, Jerusalem, April 7–11, 1968*, 46–59. Jerusalem: Yad Vashem, 1971.

Hebrew, "Mekorot le-mekhkar ha-'amidah ha-yehudit," *ha-'Amidah ha-Yehudit bi-tekufat ha-Sho'ah* (Jerusalem: Yad Vashem, 1970), 34–46.

1969

"Der oyftu fun yosef vulf [The Accomplishment of Joseph Wulf]." *Di goldene keyt* 65 (1969): 200–206.

"Der takhles fun lernen . . . (oyfn rand fun ana langfus' 'Zalts un shvebl' oyf yidish) [The Purpose of Teaching . . . Marginal Notes on Anna Langfus' (novel) *Salt and Sulphur* in Yiddish' (Tel Aviv, 1969)]." *Lebns-fragn* 210–11 (September–October 1969): 10–11.

"Le Judenrat: Sa nature et son rôle [The Judenrat: Its Nature and Role]." *Le Monde Juif* 24 (1968): 36–42; 25 (1969), 33–40. Reprinted in *Mémoire du Génocide: Un recueil de 80 articles du "Monde Juif"*, *revue du Centre de documentation Juive Contemporaine*, ed. Georges Wellers and Serge Klarsfeld (Paris: Centre de documentation juive Contemporaine, 1987), 333–46.

"Tsu der geshikhte fun yidn in kozshenits [On the History of the Jews in Kozienice]." In *Sefer koz'enits: tsum 27-tn yor-tog nokh dem groysamen khurbn fun undzer gevezener heym*, edited by Borukh Kaplinski, 31–45. Tel Aviv: Irgun yotsey koz'enits in yisroel, 1969.

"Umgloyblikhe mayses fun yener tsayt . . . [Unbelievable Deeds from That Time; on the fight against hunger in the ghetto]." *Lebns-fragn* 202–3 (January–February 1969): 8–9.

Foreword to Yerakhmiel Briks [Rachmil Bryks], *Di papirene kroyn* [*The Paper Crown*], 5–7. New York: Yerahmi'el briks bukh komitet, 1969.

1970

"A vizit in shtetl budzanov [A Visit to the Town of Budzanów]." In *Budzanover yisker-bukh*, edited by Yitskhok Ziglman, 116–20. Haifa: Budzaner landslayt in yisroel un amerike, 1970.

"Nitsokhn?! [Victory?!—on the situation of the Jews in postwar Poland]." *Lebns-fragn* 216–17 (March–April 1970): 18–19.

Foreword to Mordechaj Zajczyk, *Mi-yomano shel partizan nitzol ha-shoah* [*From the Diary of a Partisan Who Survived the Shoah*], 5–8. Tel Aviv: n.p., 1970/71.

1971

"Le-toldot Yehude Maikhov [On the History of the Jews of Miechów (and the towns of)]" "Kharshnitsah [Charsznica]" and "Kshoinz Vielki [Książ

Wielki]." In *Sefer yizkor Maikhov, Kharshnitsah, u-Kshoinz*, edited by Blumental and Ben-Azar (1971), 35–52, 232–33, 239–43.

"Yezyerne [Jezierna; history of]." In *Sefer Yezyernah / Yezyerner yisker-bukh*, edited by Yitshak Zigelman, 28–63. Haifa: Va'ad yotz'e Yezyernah be-Yisra'el, 1971.

1972

"Arum dem varshever geto-oyfshtand [On the Warsaw Ghetto Uprising]." *Lebns-fragn* 240–41 (March–April 1972): 3.

"Barash, Ephraim." *Encyclopaedia Judaica*, edited by Cecil Roth, vol. 4, 203. Jerusalem: Keter, 1972; 2nd ed., edited by Fred Skolnik and Michael Berenbaum, vol. 3 (Detroit: Macmillan Reference USA/Keter, 2007), 137.

"Der letster briv fun bendin (17.7.1943)." In *Pinkes Zaglembye*, edited by Y. Rapaport, 419–22. Melbourne: Zaglembier landsmanshaft un pinkes-zaglembye komitet in melburn, 1972. English, "The Last Letter from Bedzin," 3–4 (English section), www.jewishgen.org/Yizkor/Zaglembia/zag003E.html.

"Der yidisher khurbn in daytshe dokumentn [The Jewish *Khurbn* in German Documents]." In *Pinkes Zaglembye*, ed. Rapaport, 294–303.

"Geshikhte fun di yidn in podhayts." In *Sefer Podhaytsah*, edited by M. Sh. Geshuri, 67–83. Tel Aviv: Irgun yotz'e Podhaytsah uveha-sevivah be-Yisra'el, 1972. English trans. by Jerrold Landau, "History of the Jews of Podhajce," /www.jewishgen.org/yizkor/podhajce/pod067.html. Print-on-demand hard copy, *The Memorial Book of Podhajce, Ukraine: Translation of Sefer Podhaytsah* (JewishGen, 2013), www.jewishgen.org/yizkor/ybip/YBIP_Podhajce.html.

"Katin [Katyn; on blaming the Jews for the Soviet massacre of Polish officers]." *Lebns-fragn* 244–45 (July–August 1972): 5–7.

"M. M. Oyzerkis." In *Sefer Podhaytsah*, ed. Geshuri, 89–96 (Hebrew summary 60). English trans. by Jerrold Landau, "M. M. Oyzerkes: In memory of a forgotten Yiddish writer," www.jewishgen.org/yizkor/Podhajce/pod056.html.

"September 1939—september 1972 [on the murder of Israeli athletes at the 1972 Olympic Games in Munich, with reflections on the Nazi past]." *Lebns-fragn* 246–47 (September–October 1972), 16–17.

"Yankev glatshteyn: der lubliner [Jacob Glatstein: of Lublin]." *Kol Lublin—Lubliner shtime* (November 1972): 33–34.

1973

"Anshtaltn—Mosadot [Institutions]." In *Sefer Zikaron li-kehilat Ravah-Ruskah veha-sevivah*, edited by A. M. Ringel, 153–56. Tel Aviv: Irgun yotz'e Ravah-Ruskah be-Yisra'el, 1973.

"Rava-ruska un umgegnt [Rava-Ruska and Vicinity]." In *Sefer Zikaron*, ed. Ringel, 11–15.

"Dos drite raykh un di yidn [The Third Reich and the Jews]." *Lebns-fragn* 258–59 (September–October 1973): 13–14.

"Dos 'toyznt-yorike raykh': paradoksn fun der geshikhte [The 'Thousand-Year Reich': Paradoxes of History]." *Lebns-fragn* 252–53 (March–April 1973): 3–4; (May–June): 7–8.

"Zur Genesis der 'Endlösung der Judenfrage.' [On the Origin of the 'Final Solution of the Jewish Question']." In *Essays über Naziverbrechen Simon Wiesenthal gewidmet*, 20–35. Amsterdam: Wiesenthal-Fonds, 1973.

Foreword to Daniel Freiberg, *Finsternish oyf der erd* [*Darkness Upon the Earth*], 5–10. Tel Aviv: Hamenorah, 1973.

1974

"Di tsiln fun di geto-kemfer [The Goals of the Ghetto Fighters]." *Lebns-fragn* 264–65 (March–April 1974): 5–6.

"Nakhmen mayzil biblyografye [Bibliography of Nachman Meisel]." *Yidishe kultur* 36, no. 4 (April 1974): 29–31.

1975

"Mir veln dos keynmol nisht dergeyn: a prolegomena tsu khave rozenfarbs 'der boym fun lebn.' [We Will Never Reach It: A Prolegomena to Chava Rosenfarb's *The Tree of Life* (Tel Aviv, 1972)]." *Lebns-fragn* 276–77 (March–April 1975): 6–7.

"Yo geven, tsi nisht geven? [Was, or Was not?; on the question of aid given to Jews in wartime Poland]" *Lebns-fragn* 282–83 (September–October 1975): 12–13.

1976

"Artuski." In *Yid, mentsh, sotsyalist: y. artuski ondenk-bukh*, 85–89. Tel Aviv: Artuski bukh-komitet / *Lebens-fragn*, 1976.

"Di partey un di mishpokhe (kuryozn vegn di gilgulim fun der sovyetisher 'visnshaft') [The Party and the Family (Curiosities in the Metamorphoses of Soviet 'Science')]." *Lebns-fragn* 286–87 (January–February 1976): 5–6.

"Geshikhtlekher emes—tsi partey-'geshikhte'?: arum vidershtand-fragn unter der daytsher okupatsye [Historical Truth—or Party-'History'?: On Questions of Resistance under the German Occupation]." *Lebns-fragn* 288–89 (March–April 1976): 8–9.

"Vemen dos folk hot premirt [Whom the Nation Honors; opposing a medal given to Moshe Dayan after the Yom Kippur war]." *Lebns-fragn* 290–91 (May–June 1976): 4.

1977

"Doplte moral [Double (Standard of) Morality; on Zygmunt Klukowski and Ernst von Weizsäcker]." *Lebns-fragn* 300 (March–April 1977): 6–7.

"Kine-sine [Envy and Hatred; on the psychosis of hatred for the living]." *Lebns-fragn* 298–99 (January–February 1977): 12.

1978

"Antisemitishe propagande in sovetn-farband [Antisemitic Propaganda in the Soviet Union]." *Di tsukunft* (April 1978): 149–50.

"Erev pesakh tashag [Passover Eve 5703]—19 april 1943." *Lebns-fragn* 311–12 (April–May 1978): 4–5.

"'Nusakh Lublin.'" *Kol Lublin—Lubliner shtime* 13 (1978): 6–7 (reprint from 1962).

1979

"Hitler Redivivus: hitler is nisht geshtorbn (di 'visnshaftlekhe' rehabilitatsye fun natsishn monster) [Hitler is not Dead (the 'Scholarly' Rehabilitation of the Nazi Monster); on Henry Picker, *Hitlers Tischgespräche im Führerhauptquartier* (*Hitler's Table Talk*), 3rd ed., 1976]." *Lebns-fragn* 329–30 (September–October 1979): 7–8.

"Vos hobn mir gelernt? [What Have We Learned?]" *Lebns-fragn* 323–24 (March–April 1979): 6–7, 10.

1980

"Der nayer imazsh fun dem 'firer.' [The New Image of the 'Fuhrer']." *Lebns-fragn* 333–34 (January–February 1980): 8.

"Dertsyerishe problemen in di humanistishe gimnazyes [Pedagogical Problems in the Humanistic Gymnasia]." *Kol Lublin—Lubliner shtime* 15 (November 1980): 6–7.

"'Men vil nisht untergeyn': vegn di lodzsher geto-notitsn fun a beker a shrayber: yankev hiler—a yor nokh zayn toyt ['One Does not Wish to Perish':

On the Lodz Ghetto Notes of Writer-Baker, Jacob Hiller—A Year after His Death]." *Lebns-fragn* 335–36 (March–April 1980): 8–9.

1982

"Di migratsye fun yidishn folks-lid unter der daytsher okupatsye." In *Shmuesn*, chapter 1; and in *Folks-shtime* (September 25, 1982): 6 (reprint from 1946).

Foreword to Ruzshke Fishman-Shnaydman [Róża Fiszman-Sznajdman], *Mayn lublin: bilder funem lebns-shteyger fun yidn in farmilkhomedikn poyln* [*My Lublin: Pictures of the Lifestyle of Jews in prewar Poland*], 5–6. Tel Aviv: Y. L. Perets, 1982. Reprinted in *Kol Lublin—Lubliner Shtime* 17 (November 1982): 35.

Online Sound Recording of Blumental (YIVO Radio Program, WEVD, New York)

Radio interview of Blumental on the subject of Jewish conduct during the Holocaust. (December 17, 1967). Web page: https://yivo.org/The-Role-of-Jewish-Police-in-the-Ghettos-1967;soundrecording:https://yivo.org/cimages/47-yivo-wevd-podcast12171967.mp3. (The URL and web page are misleading; his topic was not the Jewish Police and the Judenrat.)

Writings about Blumental

[Author bio]. *Yidishe kultur* (June 1945): 13.

"Blumental, Nakhmen." *Leksikon fun der nayer yidisher literatur*, vol. 1, 324. New York: Alveltlekhn yidishn kultur-kongres, 1956.

"Competition for Textbook." *The Palestine Post* (May 27, 1949): 6.

"Kehilot Lublin be-'Kol Tzion la-Golah' [The Communities of Lublin on 'Voice of Zion for the Diaspora'; radio program in Yiddish, featuring Blumental]." *'Al ha-Mishmar* (September 11, 1952): 3.

"Kultur-khronik [Culture Chronicle; 6th Dworzecki prize awarded to Blumental]." *Lebns-fragn* 349–50 (May–June 1981): 24.

"Literatura żydowska w czasie okupacji [Jewish Literature in Time of Occupation; on talk by Blumental to Jewish Cultural Society]." *Mosty* 4, no. 25 (February 26, 1949): 7.

"Prof. nakhmen blumental [obituary]." *Lebns-fragn* 379–80 (November–December 1983): 21.

Beckerman, Gal. "The Holocaust Survivor Who Deciphered Nazi Doublespeak." *New York Times* (June 24, 2019), www.nytimes.com/2019/06/24/books/holocaust-nazi-archive.html.

Fishman-Shnaydman, Ruzshke [Róża Fiszman-Sznajdman]. "Etlekhe verter vegn nakhmen blumental [Some Words on Nachman Blumental; after his obituary]." *Kol Lublin—Lubliner Shtime* 19 (November 1984): 39–40.

———. *Mayn lublin: bilder funem lebns-shteyger fun yidn in farmilkhomedikn poyln*. Tel Aviv: Y. L. Perets, 1982.

Gliksman, Volf. "Khurbn-hitler vi opgeshpiglt in golgn-humor un sarkazm [The Hitler *Khurbn* as Reflected in Gallows Humor and Sarcasm; review of Blumental's *Verter un vertlekh*]." *Yidishe kultur* 44, no. 5 (1982): 15–17.

Kahan [Kagan], Berl. "Blumental, Nakhmen," *Leksikon fun yidish-shraybers*, 90. New York: Rayah Ilman-Kagan, 1986.

Kuhn-Kennedy, Fleur. "Autour de Nakhmen Blumental: réfléchir aux écritures de la Catastrophe dans l'après-guerre [About Nachman Blumental: Reflecting on the Writings of the Catastrophe in the Postwar Period]." *Lire une collection en yiddish Histoire et mémoire d'un monde disparu au lendemain de la catastrophe*, http://poly.hypotheses.org/250, February 19, 2014.

Nisan, Eli. "Milon le-munakhim natziyim yotz'e 'al-yede [Dictionary of Nazi Terms Published by] 'Yad va-Shem'." *Davar* (February 1, 1961): 2.

Reibel, Shlomo. "ha-Hayim ha-hevratiyim veha-tarbutiyim be-Vorshtsov ben shete milhamot ha-'olam [Social and Cultural Life in Borszczów between the Two World Wars]." In *Sefer borshtshiv*, edited by Blumental, 167–70. Tel Aviv: Y. L. Perets, 1960.

Shayntukh [Sheintuch], Yehiel. "Fun khurbn biz tsum vider-oyfboy: naye bikher un forshungen in yerusholayim [From Khurbn to Reconstruction: New Books and Studies in Jerusalem]." *Forverts* (May 11, 2012).

Shtokfish, David. "A leksikon vegn khurbn, an antologye fun galgn-humor [A Lexicon on the *Khurbn*, an Anthology of Gallows Humor; review of Blumental's *Verter un vertlekh*]." *Kol Lublin—Lubliner Shtime* 16 (November 1981): 21–22.

Trinh, Miryam. "L'écriture poétique durant la Sho'ah [Poetic Writing during the Shoah]." *Yod* 16 (December 6, 2011), http://yod.revues.org/292.

Addendum: It was announced in June 2019 that Blumental's archive of more than 200,000 German and Jewish documents of the Holocaust period had been donated by the historian's son, Miron Blumental, to the YIVO Institute for Jewish Research, which plans to digitize the collection and make it available to the public (see Beckerman, above).

Bibliography of Joseph Kermish

Scope: All locatable prewar works and postwar Yiddish writings, plus works consulted in all languages, and their publication history (in order by dates of Yiddish publication).

Books by Kermish

Lublin i Lubelskie w ostatnich latach Rzeczypospolitej (1788–1794) [*Lublin and Lublin Province in the Last Years of the Republic*]. Lublin: Wydawnictwo Zarzadu Miejskiego, 1939.

Der oyfshtand in varshever geto: 19ter april—16ter mai 1943 [*The Uprising in the Warsaw Ghetto: 19 April–16 May 1943*]. Buenos Aires: Tsentralfarband fun poylishe yidn in argentine / Yidisher historisher institut in poyln, 1948. [Translated from the Polish by Shloyme Lastik for the CJHC: *Powstanie w getcie warszawskim (19 kwietnia—16 maja 1943)* (Lodz: Centralna Żydowska Komisja Historyczna, 1946)].

[Editor]. *Mered Geto Varshah be-'ene ha-oyev: ha-dohot shel ha-general Yurgen Shtrop* [*The Warsaw Ghetto Revolt as Seen by the Enemy*]. Jerusalem: Yad Vashem, 1959; 1966.

[Editor with Blumental]. *Mul ha-oyev ha-Natzi: Lohamim mesaprim* [*Face to Face with the Nazi Enemy: Fighters Recount*] *1939–1945*, vol. 1, with joint introduction. Tel Aviv: Irgun nekhe ha-milhamah ba-Natzim, 1961 (almost entirely Yiddish narratives).

[Editor with Blumental]. *ha-Meri veha-mered be-geto Varsha: sefer mismakhim / Resistance and Revolt in the Warsaw Ghetto: A Documentary History* (Hebrew). Jerusalem: Yad Vashem, 1965.

[Editor with Blumental, Natan Eck, and Arieh Tartakower]. *Yoman geto Varsha: 6.9.1939—23.7.1942*. Jerusalem: Yad Vashem, 1968. English [with Raul Hilberg and Stanislaw Staron], *The Warsaw Diary of Adam Czerniakow: Prelude to doom* (New York: Stein and Day, 1979); introduction by Kermish, 1–24.

[Editor with Blumental]. *Kidush ha-Shem—Ketavim mi-yeme ha-Sho'ah* by Shimon Huberband. Tel Aviv: Zakhor, 1969. English, *Rabbi Shimon Huberband, Kiddush Hashem: Jewish Religious and Cultural Life in Poland During the Holocaust,* trans. David E. Fishman, ed. Jeffrey S. Gurock and Robert S. Hirt (Hoboken-New York: KTAV/Yeshiva University Press, 1987). Author of introduction to both editions.

[Editor with Shmuel Krakowski]. *Polish-Jewish Relations During the Second World War* by Emanuel Ringelblum. Jerusalem: Yad Vashem, 1974. Introduction reprinted in *The Nazi Holocaust,* vol. 5: Public Opinion and Relations to the Jews; vol. 1, ed. Michael R. Marrus (Westport: Meckler, 1989), 266-98.

[Editor with Yechiel Shzeintuch]. *Jewish Creativity in the Holocaust: Exhibition [Catalog] of Jewish Creativity in the Ghettoes and Camps under Nazi Rule (1939-1945).* Jerusalem: Yad Vashem, 1979 (Hebrew, Yiddish, and English).

[Editor with Yisrael Bialostotski]. *'Itonut-ha-mahteret ha-Yehudit be-Varshah [Underground Jewish Press in Warsaw],* 6 vols. Jerusalem: Yad Vashem, 1979-97.

[Editor]. *Ksovim fun geto* [*Writings from the Ghetto*] by Emanuel Ringelblum, 2 vols. Tel Aviv: Y. L. Perets, 1985. Hebrew [with Yisrael Gutman and Yisrael Shaham], *Yoman u-reshimot mi-tekufat ha-milhamah: Geto Varshah, September 1939—Detsember 1942* [vol. 1]; *Ketavim aharonim: yahase Polanim—Yehudim: Yanu'ar 1943—April 1944* [vol. 2] (Jerusalem: Yad Vashem-Bet Lohame ha-Geta'ot, 1992, 1994).

[Editor]. *To Live with Honor, To Die with Honor! . . . : Selected Documents from the Warsaw Ghetto Underground Archives "O.S." ["Oneg Shabbath"].* Jerusalem: Yad Vashem, 1986.

Articles by Kermish

1937

"Nieznany list patriotyczny rabina do Kościszki z rozu 1792 [An Unknown Patriotic Letter from a Rabbi to Kościuszko in 1792]." *Głos Gminy Żydowskiej* [*Voice of the Jewish Community*] I, no. 4 (October 1937): 87-88. Reprinted in *Opinia* 2, no. 5 (September 25, 1946): 18.

1938

"Reprezentacja Żydowska w Radzie Miejskiej M. St. Warszawy [Jewish Representation on the Warsaw City Council] (1919-1938)." *Głos Gminy*

Żydowskiej II, nos. 10–11 (October–November 1938): 318–22. Expanded Yiddish version, "Der yidisher representants" (1970).

1939

"Żydzi Warszawscy w Insurekcji Kościuszkowskiej (W 145 rocznięe powstania 1794 r.) [Warsaw Jews in Kościuscko's Uprising (On the 145th Anniversary of the 1794 Rebellion)]." *Głos Gminy Żydowskiej* III, nos. 5–6 (May–June 1939): 121–26.

1945

"Di arbet fun yidish-historishn arkhiv [The Work of the Jewish Historical Archive]." *Dos naye lebn* (May 5, 1945): 5.

[With Blumental]. "Khelmne [Chełmno]." *Dos naye lebn* (June 10, 1945): 3–4.

"Vi azoy bzshezshiner polyakn hobn geshpayzt di dortike yidn in geto [How Poles in Brzeziny Gave Food to the Local Jews in the Ghetto]." *Dos naye lebn* (September 14, 1945): 5.

1946

"A bashtelung fun general kaltenburger: fun der serye 'dokumentn fun yidish-historishn arkhiv' [An Order from General Kaltenburger: From the Series 'Documents from the Jewish Historical Archive']." *Dos naye lebn* (January 3, 1946): 5.

"An epos fun heldntum: di raportn fun general stroop vegn geto-oyfshtand [An Epic of Heroism: The Report of General Stroop on the Ghetto Uprising]." *Dos naye lebn* (April 23, 1946): unnumbered page; (May 17): 4; (May 24): 5; (May 31): 6. Serialized Yiddish condensation of *Der oyfshtand in varshever geto*, preceding 1946 Polish edition.

"Der talyen fun lodzsher yidntum—hans bibov [The Hangman of Lodz Jewry—Hans Biebow]." *Dos naye lebn* (March 13, 1946): 5, 7. Partial reprint as "Danyel vayskopf—a derhoybene geshtalt," in *Khalutsim in poyln: antologye fun der khalutsisher bavegung*, vol. 2, ed. Leyb Shpizman (New York: Research Institute of the Labor Zionist Movement, 1961), 508.

"3 yor tetikayt fun Ts.Y.H.K. un yidishn historishn insititut baym Ts.K. fun yidn in poyln [Three Years' Activity of the CJHC and Jewish Historical Institute of the Central Committee of Jews in Poland]." *Dos naye lebn* (March 5, 1948): 6. Partial French version, "Trois année d'activité de la Commission Centrale Historique Juive et de l'Institut Historique Juif auprès du Comité Central des Juifs en Pologne," in *Conférence européenne des commissions historiques et des centres de documentation juifs [1–10 December 1947, Paris]. Les Juifs en Europe (1939–1945): Rapports* (Paris: Éditions du Centre [de documentation Juive Contemporaine], 1949), 140–44.

"Vegn der loyfndiker arbet fun arkhiv fun der tsentraler yidisher historisher komisye [On the Current Work of the Archive of the Central Jewish Historical Commission]." *Dos naye lebn* (December 28, 1946): 5.

Foreword to Gerszon Taffet, *Zagłada Żydów Żółkiewskich,* 5–7. Lodz: Centralna Żydowska komisja Historyczna, 1946. English trans. by Piotr J. Drozdowski, *The Holocaust of the Jews of Zolkiew* (Lodz: The Central Jewish Historical Committee, 1946; mimeographed typescript), 3–6.

1947

"Tsum tsveytn mol in treblinke [For the Second Time in Treblinka]." *Dos naye lebn* (June 4, 1947): 4, 6.

"Z galerii: Niemieckich prżestów wojennych: Franz Konrad (na podstawie nicopublikowanych materiałów) [From the Gallery: German War Criminals: Franz Konrad (On the Basis of Unpublished Materials)]." *Mosty* 2, no. 62 (September 23, 1947): 3.

"Z galerii: Niemieckich prżestów wojennych." *Mosty* 2, no. 53 (August 19, 1947): 3; 2, no. 54 (August 22, 1947): 3–4.

1948

"Ankete fun 'oyneg shabes' [Questionnaire from 'Oyneg shabes']" (unsigned). *Bleter far geshikhte* I, nos. 3–4 (August–December 1948): 186–202.

"Bilans 4-ch lat działalności: C. Ż. K. H. i Żydowskiego Instytutu Historycznego [Balance Sheet on the 4th Year of Activity: CJHC and JHI]." *Mosty* 3, no. 134 (November 20, 1948): 7.

"3 yor tetikayt fun Ts.Y.H.K." (see 1947).

"Nieznane dokumenty żydiwskie z okresu powstania kwiestniowego [Unknown Jewish Documents on the Period of the April Uprising]." *Mosty* 3, no. 46 (April 19, 1948): 6, 35.

"Shtroops tshuves oyf an ankete [Stroop's Answers to a Questionnaire]" (unsigned introduction and text). *Bleter far geshikhte* I, nos. 3–4 (August–December 1948): 166–85. Hebrew trans. in *Mered Geto Varshah be-ʿene ha-oyev* (1966), 195–205. Expanded treatment, "ha-Aktsiah shel Shtrop," *Dapim le-heker ha-Shoʾah veha-mered* 1 (1st series, January–April, 1951): 69–88; English summary IV–V.

1949

"Der muzey fun poylishn yidntum [The Museum of Polish Jewry]." *Yedies: byuletin fun yidishn historishn institut in poyln* [1] (November 1949): 8.

"Der oyfshtand in vershever geto [The Uprising in the Warsaw Ghetto]." *Tsu hilf dem lerer* (March 1949): 2.

"Mekoyrim tsu der geshikhte fun oyfshtand in varshever geto." *Yidishe shriftn* (April 1949): 9–10. Expanded translation (first half only), "Sources of Documentation for the History of the Uprising" in *Mered Geto Varshah be-'ene ha-oyev* (1966), English vii–xii; Hebrew 9–16.

"Vegn a biblyografye tsu der geshikhte fun poylishn yidntum in der tkufe fun der natsyonaler katastrofe [On a Bibliography of the History of Polish Jewry in the Period of the National Catastrophe] (1939–1945)." *Bleter far geshikhte* II, nos. 1–4 (January–December 1949): 223–34.

1951

"Di tsavoa fun varshever geto." *Di goldene keyt* 9 (1951): 134–62. Partial English translation, "The Testament of the Warsaw Ghetto," *Jewish Frontier* (September 1951): 9–14. Condensations: "Di tsavoa fun varshever geto," *Yedies fun yad vashem* 1 (April 1957): 8–12; English, "Warsaw Ghetto Intellectuals on Current Questions and Problems of Survival," *Yad Washem Bulletin* 1 (April 1957): 7–11. Hebrew, "Anshe ha-ruah be-Geto Varshah—'al she'elot ha-zeman uve'ayot ha-kiyum," *Yedi'ot Yad va-Shem* 8–9 (March 1956): 2–4; 10–11 (August 1956): 15–18; 12 (January 1957): 6–8. Reprinted in *Masu'ah* 24 (1996): 74–94. Expanded English version, "Ideas on Destiny and Existence," in *To Live with Honor* (1986), 717–30.

1952

Review of Tuvia Borzykowski, *Tsvishn falndike vent* [*Amid Toppling Walls*] (Warsaw, 1949). *Dapim le-heker ha-Sho'ah veha-mered* 2 (1st series, February 1952): 158–60.

1953

"ha-Meri veha-mered be-geto [Resistance and Uprising in the Ghetto]." In *Entsiklopediyah shel Galuyot*, vol. I: Warsaw, edited by Yitshak Gruenbaum, 734–800. Jerusalem: Entsiklopediyah shel Galuyot, 1953.

"In varshever geto: emanuel ringelblum, notitsn fun varshever geto." *YIVO bleter* XXXVII (1953): 282–95. English, "Mutilated Versions of Ringelblum's Notes," *YIVO Annual of Jewish Social Science* VIII (1953): 289–301.

"Tsu der forshung vegn geto-oyfshtand [On the Research of the Ghetto Uprising]." *Di goldene keyt* 15 (1953): 134–50. Portions reprinted in "Di kley-zin" (1958).

Review of Haikah Grosman, *Anshe ha-mahteret [People of the Underground]* (Tel Aviv, 1950). *Kiem* 6, no. 1 (July 1953): 484–86. Hebrew, *Dapim le-heker ha-Sho'ah veha-mered* 2 (1st series, February 1952): 161–67.

1954

"Der arkhiv fun 'yad vashem' [The Archive of 'Yad Vashem']." *Yedi'ot Yad va-Shem* 2 (July 29, 1954): 7. Hebrew, "Arkhiyon merkazi le-toldot ha-Sho'ah veha-gevurah," 5–6.

"Hovat pirsum mekorot me'arkhiyone ha-geta'ot." *Yedi'ot Yad va-Shem* 3 (December 1954): 1. English summary, "Publication of Source-Material of Ghetto Archives Obligatory," 16.

"la-Matsav ba-hoker ha-Sho'ah [The Current State of Shoah Research]." *Yedi'ot Yad va-Shem* 1 (April 30, 1954): 8–10.

1956

"Der geto-oyfshtand un di poylishe bafelkerung [The Ghetto Uprising and the Polish Population]." *Di goldene keyt* 25 (1956): 297–311. Hebrew, "ha-oklusiya ha-Polanit veha-mered be-Geto Varshah," *Yedi'ot kibutz bet lohamei ha-geta'ot* (April 1956): 25–30. Condensed Hebrew version, "'Itonut ha-mahteret ha-Polanit 'al mered Geto Varshah," *Yedi'ot Yad va-Shem* 4–5 (June 1955): 11; "Di varshever untererdishe prese vegn geto-oyfshtand" (Yiddish summary), 22–23; "The Underground Warsaw Press on the Ghetto Uprising" (English summary), 25. English Condensation as Part V of "The Jewish and Polish Underground Press" (1957 address), 99–105.

"Mekorot ha-oyev misparim 'al gevurah Yehudit." *Yedi'ot Yad va-Shem* 6–7 (January 1956): 5–7. "Fayntlekhe makoyres dertseyln vegn yidisher gvure" (Yiddish summary), 23; "Enemy Sources on Jewish Heroism" (English summary), 32. Revised Hebrew version, "Ma'ase gevurah bilti-noda'im be-geta'ot ube-mahanot," *Davar* (April 6, 1956): 3.

1957

"The Jewish and Polish Underground Press as Sources of History." In *From Hatred to Extermination: Seven Lectures Delivered at the Second World Congress, the Section for the History of the Jewish People, August 4, 1957*, 77–105. Jerusalem: Yad Vashem, 1959.

"Vegn der untererdisher prese fun varshever geto." *Di goldene keyt* 27 (1957): 243–57. English, "On the Underground Press in the Warsaw Ghetto," *Yad Washem Studies* I (1957): 85–123. Hebrew edition (1957): 69–92. Reprinted in *International Communication Gazette* 8, no. 1 (1962): 1–21. Condensed version reprinted as Parts I & II of "The Jewish and Polish Underground Press" (1957 address), 77–95.

1958

"Di kley-zin fun di oyfshtendler in varshever geto." *Yedies fun yad vashem* 3 (September 1958): 4–6 (first half only). Complete versions: English, "Arms Used by the Warsaw Ghetto Fighters," *Yad Washem Bulletin* 3 (July 1958): 5–9; Hebrew, "Kle-zinam shel morede Geto Varshah," *Yedi'ot Yad va-Shem* 14 (August 1957): 4–5; 15–16 (April 1958): 4–5. Reprinted in Hebrew as "Neshek ha-magen," *Davar* (April 18, 1958): 3.

"Di yidishe froy in varshever geto-oyfshtand [The Jewish Woman in the Warsaw Ghetto Uprising]." *Der poylisher yid* 8–9 (1958): 34–39 (first Yiddish publication not located). Abridged Hebrew version, "ha-Lohemet ha-Yehudit be-mered geto Varshah," *Davar* (April 29, 1954): 2.

"Mit 15 yor tsurik: di shoa hot geshlogn [15 Years Ago: the Shoah Hit]." *Heymish* (April 24, 1958): 3.

1960

"Khmilniker yidn untern natsi-rezshim [The Jews of Chmielnik under the Nazi Regime]." In *Pinkes khmyelnik: yisker-bukh nokh der khorevgevorener yidisher kehile*, edited by Efrayim Shedletski, 653–92. Tel Aviv: Irgun yotz'e Khmyelnik be-Yisra'el, 1960.

1961

"Danyel vayskopf—a derhoybene geshtalt [Daniel Weiskopf—An Exalted Figure]." In *Khalutsim in poyln: antologye fun der khalutsisher bavegung*, vol. 2, edited by Leyb Shpizman, 508. New York: Research Institute of the Labor Zionist Movement, 1961 (partial reprint from 1946 "Der talyen").

"Martirologye, vidershtand un umkum fun der yidisher kehile in kalushin." In *Sefer kalushin*, edited by Aryeh Shamri et al., 315–49. Tel Aviv: Irgun yotz'e Kalushin be-Yisra'el, 1961. English trans. by Gooter Goldberg, "Martyrdom, Resistance and Destruction of the Jewish Community in Kałuszyn" (complete), www.jewishgen.org/Yizkor/kaluszyn/kal314.html; and by S. Staroswiecki, "Martyrologie, Résistance et Fin de la Communauté Juive de Kałuszyn" (first two of three parts only), www.jewishgen.org/yizkor/kaluszyn/kalf314.html.

"Tsu aykhmans rol bay der yidn-farnikhtung." *Yedies fun yad vashem* 6 (March 1961): 21–24. English, "Eichmann's Role in the Destruction of Jews," *Yad Vashem Bulletin* 10 (April 1961): 19–23. Hebrew, "Le-helko shel Aykhman ba-bitsua 'haPitron ha-Sofi.'" *Yedi'ot Yad va-Shem* 27 (1961): 15–16.

"When and by Whom was the Order for 'The Final Solution' Given?" *Yad Vashem Bulletin* 14 (March 1964): 26–31. Hebrew, "Matay ve-'al yede mi nitnah ha-pikudah 'al 'ha-pitron ha-sofi'? [Third World Congress of Jewish Studies, Jerusalem, July 31, 1961]," *Yedi'ot Yad va-Shem* 31 (December 1963), 26–30; and in ed. Shaul Esh, *'Am Yisra'el be-dorenu* (Jerusalem: ha-Universitah ha-'Ivrit, 1964), 300–313.

Preface to *Ta'arukhat Sifre-Zikaron li-kehilot Yisra'el sheharvu* [*Exhibition of Memorial Books for the Destroyed Jewish Communities*], 5–7. Tel Aviv: Agudat shohare YIVO be-Yisra'el u-Muze'on Geniza le'omanut Yehudit amamit, 1961; Hebrew, 3–4. English adaptation in foreword to *Sefer zikaron li-kehilat Skarz'ishko Kamiennah* [*Skarzysko Kaminna*], 1973.

1962

"Yad Vashem Archives' Contribution to Preparation of the Eichmann Trial." *Yad Vashem Bulletin* 11 (April–May 1962): 37–45. Hebrew, "Terumat arkhiyono ba-hahanat ha-mishpat [Eichmann]," *Yedi'ot Yad va-Shem* 28 (December 1961): 28–34.

"Yehude Varshah be-mered Koshtsyushko [Warsaw Jews in the Kościuscko Uprising]." In *Sefer ha-yovel mugash li-khevod Dr. N. M. Gelber, le-regel yovlo ha-shiv'im*, edited by Yisra'el Klausner et al., 221–29. Tel Aviv: 'Olamenu, 1962/1963. Apparently a Hebrew translation of a prewar article (original not located).

1963

"The Land of Israel in the Life of the Ghetto as Reflected in the Illegal Warsaw Ghetto Press." *Yad Vashem Studies* V (1963): 105–31. Hebrew, "Eretz Yisra'el be-haye ha-geto," in Hebrew edition (1963), 89–107. English summary as Part III of "The Jewish and Polish Underground Press" (1957 address), 95–97.

1964

"New Jewish Sources for the History of the Warsaw Ghetto Uprising." *Yad Vashem Bulletin* 15 (August 1964): 27–33. Hebrew, "Mekorot Yehudiyim hadashim le-toldot ha-mered be-Geto Varshah," *Yedi'ot Yad va-Shem* 32 (March–April 1964): 19–26.

1965

"Der khurbn [in Piotrków Trybunalski]." In *Pyetrkov Tribunalski veha-sevivah: sefer zikaron*, edited by Yaakov Malts and Naftoli (Lavy) Lau, 707–74. Tel Aviv: Pyetrkover landsmanshaft in yisroel, 1965. English, "The Destruction of the Jewish Community of Piotrkow by the Nazis during World War II," trans. P. Wollman, ed. Hassia Ben Harari and Joseph Goldberg (Tel Aviv, 1965): I–LXIII [place and date per Martin Gilbert, *The Holocaust*, 1985; listed in Robinson, *The Holocaust and After*, 1975, item 1311c, as "Israel, n.d."]. English translation reprinted in *A Tale of One City: Piotrków Trybunalski*, ed. Ben Giladi (New York: Shengold Publishers, 1991), 323–53.

"Di rol fun der untergrunt-prese in varshever geto in der tsugreytung fun bodn far a bavofntn kamf." *Unzer kiem* 49–50–51 (October 1965): 14–19. English, "The Role of the Underground Press in Warsaw Ghetto in Preparing the Ground for Armed Resistance," *Yad Vashem Bulletin* 8–9 (March 1961): 9–11. Hebrew, "Helkah shel itonut-ha-mahteret be-geto varsha be-haksharat ha-karka le-hitnagdut mezuyenet," *Yedi'ot Yad va-Shem* 25–26 (February 1961): 10–12. Condensed English version, Part IV of "The Jewish and Polish Underground Press" (1957 address), 97–99.

"Historical Sources Relating to the Warsaw Ghetto Uprising." In *ha-Meri veha-mered be-geto Varsha: sefer mismakhim / Resistance and Revolt in the Warsaw Ghetto: A Documentary History*, edited by Blumental and Kermish (1965), vii–xxxv.

1966

"ha-'Itonut ha-makhteretit shel 'Gordoniah' bi-me ha-Sho'ah be-Polin [The Underground Press of 'Gordoniah' during the Shoah in Poland]." In *'Itonut "Gordoniah" be-makhteret Geto Varshah*, edited by Arieh Avnon, 13–38. Tel Aviv: Gordoniah-Macabi ha-Tza'ir, 1966.

"Hersh berlinski—a vogiker makor tsu der geshikhte fun geto-oyfshtand [An Important Source for the History of the Ghetto Uprising]." In *D R A Y— ondenkbukh: Pola Elster, Hersh Berlinski, Eliyohu Erlikh*, 133–37. Tel Aviv: Akon Ringelblum, 1966. Included in "New Jewish Sources" (1964), 28–31.

[with Blumental] "Jews in the War Against the Nazis." In *Jewish Heroism in Modern Times: A Hanukah Anthology*, 49–88. Jerusalem: World Zionist Organization, 1966.

1967

"Di plotsker yidn untern natsi-rezshim." In *Plotsk: toldot kehilah 'atikat-yomin be-Polin*, edited by Eliyahu Eisenberg, 474–505 (Hebrew 449–73; English summary 70–75). Tel Aviv: ha-Menorah, 1967; of the last, pp. 70–73 as "The Jews of Plotzk Under the Nazi Regime," www.jewishgen.org/Yizkor/plock/plo070.html.

Foreword to M. Balberishki [Mendel Balberyszski], *Shtarker fun ayzn*, 16–19. Tel Aviv: Hamenorah, 1967. English trans. in Mendel Balberyszski, *Stronger than Iron: The Destruction of Vilna Jewry 1941–1945: an eyewitness account*, rev. and ed. by Theodore Balberyszski (Jerusalem: Gefen, 2010), xxiii–xxv.

1968

"Di rol fun di geto-oyfshtandn in kamf kegn di natsis." In *Tsuzamen: zaml-bukh far literatur, kunst, yidishe problemen un dokumentatsye*, edited by Sh. L. Shnayderman, 383–95. Tel Aviv: Leib Levin, 1974. English, "The Place of the Ghetto Revolts in the Struggle Against the Occupier," in *Jewish Resistance during the Holocaust: Proceedings of the Conference on Manifestations of Jewish Resistance, Jerusalem, April 7–11, 1968* (Jerusalem: Yad Vashem, 1971), 306–23. Hebrew, "Mekomo shel mered ha-geta'ot ba-ma'avak neged ha-kibush," in *ha-'Amidah ha-Yehudit bi-tekufat ha-Sho'ah* (Jerusalem: Yad Vashem, 1970), 241–55.

"Dos galitsishe yidntum beys der hitler-okupatsye [Galician Jewry during the Hitler Occupation]." In *Sefer galitsye: gedenk bukh*, edited by Yosef Okrutni, 9–40. Buenos Aires: Farlag "Galitsye" baym tsentral farband fun galitsyaner yidn in buenos ayres, 1968. Hebrew, "Parshat ha-Sho'ah shel Yahude Galitziyah," in *Pirke Galitsyah: sefer zikaron le-Dr Avraham Zilbershein*, ed. Yisra'el Kohen and Dov Sadan (Tel Aviv: 'Am 'oved, 1957), 428–53. Hebrew condensation, "Le-parshat ha-meri shel Yahadut Galitsyah," *Yedi'ot Yad va-Shem* 17–18 (December 1958): 3–6, 9.

"Les archives de Yad Vashem." In *D'Auschwitz a Israël: Vingt ans après la libération*, edited by Isaac Schneersohn, 419–23. Paris: Centre de documentation Juive Contemporaine, 1968.

"The Poles and the Warsaw Ghetto Uprising in the light of newly discovered documents." *Yad Vashem Bulletin* 22 (May 1968): 13–18. Hebrew, "Yahas ha-Polanim le-mered Geto Varshah (le-or teʻudot hadashim)," *Yediʻot Yad va-Shem* 39 (March 1968): 9–13.

"Umbakante notitsn fun emanuel ringelblum" (brief version). *Di goldene keyt* 64 (1968): 149–50. English, "Emmanuel Ringelblum's Notes hitherto Unpublished," *Yad Vashem Studies* VII (1968): 173–83.

1970

"Di yidishe reprezentantn in varshever shtotrat." In *Sefer ha-Shanah / Yorbukh / Yearbook* III, edited by Aryeh Tartakower, 279–93. Tel Aviv: World Federation of Polish Jews, 1970. Expanded version of "Reprezentacja" (1938).

1972

"Shoʼat yehude Kolomeyah veha-sevivah [The Destruction of the Jews of Kołomyja and Vicinity]." In *Sefer zikaron li-kehilat Kolomeyah veha-sevivah*, edited Dov Noy and Mordecai Shutzman, 267–308. Tel Aviv: Irgun yotzʼe Kolomeyah veha-sevivah, 1972.

1973

"Di endgiltike tseshterung fun varshever geto [The Final Destruction of the Warsaw Ghetto]." In *Entsiklopediyah shel Galuyot*, vol. XII: Warsaw 3, edited by Kh. Barlas et al., 383–406. Jerusalem: Entsiklopediyah shel Galuyot, 1973.

"Der oyfshtand in varshever geto in likht fun a biz itst umbakantn ofitsyeln daytshishn barikht." *Di goldene keyt* 79–80 (1973): 199–217. English, "The Warsaw Ghetto Uprising in the Light of a Hitherto Unpublished Official German Document," *Yad Vashem Studies* IX (1973): 7–27. Hebrew, "Mered Geto Varshah le-or dv"h Germani bilti-yaduʻa," in Hebrew edition (1973), 7–23. Reprinted in *Shoʼat Yehude Eropah: Reka, Korot, Mashmaʻut*, ed. Yisrael Gutman and Livia Rothkirchen (Jerusalem: Yad Vashem, 1973), 418–36. English reprinted in Gutman and Rothkirkhen, *The Catastrophe of European Jewry* (Jerusalem: Yad Vashem, 1976), 559–81. Hebrew summary, "Teʻudah rishmit natsit bilti-yaduʻa ʻal mered Geto Varshah," *Davar* (April 29, 1973): 10.

Foreword to *Sefer zikaron li-kehilat Skarz'ishko Kamiennah* [*Memorial Book of the Community of Skarzysko Kaminna*], 260–59. Tel Aviv: Irgun yotzʼe Skarz'ishko Kamiennah, 1973.

1974

"Di rol fun di geto-oyfshtandn in kamf kegn di natsis" (see 1968).

"Mekoyres vegn di khinukh problemen in geto." *Yerusholaymer almanakh* 2–3 (1974): 179–86. English, "Origins of [correctly, 'Sources Regarding'] the Education Problem in the Ghetto," *Yad Vashem Bulletin* 12 (December 1962): 28–34. Hebrew, "Mekorot li-be'ayot ha-hinukh ba-geto," *Yedi'ot Yad va-Shem* 29 (1962): 19–21. Reprinted in *ha-Yeled veha-na'ar ba-sho'ah uva-gevurah*, ed. Aryeh Bauminger, Nahman Blumental, and Yosef Kermish (Jerusalem: Kiryat Sefer, 1965), 11–16.

"The Activities of the Council for Aid to the Jews ('Zegota') in Occupied Poland [Yad Vashem Conference, Jerusalem, April 8–11, 1974]." In *Rescue Attempts During the Holocaust*, 367–98. Jerusalem: Yad Vashem, 1977. Reprinted in *The Nazi Holocaust*, vol. 5: Public Opinion and Relations to the Jews; vol. 2, ed. Michael R. Marrus (Westport: Meckler, 1989), 485–516. Hebrew, "Pe'ulah shel ha-Mo'atsah le-'Ezrat ha-Yehudim be-Polin ha-kibushah," in *Nisyonot u-fe'ulot hatsalah bi-tekufat ha-Sho'ah*, ed. Yisrael Gutman (Jerusalem: Yad Vashem, 1976), 306–30.

1975

"Di emese organizatorn fun geto-oyfshtand [The True Organizers of the Ghetto Uprising]." *Yerusholayimer almanakh* 4 (1975): 11–22. English, "Who Organized the Revolt?" (first half only), *Yad Vashem Bulletin* 4–5 (October 1959): 4–7. Hebrew, "Meholele ha-Mered," *Yedi'ot Yad va-Shem* 19–20 (May 1959): 3–4; 21–22 (December 1959): 4–5. French, "Les Veritables Initiateurs de la Revolte," *Le Monde Juif* 49: 147–48 (1993): 150–57.

"D"r filip fridman—der historiker fun khurbn [the Historian of *Khurbn*]." *Di tsukunft* (April 1975): 151–54. English, "The Founder of the Jewish Historical Commission in Poland after the Second World War," *Yad Vashem Bulletin* 6–7 (June 1960): 4–6. Hebrew, "Meyased ha-va'adah ha-historit be-Polin ahare ha-milhamah" (Memorial address, Yad Vashem, February 15, 1960), *Yedi'ot Yad va-Shem* 23–24 (May 1960): 4–6.

1977

"The Judenrat in Warsaw." In *Patterns of Jewish leadership in Nazi Europe, 1933–1945: proceedings of the Third Yad Vashem International Historical Conference, Jerusalem, April 4–7, 1977*, edited by Yisrael Gutman and Cynthia J. Haft, 75–90. Jerusalem: Yad Vashem, 1979. Reprinted in *The Nazi Holocaust*, vol. 6: The Victims of the Holocaust; vol. 1, ed. Michael R.

Marrus (Westport: Meckler, 1989), 216–31. Partial reprint as "'Judenrat' Policy and Social Tensions," in *To Live with Honor* (1986), 289–93. Hebrew, "ha-Yudenrat be-Varshah," in *Demut ha-hanhagah ha-Yehudit be-aratsot ha-shelitah ha-Natzit, 1933–1945*, ed. Yisrael Gutman (Jerusalem: Yad Vashem, 1979), 63–76.

"Rokhl Oyerbakh—di grinderin funem eydes-verk 'yad vashem' [the Founder of Eyewitness Work at Yad Vashem]." In Rohkl Oyerbakh, *Baym letstn veg*, 305–18. Tel Aviv: Yisroel-bukh, 1977.

1978

"Der kamf funem geto—oyf tsvey frontn." *Yerusholaymer almanakh* 10 (1978): 15–29. Hebrew, "ha-Ma'avak shel geto be-shete hazitot," *Yedi'ot Yad va-Shem* 30 (1963): 1–7. Condensed English translation, "The Ghetto's Two-Front Struggle," *Yad Vashem Bulletin* 13 (October 1963): 12–19. Reprinted in Hebrew as, "ha-Ma'avak ha-du-haziti shel Geto Varshah," *Mas'uah* 3 (1975): 38–47.

"Nisht bloyz kortshak aleyn . . . Vegn di dertsyers vos hobn nisht ibergelozn zeyere talmidim in zeyer letsn veg [Not Janusz Korczak Alone . . . On the Educators Who Did not Abandon Their Students on Their Final Journey]." *Di goldene keyt* 95–96 (1978): 283–89. Reprinted in *Yidish-literatur in medines-yisroel: antologye* (1991).

1980

"Tsu der geshikhte fun shvartsn bukh [On the History of the *Black Book*; Ehrenburg and Grossman (Moscow, 1944)]." *Di goldene keyt* 102 (1980): 121–29. Hebrew, "le-Toldot ketav ha-yad shel 'Sefer ha-Shahor' be-'arikhat Ilya Ehrenberg u-Vasili Grosman," *Masu'ah* 16 (1988): 197–204.

"Zhabotinskis toyt un der untererdisher prese inem varshever geto [Jabotinski's Death and the Underground Press in the Warsaw Ghetto]." *Folk un tsyen* 33 (1980): 19–20.

1982

"Yeshaye trunk." *Di goldene keyt* 108 (1982): 149–56. Reprinted as "Yeshaye trunk z"l," in Trunk, *Geshtaltn un gesheenishn [naye serye]* (Tel Aviv: Y. L. Perets, 1983), 7–16. English, "Isaiah Trunk," in Isaiah Trunk, *Łódź Ghetto: A History*, trans. and ed. Robert Moses Shapiro (Bloomington: Indiana University Press, 2006), xxi–xxviii. Condensed translation, "Isaiah Trunk (1905–1981): In Memoriam," *Yad Vashem Studies* XIV (1981): 335–40.

1983

"Daily Entries of Hersh Wasser" (Introduction). *Yad Vashem Studies* 15 (1983): 201–9. Hebrew edition (1984): 161–227.

"Umbakante briv fun zelig kalmanovitsh, fun vilner geto, tsu itsik giterman, in varshever geto [Unknown letters from Zelig Kalmanovitch, from the Vilna Ghetto, to Itzik Giterman, in the Warsaw Ghetto]." *Di goldene keyt* 110–11 (1983): 17–30.

1988

"Umbakante bleter fun perets opochinski: 'varshever geto-khronik' [Unknown letter from Perets Opochinski: 'Warsaw Ghetto Chronicle']." *Di goldene keyt* 124 (1988): 136–39.

1991

"Nisht bloyz kortshak aleyn . . . ." *Yidish-literatur in medines-yisroel: antologye*, vol. 2, 330–34. Tel Aviv: Fareyn fun yidishe shrayber un zshurnalistn in yisroel, 1991 (with photo and short bio; reprint from 1978).

Writings about Kermish

Unpublished document: "Di byografye fun d"r yosef kermish," autobiographical memoir, stating that it was written by Kermish in 1993 with later additions by his widow, Batyah (Basia) Bobker-Kermish, and translated from Hebrew to Yiddish by Carrie Friedman-Cohen and Yehiel Sheintuch of the Dov Sadan Institute of the Hebrew University; generously made available by Dov-Ber Kerler, editor of *Yerusholayimer almanakh*, in December 2010, in the form of four typeset pages in Yiddish.

"Byli uczestnicy powstania w getcie warszawskim: przygotowuią gen. Stgroopowi [They Were Participants in the Warsaw Ghetto Uprising: Preparing the Indictment Against Gen. Stroop (on Kermish's conversations with Stroop)]." *Mosty* 4, no. 67 (June 9, 1949): 3.

"Dr. Joseph Kermish z"l (1907–2005)." *Yad Vashem Quarterly Magazine* 40 (Winter 2006).

"Dr. Yosef Kermish . . ." *'Al ha-Mishmar* (June 7, 1950): 1.

"[D"r. Yosef Kermish]." *Amerikaner* (September 14, 1945): 5 (on his receiving the Order of Polonia Restituta for service as a partisan fighter and Polish Army captain).

"D"r Yosef kermish." *Yerusholaymer almanakh* 2–3 (1974): 253.

"D"r yosef kermish un prof. martin gilbert—laureatn fun k. tsetnik-prayz [Laureates of Ka-Tzetnik Prize]." *Yerusholaymer almanakh* 18 (1988): 227–28.

"ha-Ti'ud ha-Germani-Natzi mi-yeme ha-Sho'ah [Nazi-German Document during the Catastrophe]" (television lectures, Open University, Channel 1), "Modi'in [current day television schedule]." *Ma'ariv* (April 7, 1986): 14.

"ha-Ti'ud ha-Yehudi she-notzar ba-Sho'ah ve-goralo [Jewish Document Created during the Castatrophe and Its Fate]" (television lectures, Open University, Channel 1), "Modi'in [current day television schedule]." *Ma'ariv* (April 14, 1986): 14.

"Za aniszcznie stolicy i zagładę Żydów: odpowiadać będą przestępcy hitlerowscy [For the Destruction of the Capital and Extermination of the Jews: The Criminal Hitlerites Will Answer; Kermish on trial preparations]." *Mosty* 3, no. 133 (November 18, 1948): 4.

"Z działalności Żyd. Tow. Kultury [From the activities of the Jewish Cultural Society; Lecture by Kermish on conversation with Stroop]." *Mosty* 4, no. 38 (March 29, 1949): 3.

Barshteyn, Yitskhok. "Dray yidishe expertn bashuldikn . . . [Three Jewish Experts Accuse . . . ; on Kermish at Ludwik Fischer trial]." *Dos naye lebn* (February 6, 1947): 3.

Gliksman, Volf. "'Itonut ha-mahteret ha-Yehudit be-Varshah—Di untererdishe prese in varshe' [The Jewish Underground Press in Warsaw; review; vol. 3, July–October 1941]." *Yidishe kultur* 48, no. 2 (1986): 53–59.

Goldberg, Re'uven. "Kermish, Yosef." *Leksikon fun der nayer yidisher literatur*, vol. 8, 237–38. New York: Alveltlekhn yidishn kultur kongres, 1981.

Gris, Noah. "le-Ba'o shel hoker ha-Sho'ah D"r Yosef Kermish [Arrival of Shoah Researcher Dr. Joseph Kermish]." *'Al ha-Mishmar* (June 14, 1950): 2.

Shayntuch, Yehiel. "Oysshtelung vegn yidisher kultur-sheferishkayt untern natsishn rezshim [Exhibition on Jewish Cultural Creativity under the Nazi Regime]." *Yerusholaymer almanakh* 10 (1978): 83.

Silberklang, David. "Józef Kermisz (1907–2005): twórca badań nad Szoa [Author of Research on the Holocaust]." *Zagłada Żydów* 10, no. 1 (2014), 304–15 (with a summary in English).

Bibliography of Mark Dworzecki

Scope: All locatable prewar and postwar Yiddish writings (except prewar medical articles), plus works consulted in all languages, and their publication history (in order by date of Yiddish publication). The bibliography of Dworzecki's works (in Eliav, 1979) omits most Yiddish works. In the early postwar years, Dworzecki published chiefly in *Unzer vort* (Paris) and *Idisher kemfer* (New York) as listed below; largely repetitive items in *Baderekh* (Rome), *Der kval* (New York), *In gerangl* (Brussels), *Undzer veg* (Munich), *Vort* (Munich), and *Yidishe Tsaytung* (Johannesburg) are not listed.

Books by Dworzecki

Kamf farn gezunt in geto-vilne [*The Struggle for Health in the Vilna Ghetto*]. Paris: OSE farband, 1946. French, *Le ghetto de Vilna: rapport sanitaire*. Geneva: Union OSE, 1946. Adapted as chapter 5, "Kamf farn gezunt," in *Yerusholayim d'lite*. Condensed version, "In ibermentshlekhn gerangl mit toyt un umkum" (1968; see below).

Yerusholayim d'lite in kamf un umkum [*Jerusalem of Lithuania* (Vilna) *in Struggle and Extermination*]. Paris: Yidishn natsyonaln arbeter-farband in amerike / Yidishn folksfarband in frankraykh, 1948. Hebrew, *Yerushalayim de-Lita bi-meri ube-sho'ah* (Tel Aviv: Hotsa'at Mifleget po'ale Eretz Yisra'el, 1951). French, *La victoire du Ghetto*, trans. Arnold Mandel (Paris: Editions France-Empire, 1962).

Ben ha-Betarim [*Between the Parts*] (title quoted from the traditional "Covenant Between the Parts" of Genesis 15; collection of Hebrew versions of prior Yiddish articles). Tel Aviv: Kiryat Sefer, 1956.

Eyrope on kinder [*Europe without Children* (on the Nazi plan for biological subjugation of conquered peoples)]. Jerusalem: Y. L. Perets, 1961. Hebrew, *Erope le-lo yeladim* Jerusalem: Yad Vashem, 1959.

Hirshke glik: der mekhaber fun partizaner-himn [*Hirsh Glick: The Author of the Partisan Hymn*]. Paris: Undzer Kiem, 1966. French, *Hirsch Glik* (Paris: Éditions Notre Existence, 1966). Spanish, *Hirsch Glik: el Autor de "Partizaner-Himn"* (Buenos Aires: Congreso Judio Latinoamericano), 1973. Chapters 1–4 reprinted in condensed form in *Yidish-literatur in medines-yisroel: antologye* (1991).

Historia de la Resistencia Antinazi Judía, 1933–1945: Problemática y metodología, trans. from French by Roberto A. Gombert. Buenos Aires: Ejecutivo Sudamericano del Congreso Judío Mundial, 1970. French, *Histoire de la Resistance anti-Nazie juive (1933–1945): Problemes et métodologie* (typescript; Tel Aviv: n.p., 1965), for 12th International Congress of Historical Sciences, Vienna, 1965.

Vayse nekht un shvartse teg (yidn-lagern in estonye) [*White Nights and Black Days (Jewish Camps in Estonia)*]. Tel Aviv: Y. L. Perets, 1970. Hebrew, *Mahanot ha-yehudim be-Estoniyah* (Jerusalem: Yad Vashem, 1970). French, "L'histoire de la déportation et des camps en Esthonie" (PhD diss., Sorbonne, 1966).

[Coeditor]. *Yankev mansdorf in zayn dor* [*Jacob Mansdorf in His Generation*]. Tel Aviv [?]: n.p., 1960 [?].

Articles by Dworzecki

1929

"Dos bundishe shul-vezn oyf der bashuldikungs-bank: groyse gezelshaftlekher mishpet iber di tsysho-shuln in vilne (a briv fun vilne) [The Bundist School System in the Dock: Great Community Trial of the Central Yiddish School Organization in Vilna (a letter from Vilna)]." *Haynt* (November 19, 1929): 4.

1930

"A idisher prese-albom baym tsofn-yarid in poyln [A Jewish Press Album at the Northern Fair in Poland; letter regarding Jewish participation in the Northern Trade Fair / Targi Północne, 14–28 September 1930, held annually in Vilna]." *Unzer ekspres* (August 15, 1930): 16; *Haynt* (August 20, 1930): 6.

"Di ershte absolventn-konferents fun hebreyishn 'tarbut'-seminar in vilne [First Alumni Conference of Hebrew [Teachers'] Tarbut-Seminary in Vilna]." *Haynt* (January 22, 1930): 4.

"Vegn yidishn un hebreyishn pen-klub [On Yiddish and Hebrew PEN Club; within the worldwide PEN Club movement]." *Trybuna Akademicka* (September 1, 1930): 18–17 (Yiddish section with page numbers running back to front from Polish section).

"Vilne nemt oyf a kamf mit virtshaftlekhn krizis! [Vilna Fights against the Economic Crisis!; on the economic role of Vilna in Poland after World War I and the importance of the Northern Trade Fair in combating the economic crisis]." *Lubliner togblat* (August 22, 1930): 6.

1931

"Yeme ha-shitafon be-Vilnah [In the Days of Inundation in Vilna]." *ha-Tzefira* (April 29, 1931): 3.

1943

"Dos shulkind in geto un zayn gezunttsushtand [The School Child in the Ghetto and the State of His Health]." *Folksgezunt* 14 (June 1943). Manuscript in Dworzecki archive, Yad Vashem. Dworzecki's *Yerusholayim d'lite* suggests that this and the following issue of *Folkgezunt* may be in the YIVO collection, but they have not been located.

"Meditsin un meditsiner bay yidn in der tekufe fun mitlalterlekhe getos [Medicine and Medical Workers among Jews in the Period of Medieval Ghettos]." *Folksgezunt* 18 (August 1943).

1945

"A nayer koyekh in folk: di menshn fun vidershtand [A New Strength in the Nation: The People of Resistance]." *Idisher kemfer* (October 19, 1945): 3–5. Latter portion reprinted in Niger, *Kidush hashem* (New York: Tsyko bikher farlag, 1948), 509–10.

"Benkshaft tsu tsyenizm—benkshaft tsu sotsyalizm [Longing for Zionism—Longing for Socialism]." *Idisher kemfer* (August 31, 1945): 8.

"Der shos fun 'deportirtn zelbstmerder' [The Shot of the 'Deported Suicide'; on Displaced Persons]." *Idisher kemfer* (November 9, 1945): 8–9.

"Der umbakanter idisher zelner [The Unknown Jewish Soldier]." *Idisher kemfer* (November 30, 1945): 13–14.

"Di letste teg in a konsentratsye-lager [The Last Days in a Concentration Camp]." *Unzer vort* (May 25, 1945): 2.

"Di tsavoe fun di toyte [The Oath of the Dead]." *Idisher kemfer* (July 27, 1945): 10–11. Reprinted in *Unzer vort* (July 29, 1945): 3. Hebrew trans. in *Davar* (October 1, 1945): 2; and in *Ben ha-Betarim*, 30–32.

"Farshvaygn—oder dertseyln dem gantsn emes? [Remain Silent—Or Recount the Whole Truth?]." *Unzer vort* (June 22, 1945): 3. Reprinted in *Idisher kemfer* (July 20, 1945): 7–8. Hebrew trans. in *Ben ha-Betarim*, 24–29.

"Gedenk di katastrofe fun yisroel [Remember the Catastrophe of Israel; memorial poem, composed July 14, 1945 (per *Ben ha-Betarim*, 37)]." First published in *Yerusholayim d'lite* (1948), 495. Reprinted in Yiddish and/or Hebrew in *yizkor* books of at least 11 towns: Beitsh (1960), 339; Budzanov (1968), 36; Glubok (1956), 3–4; Horodlo (1960), 13 and (1966), 15; Yozefov (1975), 208; Kobylnik (1967), 20; Maytshet (1973), 288; Stolin (1952), 8; Trovits (1967), 29; Turka (1966), 312; Vishkov (1964), 243. Reprinted as "Gedenk!" in *Undzer lodzsh* 2 (1951): 74.

"Ikh gezegn zikh mit natsi-daytshland [I Take Leave of Nazi Germany]." *Unzer vort* (June 8, 1945): 2.

"Integrale idishe kultur [Integrated Jewish Culture]." *Idisher kemfer* (December 28, 1945): 6–8.

"Ir zayt ale gerekht . . . [You Are All Correct . . . ; on Jewish life in Paris]." *Idisher kemfer* (August 17, 1945): 8 [labeled "a4"], 9–10.

"Iz gekumen bialik in geto vilne . . . [Bialik Came to the Vilna Ghetto . . .]." *Unzer vort* (July 6, 1945): 3. Preview of *Yerusholayim d'lite*, 272–73.

"Kh'vil kontrolirn mayn gefil tsu poyln [I Will Control My Feelings toward Poland]." *Idisher kemfer* (September 28, 1945): 7–8. Hebrew trans. in *Davar* (October 12, 1945): 4.

"Oyf fir vegn veln mir fanandergeyn [We Will Go Our Four Separate Ways]." *Unzer vort* (September 21, 1945): 2. Reprinted in *Idisher kemfer* (October 5, 1945): 4–5, 9. Hebrew trans. in *Davar* (October 21, 1945): 2; and in *Ben ha-Betarim*, 33–36.

"Umgerikhte bafrayung . . . oyfn evakuatsye-marsh keyn dakhau [Unexpected Liberation . . . on an Evacuation March toward Dachau]." *Unzer vort* (June 1, 1945): 3.

"Vi azoy bistu geblibn lebn? [How Did You Survive?]" *Unzer vort* (August 28, 1945). Reprinted in *Parizer shriftn* 1 (October 1945): 18–25; *Idisher kemfer* (September 14, 1945): 11–13, 18. German trans. in *Pessach Buch 5766–1946*, ed. Israel Blumenfeld (Marburg: Jüdishe Rundschau, 1946), 231–41. Hebrew trans. in *Ben ha-Betarim*, 44–50.

"Vos mir hobn di kinder nit gelernt . . . . [What We Did not Teach Our Children]." *Idisher kemfer* (November 23, 1945): 12–13. Reprinted as "Vos mir hobn undzere kinder nit gelernt," *Undzer veg* [Munich] 32 (May 10, 1946): 5; *Nyu-yorker vokhnblat* (June 14, 1946): 2–3. Hebrew trans. in *Davar* (February 17, 1947): 2.

"Yitskhok grinboym derklert unz [Isaac Greenbaum Informs Us]." *Unzer vort* (August 31, 1945): 3 [signed "D. mark"].

"Zayt gegrist, ir yidishe yeshuvim [Be Welcomed, You Jewish Communities]." *Unzer vort* (31 August 31, 1945): 3.

1946

"A kinder-heym in frankraykh (oyfn nomen fun ana yarblum) [A Children's Home in France (in the Name of Anna Yarblum)]." *Idisher kemfer* (November 1, 1946): 8–9, 14.

"A tog in geto [A Day in the Ghetto]." *Di tsukunft* (July 1946): 496–500. Excerpt from *Yerusholayim d'lite*, 402–12. Reprinted as "A mes-les in geto," *Yidishe tsaytung* (April 23, 1948): 4–5. English, "A Day in the Vilna Ghetto," *Jewish Spectator* (October 1946): 16–20; reprinted in *Jewish Frontier* (May 1952): 7–12. Hebrew trans. in *Ben ha-Betarim*, 82–94.

"Biztu greyt mekhalel tsu zayn yom-kiper? [Are You Ready to Desecrate Yom Kippur?]" *Idisher kemfer* (October 4, 1946): 3–4. Reprinted in *Landsberger lager-tsaytung* (October 1946); *Shriftn* (October–November 1947): 258–62; *Rosh hashone yor-bukh* (Johannesburg 1949). English, "A Yom Kippur Homily," *Jewish Frontier* (December 1946): 10–11. Hebrew trans. in *Ben ha-Betarim*, 57–60.

"Der toyt fun d"r yankev vigodski [The Death of Dr. Jacob Wygodski]." *Ilustrirte folks-bleter* (April 1946): 20–21. Preview of *Yerusholayim d'lite*, 45–50.

"Dos kultur-vezn in vilner geto [The Cultural System in the Vilna Ghetto]." *Parizer shriftn* 2–3 (March 1946): 28–40. Preview of *Yerusholayim d'lite*, 222–36. Excerpt of 32–33 as, "Mesires nefesh fun lerers un talmidim," in *Kidush hashem*, ed. Shmuel Niger (New York: Tsyko bikher farlag, 1948), 219–20.

"Dray fun yerusholayim d'lite . . . [Three from Jerusalem of Lithuania (Vilna)]." *Unzer vort* (November 22, 1946): 3.

"Farshidn zenen geven di vegn [Varied were the Ways]." *Unzer vort* (June 21, 1946): unnumbered p. 3. Prefigures the chapters in Part 2 of *Yerusholayim d'lite*. Reprinted in *Idisher kemfer* (June 28, 1946): 8–9. Portions reprinted as "Vakh zayn," in *Kidush hashem*, ed. Shmuel Niger (New York: Tsyko bikher farlag, 1948), 730–33; and in *Der gaystiker vidershtand fun yidn in getos un lagern*, ed. Menashe Unger (Tel Aviv, 1970), 52. Hebrew, "Darkhe ha-ma'avak ha-Yehudi ba-Geta'ot" in *Metsudah* V–VI, ed. Simon Rawidowicz (1948): 519–23; and (with condensed ending) in *Ben ha-Betarim*, 51–56.

"Gezunt-shuts fun der sheyres hapleyte [Health Protection of the Survivors]." *Idisher kemfer* (February 15, 1946): 9–10. Hebrew trans. in *Davar* (March 4, 1946): 2.

"Iber idishe yishuvim in belgye [Across the Jewish Communities in Belgium]." *Idisher kemfer* (May 24, 1946): 8–9.

"Leyvik in geto [Leyvik in the Ghetto]." *Unzer vort* (June 7, 1946): 3.

"Literatur un kunst in vilne-geto [Literature and Art in the Vilna Ghetto]." *Parizer shriftn* 4 (September 1946): 18–28. Preview of *Yerusholayim d'lite*, 238–54. Preview of 18–19 as, "Literarishe oventn in vilner geto," *Eynikeyt* (April 1946): 20.

"Notitsn fun an 'umlegaln korespondent': briv fun der sholem-konferents in pariz; [Notices from an 'Illegal Correspondent': Letters from the Peace Conference in Paris]." *Idisher kemfer* (August 9, 1946): 6–7.

"Vegn unzer farfirerishn optimism [Regarding Our Treacherous Optimism]." *Idisher kemfer* (March 8, 1946): 10–12. Incorporated in part into, "Efsher vet geshen a nes? . . ." (1947).

"Vos mir hobn undzere kinder nit gelernt [What We Did not Teach Our Children]." *Undzer veg* [Munich] 32 (May 10, 1946): 5; *Nyu-yorker vokhnblat* (June 14, 1946): 2–3 (reprints from 1945).

"Yeder id in di lagern iz an iyov (a geshprekh mit h. leyvik) [Every Jew in the Camps is a Job (A Conversation with H. Leyvik)]." *Idisher kemfer* (June 14, 1946): 7–8.

"Yidish teater in vilner geto [Yiddish Theater in the Vilna Ghetto]." *Teater-shpigl* (December 1946): 5–7. Preview of *Yerusholayim d'lite*, 248–52.

1947

"Der vitenberg-tog in vilner geto [Wittenberg Day in the Vilna Ghetto]." *YIVO bleter* XXX, no. 2 (1947): 211–13. Preview of *Yerusholayim d'lite*, 442–45.

"Di daytshe meditsinishe farbrekhns farn mishpet fun ershtn internatsyonaln kongres fun doktoyrim in pariz [German Medical Crimes on Trial at the First International Congress of Doctors in Paris; September 1947]." *Shriftn* 87–88 (August–September 1949): 93–102.

"Efsher vet geshen a nes? Problemen fun geto-lebn [Perhaps a Miracle Will Occur? Problems of Ghetto Life]." *In gang* (October–December 1947): 91–93. Reprinted as "Un efsher vet geshen a nes? . . . ," *Kiem* (January 1948): 77–78. Preview of *Yerusholayim d'lite*, 85–88.

"Froyen geboyrne in beyze shoen [Women Born in Evil Times]." *Pyonern-froy* (October 1947): 12–13.

"In topeler gefangenshaft. A kapitl daytsher krigs-gefangenshaft in yor 1939 [In Double Captivity. A Chapter of German War Captivity in 1939]." *Vort* (October 10, 1947): 6.

"Let us throw the anathema against the murderer-doctors [Motion on behalf of the Jewish Medical Association of Palestine at the World Medical Association founding congress, Paris, September 16–21, 1947]." Records of the World Jewish Congress, Jacob Rader Marcus Center of the American Jewish Archives (misdated "9/30/1947"), www.trumanlibrary.org/whistlestop/study_collections/nuremberg/documents/index.php?documentdate=1947-09-30&documentid=C194-3-1&studycollectionid=&pagenumber=1. Published as, "Jetons l'anathème contre la science criminelle nazie," *Revue d'histoire de la médicine hébraïque* 1 (June 1948): 60–63. For a description of the proceedings, biographical sketch of Dworzecki, and annotated text of the motion, see Etienne Lepicard (in "Writings about Dworzecki" below).

"Peysekh in vilner geto [Passover in the Vilna Ghetto]." *Morgn zshurnal* (April 9, 1947). Reprinted in *Kidush hashem*, ed. Shmuel Niger (New York: Tsyko bikher farlag, 1948), 264–66. Reprinted in *Khurbn antologye*, ed. Shmuel Rozshanski [Musterverk series no. 41] (Buenos Aires: Literatur-gezelshaft baym yivo in argentine, 1970), 135–38.

"Sotsyale untersheydn in geto [Social Differentiation in the Ghetto]." *Di tsukunft* (March 1947): 168–72. Preview of *Yerusholayim d'lite*, 151–59. Reprinted in Polish in *Mosty* (1948).

"Tsvishn kloyster-kinder [Among Church-Children; on the opening of a Jewish kindergarten in Paris for the orphans formerly hidden in Catholic institutions in occupied Poland]." *Idisher kemfer* (July 4, 1947): 3–4.

1948

"A mes-les in geto [A Day in the Ghetto]." *Yidishe tsaytung* (April 23, 1948): 4–5 (reprint from 1946); further (October 8, 1948): 3.

"ba-Meh Madlikin? [With What May One Kindle (the Sabbath Lights)?—the opening words of the *Mishna Shabbat*; on the future of the Jewish community in Paris]." *Kiem* (December 1948), 697–700.

"Der novi fun vilner geto [The Prophet of the Vilna Ghetto; on Zelig Kalmanovitsh]." *Idisher kemfer* (September 24, 1948): 4–5. Reprinted from *Yerusholayim d'lite*, 260–64. Reprinted in *Shriftn* 99–100 (August–September 1950): 125–27, 152.

"Di untererdishe shlikhim fun geto tsu geto [The Underground Emissaries from Ghetto to Ghetto]." *Idisher kemfer* (April 1948): 3–4. Expanded version, "Getos un kontsentratsye-lagern" (1949).

"Farshidn zenen geven di vegn" and "Vakh zayn [Be Awake]." In *Kidush hashem*, edited by Shmuel Niger, 730–33. New York: Tsyko bikher farlag, 1948 (partial reprint from 1946).

"Farvos iz gevorn unzer lebn azoy vokhedik? (oyfn rand fun yisroel efroykins bukh 'a khezhbn hanefesh') [Why Has Our Life Become So Ordinary? (Marginal Notes on Israel Efroykin's Book, 'A Spiritual Account-Taking')]." *Kiem* (April 1948): 234–37. Reprinted in *Idisher kemfer* (April 9, 1948): 8–9.

"*Folksgezunt* in geto vilne [*Folksgezunt* (journal on public health) in the Vilna Ghetto]." *Folksgezunt* [Paris] (November 1948): 4.

"Geto oder vald [The Ghetto or the Woods]." *Farn folk* (April 9, 1948): 10.

"Khaneke likht in geto vilne un in di kontsentratsye lagern [Hanukkah Lights in the Vilna Ghetto and in the Concentration Camps]." *Di prese* (December 29, 1948).

"Mayn letster tog in geto [My Last Day in the Ghetto]." *Ibergang* (September 23, 1948): 3. Reprint of *Yerusholayim d'lite*, 466–72.

"'Ne'emane tsyen,' in vilner geto. Di ershte trit fun der vidershtand bavegung ['Faithful of Zion' (Zionist youth group) in the Vilna Ghetto. The First Steps of the Resistance Movement]." *Bafrayung* [Lodz] (April 19, 1948): 3–5.

"O, helf mir dertseyln vos ikh hob gezen . . . (a vort vegn der shlikhes fun eydes) [O, Help Me Recount What I Have Seen . . . (A Word about the Mission of the Witness)]." *Kiem* 9–10 (September–October 1948): 530–34. Interpretive English trans., "What I Saw," in *The Way We Think: A Collection of Essays from the Yiddish*, ed. Joseph Leftwich, vol. 2 (South Brunswick: T. Yoseloff, 1969), 420–24.

"Peysekh in vilner geto." In *Kidush hashem*, edited by Shmuel Niger, 264–66. New York: Tsyko bikher farlag, 1948 (reprint from 1947).

"Różnica socjalne w getcie wileńskim [Social Differences in the Vilna Ghetto]." *Mosty* (April 19, 1948): 34. Translation of *Yerusholayim d'lite*, 151–59.

"Un efsher vet geshen a nes? . . . ." *Kiem* (January 1948): 77–78. Reprint from "Efsher vet geshen" (1947). Preview of *Yerusholayim d'lite*, 85–88.

"Yidishe khurbn-literatur in frantsoyzish [Jewish *Khurbn*-Literature in French]." *Unzer vort* (January 23, 1948): 3.

1949

"Getos un kontsentratsye-lagern zukhn kontaktn [Ghettos and Concentration Camps Seek Contacts]." *Kiem* 2, no. 4 (April 1949): 899–904 (expanded reprint from 1948 "Di untererdishe shlikhim").

"Purim 1943 in vilner geto [Purim 1943 in the Vilna Ghetto]." *Shriftn* (Shevat–Nisan 1949): 32, 83. From *Yerusholayim d'lite*, 417–19. English, "Purim in the Vilna Ghetto," *The Jewish Digest* (February 1956): 9–10.

"Vu is geven di yidishe klole? [Where Was the Jewish Curse?; on the Red Cross]." *Idisher kemfer* (August 26, 1949): 5.

1950

"Der novi fun vilner geto." *Shriftn* 99–100 (August–September 1950): 125–27, 152 (reprint from 1948).

"Sotsyale meditsin in yisroel [Social-Medicine in Israel]." *Idisher kemfer* (July 7, 1950): 4–6.

1952

"Di 'yerusholayim-deklaratsye' vegn meditsinisher etik [The 'Jerusalem Declaration' on Medical Ethics]." *Idisher kemfer* (November 14, 1952): 4–5, 11.

1953

"Dort vu s'iz geshribn gevorn 'dos lid fun oysgehargetn yidishn folk' [There, Where 'The Song of the Murdered Jewish People' Was Written; on Yitskhok Katzenelson]." *Ilustrirte literarishe bleter* (September 1953): 3, 12, 16.

"ha-Historiografiyah shel tekufat-ha-Sho'ah [The Historiography of the Period of the Shoah]." *Davar* (December 11, 1953): 2.

1954

"Der rambam un de filozofye fun der meditsinisher etik [Maimonides and the Philosophy of Medical Ethics]." *Folksgezunt* (May–July 1954).

"Eyrope fun shklafn, on kinder [A Europe of Slaves, without Children]." *Idisher kemfer* (Pesach 1954): 71–76. Summary preview of *Eyrope on kinder* (Jerusalem, 1961).

"Lider klore, shtile [Bright, Still Poems; on Avraham Lev, *Heym un feld* (Tel Aviv, 1953)]." *Di goldene keyt* 18 (1954): 209–12.

"Oyf morgn nokh moshyekhs kumen [On the Morning after the Messiah's Arrival]." *Kiem* 7, nos. 3–4 (October–December 1954): 82–85.

"Yidishe vidershtand-pruvn in di kontsentratsye-lagern fun estland [Jewish Resistance Attempts in the Concentration Camps of Estonia]." *Folk un velt* (April 1954): 15–20.

"Yisroel efroykin [review of three books by Israel Efroykin]." *Di goldene keyt* 20 (1954): 199–212.

1955

"Borkhi nafshi . . . (di ershte nakht in erets-yisroel) [Let My Soul Bless . . . (the First Night in the Land of Israel); from Psalms 103–104 (Let My Soul Bless the Lord)]." *Di tsukunft* (June 1955): 215. Hebrew trans. in *Ben ha-Betarim*, 129–30 (dated November 16, 1949, Tel Aviv).

"Der kemfer, der zinger, der zamler . . . [The Fighter, the Singer, the Collector . . . ; memorial essay on Shmerke Kaczerginski]." In *Shmerke katsherginski ondenk-bukh*, 57–59. Buenos Aires: A kometit, 1955.

"Hamtze menuhah l'sheyres hapleyte [Grant True Rest for the Survivors; the first words of the traditional prayer for the deceased, on H. Leyvik's poetry]." *Di tsukunft* (December 1955): 493–98.

"La Pathologie de la déportation et les séquelles pathologiques des rescapés [The Pathology of Deportation and the Pathological Aftereffects of the Survivors; 3rd World Congress of Jewish Physicians, Haifa, August 11, 1955]." *Revue d'histoire de la médecine hebraïque* 30 (March 1956): 31–41.

"Patologye fun hunger in di getos [Pathology of Starvation in the Ghettos]." *Folksgezunt* 54–55 (1955).`

"Oyf di gasn fun varshe [On the Streets of Warsaw]." *Di goldene keyt* 22 (1955): 199–203.

"Vofn fun byologisher farnikhtung [Weapons of Biological Destruction]." *Ilustrirte literarishe bleter* 3–4 (March–April 1955): 18–19.

"Zey zingen oyf zeyer eygener levaye [They Are Singing at Their Own Funeral]." In *Informatsye-boygn*, 25. New York: Institut far yidishe inyonem, 1955.

1956

"ha-Profesor ha-poshe'a ha-Natzi [The Criminal Nazi Professor]: Karl Klaubarg." *Yedi'ot Yad va-Shem* 6–7 (January 1956): 2–4. Yiddish summary, "Profesor karl klauberg—der natsisher krigs-farbrekher," 23.

"Tsu aykh, brider fun payn un fun vunder [To You, Brothers of Pain and of Wonder]." *Di goldene keyt* 24 (1956): 130–33.

1957

"A blik in der eybikeyt fun yidishn kiem [A Glance at the Eternity of Jewish Existence]." *Ilustrirte literarishe bleter* (March–April 1957): 18, 20.

"In di geto-april-teg: araynfir-vort in 'Ben ha-Betarim' [In the April Ghetto Days: Introductory Word in 'Ben ha-Betarim' (1956)]." *Heymish* 10 (April–Pesach 1957).

1958

"Anton shmidt—an anti-natsisher feldfebl in vilner geto." *Yedies fun yad vashem* 3 (September 1958): 15–17. English, "Anton Schmidt—Anti-Nazi Sergeant in the Vilna Ghetto," *Yad Washem Bulletin* 3 (July 1958): 18–19, 29. Hebrew, "Anton Shmidt: ha-Germani ha-anti-Natzi be-Geto-Vilnah," *Yedi'ot Yad va-Shem* 15–16 (April 1958): 14–16; "Anton Shmidt—Feldvebel anti-Natzi be-Geto-Vilnah," *Yedi'ot Yad va-Shem* 19–20 (May 1959): 6–8.

"Der neshome-forsher (shtrikhn tsu der geshtalt fun prof. fishl shneyurson, z"l) [The Researcher of Souls (A Few Lines on the Figure of Prof. Fishel Schneerson)]." *Di goldene keyt* 31 (1958): 96–106.

"Jewish Medical Resistance During the Catastrophe." In *Extermination and Resistance: Historical Records and Source Material*, vol. 1, edited by Zvi Szner, 117–20. Haifa: Ghetto Fighters' House, 1958.

"Kh'varf op a[vrom] shulmans artikl (a briv in redaktsye) [I Reject A. Shulman's Article (accusing Dworzecki of denigrating the survivors, Yiddish, and the Diaspora)]." *Heymish* 19–20 (January 17, 1958): 16.

1959

"Antologye fun der khalutsisher bavegung [Anthology of the (Zionist) Pioneer Movement; review of Leyb Shpizman, *Khalutsim in Poyln* [*Pioneers in Poland*], vol. 1 (New York, 1959)]." *Heymish* 42–43 (December 1959): 21. Reprinted in *Nyu-yorker vokhnblat* 26, no. 534 (May 1960): 5.

"Di farbrekhns fun di natsi visnshaftler [The Crimes of the Nazi Scientists; report to the World Conference on Crime Prevention], Paris, September 10, 1959." Tel Aviv, 1960. See "Vi daytshe" (1959).

"Doktoyrim-kedoyshim in di getos [Doctor-Martyrs in the Ghettos]." *Folk un velt* (April 1959).

"Dos hot nor gezolt ersht zayn der onheyb . . . [This Would Have Been Only the Beginning (of biological destruction) . . .]." *Heymish* 35–36 (May 13, 1959): 6. Preview of the theme of *Eyrope on kinder* (Jerusalem, 1961).

"Vi daytshe gelernte un doktoyrim hoben mitgearbet mit hitler'n [How German Scholars and Doctors Collaborated with Hitler]." *Forverts* (October 11, 1959): 6, S6. Portion reprinted as "Di farbrekhns" (1961).

1960

"Antologye fun der khalutsisher bavegung." *Nyu-yorker vokhnblat* 26, no. 534 (May 1960): 5 (reprint from 1959).

"Aykhmans IVB4 geshtapo-amt tsu liqvidirn dos eyropeyishe yidntum [Eichmann's Gestapo Office IV B4 to Liquidate European Jewry]." *Heymish* 50–52 (July–September 1960): 53.

"Likht-treger fun yidishn folksshafn [The Light-Bearer of Jewish Folk Creativity; on Yiddish actor Jacob Mansdorf]." In *Yankev mansdorf*, 43–46.

"Oyf di kvorim fun yerusholayim d'lite [At the Graves of Jerusalem of Lithuania (Vilna); on Leyzer Ran, *Ash fun yerusholayim d'lite* (New York, 1959)]." *Di goldene keyt* 38 (1960): 218–20.

Foreword to A. Volf Yasni, *Di geshikhte fun di yidn in lodzsh in di yorn fun der daytscher yidn-oysrotung* [*The History of the Jews in Lodz in the Years of the German Extermination of the Jews*], 7–11. Tel Aviv: Y. L. Perets, 1960.

1961

"Der khurbn-limud in Yisroel [*Khurbn*-Studies in Israel]." *Undzer kiem* 13 (December 1961): 4–5.

"Di farbrekhns fun di natsi-visnshaftler." *Yidishe kultur* 23, no. 4 (April 1961): 4–7 (partial reprint from 1959 "Di daytshe gelernte").

"'Karyere' fun a masn-merder [Career of a Mass Murderer]." *Undzer kiem* 6 (March 1961): 3–4.

1962

"Di geshikhte vos vornt [The History that Warns; on Mordechai Tenenboym-Tamaroff]." *Undzer kiem* 14 (January 1962): 21–22.

"Di yidn in ludmir in loyf fun der geshikhte [The Jews in Ludmir in the Course of History]." *Pinkas Ludmir: Sefer-zikaron li-kehilat Ludmir* [*Volodymyr Volyns'kyi*]. Tel Aviv: Irgun yotz'e Ludmir be-Yisra'el, 1962, Yiddish 45–90; Hebrew 22–44; 607–16 (endnotes in Yiddish only).

"D"r yosef zilberberg." In *Sefer ha-zikaron Sokolov-Podliask*, edited by M. Gelbart, 658–59. Tel Aviv: Irgun yotz'e sokolov-podliask be-yisra'el, 1962 (article dated 1952; original publication not located).

"Neshome-problemen fun der sheyres-hapleyte [Psychological Problems of the Survivors]." *Almanakh fun di yidishe shrayber in yisroel*. Tel Aviv: Farband fun yidishe shrayber un zshurnalistn in yisroel, 1962, 334–45. Reprinted in *Antologye: oysgevortslte un ayngevortslte*, ed. Shmuel Rozshanski [Musterverk series no. 49] (Buenos Aires: Literatur-gezelshaft baym yivo in argentine, 1971), 242–64.

"Ven dos gezets fun dzshungel hot gehersht in di velder . . . [When the Law of the Jungle Ruled in the Fields . . .]." *Undzer kiem* 18 (May 1962): 5–7.

1963

"Adjustment of Detainees to Camp and Ghetto Life and Their Subsequent Readjustment to Normal Society." *Yad Vashem Studies* V (1963): 193–219.

"Di toytn-shtot ponar [The Death-City, Ponar (outside Vilna)]." *Undzer kiem* 31 (October 1963): 12–13.

"Dos shos fun hershl grinshpan un di 'kristal-nakht.' [The Shot by Herschel Grynszpan and 'Kristallnacht']." *Undzer kiem* 32–33 (November–December 1963): 22–23.

"4 yor katedre fun khurbn un vidershtand in universitet bar-ilan, yisroel [4 Years of the Chair for Destruction and Resistance at Bar Ilan University, Israel]." *Undzer kiem* 28 (May 1963): 9–10, 16.

"Le traitement des asthénies et des anxiétés, séquelles de la pathologie concentrationnaire et post-concentrationnaire [The Treatment of Depression and Anxiety, Aftereffects of Concentrationary and Post-Concentrationary Pathology]." (Paris, 1963). (With Louis S. Copelman.) See *Archives et manuscrits de la Bibliothèque de l'Académie nationale de médecine*, http://ccfr.bnf.fr/portailccfr/jsp/ccfr/sitemap/ead_sitemap_view.jsp?record=eadcalames%3AEADC%3ACalames-2012614126343078.

1964

"Di katsetn-patologye [Concentration Camp Pathology]." *Undzer kiem* 34 (January 1964): 14–15.

"Ikh hob getroymt tsu zayn a held fun a legende [I Dreamed of Being a Hero of a Legend; on Hirsh Glik]." *Undzer kiem* 40–41 (July–August 1964): 5–7. Early version of chapters 1 and 2, *Hirshke glik*.

"Zog nisht keynmol az du geyst dem letstn veg . . . [Never Say that You're on Your Last Journey . . . ; on Hirsh Glik]." *Undzer kiem* 43 (December 1964): 2–3. Early version of chapter 3, *Hirshke glik*.

1965

"Der letster veg fun hirshke glik [The Final Journey of Hirsh Glick]." *Undzer kiem* 47 (April 1965): 3–5. Early version of chapter 5, *Hirshke glik*.

"Der royter krayts beys di khurbn-yorn [The Red Cross During the War Years]." *Folksgezunt* [Paris] (January–February 1965).

"Der velt-tsuzamenkunft far der geshikhte fun antinatsishe vidershtand in eyrope [The World Congress for the History of Anti-Nazi Resistance in Europe; 12th International Congress of Historical Sciences, Vienna, August–September, 1965]." *Undzer kiem* 52–53 (October–November, 1965): 14–17.

"Lebn un shafn fun hirshke glik in di katsetn [The Life and Creativity of Hirsh Glick in the Camps]." *Undzer kiem* 46 (March 1965): 15–17. Early version of chapter 4, *Hirshke glik*.

"'Toytmarshn', 'toytrayzes' un 'toytshifn'—a kapitl geshikhte vegn di letste teg in di katsetn ['Death Marches', 'Death Journeys' and 'Death Ships'—A Chapter of History on the Last Days in the Camps]." *Unzer kiem* 49–50-51 (October 1965): 101–3.

1966

"Vilner vos zenen gelofn: fun ponar—fun di deportatsye-banen—fun di estishe katsetn [Vilna Jews who Ran: from Ponar—from the Deportation Trains—from the Estonian Camps; as another form of resistance]." *Di goldene keyt* 57 (1966): 198–211.

1967

"Di goyrldike konferents vegn der yidisher 'end-leyzung', [The Fateful Conference on the Jewish 'Final Solution' (the Wannsee Conference)]." *Undzer kiem* 67 (January 1967): 3–7.

"Katsetn-sistem un yidisher non-konformizm" (The Camp System and Jewish Nonconformism; from his doctoral lecture at the Sorbonne). *Undzer kiem* 72–75 (June–September 1967): 7–11.

"Yisroel beys der genosid-sakone [Israel during the Genocide Danger; on the Six-Day War]." *Undzer kiem* 76 (October 1967): 3–4.

Foreword to Tehila Tiktin-Fertig, *Mitn farvorloztn kind* [*With the Abandoned Child*], unnumbered pp. 5–6. Tel Aviv: Hamenorah, 1967.

1968

"Der yidisher oyfshtand fun oyshvits [The Jewish Uprising of Auschwitz]." *Undzer kiem* 82 (April 1968): 2–4. Reprinted in *ba-Yamim ha-hem . . . : 25 shanah le-mered ha-geta'ot / In yene teg . . . : 25ster yor-tog fun oyfshtand in di getos*, ed. Hayah Lazar (Tel Aviv: n.p., April 1968), 40–48.

"Greetings on behalf of the Committee of Organizations of Partisans, Fighters and Prisoners." In *Jewish Resistance During the Holocaust: Proceedings of the Conference on Manifestations of Jewish Resistance, Jerusalem, April 7–11, 1968*, 20–22 (Jerusalem: Yad Vashem, 1971).

"In ibermentshlekhn gerangl mit toyt un umkum [The Superhuman Struggle with Death and Extermination; on the work of the Oeuvre de Secours aux Enfants (OSE; in original Russian, OZE)]." In *In kamf farn gezunt fun idishn folk (50 yor "oze")*, edited by L. Vulman, 58–79. New

York: Velt-farband "oze," 1968 (condensed version of *Kamf farn gezunt in geto-vilne*).

"The Day-To-Day Stand of the Jews." In *Jewish Resistance During the Holocaust: Proceedings of the Conference on Manifestations of Jewish Resistance, Jerusalem, April 7–11, 1968*, 152–81; 186–90 (reply); 427–29 (debate). Jerusalem: Yad Vashem, 1971. Reprinted in *The Catastrophe of European Jewry: Antecedents—History—Reflections: Selected Papers*, ed. Yisrael Gutman and Livia Rothkirchen (Jerusalem: Yad Vashem, 1976), 367–99. Reprinted as "Daily Survival in the Ghettos and Camps," in Gutman and Rothkirchen, *The Holocaust of the European Jews* (Jerusalem: Yad Vashem, 1980), 281–90. Hebrew, "ha-'Amidah be-haye-yom-yom ba-geta'ot uve-mahanot," in *ha-'Amidah ha-Yehudit be-tekufat ha-Sho'ah* (Jerusalem: Yad Vashem, 1970), 121–43; in *Sho'at Yehude Eropah: Reka, Korot, Mashma'ut*, ed. Gutman and Rothkirchen (Jerusalem: Yad Vashem, 1973), 269–93; and in *Sho'ah u-gevurah: reka, korot, mashma'ut, mivhar ma'amarim* (Jerusalem: Yad Vashem, 1975), 13–26.

Foreword to Toni Solomon-Ma'aravi, *Teg fun tsorn* [*Days of Anger*], 7–9. Tel Aviv: Hamenorah, 1968; English iv–vii.

1969

"Dos kultur lebn in di estonishe lagern [Cultural Life in the Estonian Camps]." *Di tsukunft* (April 1969): 114–25. Preview of *Vayse nekht un shvartse teg*, 301–29.

"Lomir shvaygn [Let Us Remain Silent]." *Di tsukunft* (April 1969): 119–23. Preview of *Vayse nekht un shvartse teg*, 114–25.

"Nisht farlirn dem tseylem-ha-odem [Do not Lose the Image of Man]." *Di tsukunft* (November 1969): 369–74.

1970

"Di vos zeyer haynt iz bashotnt mitn nekhtn [Those Whose Present Lies in the Shadow of Yesterday; on L. Kurland, *Oyfn veg tsu zikh* [*On the Way Back*] (Paris, 1967)]." *Di goldene keyt* 68 (1970): 219–21.

"Farshidn zenen geven di vegn." In *Der gaystiker vidershtand fun yidn in getos un lagern*, edited by Menashe Unger, 52. Tel Aviv: ha-Menorah, 1970 (partial reprint from 1946).

"Peysekh in vilner geto." In *Khurbn antologye*, edited by Shmuel Rozshanski [Musterverk series no. 41], 135–38. Buenos Aires: Literatur-gezelshaft baym yivo in argentine, 1970 (reprint from 1947).

1971

"Der mentsh in thom (draysik yor zint vilner geto) [Man in the Abyss (Thirty Years since the Vilna Ghetto)]." *Di goldene keyt* 74 (1971): 73–82.

"Neshome-problemen fun der sheyres-hapleyte." In *Antologye: oysgevortslte un ayngevortslte*, edited by Shmuel Rozshanski [Musterverk series no. 49], 242–64. Buenos Aires: Literatur-gezelshaft baym yivo in argentine, 1971 (reprint from 1962).

1972

"Kinder fun baheltenishn [Children of Hiding Places]." *Folk un tsyen* 7–8 (March–April 1972).

1973

"Mishpahat Dvorzʹetzki [The Dworzecki Family]." In *Sefer-zikaron li-kehilat Meytshet*, edited by Ben-Tzion H. Ayalon, 211–17. Tel Aviv: Irgun yotzʹe Meytshet be-Yisraʹel uve-hutz-la-aretz, 1973. English trans. by Ron Rabinovitch, "The Dworzecky Family," www.jewishgen.org/yizkor/Molchadz/mol207.html#Page211. Print-on-demand hard copy, *Memorial Book of the Molchad (Maytchet) Jewish Community: Translation of Sefer zikaron le-kehilat Meytshet* (JewishGen, 2015), www.jewishgen.org/yizkor/ybip/YBIP_Molchad.html.

"Partizanim ve-Yehude-ha-ʻayarot be-ʻayarot Meytshet [Partisans and Forest Jews in the Forests of Maytchet]." Idem, 346–66. English trans. by Ariel Dvorjetski and Jerrold Landau, "Partisans and the Jews in the Forests of Maytchet," www.jewishgen.org/yizkor/Molchadz/mol335.html#Page346.

1974

"Dos togbukh fun lerer moyshe olitski [The Diary of Teacher Moshe Olitzki]." In *Vilner zamlbukh / Meʾasef Vilnah*, edited by Yisrael Rudnitski, 96–105. Tel Aviv: Igud ʻolami shel yotzʹe Vilnah veha-sevivah be-Yisraʹel, 1974. Hebrew condensation, "ʻYeven Metzulah' (yoman Geto-Vilnah me-et ha-moreh Moshe Olitzki)," *Korot* 6, nos. 7–8 (June 1974).

"The International Red Cross and its Policy vis-à-vis the Jews in Ghettos and Concentration Camps in Nazi-Occupied Europe." In *Rescue Attempts During the Holocaust: proceedings of the Second Yad Vashem International Historical Conference, Jerusalem. April 8–11, 1974*, 71–122. Jerusalem: Yad Vashem, 1977. Reprinted in *The Nazi Holocaust*, vol. 8: Bystanders to the Holocaust; vol. 3, ed. Michael R. Marrus (Westport: Meckler, 1989), 1133–72. Hebrew, "ha-Tselav ha-adom ha-benle'umi ve-yahaso la-Yehudim be-aratsot ha-kibush ha-Natzi be-geta'ot uve-mahanot ha-rikuz," in *Nisyonot u-fe'ulot hatsalah bi-tekufat ha-Sho'ah*, ed. Yisrael Gutman (Jerusalem: Yad Vashem, 1976), 56–87.

1991

"Zog nit keyn mol az du geyst dem letstn veg! [Never Say You Are on the Final Journey!; on Hirsh Glick, author of the partisan hymn]." In *Yidish-literatur in medines-yisroel: antologye*, vol. 1, 256–60. Tel Aviv: Fareyn fun yidishe shrayber un zshurnalistn in yisroel, 1991 (with photo and short bio; condensed reprint from 1966 *Hirshke glik*).

Online Video Recording of Dworzecki

Dworzecki's testimony at the Eichmann Trial, Jerusalem, 1961, https://youtu.be/9MfBeMc3ksc?t=216.

Writings about Dworzecki

"Berit 'Ivrit Tzarfat' [Hebrew Union of France; announcement of a lecture to be given on May 27, 1945 by Dworzecki on "ha-'Avodah ha-tarbutit be-Geto shel Vilnah" (Cultural Work in the Vilna Ghetto) (1941–1943)]." *Unzer vort* (May 25, 1945): 3.

"Derefent di gas u. n. fun artur ziglboym [Street Opened in the Name of Arthur Zygielbaum; on Dworzecki's speech representing Yad Vashem]." *Lebns-fragn* 138–39 (June–July 1963): 10.

"Dr. Mark Dworzecki and other members of the Art and History Lovers of Krakow Antiquities standing in the courtyard of the Wawel Royal Castle" (photo: date and provenance unknown; more correctly, Society of History and Antiquities of Krakow / Towarzystwo Miłośników Historii i Zabytków Krakowa), www.eilatgordinlevitan.com/krakow/krkw_pix/art/012608_47_b.gif and www.eilatgordinlevitan.com/radoshkovichi/r_images/archives/121508_34_b.gif.

"1-ter tsuzamenfor fun yidishe doktoyrim fun vilner un navaredker kant [1st Meeting of Jewish Doctors from the Vilna and Nowogródek District; May 16–17, 1937]," bilingual Yiddish–Polish program booklet. YIVO Archives, RG 29, F 143.1, http://polishjews.yivoarchives.org/archive/?p=digitallibrary/digitalcontent&id=2134#.

"Fun organizatsyoneln lebn [From Organizational Life]." *Lebns-fragn* 115–16 (May–June 1961): 22–23.

"Groyser 'undzer kiem'-ovent mit der bateylikung fun dr. m. dvorzshetski [Great 'Undzer kiem' ('Our Existence' Publishing House) Evening with the Participation of Dr. M. Dworzecki; February 4, 1967]." *Undzer kiem* 67 (January 1967): unnumbered inside front cover.

"ha-Haktzavot le-hinukh ule-tarbut [The Allocations for Education and Culture; on Dworzecki's proposal for a chair in Yiddish at the Hebrew University]." *Davar* (December 24, 1946): 1.

"Już ukazał się miesięcznik 'Mosty' nr 2 (10) [*Mosty* Monthly Ready to Appear]." *Mosty* (February/Lutego 18, 1947): 4 (listing among the anticipated contents an article by Dworzecki on Hebrew theater in the Vilna Ghetto, apparently not published).

"Khronik [Chronicle]." *Kiem* (February 1948): 63; (May 1948): 349; (June 1948): 411; (September–October 1948): 602; (November 1948): 668; (December 1948): 715; (January 1949): 795; (April 1949): 954; (June 1949): 1081; (September–October 1949): 1244.

"Literarisher ovent in tel-aviv tsum dershaynen fun bukh 'hirshke glik' [Literary Evening in Tel Aviv on the Publication of the Book 'Hirshke glik']." *Undzer kiem* 67 (January 1967): inside front cover.

"Three Authors Win Prizes for Best Works of Jewish Literature in 1957." *Jewish Telegraphic Agency* (December 27, 1957), www.jta.org/1957/12/27/archive/three-authors-win-prizes-for-best-works-of-jewish-literature-in-1957.

"Tikun toes [Errata; corrected information on the Dworzecki Prize for Holocaust literature from his widow]." *Lebns-fragn* 107–8 (November–December 1977): 19.

"Viku'ah ivrit-idish ba-agudat ha-sofrim be-Vilna [Hebrew-Yiddish Conflict in Writers Union in Vilna]." *Davar* (March 6, 1932): 2.

"Yerlekhe farzamlung fun yidishn literatn un zshurnalistn-fareyn [Annual Gathering of the Yiddish Writers and Journalists Union]." *Lebns–fragn* 70–71 (June–July 1957): 25.

Cohen, Boaz. "Dr Meir (Mark) Dworzecki: the historical mission of a survivor historian." *Holocaust Studies* 21, nos. 1–2 (2015): 24–37.

Dworzecki, H[asia]. Dworzecki bibliography in *'Iyunim bi-tekufat ha-Sho'ah: asupat ma'amarim le-zikhro shel Prof. Me'ir Dvorz'etzki z"l*, edited by Mordecai Eliav, 129–39. Jerusalem: Bar-Ilan University, 1979.

Eliav, Mordecai, ed. *'Iyunim bi-tekufat ha-Sho'ah: asupat ma'amarim le-zikhro shel Prof. Me'ir Dvorz'etzki z"l* [*Studies on the Period of the Shoah: Collected*

Papers in Memory of Prof. Meir Dworzecki, of Blessed Memory]. Jerusalem: Bar-Ilan University, 1979.

Fridman, Filip. Review of *Yerusholayim d'lite in kamf un umkum* (Paris, 1948). *Kiem* (June 1948): 406–7.

Glatshteyn, Yankev. "*Yerusholayim d'lite* [review]." In *In tokh genumen*, vol. I, 176–81. Buenos Aires: Farlag poale-tsyon hitahdut, 1960 (reprinted from his column in *Idisher kemfer*, 1949).

Heiman, Leo. "Jewish Doctors' Immortal Work in Nazi-Made Ghettos." *The Jewish Digest* (March 1960): 25–29.

Kahan [Kagan], Berl. "Dvorzshetski, Mark," *Leksikon fun yidish-shraybers*, 191–93. New York: Rayah Ilman-Kagan, 1986 (replaces the entry in NLYL).

Kaganovitsh, M. "'Yerusholayim d'lite in kamf un umkum' fun d"r m. dvorzshetski [review]." *Farn folk* 25 (June 11, 1948): 13–14.

Kaplan, Yisroel. "Yidn-katsetn in tsofn [Camps for Jews in the North (Estonia); on Dworzecki's *Vayse nekht*]." *Di goldene keyt* 72 (1971): 244–46.

Kersh, Y. "*Vayse nekht un shvartse teg* [review]." *Lebns-fragn* 226–27 (January–February 1971): 15.

Korn, Yisroel. "Dr. m. dvorzshetski—vunder fun der sheyres-hapleyte [Wonder of the Survivors]." *Forverts* (December 22, 1963): 2. Reprinted as "Dr. m. dvorzshetski—laurat fun der meditsin-akademye in frankraykh [Laureate of the Physicians' Conference in France]." *Undzer kiem* 34 (January 1964): 12–13.

Krell, Robert, and Marc I. Sherman. *Medical and Psychological Effects of Concentration Camps on Holocaust Survivors* (vol. 4 in the series, *Genocide: A Critical Bibliographic Review*), 89 (on Dworzecki). Jerusalem: Transaction Publishers, 1997.

Lepicard, Etienne. "Jewish Medical Association of Palestine. Motion to the World Medical Association ([September 16–21,] 1947)." In *Silence, Scapegoats, Self-Reflection: The Shadow of Nazi Medical Crimes on Medicine and Bioethics*, edited by Volker Roelcke et al., 315–26. Göttingen: V&R Academic, 2014.

Mark, Ber [anon.; editor]. "Biblyografishe notitsn [Bibliographical Notes]." *Dos naye lebn* (April 9, 1948): 5.

Mestl, Yankev. "Kamf farn gezunt in vilner geto [review]." *Yidishe kultur* 9, no. 2 (February 1947): 60–63.

Oyerbakh, Rokhl. "Tikun khatses [(Hebrew, Tikun Hatzot); Midnight Prayer; on Dworzecki's *Ben ha-Betarim*]." *Di goldene keyt* 27 (1957): 279–83.

Ravitch, Melekh. "Dr. mark dvorzshetski," *Mayn leksikon*, vol. 3. Montreal: a komitet, 1958, 151–52.

Shmulevitsh, Y. "Yisroyl doktor vos hot antdekt a merkvirdige arkhiv fun natsi lager in terezienshtat [Israeli Doctor Who Discovered a Notable Archive of the Nazi Camp in Theresienstadt]." *Forverts* (September 12, 1959): 2–3.

Zilbertsvayg, Zalmen. "Diana Blumenfeld-Turkov," *Leksikon fun yidishn teater*, vol. 4, 3179–91. New York: Yidisher aktyorn yunye in amerike, 1963.

General Bibliography

Scope: Works consulted—other than those in the five preceding bibliographies of works by and about specific "Yiddish historians of the Holocaust."

"Argentina." *American Jewish Yearbook 1951* (New York: American Jewish Committee, 1952), 221–22.

"A ringele in der keyt [A Ring in the Chain]." *Dos naye lebn* (Yubiley oysgabe 1947): 1.

"Biblyografye fun di shriftn fun prof. ber (bernard) mark [Bibliography of the Writings of Prof. Ber Mark]." *Bleter far geshikhte* XXVI (1988): 240–360.

Bleter vegn vilne: zamlbukh [Pages on Vilna: Compendium]. Lodz: Tsentraler yidisher historisher komisye in poyln, 1947.

Die Judenpogrome in Russland, 2 vols. Cologne-Leipzig: Zionist Organisation, 1910.

"Dos zamlbukh Oyshvits [The Auschwitz Compendium]." *YIVO bleter* XXVII, no. 1 (Spring 1946): 194–97.

"Ekspertize fun mgr. arn ayzenbakh: der umkum fun di yidn in 'varte-land' un di rol fun lodzsher talyen hans bibov [The Expertise of Magister Artur Eisenbach: The Extermination of the Jews in the "Warthegau" and the Role of Lodz Hangman Hans Biebow]." *Dos naye lebn* (April 28, 1947): 3.

"Farshartkn unzer onteyl in der sotsyalistisher boyung: barikht-referat fun y. lazebnik [Strengthen Our Participation in Building Socialism: Report by Y. Lazebnik]." *Dos naye lebn* (November 21, 1949): 6.

"Fun der tetikayt fun di yivo-fraynd in yisroel." *Yedies fun YIVO* 46 (September 1952): 3; English, "Activity of Friends of YIVO in Israel," *News of the YIVO* 46 (September 1952): 5*.

"Hartsike oyfname far d"r rafoel mahler in vlotslav: derefenung fun kurs fun yidisher geshikhte [Hearty Reception for Dr. Raphael Mahler in Wrocław: Opening of Course on Jewish History]." *Dos naye lebn* (September 28, 1947): 5.

"Jewish Teachers Seminary Celebrates First Degree-Granting Program." *Jewish Telegraphic Agency* (January 10, 1962), www.jta.org/1962/01/10/archive/jewish-teachers-seminary-celebrates-first-degree-granting-program.

"Martin Broszat and Saul Friedländer: A Controversy about the Historicization of National Socialism." *Yad Vashem Studies* 19 (1988): 1–47.

Payn un gvure in der yidisher over in likht fun der kegnvart [*Pain and Heroism in the Jewish Past in Light of the Present*]. Warsaw: Dror, July–August 1940.

Pinkes: a fertlyoriker zshurnal for yidisher literaturgeshikhte, shprakhforshung, folklor un biblyografye, band 1 [*Chronicle: A Quarterly Journal for Yiddish Literary History, Linguistics, Folklore and Bibliography, vol. 1*] 1927–1928. New York: YIVO amerikaner sektsye, 1928.

"Program of the Twenty-Third Annual Conference of the YIVO." *News of the YIVO* 30 (December 1948): 6*.

Prospekt fun di oysgabn fun der tsentraler yidisher historisher komisye in poyln [*Prospectus of the Publications of the Central Jewish Historical Commission in Poland*]. Warsaw-Lodz-Krakow: Tsentraler yidisher historisher komisye in poyln, 1947.

"Protokol fun der zitsung fun prezydyum fun der historisher komisye, 29ster april 1938 [Minutes of the Meeting of the Presidium of the Historical Commission]." *YIVO bleter* XLVI (1975): 301–2.

"Rede fun B. Mark oyf der geto-akademye in varshe [Speech of Ber Mark at the Ghetto Conference in Warsaw]." *Dos naye lebn* (May 3, 1946): 6.

"Sesye funem veltrat fun yad-vashem [Session of the World Council of Yad Vashem; 19 April 1956]." *Yedi'ot Yad va-Shem* 10–11 (August 1956): 30–33; Hebrew 7–12, 14; English 35.

Tsaytshrift far yidisher geshikhte, demografye un ekonomik, literatur-forshung, shprakhvisnshaft un etnografye [*Periodical for Jewish History, Demography and Economics, Literary History, Linguistics and Ethnography*] II–III. Minsk: Institut far vaysruslenisher kultur—yidisher sekstye, 1928.

"Tsen yor zaml-, forshung-, un farlag-arbet vegn geshikhte fun yidn in poyln [Ten Years Collection-, Research-, and Publishing-Work on the History of Jews in Poland]." *Bleter far geshikhte* VII, nos. 2–3 (April–August 1954): 8, 9, 11, 13, 18.

"Visnshaftlekhe zitsungen fun der tsentr. yid. historisher komisye [Academic Meetings of the CJHC]." *Dos naye lebn* (November 1, 1946): 9.

"YIVO tetikayt in medines-yisroel" / "Activities of the 'Friends of YIVO' in Israel." *Yedies fun YIVO / News of the YIVO* 50 (September 1953): 4; English 4*.

Abramson, Henry. "Historiography on the Jews and the Ukrainian Revolution." *Journal of Ukrainian Studies* 15, no. 2 (Winter 1990): 33–45.
Adorno, Theodor W. "Commitment." In *Aesthetics and Politics*, edited by Ernst Bloch et al., 77–95. London: New Left Books, 1977.
Aharony, Michal. *Hannah Arendt and the Limits of Total Domination: The Holocaust, Plurality, and Resistance.* New York: Routledge, 2015.
Aleksiun, Natalia. "From Galicia to Warsaw: Interwar Historians of Polish Jewry." In *Warsaw. The Jewish Metropolis*, edited by Glenn Dynner and François Guesnet, 370–89. Leiden: Brill Academic Publishing, 2015.
———. "Polish Jewish Historians Before 1918: Configuring the liberal East European Jewish intelligentsia." *East European Jewish Affairs* 34, no. 2 (2004): 41–54.
———. "The Central Jewish Historical Commission in Poland 1944–1947." *Polin* 20 (2007): 75–97.
———. "The Vicious Circle: Jews in Communist Poland, 1944–1956." *Studies in Contemporary Jewry* XIX (2003): 157–80.
Aleksiun-Madrzak, Natalia. "Ammunition in the Struggle for National Rights: Jewish historians in Poland between the Two World Wars." PhD diss., New York University, 2010.
An-ski, Sh. *Khurbn galitsye: der yidisher khurbn fun poyln, galitsye un bukovina fun tog-bukh* [*The Jewish Khurbn in Poland, Galicia and Bukovina from (My) Diary*] *1914–1917* in his *Gezamlte shriftn*, vols. 4–6. Vilna-Warsaw-New York: Farlag an-ski, 1921–22.
Apfelbaum, Emil. *Maladie de famine: Recherches cliniques sur la famine exécutées dans le ghetto de Varsovie en 1942.* Warsaw: American Joint Distribution Committee, 1946.
Applegate, Celia. "A Europe of Regions: Reflections on the Historiography of Sub-National Places in Modern Times." *American Historical Review* 104, no. 4 (October 1999): 1157–82.
Arendt, Hannah. "Eichmann in Jerusalem—I." *The New Yorker* (February 16, 1963): 40–113; "Eichmann in Jerusalem—III" (March 2, 1963): 40–91.
———. *Eichmann in Jerusalem. A Report on the Banality of Evil.* New York: The Viking Press, 1963.
———. "Social Science Techniques and the Study of Concentration Camps." *Jewish Social Studies* XII (January 1950): 49–64.
Ayzen, A. [Avrom Ajzen]. *Dos gaystike ponem fun geto* [*The Spiritual Face of the Ghetto*] (Mexico [City]: Yidishe kultur-tsenter in Meksike, 1950).
Ayzenbakh, A. [Artur Eisenbach]. "A vikhtiker historisher dokument tsu der geshikhte fun yid. vidershtand bavegung in galitsye [An Important

Historical Document on the History of the Jewish Resistance Movement in Galicia]." *Dos naye lebn* (March 11, 1949): 4.

Baár, Monika. *Historians and Nationalism: East-Central Europe in the Nineteenth Century.* Oxford: Oxford University Press, 2010.

Baker, Zachary M. *Essential Yiddish Books: 1000 Great Works from the Collection of the National Yiddish Book Center: Introduction.* (N.p., n.p., [2004]), www.yiddishbookcenter.org/collections/digital-yiddish-library/1000-essential-yiddish-books.

Balaban, Majer [Meyer/Meir]. *Die Judenstadt von Lublin* [*The Jewish City of Lublin*]. Berlin: Jüdischer Verlag, 1919; Yiddish, *Di yidn-shtot lublin* (Buenos Aires: Tsentral farband fun poylishe yidn in argentine, 1947).

———. "Unzere kunst—un kultur—oytseres [Our Art—and Culture—Treasures]." *Literarishe bleter* (October 18, 1929): 818–20; (October 25, 1929): 839–40; (November 1, 1929): 860–61; (November 15, 1929): 903–4; (November 22, 1929): 913–15.

———. *Yidn in poyln* [*Jews in Poland*]. Vilna: Kletskin, 1930.

Baron, Salo. "Opening Remarks [at conference on 'Problems of Research in the Study of the Jewish Catastrophe 1939–1945,' New York, April 3, 1949]." *Jewish Social Studies* XII, no. 1 (January 1950): 13–16.

Bauer, Yehuda. *Rethinking the Holocaust.* New Haven: Yale University Press, 2001.

———. *The Jewish Emergence from Powerlessness.* Toronto: Unversity of Toronto Press, 1979.

———. "The Problem of Non-Armed Jewish Reactions to Nazi Rule in Eastern Europe." In *New Currents in Holocaust Research*, edited by Jeffry M. Diefendorf, 55–68. Evanston: Northwestern University Press, 2004.

———. *They Chose Life: Jewish Resistance in the Holocaust.* New York: American Jewish Committee, 1973.

Bauer, Yehuda and Malcolm Lowe, "Introduction." In *The Holocaust as Historical Experience*, edited by Yehuda Bauer and Nathan Rotenstreich, vii–xiv. New York: Holmes & Meier, 1981.

Bauer, Yehuda and Aharon Weiss. "Historiography of the Holocaust." *Encyclopaedia Judaica 1977/78 Year Book*, edited by Pinchas Hacohen Peli, 218–21. Jerusalem: Keter, 1979.

Bayder, Khaym [Chaim Beider]. *Leksikon fun yidishe shrayber in ratn-farband* [*Lexicon of Yiddish Writers in the Soviet Union*], edited by Boris Sandler and Gennady Estraikh. New York: Alveltlekhn yidishn kultur-kongres, 2011.

Bédarida, François and Renée. *La Résistance spirituelle 1941–1944: Les Cahiers clandestins du Témoignage chrétien.* Paris: Michel, 2001.

Beinfeld, Solon. "Health Care in the Vilna Ghetto." *Holocaust and Genocide Studies* 12, no. 1 (Spring 1998): 88–98.

———. "Life in the Ghettos of Eastern Europe." In *Genocide: Critical Issues of the Holocaust*, edited by Alex Grobman and Daniel Landes, 173–89. Los Angeles-Chappaqua: Rossel Books, 1983.

———. "The Cultural Life of the Vilna Ghetto." *Simon Wiesenthal Center Annual* 1 (1984): 5–25.

Bemporad, Elissa. *Becoming Soviet Jews: The Bolshevik experiment in Minsk*. Bloomington: Indiana University Press, 2013.

Berg, Nicolas. "Joseph Wulf, A Forgotten Outsider Among Holocaust Scholars." In *Holocaust Historiography in Context: Emergence, Challenges, Polemics and Achievements*, edited by David Bankier and Dan Michman, 167–206. Jerusalem: Yad Vashem, 2008.

Bernfeld, Shimon. "Knekhtshaft un bafrayung fun yidishn folk: a historish bild [Slavery and Liberation of the Jewish People: A Historical Picture]." *Dos leben* (April 1905): 4–17; (May 1905): 59–74.

———. *Sefer ha-Dema'ot [Book of Tears]*, 3 vols. Berlin: Eshkol, 1923–26.

Berning, Cornelia. *Vom "Abstammungnachweis" zum "Zuchtwart": Vokabular des Nationalsozialismus [Vocabulary of Nazism]*. Berlin: De Gruyter, 1964.

Bernstein, Michael André. *Foregone Conclusions: Against Apocalyptic History*. Berkeley: University of California Press, 1994.

Bernstein, Mordechai V. *Nisht derbrente shaytn [Unburnt Embers]*. Buenos Aires: YIVO, 1956.

Bettleheim, Bruno. "Individual and Mass Behavior in Extreme Situations." *Journal of Abnormal and Social Psychology* XXXVIII (1943): 417–52.

———. *The Informed Heart: Autonomy in a Mass Age*. New York: Free Press of Glencoe, 1960.

Biderman, Israel M. *Mayer Balaban: Historian of Polish Jewry*. New York: Dr. I. M. Biderman Book Committee, 1976.

Bikl, Shloyme. "Di tsaytshrift 'Di yudishe (idishe) velt,' [The Periodical 'The Jewish World']." In *Pinkes far der forshung fun der yidisher literatur un prese*, vol. 1, edited by Shloyme Bikl, 122–70. New York: Alveltlekhn yidishn kultur-kongres, 1965.

———. [editor] *Di yidishe esey: a zamlung [The Yiddish Essay: A Collection]*. New York: Farlag matones, 1946.

Bloxham, Donald and Tony Kushner. *The Holocaust: Critical Historical Approaches*. Manchester: Manchester University Press, 2005.

Borokhov, Ber. "Di biblyoteyk fun'm yidishn filolog: firhundert yor yidishe shprakhforshung [The Bibliography of the Yiddish Philologist: Four Hundred Years of Yiddish Linguistics]." In *Der pinkes: yor-bukh far der geshikhte fun der yidisher literature un shprakh, far folklor, kritik un biblyografye*, edited by Sh. Niger, separate pp. 1–66. Vilna: Kletskin, [1913].

Brenner, Michael. *Prophets of the Past: Interpreters of Jewish History*. Princeton: Princeton University Press, 2010.

Broszat, Martin. "A Plea for the Historicization of National Socialism." In *Reworking the Past: Hitler, the Holocaust, and the Historians' Debate*, edited by Peter Baldwin, 77–87. Boston: Beacon Press, 1990.

Browning, Christopher R. *Remembering Survival: Inside a Nazi Slave-Labor Camp*. New York: Norton, 2010.

Calvör, Caspar. *Gloria Christi*. Leipzig, 1710.

Cherikover, E. [Eliyohu/Elias Tcherikower]. *Antisemitizm un pogromen in ukrayine 1917–1918: tsu der geshikhte fun ukrayinish-yidishe batsyungen* [*on the History of Ukrainian-Jewish Relations*]. Berlin: Mizrekh-yidishn historisn arkhiv, 1923.

———. "Ber Borokhov—vi ikh ken im [As I Know Him]." *Literarishe bleter* (December 23, 1927): 999–1000; (December 30, 1927): 1023–24.

———. "Di maskilim, nikolay der ershter un di idishe masen [The Maskilim, Nicholas I, and the Jewish Masses]." *Di tsukunft* (July 1939): 409–13.

———. *Di ukrayiner pogromen in yor 1919* [*The Ukrainian Pogroms in 1919*]. New York: YIVO, 1965.

———. "Di yidishe historishe visnshaft in mizrekh-eyrope [Jewish Historical Scholarship in Eastern Europe; Russian-Jewish only]." *YIVO bleter* I, no. 2 (February 1931): 97–113.

———. [editor] *Geshikhte fun der yidisher arbeter-bavegung in di fareynikte shtatn* [*History of the Jewish Labor Movement in the United States*], 2 vols. New York, 1943, 1945.

———. Preface to *Historishe shriftn* I (Warsaw, 1929): unnumbered pp. i–ii.

———. "Yidishe buntn gegen di gezeyres fun nikolay dem ershtn [Jewish Rebellions against the Decrees of Nicholas I]." *Di tsukunft* (March 1939): 175–79.

———. "Yidishe historiografye [Jewish Historiography]." *Algemeyne entsiklopedye*, vol. Yidn I, 284–302. Paris: Dubnov-fond, 1939.

———. "Yidishe martirologye un yidishe historiografye." *YIVO bleter* XVII, no. 2 (March–April 1941): 97–112. English, "Jewish Martyrology and Jewish Historiography," *YIVO Annual of Jewish Social Science* 1 (1946): 9–23.

———. [editor] *Yidn in frankraykh* [*Jews in France*], 2 vols. New York: YIVO, 1942.

Cohen, Beth. "The Myth of Silence: Survivors tell a different story." In *After the Holocaust: Challenging the Myth of Silence*, edited by David Cesarani and Eric J. Sundquist, 181–91. London: Routledge, 2011.

Cohen, Boaz. *Israeli Holocaust Research: Birth and Evolution*, trans. Agnes Vazsonyi. Abingdon-New York: Routledge, 2013.

———. "Representing the Experiences of Children in the Holocaust." In *"We Are Here": New Approaches to Jewish Displaced Persons in Postwar Germany*, edited by Avinoam J. Patt and Michael J. Berkowitz, 74–97. Detroit: Wayne State University Press, 2010.

———. "Setting the Agenda of Holocaust Research: Discord at Yad Vashem in the 1950s." In *Holocaust Historiography in Context: Emergence, Challenges, Polemics and Achievements*, edited by David Bankier and Dan Michman, 255–92. Jerusalem: Yad Vashem, 2008.

Cole, Tim. "Ghettoization." In *The Historiography of the Holocaust*, edited by Dan Stone, 65–87. Basingstoke: Palgrave Macmillan, 2004.

Dawidowicz, Lucy S. *The Holocaust and the Historians*. Cambridge: Harvard University Press, 1981.

———. *The War Against the Jews, 1933–1945*. New York: Holt, Rinehart and Winston, 1975.

Deletant, Dennis, and Harry Hanak. *Historians as Nation-Builders: Central and South-East Europe*. Basingstoke: Macmillan, 1988.

Dinaburg, B. [Ben-Zion Dinur]. *Idishe geshikhte (historishe khrestomatye)* [*Jewish History (Historical Chrestomathy)*]. Petrograd-Kiev: Mefitse Haskalah be-Yisraèl, 1919.

Diner, Dan. "'Rupture in Civilization,' On the Genesis and Meaning of a Concept in Understanding." In *On Germans and Jews under the Nazi Regime: Essays by three generations of historians: A festschrift in honor of Dov Kulka*, edited by Moshe Zimmermann, 33–48. Jerusalem: Hebrew University Magnes Press, 2006.

Diner, Hasia R. *We Remember with Reverence and Love: American Jews and the Myth of Silence after the Holocaust, 1945–1962*. New York: New York University Press, 2009.

Dlin, Elly [Elliott]. "Meanings of the Holocaust: Lecture 1: Is the Holocaust Unique?" (July 7, 2008), www.jewishagency.org/meanings/content/24039.

Dobroszycki, Lucjan. "YIVO in Interwar Poland: Work in the Historical Sciences." In *The Jews of Poland Between Two World Wars*, edited by Yisrael Gutman et al., 495–518 Hanover: Brandeis University Press, 1989.

Dold, Maria. "'A Matter of National and Civic Honour': Majer Bałaban and the Institute of Jewish Studies in Warsaw." *East European Jewish Affairs* 34, no. 2 (2004): 5–72.

Dreksler, Adina, and Michael Berenbaum. "Spiritual Resistance in the Ghettos and Concentration Camps." *Encyclopaedia Judaica*, 2nd ed., edited by Fred Skolnik and Michael Berenbaum, vol. 19, 360–65. Detroit: Macmillan Reference USA/Keter, 2007.

Dubnov, Shimen. "Der itstiker tsushtand fun der yidisher historiografye [The Present State of Jewish Historiography]." In *Tsum hundertstn geboyrntog fun shimen dubnov*, edited by Nakhmen Mayzil, 73–75. New York: YKUF, 1961.

———. "Di drite haydmatshine: historishe hagdome [The Third Wave of Massacres: Historical Introduction]." In Eliyohu Cherikower, *Antisemitizm un pogromen in ukrayine 1917–1918: tsu der geshikhte fun ukrayinish-yidishe batsyungen*, 9–15. Berlin: Mizrekh-yidishn historisn arkhiv, 1923.

———. *Dos bukh fun mayn lebn [The Book of My Life]*, 3 vols. Buenos Aires: alveltlekher yidisher kultur-kongres, 1962.

Duker, Abraham. "'Evreiskaia Starina' [The Jewish Antiquarium]: A Bibliography of the Russian-Jewish Historical Periodical." *Hebrew Union College Annual* VII–IX (1931–32): 525–603.

Efroykin, Y[isroel]. "Kedushe un gvure bay yidn amol un haynt [Holiness and Heroism among Jews in the Past and Today]." *Kiem* 4 (April 1948): 257–65 (further portions in May and July–August issues).

———. *Kedushe un gvure bay yidn amol un haynt: gezeyres tash–tashah*. New York: Farlag oyfn sheydveg, 1949.

Eisenbach, Artur. "Jewish Historiography in Interwar Poland." In *The Jews of Poland Between Two World Wars*, edited by Yisrael Gutman et al., 453–93. Hanover: Brandeis University Press, 1989.

Ek [Eck], Natan. *ha-To'im be-darkhe ha-mavet [Wandering on the Roads of Death]*. Jerusalem: Yad Vashem, 1960.

———. "Matarot ha-hoker ha-histori shel Yad va-Shem [The Goals of Yad Vashem's Historical Research]." *Yedi'ot Yad va-Shem* 4/5 (June 1955): 10; English summary 25.

Ek, Nosn [Natan Eck]. "Di gefalene in yidishn krig [Those Who Fell in the Jewish War]." *Unzer vort* (April 19, 1945): 1.

Endelman, Todd M. "The Legitimization of the Diaspora Experience in Recent Jewish Historiography." *Modern Judaism* 11 (1991): 195–209.

Engel, David. *Historians of the Jews and the Holocaust*. Stanford: Stanford University Press, 2010.

Engelking-Boni, Barbara, and Jacek Leociak, *The Warsaw Ghetto: A Guide to the Perished City*. New Haven: Yale University Press, 2009.

Erik, Max. *Di geshikhte fun der yidisher literatur fun di eltste tsaytn biz der haskole-tkufe, fertsenter-akhtsenter yorhundert* [*The History of Jewish Literature from the Oldest Times to the Period of the Haskalah*]. Warsaw: Kultur-lige, 1928.

Esh, Shaul. "The Dignity of the Destroyed: Towards a Definition of the Period of the Holocaust." *Judaism* 2, no. 11 (Spring 1962): 99–111. Reprinted in *The Catastrophe of European Jewry*, ed. Yisrael Gutman and Livia Rothkirchen. Jerusalem: Yad Vashem, 1976, 346–66.

Feldman, Yael S. "'Not as Sheep Led to Slaughter'?: On Trauma, Selective Memory, and the Making of Historical Consciousness." *Jewish Social Studies* 19, no. 3 (Spring–Summer 2013): 139–69.

Fishman, David E. *The Rise of Modern Yiddish Culture*. Pittsburgh: University of Pittsburgh Press, 2005.

Fishman, Joshua A. "Attracting a Following to High-Culture Functions for a Language of Everyday Life: The Role of the Tshernovits Language Conference in the 'Rise of Yiddish.'" In *Never Say Die! A Thousand Years of Yiddish in Jewish Life and Letters*, edited by Joshua A. Fishman, 369–94. The Hague: Mouton, 1981.

———. *Ideology, Society & Language: The Odyssey of Nathan Birnbaum*. Ann Arbor: Karoma Publishers, 1987.

———. [editor] *Shtudyes vegn yidn in poyln 1919–1939 / Studies on Polish Jewry 1919–1939: The interplay of social, economic, and political factors in the struggle of a minority for its existence*. New York: YIVO, 1974.

Frankl, Viktor. *Man's Search for Meaning: An Introduction to Logotherapy*. New York: Washington Square Press, 1963.

Friedländer, Saul. "Some Reflections on the Historicization of National Socialism." In *Reworking the Past: Hitler, the Holocaust, and the Historians' Debate*, edited by Peter Baldwin, 88–102. Boston: Beacon Press, 1990.

———. "Trauma, Memory and Transference." In *Holocaust Remembrance: The Shapes of Memory*, edited by Geoffrey H. Hartman, 252–63. Oxford: Blackwell, 1994.

Friedman, Susan W. *Marc Bloch, Sociology and Geography: Encountering Changing Disciplines*. Cambridge: Cambridge University Press, 1996.

Fuchs, Harald. *Der Geistige Widerstand Gegen Rom in der Antiken Welt* [*Spiritual Resistance against Rome in the Ancient World* (1938)]. Reprint, Berlin: Walter de Gruyter, 1964.

Gelbman, Sh. Y. *Sefer Moshi'an shel Yisra'el* [*The Book of the Deliverer of Israel*] (biography of Satmar Rebbe Joel Teitelbaum), 9 vols. Kiryas Yo'el: Sh. Y. Gelbman, 1987–.

Gets [Gerlits], Menahem. *Yerushalayim shel ma'lah* [*The Heavenly Jerusalem*]. Jerusalem: Hotsa'ah ha-Ganzakh ha-Haredi, 1973; expanded Yiddish translation, Menakhem Mendil Gerlits, *Di himldige shtot: yerusholayim shel male*, 3 vols. (Jerusalem: Oraytah, 1979–80).

Gideman, Morits [Moritz Güdemann]. *Idishe kultur-geshikhte in mitlalter (idn in daytshland dos XIV un XV yorhundert)* [*Jewish Cultural History in the Middle Ages (Jews in Germany in the 14th and 15th Century)*]. Berlin: Klal-farlag, 1922. Trans. Nokhem Shtif from *Die Geschichte des Erziehungswesens und der Cultur der abenländischen Juden während des Mittelalters und der neueren Zeit*, vol. 3 (Vienna, 1888).

Gilbert, Martin. *The Holocaust: A History of the Jews of Europe during the Second World War*. New York: Henry Holt and Company, 1985.

Ginzburg, Shoyl [Saul Ginsburg; signed, "G—g"]. "A bletil yudishe geshikhte tsum 200-yorigen yubileyum fun peterburg [A Page of Jewish History on the 200-Year Jubilee of St. Petersburg]." *Der fraynd* 108 (May 27, 1903): 2–3.

———. "Di haskole un ihre moderne kritiker [The Haskalah and Its Modern Critics]." *Di Tsukunft* (December 1939): 719–21.

———. "Unzer veg" [Our Way; unsigned]. *Di idishe velt* 1 (March 23, 1912): 1–6.

———. "Vi azoy men shraybt bay unz geshikhte [How History is Written by Us]." *Di Tsukunft* (November 1939): 662–65.

Ginzburg, Shoyl and Peysekh Marek. *Yidishe folkslider in rusland* [*Yiddish Folksongs in Russia* (Moscow, 1901)]. Reprint, ed. Dov Noy. Ramat Gan: Bar-Ilan University Press, 1991.

Goldberg, Amos. "The History of the Jews in the Ghettos: A Cultural Perspective." In *The Holocaust and Historical Methodology*, edited by Dan Stone, 79–100. New York: Berghahn, 2012.

Goldsmith, Emanuel S. *Architects of Yiddishism at the beginning of the Twentieth Century*. Rutherford: Fairleigh Dickinson University Press, 1976.

Gottesman, Itzik Nakhmen. *Defining the Yiddish Nation: The Jewish Folklorists of Poland*. Detroit: Wayne State University Press, 2003.

Gottlieb, Roger S. "The Concept of Resistance: Jewish Resistance During the Holocaust." *Social Theory and Practice* 9, no. 1 (Spring 1983): 31–48.

Greenbaum, Alfred Abraham. *Jewish Scholarship and Scholarly Institutions in Soviet Russia 1918–1953*. Jerusalem: Hebrew University, 1978.

Greenberg, Irving. "Voluntary Covenant." In *Perspectives* (pamphlet). New York: National Jewish Center for Learning and Leadership, October 1982.

Grosman, Khayke. "Di geshikhte fun a bavegung [The History of a Movement]." *Yedies fun yad vashem* 1 (April 1957): 21–22.

Gruber, Monique. "La Résistance spirituelle, fondement et soutien de la Résistance active. L'exemple des Cahiers clandestins du Témoignage chrétien [Spiritual Resistance, Foundation and Support for Active Resistance. The Example of the Clandestine Pamphlets of Christian Testimony] (1941–1944)." *Revue des Sciences Religieuses* 78, no. 4 (2004): 463–87.

Grumet, David. "Yves de Montcheuil: Action, Justice, and the Kingdom in Spiritual Resistance to Nazism." *Theological Studies* 68 (2007): 618–41.

Gutman, Yisrael. "Kiddush ha-Shem and Kiddush ha-Hayim [Sanctification of the Holy Name (self-sacrifice) and Sanctification of Life (self-preservation)]." *Simon Wiesenthal Center Annual* 1 (1984): 185–202.

———. *Mered ha-netsurim: Mordekhai Anilevitch u-milhemet geto Varshah* [*Revolt of the Besieged: Mordechai Anilevitch and the War of the Warsaw Ghetto*]. Merhavyah: Sifriyat po'alim, 1963.

———. "The Judenrat as a Leadership." In *On Germans and Jews under the Nazi Regime: Essays by Three Generations of Historians: A Festschrift in Honor of Otto Dov Kulka*, edited by Moshe Zimmermann, 313–35. Jerusalem: Hebrew University Magnes Press, 2006.

Gutman, Yosef. "Referatn un retsenzyes [Reports and Reviews]." *YIVO bleter* XXX, no. 2 (Winter 1947): 291–96.

Habermann, A. M., ed. *Gezerot Ashkenaz ve-Tzarfat* [*(Evil) Decrees of Germany and France*]. Jerusalem: Sifre Tarshish be-siyu'a Mosad ha-Rav Kuk, 1945.

Habermas, Jürgen. *Eine Art Schadensabwicklung* [*A Kind of Claims Settlement*]. Frankfurt a. M.: Suhrkamp, 1987.

Hadda, Janet. "Imagining Yiddish: A Future for the Soul of Ashkenaz." *Pakn Treger* 41 (Spring 2003): 10–19.

Handlin, Oscar. "Jewish Resistance to the Nazis." *Commentary* 34 (1962): 398–405.

Harshav, Benjamin. *Language in Time of Revolution*. Berkeley: University of California Press, 1993.

Henry, Patrick. "Introduction." In *Jewish Resistance Against the Nazis*, edited by Patrick Henry. Washington, DC: The Catholic University of America Press, 2014.

Heshl, Avrom Yehoshue [Abraham Joshua Heschel]. *Kotsk*, 2 vols. Tel Aviv: Hamenorah, 1973.

Hilberg, Raul. *The Destruction of the European Jews*. Chicago: Quadrangle, 1961.

———. "The Ghetto as a Form of Government: An Analysis of Isaiah Trunk's *Judenrat*." In *The Holocaust as Historical Experience*, edited by Yehuda Bauer and Nathan Rotenstreich, 155–71. New York: Holmes & Meier, 1980.

Hill, Leonidas E. "The Nazi Attack on un-German Literature." In *The Holocaust and the Book: Destruction and Preservation*, edited by Jonathan Rose, 9–46. Amherst: University of Massachusetts Press, 2001.

Hirshoyt, Y[ehiel] [Julian Hirshaut]. "*Bleter far geshikhte* fun umkum un oyfshtand [*Pages of History* of Extermination and Uprising; review of *Dapim*]." *YIVO bleter* XXXVI (1953): 309–13.

Hoffschulte, Martina. *"Deutsche Hörer!": Thomas Manns Rundfunkreden (1940 bis 1945) im Werkkontext* [*German Listeners!: Thomas Mann's Radio Addresses (1940 to 1945) in Work Context*]. Münster: Telos, 2004.

Horn, Mauritsi [Maurycy]. "Visnshaftlekhe un editorishe tetikayt fun der tsentraler yidisher historisher komisye baym TsKY"P un funem yidishn historishn institut in poyln in di yorn [Scholarly and Editorial Activity of the Central Jewish Historical Commission of the CCJP and of the Jewish Historical Institute in Poland in the Years] 1945–1950." *Bleter far geshikhte* XXIV (1986): 143–59.

Jockusch, Laura. "Chroniclers of Catastrophe: History Writing as a Jewish Response to Persecution before and after the Holocaust." In *Holocaust Historiography in Context: Emergence, Challenges, Polemics and Achievements*, edited by David Bankier and Dan Michman, 135–66. Jerusalem: Yad Vashem, 2008.

———. "Collect and Record! Help to Write the History of the Latest Destruction! Jewish Historical Commissions in Europe 1943–1953." PhD diss., New York University, 2007.

———. *Collect and Record! Jewish Holocaust Documentation in Early Postwar Europe*. New York: Oxford University Press, 2012.

Jockusch, Laura and Gabriel N. Finder, *Jewish Honor Courts: Revenge, Retribution, and Reconciliation in Europe and Israel after the Holocaust*. Detroit: Wayne State University Press, 2015.

Joffe, Judah, and Yudel Mark, *Groyser verterbukh fun der yidisher shprakh* [*Great Dictionary of the Yiddish Language*], 4 vols. New York: Komitet farn groysn verterbukh fun der yidisher shprakh, 1961–80.

Joyner, Charles. *Shared Traditions: Southern History and Folk Culture*. Urbana: University of Illinois Press, 1999.

Kalmanovitsh, Zelig. "A nay verk iber der geshikhte fun yuden [A New Work on the History of the Jews; review of *Istoria Evreev v Rossia* (Moscow, 1914)]." *Di yudishe velt* 1, no. 2 (February, 1915): 199–207; 1, no. 3 (March 1915): 338–54.

Kaplan, Louis. " 'It Will Get a Terrific Laugh': On the Problematic Pleasures of Politics of Holocaust Humor." In *Hop on Pop: The Politics and Pleasures of Popular Culture*, edited by Henry Jenkins et al., 343–56. Durham: Duke University Press, 2002.

Kaplan, Yisroel. *Dos folks-moyl in natsi-klem: reydenishn in geto un katset* [*The People's Tongue in the Nazi Vise: Sayings in the Ghettos and Camps*]. Munich: Tsentraler historisher komisye baym Ts.K. fun di bafrayte yidn in der amerikaner zone in daytshland, 1949.

Karlip, Joshua M. "Between Martyrology and Historiography: Elias Tcherikower and the making of a pogrom historian." *East European Jewish Affairs* 38, no. 3 (December 2008): 257–80.

———. *The Tragedy of a Generation: The Rise and Fall of Jewish Nationalism in Eastern Europe*. Cambridge: Harvard University Press, 2013.

Kasov, Shmuel [Samuel Kassow]. "Zalmen reyzen un zayn gezelshaftlekh-politish arbet: [Zalman Rejzen and His Communal-Political Work] 1915–1922." *YIVO bleter* New Series II (1994): 67–97.

Kassow, Samuel. "Historiography: An Overview." *The YIVO Encyclopedia of Jews in Eastern Europe*, www.yivoencyclopedia.org/article.aspx/Historiography/An_Overview.

———. "Travel and Local History as a National Mission: Polish Jews and the Landkentenish Movement in the 1920s and 1930s." In *Jewish Topographies*, edited by Julia Brauch et al., 241–64. Aldershot-Burlington: Ashgate, 2008.

———. *Who Will Write Our History? Emanuel Ringelblum, the Warsaw Ghetto, and the Oyneg Shabes Archive*. Bloomington: Indiana University Press, 2007, 2018.

Katsherginski, Sh. [Shmerke Kaczerginski]. *Khurbn vilne: umkum fun di yidn in vilne un vilner gegnt* . . . [*Khurbn Vilna: Extermination of the Jews in Vilna and Vilna Region*]. New York: CYCO, 1947.

Kazdan, Kh. S. *Di geshikhte fun Yidishn shulvezn in umophengikn Poyln* [*The History of the Yiddish School System in Independent Poland*]. Mexico [City]: Gezelshaft "Kultur un Hilf," 1947.

———. *Fun kheder un 'shkoles' biz tsysho (tsentraler yidisher shul organizatsye)* [*From Religious Schools to TsYSho (Central Yiddish School Organization)*]. Mexico [City]: Shloyme Mendelson Fond, 1956.

Keele, Alan F. "Six Authors in Search of a Character: The importance of Helmuth Hübener in post-war German literature." Guest Faculty Essay in *Perspectives–Student Journal of Germanic and Slavic Languages* 12 (Winter 2004), formerly online at http://germslav.byu.edu/perspectives/w2004.php.

Kempter, Klaus. "'Objective, Not Neutral': Joseph Wulf, a Documentary Historian." *Holocaust Studies* 21, nos. 1–2 (October 2015): 38–52.

Kenan, Orna. *Between Memory and History: The Evolution of Israeli Historiography of the Holocaust, 1945–1961*. New York: Peter Lang, 2003.

Kerenji, Emil. *Jewish Responses to Persecution (Vol. IV) 1942–1943*. Lanham: AltaMira Press, 2015.

Korman, Gerd. "The Holocaust in American Historical Writing." *Societas* 2 (1972): 251–70.

———. "Warsaw Plus Thirty: Some Perceptions in the Sources and Written History of the Ghetto Uprising." *YIVO Annual of Jewish Social Science* XV (1974): 280–96.

Kostanian-Danzig, Rachel. *Spiritual Resistance in the Vilna Ghetto*. Vilnius: The Vilna Gaon Jewish State Museum, 2002.

Kovner, Abba. "Discussion." In *The Holocaust as Historical Experience*, edited by Yehuda Bauer and Nathan Rotenstreich, 250–52. New York: Holmes & Meier, 1980.

Kugelmass, Jack and Jonathan Boyarin. *From a Ruined Garden*, 2nd expanded ed. Bloomington: Indiana University Press, 1998.

———. "Yizker Bikher and the Problem of Historical Veracity: An Anthropological Approach." In *The Jews of Poland Between Two World Wars*, edited by Yisrael Gutman et al., 519–36. Hanover: Brandeis University Press, 1989.

Kuznitz, Cecile Esther. *YIVO and the Making of Modern Yiddish Culture: Scholarship for the Yiddish Nation*. New York: Cambridge University Press, 2014.

Lacquer, Walter. *The Terrible Secret: Suppression of the Truth about Hitler's "Final Solution."* Boston: Little, Brown, 1980.

Langer, Lawrence L. *Admitting the Holocaust: Collected essays*. New York: Oxford University Press, 1996.

Leff, Lisa Moses. "Rescue or Theft? Zosa Szajkowski and the Salvaging of French Jewish History." *Jewish Social Studies* 18, no. 2 (2012): 1–39.

Leshtshinski, Yankev [Jacob Lestshinsky]. *Di yidishe katastrofe: di metodn fun ir forshung* [*The Jewish Catastrophe: The Methods for Its Study*]. New York: Institut far idishe inyonim funm idishn amerikaner un velt-kongres, 1944.

Lestschinsky, Jacob. *Crisis, Catastrophe, and Survival: A Jewish Balance Sheet, 1914–1948*. New York: Institute of Jewish Affairs of the World Jewish Congress, 1948.

Lewinsky, Tamar. "Dangling Root? Yiddish Language and Culture in the German Diaspora." In *"We Are Here": New Approaches to Jewish Displaced Persons in Postwar Germany*, edited by Avinoam J. Patt and Michael J. Berkowitz, 308–34. Detroit: Wayne State University Press, 2010.

Lindenthal, Jacob Jay. "The Epidemiological Status and Health Care Administration of the Jews Before and During the Holocaust." In *Jewish Medical Resistance in the Holocaust*, edited by Michael A. Grodin, 1–33. New York: Berghahn Books, 2014.

Lipstadt, Deborah E. "America and the Memory of the Holocaust, 1950–1965." *Modern Judaism* 16, no. 3 (October 1996): 195–214.

Loose, Ingo. "Die Bateiligung deutscher Kreditinstitute an der Vernichtung der ökonomischen Existenz der Juden in Polen [The Participation of the German Credit Institute in the Destruction of the Economic Existence of the Jews in Poland] 1939–1945." In *Die Commerzbank und die Juden, 1933–1945*, edited by Ludolf Herbst and Thomas Weihe, 223–71. Munich: C. H. Beck, 2004.

———. *Kredite für NS-Verbrechen: Die deutschen Kreditinstitute in Polen und die Ausroubung der polnischen und judischen Bevölkerung* [*Credit for Nazi Criminals: The German Credit Crimes: The German Credit Institute in Poland and the Extermination of the Polish and Jewish Population*] 1939–1945. Munich: Oldenbourg, 2007.

Mahler, Rafoel. "Di forshung fun der letster yidisher martirologye oyf naye vegn [Research on the Recent Jewish Martyrology on New Paths]." *Yidishe kultur* 11, no. 2 (February 1949): 1–8.

———. *Historiker un vegvayzer* [*Historians and Guides*]. Tel Aviv: Yisroelbukh, 1967.

———. "Yidish un hebreyish in likht fun der hayntiker virklekhkayt [Yiddish and Hebrew in Light of the Present Reality]." *Yidishe kultur* 9, no. 6 (June 1947): 12–20.

Mahler, Rafoel, and Emanuel Ringelblum, eds. *Geklibene mekoyrim tsu der geshikhte fun di yidn in poyln un mizrekh-eyrope* [*Collected Sources on the History of the Jews in Poland and Eastern Europe*], 2 vols. Warsaw: Kulturlige, 1930.

Mann, Thomas. *Listen, Germany!: Twenty-Five Radio Messages to the German People Over BBC*. New York: A. A. Knopf, 1943.

Mark, B[er]. "25 bikher 'dos poylishe yidntum' [25 Books 'The poylisher Yidntum' (series)]." *Dos naye lebn* (December 14, 1947): 4 (unsigned, but with companion article signed by the editor, B. Mark).

———. *Dokumentn un materyaln vegn oyfshtand in varshever geto* [*Documents and Materials on the Uprising in the Warsaw Ghetto*]. Warsaw: Yidish bukh, 1953.

———. *Dos bukh fun gvure: oyfshtand fun varshever geto* [*The Book of Heroism: The Uprising in the Warsaw Ghetto*] (cover title: *Khurves dersteyln* [*Ruins Recount*]). Lodz: Dos naye lebn, 1947. Expanded version of *Der oyfshtand in varshever geto* (Moscow: Der emes, 1947).

———. "Problemen fun der forshung fun di vidershtand-bavegungen in di getos [Problems of Research on the Resistance Movement in the Ghetto]." *Yedies: byuletin fun yidishn historishn institut in poyln* [2] (November 1950): 2.

———. *Tsvishn lebn un toyt* [*Between Life and Death*]. Warsaw: Yidish bukh, 1966.

Marrus, Michael R. *The Holocaust in History*. Hanover: University Press of New England, 1987.

Mashbaum, Yael Weinstock. "Spiritual Resistance During the Holocaust: 'What We Value,'" www.yadvashem.org/articles/general/spiritual-resistance-during-the-holocaust.html.

Matthäus, Jürgen, et al. "Introduction." In *Jewish Responses to Persecution (Vol. I) 1933–1938*, edited by Jürgen Matthäus and Mark Roseman. Lanham: AltaMira Press, 2010.

Mayzil, Nakhmen [Nachman Meisel]. "Yidn-visnshaft oder yidishe visnshaft [Scholarship on Jews or Jewish Scholarship; on YIVO's publication, "Dos tsveyte yor aspirantur" (Vilna, 1938)]." *Literarishe bleter* (December 3, 1937): 779–80.

McCumber, John. "The Holocaust as Master Rupture: Foucault, Fackenheim, and 'Postmodernity.'" In *Postmodernism and the Holocaust*, edited by Alan Milchman and Alan Rosenberg, 239–64. Amsterdam-Atlanta: Rodopi, 1998.

Melezin, Abraham. "Demografishe farheltnishn in di getos in poyln [Demographic Conditions in the Ghettos in Poland]." *Gedank un lebn* V, nos. 1–4 (January–December 1948), 86–100.

Mendelson, Shloyme [Shlomo Mendelsohn]. "Vi azoy lebn poylishe yidn in di getos [How the Polish Jews Are Living in the Ghettos]." *YIVO bleter* XIX, no. 1 (January–February 1942), 1–27.

Meyer, Michael A. "Two Persistent Tensions within Wissenschaft Des Judentums." *Modern Judaism* 24, no. 2 (May 2004): 105–19.
Michman, Dan. "Is There an 'Israeli School' of Holocaust Research?" In *Holocaust Historiography in Context: Emergence, Challenges, Polemics and Achievements*, edited by David Bankier and Dan Michman, 37–66. Jerusalem: Yad Vashem, 2008.
———. "Research on the Holocaust in Belgium and in General: History and Context." In *Belgium and the Holocaust: Jews, Belgians, Germans*, edited by Dan Michman, 3–38. Jerusalem: Yad Vashem, 1998.
Mirski, M. [Mikhl Mirsky]. "Moskve [report on the Moscow Conference of Foreign Ministers, December 1945]." *Dos naye lebn* (January 3, 1946): 1.
Mitelberg, A. "Bikher-monument [Monument of Books]." *Oyfn shvel* (January 1952): 15.
Morreall, John. "Humor in the Holocaust: Its Critical, Cohesive, and Coping Functions." *Holocaust Teacher Research Center* (November 11, 2001), www.holocaust-trc.org/humor-in-the-holocaust.
Myers, David N. "'*Mehabevin et ha-Tsarot*': Crusade Memories and Modern Jewish Martyrologies." *Jewish History* 13, no. 2 (Fall 1999): 49–64.
———. *Re-Inventing the Jewish Past: European Jewish Intellectuals and the Zionist Return to History*. New York: Oxford University Press, 1995.
———. "Remembering the Satmar Movement's Chronicler." *Tablet Magazine* (April 3, 2015), http://tabletmag.com/scroll/190062/remembering-the-satmar-movements-chronicler. Yiddish, "Der historiker un arkhivist fun satmar," *Der yid* (April 15, 2015).
———. "The Ideology of Wissenschaft des Judentums." In *History of Jewish Philosophy*, edited by Daniel H. Frank and Oliver Leaman, 706–20. London: Routledge, 1997.
Nalewajko-Kulikov, Joanna. "The Last Yiddish Books Printed in Poland." In *Under the Red Banner*, edited by Elvira Grözinger and Magdalena Ruta, 111–34. Wiesbaden: Harrasowitz Verlag, 2008.
Nathans, Benjamin. "On Russian-Jewish Historiography." In *Historiography of Imperial Russia: The Profession and Writing of History in a Multinational State*, edited by Thomas Sanders, 397–432. Armonk: M. E. Sharpe, 1999.
Netzer, Shlomo. "The Holocaust of Polish Jewry in Jewish Historiography." In *The Historiography of the Holocaust Period: Proceedings of the Fifth Yad Vashem International Historical Conference* (Jerusalem, March 1983), edited by Yisrael Gutman and Gideon Greif, 133–48. Jerusalem: Yad Vashem, 1988.

Niger, Shmuel, ed. *Kidush hashem*. New York: Tsyko bikher farlag, 1948.
Novick, Peter. *That Noble Dream*. Cambridge: Cambridge University Press, 1988.
Novik, P. *Eyrope—tsvishn milkhome un sholem: rayze-bilder, batrakhtungen* [*Between War and Peace: Travel Scenes, Reflections*]. New York: YKUF, 1948.
Novitch, Miriam. *Spiritual Resistance: Art from Concentration Camps—With Essays by Miriam Novitch, Lucy Dawidowicz, and Tom L. Freudenheim*. Philadelphia: Jewish Publication Society of America, 1981.
Ostrower, Chaya. "Humor as a Defense Mechanism in the Holocaust," www.academia.edu/554260/Humor_as_a_Defense_Mechanism_in_the_Holocaust, with response/comment by Bella Bryks-Klein, Academia: Beit Berl Academic College, https://beitberl.academia.edu/Departments/Psychology/Documents.
———. *It Kept Us Alive: Humor in the Holocaust*. Jerusalem: Yad Vashem, 2014.
Oyerbakh, Rokhl [Rachel Auerbach]. *Oyf di felder fun treblinke* [*On the Fields of Treblinka*]. Warsaw-Lodz: Tsentraler yidisher historisher komisye in poyln, 1947.
Pächter, Heinz, et al. *Nazi-Deutsch: A Glossary of Contemporary German Usage*. New York: Frederick Ungar, 1944.
Pat, Yankev. *Ash un fayer: iber di khurves fun poyln* [*Amid the Ruins of Poland*]. New York: Tsyko bikher farlag, 1946). *Ashes and Fire*, trans. Leo Steinberg. New York: International Universities Press, 1947.
Person, Katarzyna. "The Initial Reception and First Publications from the Ringelblum Archive in Poland, 1946–1952." *Gal-Ed: On the History and Culture of Polish Jewry* 23 (2012): 59–76.
Petropoulos, Jonathan. "The Nazi Kleptocracy: Reflections on Avarice and the Holocaust." In *The Holocaust in International Perspective*, edited by Dagmar Herzog, 29–38. Evanston: Northwestern University Press, 2006.
Pine, Lisa. "Gender and Family." In *The Historiography of the Holocaust*, edited by Dan Stone, 364–82. New York: Palgrave Macmillan, 2004.
Pinson, Koppel S. "Simon Dubnow: Historian and Political Philosopher." In *Nationalism and History: Essays on Old and New Judaism by Simon Dubnow*, edited by Koppel S. Pinson, 3–65. Philadelphia: Jewish Publication Society, 1958.
Pohl, Dieter. "The Robbery of Jewish Property in Eastern Europe Under Nazi Occupation, 1939–1942." In *Robbery and Restitution: The Conflict Over Jewish Property in Europe*, edited by Martin Dean et al., 68–80. New York: Berghahn Books, 2007.

Poliakov, Léon. *L'étoile jaune* [*The Yellow Star*]. Paris: Éditions du Centre, 1949. Yiddish, *Di gele late* [*The Yellow Badge*]. (Paris: Farlag fun tsenter, 1952).

Reitlinger, Gerald. *The Final Solution: The Attempt to Exterminate the Jews of Europe: 1939–1945*. New York: Beechurst Press, 1953.

Reyzen, Z. [Zalman Rejzen], ed. *Pinkes far der geshikhte fun vilne in di yorn fun milkhome un okupatsye* [*Chronicle of the History of Vilna in the Years of War and Occupation*]. Vilna: Historish-etnografisher gezelshaft oyfn nomen fun sh. an-ski, 1922.

———. *Leksikon fun der yidisher literatur un prese*. Warsaw: Tsentral, 1914.

———. *Leksikon fun der yidisher literatur, prese un filologye*, 4 vols. Vilna: Kletskin, 1926–29.

Ringelblum, Emanuel. "Der internatsyonaler kongres fun historishe visnshaft in varshe un di yidishe visnshaft [The International Congress of Historical Sciences in Warsaw and Jewish Scholarship]." In *Kapitlen geshikhte fun amolikn yidishn lebn in poyln* by Emanuel Ringelblum, edited by Yankev Shatski, 467–83. Buenos Aires: Tsentral farband fun poylishe yidn in argentine, 1953 (first published in *Di tsukunft*, April 1934, 223–28).

———. "Vegn yidishe altertimlekhkaytn in poyln [On Jewish Antiquities in Poland]." *Literarishe bleter* 7, no. 33 (August 15, 1933): 615–16.

———. "Yidishe malbushim in poyln sof 18 y"h [Jewish Clothes in Poland, Late 18th Century]." *Fun noentn over* I, no. V (1938): 17–20.

Robinson, Jacob. *And the Crooked Shall be Made Straight*. New York: Macmillan, 1965.

———, assisted by Mrs. Philip Friedman. *The Holocaust and After: Sources & Literature in English*. Jerusalem: Israel Universities Press, 1973.

Roland, Charles G. *Courage Under Siege: Starvation, Disease, and Death in the Warsaw Ghetto*. Oxford: Oxford University Press, 1992.

Roskies, David. "The Holocaust According to Its Anthologists." *Prooftexts* 17, no. 1 (January 1997): 95–113.

———. "What Is Holocaust Literature?" In *Jews, Catholics, and the Burden of History*, edited by Eli Lederhendler, 157–212. Oxford: Oxford University Press, 2005.

Roth, Cecil. "Historiography." *Encyclopaedia Judaica*, edited by Cecil Roth, vol. 8, 551–69. Jerusalem: Keter, 1972.

Rozett, Robert. *Approaching the Holocaust: Texts and Contexts*. London: Valentine Mitchell, 2005.

———. "Jewish Resistance." In *The Historiography of the Holocaust*, edited by Dan Stone. New York: Palgrave Macmillan, 2004, 341–63.

Rudavsky, Joseph. *To Live with Hope, To Die with Dignity: Spiritual resistance in the ghettos and camps*. Mahwah: Center for Holocaust and Genocide Studies, Ramapo College of New Jersey, 1987.

Sauder, Gerhard. *Die Bücherverbrennung [Book Burning]: Zum 10. Mai 1933*. Munich: Hanser, 1983.

Schöne, Albrecht. *Göttinger Bücherverbrennung [Book Burning in Göttingen] 1933: Rede am 10. Mai 1983 zur Erinnerung an die "Aktion wider den undeutschen Geist."* Göttingen: Vandenhoeck u. Ruprecht, 1983.

Schorsch, Ismar. "The Lachrymose Conception of Jewish History." In *From Text to Context: The Turn to History in Modern Judaism*, 376–88. Hanover: Brandeis University Press, 1994.

Schroeter, Gudrun. *Worte aus einer zerstörten Welt [Words from a Destroyed World]: Das Ghetto in Wilna*. St. Ingbert: Röhrig Universitätsverlag, 2007.

Schulman, Elias. "'The Pogroms in the Ukraine in 1919' [review of Tcherikower, New York, 1965]." *Jewish Quarterly Review* 57, no. 2 (October 1966): 159–66.

Schwarz, Jan. "A Library of Hope and Destruction: The Yiddish Book Series Dos poylishe yidntum, 1946–1966." *Polin* 20 (2007): 173–96.

———. *Survivors and Exiles: Yiddish Culture After the Holocaust*. Detroit: Wayne State University Press, 2015.

Seltzer, Robert M. *Simon Dubnow's "New Judaism": Diaspora Nationalism and the World History of the Jews*. Leiden: Brill, 2014.

Shalit, Moyshe. "Shoyl ginzburgs histor. verk, 3 bender, nyu-york 1937 [Saul Ginsburg's Historical Works, 3 volumes]." *Fun noentn over* IV (1937): 339–42.

Shandler, Jeffrey. *Adventures in Yiddishland: Postvernacular Language and Culture*. Berkeley: University of California Press, 2006.

———. [editor] *Awakening Lives: Autobiographies of Jewish Youth in Poland Before the Holocaust*. New Haven: Yale University Press, 2002.

Shanes, Joshua. "Yiddish and Jewish Diaspora Nationalism." *Monatshefte* 90, no. 2 (Summer 1998): 178–88.

Shapiro, Robert Moses, and Tadeusz Epsztein, eds. *The Warsaw Ghetto: Oyneg Shabes- Ringelblum Archive: Catalog and Guide*, trans. Robert Moses Shapiro. Bloomington: Indiana University Press, 2009.

Shatski, Yankev [Jacob Shatzky]. "A naye idishe teater-geshikhte [A New Yiddish Theater History]." *Tealit* 1, no. 3 (January 1924): 23–32.

———. "Di ershte geshikhte fun yidishn teater: tsu d"r y. shipers verk [The First History of Jewish Theater: On Dr. Y. Schiper's Work]." *Filologishe shriftn* II (Vilna, 1928): 215–64.

———. [editor] *Kapitlen geshikhte fun amolikn yidishn lebn in poyln* [*Chapters of the History of Former Jewish Life in Poland*] by Emanuel Ringelblum. Buenos Aires: Tsentral farband fun poylishe yidn in argentine, 1953.

———. "Problemen fun yidisher historyografye." *Di tsukunft* (March 1955): 121–26.

———. "Referatn un retsenzyes: yisker-bikher." *YIVO bleter* XXXVII (1953): 264–82. English, "Review of Yizker Books—1953," in *Memorial Books of Eastern European Jewry: Essays on the History and Meanings of Yizker Volumes*, ed. Rosemary Horowitz (Jefferson: McFarland, 2011), 54–67.

———. "Referatn un retsenzyes: yisker-bikher." *YIVO bleter* XXXIX (1955), 339–55. English, "Review of Yizker Books—1955," in *Memorial Books of Eastern European Jewry*, ed. Horowitz, 68–80.

Shaykovski, Z. [Zosa Szajkowski]. "Yidn in eyrope forshn zeyer umkum [Jews in Europe Research Their Extermination], 1939–1946." *YIVO bleter* XXX, no. 1 (Fall 1947): 99.

Shedletsky, E. "Baratung in der tsentraler yidisher historisher komisye [Conference of the CJHC; August 12, 1945, Lodz]." *Dos naye lebn* (August 20, 1945): 6.

———. "Tsveyte visnshaftlekhe baratung fun der tsen. yidisher historisher komisye in poyln [Second Academic Conference of the CJHC; September 19–20, 1945, Lodz]." *Dos naye lebn* (October 13, 1945): 5.

Shiper, Yitskhok [Ignacy Schiper]. *Geshikhte fun yidisher teater-kunst un drame fun di eltste tsaytn biz 1750* [*History of Jewish Theatrical Arts and Drama from the Oldest Times to 1750*], 2 vols. Warsaw: Kultur-lige, 1923, 1925.

Shmeruk, Chone. "Hebrew-Yiddish-Polish: A Trilingual Jewish Culture." In *The Jews of Poland Between Two World Wars*, edited by Yisrael Gutman et al., 285–311. Hanover: Brandeis University Press, 1989.

Shnayderman, Sh. L. [S. L. Shneiderman]. *Tsvishn shrek un hofenung (a rayze iber dem nayem poyln)* [*(A Journey across the New Poland)*]. Buenos Aires: Tsentral farband fun poylishe yidn in argentine, 1947. English, *Between Fear and Hope*, trans. Norbert Guterman (New York: Arco, 1947).

Shneer, David. "A Study in Red: Jewish Scholarship in the 1920s Soviet Union." *Science in Context* 20, no. 2 (June 2007): 197–213.

Shneiderman, S. L., ed. *Warsaw ghetto, a diary by Mary Berg*. New York: L. B. Fischer, 1945.

Shoshkes, Khaym. *Poyln—1946 (Ayndrukn fun a rayze)* [*(Impressions from a Journey)*]. Buenos Aires: Ts.F.P.Y.A., 1946.

Shpizman, Leyb [Leib Spizman]. "Yidn in zaglembye beys der itstiker milkhome [Jews in Zagłębie Dąbrowskie during the Present War]." *YIVO bleter* XIX, no. 2 (March–April 1942): 221–31.

———. *Di yidn in natsi-poyln*. New York: Idisher kemfer, 1942.

Shtaynboym, Yisroel. *Di geshikhte fun yidishn lerer-seminar un folks-universitet in nyu-york* [*The History of the Jewish Teachers' Seminary and People's University in New York*]. Jerusalem: n.p., 1979.

Shtif, N. "Vegn a yidishn akademishn institute [On a Yiddish Academic Institute]." In *Di organizatsye fun der yidisher visnshaft*, 19–22. Vilna: YIVO, 1925.

Shulman Eliyohu [Elias Schulman]. "Di tsaytshrift 'Di yudishe (idishe) velt.' [The Periodical 'The Jewish World']." In *Pinkes far der forshung fun der yidisher literatur un prese*, edited by Shloyme Bikl, 122–70. New York: Alveltlekhn yidishn kultur-kongres, 1965.

Simon, Ernst. "Jewish Adult Education in Nazi Germany as Spiritual Resistance." *Leo Baeck Institute Yearbook* I (1956): 68–104.

Smith, Mark L. "Joseph Wulf—The Path Not Taken: His early career in Yiddish Holocaust studies." Invited conference paper for "Joseph Wulf: A Polish-Jewish Historian in Western Germany," joint project of Zentrum für Literatur- und Kulturforschung (Berlin) and Centre de Recherches Historiques, École des Hautes Études en Sciences Sociales (Paris); Polish Academy of Sciences, Paris (February 16, 2018), https://savoirs-inclass ables.ehess.fr.

———. "No Silence in Yiddish: Popular and Scholarly Writing about the Holocaust in the Early Postwar Years." In *After the Holocaust: Challenging the Myth of Silence*, edited by David Cesarani and Eric J. Sundquist, 55–66. London: Routledge, 2011.

Smoliar [Smolar], Hersh. "The Lambs Were Legend—The Wolves Were Real: A new look at the charge of Jewish passivity in the Ghettoes." *Jewish Currents* (April 1959): 7–11.

Smolyar [Smolar], Hersh. *Oyf der letster pozitsye mit der letster hofenung* [*At the Last Position with the Last Hope*]. Tel Aviv: Y. L. Perets, 1982.

Steinschneider, Moritz. *Die geschichtsliteratur der Juden in druckwerken und handschriften* [*The Historical Literature of the Jews in Printed Works and Manuscripts*]. Frankfurt a. M.: J. Kauffman, 1905.

Storm, Eric. "Regionalism in History, 1890–1945: The Cultural Approach." *European History Quarterly* 33, no. 2 (2003): 251–65.

Suchoff, David. "A Yiddish Text from Auschwitz: Critical History and the Anthological Imagination." *Prooftexts* 19, no. 1 (January 1999): 59–69.

Suhl, Yuri, ed. *They Fought Back: The Story of Jewish Resistance in Nazi Europe*. New York: Schocken, 1967.

Taytlboym [Teitlbaum], Dora. *Mitn ponem tsum lebn: rayze-ayndrukn* [*Facing Life: Travel Impressions*]. Paris: Oyfsnay, 1952.

Tec, Nechama. "Jewish Resistance: Facts, Omissions, and Distortions." Miles Lerman Center for the Study of Jewish Resistance, United States Holocaust Memorial Museum (1997), www.ushmm.org/m/pdfs/Publication_OP_1997-02.pdf. Republished in *Jewish Resistance Against the Nazis*, ed. Patrick Henry (Washington, DC: Catholic University of America Press, 2014), 40–70.

Tenenboym, Yosef. "D"r yankev shatski—polihistor un historiograf (an opshatsung) [(An appreciation)]." In *Shatski-bukh*, edited by Y. Lifshits, 29–44. New York: YIVO, 1958.

Trachtenberg, Barry. *The Revolutionary Roots of Modern Yiddish, 1903–1917*. New York: Syracuse University Press, 2008.

Tsinberg, Yisroel [Israel Zinberg]. *Di geshikhte fun literatur bay yidn* [*The History of Literature among Jews*], vol. VI: *Alt-yidishe literatur fun di eltste tsaytn biz der haskole-tkufe* [*Old Yiddish Literature from the Oldest Times to the Haskalah Period*]. Vilna: Farlag Tomor, 1935.

———. "Tsu der geshikhte fun der yidisher folks-dramatik [On the History of the Yiddish Popular Drama]." *Bikher velt* 2, no. 1 (January 1, 1929): 31–41; 2, no. 3 (March 1, 1929): 22–30.

Turkov, Yonas [Jonas Turkow]. *Nokh der bafrayung (zikhroynes)* [*After the Liberation (Memoirs)*]. Buenos Aires: Tsentral-farband fun poysishe yidn in argentine, 1959.

Tych, Feliks. "The Emergence of Holocaust Research in Poland: The Jewish Historical Commission and the Jewish Historical Institute (ŻIH), 1944–1989." In *Holocaust Historiography in Context: Emergence, Challenges, Polemics and Achievements*, edited by David Bankier and Dan Michman, 227–44. Jerusalem: Yad Vashem, 2008.

Unger, Menashe. *Der gaystiker vidershtand fun yidn in getos un lagern* [*Spiritual Resistance of Jews in Gettos and Camps*]. Tel Aviv: ha-Menorah, 1970.

US Holocaust Memorial Museum. "Spiritual Resistance in the Ghettos." *Holocaust Encyclopedia*, www.ushmm.org/wlc/en/article.php?ModuleId=10005416.

Vaynraykh, M. [Max Weinreich]. Foreword to Ezriel Presman [Israel Pressman], *Der durkhgegangener veg* [*The Road Traveled*], iii–iv. New York: YIVO, 1950. English, "Roads That Passed: Russia, My Old Home," trans. Philip Desind, *YIVO Annual of Jewish Social Science* 22 (1995): 4–5.

———. "Hitlers profesorn: der kheylek fun der daytsher visnshaft in daytshlands farbrekhns kegn yidishn folk." *YIVO bleter* XXVII, no. 1 (Spring 1946): 1–160; XXVII, no. 2 (Summer 1946): 209–312. English, *Hitler's Professors: The part of scholarship in Germany's crimes against the Jewish people* (New York: YIVO, 1946).

———. "Tsu der geshikhte fun der eltere ahashverush-shpil [On the History of the Older Ahasuerus Plays]." *Filologishe shriftn* II (Vilna, 1928): 425–28.

Virshubski [Wirszubski], A. "Dos folksgezunt un der meditsinisher lebnsshteyger in vilne beys der daytsher okupatsye [Public Health and Medical Lifestyle in the Vilna Ghetto during the German Occupation] (18 september 1915—1 yanuar 1919)." In *Pinkes far der geshikhte fun vilne in di yorn fun milkhome okupatsye*, edited by Z. Reyzen, 81–108. Vilna: Historish-etnografisher gezelshaft oyfn nomen fun sh. an-ski, 1922.

Vishnitser [Wischnitzer], Mark. "Der historiker-krayz baym YIVO [The Historians' Circle at YIVO]." *YIVO bleter* XXVII, no. 2 (1946): 371–79; XXIX, no. 2 (1947): 273–82; XXXIII (1949): 225–34.

von Fransecky, Tanja. *Flucht von Juden aus Deportationszügen in Frankreich, Belgien und den Niederlanden [Flight of Jews from Deportation Trains in France, Belgium and the Netherlands]*. Berlin: Metropol Verlag, 2014.

Waxman, Meyer. *A History of Jewish Literature*, vol. 4. New York: Block, 1941.

Weinreich, Max. "Israel Zinberg 1873–1943 [*sic*; d. 1938]." *Historia Judaica* VI, no. 1 (April 1944): 101–2.

Weitzman, Lenore J. "Living on the Aryan Side in Poland: Gender, Passing, and the Nature of Resistance." In *Women in the Holocaust*, edited by Dalia Ofer and Lenore J. Weitzman, 187–222. New Haven: Yale University Press, 1998.

———. "Women of Courage: The Kashariyot (Couriers) in the Jewish Resistance During the Holocaust." In *New Currents in Holocaust Research*, edited by Jeffry M. Diefendoff, 112–52. Evanston: Northwestern University Press, 2004.

Wieviorka, Annette. *The Era of the Witness*. Translated by Jared Stark [original French edition, 1998]. Ithaca: Cornell University Press, 2006.

Wisse, Ruth R. *The Modern Jewish Canon: A Journey Through Language and Culture*. New York: The Free Press, 2000.

Wohl, Samuel. *Mayn rayze keyn varshe [My Journey to Warsaw]*. New York: n.p., 1947.

Yasni, A. Volf. *Di geshikhte fun yidn in lodzsh in di yorn fun der daytsher yidn-oysrotung [The History of the Jews in Lodz in the Years of the German Extermination of the Jews]*, 2 vols. Tel Aviv: Y. L. Perets, 1960, 1966.

———. "Tsvantsik yor 'yidisher historisher institut' in poyln [Twenty Years of 'Jewish Historical Institute' in Poland]." *Lebns-fragn* 154 (March 1965): 6–7.

Yefroikin [Efroykin], Israel. "The Lie of Jewish Cowardice." *The Jewish Digest* (March 1957): 17–20; "condensed from *Jerusalem*, Larrea 744, Buenos Aires, Argentina, translated exclusively for The Jewish Digest by Annabelle Sinai."

Yerushalmi, Yosef Hayim. *Zakhor*. Seattle: University of Washington Press, 1982.

Zenderland, Leila. "Social Science as a 'Weapon of the Weak': Max Weinreich, the Yiddish Scientific Institute, and the Study of Culture, Personality, and Prejudice." *Isis* 104 (2013): 742–72.

Zipperstein, Steven J. "Ashkenazic Jewry and Catastrophe: A Review Essay." *Polin* 1 (2004): 327–35.

Zuckerman, Yitzhak ("Antek"). *A Surplus of Memory: Chronicle of the Warsaw Ghetto Uprising*, translated and edited by Barbara Harshav. Berkeley: University of California Press, 1993.

Zunz, Leopold. *Die gottesdienstlichen Vorträge der Juden*, 2nd ed. Frankfurt a. M.: J. Kauffmann, 1892.

INDEX

Page numbers in *italics* indicate illustrations. Specific works generally will be found under the author's name.

Academie Nationale de Medecine, France, 59–60
Academy for Jewish Research, 61
Adler, Alfred, 43
Adorno, Theodor, 65
Aharony, Michal, 276
Ajzen, Abraham, 264n139; *Dos gaystike ponem fun geto* (*The Spiritual Face of the Ghetto*; 1950), 260
Aleichem, Sholem, 287
Aleksandrov, Hillel, 111n156
Aleksium, Natalia, 64, 167, 294, xivn2
'Al ha-Mishmar (newspaper), 54
Alltagsgeschichte (history of everyday life), contextualization of Holocaust by study of, 194–95, 210–14
American Historical Association, 208
American Historical Review, 88
American Joint Distribution Committee ("the Joint"): banned in Poland, 181; Friedman as educational director of D.P. camps, US Zone, Germany, 55n115, 101, 121–22, 135, 150, 181; "starvation disease" research of Warsaw Ghetto doctors published by, 193
Amidah ("standing up against" as a form of resistance), 247, 250, 269, 270, 273, 274, 276, 277
Amolike yorn (Bygone Years; proposed journal), 10–11
Anielevitch, Mordechai, 258, 286

Annales school, France, 24, 219
An-sky, S., 76, 197, 287; *The Enemy at his Pleasure*, 187
anti-lachrymose approach of Yiddish historiography, xiv, xvi, 62, 63–69, 75–76, 82–83, 229, 290, 315–16
Arendt, Hannah, 3, 103, 117, 209, 235–36, 238, 243, 247, 274, 276, 283, 286, 287, 288; *Eichmann in Jerusalem* (1963), 191
Argentina: *Argentiner YIVO shriftn*, 111; end of Yiddish cultural life in, 160; Leyb-Hoffer Prize, Argentine branch of World Conference for Jewish Culture, 60; *Dos poylishe yidntum* series, 122–23
arms, Jewish resistance and lack of/difficulty of obtaining, 234n30, 237, 240–41
Aroni, Samuel, xvi
Artuski, Issachar, 48, 50, 57
Asch, Sholem, 78, 287
Association of Writers, Journalists and Artists in postwar Polans, 162
Auerbach, Rachel, 29, 35, 37, 40, 41, 42, 45n76, 49, 60, 101, 105, 109, 164, *176*, 186, 188, 272
Auschwitz: Frankl's memoir of, 253; Friedman's monograph on, 122–23, 145–46, 158, 165, 170; personal accounts, preservation of, 142
autobiographical authors, Yiddish historians encouraging, 133–36
awards and prizes won by Yiddish historians, 59–61, 226, 279–80

Baker, Zachary, 301
Bałaban, Meyer, 9n25, 11, 22n3, 26, 43, 91, 141, 199, 220, 302n82
Balberyszski, Mendel, 133, 178
Baldwin, Peter, xv
Band, Arnold, xv
Bar-Ilan University, Israel, chair of Holocaust studies at, 38, 295–96
Baron, Jeanette M., 40–41
Baron, Salo M.: on continuity of Jewish historical experience, 199–200; on Friedman, 61, 84–85; Friedman and, 22n3, 23n4, 35; journals edited by, 112n157, 114; lachrymose and martyrological approaches critiqued by, xiv, 64, 66, 69, 72, 78–79, 290; as synthetic historian, 221; wife and, 40–41
Bass, Hyman G., 280n1
Bauer, Yehuda, 234, 274, 276, 282, 283, 286, 288, 292; *They Chose Life: Jewish Resistance in the Holocaust* (1973), 272–73, 285
Beider, Chaim, 310
Beinfeld, Solon, 299
Ben-Gurion, David, 44
Berenbaum, Michael, xv, 275
Berg, Mary, 35
Berg, Nicholas, 306
Berlin Airlift, 125
Bernfeld, Shimon, 77, 79, 309; *Sefer ha-Demaʿot* (*Book of Tears*; 1923-26), 82
Bernstein, Tatiana, 40
Bershadskii, Sergei, 8n24
Bet Lohame ha-Getaʿot (Ghetto Fighters' House or GFH), Israel, 29–30, 34, 47, 160, 218
Bettelheim, Bruno, 3, 235–36, 247, 283, 284, 286–88; *The Informed Heart* (1960), 286
Beys Yaakov schools, 94
Bialik, Chaim Nachman, "In the City of Slaughter" (1903), 187
Bickel, Shlomo, 148–49; *The Yiddish Essay* (1946), 309

Biderman, I. M., 141
Biebow, Hans, 168n21
Biographical Dictionary of Modern Yiddish Literature (1956–81/1986), 310
Black Book, Jewish Anti-Fascist Committee, Soviet Union, 111n156
Bleter far geshikhte (*Pages for History*; journal), 33n33, 111, 132, 172, 181–82
Bloch, Marc, 219
Bloxham, Donald, 297–98
Blumenfeld, Diana, 60
Blumental, Nachman, 27–28; anti-lachrymose approach of, 65–66; autobiographical authors, encouragement of, 133–35; bibliography, 359–80; camps visited by, 165–66; CJHC/JHI and, 28, 48, 126, 127, 165; continuities, pursuit of, 108–9; on continuity of Jewish historical experience, 200; Dawidowicz's reliance on, 219; death of, 160; Diaspora, historical validation of life in, 291; dual objective/subjective perspective, 150, 154, 155, 156–57; Dworzecki and, 34, 35; everyday life, study of, 213; as folklorist, 27, 44, 67, 94, 104, 142, 188, 299; Friedman and, 27–28, 37, 100–101, 302n83; Galicia, advantages of origins in, 22n3; general Jewish historical work by, 115n166; German versus Jewish sources, use of, 185, 187–90, 192n117; on Holocaust history as Jewish history, 165–66, 192; humor and ridicule, on Jewish use of, 267–68, 275, 302–4; imperative to publish, 127, 128; *Innocent Words* (1947), 189; Israel, migrating to, 29–30, 34–35, 85, 181; in Israel, 29–30; Jewish resistance/passivity, defending/explaining, 230, 231, 232, 235, 238, 240–46; on Jewish unarmed resistance, 257, 265, 267–69, 271, 274, 275, 277;

on Judenrat, 208; Kermish and, 28, 29–30, 34–35, 37, 39, 288; lexicon of Yiddish in Nazi period, 111, 149, 159–60, 188–90, 299–300; Lodz Ghetto, on books recovered from, 82; loss of family members in Holocaust, 154; material culture and, 217, 218; "Myth of Silence" refuted by, 120; Nazi war criminals, pursuit of, 168; original language research, historians' use of/failure to use, 294, 299–304; photos of, *28, 176*; political stance of, 87, 93–94; popular diffusion of Jewish knowledge, commitment to, 103–5; *Dos poylishe yidntum* series, publishing in, 122; prizes and awards, 60; as public figure, 54, 56, 57, 58, 60; publishing venues, 52–53 (table); on religious topics, 215, 216; on reparations, 228; Shildkroyt, posthumous Festschrift for, 40; solicitation and use of personal accounts, 143, 145, 148; Soviet hegemony and politicization of scholarly work, 175n45, 177, 178–79, 181–82; specialized focus of, 67; survival of Nazi occupation by, 84; translations of work of, 281, 298; Trunk and, 29–30, 58; *Tsurikblikn (Backward Glances*; 1973), 108–9; *Verter un vertlekh (Words and Sayings*; 1981), 189; on victim/survivor self-expression, 124–25, 126; Yad Vashem and, 34, 104–5, 187, 189, 295; Yiddish language and, 43, 47–48, 49, 87, 103–4; YIVO and, 27, 30, 58, 104; *yizkor* books and, 136, 137, 138 (map), 139 (table), 140–45, 148, 154, 156–57, 224n233, 231, 268; in *Yunger historiker krayz*, 173n35

Borochov, Ber, 6, 44, 89, 308n106

Boyarin, Jonathan, 137, 142

Braude, Markus, and Braude Schools, 87, 94

Broszat, Martin, 151, 194n123

Browning, Christopher, 148, 297

Buber, Martin, 251, 252n95

Bühler, Josef, 168

Bund: General Jewish Labor Bund, 38, 44; in Israel, 48, 57; in Poland, 91–92, 93, 95, 97, 126, 131, 181

bystander history, 166, 224

Cahiers du Témoignage crétien (Booklets of Christian Witness), 252–53

Calvör, Caspar, 16n54

cantonists, 72–73, 208

"Catastrophe" or "Destruction," as Yiddish historians' English term for Holocaust, xi

Central Historical Commission, Munich, 296–97

Central Jewish Historical Commission of Poland (CJHC; later Jewish Historical Institute [JHI]), xvii, 7, 162–64; anti-lachrymose approach of, 65; antisemitic agitation in Poland and, 32, 33; Auerbach and, 29; Blumental and, 28, 48, 126, 127, 165; directors of Jewish Historical Institute, 32; Dworzecki and, 33–34, 83; Friedman and, 22, 24, 79, 90, 100–101, 127, 143, 145, 165, 294, 297; German versus Jewish sources, use of, 182–83, 186–87, 188; Holocaust history as Jewish history for, 162–64, 165, 167, 168, 170–71, 197–98; imperative to publish at, 127–28; Judenrat, honor courts on former members of, 228–29; Kermish and, 29, 49, 122, 143–44, 150, 165; Lestschinsky and Tcherikower, work of, 197; material culture and, 218; Nazi war criminals, pursuit of, 167–73, 180; Polish Academy of Sciences, absorption by, 182; post-Holocaust archival initiative, 67n18; semi-official status of, 225–26; solicitation and use of personal accounts, 143–44;

Central Jewish Historical Commission of Poland (*cont'd*)
Soviet hegemony and politicization of scholarly work of, 173–82, *176*; Trunk and, 27, 29; victim/survivor self-expression and, 124; Yasni and, 57

Centre de documentation Juive Contemporaine, Paris, Friedman as research director of, 101, 150

characteristics of Yiddish Holocaust historians, xvi–xvii, 62–115; anti-lachrymose approach of, xiv, xvi, 62, 63–69, 75–76, 82–83, 229, 290, 315–16; continuities, pursuit of, 62, 63, 108–10; early focus on Holocaust compared to absence of other Jewish historians, 63–64, 110–15; geographic focus of, 85–86; martyrological approach and, 69–76, 79–83; personal inclinations and affinities, continuity of, 100–107; political stances of, 86–100; reintegration into Jewish society postwar, 85; survival of Nazi occupation by, 22, 83–85, 110–15; Yiddish literature, lachrymose/martyrological approach of, 76–79

Chełmno extermination camp, *28,* 124, 165–66

Cherikover, Elias, 203n3, 302n82

Chmielnicki Uprising (1648), 73, 78, 221

Chwolson, Daniel, 9n26

CJHC. *See* Central Jewish Historical Commission of Poland

Cohen, Boaz, 64, 274n175, 277, 294, xivn2

Cole, Tim, 282

collective memory, 74

collective mutual aid in camps and ghettos, 269–70

collective responsibility, Nazi imposition of, 237–38

Communism: history, Marxist interpretation of, 24, 89–90, 95, 229, 261; Mahler, Marxism of, 132n76;

political stance of Yiddish historians and, 90, 95, 132n76; Soviet hegemony and politicization of scholarly work, 174, 175–80; Yiddish historians and Iron Curtain, 27, 29, 31–33, 85. *See also* Russia/Soviet Union

comparison of Holocaust with other catastrophes, 194, 195–98

Conference on Material Claims Against Germany, 310

Congress for Jewish Culture, 310

Congress of Liberated Jews in the US Zone of Germany, 158

continuity of Jewish historical experience, contextualization of Holocaust within, 194, 198–210

Crusades, Jewish accounts of, 71, 77–78, 197, 224

Czacki, Tadeusz, 8n24

Czerniaków, Adam, 42, 105, 239

Dapim (*Pages*; journal), 47–48, 274

Datner, Szymon, 32, 110, 134

Davar (*Word*; journal), 96, 98

Dawidowicz, Lucy, 21, 64, 234, 277, 303; *The War Against the Jews* (1990), 219

debilitation, Jewish resistance and problem of, 238–39

deception, Jewish resistance and problem of, 239

De-Nur, Yehiel (né Feiner; Ka-Tsetnik), 108

"Destruction" or "Catastrophe," as Yiddish historians' English term for Holocaust, xi

Diaspora: historical validation of life in, 283–93; "negation of the Diaspora" stance, 88, 291

Diaspora nationalism, 86–87, 88, 90, 92, 93, 97, 163, 227, 314

Diner, Dan, 63

Diner, Hasia, 64, 114n165

Dinur, Ben-Zion, 5, 49, 114, 229, 295

disorientation, Jewish resistance and problem of, 239

Displaced Persons (D.P.) camps:
American Joint Distribution
Committee camps, US Zone,
Germany, Friedman as educational
director of, 55n115, 101, 121–22, 135,
150, 181; literature of, 128–29, 135,
146; resettlement of most inhabitants
by 1950, 227; Schwarz's *The Redeemers*
(1953) on, 132
"divide and rule" tactics and problem of
Jewish resistance, 239–40
Dlin, Elly, 195
D.P. camps. *See* Displaced Persons (D.P.)
camps
Dreksler, Adina, 275
Dror Labor-Zionist movement, 309
dual objective/subjective perspective of
Yiddish historians, 149–59
Dubnow, Simon: appeal for Jewish
documents, 67n18; on audience
for YIVO works, 131; current
availability of texts, 302n82; Diaspora
life, historical validation of, 287;
martyrological approach of, 70–71;
on non-Jewish sources, 183; popular
history, Yiddish historians writing for,
56; prewar Yiddish historical work
and, 9, 10, 15–16, 19; as synthetic
historian, 221; Trunk compared, 204;
Velt geshikte fun yidishn folk (*World
History of the Jewish People*; 1948-
1956), 290n41; Yiddish language and,
41; Yiddish studies and, 309; *yizkor*
books and, 141
Dworzecki, Hasia, 41n64, 109
Dworzecki, Mark, 30–31; anti-
lachrymose approach of,
82–83; autobiographical authors,
encouragement of, 135–36; Bar-Ilan
University, chair of Holocaust studies
at, 38, 295–96; bibliography, 396–415;
Blumental and, 34, 35; CJHC/
JHI and, 33–34, 83; continuities,
pursuit of, 109–10; on continuity of
Jewish historical experience, 199;
Dawidowicz's reliance on, 219; death
of, 159; Diaspora, historical validation
of life in, 291; D.P. camps, literature
of, 128–29; dual objective/subjective
perspective, 153, 154; Efroykin and,
259–60; Eichmann trial (1961), as
witness at, 3, 84, 117, 169, 247, 298;
on Estonian Nazi camps, 147–48, 149,
269; *Europe Without Children* (1958),
106–7; everyday life, study of, 213–14;
*The Fight for Health in the Vilna
Ghetto* (1946), 106; Friedman and,
33–34, *34, 37*, 38, 51, 83, 135, 261–62;
general Jewish historical work by,
115n166; *Hirshke glik* (1967), 57,
125–26, 147; on Holocaust history as
Jewish history, 164, 192; imperative to
publish, 128–29; in Israel, 38, 50–51,
85, 99; on Jewish position in Poland,
99; Jewish resistance/passivity,
defending/explaining, 230n14, 235,
240–42, 244, 245; Jewish unarmed
resistance, influencing other authors
regarding, 265–68, 271–77; on
Jewish unarmed resistance, 246–50,
253–65, 269–70; *Kamf farn gezunt
in geto-vilne* (*Fight for Health in the
Vilna Ghetto*; 1946), 33, 261; Kermish
and, 34, 35, 98; languages used by,
42, 43–45, 50–51, 87; on Leivick's *Di
khasene in fernvald* (*The Wedding
in Föhrenwald*), 81–82; loss of wife
and family members in Holocaust,
83, 84, 109–10; material culture and,
217; medical history, research on,
105–7, 199, 253–54; "Myth of Silence"
refuted by, 121; original language
research, historians' use of/failure to
use, 294, 300, 306; in Paris, 31, 33–34,
52, 54–55, 57, 60, 83–84, 85, 98, 106,
121, 164, 170, 227, 256, 261, 291;
photo of, *30*; political stance of, 87,
97–99, 291; prizes and awards, 59–60;
as public figure, 54–55, 56–57, 59–60;
publishing venues, 52–53 (table);

Dworzecki, Mark (cont'd)
on reintegration of survivors into civil society, 85; on religious topics, 215; "Remember the Jewish Catastrophe" (poem; 1948), 140; on reparations, 228, 310; on righteous gentiles, 289; solicitation and use of personal accounts, 147–48, 149; specialized focus of, 67–68; survival of Vilna Ghetto by, 31, 83, 84, 98, 105, 124, 242; trains, on escapes from, 306; translations of work of, 281, 298; Trunk and, 31, 255n104; on victim/survivor self-expression, 124, 125–26, 127; Vilna Ghetto, studies of, 31, 33–34, 37, 57, 59, 83, 98, 105–7, 124, 128, 135–36, 147, 153, 199, 208, 215, 241, 248, 249, 253–55, 261, 270, 275, 289, 298; on women's involvement in Jewish resistance, 305; World Medical Association addressed by, 106, 170; Yad Vashem and, 35, 39, 57; *Yerusholayim d'lite in kamf un umkum* (*Jerusalem of Lithuania in Struggle and Extermination*; 1948), 33, 147, 261, 262, 266, 271, 273, 277, 289, 298, 299, 300, 305; on Yiddishism, 43–45, 50–51, 97; Yiddish studies and, 309; YIVO and, 44; *yizkor* books and, 137–40, 138 (map), 139 (table), 154

Eber, Ada (wife of Philip Friedman), 40, 45n77, 171, 174
Eck, Natan, 35, 49, 114n163, 255–57, 272, 274
Edelman, Marek, 186
Efron, John, xiv
Efroykin, Israel, 233, 258–60, 265; *Kedushe un gvure bay yidn amol un haynt* (Holiness and Heroism among Jews in the Past and Today; 1949), 259
Eichmann, Adolf: Kastner Affair and, 205; trial (1961), 3, 84, 117, 169, 191, 209, 233, 235, 237, 247, 290n42, 298

Eisenbach, Artur, 29n23, 32, 33n33, 110, 168n21, 185
Ekonomishe shriftn (*Economic Writings*; YIVO series), 15
Encyclopaedia Judaica, xiv–xv, 275
Encyclopedia of Jewish Communities (*Pinkas ha-Kehillot*) project, 39, 113, 137n198
Encyclopedia of the Diaspora project, Yiddish (*Entsiklopediyah shel Galuyot*), 39, 49, 137n198
Encyclopedia of the Holocaust (1990), 276
Endelman, Todd, 283–88, 291–93
Engel, David, 64
Entsiklopediyah shel Galuyot (*Encyclopedia of the Diaspora*) project, 39, 137n198
Erik, Max, 308–9, 310
Esh, Shaul, 189n107, 234, 256, 272, 273, 274
Estonia, Nazi camps in, 147–48, 149, 269
everyday life, history of (*Alltagsgeschichte*), contextualization of Holocaust by study of, 194–95, 210–14
Evreiskaia Starina (*Jewish Heritage*; journal), 70
eyewitnesses. *See* survivors of Holocaust

Feigenbaum, Moshe, 296n60
Feuchtwanger, Lion, 157
Filologishe shriftn (journal), 14, 15
Finder, Gabriel N., 228n9
Finkelstein, Chaim, 76
Fischer, Ludwik, 168
Fishman, Joshua, 10, 203
Föhrenwald D.P. Camp, 81–82
Folksgezunt (journal), 199
Forverts (newspaper), 300
France: Academie Nationale de Medecine, 59–60; Annales school, 24, 219; Centre de documentation Juive Contemporaine, Paris, Friedman as research director of, 101, 150; Dworzecki in Paris, 31, 33–34, 52,

54–55, 57, 60, 83–84, 85, 98, 106, 121, 164, 170, 227, 256, 261, 291; spiritual resistance, concept of, 247, 252–53, 258; Survivors Union, 31; Tcherikower escaping Nazis in, 118–19

Frankl, Viktor, *Man's Search for Meaning* (1946), 253, 269

Fransecky, Tanya von, 306

Der fraynd (newspaper), 10n30

Friedländer, Saul, xv, 151, 152, 159, 194n124, 210

Friedman, Philip, 22–25; American Joint Distribution Committee, as educational director of D.P. camps, US Zone, Germany for, 55n115, 101, 121–22, 135, 150, 181; anti-lachrymose approach of, 65, 66, 72, 73, 76; Auschwitz monograph of, 122–23, 145–46, 158, 165, 170; autobiographical authors, encouragement of, 134, 135; bibliography, 325–40; Blumental and, 27–28, 37, 100–101, 302n83; at Centre de documentation Juive Contemporaine, Paris, 101, 150; CJHC/JHI and, 22, 24, 79, 90, 100–101, 127, 143, 145, 165, 294, 297; comparison of Holocaust with other catastrophes, 195–96; continuities, pursuit of, 108; on continuity of Jewish historical experience, 198, 202; Dawidowicz's reliance on, 219; death of, 35, 38, 39–40, 61, 159, 164, 196, 209, 295; Diaspora, historical validation of life in, 202, 290–91; dual objective/subjective perspective, 150–53, 157–59; Dworzecki and, 33–34, *34, 37*, 38, 51, 83, 135, 261–62; early disinterest of Jewish historians in Holocaust and, 64; Ada Eber and, 40; *Extermination of Polish Jews* (1945), 169–70; general Jewish historical work by, 115n166; *German Crimes in Poland* (1946), chapter in, 167–68, 169; German versus Jewish sources, use of, 184–85; *Guide to Jewish History under Nazi Impact* (1960), 181, 102; on Holocaust historiography, 100–102, 115, 146, 249–50; on Holocaust history as Jewish history, 165–67, 170, 171, 174, 175, 190–91, 192–93, 292; humor and ridicule, on Jewish use of, 302n83; imperative to publish, 127; importance in Yiddish historiography, xiv, 61; Israel visited by, 36–37, 38, 53, 192; Jewish resistance/passivity, defending/explaining, 230–31, 233, 234–35, 236, 239–43; on Jewish unarmed resistance, 249–50, 264–66; Kermish and, 28, 29, 36–37, 39–40, 95, 98, 100–101, 105; languages used by, 42–43, 45–46, 47, 87; loss of family members in Holocaust, 84–85; Mahler and, 171; Ber Mark and, 37n47; martyrological approach and, 73, 79–80; *Martyrs and Fighters* (1954), 91, 229n11, 281, 282; material culture and, 217; "Myth of Silence" refuted by, 118–20, 121–22; on November uprising (1830), 227n6; at Nuremberg Trials, 85, 168; organization of Jewish historical field and, 100–102; original language research, historians' use of/failure to use, 294; photos of, *23, 176*; on Polish High Commission to Investigate the German Crimes in Poland, 165, 167–68; political stance of, 87–90; on popular historical scholarship, 131–32; *Dos poylishe yidntum* series, publishing in, 122–23; programmatic outlines for Holocaust research, 101–2; as public figure, 53–56, 57, 61, 226; publishing venues, 52–53 (table); regionalism supported by, 24–25, 88–89, 219–22; on religious topics, 215; on righteous gentiles, 166, 289–90; *Roads to Extinction* (1980), 92n91, 118; solicitation and use of personal accounts, 1, 143–46, 148–49;

Friedman, Philip (cont'd)
  Soviet hegemony and politicization of scholarly work, 174, 175–80, 229; specialized focus of, 68; survival of Nazi occupation by, 84, 114, 289; on synthetic approach, 219–22; *Their Brothers' Keepers* (1957), 166, 281, 282, 289–90; translations of work of, 281, 288, 298; Trunk and, 25–27, 35, 36, 39–40, 91, 92n91, 93, 209; United States, emigrating to, 35, 85, 227, 291; University of Lodz, professorship at, 226; on victim/survivor self-expression, 123–24, 125; on Warsaw Ghetto/Uprising, 146, 264–65; Yad Vashem and, 102, 192; YIVO and, 24, 25, 37, 55, 88, 100, 102, 113, 295; *YIVO bleter* and *YIVO Annual* (1953) co-edited by, 39; *yizkor* books and, 89, 136, 137, 138 (map), 139 (table), 140, 141, 144, 220, 221, 222
Friedman, Tuviah, 228
Fuchs, Harold, 250–51
Fun letstn khurbn (From the Last Extermination; journal), 246
Fun noentn over (The Recent Past; journal), 11, 15

Galicia, advantages of origins in, 22n3
Gar, Joseph, 135, 153, 221–22
Gedank un lebn/The Jewish Review, 111–12
geistiger Widerstand, 247, 250, 251–52nn93–94, 258
Gelber, Nathan Michael, 110, 141
gender. *See* women
General Jewish Labor Bund, 38, 44
German Crimes in Poland (1946), 167–68, 169
German versus Jewish sources, 182–90, 191
Germany: American Joint Distribution Committee, US Zone, Friedman as educational director of D.P. camps of, 55n115, 101, 121–22, 135, 150, 181; Berlin, prewar Yiddish historical practice in, 11; Central Historical Commission, Munich, 296–97; Congress of Liberated Jews in the US Zone of, 158; illusive Jewish belief in German civilization and rationality, 243–44; intentionalist approach to WWII behavior in, 69–70; "Jewish Question" in, 16–17; reparations agreement between Israel and West Germany (1952), 228, 310; spiritual resistance, concept of, 247, 250–52, 258
Gessen, Julius, 9n25, 9n28
Getz, Menahem, 214n194
Ghetto Fighters' House (Bet Lohame ha-Geta'ot; GFH), Israel, 29–30, 34, 47, 160, 218
Gilbert, Martin, 59, 234, 297–98
Ginsburg, Saul, xiii–xiv, 3n4, 4, 9–11, 13, 15, 72–73, 132, 141, 209, 287, 302n82, 309
Glatstein, Jacob, 261
Glik, Hirsh, 57, 125–26, 147
Goldberg, Amos, 292, 299
"golden chain" metaphor in Yiddish literature, 124, 160–61, 272
Di goldene keyt (The Golden Chain; journal), 49, 106, 206, 272
Goldhar-Mark, Esther, 41n64
Górniewicz, Józef, 168
Göth, Amon, 168
Grade, Chaim, 123, 175n45
Graetz, Heinrich, 56, 80, 119, 158, 221, 309
Grayek, Stefan, 186
Great Dictionary of the Yiddish Language, 311
Greenberg, Eliezer, 287
Greenberg, Irving, 99
Gringauz, Samuel, 158
Gris, Noah, 54
Grosman, Moyshe, 53n107
Grossman, Chaika, 257–58
Gruss, Noe, 167

Gumplowicz, Ludwik, 9n26
Gutman, Israel, 208, 273; *The Jews of Warsaw, 1939–1942* (1983), 286
Guttmann, Josef, 287
Gypsies, 196

Habermann, A. M., 77–78
Habermas, Jürgen, 63
Handelsman, Marceli, 29n23
Handlin, Oscar, 233n26
Hannover, Natan Note, *Yeven Metzulah* (*Deep Mire*; 1653), 73, 128
Haskalah (Jewish Enlightenment), 23, 67, 259
Haynt (*Today*; newspaper), 18–19, 44, 76, 89
Hebrew language: conflict over use of Yiddish versus, 43–45, 50–51, 97; historical practice in, 5; Holocaust, Yiddish/Hebrew use of/terms for, xi; religious Jews generally writing in, 214; vernacular, doubts about future as, 5–6
Hebrew University, xv, 5, 15, 50, 113, 114, 249, 295
Helsinfors Zionist conference (1906), 87
Henry, Patrick, 236
Heschel, Abraham Joshua, xviii
Hesemeyer, Eilert, 168
Hilberg, Raul, 3, 69, 193n120, 209, 234, 236, 238, 247, 283, 284, 287, 288, 292, 313; *The Destruction of the European Jews* (1961), 117, 191, 284
Hillgruber, Andreas, 194n122
Hirshaut, Julian, 47–48, 302n82
Histadrut Labor Federation, 94
"Historical Jewish Press" (online source), 312
historical materialism, 89
Historikerstreit, 193–95
Historishe shriftn (*Historical Writings*; YIVO series), 13, 15, 20, 70–71
Hitler, Adolf, 69, 155, 171, 245, 256, 303
Holocaust historiography: accepted truths opposed by Yiddish historians, 3–4; early absence of non-Yiddish Jewish historians in, 63–64, 110–15; final link in chain of transmission, Yiddish historiography as, 159–61, 314–15; Friedman on organization of, 100–102, 115, 146, 249–50; relationship to mainstream Jewish history, 113–15; as rupture versus continuity, 62, 63; survivors, Yiddish historians as, 22, 83–85, 110–15; Yiddish/Hebrew use of/terms for Holocaust, xi; Yiddish language and, 110–15. *See also* public discourse on Holocaust; survivors of Holocaust; Yiddish historians of the Holocaust
Holocaust history as Jewish history, xvii, 162–224, 317; CJHC and, 162–64, 165; comparison with other catastrophes, contextualization by, 194, 195–98; continuity of Jewish historical experience, contextualization by, 194, 198–210; Diaspora, historical validation of life in, 283–93; German versus Jewish sources, use of, 182–90, 191; *Historikerstreit*, moral issues raised by, 193–95; history of everyday life (*Alltagsgeschichte*), contextualization by study of, 194–95, 210–14; Nazi war criminals, Yiddish historians' pursuit of, 167–73, 180; perpetrator/bystander studies versus, 3, 68, 69, 71, 106, 114, 165–67, 169–71, 180–83, 193n120, 195, 210, 218, 224, 228, 232, 282, 315, 318; recognition of Jewish experience as normative basis for Holocaust research, 190–93; religious and material culture, Yiddish historians' omission of, 214–18; Soviet hegemony and politicization of scholarly work, 173–82; struggle for Jewish orientation, 164, 165–82; synthetic history, lack of, 218–24; transmission of approach to broader academic culture, 298–99

honor courts, 228–29
Horn, Maurycy, 167
Höss, Rudolf, 168, 179
hostile surrounding population, Jewish resistance and problem of, 241
Howe, Irving, 287
Huberband, Shimon, 105, 130, 141, 215–16
humor and ridicule, Jewish use of, 267–68, 275, 302–4
hurban, as Hebrew term for Holocaust, xi

Idisher kemfer (*Jewish Fighter*; journal), 56, 88, 98, 248
Di idishe velt (*The Jewish World*; journal), 10
"Index to Yiddish Periodicals" (online source), 312
Institute for Belorussian Culture, 7
Institute for Jewish Studies, Warsaw, 11, 27
International Congress of Historians, 24, 89
International Red Cross, 281
Israel: anti-Yiddish period in, 44–45, 51, 58n128; Bar-Ilan University, chair of Holocaust studies at, 38, 295–96; Bund in, 48, 57; Eichmann trial (1961) in, 3, 84, 117, 169, 191, 209, 233, 235, 237, 247, 290n42, 298; Friedman visiting, 36–37, 38, 53, 192; Friends of YIVO in, 30, 56, 151; GFH (Ghetto Fighters' House; Bet Lohame ha-Geta'ot), 29–30, 34, 47, 160, 218; Hebrew University, xv, 5, 15, 50, 113, 114, 249, 295; Jewish historical practice in, xv; Kastner, Rudolph, and Kastner Affair (1954-55), 205, 206; "negation of the Diaspora" stance in, 291; reparations agreement with West Germany (1952), 228, 310; Yiddish historians migrating to, 29–30, 34–35, 38, 54, 85, 92, 227. *See also* Union of Yiddish Writers and Journalists; Yad Vashem

Jerusalem School of historians, xv, 2, 15–16
Jewish badges, research on, 166, 169
Jewish Book Annual, 279
Jewish Book Council, 279
Jewish Frontier (journal), 56
Jewish Historical-Ethnographic Society, 9
Jewish Historical Institute (JHI). *See* Central Jewish Historical Commission of Poland
Jewish history, Holocaust history as. *See* Holocaust history as Jewish history
Jewish leadership: Jewish resistance and problem of, 242; Judenrat as, 207–9
"Jewish Question," 9, 16–18, 228
Jewish resistance, xvii, 230–46; Blumental on, 230, 231, 232, 235, 238, 240–46; criticisms of passivity, 3, 103, 117, 191, 209, 229–37, 283, 284; "divide and rule" tactics, 239–40; Dworzecki on, 230n14, 235, 240–42, 244, 245; Friedman on, 230–31, 233, 234–35, 236, 239–43; German/Nazi actions, Jewish experience of, 237–40; German versus Jewish sources, use of, 185, 186; internal problems of Jewish community and, 241–46; Kermish on, 231–32, 237, 240; "psychological readiness" for, 201–3; responses to critiques of, 238–46; Ringelblum on, 231–32, 258; "sheep to the slaughter," 230, 232, 272; trains, escapes from, 306; Trunk on, 72, 209–10, 230–31, 233, 234–35, 236, 238–41, 243–45; weapons, lack of/difficulty of obtaining, 234n30, 237, 240–41; women's involvement in, 95, 125, 264, 304–6; Yad Vashem Conference on, 39, 232, 247, 270–71, 272, 274, 303; Yiddish historians' focus on, 230, 316. *See also* Jewish unarmed resistance; Warsaw Ghetto Uprising
Jewish Social Studies, 114

Jewish State Museum, Vilnius, 275–76
Jewish Teachers' Seminary and People's University, New York, 45–47, 111–12, 291
Jewish unarmed resistance, 246–78; as *Amidah* ("standing up against"), 247, 250, 269, 270, 273, 274, 276, 277; Blumental on, 257, 265, 267–69, 271, 274, 275, 277; as collective mutual aid, 269–70; Dworzecki influencing other writers on, 265–68, 271–77; Dworzecki on, 246–50, 253–65, 269–70; Efroykin on, 258–60; Friedman on, 249–50, 264–66; humor and ridicule, Jewish use of, 267–68, 275, 302–4; Kermish on, 266–67, 271, 275; as *Kidush ha-Hayim* ("the sanctification of life"), 247, 255–57, 273, 274; medical resistance in Vilna Ghetto, 33, 105–6, 253–54, 261; redefining concept of resistance through, 246–50; as spiritual resistance, 247, 250–53, 258–66, 270, 274–76; Trunk on, 262–64, 265, 271, 275; at Yad Vashem Conference on Jewish resistance, 270–71, 272, 274, 303
Jewish versus German sources, 182–90, 191
JHI (Jewish Historical Institute). *See* Central Jewish Historical Commission of Poland
Jockusch, Laura, 64, 80, 228n9, 294, xivn2
"the Joint." *See* American Joint Distribution Committee
Jost, Marcus, 221
Joyner, Charles, 210–11n183
Judenräte: Dworzecki on membership of Vilna Judenrat, 37; honor courts on former members of, 228–29; as Jewish leadership, 207–9; Trunk on ideology of, 204–7; Trunk's *Judenrat* (1964), 58, 60–61, 91, 103, 142, 147, 209–10, 223–24, 236, 280–81, 282, 284–85, 292, 294, 313

Kaczerginski, Shmerke, 175n45; *Khurbn vilne* (*Destruction of Vilna*; 1947), 83
Kagan, Berl, 310
Kaganovitsh, Moyshe (Moshe Kahanovitsh), 135, 203n82, 261
Kalmanovitch, Zelig, 19–20, 129, 258
Kamiński, Franciszek, 84n70
Kaplan, Israel, 146
Kaplan, Louis, 303–4
Karlip, Joshua, 74
Kassow, Samuel, xv, 258
Kastner, Rudolph, and Kastner Affair (1954-55), 205, 206, 207
katastrofe, as Yiddish term for Holocaust, xi
Ka-Tsetnik (Yehiel De-Nur, né Feiner), 108
Katzmann, Friedrich, 184–85
Katznelson, Yitskhok, 213; "Song of the Murdered Jewish People," 125–26
Kent, Martin, 54n108, 297
Kermish, Joseph, 28–30; anti-lachrymose approach of, 65; autobiographical authors, encouragement of, 133, 134; bibliography, 381–95; Blumental and, 28, 29–30, 34–35, 37, 39, 288; camps visited by, 165–66; CJHC/JHI and, 29, 49, 122, 143–44, 150, 165; comparison of Holocaust with other catastrophes, 197–98; continuities, pursuit of, 109; on continuity of Jewish historical experience, 201–2; Dawidowicz's reliance on, 219; documentary and archival aspects of history, inclination toward, 105; dual objective/subjective perspective, 150, 154, 156; Dworzecki and, 34, 35, 98; everyday life, study of, 213; final Holocaust works of, as end of Yiddish historical practice, 4–5; Friedman and, 28, 29, 36–37, 39–40, 95, 100–101, 105; Galicia, advantages of origins in, 22n3; general Jewish historical work by, 115n166;

Kermish, Joseph (*cont'd*)
German versus Jewish sources, use of, 183, 185, 186, 187–88; on Holocaust historiography, 115; on Holocaust history as Jewish history, 165–66, 170–71, 183; imperative to publish, 128, 129–31; Israel, migrating to, 29–30, 34–35, 54, 85, 181; Jewish resistance/passivity, defending/explaining, 231–32, 237, 240; on Jewish unarmed resistance, 266–67, 271, 275; on Kościuszko's Jewish adherents, 225, 226; languages used by, 43, 47, 49, 87; on "the lesson" of the Holocaust, 229; Mahler and, 171; material culture and, 217, 218; "Myth of Silence" refuted by, 120; Nazi war criminals, pursuit of, 168, 170–71; original language research, historians' use of/failure to use, 294, 301, 307; photos of, *28, 176*; political stance of, 87, 94–97; *Dos poylishe yidntum* series, publishing in, 122; prizes and awards, 59, 226; as public figure, 54, 56, 57, 59, 226; as public historian, 29; publishing venues, 52–53 (table), 160; on religious topics, 215, 216; on righteous gentiles, 289; Ringelblum and, 96, 105, 109, 213, 231–32, 266, 275n177; solicitation and use of personal accounts, 143–44, 148; Soviet hegemony and politicization of scholarly work, 175n45, 177, 181; specialized focus of, 68; survival of Nazi occupation by, 84, 111, 289; on thefts of Jewish property, 307; translations of work of, 281, 288, 298; Trunk and, 29–30, 37–38, 40, 92, 102, 130–31, 160; on victim/survivor self-expression, 124; Warsaw City Council, research on Jewish members of, 94–96; on Warsaw Ghetto/Uprising, 109, 122, 129–31, 140, 185, 186, 187, 201, 206, 215, 257, 260n126, 263, 266–67, 286; on women's involvement in Jewish resistance, 305–6; Yad Vashem, 34–35, 59, 96, 105, 129–30, 187, 218, 295; Yiddish studies and, 309; YIVO and, 30; *yizkor* books and, 136, 137, 138 (map), 139 (table), 140, 266–67, 298

khurbn, as Yiddish term for Holocaust, xi
ha-Kibutz ha-Me'uhad (United Kibbutz Movement), 48
Kidush ha-Hayim ("the sanctification of life"), 247, 255–57, 272, 273, 274
Kidush ha-Shem (self-sacrifice; sanctification of the name), 265, 273
Kiem (*Existence*; journal), 258
Kiln, Abraham, 280n1
Kon, Pinkhas, 13n41
Korman, Gerd, 280
Korn, Ludwik, 168
Kościuszko, Tadeusz, 95, 129, 225, 226
Kosover, Mordecai, 280n1
Kovner, Abba, 232
Kraushar, Alexander, 9n26
Kruk, Herman, 267
Kugelmass, Jack, 137, 142
Kuhn-Kennedy, Fleur, 300
Kuperstein, Isaiah, *36*
Kurland, Leyb, 213
Kushner, Tony, 297–98
Kutno, Trunk's history of, 91, 93, 108, 140, 153–54, 183
Kuznitz, Cecile Esther, 18n59

Labor Zionist Hashomer Hatzair party, 34
Lacquer, Walter, *The Terrible Secret* (1980), 286
Landkentnish (*Knowing the Land*; journal) and *Landkentnish* movement, 15, 24, 26, 42, 88, 100
law, Jewish resistance and loyalty to, 242–43
Lawson, Tom, *Debates on the Holocaust* (2010), 274
Lazebnik, Joel, 173, 181
leadership, Jewish. *See* Jewish leadership
Dos leben (*Life*; journal), 10n30
Lebns-fragn (*Life Questions*; journal), 48, 92, 93

Leftwich, Joseph, 287
Lehman, Shmuel, 126
Leivick, H., *Di khasene in fernvald* (*The Wedding in Föhrenwald*; 1949), 81–82, 192
Leon Johnson Award, 280nn1–2
"the lesson" of the Holocaust, Yiddish historians not seeking, 114n163, 229
Lestschinsky, Jacob, 81, 197, 230n14
Levite, Abraham, 143–44n123
Lindenthal, Jacob Jay, 288
Linder, Menachem, 24–25
Literarishe bleter (*Literary Pages*; journal), 15, 18, 27, 35, 55, 93, 104
Lodz Friends of YIVO, 24, 27, 100
Lodz Ghetto: autobiographical authors, encouragement of, 135; books recovered from, 82; difficulty of resistance in, 241; literary productivity in, 124, 200; Nazi war criminals, post-war pursuit of, 168n21; Rosenblum's drama about, 58; solicitation and use of personal accounts, 143; Trunk's history of, 51–53, 147, 184, 204, 212–13, 235, 280, 285, 294, 299, 300, 313; Yasni's history of, 57
Lodzsher visnshaftleke shriftn (*Lodz Scholarly Writings*; journal), 100
Loose, Ingo, 300
Lubliner shtime (*Lublin Voice*; newspaper), 93
Lubliner togblat (*Lublin Daily Paper*; newspaper), 93, 104

Magnus, Judah, 252n95
Mahler, Raphael: on aims of CJHC, 171–72; current availability of texts, 302n82; emigration to United States (1937), 12, 32, 110, 111; Friedman and, 22, 24, 89n81; *Gedank un lebn*/*The Jewish Review*, on editorial board of, 112n157; at Jewish Teachers' Seminary and People's University, New York, 45n78; lachrymose approach critiqued by Trunk, 67; Marxism of, 24, 132n76; regional studies by, 220; Ringelblum and, 102–3, 172; Trunk's work reviewed by, 72; Yiddish language and, xiv, 12, 42, 111; Yiddish language championed by, xiv; Yiddish studies and, 309; *yizkor* books and, 141
Maimonides, 205n166
Mandeslberg-Shildkroyt, Bella, 40, 141
Mann, Thomas, 251
Mapai party, 51, 206
Mark, Ber (Bernard), 32, 37n47, 41n64, 90, 95, 110, 175n45, 180, 213, 261, 286, 294
Marrus, Michael, 64, 273
martyrological approach, 69–76, 79–83
Marxist interpretation of history, 24, 89–90, 95, 229, 261
Mashberg, Michael, 36
material studies: in prewar Yiddish historical practice, 67; Yiddish Holocaust historians generally ignoring, 216–18
Matthäus, Jürgen, 281
McCumber, John, 63
medical history: Dworzecki's research on, 105–7, 199, 253–54; Nazi medical research, ethics of using, 193; Ringelblum on Jewish doctors in Poland, 199n138; Trunk on diseases and mortality rates in Warsaw Ghetto, 203–4, 288; Vilna Ghetto, medical resistance in, 33, 105–6, 253–54, 261; Warsaw Ghetto, clandestine medical school in, 199; Warsaw Ghetto, "starvation disease" research from, 193
Meisel, Basya, 27n19
Meisel, Nachman, 18, 28, 54n109
Melezin, Abraham, 112n157
memory, 74, 77, 83, 229
Mendelsohn, Shlomo, 75, 112
Menes, Abraham, 110, 309
Metsudah (*Fortress*; journal), 248
Meyer, Michael, 17–18

Michel, Henri, 280–81
Michman, Dan, 114, 273, 295, 296
Milton, Sybil, 305
Mirsky, Mikhl, 173, 175–79
Mitelberg, Abraham, 123
Morreall, John, 303
Mosty (*Bridges*; journal), 34
Motzkin, Leon, 197
Muzikant, B., 10n30
Myers, David N., xv, 17, 77–78, 81
"Myth of Silence," xvii, 64, 117–23

Dos naye lebn (*New Life*; newspaper), 79, 167, 173, 179, 180
Nazis and Nazism: Friedman comparing Communism to, 90; prewar Yiddish historical responses to, 19; question of Jewish resistance and Jewish experience of German/Nazi actions, 237–40; Ringelblum perishing under, 31–32; Yiddish historians' personal survival of, 22, 83–85, 110–15; Yiddish historians' pursuit of war criminals, 167–73, 180, 228
"negation of the Diaspora" stance, 88, 291
Netzer, Shlomo, 167
Neugroschel, Joachim, 36
New Frontier (journal), 92n91
News of Yad Vashem, 129–30
Nicholas I (tsar), 14, 208
Niger, Shmuel, 65n13, 77–78; *Kidush hashem* (anthology, 1948), 248
Nimtzovitch, Itzhak, 59
Nissenbaum, Isaac, 255, 257, 272
Nolte, Ernst, 194n122
nonviolent resistance. *See* Jewish unarmed resistance
Nordau, Max, 185
November uprising (1830), Poland, 226–27
Novershtern, Avrom, xiv
Novick, Peter, 213
Novitch, Miriam, 218n211
Nuremberg Trials, 85, 168, 213

objective/subjective perspective of Yiddish historians, 149–59
Olitski, Moshe, 270; *Yeven Metzulah—Book 2,* 128
Opatoshu, Joseph, 158
OPE (Society for the Dissemination of Enlightenment among the Jews), 10
Operation Reinhard, 213
optimism, and Jewish resistance, 244–45
Orenstein, Benjamin, 55, 135, 146, 158
Orshanskii, Ilia, 9n25, 9n28
ORT, banned in Poland, 181
Ostrover, Chava, *It Kept Us Alive* (2014), 303–4
Oyfn sheydveg (*At the Crossroads*; journal), 258
Oyneg Shabes project, Warsaw Ghetto, 25, 29, 31, 65, 105, 128, 129, 175, 203, 215, 271, 275n177, 281

Parizer shriftn (*Parisian Writings*; journal), 254
passivity, Jewish. *See* Jewish resistance
Pat, Jacob, 163, 174–76
PEN Club movement, 44
Peretz, Y. L., 287
perpetrator history, 3, 68, 69, 71, 106, 114, 165–67, 169–71, 180–83, 193n120, 195, 210, 218, 224, 228, 232, 282, 315, 318
Person, Katarzyna, 300–301
Petropoulos, Jonathan, 307
Pilsudski, Jozef, 19
Pine, Lisa, 305
Pinkas ha-Kehillot (*Encyclopedia of Jewish Communities*) project, 39, 113, 137n198
Pinkes (journal), 13n42
Pinson, Koppel, 114n165
Piotrków-Trybunalski, 91, 267, 298
Płock: Kermish's *yizkor* book on, 267; Trunk's 1936 monograph on Jews of, 18–19, 44, 72, 93, 103, 183, 216
pogroms, historical studies of, 68, 70–71, 73, 74, 76, 80, 163, 187, 197, 228

Pohl, Dieter, 307
Poland: antisemitic agitation post-war in, 32, 33, 85, 99, 164, 225; Bund in, 91–92, 93, 95, 97, 126, 131, 181; geographic focus of Yiddish historians on, 85–86; Institute for Jewish Studies, Warsaw, 11, 27; Jewish nationalisms in, 86–87; November uprising (1830), 226–27; Operation Reinhard, 213; post-war possibility of rebuilding Jewish communal life in, 162, 225–27; prewar Yiddish historical practice in, 11–13, 14; publicly strained relations between Western and Warsaw historians, 37n47; Soviet hegemony and politicization of scholarly work in, 173–82; Stalinist takeover of, 33, 85, 90, 95, 163–64; Yiddish historians and Iron Curtain, 27, 29, 31–33, 85; Yiddish historians' departures from, 85. *See also* Central Jewish Historical Commission of Poland
Poliakov, Léon, 69, 150, 169n23, 193; *Das Dritte Reich und die Juden* (with Joseph Wulf; 1955), 191; *Harvest of Hate* (1951), 190
Polish Academy of Sciences, 182
Polish High Commission to Investigate the German Crimes in Poland, 165, 167
Polish-Jewish nationalism, 86–87, 88–89, 93, 94, 95, 96, 98–99
political stances of Yiddish Holocaust historians, 86–100. *See also specific political parties and positions*
Ponar mass murder site, 83, 84, 244, 298
prewar Yiddish historical practice, xvi, 4–20; anti-lachrymose approach of, 62, 66–67; audience for, 15–16, 55; as dissident and populist undertaking, 8–11; engaged scholarship, tradition of, 16, 18–19; geographical centers of, 9, 11–13, 66; internal aspects of Jewish history, focus on, 19–20; "Jewish Question" and, 9, 16–19; material studies in, 67; multiple languages, contexts, and identities of historians, 5, 6–8; post-Enlightenment origins, 4–6; as transnational and pan-Yiddish enterprise, 13–15; university education and scholarly connections, 12–13, 17, 18; WWI and Russian revolution, 10–11; Yiddish historians of the Holocaust, prewar writings of, 18–19; YIVO and, 5, 7, 12, 13, 14, 15, 18
Pribram, Alfred Francis, 23n4
prizes and awards won by Yiddish historians, 59–61, 226, 279–80
"psychological readiness" and continuity of Jewish experience, 201–3
publications: CJHC publications mainly in Polish, 226; imperative to publish, 127–31; online sources, 312; translations of works of Yiddish historians, 51–53, 160n195, 279–83, 287–88; Warsaw Ghetto underground press, 37–38, 97, 105, 130–31, 201, 206, 263, 306; Yiddish historians, publishing venues for, 52–53 (table), 132–33, 160; Yiddish publications, rise and fall of market for, 159–60
public discourse on Holocaust, xvii, 116–61; autobiographical authors, encouragement of, 133–36; Blumental's lexicon of Yiddish in Nazi period and, 149, 159–60; dual objective/subjective perspective, 149–59; early absence of non-Yiddish Jewish historians in, 63–64, 110–15; final link in chain of transmission, Yiddish historiography as, 159–61, 314–15; imperative to publish, 127–31; lay-professional partnership, encouragement of, 131–49; "Myth of Silence," xvii, 64, 117–23; popular scholarship, emphasis on, 131–133; solicitation and use of personal accounts, 142–49; victims and survivors, literary productivity of, 116–17, 123–27;

public discourse on Holocaust (*cont'd*)
  yizkor books, reviewing and writing for, 39, 51, 108, 109, 115n166, 136–42, 138 (map), 139 (table)
public figures, Yiddish historians as, 53–61, 225–26

Ranke, Leopold von, 196, 212, 213
Rapoport-Albert, Ada, 71
Ravitch, Melech, 55, 109
Rawidowicz, Simon, 248
Red Cross, 281
regionalism, Jewish: Friedman supporting, 24–25, 88–89, 219–22; Trunk supporting, 26–27, 220, 222–24
Reitlinger, Gerald, 228–29, 234; *The Final Solution* (1954), 69, 190–91, 193
Rejzen, Zalmen, 76, 310
religious topics, Yiddish historians seldom addressing, 214–16
reparations, 228, 310
resistance, Jewish. *See* Jewish resistance; Jewish unarmed resistance
Résistance spirituelle, 247, 250, 252, 253n98, 258
ridicule and humor, Jewish use of, 267–68, 275, 302–4
righteous gentiles, 70, 166, 288–90
Ringelblum, Emanuel: current availability of texts, 302n82; Friedman and, 22, 24; on Jewish doctors in Poland, 199n138; on Jewish passivity/resistance, 231–32, 258; on Jews writing their own history, 171; Kassow's study of, xv, 31n31, 258n117; Kermish and, 29n23, 96, 105, 109, 213, 231–32, 266, 275n177; letter on "Jewish cultural work in the ghettos of Poland," 112; Linder and, 25; Mahler and, 102–3, 172; Marxism of, 24, 89–90; Nazis, perishing under, 31–32; *Notes*, 31, 109, 128, 130, 160, 231, 303; Oyneg Shabes project and, 31, 65, 128, 175, 203, 215, 275n177; publication of works of, 128; Trunk and, 26, 102–3; on victim/survivor urge to self-expression, 123–24; on women in Warsaw Ghetto, 304; Yiddish language and, xiv, 12, 42; Yiddish studies and, 310; *yizkor* books and, 141
Ringelblum Archive, 31, 56, 124, 128, 129, 175, 187, 215, 301
Ringelheim, Joan, 305
Robinson, Jacob, 191n115
Roland, Charles, 288
Roseman, Mark, 281
Rosenblum, Shammai, 58
Roskies, David, 78, 299
Rost, Nella, 178
Rozett, Robert, 152, 276, 277
Rudavsky, Joseph, *To Live with Hope, To Die with Dignity* (1978), 274–75
Rumkowski, Mordechai, 174, 200, 244n74
Runes, Dagobert, 114n165
Russia/Soviet Union: Black Book, Jewish Anti-Fascist Committee, 111n156; hegemony of, and politicization of scholarly work, 173–82; Jewish nationalism and particularism, efforts to eradicate, 164; Poland, Stalinist takeover of, 33, 85, 90, 95, 163–64; prewar Yiddish historical practice in, 9, 12–13, 14; revolution of 1917, 10; suppression of non-Russian languages, after 1929, 14n43, 98; Yiddish historians and Iron Curtain, 27, 29, 31–33, 85. *See also* Communism

"the sanctification of life" (*Kidush ha-Hayim*), 247, 255–57, 272, 273, 274
Schiper, Isaac, xiv, 12, 14, 22n3, 42, 141, 220, 227n6, 309, 310
Schmidt, Anton, 289
Schneerson, Isaac, 150
Schorr, Moses, 9n25, 11, 22n3, 42
Schroeter, Gudrun, 276–77, 300
Schulman, Elias, 10n30, 48, 302n82
Schulweis, Harold, 289–90

Schwartz, Jan, 294
Schwarz, Leo, *The Redeemers* (1953), 132
self-sacrifice *(Kidush ha-Shem;* sanctification of the name)*, 265, 273
Sfard, Dovid, 175
Shandler, Jeffrey, xiii, 293
Shapiro, Robert Moses, *36,* 53
Sharrett, Moshe, 206
Shatzky, Jacob, xiv, 3n4, 12, 14, 29n23, 45n78, 73, 110, 111, 141, 202, 221, 222–23, 302n82, 309, 310, 314
Shayevitsh, Simkhe Bunin, 200
Shazar, Zalman, 209
"sheep to the slaughter," 230, 232, 272
Sheintuch, Yehiel, 300
shelilat ha-galut (negation of the exile), 229
Shnayderman, Shmuel-Leyb, 35, 168
Shner, Tzvi, 48
Sho'ah, as Hebrew term for Holocaust, xi
Shoshkes, Chaim, 175
Shpizman, Leyb, 75, 112
Shtif, Nokhem, 3n4
Shul-kult movement, 94
silence, myth of, xvii, 64, 117–23
Simon, Ernst (Akiba), 251–52
Singer, Isaac Bashevis, 310
Sloan, Jacob, 303
Smoliar, Hersh, 182, 233
Sobibór, 178
Society for the Dissemination of Enlightenment among the Jews (OPE), 10
Society of Friends of History, Warsaw, 96
Society of History and Antiquities, Krakow, 99
Society of Lublin Survivors, 160
Sokołów Podlaski Ghetto, 128
Soviet Union. *See* Russia/Soviet Union
Spiegel, Isaiah, 213
spiritual resistance, Jewish unarmed resistance as, 247, 250–53, 258–66, 270, 274–76
Stalin, Joseph, 90, 181–82

Stalinist takeover of Poland, 33, 85, 90, 95, 163–64
Steinschneider, Moritz, 308n106
Strigler, Mordecai, 123
Stroop, Jürgen, 184–86, 213
subjective/objective perspective of Yiddish historians, 149–59
Suhl, Y., *They Fought Back* (1967), 288
suicide in ghettos, 260
survivors of Holocaust: dual objective/subjective perspective of Yiddish historians, 149–59; Dworzecki on reintegration into civil society, 85; on Jewish passivity and Jewish resistance, 232–33, 248; literary productivity of, 116–17, 123–27; solicitation and use of personal accounts of, 142–49, 296–98, 315; Yad Vashem, between Israel historians and survivor-historians at, 49, 105, 113–14; Yiddish historians of Holocaust as, 22, 83–85, 110–15
Survivors Union, France, 31
Sutzkever, Avrom, 50, 106, 175n45
synthetic history, Yiddish historians' lack of, 218–24
Szabad, Cemach, 107
Szajkowski, Zosa, 113, 142, 218

Tabakman, Israel, 49
Tabaksblat, Israel, 146–47
Taffet, Gerszon, 134, 289
Tarbut school system, 94, 97–98
Tarfon, Rabbi, 137
Tcherikower, Elias: Efroykin and, 258; Friedman on, 79–80; on Jewish catastrophe (1941), 73–76, 82, 112, 118–19, 287, 308; pan-Ashkenazi approach of, xiv; on pogroms, 68, 70–71, 73, 74, 76, 80, 163, 197, 228; prewar historiography and, 6, 14–15, 19, 20; translations of, 287–88; Yiddish studies and, 309, 310
Tec, Nechama, 236
Tenenbaum, Joseph, 193

theft of Jewish property by Germans, 228, 307
Tokarz, Wacław, 29n23
Tolstoy, Leo, 157
trains, escapes from, 306
translations of works of Yiddish historians, 51–53, 160n195, 279–83, 287–88, 298
transmission of Yiddish historians' works to broader culture, xviii, 279–312; final link in chain, Yiddish historiography as, 159–61, 314–15; Holocaust history as Jewish history, 298–99; humor and ridicule, Jewish use of, 267–68, 275, 302–4; importance and significance of, 307–8; original language research, historians' use of/failure to use, 293–308; scholarly absorption of ideas, 283–93; scholarly succession/intellectual heirs, paucity of, 295–96; solicitation and use of personal accounts, 296–98; translations of work, 51–53, 160n195, 279–83, 287–88, 298; women's involvement in Jewish resistance, 304–6; Yiddish studies, as scholarly field, 308–12
Treblinka, 166, 178, 259, 267
trilingualism of Yiddish historians, 40–43
Trinh, Miryam, 300
Trunk, Gabriel, 37, 92n91, 120, 149n155
Trunk, Isaiah, 25–27; anti-lachrymose approach of, 65, 67, 82; on Arendt's *Eichmann in Jerusalem*, 191; bibliography, 341–58; Blumental and, 29–30, 58; CJHC/JHI and, 27, 29; comparison of Holocaust with other catastrophes, 196; continuities, pursuit of, 108; on continuity of Jewish historical experience, 199, 203–10; Dawidowicz's reliance on, 219; death of, 160, 295; Diaspora, historical validation of life in, 202; on diseases and mortality rates in Warsaw Ghetto, 203–4, 288; dual objective/subjective perspective, 151–52, 155–56; Dworzecki and, 31, 255n104; in *Encyclopaedia Judaica* (2007), xv; engaged approach to Jewish history, calling for, 18–19; everyday life, study of, 211–12; Friedman and, 25–27, 35, 36, 39–40, 91, 92n91, 93, 209; general Jewish historical work by, 115n166; German versus Jewish sources, use of, 183–84, 186, 191; on ghetto suicides, 260n126; on Holocaust history as Jewish history, 166, 191–92, 292; imperative to publish, 128, 130–31; Israel, migrating to, 29–30, 85, 92, 181; in Israel, 29–30, 295; Jewish resistance/passivity, defending/explaining, 72, 209–10, 230–31, 233, 234–35, 236, 238–41, 243–45; *Jewish Responses to Nazi Persecution* (1979), 82, 103, 145, 147, 156, 160, 215, 281; on Jewish unarmed resistance, 262–64, 265, 271, 275; *Judenrat* (1964), 58, 60–61, 91, 103, 142, 147, 209–10, 223–24, 236, 280–81, 282, 284–85, 292, 294, 313; on Judenrat as Jewish leadership, 207–9; on Judenrat ideology, 204–7; Kermish and, 29–30, 37–38, 40, 92, 102, 130–31, 160; Kutno, history of, 91, 93, 108, 140, 153–54, 183; *Lodz Ghetto*, 51–53, 147, 184, 204, 212–13, 235, 280, 285, 294, 299, 300, 313; loss of family members in Holocaust, 85, 120; Mahler and, 171; Ber Mark and, 37n47; material culture and, 217; "Myth of Silence" refuted by, 120; Nazi war criminals, pursuit of, 168, 169; North America, move to, 35, 85; on November uprising (1830), 226–27; original language research, historians' use of/failure to use, 294, 300, 307; photo of, *26*; Piotrków-Trybunalski, history of, 91, 267, 298; Płock, 1936 monograph on Jews of, 18–19, 44, 72, 93, 103, 183, 216; political stance of,

87, 90–93; prizes and awards, 60–61, 279–80; as public figure, 56, 58–59, 60–61; publishing venues, 52–53 (table), 160; regionalism, support for, 26–27, 220, 222–24; on religious topics, 215; solicitation and use of personal accounts, 145, 146–47, 148; Soviet hegemony and politicization of scholarly work, 181; specialized focus of, 67; *Studies in Jewish History in Poland,* 108; survival of Nazi occupation by, 84, 114; synthetic account of Holocaust in Yiddish encyclopedia, 218–19; on synthetic approach, 222–24; on thefts of Jewish property, 307; translations of work of, 280–81, 288, 298; understated approach of, 102–3; on victim/ survivor self-expression, 126; on Warthegau region labor camps and ghettos, 93, 146, 183–84, 257, 297, 300, 301n77; Yad Vashem and, 58; Yiddish language and, 42, 43, 47–48, 87; YIVO and, 3n3, 26, 27, 30, *35, 36,* 56, 58, 59, 92–93, 98, 295; *yizkor* books and, 137, 138 (map), 139 (table), 140, 141, 142, 203, 207, 222–23

Trunk, Yehiel Yeshaye, 26n13
Trunk, Yitskhok Yehuda, 25n13, 153
Tsanin, Mordechai, 51
Di Tsayt (*Time;* journal), 44n71
Tsaytshrift ("*Periodical*"), 13–14
Di tsukunft (*The Future;* journal), 13, 14–15, 92, 220
TsYShO movement, 94, 104
Turkow, Jonas, 162
Tych, Feliks, 32n32, 165, 166
ha-Tzefira (*The Dawn;* journal), 44n71
Tzvi Kessel Prize for Jewish Literature, Mexico, 60

Uebersberger, Hans, 23n4
unarmed resistance. *See* Jewish unarmed resistance
Undzer kiem (*Our Existence;* journal), 295

Unger, Menashe, 215
Union of Yiddish Writers and Journalists, Israel, 44, 50, 57, 60, 160, 309; *Yiddish Literature in the State of Israel* (anthology; 1991), 309
"unique" status of Holocaust, 194, 195–98
United Kibbutz Movement (ha-Kibutz ha-Me'uhad), 48
United States: Jewish Teachers' Seminary and People's University, New York, 45–47, 111–12, 291; prewar Yiddish historical practice in, 12, 13, 14; Yiddish historians migrating to, 32, 35, 85; YIVO in New York, 12, 35, *36,* 55, 56, 58, 74, 88, 92, 112, 217
unpreparedness and problem of Jewish resistance, 245–46
Unzer tsayt (*Our Time;* journal), 92
Unzer vort (*Our Word;* journal), 98, 248, 256
US Holocaust Memorial Museum, 275, 281

Der veker (*The Awakener;* newspaper), 201
Vilna: conflict between proponents of Yiddish and Hebrew in, 43–44, 97; Northern Trade Fair, 98–99; prewar Yiddish historical practice in, 12–13, 14; YIVO in, 12, 14, 88, 111
Vilna Ghetto: Balberyszski's account of, 133; Dworzecki's studies of, 31, 33–34, 37, 57, 59, 83, 98, 105–7, 124, 128, 135–36, 147, 153, 199, 209, 215, 241, 248, 249, 253–55, 261, 270, 275, 289, 298; Dworzecki surviving, 31, 83, 84, 98, 105, 124, 242; impossibility of armed resistance in, 241; Kruk's account of, 267; medical resistance in, 33, 105–6, 253–54, 261; *Parizaner lid* (Partisan Hymn) of, 57, 125–26; Anton Schmidt's work in, 289; Schroeter's study of, 276; suicide in, 260
Vinaver, Maxim, 9n25, 9n28

Visnshaftlekher krayz (Academic Circle) of the Society of Friends of YIVO, Lodz, 24
von Fransecky, Tanya, 306
von Ranke, Leopold, 196, 212, 213

Warsaw City Council, Kermish's research on Jewish members of, 94–96
Warsaw Ghetto: autobiographical authors, encouragement of, 134, 135; Berg diary, 35; Diana Blumenfeld surviving, 60; clandestine medical school in, 199; Czerniaków diary, 42; destruction of, 184–86; everyday life, study of, 213; Friedman on, 146, 264–65; Gutman on, 286; Kermish on, 109, 122, 129–31, 140, 185, 186, 187, 201, 206, 215, 257, 260n126, 263, 266–67, 286; *Kidush ha-Hayim* ("the sanctification of life") in, 247, 255, 256; literary productivity in, 124, 126, 200; Nazi war criminals, postwar pursuit of, 168; Oyneg Shabes project, 25, 29, 31, 65, 105, 128, 129, 175, 203, 215, 271, 275n177, 281; "psychological readiness" in, 203; "starvation disease" research from, 193; suicide in, 260n126; taxation in, 201; Trunk on diseases and mortality rates in, 203–4, 288; Trunk's loss of family members in, 85; underground press publications, 37–38, 97, 105, 130–31, 201, 206, 263, 306
Warsaw Ghetto Uprising, 56, 59, 90, 95, 96, 105, 122, 180–81, 185–88, 230–31, 234, 240, 256–58, 262–66, 286
Warthegau, Trunk on labor camps and ghettos of, 93, 146, 183–84, 257, 297, 300, 301n77
Waxman, Meyer, *A History of Jewish Literature* (1941), 310
weapons, Jewish resistance and lack of/ difficulty of obtaining, 234n30, 237, 240–41

Weinreich, Max, 14, 44n72, 74, 83, 112, 133, 202–3; *Hitler's Professors* (1946), 170
Weinreich, Uriel, 114n165
Weinryb, Bernard, 45n78, 112
Weiss, Aharon, 283, 286, 288
Weiss, Isaac Hirsch, 214
Weitzman, Lenore, 304
Werner, Alfred, 150
Wiener, Mark, 302n82
Wiesenthal, Simon, 150, 228
Wieviorka, Annette, 297
Wirszubski, Abraham, 107
Wischnitzer, Mark, 110, 112
Wischnitzer, Rachel, 110
Wisse, Ruth, 76–77
Wissenschaft des Judentums, 2, 16–19, 67
Wohl, Samuel, 175n45
women: Jewish resistance, involvement in, 95, 125, 264, 304–6; lack of, as Yiddish historians of the Holocaust, 40–41; Yiddish historians on, 304–6
World Conference for Jewish Culture, 60
World Congress of Jewish Studies, 292
World Federation of Polish Jews, 59
World Medical Association, Dworzecki addressing, 106, 170
world opinion, illusive Jewish belief in, 243–44
Wulf, Joseph, 168, 306–7; *Das Dritte Reich und die Juden* (with Léon Poliakov; 1955), 191
Wygodski, Jacob, 107

Yad Vashem, 7, 34–35; Blumental and, 34, 104–5, 187, 189, 295; commemorative aims of, 229; conflict with survivor-historians at, 49, 105, 113–14; Dworzecki and, 35, 39, 57; Friedman and, 102, 192; German versus Jewish sources, use of, 187–88; ghettos, joint commemoration of, 57; Holocaust historiography of, 113–14; Holocaust history as Jewish history and, 187–88, 192; Jewish resistance, Conference on,

39, 232, 247, 270–71, 272, 274, 303; joint projects with YIVO, 37, 57, 102, 113, 121–22; Ka-Tsetnik Prize, 59; Kermish and, 34–35, 59, 96, 105, 129–30, 187, 218, 295; material culture and, 218; post-Holocaust archival initiative, 67n18; publication imperative of, 129–30; spiritual resistance, adoption of Dworzecki's redefinition of, 275; Trunk and, 58; Yiddish language and, 49

Yasni, A. Wolf, 57, 110, 172–73, 296n60, 302n82

Yavetz (Jawitz), Ze'ev, 214

Yedi'ot Yad va-Shem/Yedies fun yad vashem (News of Yad Vashem; journal), 49

Yerushalmi, Yosef Hayim, 74, 157; *Zakhor* (1982), 119

Yerusholayimer almanakh (journal), 59

Yiddish Book Center, Amherst, Massachusetts, 301

Yiddish encyclopedia (*Algemeyner entsiklopedye*), 2, 20, 46, 60, 66, 74, 218–19, 235, 263, 280

Yiddish historians emigrating during interwar period, 110–11

Yiddish historians of the Holocaust, xiii–xviii, 21–61, 313–18; accepted truths of Holocaust historiography opposed by, 3–4; audience for, 55–56, 69, 131–42, 314; defined, 22; embrace of Yiddish defining sphere of Holocaust discourse, 21, 40–53; engaged scholarship, heritage of, 16, 18–19, 225; Iron Curtain and, 27, 29, 31–33, 85; lack of scholarly attention to, 2–3, 282; personal and professional relations between, 33–40, *34, 36*; prizes and awards won by, 59–61, 226, 279–80; as public figures, 53–61, 225–26; publicly strained relations between Western and Warsaw historians, 37n47; publishing venues, 52–53 (table); significance of, 1–2, 21; as specific group, 21; survival of Nazi occupation by, 22, 83–85; women, lack of, 40–41. *See also* characteristics of Yiddish Holocaust historians; Holocaust history as Jewish history; Jewish resistance; Jewish unarmed resistance; prewar Yiddish historical practice; public discourse on Holocaust; transmission of Yiddish historians' works to broader culture; *specific historians*

Yiddish language: academic Yiddish of Yiddish historians, 311; Blumental's lexicon of Yiddish in Nazi period, 111, 149, 159–60, 188–90, 299–300; commitment of prewar Yiddish historians to, 8–9; disparaged as folk idiom, 2; ending of writing and publication in, 4–5, 159–61, 314–15; German othering of, 16–17; Hebrew and Yiddish, conflict over use of, 43–45, 50–51, 97; Hebrew vernacular, doubts about future of, 5–6; Holocaust, Yiddish/Hebrew use of/terms for, xi; Holocaust historiography and, 110–15; Israel, anti-Yiddish period in, 44–45, 51, 58n128; multilingual Jewish culture, gradual demise of, 279–80; original language research, historians' use of/failure to use, 293–308; political stance and use of, 87; postvernacular, xiii, 8, 293; postwar scholarly journals in, 111–12; publishing venues, 52–53 (table), 132–33, 160; sphere of Holocaust discourse, Yiddish historians' use of Yiddish defining, 21, 40–53; trilingualism of Yiddish historians, 40–43

Yiddish literature, lachrymose/ martyrological approach of, 76–79

Yiddish Scientific Institute. *See* YIVO

Yiddish studies, as scholarly field, 308–12

Yiddish Writers and Journalists Union. *See* Union of Yiddish Writers and Journalists

Yidishe kultur (*Yiddish Culture*; journal), 54n109, 94, 172

Yidishe shprakh (*Yiddish Language*; journal), 111, 149, 189

YIVO Institute for Jewish Research (originally Yiddish Scientific Institute), 7; audience of, 131–32, 142; autobiography contests, 133; Blumental and, 27, 30, 58, 104; divergence of Jewish scholarship with founding of Hebrew University and, xv; Dworzecki and, 44; Friedman and, 24, 25, 37, 55, 88, 100, 102, 113, 295; ghettos, joint commemoration of, 57; Historians' Circle, 88, 93, 112–13; Holocaust historiography of, 112–13; Israel, Friends of YIVO in, 30, 56, 151; joint projects with Yad Vashem, 37, 57, 102, 113, 121–22; Judenrat Colloquium (1967), 58; Kermish and, 30; Lodz Friends of YIVO, 24, 27, 100; in New York, 12, 35, *36*, 55, 56, 58, 74, 88, 92, 112, 217; personal relations between Yiddish historians and, 36; post-Holocaust archival initiative, 67n18; prewar Yiddish historical practice and, 5, 7, 12, 13, 14, 15, 18; "psychological readiness" through, 202–3; Tarbut seminary papers at, 98; Tcherikower and, 74; Trunk and, 3n3, 26, 27, 30, 35, *36*, 56, 58, 59, 92–93, 98, 295; in Vilna, 12, 14, 88, 111. *See also specific journals*

YIVO Annual, 39, 92, 287–88

YIVO bleter (*YIVO Pages*; journal), 15, 39, 92, 93, 112, 132, 286

yizkor books: Blumental and, 136, 137, 138 (map), 139 (table), 140–45, 148, 154, 156–57, 224n233, 231, 268; defined, 136; Dworzecki and, 137–40, 138 (map), 139 (table), 154; Friedman and, 89, 136, 137, 138 (map), 139 (table), 140, 141, 144, 220, 221, 222; information about Yiddish historians derived from, 27n19, 30n28; Kermish and, 136, 137, 138 (map), 139 (table), 140, 266–67, 298; regionalism/synthetic history and, 220, 221, 222; reviewing and writing for, 39, 51, 108, 109, 115n166, 136–42, 138 (map), 139 (table); tragic focus of, 64; Trunk and, 137, 138 (map), 139 (table), 140, 141, 142, 203, 207; Yiddish studies and, 311

Yunger historiker krayz (Young Historians Circle), 12, 24n8, 26, 40, 92, 171, 172n35

Zachariasz, Shimon, 175
Zaderecki, Tadeusz, 84
Zenderland, Leila, 202–3
Zilberman, Yosef, 128
Zinberg, Israel, xiii–xiv, 3n4, 9, 10, 13, 14, 141, 302n82, 308–10
Zionism, 86–88, 95, 96, 97, 98, 99, 229, 291
Zipperstein, Steven J., 71
Zuckerman, Yitzhak, 105
Zunz, Leopold, 16, 80
Zygielbojm, Shmuel (Artur), 57, 91, 126